D1550092

THE WONDERFUL STORY OF LONDON

THEIR FINEST HOUR

On December 29, 1940, successive waves of German aircraft showered innumerable fire bombs on the heart of London. Acres of buildings were gutted and St. Paul's Cathedral was ringed by an inferno. Miraculously, it escaped serious damage and stood out triumphant, symbol of London's heroism, above fire and smoke.

THE WONDERFUL STORY OF LONDON

General Editor
HAROLD WHEELER
HON.D.LITT., F.R.HIST.S.

THIRD EDITION
EDITED BY
B. WEBSTER SMITH

ODHAMS PRESS LIMITED
LONG ACRE, LONDON

First Published 1936
Second Edition 1950
Third Edition 1956

MADE AND PRINTED IN GREAT BRITAIN BY
ODHAMS (WATFORD) LTD., WATFORD, HERTS

CONTENTS

YEOMEN OF THE GUARD

Founded in 1485 as " Yeomen of the Guard of our Lord the King " to act as personal bodyguard to the monarch, this corps is one of the oldest of its kind still existing. Its duties are now ceremonial only.

INTRODUCTION

THERE are over a dozen Londons. If you have a sufficiently large map you may perhaps discover the little dots that represent the minor owners of that name. It will take time, for the territories in which they are situated are as wide apart as the Orkney Islands and Canada, Argentina and Spanish Guinea, the United States and Chile.

Some have thought it well to prefix New to their designation; others have not altered it by jot or tittle. All have seen fit to honour the big dot which stands for the largest city in the world, though the naming after it of a reef in the South China Sea is none too delicate a compliment, however well intended. London itself cannot complain of this duplication because it consists of quite a number of Londons.

The capital of the British Empire started without pretensions and without promise. There has been much argument as to the how and when of the matter, and even as to exactly where the first little human group settled down. The men, women and children who comprised it were rough, unlettered folk given to fishing and hunting.

In a day of few needs and no wants, they were doubtless satisfied if they had a measure of protection and comfort. The wild beasts with whom these early inhabitants shared the wooded and watery waste were anything but friendly. Often enough, it is to be feared, the cupboard was bare and the fire fitful. Vigilance was the price exacted for life. There was no money, which was perhaps a blessing. The days when a leasehold in Oxford Street with a frontage of 24 feet would be sold for nearly £100,000 were far distant.

From Then to Now has been no easy passage for the Londoner. He has endured much since he cast aside his shaggy coat for a variety of costumes. Be it added that he has also achieved a great deal. His city has been battered and burned, plague has desolated it, kings have sought to take away its freedom, there has been strife within and without, and bombs have rained from the sky. But while the Londoner has barred his gates in the face of the invader, he has also flung them open to the refugee and the exile. His purse-strings have been tied loosely for such as these. He has built, torn down and reconstructed with a mighty stubbornness, and hated and loved with equal fervour.

Riches and rags, saint and sinner, the famous and the infamous have trodden London streets. While martyrs were being fed to the flames at Smithfield the gallows were busy at Tyburn and prisoners were being tortured in the Tower and beheaded on Tower Hill. Yet only a stone's-cast from the place of burning monks were praying for souls in the priory of St. Bartholomew-the-Great, and physicians were attempting to heal broken bodies in the nearby hospital. Both had been founded by a king's jester. It is significant that the very name of Tyburn has been wiped out, that the place where the executioner's block stood on Tower Hill is now a garden, and that what remains of the ancient Norman church and a vastly greater Barts' continue their beneficent work. The good endures.

The neighbouring prison of Newgate has disappeared, though part of the wall of the graveyard once nicknamed Dead Man's Walk stands in Amen Court, and some of the stones were used to build the Central Criminal Court. In 1785, between February and December, ninety-six people suffered the extreme penalty at Newgate. Into this den, where young and old, male and female, drunk and sober, ill and well were herded together, Elizabeth Fry, the wife of a London merchant, brought hope. Following her exertions, frowned on at first, reform was substituted for torture. The Old Bailey has given place to the Central Criminal Court. " Defend the children of the poor, and punish the wrongdoer," so reads the inscription over the main entrance. The floor of the Bench is still strewn with herbs once used to keep away gaol-fever, but that is only a reminder of less humanitarian days and bullying ways. Transportation for life for stealing an apron, fourteen years for filching a pair of shoes, hanging for stealing a horse, were typical sentences of the bad old times.

If the bell of St. Sepulchre's Church has tolled for the condemned, peals have made merry often enough. Certainly Londoners did not always take their pleasures sadly. On the birth of the baby who became Edward III the conduit in Chepe—now known as Cheapside—ran with wine instead of water, and for fear that any citizen should go thirsty the supply was supplemented by a tun of the same vintage.

Pageantry and more serious business has fallen to the lot of London's river. There was a day when a certain fiery fellow of the name of Francis Drake sailed up the Thames in the worm-eaten *Golden Hind*, the first English ship to plough its way round the world. When the Spanish Armada threatened, London contributed a fleet of thirty armed merchantmen manned by 2,180 sailors, and paid every penny of the cost. In 1858 *The Great Eastern*, the mightiest liner of her time, was launched at Millwall, and in 1912 H.M.S. *Thunderer*, the last big ship for the Navy to be built on the banks of the Thames, was completed.

There is romance enough and to spare in grey old London. Whittington and his cat, Gresham and his grasshopper, the Old Lady of Threadneedle Street, the meetings in a coffee-house which led to the formation of Lloyd's, the early zoo in the Tower, the building of St. Martin-in-the-Fields because a King disliked funerals, the waxworks in Westminster Abbey, the stuffed body of Jeremy Bentham sitting in a glass case in University College—these and many other quaint and curious matters are dealt with in the following pages. HAROLD WHEELER.

This book was first published before the Second World War and was revised by me after the war at the publisher's request, so as to bring it up-to-date by incorporating the effects of that terrible cataclysm upon the metropolis. In order to achieve this, certain excisions had to be made and a new chapter was added outlining the fortunes of the great city during those fateful years when it was the corner-stone of Britain's resistance to the Hitler domination of Europe.

The impress of this war upon London was indeed terrific. Terrible and deep are the scars which she bears in consequence, honourable though they are as memories of her war service and of the devotedness, cheerful endurance and stubborn will to win of her vast population. But time passes quickly and the great events of 1939 to 1945 have already receded into the background. After a long period of frustration a new London is emerging from the wreck of the old. Further revision of the book has therefore become necessary, and in this edition the text has been brought up-to-date and many new illustrations have been included. It is hoped that these steps will not render the work less attractive to the many people who have received earlier editions so favourably.

B. WEBSTER SMITH.

London Museum

THE ROMAN CITY OF LONDON

In the foreground is Southwark, from which a timber bridge leads to the walled city built on two small hills. Situated in the centre of the city stands the basilica, then probably the largest building in Britain.

LONDON THE ROMANS KNEW

Like that of a foundling, the very name of the world's mightiest city is wrapped in mystery. All we dare assert without fear of contradiction is that Tacitus, the Roman historian who died about A.D. 120, refers to the place as Londinium. The name may have been derived from the Celtic words *Llyn* or *Lin*, meaning a pool, and *din* or *deen*, a fortified place, stronghold, hill or mount; or it may not. Nobody knows.

There have been many Londons, but each has remained true to the parent site. In early days, "London" meant what to-day we call "the City"; Westminster, Islington, Stepney, were all outside London proper and it was not until Stuart times that any really great expansion of the capital began.

Julius Cæsar probably entered Londinium, which lay directly on his route from Kent to St. Albans.

His first landing (55 B.C.) was at once a skirmish and an expedition for the purpose of finding out something about the characteristics of the hardy warriors who aided and abetted their kinsmen in Gaul, and who as auxiliaries were additional thorns in the flesh of the legions.

The general crossed with no more than two legions (about 10,000 men) and some cavalry, which suggests that he either did not anticipate serious opposition or that conquest was not intended. He left with a high regard for the military prowess of the barbarians. In battle they drove their chariots, which had scythes fixed to the wheels, in all directions, fought like fiends, and sought to break the ranks of the enemy. They would then leap from their chariots and engage on foot. "The charioteers in the meantime," adds Cæsar, "withdraw some little distance from the battle, and so place themselves with the chariots that if their masters are overpowered by the number of the enemy they may have a ready retreat at hand. Thus they display in battle the speed of horse and the firmness of infantry."

In the spring of the following year the great Proconsul visited Britain again. This time his army was considerably augmented, for he took with him five legions and 2,000 cavalry, about 27,000 men in all. During his advance he found the number of the people "countless" and of their cattle "great." Their buildings were "exceedingly numerous." "They use either brass or iron rings, determined at a certain weight, as their money. Tin is produced in the midland regions; in the maritime iron, but the quantity of it is small; they employ brass, which is imported. As in Gaul there is timber of every description except beech and fir. They do not regard it lawful to eat the hare, and the cock, and the goose; they, however, breed them for amusement and pleasure." The reference to tin being worked in the interior is incorrect.

The warrior-author adds that " most of the inland inhabitants do not sow corn, but live on milk and flesh, and are clad with skins. All the Britons, indeed, dye themselves with woad, which occasions a bluish colour, and thereby have a more terrible appearance in fight. They wear their hair long, and have every part of their body shaved except their head and upper lip."

Exactly where he crossed the Thames, " which river can be forded in one place only, and that with difficulty," is unknown, but Brentford has been suggested. At St. Albans he secured the submission of the British chieftain, Cassivelaunus, but the British were not conquered and the tribute imposed was never paid.

In A.D. 43, nearly ninety years after the second visit of Julius Cæsar, the emperor Claudius himself took part in a new expedition. He and his successors firmly held the country for the next four centuries. The first result of this increased intercourse with the Continent was that Londinium became an important trading and government centre. The Romans made it their administrative capital, and its growth in population and luxury soon outstripped that of any other town in Britain.

In A.D. 61 tempestuous Boudicca—the Boadicea of our childhood—flamed her fiery way from the once tribal capitals of Colchester and St. Albans to London. Why the Queen of the Iceni revolted is not crystal clear. There are dark tales of the horse-whipping of herself and the violation of her daughters, of a loan by the Roman philosopher Seneca of 10,000,000 sesterces (over £80,000) at high interest and its sudden recall, of property given to British chiefs which had been treacherously sold.

When news of the rising reached Suetonius

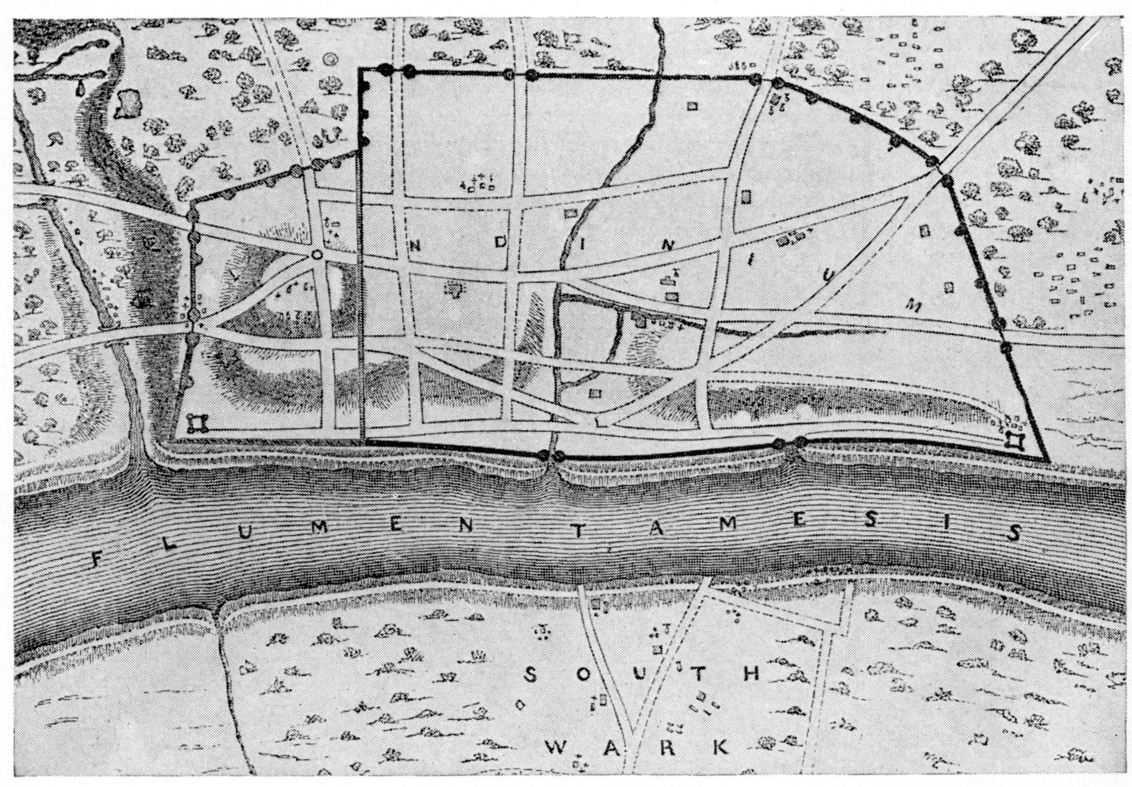

THE WALLED CITY OF ROMAN LONDON

Londinium, later named Augusta, covered an area of 330 acres. The river bank area was by far the most densely populated, the northern half of the city being for long only thinly covered with houses.

Paulinus, the Roman Governor, he hurried from Wales to defend London. The legion ordered to join him failed to appear. Exhausted and footsore, his men were in no condition to fight a victorious army, and so the city was left to fend for itself. " Neither the tears nor the entreaties of the stricken citizens," we are told, " bent him from his purpose." The inhabitants were put to the sword and their homes to the torch by Boudicca's followers. It is said that 70,000 people perished. Remains of the fire exist in a layer of burnt earth ten to thirteen feet beneath the present surface.

The conqueror's triumph was short-lived. The revolt was crushed, but the three-fold sequel was ironic. According to the story, and perhaps in fact, the Queen took poison; the leader who had failed to bring reinforcements committed suicide; the Governor-General was recalled. London alone was victorious. She arose from her ashes, and the living took the place of the dead. To-day, cast in bronze, Boudicca from her chariot on Westminster Bridge still urges the wild tribesmen to battle.

Donald McLeish

ROMAN LONDON'S MILESTONE

Supposed to have been the milestone in the forum of Londinium from which distances were measured.

Life in the City

The Romans constructed the first Thames Embankment. Great baulks of oak, the framework of the wharves where craft loaded and unloaded, have been discovered. Watling Street, begun by the conquerors before the incursion of Boudicca but surely based on an ancient track-way, extended from Dover, through Canterbury, Rochester, London, St. Albans, Dunstable, Towcester and High Cross to Chester. London Stone, fixed in the ruined wall of St. Swithin's Church, Cannon Street, is said to be the milliarium or milestone from which the roads radiated and the distances on them were measured. It once stood on the south side of the thoroughfare, " fixed deeply in the ground, fastened with bars of iron and otherwise so strongly set that if carts do run against it through negligence the wheels be broken and the stone itself unshaken. The cause why this stone was set there, the time when, or other memory hereof is none." Thus wrote John Stow in the reign of James I, and there is nothing to add to his information in the days of Elizabeth II.

There is reason to believe that the forum or market place and the basilica used for municipal purposes and courts of justice were in the neighbourhood of Leadenhall Market. Their area was perhaps 450 feet by 350 feet. The basilica was then the biggest building in Britain. A wooden bridge almost certainly crossed the Thames close to the present London Bridge. A fine bronze head of Hadrian, fished up from the bed of the Thames, may be the fragment of a statue that stood on the old wooden bridge. Perhaps it was erected to commemorate the Emperor's visit in A.D. 120.

What manner of life was led by the folk of these times? Not so markedly different, we suspect, from that of a small provincial town of to-day, minus many of its amenities and most of its mechanisation. The Romans ruled with a firm but not unkindly hand.

While excavations for the rebuilding of the Bank of England were progressing, the disturbing shovel of the excavator brought to light evidence of vanity not usually associated with that highly respectable and prosaic institution. The objects included a spoon with a tiny bowl of gold, apparently for scooping lipstick from a narrow bottle, and bronze hairpins. Buttons and buttonholes had not been invented, but the safety-pin, called a fibula, had been used long before the coming of the Romans. Some of the pins, cast in bronze, were highly decorative. Bronze mirrors reflected faces pretty and plain; little lamps of burnt clay flickered feebly at night. Red glazed ware of Gaul, incorrectly known as Samian, and a pipeclay statuette of Venus are eloquent of culture, a basin for mixing and pounding food, of domesticity, an iron boat hook, of commerce. A quern stone for grinding corn was dug up in Prince's Street.

Within the city the frail little houses of wattle were doubtless swept away, though we may be sure that outside the square mile so easy a method of building held sway for many a long day after the introduction of brick, rubble and stone. Water was supplied to the new houses in London proper through lead pipes. There was central heating, the hot air circulating in the walls and under the floors by means of flues known as hypocausts. These were fed by a wood-burning furnace placed outside the building at a rather lower level.

Rooms were plastered and brightly coloured,

ROMAN PAVEMENT
Found during excavations in Bucklersbury, nineteen feet below the present street level. Now in Guildhall.

and sometimes pictures were painted on the walls. Special attention was given to the tessellated pavements that occupied the place of the carpets of a later age. Many of the patterns were both elaborate and pictorial, and were carried out in brick, slate, chalk and other materials, the little pieces being called *tessaræ*. There may have been an upper floor to some of the houses, though this is doubtful. A bathroom was as necessary to a Roman gentleman as it is indispensable to the decent citizen of to-day. A well-preserved specimen of a Roman bath is to be seen near the Strand, and its story is told in the chapter dealing with that street.

Articles of a Roman Household

Pottery was used for domestic and artistic purposes, then as now. Babies drank from little earthenware feeding-bottles. Some of the articles used in a household were imported, but many were made at home. Glass for the most part came from abroad. Lamps were fashioned of earthenware, lead, iron and bronze. Metal tools and instruments were rich in variety. They varied from shears remarkably similar to those of the spring type used by gardeners in our own time to spurs for fighting-cocks. Pen, ink and parchment or styles and tablets fitted with wax sheets were used for writing.

The first picture of London is on a gold medallion of Constantius Chlorus struck in the Roman city of Trier, in north-eastern Gaul. The father of Constantine the Great is shown on horseback, being welcomed with outstretched arms by a figure representing London kneeling before a gate of the walled city. In the foreground four soldiers are sitting in the beaked war galley which had brought the general across the Channel.

The presence of Constantius, to whom had been assigned the care of the western provinces of the Empire, was due to a revolt. Carausius, in command of a Roman fleet charged with the suppression of Frankish pirates, had seized Boulogne and Britain and assumed the title of Augustus. He became so powerful that the two Emperors Diocletian and Maximian could do no other than acknowledge him as colleague, a triumph which he celebrated by setting up a mint in London and having medallions struck bearing portraits of the trio and the legend "Carausius and his brothers."

The usurper was murdered by Allectus, his

chief lieutenant, who retained power until Constantius took vigorous and decisive action in 296; Allectus being defeated and slain.

The Roman Wall

It is probable that the Roman wall (fragments of which still occur on Tower Hill, in Cripplegate, and elsewhere, mostly underground) was built as a result of this menace. It ran for about three miles, fronting the Fleet river on the west, the Wall brook on the east, and what are now Moorfields and Aldersgate Street on the north. The land faces were erected first, followed by a wall along the river front. It was about nine feet thick at the base, about twenty feet high, and the relics showed signs of its having been hastily and imperfectly built. To strengthen it, thirty strong bastions were built outside it, a perfect example of which still exists at St. Giles's, Cripplegate.

UNEARTHING THE MITHRAS TEMPLE
While digging the foundations of the new Bucklersbury House, the walls and chambers of a Temple of Mithras, dated second century A.D., were found.

Discovery of a Mithras Temple

While excavating the site for Bucklersbury House, Wallbrook, in September, 1954, the remains of a Roman Temple of Mithras were uncovered. They probably date from the second century A.D. They comprised a basilica sixty feet long and twenty feet wide, divided by pillars into three parts. Some wonderfully preserved statuary was also unearthed, including a head of the god in white marble, which had been socketed for attachment to a statue. There were also found a beautifully chiselled head of the bearded god Serapis, a figure of Silenus riding on an ass, with a wine cup in his hand, also a statuette of a woman. It was impossible to preserve this unique memorial of Roman London on its original site, because the new building had to be erected above it; but a new home for the Temple was found on an ajacent site, mainly through the generosity of the owners.

The growing importance of London is proved by several significant facts. In the fourth century she received the name of Augusta, in 360 the Roman general Lupicinus arrived there to "deliberate upon the aspect of affairs" and plan a campaign against invaders, and in 368 the more famous Theodosius, the father of Theodosius the Great, made a joyful and triumphant entry following "disasters" of which we have no knowledge.

Sea Rovers Fall on Britain

For some four hundred years Londoners and their fellow-countrymen had the benefit of the schooling of Rome and the disability of being in leading-strings. Of the beneficent results of Rome's rule much has been written; but the unity she brought about was a unity imposed by a conqueror on the conquered.

They intermarried with the Latins, went about their lawful occasions, progressed in culture and material gain, taking the defence of their land by the legions for granted and as eternal. Any notion of the withdrawal of the garrisons probably never entered their heads. Such affairs as those of Carausius and his traitorous satellite were common in a military empire when the central power was so far away and otherwise occupied; but they were merely episodes, the end of which became inevitable as soon as Cæsar or his deputy chose to take them seriously.

But Rome herself was in the throes of a death-struggle and could no longer worry about her outlying possessions, no matter how valuable; and that she valued Britain greatly there is abundant proof. But, hard pressed by foes from within and without, she decided to abandon the island in the far north-west, and recalled her legions at the very moment when barbarian tribes from north, west and east were attacking it. The islanders were told to defend themselves;

but the softening influence of Roman control had left them in no condition to do so.

Picts and Brigantes came from Caledonia (Scotland), Scots from Ireland; from Wales, Celts; from Jutland, Jutes; Angles from Schleswig and Saxons from Holstein raided and plundered. Some had already set a disturbing precedent long before the dust had fallen from the uplifted sandal of the last departing warrior. Rome, which had dealt so adequately with such marauders, vouchsafed no answer to the pathetic appeal for help: "The barbarians drive us to the sea and the sea drives us back to the barbarians."

The existence of Hengist and Vortigern, whose deeds of daring thrilled us in the class-room, is now open to doubt. Certainly those who came showed no intention of departing. Indeed, the Anglo-Saxons arrived in ever-increasing numbers, a compound of bloody-minded pirates and Pilgrim Fathers, as Prof. G. M. Trevelyan wittily suggests. If London was seriously affected we do not know it. It is said on somewhat dubious authority that in 457 many of the Britons who succeeded in escaping from defeat at Crayford in Kent sought refuge in the city. From that year until the dawn of the seventh century the story of London is unknown.

The "Anglo-Saxon Chronicle," that store-house of information probably inspired by Alfred, makes no reference to disaster over-taking her, so one may perhaps presume that she carried on in a rather down-at-heel kind of way. She could do no other amid the distractions of a harassed age. Two battered draughtsmen cut from the shoulder-blade of an ox and used by the invaders, some charred beams believed by some to be remains of the original Saxon church of All Hallows, Barking; a cross-head unearthed in the churchyard of St. John's, Walbrook; and a miscellaneous collection of weapons are scarcely sufficient evidence on which to base a record.

In 604 there is news of the city. Three years before, Augustine had been ordered by the Pope to make London the seat of an arch-bishopric, but the missionary chose Canter-bury, and in 604 consecrated Mellitus "to preach baptism to the East-Saxons." King Ethelbert built the first St. Paul's, but the bishop was also instructed to convert the temples "from the worship of devils to the service of the true God."

Donald McLeish

BASTION OF THE ROMAN WALL

To be seen in the churchyard of St. Giles', Cripplegate. The Roman Wall was apparently from eight to nine feet thick at the base and about twenty feet high. Bastions were fortified points in the walls.

THE TOWER OF LONDON
This aerial photograph shows clearly the plan of the Tower. In the centre is the Keep built by William the Conqueror; round this are the two fortified walls added later, with the moat surrounding all.

CASTLE OF THE CONQUEROR

It is nearly ten o'clock at night. Her Majesty's Tower of London, by day a show-place for the million, now stands silent and aloof, as if it were brooding in the darkness over its sombre memories. The measured tread of an armed sentry, the clang of a rifle butt on stone—these are the only sounds which break the stillness of its peace.

Suddenly, deep within its massive walls, there comes the cry :

" Escort for the Keys! "

In the Inner Ward, upon the stony rise that leads to Tower Green, appears a figure straight from England's storied past. Clad in a long red cloak of antique cut, coiffed with hat of Tudor style, he bears in one hand an ancient lantern lit with tallow dip, in the other the most famous bunch of keys in the world. It is the Chief Warder of the Tower, come to perform a time-honoured ceremony that has taken place each night for no one knows how many centuries.

Four stalwart Guardsmen, with rifles and fixed bayonets, and commanded by a sergeant, stand ready to receive him. He places himself in their midst. A sharp word of command, and the party marches down the slope on its way to the gate which separates the Tower from the outside world.

The sentries stationed on the route come to attention and present arms; a passer-by halts, and raises his hat as Her Majesty's Keys go by.

With befitting solemnity the Chief Warder locks the barrier gate. Then with his escort he marches back down the hill. At the Middle Tower, which in former days defended the main landward entrance to the Tower of London, he swings to the heavy doors, shoots home the bolts, and turns the keys in their locks. At the Byward Tower across the moat he repeats the process.

The party marches on. As they approach the cavernous entrance to the Bloody Tower, a challenge rings out :

" Halt! Who comes there? "

" The Keys! " is the reply.

" Whose Keys? "

Donald McLeish

THE CASTLE BUILT BY THE CONQUEROR

The White Tower, so called from the colour of the stone from Caen in Normandy of which it was built, was erected by Gundulf, Bishop of Rochester, for William I. It was designed as a self-contained fortress.

" Queen Elizabeth's Keys."

" Advance, Queen Elizabeth's Keys. All's well."

The Keys are borne beneath the threatening portcullis into the Inner Ward, where the main guard of the Tower is drawn up in their honour.

" Guard and escort, present arms! "

In the silence which follows the Chief Warder steps forward two paces, raises his hat, and cries : " God preserve Queen Elizabeth! "

And the guard and escort respond " Amen! "

The nightly ritual is over. Another link has been forged in a chain that goes back at least six hundred years. As in the days of the Plantagenet kings, and ever since, Her Majesty's Tower of London is secured until the following morning against all save those who hold the password.

The Yeomen Warders of the Tower will tell you that the ceremony of " the Keys " began in 1322, when one John of London became Constable. That it goes back so far is certain, but it may easily be far more ancient, for at that date the Tower of London was already old.

The story of the Tower begins in 1066, when William of Normandy, having defeated and slain Harold the Saxon at Senlac field, marched north to Berkhamsted in Hertfordshire, and there received the submission of the citizens of London. The Conqueror, having granted a charter to the most important city in his new dominions, proceeded thither for his coronation, and tradition says that he pitched his camp on the very spot where now the White Tower stands. Historians surmise that he built there at once the typical Norman castle of his day—a timbered fort on a mound surrounded by a wooden palisade.

London was then, as now, the key to England, and William must have decided that the safety and loyalty of so important a city must be adequately safeguarded. About 1078 there began to rise on Tower Hill the walls of the grim stone keep which for the past seven centuries has been known as the White Tower, or in early days *La Tour Blanche*.

The Impregnable White Tower

Yet by far the most interesting exhibit on Tower Hill is the Tower of London itself, " the most perfect example of a medieval fortress " existing in England. And the fairest jewel in this crown of medieval architecture is the White Tower.

The White Tower is absolutely unique; there is not another like it in the whole country. Contrary to general belief, the Normans did not build stone castles, save in very exceptional circumstances. Actually only four were built in the reign of William the Conqueror.

Of those very few, only the White Tower remains intact. The rest have long since crumbled into ruin. The White Tower is perfect, or very nearly so. Save that Sir Christopher Wren, or someone of his time, enlarged the windows and faced some of the stones, it remains in shape and form the same massive and impregnable building which Gundulf, the warrior-monk (who in 1077 became Bishop of Rochester) slowly erected for his royal master during the closing years of the eleventh century. And it is still in use.

Feel the security of those mighty walls enclosing you, and then in your imagination fill the ground floor with soldiers, Norman soldiers encased in body armour, in garrison here to defend the King's majesty against attack by foreign foes, but also and perhaps even more to overawe the proud and turbulent city of London. These huge, lofty chambers, one of which is ninety feet long, are fitting apartments for medieval soldiery. Even the wall which divides them is eight feet thick, as you can see by its low, rounded arches.

Pass to the second floor and picture to yourself Henry I, fiercest of the fiery Plantagenets, or Richard of the Lion Heart, carousing with gay abandon in the Banqueting Hall. With his garrison below and his guards looking out from the four turrets of the Tower, any monarch, however hated by his people, could feel secure in such a fortress, could laugh at the very thought of attack.

History would have proved him right. No enemy ever attempted seriously to besiege the Tower of London. There were one or two half-hearted attempts to cannonade it, and in 1381 Wat Tyler and his men actually possessed themselves of the fortress for a few hours; but the greatest peril the Tower ever stood in was from German bombs during the World Wars. Fortunately they did it no damage, though there were many heavy raids on the commercial and dock area which surrounds the Tower.

Alongside the Banqueting Hall is the Royal Chapel of St. John. Cold and bare its Norman arches look to-day, for nearly 400 years ago its richness was despoiled, and its " crosses, images, plate and gold " were melted down by order of the young King Edward VI, son of Henry VIII, whose advisers burned with zeal for religious reform.

But for over 400 years before that date the monarchs of England had knelt in the dim religious light of this austerely simple chapel, and paid their homage to the only Overlord whom they acknowledged. Even in its bareness it remains the most perfect example of a Norman fortress chapel in the country.

Where Kings Sat in Council

For the imaginatively-minded the third floor is the most exciting of all. Here it was the custom of the King of England to sit in council with his peers, and many a decision fraught with destiny for England has been arrived at in this chamber. From the *Magnum Concilium*, as it was called, developed the courts which administered the King's justice—the Court of the King's Bench and the Court of Common Pleas. These courts were originally held in the Tower, but afterwards began to move round the country following the King as he travelled from place to place.

On this floor, too, the early monarchs confined their noblest prisoners. The first of these, so far as is known, was the man who found the money to build the Tower, Ranulf Flambard, Bishop of Durham, the well-hated Justiciar of William Rufus. He also achieved the distinction of making the first successful escape from its walls. Thrown into prison by Henry I on his accession, Flambard did not brook confinement long. According to the popular legend, a length of rope was smuggled in to him concealed in a flagon or barrel of wine. The wily bishop invited his gaolers to drink with him, plied them with liquor and then, as they lay snoring in drunken slumber, crawled through a narrow window 65 feet above ground —you can see it still, for it is one that the restorers overlooked—and slid down his rope to safety and freedom.

The story says he fell at the bottom and hurt himself badly. But he got away to France for all that. Centuries later another prisoner, a Welshman pining for his native hills, tried to emulate the Justiciar's feat. He, poor wretch, had no stout rope but only knotted sheets and blankets upon which to rely, and his mangled body was found next morning at the foot of the Tower walls.

Royal Poet in the Tower

From Agincourt in 1415 the young King Henry V returned to England in triumph, bearing with him a number of distinguished prisoners. Among them was Charles, Duke of Orleans, a scion of royal rank and a poet of no mean order.

Royal captives taken on the field of battle were worth big money in those days. Henry valued Charles of Orleans at 300,000 crowns. It took twenty-five years to convince France that he was worth that amount, in spite of Joan of Arc's belief that he was one of the chosen deliverers of her country, and that if he could return all would be well.

During that quarter of a century Charles was resident in the Tower, though not kept in strict confinement, and in it he composed large numbers of those elegant ballads and rondels which have kept his name famous.

Forty-five years after his departure to France the Council Chamber was to witness perhaps the most shocking example of royal baseness ever seen within its walls.

Richard Crookback, Protector of England and guardian of the two hapless Princes whose foul murder he was plotting, thought it prudent in scheming his way to the Crown of England to remove from his path all who might hinder his royal ambitions. Among these was William, Baron Hastings, who had refused him allegiance after the death of Edward IV. Pretending friendliness, Richard summoned Hastings to a meeting of the Council on June 13, 1483.

Little did the noble lord imagine, as he made his way up the narrow circular stairs leading to the Council Chamber, that the seemingly solid wall was filled with armed men lying in wait to compass his death.

The council meeting opened. Richard, feigning anger at some remark made by Hastings, brought down his fist with a crash upon the table.

It was the agreed signal. Cries of " Treason! Treason! " re-echoed through the Keep, and the clash of arms was heard on the stairway. Soldiers burst into the Council Chamber and seized Lord Hastings.

Accusing him of treacherous plotting, Richard exclaimed :

" By God, I will not dine until thy head is struck from thy shoulders! "

The wretched peer was hurried downstairs; a log of timber used for odd repairs was made to serve as a block, and beneath the walls of the Keep his head was struck from his body.

Hastings was by no means the first man to be beheaded in the Tower of London. That distinction belongs, so we are told, to Sir Simon Burley, who suffered in the reign of Richard II. Long before his day, however, death in many a grim form had been busy in the Tower.

Torture Chambers in the Keep

Before leaving the Keep, descend for a while to its dungeons—those inevitable appendages of every medieval fortress. It is only comparatively recently that these have been shown to the public. Their opening disposed of the ghastly tales which used to be in circulation of medieval captives shrieking with fear as the muddy waters of the Thames rose inch by inch to drown them in their cells.

There are no cells save one, called " Little Ease," a horrible little hole 4 feet square, so called because in it a prisoner was unable to sit, stand or lie down in comfort. It was situated in the passageway between the two huge vaulted chambers which comprise the dungeons. These for the most part stand above ground, while the Thames at high tide does not rise to within 20 feet of the level of their floors.

For all that, these gloomy dungeons have beyond doubt many a time and oft resounded to the shrieks of terror-stricken prisoners; but it was a grimmer fear by far than that of death by drowning which provoked those cries of anguish.

Here—and here alone in the Tower, if report

speak truly—were prisoners subjected to torture. On the floor above you may still see some of the implements which were used; the bilboes that shackled the ankles, the thumbscrew, and the dreaded "Scavenger's Daughter," an appliance of iron which held the neck, wrists and ankles of the victim. The name is a corruption of that of the inventor, Sir William Skevington, Lieutenant of the Tower in the reign of Henry VIII. In the crypt of St. John's Chapel, popularly known as "Raleigh's Cell," though the famous Elizabethan was never confined there, is exhibited a tiny model of the rack, half an hour of which reduced Guy Fawkes from brazen obduracy to an agonised readiness to confess the misdeeds of himself and his fellow-conspirators.

Functions of the Tower

Guy Fawkes was among the last of those "put to the question" in the Tower, but before his day the torturer was for centuries kept busy in the dungeons of the Keep. King John—and other English monarchs—there drew the teeth and peeled off the nails of Jews alleged to possess hidden stores of gold; those who clipped the edges of coins paid the penalty of their crime according to barbarous medieval standards; and the reign of Henry VIII saw religion made a cause for mutilation.

Horrible as are the deeds which have been committed within its walls, the Conqueror's castle—never, indeed, called "castle," but from its birth the Tower of London—must not be thought of primarily as a place of imprisonment and torture. Those indeed were the least of its functions, being merely incidental to the fact that it was a fortress.

John Stow, who in his time knew more about London than any man living, wrote about 1600 that the Tower was "A citadel to defend or command the City; a royal palace for assemblies or treaties; a prison of State for the most dangerous offenders; the only place of coinage for all England; the treasury of the ornaments and jewels of the Crown; and the general conserver of the most ancient records of the King's Courts of Justice."

Housed the Royal Menagerie

This list by no means exhausts the many uses to which the Tower has been put during its long life. Until a disastrous fire broke out on October 30, 1841, in the Bowyer Tower, it was the chief royal armoury, while for almost six hundred years it housed the royal menagerie.

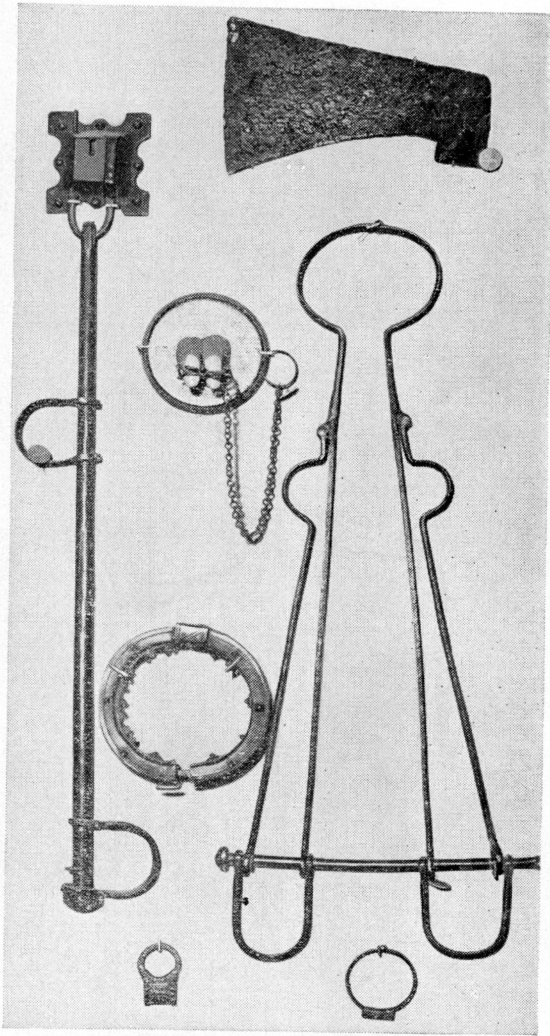

TORTURE INSTRUMENTS
Preserved in the crypt of the Chapel of St. John, together with the blade of an execution axe.

In 1235 the Emperor Frederick sent Henry III three leopards—a tasteful compliment to the royal arms. A few years later an elephant arrived—the first seen in England since the days of the Romans. Polar bears, tigers, lions and other strange and fearful wild beasts followed, until Tower Hill became a popular resort for Londoners, who came there to "see the lions," according to the phrase they coined.

It was not until 1834 that the menagerie was transferred to the present Zoo in Regent's Park. The Lion Tower in which it was housed has been completely demolished; it stood on the ground where visitors now buy

MOST PERFECT FORTRESS CHAPEL IN ENGLAND

The Chapel of St. John in the White Tower was built about 1080, and is a unique gem of pure Norman architecture. It consists of a nave and aisles of four bays, and an apse with five arches giving on to an ambulatory. It is quite small, being only 55 feet 6 inches long by 31 feet wide. The plain heavy columns carry carved capitals, some of which have a T-shaped figure only found in early Norman work. Above the arches, which are devoid of ornament, is a clerestory with a gallery which continues the wall passages of the rooms on the second floor of the Tower. The fittings in the chapel are modern; the glass in the windows belonged to Horace Walpole. Its "crosses, images, plate and gold" were melted down by order of Edward VI, whose advisers burned with zeal for religious reform and austerity.

their tickets. That is why the first tower one comes to is the Middle Tower; it was midway between the Lion Tower and the Byward Tower.

The Royal Observatory had its birth in the Tower, for it was there that John Flamsteed, appointed by royal warrant in 1674 " astronomical observator," carried out his observations until the special observatory buildings were erected in Greenwich Park.

Legend says that the turret in the White Tower which he occupied was the one in which King John imprisoned the most beautiful girl in England, Maud Fitzwalter, because she persistently refused to become his mistress, and did her to death by means of poisoned food.

A Royal Tradition

Until Cromwell, burning with republican fervour, destroyed the royal apartments at the Tower, the English monarchs were regularly in residence there. In particular, it was traditional that they should spend the night before their coronation in the venerable fortress.

A dark and gloomy residence it must have been, by all accounts. In all its dozen huge rooms there are only three fireplaces, or possibly four.

To-day the Tower still retains two of its original uses; it houses a garrison and the regalia are lodged in the Wakefield Tower. By virtue of these functions it is unique as the oldest building in the world still used for its original purposes.

The " mystery " of the Royal Mint ceased to be practised there in 1810, and the State papers were transferred to the Public Record Office in 1866. But even now the Tower is occasionally used as a prison. William the Conqueror's Tower was an isolated stone keep, self-sufficient and with no defence save its own stout walls. It stood just outside the walls of London City, and some distance from the Thames. It had no moat, and its only entrance (now blocked up) was high up in the wall facing the river.

His sons, William Rufus and Henry I, it is believed, began to ring it round with the ramparts which now form the turreted wall enclosing what is called the Inner Ward. Richard I spent a lot of money on the fortress, but it was Henry III who, by erecting the outer wall with its fortifications, transformed the Conqueror's idea and left us the Tower as we know it to-day.

His revolutionary plan was to extend the Tower down to the Thames, thus turning it into a water fortress. At immense cost, and greatly to the discontent of the Londoners, who had to bear most of the expense, he constructed Tower Wharf along the low muddy banks of the river, made in it an entrance to the Tower and then ringed the entire fortress with water by constructing an enormous moat supplied from the Thames.

The entrance to the Tower from the river was made directly opposite the only entrance to the Inner Ward, the portcullised archway beneath the Bloody Tower. It was closed by a water gate, later to acquire a dreadful renown under the sinister name of Traitors' Gate.

To defend the water gate, Henry built over it a tower. On St. George's Day, 1240, disaster overcame the work; both wharf and water gate crashed to ruin.

Henry III at once began rebuilding, and this time so strongly that his work stands to this day. The archway which he constructed over the water gate is one of the most interesting architectural features in the Tower, for though it has a span of sixty-one feet it has no keystone. Each stone along the lowest course is locked to its neighbour by a cog.

Though some buildings have been destroyed, a number altered, and many added since the days of Henry III, the general plan of the fortress has remained untouched. An airman flying over the Tower to-day views substantially what an observer would have seen in 1250, the main exception being that the Royal Palace, which extended from the Keep to the south-east corner of the fortifications, has disappeared.

In the centre stands the White Tower, grim and completely isolated, save that a fragment of what was once the royal wardrobe stands in jagged ruin beneath the south-east turret.

Wall With Thirteen Towers

The spacious Inner Ward is enclosed by a hexagonal wall from which rise thirteen towers. The two most famous—the Bloody Tower and the Wakefield Tower—face the Thames.

It is impossible to look upon the gateway beneath the Bloody Tower without emotion. Some of the greatest, the wisest and the most faithful of England's sons and daughters, as well as an unconscionable number of distinguished rogues and villains, have passed beneath that portal to their deaths. It speaks of the tyranny of monarchs, of the savagery of religious fanaticism, of faithless treachery, and

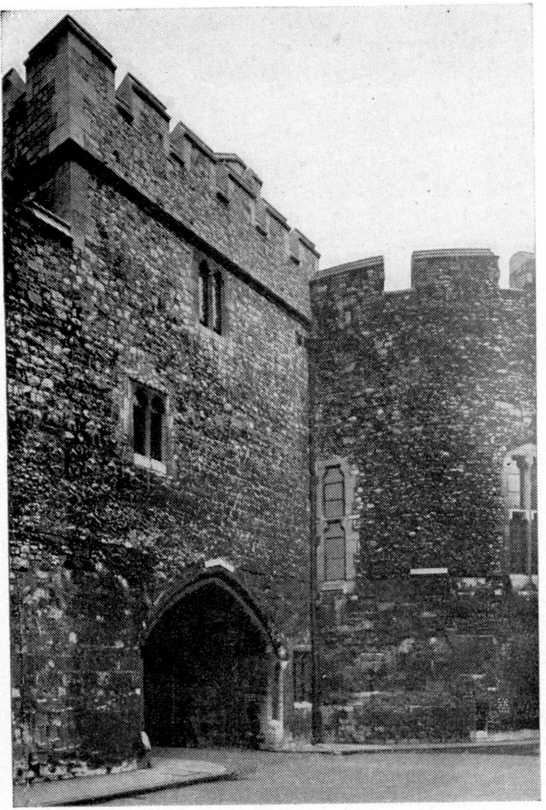

THE BLOODY TOWER
Where probably the little Princes were murdered. On the right is part of the Wakefield Tower.

of base revenge. It is the frontispiece for a volume written in blood.

It has witnessed innumerable scenes of an enduring pathos. Before it stood, on May 2, 1536, pretty Anne Boleyn, so lately the darling of a king, now a terrified, hysterical woman, with the shadow of the axe already falling on her slender neck.

Elizabeth in the Tower

Eighteen years later her daughter, Elizabeth, also stood before the fatal entrance in almost equal peril of her life; but young though she was—not yet twenty-one years of age—Elizabeth could put a bold face on an unhappy situation.

It was raining on that Palm Sunday when with her escort she came to the Tower. The tide was low; a bank of glistening mud lay between the barge and the landing place. The story goes that she was fiercely angry at being brought to the water gate—the way traitors came—and that she sprang out on the mud, sat her down upon one of the wet stones, and refused to budge.

" Better sit here," she remarked with mordant humour, " than in a worse place."

Tudor though she was, Elizabeth could know fear, and the two months she spent in the Tower were months of real terror for her. If legend is to be believed, she quickly recovered upon her release. After attending a thanksgiving service in the church of All Hallows Steyning (of which the tower can be seen in Star Alley), she sat down to a hearty meal of pork and peas at the " King's Head "— later rebuilt as the " London Tavern "— next door.

Execution of Sir Thomas More

Most pathetic of all entries to the Tower was that of the gentle Sir Thomas More, formerly Lord Chancellor, after his condemnation in Westminster Hall. His grandson wrote of it :

" When Sir Thomas was now come to the Tower Wharf, his best-beloved child, my Aunt Roper, desirous to see her father, whom she feared she would never see in this world after, to have his last blessing, gave there attendance to meet him; whom, as soon as she had espied, she ran hastily unto him, and without consideration or care for herself, passing through the midst of the throng and guard of men, who with bills and halberts compassed him around, there openly in the sight of them all embraced him, and took him about the neck and kissed him, not able to say any word but ' Oh, my father ! Oh, my father ! ' "

When she had said farewell, and More had passed on, she rushed back " like one who had forgot herself, ravished with the entire love of so worthy a father," and clung to him and kissed him again, " whereat he spoke not a word, but carrying still his gravity, tears fell also from his eyes; yea, there were very few in all the troop who could refrain hereat from weeping, no, not the guard themselves."

A great and spirited people, these English of Tudor days. The aged John Fisher, Bishop of Rochester and friend of Thomas More, committed to the Tower because he did " openly declare in English that the King, our sovereign Lord, is not supreme head of the Church of England," could write a piteous letter to the chancellor, Thomas Cromwell, begging for another blanket to keep warmth in limbs racked with rheumatism; but when at five o'clock on a June morning they woke him to tell him he must die at nine, he answered,

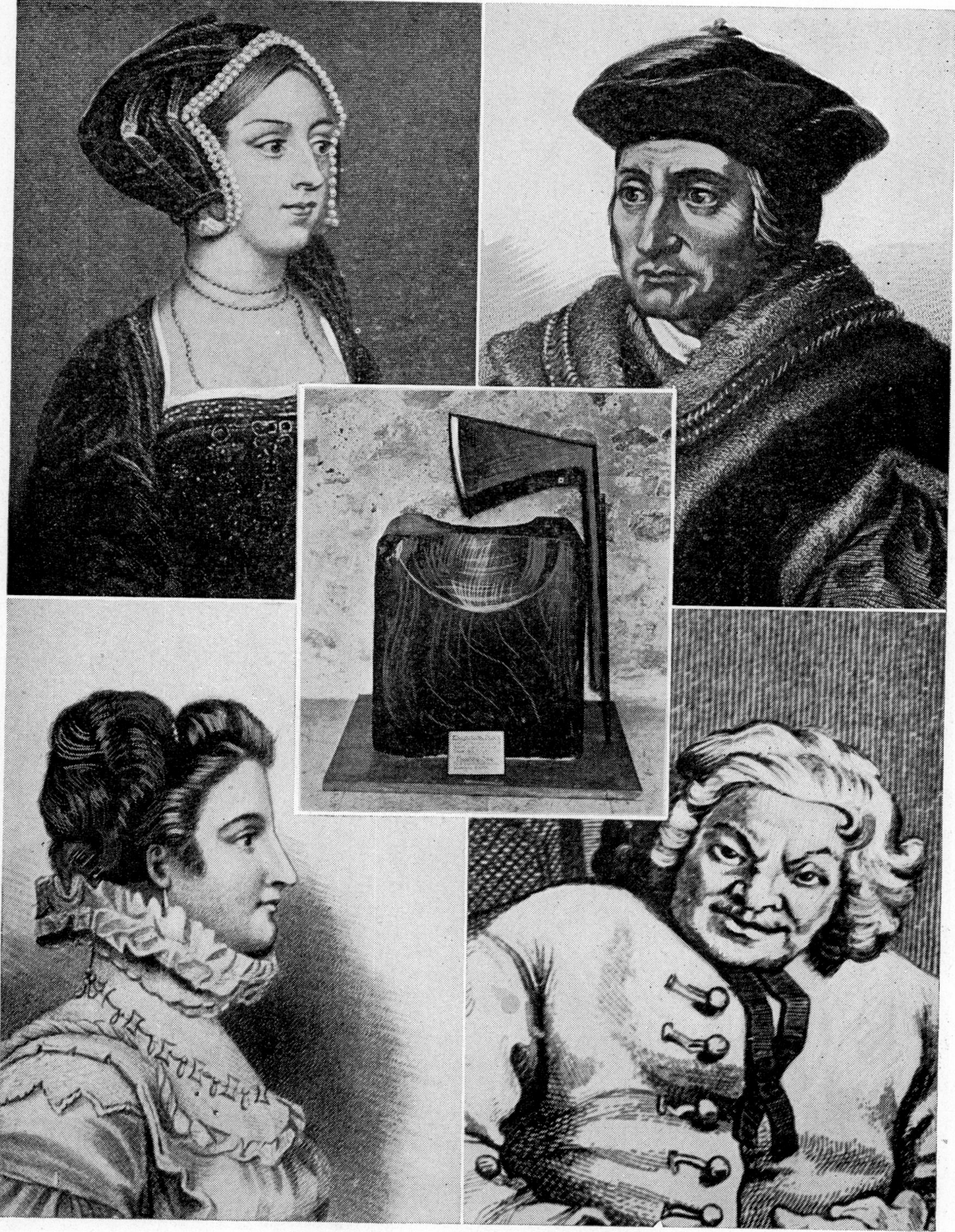

VICTIMS OF THE EXECUTIONER'S AXE
Top left, Anne Boleyn, wife of Henry VIII; right, Sir Thomas More. Lower left, Lady Jane Grey; right, Simon Lord Lovat, the last to suffer on the block. Centre, the block on which Lovat died.

" Well, then, let me by your patience sleep an hour or two, for I have slept very little this night, and yet, to tell you the truth, not from any fear of death, I thank God, but by reason of my great weakness and infirmity."

Saddest Spot on Earth

More and Fisher are among those who lie buried in the little church of St. Peter ad Vincula which stands within the Inner Wall, and is the only church outside Rome dedicated to St. Peter " in chains." " In truth," wrote Lord Macaulay, " there is no sadder spot on earth than this little cemetery. Death is there associated, not, as in Westminster Abbey and St. Paul's, with genius and virtue, with public veneration and with imperishable renown; not, as in our humblest churches and churchyards, with everything that is most endearing in social and domestic charities; but with whatever is darkest in human nature and in human destiny, with the savage triumph of implacable enemies, with the inconstancy, the ingratitude, the cowardice of friends, with all the miseries of fallen greatness and of blighted fame."

Within the chancel are the graves of fifteen of noble blood whose names are writ on the darker pages of English history, and of whom all but two died upon the block. " Here lieth," wrote Stow, " before the high altar in St. Peter's Church, two dukes, between two queens, to wit, the Duke of Somerset and the Duke of Northumberland between Queen Anne and Queen Catherine, all four beheaded."

The axe was kept busy in Tudor days, and it was then that the Tower of London acquired its sinister reputation as the place of execution for those noble enough to be spared the indignity of the hangman's rope. If you regard the dates upon the narrow tombs within the chancel rails, you will see that ten of them fall within a period of eighteen years.

The Nine Days' Queen

Among them is that of Lady Jane Grey, the hapless child of sixteen who was for nine days most unwillingly the Queen of England. No more innocent victim ever came to the block on Tower Green, and few wiser or more brave. She did not even know, so the story

HIGH ALTAR OF ST. PETER AD VINCULA

Built in the twelfth century and rebuilt in the sixteenth, this little church contains the remains of many who suffered on Tower Hill. Beneath the altar lies James, Duke of Monmouth, who rebelled against James II.

runs, how to place her head for the fatal stroke. Yet she tied with her own hands a handkerchief to cover her eyes, refusing the headsman's aid.

Courage of another sort was shown by the aged Countess of Salisbury, brought hither for execution in 1541 because Henry VIII was unable to wreak vengeance on her famous son, Cardinal Pole.

She refused to lay her head upon the block. "So should traitors do, and I am none," she declared resolutely. Defying the headsman, she ran from him with shrieks, so that, in the language of the time, he was "compelled to fetch her off slovenly."

Tradition says that on the anniversary of her death her spirit may be seen running round the place of execution, pursued by a ghostly executioner with axe in hand.

CARVED BY UNKNOWN HANDS

The upper carving, dated 1570, bears the name and arms of Peverel. The lower refers to Lady Jane Grey.

Carvings made by Prisoners

How prisoners whiled away the dreary hours and maintained their courage may best be seen in the Beauchamp Tower, which stands nearly opposite the site of the block upon which those of royal or noble blood suffered. In the room which is shown to the public are nearly one hundred inscriptions carved in the stone of the walls. Some are but crudely scratched initials or names; others are elaborate sculptures, many showing considerable artistic skill.

Most brief, most pathetic is the single word JANE, which is carved in two separate places, and was cut, it is thought, by her boy husband, Lord Guilford Dudley, some say while he was waiting to be called to execution. The Lady Jane Grey was never lodged in this tower, but in the house of the Gentleman Jailer below the Green. All five Dudley brothers were, and one of them, John, Earl of Warwick, amused himself by cutting a puzzle picture, the Dudley Rebus, the meaning of which has never been completely deciphered.

Many philosophic utterances, signed and unsigned, are to be read on these tragic walls. "Be wyse ande pacyente in troble," wrote William Rame in 1559. "Hope in God," an unknown hand has scratched. Charles Bailly, an adherent of Mary Queen of Scots, in prison comes to the conclusion that "Wise men ought circumspectly to see what they do, to examine before they speake, to prove before they take in hand, to beware whose company they use, and above all things to whom they truste." The last clause suggests that Bailly had been over-confident in trust. Perhaps a similar experience induced Thomas Clarke to write a few years later, "Hit is the poynt of a wise man to try and then trust, for hapy is he whome fyndeth one that is just." Imprisonment in the Tower prompted, it seems, much moralising.

Raleigh in the Tower

Not all prisoners spent their time carving inscriptions. Sir Walter Raleigh, who in all spent eighteen years in the Tower, wrote the first part of a *History of the World*, made experiments in chemistry, and enjoyed the society of his many friends.

"Hither came to him," wrote a nineteenth-century author, "the wits and poets, the scholars and inventors of his time; Jonson and Burrell, Hariot and Pett; to crack light jokes; to discuss rabbinical lore; to sound the depths of philosophy; to map out Virginia; to study the shipbuilder's art."

"None but my father would keep such a bird in such a cage," sighed Prince Henry, whose early death may have completely altered English history, for he was far wiser than his ill-fated brother Charles.

Raleigh had several terms of imprisonment in the Tower. A number of cells are connected with his name, most of them probably incorrectly, but he was certainly incarcerated in the Bloody Tower for thirteen years. When his health broke down through close confinement he was allowed to exercise upon the ramparts leading from the Bloody Tower to the Bell Tower, and to live in the Garden

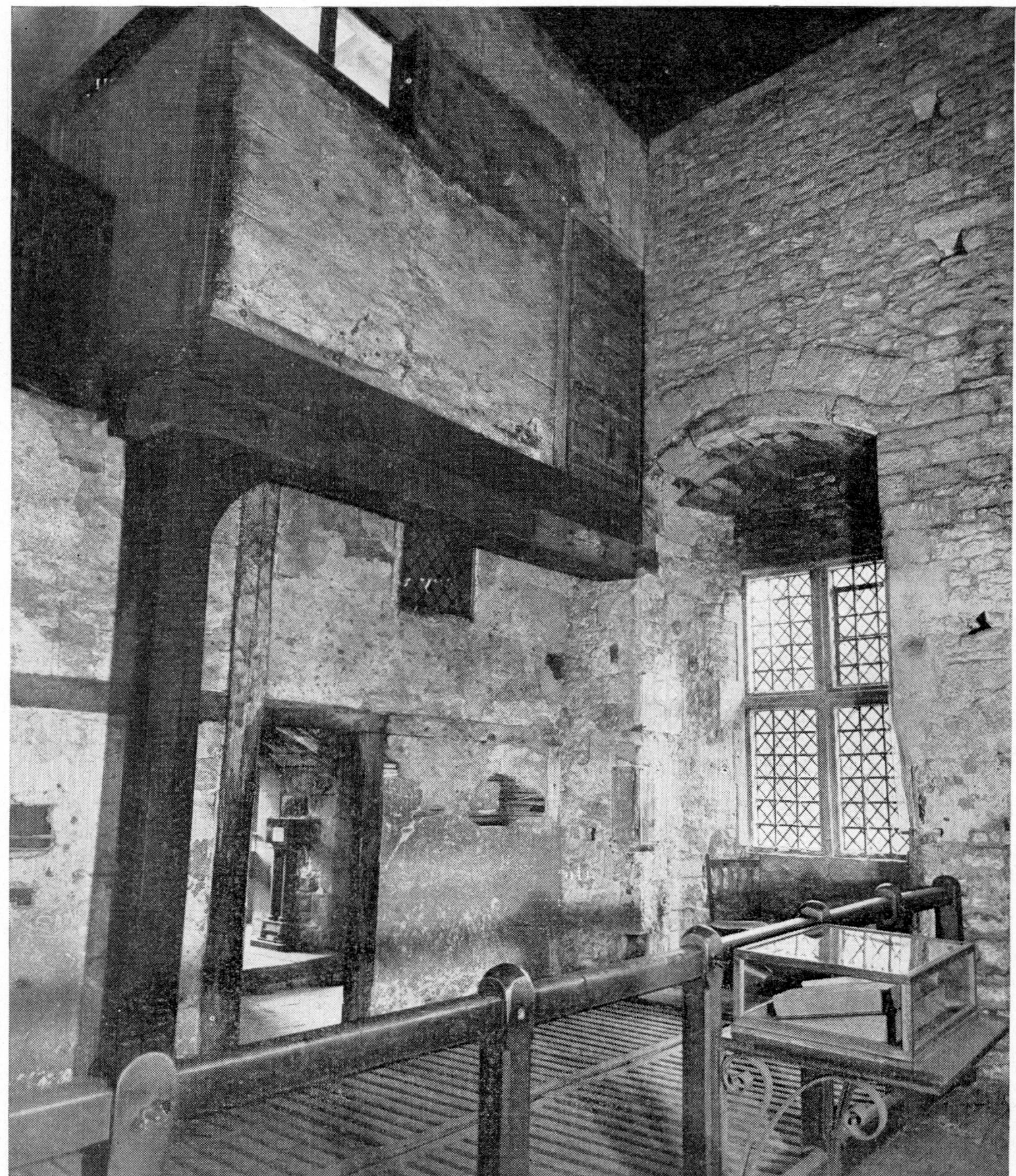

GRIM INTERIOR OF THE BLOODY TOWER

Built during the second half of the fourteenth century, the Bloody Tower was known originally as the Garden Tower, owing to its proximity to the open space where stood formerly the Constable's garden. The Tower probably gained its grim sobriquet shortly after 1483, the year in which the little Princes, Edward V and his brother the Duke of York, were imprisoned there and murdered, as all men believe, by their uncle, Richard, Duke of Gloucester. Among notable later captives confined in the Bloody Tower were Sir Walter Raleigh and Archbishop Laud, who was executed in 1645. While a prisoner, Laud was asked by Wentworth, Earl of Strafford, to bless him as he went to execution. The archbishop put his hands out of the heavily barred window, gave the blessing and, overcome with emotion, fell fainting to the floor. The Bloody Tower contains one of the few working portcullises extant.

House, a more pleasant building long since demolished.

The crews of passing ships, when they saw the well-known figure pass along the walls, would break into cheers for one who, whatever his faults, was among the greatest colonisers of his time.

Few quarters of the Tower of London are without their tale of blood, but the small, squat, immensely strong Bloody Tower has outrun them all, not merely in its quota of " black and midnight murder," but in every type of sombre association.

Built during the reigns of Edward III and Richard II, it had for many years no evil reputation. It was originally known as the Garden Tower, and was, no doubt, a comparatively pleasant spot.

Murder of the Princes

Then in May, 1483, Richard, Duke of Gloucester, brought the young boy King Edward V to London and lodged him in the Tower, there to await the time when he might be crowned with all due ceremony.

Four weeks later the little Duke of York came to join his brother. Why their mother, who was under no illusion about the character of the Duke of Gloucester, ever gave him up must remain a mystery. Sir Thomas More, who wrote one of the only two contemporary accounts of the episode, says she was told that " the King lacketh a playfelowye."

Whatever the reason, Elizabeth Woodville surrendered him to his uncle, Gloucester, who received him with " many lovynge wordys " and conducted him " through the citie honourably unto the Tower."

Probably the rest of the story must remain shrouded in mystery for all time, though few people now have any doubts as to what happened. The little Princes went into the Tower, and were never seen free again. Sir Thomas More, who was a boy at the time, has related in detail the story of their end. The upright and honest Constable of the Tower was replaced at a moment's notice by a creature of Richard's. Then, one morning very early, three hired assassins crept along the top of the inner wall, up the dark and narrow stone staircase, and into the room where the two boys were sleeping.

One they suffocated with a pillow; the other, who awaked, was stabbed to death. The bodies were hastily buried " at the stayre foote metely depe in the grounde under a great heape of stones."

In that same place were found two hundred years later the bones of two young boys. Charles II, believing them to be the remains of Edward V and his brother, had them removed to Westminster and there given royal burial in the Abbey.

The scientific historian of the twentieth century believes nothing that is not based on indisputable material evidence. The fact that Sir Thomas More, a man of the highest integrity and who moved in the best informed circles of his day, had accepted as true the confession signed by the three murderers, was not deemed sufficient. He expressed his doubts as to whether Richard III ever contrived the death of the two princes, and suggested that Henry VII might be the guilty one.

To satisfy any doubts, in the summer of 1933 the remains were taken from the marble urn in which they reposed in Westminster Abbey and examined by an anatomist of the highest authority in the presence of distinguished witnesses.

His conclusion was that they were the bones of two boys, apparently related, of whom one was about twelve, the other between nine and eleven, but most probably about ten. If the young princes were murdered in August, 1483, Edward was then twelve years and nine months old, while Richard, his brother, was within a few days of his tenth birthday.

Evidence that was Forgotten

And there the matter rests, save that in the library at Lille in Northern France was found some time ago a forgotten manuscript written by an Italian priest who was in London when Richard Crookback rode in state through its streets to accept the crown he had been " offered."

In that manuscript it is told how the net closed round the two hapless youngsters. At first they had their own servants to wait upon them; then these were withdrawn and replaced by strangers.

When they first went to live in the Tower they were allowed to play at will on the open spaces within its frowning walls. Then this liberty was denied them, and they were kept indoors under close restraint.

For a while their wistful, young faces were to be seen peering through the closely barred, narrow windows. Then came a day after which no man ever saw them more. . . .

TRAITORS' GATE OF ABANDONED HOPE
The famous gate through which so many noble captives passed after trial and sentence in Westminster Hall. The river does not now reach the gate, but a ring to which the barges were moored still exists.

The boy king, so the Italian says, knew full well his doom was fixed, and that there was no escape. Every day the poor little lad confessed his sins—what sins could have been possible at such a time and in such a place?—that he might be ready to meet his God.

Smiles Brought Curses

The Italian tells us, too, that the moment the whisper ran round London of the deed that had been done, men's hearts turned like flint against Richard, and that when he smiled upon them in their streets the citizens averted their gaze and cursed him under their breath.

Another unexplained mystery occurred about a hundred years later. Henry Percy, eighth Earl of Northumberland, whose elder brother had been executed for conspiring on behalf of Mary Queen of Scots, fell under Elizabeth's displeasure and was thrown into the Tower.

One night the alarm was raised. The Lieutenant of the Tower was called to the Earl's room, where he found him lying in a pool of blood. He had been stabbed to death. The official account said suicide, but . . .

There was no question about suicide when Sir Thomas Overbury met his end here in 1613. No more disreputable scandal has ever stained the pages of English history. Overbury, friend and adviser of King James I's favourite, Robert Carr, Earl of Rochester, had made the fatal mistake of incurring the hatred of a most unscrupulous woman.

Plied with Powdered Diamonds

Rochester fell in love with the young and beautiful but depraved Countess of Essex, and proposed to marry her when she could get a divorce from her husband. Overbury opposed the marriage. The lady was furious; after canvassing other less wicked means of getting rid of him, she had him committed to the Tower and set to work to ensure that "he should return no more to this stage." To achieve her end, accomplices within and without the Tower were bribed, and a system of slow poisoning was begun. But Overbury's constitution was robust and though his would-be murderers, according to their own later confession, plied him with arsenic, cantharides, lunar caustic, mercury and even powdered diamonds, all these together failed to kill him.

They resorted to stronger measures, and in September a clyster put an end to Overbury's sufferings. He was hastily buried,and it was given out that he had died of a loathsome and contagious disease. A few days later Rochester, now Earl of Somerset, married his Countess amidst revels which lasted for weeks.

Twelve months later the story leaked out. The four minor characters in the tragedy were hanged, but the Earl and Countess of Somerset, thanks to royal favour, were pardoned. Such was justice under the Stuarts.

End of Judge Jeffreys

It was another Stuart who sent Judge Jeffreys to conduct the "Bloody Assizes" in the west after Monmouth's unhappy attempt to gain the Crown. When his royal master fled from England, Jeffreys thought it also time to go, but he was less fortunate than James II.

A law clerk spied him peering out of the window of a tavern in Wapping, and had him arrested. Shaking with terror, Jeffreys was conveyed to the Tower through a raging mob howling for his death. He very narrowly escaped lynching, but survived to die a natural death in the Bloody Tower on April 18, 1689.

The Wakefield Tower, now daily thronged with visitors who come to see the Crown Jewels, is not without its sombre memories, for tradition says that in the very room in which the regalia are now kept the wretched half-saint, half-imbecile King Henry VI was murdered as he knelt in prayer. It is significant that Richard, Duke of Gloucester, was present in the Tower that same night.

On May 21, the anniversary of Henry's death, three lilies, tied with Eton blue ribbon, are every year placed on the stone inscribed with his name in the Wakefield Tower. Henry VI founded Eton College, and the school remains mindful of "her Henry's holy shade."

The British regalia are the only Crown Jewels in the world displayed for public exhibition. The crowns and most of the other pieces are comparatively modern, for Cromwell destroyed the ancient regalia. Only the anointing spoon and the ampulla, or eagle of gold, are really old, and both of these have been restored. Some of the pieces of royal plate date from the sixteenth century.

The Imperial State Crown was made for the coronation of Queen Victoria in 1838, and has been twice altered, on the latter occasion so that one of "The Stars of Africa" cut from the Cullinan diamond might be inserted in the front. The other "Star of Africa," the largest cut diamond in the world, is in the royal sceptre.

Many of the jewels in the Imperial State Crown—there are over 3,200 altogether—were taken from older crowns. Among them is a ruby which, presented to the Black Prince in 1367, was worn by Henry V at Agincourt.

The oldest pieces of the present regalia were made for the coronation of Charles II. Barely eleven years after they had been fashioned, a daring attempt was made to steal them. The Crown Jewels were then, and for long afterwards, housed in the Martin Tower, which stands at the north-east corner of the inner wall.

One day in April, 1671, a "parson" and his "wife" called upon Mr. Talbot Edwards, the custodian, who had the right to show the regalia to the public upon payment of a fee. After the pair had viewed the jewels, "Mrs. Blood" was seized with a sudden attack of faintness, and her "husband" requested that she might be allowed to rest awhile to recover.

Mrs. Edwards, the keeper's wife, was kindness itself. She took the lady up to lie on her own bed, brought brandy and restoratives, and looked after her with the utmost consideration.

When "Mrs. Blood" had sufficiently revived, she and her "husband" were, not unnaturally, profuse in their thanks, and a few days later they returned to the Tower with a little present—four pairs of white gloves for Mrs. Edwards.

Parson Blood Proposes Marriage

Such civilities invited friendship, and it was not long before Parson Blood was on such good terms with the Edwards that he was proposing a marriage between their pretty daughter and his nephew, a young fellow whom he described as having an income of two or three hundred pounds a year—a very tidy competence in those days. The proposal was readily accepted, and May 9 was fixed for a first meeting of the young pair. At seven o'clock in the morning on the appointed day, Parson Blood arrived with three male companions. His wife, he explained, had been delayed and he suggested

CROWN JEWELS IN WAKEFIELD TOWER

The Wakefield Tower, which dates from the fourteenth century, adjoins the Bloody Tower. Here the Royal Regalia have been kept since 1841. On the topmost tier is seen the Imperial State Crown, made for Queen Victoria. It contains over 3,200 jewels, some of which were taken from older crowns.

they should not go upstairs until she arrived. While they were waiting, would Mr. Edwards be so kind as to show his nephew and friends the regalia, which they had never seen? One of them would watch for Mrs. Blood.

Stealing the Crown

The old man—he was seventy-seven years of age—would be only too pleased. He conducted them at once to the jewel room, and led them in. As he closed the door, the three villains sprang upon him, threw a cloak over his head, and then forced a gag into his mouth.

Talbot Edwards, for all his age, had plenty of courage. Told that he would be killed if he made a sound, he made as much as he could. One of the ruffians knocked him down with a mallet; he lay as one dead.

Then Blood took the crown, his companion Parrot the orb, while the third robber began to file through the sceptre, this being too large for easy concealment. But they were suddenly disturbed.

By an extraordinary coincidence, Talbot Edwards' son, a soldier who had been serving abroad, had quite unexpectedly come home on leave. Seeing a stranger—the sentry whom Blood had left on guard—he naturally assumed him to be a visitor wanting to see the regalia, and offered to show him upstairs.

The sentry took fright and rushed to the jewel room to warn the robbers. The son followed him; Talbot Edwards, ridding himself of the gag, began lustily to shout "Treason! Murder!" His daughter, hearing his cries, ran out and gave the alarm.

Flung Away the Sceptre

Blood made a bold attempt to get away with the spoils. Abandoning the sceptre, he and his accomplices rushed off with the crown and the orb. A warder who attempted to stop them was shot at, and for a time they evaded pursuit by pretending to be in chase of the robbers.

"It was a gallant attempt, however unsuccessful; it was for a crown," was Blood's comment when he was finally overpowered.

Apparently, Charles II took the same humorous view, for Blood, instead of going to the scaffold, was not only pardoned but estates he had forfeited were returned to him. There have been those who have suggested that the

Merry Monarch was privy to the attempt on the Crown Jewels, and was to have received his share of the proceeds had the robbery been successful.

Countless other tales could be recorded of the Tower, where every turret has its story, every stone its memory.

One of the very few stories with a happy ending has its scene in the King's House, that beautiful Tudor building which stands between the Bloody Tower and the Bell Tower, so called because it carried the alarm bell of the fortress. This bell is still used every night at sunset to ring curfew.

Saved by a Woman's Daring

What is now the Governor's drawing-room was once the Council Chamber. Next to this room is a very much smaller one. In this Lord Nithsdale, a Scottish peer who had taken part in the Jacobite rebellion of 1715, was confined after being sentenced to death.

The night before he was to have been executed he escaped. The story is a familiar one, but it will always bear retelling, for it is that of a woman's love inspiring her to fearless courage.

Lady Nithsdale, who had followed her husband to London on hearing of his capture at Preston, tried by every legal means to obtain his pardon. When these failed, she did not despair, but set to work to make herself popular among the guards placed in charge of him, and to spread the belief among them that his pardon was only a matter of time.

The day before her husband was to die she came with two friends to pay him a final visit. Trusting that the favourable impression she had made among the gaolers would render them somewhat lax, and relying upon the fact that many people were coming and going in the house, she staked all upon a daring plan.

She with two friends came to the room where her husband was confined. Quickly they disguised him as a woman, dressing him in petticoats, hood and muffler.

When all was ready, they opened the door, and two weeping women issued forth into the outer chamber. Then, in Lady Nithsdale's own words, "the guards opened the door, and I went downstairs with him, still conjouring him to make all possible dispatch. As soon as he had cleared the door I made him walk before me, for fear the sentinel should take notice of his walk, but I continued to press him to make all dispatch he possibly could. At the bottom of the stairs I met my dear Evans (her faithful Welsh serving-maid) into whose hands I confided him."

Then, in order that her husband might get clear away, this courageous woman actually returned to her husband's prison chamber, and for a considerable time held an imaginary conversation with him, imitating his voice and pacing up and down the room with his step.

At last—and what superb acting this final scene must have required!—"I opened the door and stood half in it, that those in the outward chamber might hear what I said, but held it so close that they could not look in. I bade my lord formal farewell. . . ."

Lord Nithsdale made good his escape; his heroic wife was arrested, but happily pardoned, and the devoted pair lived together in Italy for thirty-two years.

By that time the long reign of the block on Tower Hill was over. The last head to fall under the executioner's axe was that of Simon Fraser, twelfth Baron Lovat, who, after a long life stained by every variety of treacherous crime, came to a well-merited end in 1747.

Hogarth sketched the aged rogue—he was about eighty at the time—as he was being borne to trial in a litter. Lovat is shown ticking off on his fingers the names of the clans who had taken part in the rebellion, no doubt with the possible idea of gaining a pardon by betraying them, for double-dealing was his special forte.

Jest from the Scaffold

On this occasion it availed him nothing, and accepting the inevitable he went to his death with a jest on his lips. As he stood on the scaffold, a stand bearing spectators collapsed. "The mair mischief the mair sport," he chuckled.

Then, as he laid his head upon the block, he murmured the old Latin saw, *Dulce et decorum est pro patria mori* (Sweet and proper is it to die for one's country).

Since those days the Tower has known many vicissitudes, though chiefly of a more peaceful nature. State prisoners continued to be lodged there until 1820, when the Cato Street conspirators, who had plotted the assassination of the members of the Cabinet, were confined within its walls. This practice was resumed during the World Wars of 1914–18 and 1939–45.

In 1792, when England was seething with popular discontent, the Tower was hurriedly fortified against the possibility of a siege, but nothing came of it. In 1830, when the agitation for the Reform Bill was at its height, the Duke of Wellington had the moat cleaned out, deepened and filled with water. His political opponents declared he was preparing the fortress against an attack by the Reformers.

Thirteen years later the moat was filled in, and became, as we know it to-day, a parade ground and lawns. This was two years after the great fire of 1841, which destroyed the armouries, almost reached the regalia, and threatened the entire fortress with destruction.

Neglect of the Tower

During the first half of the nineteenth century the Tower reached the lowest depths of neglect. Harrison Ainsworth wrote his famous romance, *The Tower of London*, very largely to stir the public out of their apathy, and to prevent Britain's most venerable medieval fortress from being allowed to crumble into ruin.

His book had very considerable effect, and during the past eighty years or so increasing care has been taken of the building, while the number of visitors has grown steadily, until now, during the summer months, an average of 4,000 a day view the Tower and its treasures. As popular demand has increased, more and more of the fortress has been thrown open to public exhibition, and there are few spots of surpassing interest into which the curious may not now penetrate.

It is not possible to show the whole, for large parts of the Tower are inhabited. Including the infantry regiment which is stationed there—usually a battalion of Guards—between 700 and 800 people live within its walls. The Constable of the Tower, whose office stretches back in an unbroken line to the Conqueror's day, is not now resident, but the Resident Governor occupies the Queen's House.

Nearby dwell the Yeomen Warders of the Tower, whose picturesque red and black Tudor uniforms form one of the main attractions for many visitors. Thirty-seven of these are always on duty during the day. They are all retired warrant officers or non-commissioned officers of high rank with magnificent army records, and a finer set of men it would be difficult to discover.

They are worthy upholders of an aged and honourable tradition, their corps being the oldest in England still performing its original duties. How old it is no one knows, but certainly far older than the Queen's Bodyguard of the Yeomen of the Guard, which was founded in 1485, and with which it is often confused.

The Warders of the Tower are honorary members of the Queen's Bodyguard, but they are a distinct corps, with their own distinctive duties and privileges. Their uniform, granted them as a reward for their devotion to the Lord Protector Somerset when he was imprisoned in the Tower, closely resembles that of the Yeomen of the Guard, but lacks the cross-belt which the latter wear in full dress.

The community living in the Tower is self-contained, with its own ruler, its own regulations, its chaplain, medical officer and even coroner. It is not in the City of London, but constitutes a " liberty," an ancient right which every three years is asserted on Ascension Day by the traditional ceremony of " beating the bounds."

After a service in St. Peter's Church, a procession forms up on the parade ground. Included in it are the Yeoman Jailer, bearing the processional axe (not the execution axe, as is so often said), which in former days was borne before a prisoner, the edge towards him if he was condemned to death; a painter, who marks the bounds; and the warders in full dress uniform with halberds.

As the painter marks each bound with a red " broad-arrow " upon a white ground, the chaplain declares solemnly, " Cursed be he who removeth his neighbour's landmark." The bounds extend to St. Katharine's Docks, and it lies within the power of the Tower authorities to close the road leading from Tower Bridge.

Garden on Site of Block

A scheme has been on foot for some time to transform the whole of Tower Hill into a public open space and this was incorporated also in the post-war rebuilding plan. Already much has been done to brighten the environs of the ancient fortress. The place of public execution is now a pleasant garden. No longer do people fight for front seats to witness a traitor's death; they merely sit and sun themselves in comfort.

The happiest transformation has been that of Tower Wharf. In the days of Edward III it was a crime punishable by death to bathe in the Thames anywhere near the Tower. Six hundred years later—in July, 1934—a stretch of the foreshore beneath its walls was opened as a bathing and paddling beach for children. So now children's laughter renders joyous a spot once pregnant with tragedy.

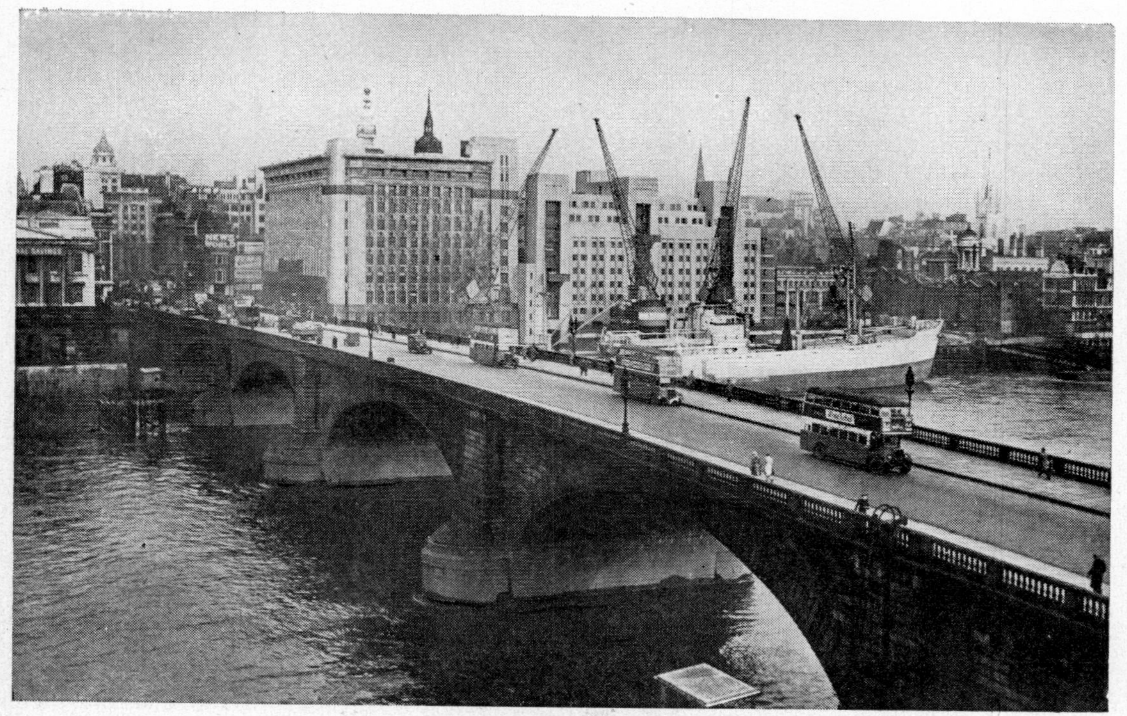

LONDON BRIDGE

John Rennie's graceful structure, opened in 1831 by King William IV. On the left is seen Fishmongers' Hall, on the right Adelaide House. Behind the latter, in Lower Thames Street, is Billingsgate Market.

LONDON BRIDGE IS BROKEN DOWN

THE old rhyme may not be so familiar to the present generation, but most elderly folk will recall it with affection. Londoners or provincials, they all sang it, and they all played nursery games to its refrain:

London Bridge is broken down,
Dance o'er my lady Lea;
London Bridge is broken down,
With a gay lady.

How shall we build it up again,
Dance o'er my lady Lea;
How shall we build it up again,
With a gay lady?

What the words meant they had no idea, nor did they bother to find out. " London Bridge " had for them no terrestrial significance; it belonged to the great enchanted world of make-believe, wherein lived little Jack Horner, Jack the Giant Killer, and Cinderella.

Later they learned better. They found out that there was a real London Bridge. The history books gave here and there brief and tantalising glimpses of a fascinating old structure which had houses and shops on it, and a tower on which traitor's heads were impaled—sometimes, one learned, adorned in mockery with paper crowns.

And there for many the matter ended. The " London Bridge " of the nursery rhyme ceased to attract, and the reality, even to those acquainted with it, proved of little interest. This is not surprising, for the present bridge has little romance to boast of, and Old London Bridge, the pride of the City for nearly six centuries, scene of countless historic events and the subject of innumerable legends, stories, verses and proverbs, has disappeared so completely from the face of the earth that hardly a stone remains. It was demolished in 1832, and the greater part of its fabric was simply thrown into the river.

So unsentimentally did those in charge of the demolition proceed that when they came across the bones of the twelfth-century builder they pitched them into the Thames as well. Thereby they did an unworthy thing. Let us remember that it was " reform " year.

One or two precious fragments of the old bridge escaped the general destruction. In a court at Guy's Hospital in St. Thomas's Street may be seen one of the stone alcoves which adorned its parapets during its later years. Two more are to be found in a far corner of Victoria Park in the East End. Very little else escaped destruction.

In 1920, during demolitions prior to the erection of Adelaide House at the north end of London Bridge, an arch of the old structure was laid bare by the excavator's pick. No funds were available to preserve this, but two of the stones were placed in the churchyard of St. Magnus the Martyr in Lower Thames Street. The road to the old bridge passed through this yard, and when Sir Christopher Wren rebuilt the church after the Great Fire of London he left a passageway under its tower for pedestrians. The Fishmongers' Company treasures a chair made of wood from the old bridge.

OLD LONDON BRIDGE
London Bridge as it appeared about 1616. Note the piers on which it was built and the gateway.

London has to-day so many thoroughfares over the Thames that it is difficult to imagine a time when it possessed only one. For centuries it must have been far more difficult to imagine London with more than one.

Built of Timber

London was born of its bridge. The town grew up in the first instance round the point nearest to the sea at which the river could be crossed. It is said, though on doubtful authority, that there was a bridge near the site of the present structure when the Romans came in A.D. 43. It is certain that the Romans had not been long in the country before they found it necessary to build a bridge that could connect London with their Kentish highway.

Whenever placed in position, the original bridge was built of timber, as were all which followed it for the next thousand years. How many different bridges there were during this period no one can say, but it is certain that there were several.

Olaf the Good of Norway destroyed one about 1014, when he was assisting King Ethelred against the Danes. The story is told in " Saint Olaf's Saga," compiled by Snorre Sturlason of Iceland in the thirteenth century :

Attacked by a Fleet

" They steered first to London, and sailed into the Thames with their fleet; but the Danes had a castle within. On the other side of the river is a great trading place, which is called Southwark. There the Danes had raised a great work, dug large ditches, and within had built a bulwark of stone, timber, and turf, where they had stationed a strong army. King Ethelred ordered a great assault; but the Danes defended themselves bravely and King Ethelred could make nothing of it. Between the castle (possibly on the site of the future Tower of London) and Southwark there was a bridge, so broad that two waggons could pass each other. On the bridge were raised barricades, both towers and wooden parapets, in the direction of the river, which were nearly breast high; and under the bridge were piles driven into the bottom of the river. Now when the attack was made the troops stood on the bridge everywhere, and defended themselves. King Ethelred was very anxious to get possession of the bridge, and he called together all the chiefs to consult how they should get the bridge broken down. Then said King Olaf he would attempt to lay his fleet alongside of it, if the other ships would do the same. It was then determined in this council that they should lay their war forces under the bridge; and each made himself ready with ships and men.

" King Olaf ordered great platforms of floating wood to be tied together with hazel bands, and for this he took down old houses; and with these, as a roof, he covered over his ships so

IN MEMORY
A baluster from old London Bridge on a tomb in the cemetery at Gravesend.

widely that it reached over the ships' sides. Under this screen he set pillars so high and stout that there was both room for swinging their swords, and the roofs were strong enough to withstand the stones cast down upon them. Now when the fleet and men were ready, they rowed up the river; but when they came near the bridge there were cast down upon them so many stones and missiles, such as arrows and spears, that neither helmet nor shield could hold out against it; and the ships themselves were so greatly damaged that many retreated out of it. But King Olaf, and the Northmen's fleet with him, rowed quite up under the bridge, laid their cables around the piles which supported it, and then rowed off with all the ships as hard as they could down the stream. The piles were thus shaken at the bottom, and were loosened under the bridge. Now as the armed troops stood thick of men upon the bridge, and there were likewise many heaps of stones and other weapons upon it, and the piles under it being loosened and broken, the bridge gave way; and a great part of the men upon it fell into the river, and all the others fled, some into the castle, some into Southwark.

"Thereafter Southwark was stormed and taken. Now when the people in the castle saw that the River Thames was mastered, and that they could not hinder the passage of ships up into the country, they became afraid, surrendered the tower, and took Ethelred to be their king. So says Othar Svarte :

"London Bridge is broken down,
Gold is won, and bright renown.
Shields resounding,
War-horns sounding,
Hildur shouting in the din!
Arrows singing,
Mail-coats ringing—
Odin makes our Olaf win!"

Another bridge collapsed during heavy floods in 1091 and a third was destroyed by fire in 1136. Some years later a London priest, Peter, Chaplain of St. Mary Colechurch in Cheapside, conceived the idea of building a bridge in stone. Such an idea is commonplace to us, but it was revolutionary then.

In spite of opposition, Peter persisted, and in 1176 made a start. To overcome the difficulty of foundations in the soft muddy bed of the river, he drove wooden piles deep into it, laid on them planks of timber 10 inches thick, and on top of these placed the main foundations of his stone piers.

Many Workmen Drowned

For long he was sadly hampered by lack of money. Then Henry II imposed a tax on wool and gave him the proceeds. From this arose the legend that the bridge was built on woolpacks.

Year after year the work went on. It was both slow and dangerous. As pier after pier was erected the rush of the tide through the arches grew ever swifter. Every now and then workmen were swept away and drowned. It is quite possible that over 200 perished during the building.

Peter himself did not live to see the completion of his masterpiece. He died in 1205 and was laid to rest in the little church he had

ALCOVE AT GUY'S
One of the alcoves from old London Bridge, now in a courtyard at Guy's Hospital in south London.

erected on one of the central piers, a church dedicated to St. Thomas Becket, who had been baptised in St. Mary Colechurch, and who, after his canonisation in 1172, was regarded by Londoners as their patron saint.

Three or four years later the last stone was laid, and London Bridge, which had taken thirty-three years to build, was complete. It was 905 feet 10 inches long and 20 feet wide above the arches, of which there were twenty. Each of its nineteen piers was protected by "starlings," which were frameworks of wood on timber piles, designed to protect the stonework from erosion by the tidal waters. Towards the northern end there was a drawbridge protected by a tower, to allow for the passage of ships.

Houses on the Bridge

How soon people began to build houses on the bridge is a matter of dispute, but it seems to have been quite early. In 1212 or 1213 a terrible disaster occurred. A fire broke out in Southwark, and, as was usual in those days of timber houses, spread with alarming rapidity.

Large numbers of people crowded on to London Bridge, either to view the sight or to escape from the flames. While they watched, fire broke out on the northern bank. According to old accounts the flames crept down to the bridge and seized upon the double row of houses thereon, thus completely trapping the people and creating a fearful panic.

Boats which rushed to the scene were sunk beneath the weight of those who endeavoured to escape, and it is recorded that 3,000 people perished.

Five Arches Swept Away

Another disaster, happily unattended by loss of life, took place in 1281, when five of the arches collapsed. The bridge had been neglected for many years, and was almost in a ruinous condition, thanks to Queen Eleanor, wife of Henry III, who had spent the very considerable income willed by pious Londoners for its upkeep upon her own personal affairs.

Some people believe that the old nursery rhyme dates from this event, though others think it had its origin when Olaf of Norway pulled down the old timber bridge.

After 1281 the structure was better looked after, and it was during the four succeeding centuries that it assumed the aspect which has rendered it so famous. During this time it was bridge, town and fortress.

Houses of timber were built along it from end to end, save that three open spaces, of which the longest was 50 feet, were preserved. The

LONDON BRIDGE IS BROKEN DOWN

The demolition of old London Bridge, from a print of January, 1832. The aged structure was torn down with great haste, as the rush of water between its piers was endangering the new bridge.

LONDON'S SECOND BRIDGE
The opening of Westminster Bridge in 1750 gave London its second thoroughfare across the Thames. Rebuilt in 1862, the bridge now carries an endless stream of motor, horse and pedestrian traffic.

houses hung precariously half on and half off the bridge, their backs over the stream and supported by struts. As storey was piled on storey, each as a rule projecting farther out than the one below, the fronts of the two rows of houses were at best only a few feet apart, and in places actually met.

According to Norden, who published a view of the bridge about 1624, it was "adorned with sumptuous buildings and statelie and beautiful houses on either side, inhabited by wealthy citizens, and furnished with all manner of trades, comparable in itself to a little city, whose buildings are so artificially contrived, and so firmly combined as it seemed to be more than an ordinary street, for it is as one continual vault or roof, except certain void spaces reserved from buildings for the retire of passengers from the danger of carts, cars, and droves of cattle usually passing that way."

Importance of the Bridge

The road across the bridge was a cobbled, miry thoroughfare only twelve feet wide. And this was London's only exit to the south-east, for many reasons the most important way out of the city. It was the road by which "Kings set out on many an overseas adventure at Calais or Crecy, Poictiers or Agincourt: over which Lord Mayors and all the great officers of the City rode out in splendour as far as Blackheath to greet the returning hosts or welcome newcomers of distinction. . . ."

It was also a favourite social rendezvous, a great place for joustings and tournaments, a standing-ground for pedlars, and on occasion the scene of furious brawls or even civil strife. It is not surprising to read that people used to be crushed to death when the bridge was crowded, that they not infrequently fell or were pushed over the parapet, or that in the all too numerous fires they were often trapped and burned to death.

Danger of the Arches

But dangerous as was life on occasion upon the bridge, the casualties beneath it were probably far more numerous. So narrow were the arches that the bridge acted as a dam against the river tides. The water piled up against the piers and roared through the arches at tremendous speed, falling as much as six feet and creating dangerous whirlpools and eddies. Beneath one of the arches Peter Morrice, a Dutchman, built a water-wheel in 1588 to supply the city with water. Eventually

THE EMBANKMENT AND THE

The new Waterloo Bridge, built of reinforced concrete, was opened on August 11, 1942. On the left of the bridge may be seen the Embankment and Cleopatra's Needle, backed by Shell-Mex House and the Savoy

five of these contrivances were erected. In time it became a well-known saying that " London Bridge was made for wise men to go over and fools to go under."

Among the strangest of the buildings on the bridge was Nonesuch House, a timber structure brought from Holland in Queen Elizabeth's reign, embellished with cupolas and turrets, and erected without a single nail, wooden pegs and dovetailing being used instead. " Each front," we are told, " was ornamented with a profusion of transom casement windows, with carved wooden galleries before them, while richly-sculptured wooden panels and gilded columns were to be found in every part of it."

The southern end of the bridge achieved a grim notoriety from the custom of impaling on the turrets of the gate the heads of traitors and other executed persons. So far as is known the first head to be impaled on London Bridge was that of the Scottish patriot Wallace in 1305.

There were at one time two gates at the Southwark end, with a drawbridge between. The Great Stone Gate fell down in 1437, and thereafter the heads were fastened on the " new " stone gate.

During the eighteenth century the aged structure became a public nuisance, both because it was so constantly needing repair and also because it had become so inadequate for London's traffic needs.

Yet the City Fathers could not make up their minds to replace it. The opening of Westminster Bridge in 1750 produced a volume of criticism of London Bridge; seven years later the houses were removed, the roadway was extended to thirty-one feet wide and a seven-foot pavement was made on either side.

Lightened and widened, the venerable structure lasted another seventy years or more. Even when its end was finally decreed, many could not believe the news. Readers of Charles Dickens will remember the opinion of the coalheavers of Scotland Yard that " if the Lord Mayor contemplated any such dark design, he would just be clapped up in the Tower . . . and then killed for high treason."

On March 15, 1824, the first pile of the new bridge was driven in. It was the Sailor King,

NEW WATERLOO BRIDGE
Hotel. Behind the left-hand arch are Somerset House and King's College. A number of the City churches, St. Paul's Cathedral and Faraday House can also be seen. On the right are wharves and warehouses.

William IV, who on August 1, 1831, declared open the bridge we use to-day.

All London went *en fête*. The new King was exceedingly popular, and his queen, Adelaide, who came with him, was greatly beloved. The royal party came by barge from Somerset House between serried rows of gaily painted and decorated craft. One hundred bands were massed to give appropriate music, and for seven hours artillery salutes roared over the thronged but unruffled Thames.

Designer of London Bridge

The new bridge, which had five arches only in place of the twenty of old London Bridge, was designed by John Rennie the elder, who was responsible also for the first Waterloo Bridge. He died in 1821, long before construction was begun, and his two sons, John and George, took charge.

The new bridge cost about £500,000, but three times that amount was spent on making suitable approaches to it from either bank. It was far higher than the old bridge, the level of which can be judged either from the churchyard of St. Magnus the Martyr or from Southwark Cathedral, the purlieus of which are now well below street level.

One of the most beautiful of the bridges across the Thames, London Bridge to-day gets little appreciation, chiefly because it is quite the most difficult to see. On either side the river wharves prevent access to the bank, and though a clear view may be obtained from Tower Bridge, it is rather too distant for full appreciation.

Built entirely of granite, the bridge is 928 feet long and 63 feet wide. Its original width was 54 feet, but in 1903–4 the pavements were extended beyond the width of the piers.

Though it can never attain the fame of Old London Bridge, the present one has an important geographical significance. It is the dividing line between east and west London, and it is the highest point attained by ocean-going steamers of any size.

Only small steamers, barges, lighters and boats can go " above bridge," but " below bridge " one is immediately in the region of docks and wharves. In this respect London

Bridge is a unique feature of the world's greatest city.

The days when London was served by a single bridge are now receding into the remote past. It is over 200 years since the old Westminster Bridge (rebuilt 1846–62) was thrown across the river. Old Waterloo Bridge, so called because it was opened on the anniversary of the historic battle which freed Europe from the terror of Napoleon, dated from 1817, Southwark Bridge from 1819. The latter was rebuilt by the Corporation of London in 1921; the demolition of the former, which was necessitated by the subsidence of two piers, was begun by the London County Council in 1934. It was replaced by a bridge of five spans in reinforced concrete, faced with Portland stone, which was opened to traffic on August 11, 1942.

There were many regrets over the passing of Waterloo Bridge, which, designed by George Dodd and constructed by John Rennie, was held by not a few to be the finest structure of its kind in Europe. Its huge blocks of grey granite, impressive both in size and strength, yielded but slowly to the demolition gangs. The new bridge, though admirably utilitarian, and impressive in its vast sweep, is not an artist's substitute for Rennie's masterpiece.

London's most picturesque bridge, Tower Bridge is comparatively modern; it was constructed by the Corporation of London and opened in 1894. The raising of its giant bascules, which have a span of 200 feet, is a sight of never-failing interest.

Among London's newest Thames bridges are Lambeth Bridge, opened in 1932, Twickenham Bridge (1933), Chiswick Bridge (1933). Altogether there are now, in the area controlled by the Port of London Authority, over twenty bridges.

Tunnelling beneath the river presents peculiar difficulties, as the projectors of the original Thames tunnel found to their cost. The idea was mooted in 1823 by Mark Isambard Brunel,

LONDON'S MOST INTERESTING BRIDGE

Visitors throng to see the raising of the bascules of Tower Bridge. The massive towers are 120 feet high from the river piers, and the raised footway is 142 feet above high water.

LAMBETH BRIDGE AND PALACE

The present bridge, opened in 1932, replaced what has been described as the cheapest and ugliest bridge ever built. It was a suspension bridge, constructed in 1862, and carrying only two lines of traffic.

father of the more famous I. K. Brunel, and backed by, among other influential persons, the Duke of Wellington.

Brunel, who was assisted by his son, was unhappily advised by the geologists he consulted, for they told him to keep far too close to the bed of the river. Soon after work was commenced in March, 1825, subsidences and irruptions of water began to endanger the lives of those engaged upon the project. Thanks to Brunel's consummate genius, the tunnel was pushed to the centre of the river without fatal accident, but on August 12, 1828, a terrible catastrophe occurred. The river burst into the workings, several men were drowned, and owing to the ensuing public alarm and a lack of funds the whole project was abandoned for seven years.

First Thames Tunnel Completed

Work was resumed in 1835. Four times during the next six years the Thames poured threateningly into the tunnel, but each time, so skilfully had Brunel guarded against the danger, all the men at work were safely withdrawn. At last, on August 13, 1841, the great engineer descended at Wapping into the tunnel which had cost so much in life, labour and money, and emerged at Rotherhithe, the first man ever to traverse the Thames by an underground route.

The Thames Tunnel was formally opened in 1843; 1,200 feet in length, it remained a public thoroughfare only until 1866, when it was acquired by the East London Railway; it is still used by London Transport.

All the other Thames tunnels are modern. Two cater for foot passengers and vehicles, two for foot passengers only, and five for tube trains. Of the first mentioned the Blackwall Tunnel (1897), connecting Poplar with Greenwich, is 1 mile 279 yards long, of which 377 yards are beneath the river; the Rotherhithe Tunnel (1908) is 1 mile 332 yards long, with 474 yards beneath the river. The tunnels for pedestrians only are at Greenwich and Woolwich, and are respectively 406 and 552 yards long. On the river above the latter plies a free passenger and vehicle ferry.

Subway for Omnibuses

Another tunnel, the Tower Subway, was opened in 1870 to relieve the congestion of the London streets. It caused a sensation at the time, for its designers, P. W. Barlow and J. G. Greathead, astonished everybody by keeping a dual promise to construct it within twelve months at the surprisingly low cost of £16,000. Profiting by Brunel's errors, they drove deep into the impermeable London clay, bored their tunnel at an average depth of 30 feet below the river bed, and, far from being troubled by irruptions of the Thames, had to send down water to the workmen to enable them to mix their cement. The tunnel, 1,340 feet long, first carried a light railway bearing a passenger omnibus, and was later used for pedestrians. It was closed up when Tower Bridge was opened.

In 1936 work began on a tunnel between Dartford and Purfleet. This scheme, originally sanctioned in 1930 but held up, first by trade depression and then by the war, will provide a much-needed link between north and south banks of the Thames estuary.

The tunnel, which is to be rather more than a mile in length, will connect on the north bank with the Purfleet-Grays Road, on the south with the Folkestone and Dartford bypass roads.

It will considerably ease the demands on Blackwall and Rotherhithe tunnels, both of which are badly congested. In December, 1938, the Highways Committee of the L.C.C. recommended that Blackwall Tunnel should be duplicated forthwith, at a total cost of £3,122,000, to be spent over nine years; this scheme, like a number of other projects, was shelved on the outbreak of the war.

Since 1914 the tunnel traffic has quadrupled, while it has become necessary to add new ferry boats at Woolwich, so greatly has the traffic there increased.

BLACKWALL TUNNEL

Opened on behalf of Queen Victoria by the Prince of Wales in 1897; links Poplar with East Greenwich.

This is mainly due to the Royal Arsenal, which owes its origin to an accident. In 1716 the Government gun-foundry was at Moorfields, and several distinguished visitors were watching the casting of a cannon. Among the company was Andrew Schalch, a Swiss, who noticed that the moulds were damp. No notice was taken of his warning that when the metal was poured there would be an explosion, and the inevitable happened. Schalch escaped, was made master-founder, and chose Woolwich for the new Arsenal.

London's traffic has always been a serious problem, and to-day a vast number of vehicles on cross-country journeys is compelled to pass through London in order to cross the river. It is probable that in the near future several new bridges and tunnels will have to be undertaken; for even though the railway bridges at Charing Cross and Blackfriars may be demolished and one great terminus be built at Waterloo, this will merely add to the enormous traffic by road.

THE POOL OF LONDON

The Pool is that stretch of the Thames between Tower Bridge and London Bridge from which this view was taken. The Tower Bridge opens in order to allow the large ocean-going ships to enter the Pool.

CORONATION OF HENRY IV

The first English King to be crowned in Westminster Abbey was Harold, who in 1066 seized the throne after the death of Edward the Confessor. Henry IV became King by the will of the people, not by succession.

WESTMINSTER'S HALLOWED FANE

THE spirit of England through the ages is epitomised in Westminster Abbey as nowhere else.

Why should this be? How is it that Wren's mighty church on Ludgate Hill and the storied battlements of the great Tower that stands guard over London's river are less mentioned in this connection? Why was it that, as he was about to engage in one of the most important naval battles in history, Nelson's thoughts flashed back to Westminster Abbey? Why did King Edward IV, writing to the Pope more than three hundred years before Trafalgar, speak of the Abbey " as placed before the eyes of the whole world of Englishmen," and add that any benefit it received would be " welcome to all of English blood? "

Why did the republican, priest-hating followers of Oliver Cromwell consider the resting-place of kings and monks a fit sepulture for their hero? How was it that Cromwell, who thought so little of turning cathedrals into stables, originated the custom of laying great commoners to rest in the Abbey by interring there the remains of Admiral Blake?

Lastly, how did it come about that, though St. Paul's is the traditional burial-place of famous soldiers and sailors, the grave of the Unknown Warrior is in the nave of Westminster Abbey?

The answers to these questions are not immediately obvious, nor can they be expressed in a single sentence.

St. Paul's is the Abbey's nearest rival; but whereas the latter is indeed " placed before the eyes of the whole world of Englishmen," the former belongs in a very special sense to London alone. The church on Ludgate Hill is a cathedral, in which the Bishop of London has his throne, but the Abbey is not a cathedral (though it was so for a short period), and as a Royal Peculiar claims exemption from both episcopal and archiepiscopal authority. The antiquity of this claim is given expression in a beautiful legend which tells how the first church at Westminster was dedicated.

It happened in this wise. One night, in the year A.D. 616, a few days after the builders had put the finishing touches to the fabric, a fisherman on the Surrey side of the Thames met a stranger who asked to be ferried across the river. What is now Westminster was then an island in the marshes formed by the Thames and two streams that have their source in the Highgate hills. Having disembarked his passenger at Thorney, or Isle of Thorns, as the place was called, the fisherman saw the stranger enter the new church, which thereupon "suddenly seemed on fire with a glow that enkindled the firmament." At the same time choirs of angels were heard to burst into song, and the walls of the church were sprinkled with holy oil and water.

Dedicated by St. Peter

The astonished fisher awaited the return of the stranger, who announced himself as St. Peter and gave instructions that Mellitus, then Bishop of London, should be told that the dedication ceremony had been carried out by the Saint himself. He rewarded the fisherman with a miraculous draught of salmon, for the Thames was then no muddied stream, assuring him that he and his fellows should never lack fish as long as they gave a tithe of what they caught to the new church, and abstained from casting their nets on a Sunday.

It is said that it was upon hearing this legend that Edward the Confessor decided to build a church on the same site in lieu of a vow he had taken to make a pilgrimage to Jerusalem, and it was probably due to implicit belief in the story that the Thames fishermen for many centuries contributed a tithe of their catches to the monks of the Abbey. The legend has a further interest in that it records the Abbey's claim to date from the seventh century, like St. Paul's.

The fact that the Abbey was free from the control of London's Bishop reminds us of an even more important point, namely that it was well outside the boundaries of the City, and therefore not subject to the jurisdiction of its authorities.

The citizens of London were ever jealous of their privileges, and constantly at loggerheads with monarchs who attempted any deprivation or restriction of them. Thus, while it was highly advisable for the king to have his main residences near the chief centre of the country's wealth, it was not considered wise for him to make his home within its walls.

Westminster, being within easy reach of the City yet outside it, and being also at a point where the Thames was crossed by a much-used ford, was an obvious site for a king's palace. Edward the Confessor had his residence a little to the east of the Benedictine monastery, and he had no hesitation in choosing Westminster (i.e., the Monastery west of London) as the site of his new church. Thus was forged the first link in the long chain that connects the Abbey with royalty.

The extent of the Abbey's indebtedness to the Confessor is difficult to over-emphasize. He was regarded with respect by both the English and the Normans: by the former because he was the last Anglo-Saxon king of the old line, and by the latter because he had promised the crown to William of Normandy, whose cousin he was. His monk-like virtues made him an object of reverence long before his canonisation by Pope Alexander III, when he became "the Confessor," which means one who has suffered for his religion. The Abbey which he had built, and before whose altar his remains were placed, was inseparably connected with his name and therefore came to be regarded as a church apart. It occupied practically the whole of the ground covered by the present building, and was the first cruciform church erected in England.

Parliament in Abbey

No doubt William the Conqueror thought of the Abbey as the Confessor's church when he decided that he would be crowned there; and it was Henry III's desire that his body should lie beside the hallowed bones of the Confessor that induced him to choose the Abbey as his burial-place.

Henry III had a marked affection for Westminster. He spent immense sums of money on the reconstruction of the choir of its church, on the monastery, and on the royal palace, and he placed the Law Courts there, thus taking the first step towards making Westminster the political capital of England. In those days the abbots of the more important monasteries played a leading part in political life, and it is therefore not surprising that the early Parliaments frequently met in the Chapter

Donald McLeish

WESTMINSTER ABBEY

The west front, showing the twin towers. These were designed by Sir Christopher Wren, who built the lower portions. The upper parts were completed after his death. The west entrance of the Abbey gives direct into the nave, where the Unknown Warrior is buried. In the right-hand tower is the Warrior's Chapel. The castellated building contains the Jerusalem Chamber. On the left is St. Margaret's Church, which since 1614 has been the place of worship of members of the House of Commons. The column in the foreground commemorates former scholars of Westminster School who died in the Crimean War.

THE CONFESSOR'S TOMB
Covered with a gorgeous cloth of crimson and gold, it stands in a chapel behind the high altar.

House and Cloisters of the Abbey. More than one abbot shared the confidence of kings. The monastery of St. Peter in Westminster assumed a political as well as a religious significance.

Shrine Encrusted with Jewels

In order to guard the remains of the Confessor more fitly, Henry erected a magnificent shrine to house them. It was encrusted with jewels and gold, which the King subsequently pawned "for the pressing needs of this realm," but redeemed within a year, as he had promised to do. Henceforth pilgrims in bare feet and wearing sackcloth next to the skin, shuffled to the hallowed spot, there to pray beneath the body of the saint, for the remains reposed in a stone sarcophagus supported by slender pillars. At each corner under the cornice were movable blocks of stone. By taking them out objects could be passed from one side of the structure to the other, touching the coffin as they did so, and thus acquiring sanctity. King James II had the original casket enclosed within another.

The screen of the shrine is divided into fourteen different compartments. One of the sculptures shows the Confessor in bed with a thief kneeling at the money chest. The story goes that a servant entered the King's chamber when he believed the monarch to be asleep and helped himself to a considerable sum from the coffer which Hugoline, the King's chamberlain, had forgotten to lock. On his third appearance Edward exclaimed, "You are too covetous, youth; take what you have and fly, for if Hugoline come, he will not leave you a single doit." When the chamberlain appeared and discovered the theft the King pretended to be ignorant of what had happened. "Be at peace," replied the monarch after he had been told, "perhaps he who has taken it has more need of it than ourselves : let him have it, what remains is sufficient for us."

Peace of Abbey Precincts

To-day there hangs above the shrine a great cloth of crimson and gold, the offering of King Edward VII. Lest it be thought that only the high and mighty have contributed to the grandeur of the fane, be it added that the two silver-gilt candlesticks at the high altar were the gift of one Sarah Hughes, whose claim to fame was no more than that of a humble housekeeper who gave of her best.

The sense of holy peace which even to-day must impress the most casual visitor to the Abbey's precincts is a precious legacy from the members of the Benedictine community who dwelt there for at least six hundred years before the Reformation. Not all the kings who lived at Westminster were as pious as the Confessor and Henry III. Many times St. Peter's fell into ruin, but no matter what the condition of the church the monks remained faithful to it, keeping alive its sacred traditions and associations. Can we doubt that, had they not been there, the Abbey would never have attained the place it occupies in the minds of all Englishmen to-day?

Let him who would capture the real spirit of the Abbey visit the remains of its monastic buildings early in the morning before the crowds of impatient sightseers have had time to disturb their stillness and send the ghosts of the Norman monks scurrying into their secret hiding-places.

Let him, if possible, choose a day in late spring or early summer when the sun will have slightly warmed the mellow stone. Resisting the temptation to reach the monastic building through the church itself, he should enter Dean's Yard from Victoria Street, and pass thence by way of Little Dean's Yard and the Dark Cloister to the north side of Cloister Garth.

Lawns and Flowers

Let him stand in the North Cloister and look southwards across the soft greenness of the lawn to the flowers that bloom on the roof of the South Cloister. All memory of the scurrying buses and hurrying crowds of Victoria Street will fade from his mind, to be replaced by vivid pictures of the fourteenth-century monks who once worked and prayed in this very place, and he will begin to realise how much the Abbey owes to the Benedictine community of St. Peter's, Westminster. The Abbey is essentially a product of the monastic spirit of the Middle Ages, and no amount of thought on the part of present-day architects and builders could produce its like.

In the fourteenth century bookcases lined the walls of the North Cloister, for it was then a library in which the monks used to write and study. The prior had his seat there, while the senior monks had each a little desk and a stool. The West Cloister, built between 1350 and 1370, was the monastery school, where the masters of the novices gave elementary instruction to the boys of the neighbourhood, some of whom would in time take Benedictine vows. The boys used to play marbles on the stone benches, and the holes they used for this purpose can still be seen.

At the other end of this cloister, in a recess beneath an arch near the Refectory door, the monks performed their ablutions before meals. They kept their towels in four niches in the wall of the South Cloister.

In the East Cloister, part of which dates from the middle of the thirteenth century, may be seen the stone bench before which the Abbot used to kneel on Maundy Thursday, to wash the feet of his fellow monks. Thus was commemorated the similar service performed by Christ for His disciples.

Let into the floor at the southern end is a massive blue stone under which are said to rest the remains of the Abbot and twenty-six monks who fell victims of the Black Death in 1349. It is commonly known as " Long Meg," but the reason why is forgotten.

Not far away is the entrance to the Pyx Chapel, where were kept the standard pieces of gold and silver by which coinage was annually tested. Dating from the eleventh century, it was once used as a chapel, as its stone altar proves, but it has been Crown property since the Reformation. It was for long the royal treasury, but in 1303, during the absence of Edward I in Scotland, wealth to the value of £2,000,000 mysteriously disappeared. When repairing the Abbey in the nineteenth century, Sir Gilbert Scott found nailed to the door strips of the skin of a man who had been flayed alive. The Abbot and forty-eight of the brethren were suspected of having abetted the criminal, so perhaps his skin was exhibited as a reminder of what might happen to them were the robbery to be repeated. The Crown Jewels and regalia were kept in the Pyx Chapel until 1643, when they were forcibly removed by Parliament.

The eight-sided Chapter House has always been considered one of the principal glories of Westminster Abbey. Built between 1250 and 1253, it was originally intended to be used only as a Council Chamber for the members of the Benedictine community, but four years after its completion the King's advisers assembled here to discuss affairs of state, and from 1377 until 1547 the Commons of England held their meetings within its walls. This house may therefore justly be called the birthplace of English liberty, for it was here that the Commons discussed their grievances and made plans to force the will of the people on the kings and their nobles. Their last sitting in this house took place on the day of Henry VIII's death, when they attainted the Duke of Norfolk.

Where Monks were Flogged

The monks met here periodically, not only to discuss secular business, but also to administer punishment to those of the elder brethren who had transgressed. The offenders were flogged near the central pillar in front of their fellows.

In 1850 the Chapter House came under the absolute control of the Crown and was used as a storehouse for State papers. To fit it for this purpose wooden galleries were erected all round the walls and a wooden floor was put in. When the latter was taken up in the later years of the nineteenth century the beautiful old tiled pavement was discovered to be almost as perfect as when first laid down six hundred years earlier. So that these tiles may not be damaged by heavy boots all visitors are required to put on sandals before they are permitted to enter. The building was restored in 1867 after the removal of the documents.

Beneath the floor of the Chapter House is a crypt which was once a royal strong-room. Because of the thickness of its walls—17 feet in places—the Coronation Chair was kept there during the First World War; from 1939–45 it was removed from London.

The Coronation Chair

About the Stone of Scone, immediately beneath the seat of the Coronation Chair, there is much mystery and many absurd stories are told as to its origin and wanderings. It certainly ended up in Scotland, where it was used at the coronation of Scottish kings; hence it acquired a national significance which Edward I sought to destroy by bringing the stone to England.

The first English king to use it was Edward II in 1308. Since then almost every English monarch has sat on it to be crowned. Even Cromwell had it taken to Westminster Hall when he was proclaimed Lord Protector. Queen Victoria used the ancient chair twice : when she was crowned and at her Jubilee in 1887.

SIR THOMAS HUNGERFORD

A fourteenth-century Speaker of the House of Commons, which from 1377 to 1547 met in the beautiful Chapter House of Westminster Abbey.

To the amazement and disgust of all England, the Stone was stolen from the Abbey by four misguided young Scottish Nationalists on Christmas Day, 1950. It was taken to the ruined Abbey of Arbroath, where Scottish kings had formerly been crowned, but was eventually returned to Westminster on April 13, 1951. The offenders confessed, but the government wisely decided not to prosecute them.

To the south of the Chapel of the Pyx, and underneath the old monastic Dormitory, is the Undercroft, one of the most ancient parts of the Abbey, having been built in the latter half of the eleventh century. The two northern bays were probably used as the monks' common room. There they would congregate to warm themselves before the only fire the Abbey boasted. One of the other bays probably formed their shaving house.

Unique Bell in Undercroft

The Undercroft is now a museum. Among its many interesting exhibits may be noted the bell which bears the inscription, "Thos. Lester Made Me. 1742," and which used to hang outside the South Transept. It was last rung on November 11, 1918, the day of the signing of the Armistice which preluded the end of the War. Beside it rests the only medieval refectory bell in England. It summoned the monks to meals.

Leaving the Undercroft, we pass along the Dark Cloister, and turning down a vaulted passage enter what is perhaps the most charming part of the monastic buildings, the Little Cloister. Its inside walls are about six hundred years old but the houses round it were rebuilt in the seventeenth century. In the days of the monks this cloister was surrounded by the infirmary buildings, remains of which can be seen in the canons' gardens. The old infirmary chapel was the scene of a dramatic fight between the Archbishops of Canterbury and York in 1176. Each claimed precedence over the other, but it was finally agreed that the former should be Primate of All England and the latter merely Primate of England, designations which are still retained. In the same place Henry III pledged himself to observe Magna Carta.

On the east wall is a seventeenth-century inscription concerning one who "through the spotted veil of the smallpox, render'd a pure and unspotted soul to God."

Near the entrance to the Cloister is Litlyngton's Tower, formerly the residence of a Mr. Dare who had, while living there, a servant called Emma. She afterwards became Lady Hamilton and Nelson's mistress.

England's First Printed Book

The open space at the southern end of the Dark Cloister is Little Dean's Yard, which is surrounded by the buildings of Westminster School. The most celebrated of these are Ashburnham House, once the prior's house but now the school library, and the Great Hall of Westminster School, where the ceremony of tossing the pancake takes place every Shrove Tuesday.

Dean's Yard, which we enter from the north-west corner of Little Dean's Yard, was formerly the site of many monastic buildings, including the brewhouse, the granary and the almonry. In the last-mentioned Caxton kept the press which turned out the first book that was ever printed in England.

"There was an old chapel," says Stow, "over against which the Lady Margaret, mother to King Henry VII, erected an alms-house for poor women, which is now turned into lodgings for the singing-men of the college. The place wherein this chapel and alms-house stood was called Eleemosynary or Almonry, now corruptly the Armbry, for that the alms of the abbey were there distributed to the poor, and therein Islip (actually Milling), Abbot of Westminster, erected the first press of book-printing that ever was in England, about 1471, where William Caxton, citizen and mercer of London, who first brought it into England, practised it." A high ecclesiastic, on hearing the news, is said to have given vent to his feelings by remarking that "If we do not destroy that dangerous invention it will destroy us." He proved a false prophet.

South of the Dean's Yard is College Street, which follows the course of Tyburn Stream. This stream ran along the boundary wall of the old monastery, turned the Abbot's mill, and was the waterway by which the monks towed boats loaded with building materials and food from the Thames to their home.

Just off the north-east corner of this yard is the Dean's Court with the Deanery, once the Abbot's house, on its east side. It was formerly known as Cheynegates because a massive chain guarded the entrance to the courtyard.

CORONATION CHAIR
Beneath the seat is seen the famous Stone of Scone, brought from Scotland by Edward I.

Prophecy that came True

Next to the Deanery is the Jerusalem Chamber, built by Abbot Litlyngton in the fourteenth century. Access to it is gained through a small room known as the Jericho Parlour. It contains some beautiful linen-fold panelling. The Dean and Chapter have used the Jerusalem Chamber as a council room ever since the real Chapter House ceased to be their property. Henry IV died in this room of an illness which came upon him when he was in the Abbey kneeling in prayer before the Confessor's Shrine. "Wherefore they for his comfort," writes the chronicler Fabyan, "bore him into the Abbot's place, and lodged him before the fire, where he lay in great agony a certain time. At length, when he was come to himself, not knowing where he was, he freined (asked) of such as were about him what place it was. The which showed to him that it belonged to the Abbot of Westminster; and, for he felt himself so sick, he commanded to ask if that Chamber had any special name. Whereunto it was answered that it was named Jerusalem. Then said the King, 'Laud be to the Father of Heaven, for now I know that I shall die in this Chamber, according to the prophecy made of me before said, that I should die in Jerusalem.'" Henry's body was buried in Canterbury Cathedral.

Regalia Brought to Abbey

On the eve of a coronation the regalia is brought from the Tower and deposited in the Jerusalem Chamber, watched by Yeomen of the Guard. In this way the ancient right of the Abbey to keep the regalia is maintained, for Edward the Confessor is said to have left his crown and other symbols to the Abbey on the understanding that they should never be allowed to leave the church.

As we have seen, the oldest parts of the monastic buildings date from about the middle of the eleventh century, being the remains of Edward the Confessor's Abbey, which was dedicated on Childermas Day (December 28), 1065. But it is fairly certain that monks of the Order of St. Benedict had a monastery at Westminster at least three hundred years before that date. The church they used was the one St. Peter dedicated in so unorthodox a manner. It is supposed to have been built by the orders of Sebert, King of the East Saxons, in the early years of the seventh century.

The charter of King Edgar (944–975), who is stated to have reconstructed the church and to have richly endowed the monastery under the good influence of St. Dunstan, alludes to "The church of St. Peter, said to be built pursuant to the directions of King Ethelbert, by his nephew Sebert, under whose government London was then, in a certain terrible uncultivated place called 'Thorney' from the thorns growing there." The Confessor's charter also mentions Sebert as the founder: nevertheless historians profess considerable doubt on this point. A fourteenth-century tomb which is supposed to be that of King Sebert is in the South Ambulatory.

Nothing now remains of the church known as Sebert's, and very little of that built by the Confessor, although parts of the monastic buildings erected by the latter still stand, and foundations discovered below the nave in 1931 were identified as belonging to Edward's church. The Confessor died a few days after its consecration, and was buried with great ceremony before the high altar. His successor, Harold, the last of the Saxon kings, was the first monarch to be crowned in the Abbey; but before the year (1066) was out Harold had died at Senlac, and Norman William had sat in the Coronation Chair.

The Conqueror's accession to the throne was marked by a distressing incident. Soon after the coronation ceremony had begun some of William's guards, mistaking the wildly enthusiastic acclamations within the Abbey for the battle cries of Englishmen intent on the assassination of the Norman usurper, set fire to all the houses near the Abbey. The English, on the other hand, jumping to the conclusion that they had been lured unarmed to the Abbey so that they might the more easily be massacred, rushed from the ceremony to extinguish the fires and to search for weapons wherewith to defend themselves. The Abbey was thus left empty, save for some terror-stricken priests and William himself. The latter insisted that the service should go on in spite of the commotion, and he was duly crowned, though in a somewhat hasty fashion.

Massacre at Coronation

A much more serious riot marked the coronation of Richard I in 1189. The King had issued an order to the effect that no Jews were to enter the Abbey or Westminster Hall on the day of the ceremony, but some of them were so enthusiastic in their desire to witness the pageantry and to express their loyalty that they were foolhardy enough to allow themselves to be seen in the crowds that thronged the streets in the vicinity of these two places. Some trifling incident having occurred to arouse the passions of the mob, a terrible massacre of non-Gentiles began. Those who escaped the sword in the streets were pursued and burnt alive in their homes.

Ironically enough, Henry III made use of Jewish money when he started the task of reconstructing the greater part of the Abbey in 1245. A quarter of a century before that date the same monarch had laid the foundation stone of a chapel, which he dedicated to Our Lady, on the site now occupied by Henry VII's Chapel. There his wife, Queen Eleanor, was crowned amidst scenes of great magnificence. He himself was first crowned at the Abbey of Gloucester in 1216, and for the second time at Westminster Abbey just four years later.

CHOIR OF WESTMINSTER ABBEY

The gorgeous altar and reredos were designed by Sir Gilbert Scott and erected in 1867. Beneath the pavement on either side of the altar are bases of pillars of Edward the Confessor's church.

According to Matthew Paris, the King's orders in 1245 concerning "the Church of St. Peter, at Westminster," were that it "should be enlarged, and the tower with the eastern part overthrown, to be built anew and more handsome, at his own charge, and fitted to the residue or western part." Twenty-four years later the church was again opened for divine service, the whole of the eastern portion as well as the Chapter House, together with that part of the cloisters by which it was entered, having been completed. The consecration ceremony was made the occasion for the removal of the hallowed bones of Edward the Confessor from the choir to an impressive shrine behind the high altar.

The mosaic pavement of the sanctuary, the gift of Abbot de Ware, was laid about the year 1268. When intact it must have been of remarkable beauty, as can be gathered from an inspection of Holbein's "Ambassadors," in which it figures. Italian workmen, brought from Rome, laid the little pieces of serpentine, porphyry, jasper, alabaster, touchstone and basanite with loving care. A sculptured head believed to represent de Ware is to be seen in the South Transept.

If Henry III intended—as appears probable from Paris's account—that the Abbey should be left with a new Gothic eastern part (including tower, apse, transepts and choir) adjoining the old Norman nave, he must have had a curious taste in architecture, since the composite building presented an extremely incongruous appearance. Whatever his intentions, the foundation stone of the new nave was not laid until March 3, 1376, more than a century after his death. The building operations were begun by Abbot Litlyngton, who was fortunately placed in being able to use a large sum of money which had been left for the purpose by his predecessor, Simon Langham.

In 1378 the Abbey, which possessed the right of sanctuary, was desecrated by a triple murder. According to the old chronicles, two young esquires, Frank de Haule and John Schakell, who had been imprisoned in the Tower of London by John of Gaunt, made their escape and, pursued by the Tower Constable and fifty soldiers, sought refuge in the Abbey. Mass was being celebrated when the soldiers burst into the choir in search of the prisoners. One escaped them, but the other was hacked to death at the prior's stall, the victim's servant and one of the monks also falling under the blows of the assassins' axes. The crime was regarded with such horror that the Abbey was closed for four months, and the sitting of Parliament was suspended. The assassins were excommunicated by the Archbishop of Canterbury, while their principal victim, being regarded as a martyr, was accorded burial in the South Transept.

King's Jawbone as Memento

In 1766 a Westminster boy put his hand into the tomb of Richard II, then in a neglected condition, and pulled out the King's jawbone. A companion who witnessed the deed boxed his ears and confiscated the treasure. It remained in his family until 1906, when one of his descendants returned it to the Dean and the missing bone was restored. Richard II is the only English monarch known with certainty to have been married while King of England in Westminster Abbey, though George VI was married there when Duke of York in 1923.

By the beginning of the fifteenth century the outside walls of the nave had been completed up to the level of the triforium, but no further progress was made owing to lack of funds. Fortunately, Henry V, being more pious than his father, granted 1,000 marks a year to the building fund and the work continued under the supervision of Richard Whittyngton. But it was not until near the end of the century that the nave was roofed in by Abbot Esteney. Between 1500 and 1532 Abbot Islip paved the nave and effected a number of other important improvements.

Abbey's Own Flag

Two centuries after Islip's death the nave was finally completed by the erection of the two western towers, which are said to have been designed by Sir Christopher Wren, who undoubtedly suggested the addition of a tower, steeple or dome on the squat lantern over the central crossing. In one of the towers is a clock with one hand. Incidentally, it may be mentioned that the Abbey has its own flag. It incorporates the red and white rose of the Tudors, the cross and fine gold martlets of St. Edward the Confessor, and the Royal Arms as they were at the time of Queen Elizabeth.

Abbot Islip will always be remembered in connection with Henry VII's Chapel, but the name of the architect is unknown. Work was begun in 1503, after the chapels of Our Lady and St. Dunstan had been demolished to make room for it. "One of the Statelyest and Daintiest Monuments of Europe both for the Chappell and for the Sepulcher," says Bacon. Others referred to it as the wonder of the world, forgetting the other seven wonders. It remains to-day the most beautiful Perpendicular Gothic building. The superb tracery of the vaulting is without peer. The monarch whose name it bears intended it as a burial place for Henry VI, and received a permit from Pope Julius II to remove the royal bones from Windsor. He also sought canonisation for his namesake, but the necessary fees were deemed too costly, and so the King decided that in due course the chapel should be his own last resting-place. Henry VI had gone so far as to choose the exact spot for his own interment. With his feet he measured out the necessary length and commanded a mason "to marke out there the place."

In his will Henry VII gave detailed instructions concerning his statue. It was to represent him kneeling, in full armour, and holding the crown he had won from Richard III on

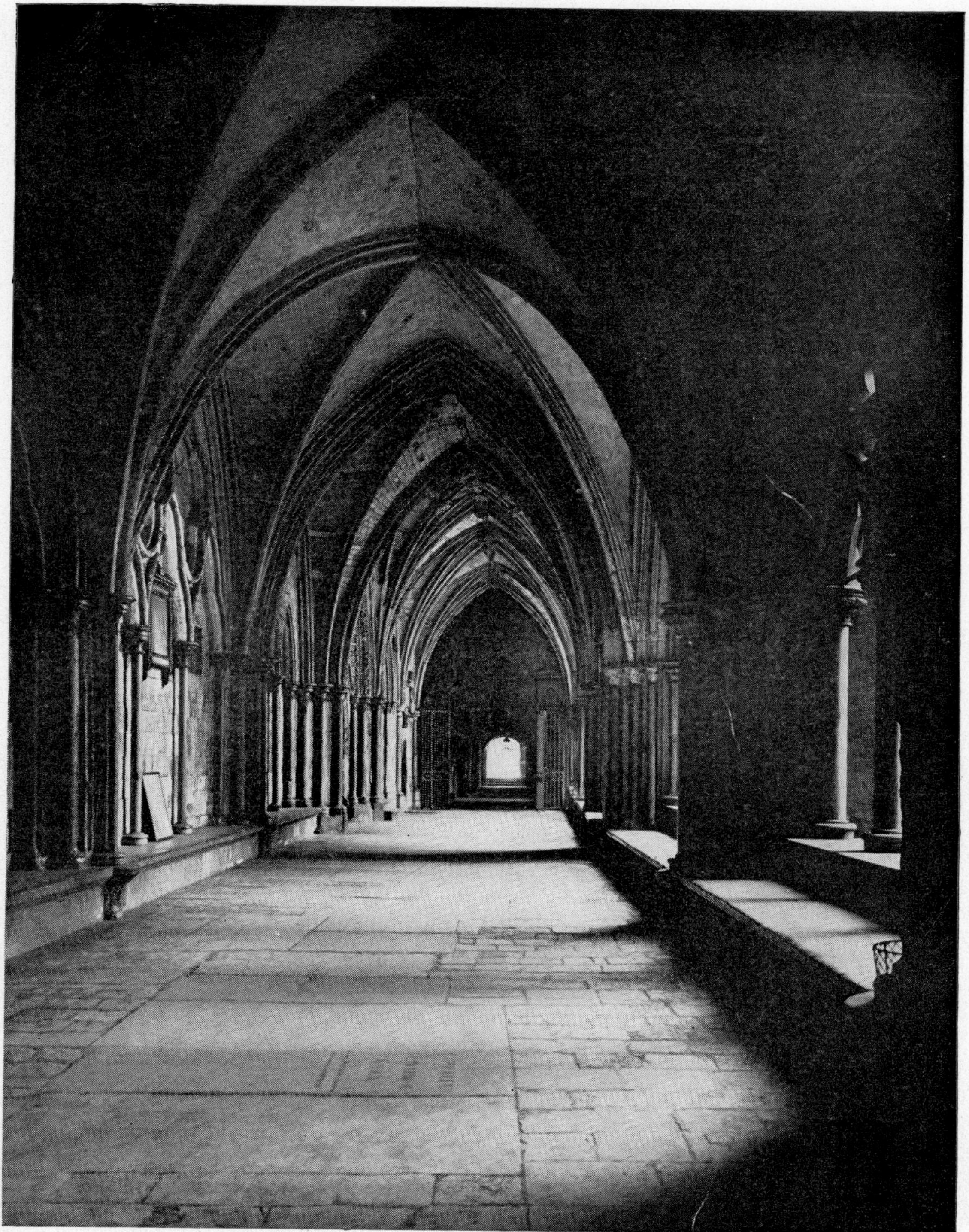

SACRED PEACE OF THE CLOISTERS

Begun in the thirteenth century and completed in the fourteenth, the cloisters of Westminster Abbey still retain the spirit of the monks who once walked and worked in their shade. On the stone floor and benches hay, straw and rushes were placed for warmth, while lamps suspended from the roof gave light.

Bosworth Field. He also requested that his funeral should be devoid of "dampnable pomp and outrageous superfluities," but those in charge of the ceremony do not appear to have respected his desire for simplicity, but rather to have spared no effort to make the pageant as impressive as possible.

Queen Elizabeth's Ring

Henry's companions in death include Queen Elizabeth, Queen Mary I, Mary Queen of Scots, Queen Mary II, Queen Anne, Edward VI, James I, Charles II, William III and George II. Near Queen Elizabeth's tomb is a pathetic relic. It is, says the inscription, "The ill-fated ring which was given by Queen Elizabeth to her favourite, Robert Devereux, Earl of Essex, with a promise of clemency should he return it to her when in need. His attempt to do so some years after was frustrated and led to his execution."

The chapel has served as the Chapel of the Order of the Bath since 1725, and the banners of the Knights Grand Cross make a colourful display. At the installation of a knight he draws his sword and hands it to the Dean, who places it upon the altar and, on returning it, pronounces what is known as the Admonition: "I exhort and admonish you to use your sword to the glory of God, the defence of the Gospel, the maintenance of your Sovereign's right and honour, and of all equity and justice, to the utmost of your power."

HENRY VII's CHAPEL

Built on the site of the original Lady Chapel of Henry III as a memorial to Henry VI.

It was formerly the custom for the King's cook to address each knight after the conclusion of the ceremony with the words, "Sir knight, the great oath that you have taken, if you keep it, will be great honour to you, but if you break it I have power, by virtue of my office, to hack the spurs from your heels." For this kindly speech he exacted the sum of four guineas!

Among the ninety-five saints whose effigies grace the building are St. Dunstan holding the devil's nose very securely with a pair of pincers; St. Matthew with a pair of spectacles reading the Bible; and St. Wilgefort with the beard that she miraculously grew when she prayed that her beauty might not be a snare to her.

A window for the chapel was being made for presentation by the magistrates of Dort, Holland, when news was received of Henry VII's death. It found its way to Waltham Abbey instead, and was later taken out and removed to New Hall, Essex. From thence it went to Copt Hall, and in 1758 to St. Margaret's Church, Westminster, a few yards from its originally intended destination.

Henry VIII Despoils St. Peter's

Henry VIII did not forget Westminster Abbey when he turned his attention to the monasteries of England. Covent Garden, much of Belgravia, and parts of Hampstead formerly included in its endowments were ruthlessly taken away. Fortunately the Abbey was spared the fate of so many monastic and sacred buildings. "The chief source of profit was the lead with which the monasteries were mostly covered," writes Cardinal Gasquet. "It was stripped from the roof of the finest church without hesitation and melted at a fire made, probably, with the wood of the stalls, screen-work or wood. . . . Bands of workmen went from place to place throughout the country, lit their fires in the naves or chancels of abbey churches, and occupied themselves for days, and even in some cases for weeks, in melting the coverings of roofs, and the gutters, spouts and pipes from the building into pigs and fodders, the sale of which might add a few pounds to the royal plunder."

In 1540 Abbot Boston and twenty-four other members of the Order of St. Benedict were turned out, to make room for the first Dean of Westminster, William Benson. Shortly afterwards the King made Thomas Thirlby Bishop of Westminster, St. Peter's Church then becoming the cathedral of the new diocese. Thirlby allowed the buildings to fall into a ruinous state, and appropriated the Abbey's revenues for unlawful purposes. This displeased Edward VI so much that in 1550 he dissolved the bishopric by Letters Patent and transferred Thirlby to the See of Norwich, at the same time vesting the government of the church in a Dean and twelve Prebendaries. Part of its revenues was transferred to St. Paul's Cathedral, whence the saying, "Robbing Peter to pay Paul."

Cathedral Becomes Abbey Again

Queen Mary did not lose much time in getting rid of the Dean and restoring the monastery with fourteen monks presided over by Abbot John Feckenham, formerly Dean of St. Paul's. Feckenham was present, in his capacity as Abbot, at the coronation of Queen Elizabeth, who was the last English monarch to receive the Crown according to the rites of the Roman Catholic Church.

In 1560 Queen Elizabeth restored the Dean and Chapter, at the same time turning St. Peter's into a collegiate church, which it has remained ever since. As then constituted, the college (Westminster School) had room for only forty boys.

During Charles I's reign and the Protectorate of Oliver Cromwell the Abbey did not fare very well. It was once attacked by a huge mob, which was only with great difficulty forced to retreat, and the edifice suffered damage at the hands of too zealous reformers.

Samuel Pepys witnessed Charles II's coronation in 1660 from "a great scaffold across the north end of the Abbey." He records his pleasure "to see the Abbey raised in the middle all covered with red, and a throne (that is, a chaire) and footstoole on top of it; and all the officers of all kinds, so much as the very fidlers, in red vests."

The Abbey had fallen into a bad state of disrepair towards the end of the century, and in William of Orange's reign Parliament was induced to make an annual grant towards its reconditioning. In 1738, however, it became necessary to petition Parliament for more money, which was obtained only with great difficulty. Twelve years later an earthquake caused the collapse of one of the piers on the north side, and in 1803 a fire broke out at the junction of the four timber roofs. Damage to the extent of £3,500 was done, but the consequences might easily have been more serious.

In 1806 the neglected condition of the Abbey aroused so much criticism that Parliament made grants amounting to about £42,000 for this purpose between 1807 and 1822. To-day the historic building is again seriously in need of attention. A Restoration Fund, amounting to about £1,000,000, has been raised by public subscription, and with this money it is hoped that the ancient glories of the Abbey will be restored.

The coronation of King George IV in 1821, which cost £238,238, was marked by a tragic incident at the doors of the Abbey. While Prince of Wales, he had quarrelled with his wife, Caroline of Brunswick, and not wishing her to be his consort on the throne had offered her £50,000 a year on condition that she renounced her royal rights. She refused the annuity and openly defied her husband by making a triumphal entry into London, whereupon the Government commenced divorce proceedings against her; but the popular outcry against this step was so great that it was found advisable to drop the obnoxious Bill.

No notice was taken of the unhappy Queen when the preparations for her husband's coronation were being made; but on the day of the ceremony, Caroline arrived at the Abbey doors to insist on her rights as the Queen of England. Not only was she refused admission, but George IV's minions considered it necessary to treat her with disgusting brutality. Less than three weeks after this shameful incident the unfortunate woman, who had always been more sinned against than sinning, died at Brandenburg House, heartbroken at the treatment she had received.

Helped by Queen Victoria

The ceremonies at the coronation of Queen Victoria in 1838 were very different from those formerly witnessed on such occasions. Following the examples of simplicity and economy set by Queen Adelaide, consort of William IV, seven years previously, she dispensed with the customary banquet in Westminster Hall and with the feudal services which it entailed.

A trivial incident revealed the young Queen's character in a most favourable light. When Lord Rolle, an infirm veteran, was retreating backwards from the throne after swearing allegiance, he stumbled and fell.

The witness we have just quoted says that "in an instant a dozen arms and hands were extended to assist him to rise; conspicuous among the number being those of the youthful maiden Queen herself, who quickly rose to go towards him as by a feminine instinct, the latter triumphing, at such a moment, over all the pageantry which surrounded her."

Until Princess Mary (Princess Royal) was married in the Abbey in 1922, only one daughter of a reigning Sovereign had given her hand in the building since 1269, when Edmund Earl of Lancaster, second son of Henry III, took unto himself a wife in the person of Aveline de Fortibus. On November 20, 1947, the Princess Elizabeth, whose father, King George VI had himself been married in the Abbey, was wedded to Lieutenant Philip Mountbatten, Duke of Edinburgh. Her Coronation as Queen Elizabeth II only five and a half years later will long remain an unforgettable scene of splendour which, thanks to the miracle of television, was seen by millions of people.

The custom of distributing Maundy Pence on the Thursday immediately preceding Good Friday is six centuries old, and was associated in former days with the washing of the feet of as many poor men as the King was years old. James II was the last monarch to perform the original ceremony; the minting of special coins had come into operation in the previous reign, that of Charles II. The required Maundy Pence is struck in silver pennies, twopenny, threepenny and fourpenny pieces as required for the King's age. In addition, £1 15s. to each woman and £2 10s. to each man is given in lieu of clothing and £1 and £1 10s. respectively in lieu of provisions. The material comforts were once paid in kind, but while food presented few problems the difficulties which arose in the matter of garments may be appreciated. Maundy is a corruption of an old Middle English word meaning something that is commanded.

MODEL OF QUEEN MARY II

This wax effigy of Queen Mary II, consort of King William III and eldest daughter of James II, is only one of several in Westminster Abbey.

Abbey's Waxwork Effigies

To modern minds the most grotesque objects in the Abbey are a number of wax effigies which remind one of Madame Tussard's exhibition in Baker Street. Some of the figures were carried in the funeral processions of the people whom they represent, and were afterwards placed on a catafalque near the grave. The first king to be featured in this way was Edward I, but the figure disappeared long since. Those which remain include Queen Elizabeth I, King William III and Queen Mary II—the only memorials of them in the church—Charles II, Queen Anne, the Earl of Chatham, and Nelson. The last-mentioned was buried in St. Paul's Cathedral, where his tomb and funeral car caused so much wonder that those in authority set up a counter-attraction in an attempt to recapture popular favour. In those days part of the emoluments of the minor canons, lay-clerks and organist was derived from what was called tomb-money; in other words, fees for showing the public the various sights.

La Belle Stuart's Stuffed Parrot

The figure of Chatham was modelled from life by Mrs. Patience Wright, and was originally shown at her exhibition of waxworks in Cockspur Street. Nearby is *La Belle Stuart*, who eloped with the Duke of Richmond and Lennox to escape the attentions of Charles II and by her side is a stuffed West African grey parrot which was her companion for forty years. Westminster boys of an earlier generation were wont to refer to these figures as the Ragged

CHAPEL OF HENRY VII

The beautiful interior of the most exquisite chapel in the Abbey, showing the banners of the Knights of the Bath, the bronze gates and the marvellous fan-tracery work in the roof. Fragments only remain of the original stained glass in the windows. Many of the stalls date from 1725, when the Chapel was arranged for the installation of the Knights of the Bath. The banners of the Knights make a gorgeous display.

Regiment, but a number of them have been carefully renovated in recent years. Some of the likenesses are declared to be excellent, particularly those of Charles II and Nelson.

Three Centuries Unburied

Of all those who found sepulture in the Abbey the body of Queen Katherine of Valois took longest in the burying. She died a widow at Bermondsey Abbey in 1437 and was interred in the Lady Chapel of the Abbey. When Henry VII pulled the building down to make room for the chapel named after him the coffin was placed by the side of her husband's tomb, and there remained for nearly three centuries. Pepys and many another were shown the remains. " I had the upper part of her body in my hands, and I did kiss her mouth, reflecting upon it that I did kiss a Queene," the diarist confided.

Orders were issued in 1778 for the coffin to be given decent burial, but it remained above ground for several years before it was put beneath the Villiers' monument in the Chapel of St. Nicholas. Finally, Dean Stanley had it placed in the Chantry Chapel of Henry V. A tomb of black marble marks the resting place of Elizabeth Tudor, child of Henry VII, whose little body was carried to the Abbey in a chair.

Folk wise and otherwise, famous and infamous, of good report and ill have been buried and commemorated among the kings.

The interment of John Broughton, pugilist and founder of the modern prize-ring, is attested by a tablet and a gravestone. Of infinitely pathetic appeal is a little memorial tablet in the Cloisters bearing the words " Jane Lister. Dear Childe."

Poet Buried Standing

One grave may contain relics of priceless worth, though it is more likely that they have turned to dust like the body of the great dramatist which was buried with them. Into the hole that was dug to contain Edmund Spenser's coffin Ben Jonson, Beaumont, Fletcher and probably Shakespeare dropped pens and poems in token of their regard. In due course Ben Jonson himself was interred nearby in a standing position. Many years later a grave-digger engaged on his mournful task came across the skull and leg bones of the poet.

There is presumably unconscious humour in some of the monuments. General Wolfe, for instance, is represented naked but supported by an officer in full regimentals, and Sir Cloudesley Shovel is shown in a Roman toga but wearing a periwig.

The face of the bust of Admiral Sir Peter Warren is pitted with smallpox. On the monument to Lieut.-Colonel Roger Townshend the British troops who fought with him in 1759 at Ticonderoga, in America, are shown wearing Roman dress. The epitaph to Gilbert Thornburgh, Gentleman of the Cellar, records that he was " formerly an earthly now a heavenly courtier."

Jonas Hanway, the first man in England to carry an umbrella, had a monument to his memory erected in the Abbey. He was a humanitarian, founder of the Marine Society for poor boys training for the sea. He was also a traveller, but only an indifferent author. " Jonas," said Dr. Johnson of him, " acquired some reputation by travelling abroad, but lost it all by travelling at home."

Abbey's Most Visited Spot

The Poets' Corner, as the South Transept is called, is one of the most visited spots in the Abbey. Here are the graves of many distinguished British authors, together with busts and memorials of others whose remains are interred elsewhere. Not by any means all are poets; in early days the western wall was called the " learned " or " historical " side on account of the scholars there buried.

English literature from Chaucer to Kipling is represented in Poets' Corner. Curiously enough, the author of the *Canterbury Tales*, though justly regarded as the Father of English poetry, did not receive Abbey burial on account of his poetic ability. Oppressed in his old age by poverty, he was given the appointment of Clerk of the Works at Westminster, and had a house in the monastery garden. It was as a dweller in the Abbey precincts that he was buried at the entrance to St. Benedict's Chapel.

For nearly a century and a half a leaden plate, " whereon," says Caxton, " was wreton his epitaphye, maad by a Poet-laureate," remained the only memorial to Chaucer. The epitaph was in Latin, Surigonius of Milan being Italian. In 1555 a poet called Nicholas Brigham obtained permission to present the marble tomb now to be seen. Whether Chaucer's remains rest beneath it is doubtful. Above the tomb is a modern window, presented by an American, containing portraits of Chaucer

POETS' CORNER

The South Transept, long sacred to those who have illuminated literature and scholarship. On the floor is seen the plain stone slab bearing the name of Thomas Hardy, who was buried here in 1928.

and John Gower, a contemporary poet who equalled if he did not surpass the former in contemporary reputation.

" Died for Lack of Bread "

Near Chaucer's grave is that of Edmund Spenser, author of the *Faerie Queene*, of whom a friend recorded that " he died for lack of bread in King Street (Westminster)." As has been previously told, many literary celebrities of the day cast poetic tributes into the grave.

John Milton, greatest of all English writers of epic poetry, died after the restoration of the Stuarts, to whom his name was anathema on account of his anti-Royalist pamphlets, and it was not until 1737 that a memorial to him was placed in the Abbey. " I have seen erected in the church," said Dr. Gregory to Dr. Johnson, " a bust of that man whose name I once knew considered as a pollution of its walls." Milton is buried in St. Giles's, Cripplegate. It was Milton who wrote of Shakespeare :

" What needs my Shakespeare for his honour'd bones
The labour of an age in piled stones? "

a protest which recurs to the mind when regarding the " preposterous monument," as Horace Walpole describes it, which the bad taste of the eighteenth century erected in 1740. Shortly after Shakespeare's death there was a popular agitation to have him re-buried in Poets' Corner, but the idea came to nothing.

Two Famous Scotsmen

Burns was among those who had to wait long for the obvious sign of national recognition; it was eighty-nine years after his death that the present bust was erected. The cost was met by shilling subscriptions, given by the poorest as well as the wealthiest among his admirers. Sir Walter Scott did not have to wait quite so long. His memorial, a replica of the Chantrey bust at Abbotsford, was placed in position sixty-five years after his death.

Nowadays recognition is more prompt. Beside the remains of Charles Dickens repose the ashes of Thomas Hardy, whose heart was buried on the same day (January 16, 1928) in the beautiful little churchyard of Stinsford, the " Mellstock " of *Under the Greenwood Tree.*

One of the pall-bearers at Hardy's funeral was Rudyard Kipling, who eight years later was himself laid to rest alongside Hardy. In 1934 a bust was unveiled in honour of the centenary of Adam Lindsay Gordon, poet of Australia, the only Dominion writer so far to be accorded a place in the Abbey. It stands near the bust of Alfred Lord Tennyson, whose exquisite short poem *Crossing the Bar* was set to music and sung for the first time at the author's funeral.

The Poet's Corner has a widespread appeal. In the nave is a simple tomb the appeal of which is universal. For those of our generation in particular there is no more hallowed spot than the grave of the Unknown Warrior, one of " the many multitudes who during the Great War of 1914–1918 gave the most that man can give, life itself," as the simple but dignified slab records.

The body of the Unknown Warrior was brought from France and laid in Westminster Abbey on November 11, 1920. On its way from Victoria Station the coffin, borne on a gun carriage, was halted in Whitehall for the unveiling of the Cenotaph. In the procession walked as chief mourner King George V, accompanied by the Prince of Wales and the Duke of York. In the nave, where stood a guard of honour consisting of one hundred wearers of the V.C., four Queens beheld the arrival of the one who came to represent " those warriors, who died unknown in the Great War."

For a week after the interment a countless host of sorrowing pilgrims filed past the open grave. Late at night on November 18 silver sand from the Isle of Thorney was arranged round the coffin, one hundred sacks of earth from the battlefields was placed upon it, and the grave was sealed up. The " Padre's Flag," the Union Jack from Ypres which had been draped over the coffin on its memorable journey, was hung from a neighbouring column.

Nearly twelve years later, on June 24, 1932, King George's eldest son dedicated the Southwest Tower, formerly the Baptistery, as the Warriors' Chapel, to the memory of all those, men and women, who lost their lives during the Great War. The Abbey was repeatedly hit by German bombs during the air raids of the Second World War. Several showers of incendiary bombs fell upon it in 1940 and 1941, but all were successfully mastered, except on the night of May 10, 1941, when the roof of the lantern was completely destroyed, debris showering down upon the floor of the Abbey inside; the buildings of Westminster School and of the Chapter Library were also burnt. In earlier raids the Deanery was completely destroyed, except for the Islip Rooms. The Chapel of Henry VII was seriously damaged outside and inside by a high explosive bomb on September 27, 1940, but this priceless architectural gem has since been very cleverly restored.

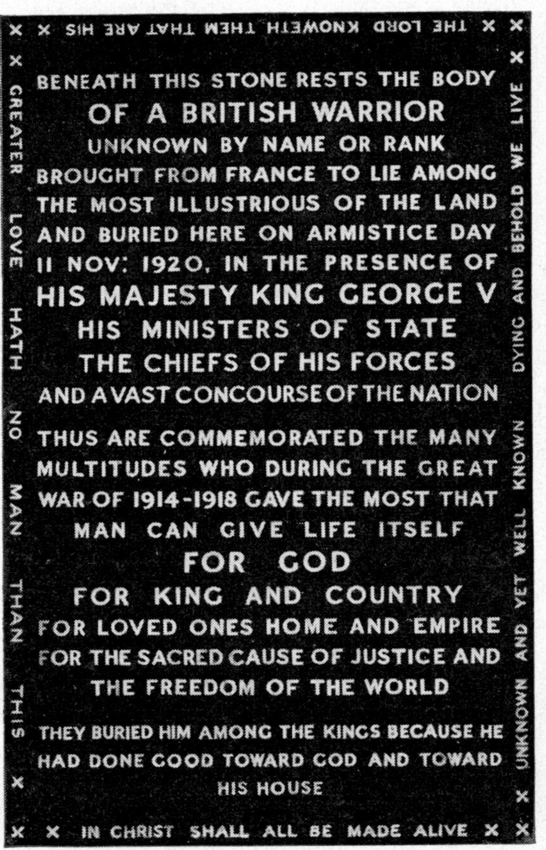

GRAVE OF THE UNKNOWN WARRIOR
The Unknown Warrior rests in the nave of the Abbey, his tomb marked by this simple slab of stone.

BUCKINGHAM PALACE FROM THE AIR

An aerial view showing the quadrangular shape of the building, and the gardens, which with the lake occupy about forty acres. In front of the palace stands the imposing Queen Victoria memorial.

PALACES PAST AND PRESENT

ONE does not usually associate St. James's Palace with lepers, Buckingham Palace with silkworms, Kensington Palace with asthma, and Whitehall and Hampton Court with the breaking of the tenth commandment. Too much history has been made, and too many far-reaching decisions have been taken in these homes of kings to suggest any such connections. Yet they exist.

" Our Court of St. James's," to which foreign ambassadors are accredited, and where each Sovereign is proclaimed on his or her accession, occupies the site of a leper hospital. The institution, says Stow, was founded " by the citizens of London, before the time of man's memory, for fourteen sisters, maidens, that were lepers, living chastely and honestly in divine service." The date was probably 1100, and the lazar-house was dedicated to St. James the Less, Bishop of Jerusalem.

In the year of his marriage to Anne Boleyn, Henry VIII demolished this structure, and having laid out " a faire parke for his greater comoditie and pleasure " erected there a " goodly manor." Bluff King Hal was a great lover of palatial residences (not always his own), even though he was not a very successful home-maker.

Henry VIII did not lack for other homes. Not far away stood York Place, the palatial residence of Wolsey until his disgrace in 1530. The king seized York Place, renamed it Whitehall Palace, and soon moved there himself; and it was not until Whitehall Palace was destroyed by fire in the closing years of the seventeenth century that the Court again took up its residence at St. James's. The throne was then held jointly by William and Mary.

The only parts of Henry VIII's building that now remain are the clock-tower and gateway facing St. James's Street, the Royal Chapel and a fragment of the Presence Chamber, the rest having been destroyed by fire in 1809. As it stands, the edifice is remarkable neither for beauty nor dignity. Its main interest for the present generation lies in the fact that the western wing, known as York House, was for many years the residence of King Edward VIII when Prince of Wales.

It has far fewer historical associations than Whitehall, although four kings were born within its walls and in the little chapel many members of the Royal Family have been married, including Queen Victoria and King George V, then Duke of York.

There Charles I spent the night before his execution and took a long last farewell of his children. Thence he walked across the Park to the Scaffold in Whitehall. A contributing cause of his unpopularity was that he had placed the palace at the disposal of his mother-in-law, Marie de Medici, who was subsequently voted a large sum of money by Parliament to leave the country.

ST. JAMES'S PALACE
The Gateway and Clock Tower, part of the original building designed, it is believed, by Hans Holbein.

Duke of Cumberland's Secret

The most sensational story connected with the building is that of the death in 1810 of Sellis, an Italian servant of the Duke of Cumberland. He was found one morning in his apartment with his throat cut, and rumour hinted that the Duke, who was extremely unpopular with the people, had murdered him. Cumberland's version of the affair was that Sellis had entered his master's bedroom in the middle of the night and had attempted to assassinate him, and that failing to accomplish his purpose he had then retired to his own room and committed suicide. The verdict of the coroner's inquest was *felo de se*, but many people were of a different mind, and so strong did the popular feeling become that after Cumberland succeeded to the throne of Hanover he rarely visited England.

Queen Elizabeth II is the sixth monarch to take up residence at Buckingham Palace, although the original Buckingham House was occupied by George III, who bought it in 1762 from Sir Charles Sheffield, who was heir to the Duke of Buckingham, its builder. Upon the front of the house was inscribed in Latin the motto, "The household gods delight in such a situation."

King Who Kept Silkworms

In the seventeenth century the site it occupies was a place of recreation known as Mulberry Gardens. According to Evelyn, the diarist, it was " the only place of refreshment about the town for persons of the best quality to be exceedingly cheated at "; and Samuel Pepys described it as " a silly place, with a wilderness somewhat pretty."

The gardens got their name in a curious way. James I, in an attempt to create a new home industry, purchased the land in 1609 and planted 5 acres with mulberry trees to feed silkworms which were to supply English weavers with silk. The project failed and a public park replaced the gardens, but it is said that some of the three-hundred-year-old trees are still alive and bearing fruit.

Thirteen years after he had purchased Buckingham House, George III settled it on his wife, Queen Charlotte, and it was for some

BUCKINGHAM HOUSE IN THE EIGHTEENTH CENTURY
Built by John Sheffield, Duke of Buckingham, in 1703, and bought by George III some sixty years later. The picture shows the house as it was in 1753. It was practically rebuilt by George IV.

years afterwards known as the Queen's House.

George IV, who was the only child of the numerous family of the royal couple not to be born in their favourite residence, decided to reconstruct it completely. Nash, the designer of Regent Street, was told to go ahead, which he proceeded to do to such purpose and with so little reference to the authorities that in 1828, three years after the work was started, a Select Committee was set up to inquire into the matter. Parliament had only authorised repairs and improvements to an existing building, whereas a new one was being erected. When it was ready for occupation over £750,000 had been spent on it and George IV and his successor were dead. Further additions at a cost of £150,000 were made in the early years of Queen Victoria's reign.

Costly Marble Arch

In front of the central entrance stood the Marble Arch, originally intended as a monument to Nelson. It was based on the Arch of Constantine at Rome, and cost about £80,000.

The Arch, which was too small for the State Coach to pass through, was removed to its present position in 1851; its gates are opened only for the reigning monarch.

Two years after his accession King George V employed Sir Aston Webb to build a new east front for Buckingham Palace. The work, costing £60,000, was completed in the extraordinarily short space of four months. The Palace was bombed and damaged during the German air raids of 1940.

Palace Built by Duchess

Marlborough House, which overlooks St. James's Palace, owes its existence to the beautiful and imperious Sarah Churchill, first Duchess of Marlborough, whose husband spent £50,000 on the place. The Dutch bricks of which it was built were brought to England as ballast in transports returning from Holland after taking over soldiers for the Duke's army.

The Duchess laid the foundation stone in 1709. Her architect was none other than Sir Christopher Wren, who built the house in two storeys. The building has been altered considerably. Outside, Wren indulged his love of stone dressings and balustrades; within, the east and west walls of the staircase and the main saloon gave the French artist Louis Laguerre ample scope for frescoes commemorating Marlborough's victories, and landscapes of Mons and Antwerp. He covered 500 square yards with them. The house remained in the Marlborough family until 1817, when it became the residence of Princess Charlotte and Prince Leopold. The latter signed the deed of acceptance of the Belgian throne there, and by so doing became first King of the Belgians.

IN VICTORIAN DAYS
Queen Victoria was the first sovereign to make Buckingham Palace her regular town residence. King Edward VII was born in the palace in 1841 and died there in 1910. A view taken in 1861.

The next occupant, the Dowager Queen Adelaide, widow of King William IV, gave a sumptuous dinner to celebrate Queen Victoria's marriage. The Prince of Wales brought his beautiful Danish bride to Marlborough House in 1863, and resided there until his accession. King George V was born in the mansion in 1865 and lived in it till 1910, when he ascended the throne, and the Queen Mother returned to the house she had occupied for so long.

On Queen Alexandra's death the place was modernised and renovated for the Prince of Wales (later King Edward VIII), but he preferred York House to the great rambling place of over 200 rooms. So it remained with drawn blinds until 1936, when Queen Mary entered into residence and chose as her personal apartments those used by George V, and there she lived until her death in 1953.

The Sheraton Room, which appears at first sight to be a library, is noted for false book-shelves and book-backs that conceal cupboards and doors. *Boyle on Steam*, *Shutters on Draughts* and *Johnson's Contradictionary* are included in the titles of these spurious volumes, while *The Passage Out* humorously indicates an exit.

Kensington Palace

William III suffered much from asthma, and when he was informed that the air of Kensington would afford him relief from this complaint he bought Nottingham House, which Lord Chancellor Finch had built on the site of the present building. The King gave £20,000 for it. Then he called in Sir Christopher Wren and directed him to reconstruct the house after the manner of Versailles.

Before Wren's design had been completed William's consort, Queen Mary, died of small-pox in the palace, and eight years later the King himself expired within its walls. His successor, Good Queen Anne, had a great fondness for the place, and she spent much of her time in directing the laying out of new gardens beside her predecessor's Dutch flower-beds. It was during her reign that Wren, then in his seventy-fifth year, built the charming Orangery. Queen Anne died there, of apoplexy brought on by over-eating.

Origin of the Serpentine

George I was rarely in residence at the palace, most of his time being spent either at St. James's or at his Hanoverian Court, but his daughter-in-law, Caroline, wife of George II, was devoted to Kensington. Like Anne, she was very interested in the gardens, and employed William Kent to lay out anew William of Orange's flower-beds. She also appropriated 100 acres from Hyde Park, created the sheet of water known as the Serpentine by widening the bed of the River Westbourne, and made the famous Broad Walk. By her orders Kensington Gardens were opened to the public on Saturdays, but visitors had to wear "full dress!"

George II made considerable alterations to the building, including an addition which he used as a nursery for his children. He employed as governess the Countess Deloraine, about whom Horace Walpole relates an amusing anecdote.

The Countess was playing cards with the King when suddenly one of the royal children pulled her chair from under her, so that she fell to the floor. She, " being provoked that her monarch was diverted with her disgrace, with the malice of a hobby-horse gave him just such another fall. But, alas! the monarch, like Louis XIV, is mortal in the part that touched the ground, and was so hurt and angry, that the Countess is disgraced, and her German rival remains in the sole and quiet possession of her royal master's favour." As the Countess was exceedingly pretty her disgrace probably did not last very long.

Home of an Unwanted Wife

George III never resided at Kensington Palace during his long reign, but it was for a time the home of Princess Sophia, who was blind and exceedingly patient. A resident of a very different type was Caroline, Princess of Wales, the unwanted wife of the future George IV. She lived in the palace between the years 1810 and 1814, and there entertained an extraordinarily diverse collection of people, including Sir Humphry Davy, the inventor of the safety-lamp for miners which bears his name, and the Rev. Sydney Smith, who by his wit helped to reform many abuses.

Five years after Princess Caroline had left Kensington, in May, 1819, the Duchess of Kent there gave birth to the future Queen Victoria, who remained at the palace for the greater part of her infancy and youth.

Queen Victoria's Early Visitors

It was at about five o'clock on the morning of June 20, 1837, that the Archbishop of Canterbury and Lord Conyngham arrived to inform Princess Victoria that she had become Queen of England. The servants were at first apparently not disposed to disturb their mistress, but when the Archbishop said, " We are come to the *Queen* on business of state, and even her sleep must give way to that," they hastened their movements. A few minutes later Victoria appeared attired only in a night-gown, a shawl and a pair of slippers. Her first action on receiving the news of her accession was to burst into tears, her second to ask the Archbishop to pray for her.

At 11.30 on the same morning she held her

PRIVATE CHAPEL OF BUCKINGHAM PALACE

Formerly a conservatory, the chapel was consecrated in 1843. In it many royal weddings and christenings have taken place. It was wrecked by a German bomb in September, 1940.

BRITISH MONARCH'S LONDON HOME

When the Sovereign is in residence at Buckingham Palace the Royal Standard is flown, and the Guard is changed daily in the courtyard before the east front. The Palace faces St. James's Park.

first Council in the palace. So well did she act her part that the Duke of Wellington told her that he could not have desired to see his own daughter perform it better.

Wolsey's Country House

Less than a month later the Queen moved to Buckingham Palace, and though her regret is recorded in her diary she never returned to Kensington. The Duchess of Kent resides in one quarter of the Palace. Another part is now used to house the London Museum, which was formerly at Lancaster House.

Hampton Court Palace was the fulfilment of a great ambition that brought great sorrow. It was in 1514 that Cardinal Wolsey, then near the height of his power, decided to build himself a country house to which he could retire from time to time and escape from the cares of his office as the chief minister of the Crown. Three considerations governed his choice of a site : in the first place, it had to be well outside the suburbs of London; in the second, it had to be easily accessible from London; and in the third, it had to be in a healthy district.

In those days London's main thoroughfare was the Thames, all important buildings, including York Place, the great Cardinal's town residence, being built near its bank, so that there was no question but that the site should be a riverside one. Wolsey would then be able to travel comfortably by barge to and from York Place. As for the third consideration, the prelate took no risks. He consulted the most eminent physicians in England, and paid them a doubtful compliment by asking the opinions of graduates of Padua, then the most celebrated medical school in Europe. The "extraordinary salubrity" of Hampton Court made the committee of learned advisers decide in its favour.

Two Thousand Rabbits

Thus it came about that Wolsey purchased a ninety-nine years' lease of the manor of Hampton, together with the lands that surrounded it, from the Knights Hospitallers of Jerusalem, in whose possession the property had been for over three centuries. One of the terms of the agreement was that when the lease expired there should be a thousand pairs of conies in the warren, otherwise the then owner would have to pay fourpence for every couple that was missing.

Few, if any, of his contemporaries can have been more concerned about their health than was the Lord Cardinal. In an age when sanitation was not much thought of and when personal cleanliness was little regarded, he employed considerable ingenuity and large sums of money in ensuring that the drainage system of his new residence should be as perfect as possible, and that it should have a permanent supply of the best water obtainable. His painstaking efforts and foresight were rewarded. For hundreds of years the inhabitants of the Palace remained perfectly healthy while epidemics of smallpox, cholera, and the plague were raging in London and its suburbs.

So efficiently did he lay down his drains that they remained in use until 1871, and so skilfully and sturdily did his masons build the water-house over the spot where the crystal clear liquid bubbled up through the sand that it may be seen to-day almost precisely as it was over four centuries ago.

Covetous Henry VIII

Henry VIII coveted Hampton Court. Assuring him that " it had always been intended as a gift to his Grace," the mighty Cardinal left it, but took with him seventy-two wagon-loads of furniture. The King's workmen demolished a great part of the Palace, and years after Dutch William transformed it still further, so that although it is often referred to as Wolsey's Palace, it is far from being his in any real sense. But the Tudor water-house he erected at the top of Kingston Hill is truly his : none has thought fit to alter it in any way.

It is hardly possible that there is anywhere in Britain another such water-house, at once so ancient and so beautiful. Screened by trees from the eyes of curious passers-by, it stands in the peaceful seclusion of the grounds of a private house, emitting from its quaint little windows the sweet, sleepy notes of softly running water.

None save the privileged may unlock the door, descend the worn steps, and pass along the dark vaulted passage that leads to the chapel-like room where a cistern receives the water which sings as it bursts from the sand. It is a veritable Temple of the Water-god, for we moderns who draw our water from machine-made taps have none of our ancestors' reverence for the precious liquid.

Coombe Springs, as it is called, is three or four miles from Hampton Court, and the question of the means by which the water was to be conveyed thither presented the Tudor workmen with a pretty engineering problem. They solved it by laying lead pipes all the way from Kingston Hill to the Palace.

Cardinal as Architect

Wolsey was to a large extent his own architect. " The furniture," we are told, " was as noble as the building; the hangings of the chambers were of wonderful value, there were 280 silk beds for the reception of strangers only,

MARLBOROUGH HOUSE

Built by Sir Christopher Wren for the victor of Blenheim, it stands opposite St. James's Palace. King Edward VII, as Prince of Wales, lived here for forty years. Later, Queen Alexandra occupied it.

BIRTHPLACE OF QUEEN VICTORIA

Kensington Palace, bought by William III and reconstructed for him by Sir Christopher Wren. Here were born Queen Victoria and Queen Mary. The former lived here until her accession to the throne in 1837.

and the place glistened with vast quantities of gold and silver plate."

Describing a "most sumptuous supper" he had at Hampton Court, Sebastian Giustinian, the Venetian Ambassador, declares that "the like of which, I fancy, was never given by Cleopatra or Caligula; the whole banqueting hall being so decorated with huge vases of gold and silver, that I fancied myself in the tower of Chosroes (of Persia), when that monarch caused Divine honours to be paid to him." After the repast twelve male and twelve female dancers appeared, "all over covered with cloth of gold."

Where Henry VIII Played Tennis

Henry VIII entered into residence there in 1529, and immediately commenced to enlarge the Palace and to build a "Close Tennys Play." It is the oldest tennis court in the world still in use.

The King brought his second wife, Anne Boleyn, to Hampton Court for her honeymoon. It was there that, in 1536, she discovered Jane Seymour in the King's arms, but jealousy did not for long gnaw her heart because only four months later she was executed on Tower Hill. Her rival followed her to the grave towards the close of the following year, a fortnight after she had rejoiced her husband by presenting him with a son the future King Edward VI.

It is related that a few days before Jane gave birth to the boy the doctors discovered that mother and child could not both live: one would have to be sacrificed to the other. When they asked the King whom they should save, he brutally replied, "The infant by all means, for another wife is easily got, but not so another child.'

Ghosts of Hampton Court

Jane Seymour is one of the many ghosts that are alleged to stalk about the Palace in the early hours of the morning. She is seen, dressed in a shroud and with a candle in her hand, making her way towards the room—long since demolished—in which Anne Boleyn discovered her in the royal tyrant's arms.

It is said that the ghost of Anne Boleyn may sometimes be seen rushing wildly along the Haunted Gallery, screaming as it goes. In her hasty nocturnal perambulations she may perhaps run into the ghost of Mrs. David Penn, Edward VI's nurse, which is also alleged to frequent the same part of the Palace.

Although she was buried in the sixteenth century, Mrs. Penn's ghost did not manifest itself until 1829, in which year her grave in Hampton Parish Church was disturbed. It was stated to be very active towards the end of the nineteenth century, even going so far as to frighten a sentry into a fit.

Anne of Cleves, having had the good fortune to escape alive after only six months as Henry's consort, did not have a great deal to do with Hampton Court.

The royal Bluebeard's fifth wife, Catherine Howard, was married in the Holy Day Closet of the Palace. Fifteen months later, on All Souls' Day, 1541, she was arrested in her private apartments on a charge of high treason. The evidence was provided by Archbishop Cranmer, who endeavoured to induce Catherine to confess to pre-marital unchastity. Like Anne Boleyn, she was executed in the Tower.

Royal Honeymoon Retreat

Mary Tudor spent her honeymoon with Philip II at Hampton Court. An old story relates that the Spanish king there suffered the humiliation of being publicly slapped in the face by Lady Acton, a famous beauty. His offence was that he had attempted to kiss her.

Queen Elizabeth passed carefree days at Hampton Court, dancing, flirting with her courtiers or watching dramatic performances.

James I and Charles I lived a good deal at this palace, and here the former lectured the Puritan ministers at the abortive Hampton Court Conference in 1604. Forty-five years later printed announcements of a great sale of the Martyr King's possessions defaced the walls. Cromwell made Hampton Court one of his principal residences, but not having much appreciation of art he sold the greater part of its collection of pictures, as well as a large number of royal relics. One of Henry VIII's canes fetched the sum of five shillings. Had he been present in spirit Bluff King Hal would no doubt have been surprised at the low value put upon his walking-stick, but he would have been even more astonished had he been privileged to read Mrs. Cromwell's housekeeping accounts. That most estimable matron believed in making

Donald McLeish

DUTCH GARDEN AT KENSINGTON PALACE

Originally designed by William III, and relaid by Caroline, wife of George II, the garden with its central lily-pond, flagged paths and brilliant flower beds screened by lime trees is an exquisitely beautiful retreat.

Donald McLeish

GREAT GATEHOUSE AT HAMPTON COURT

One of the most striking parts of the original building erected by Cardinal Wolsey. The stone bridge in front, crossing the moat, was added by Henry VIII, and is adorned with copies of the "Kynges Beestes."

money go a long way, and her favourite method of ensuring that it did so was to economise on food. She watched her servants as a cat watches a mouse, lest they should steal or waste anything. Henry VIII, on the other hand, was extraordinarily lavish where food and drink were concerned. His great kitchen—100 feet long, 38 feet broad, and 40 feet high—contained an enormous staff which dealt with £300,000 worth of food every year, while his annual expenditure on drink was £50,000.

Gallons of Ale for a Duchess

We cannot fail to be awestruck when we read that the Great Master of the Household was allotted ten gallons of ale and six quarts of wine at each of the two main meals of the day. The Lord Chamberlain only received four gallons of ale and a quart and a half of wine at each of his meals, but even so, it is hard to believe that he was always in a fit state to "censor" the King's entertainments, a duty still demanded of his office.

The female members of Henry's Court were far from being teetotallers. A duchess was allowed three gallons of ale and a pitcher of wine every day, in addition to what she could drink while actually at table.

Dining in Private not Allowed

Adjoining the Wine Cellar is the "Drynkynge House," to which all the members of the King's household went to receive their allowances of ale and wine, and which was used as a "bar." The Court players and musicians were in the habit of retiring there after their work was finished.

Henry VIII insisted that all in attendance at Court should dine together in the Great Hall. He did this, not out of any desire for company, but in order that he might the more easily keep his eye on the powerful nobles, whose presence he also insisted upon. In the "Ordinances of Eltham" (regulations for the King's household drawn up by Wolsey) are mentioned with disapproval those "noblemen, gentlemen, and others who do much delight and use to dyne in corners and secret places."

It was to provide a suitable dining-room for himself and his nobles that King Hal built the Great Hall, the open timber roof of which reminds one of Westminster Hall. The arrival from the kitchen of each course of the banquets that were given was heralded by pipes and trumpets in the Minstrels' Gallery.

Plays in Great Hall

In the Great Hall were staged, for the enjoyment of Queen Elizabeth, the plays of Shakespeare and his fellow-dramatists. Shakespeare's own company acted here, and he may have taken a part himself. In 1718, after it had ceased to be used as a communal dining-room, the Great Hall was fitted up as a theatre, and in the same year a play called *Henry VIII; or the Fall of Wolsey* was presented. Eighty years later the stage fittings were removed.

We can hardly doubt that Oliver Cromwell knew something of the history of Hampton Court, and the thought of Henry's feasts and Elizabeth's dancing and play-watching must have revolted his Puritan soul. One of his few relaxations was listening to music, and John Milton is said to have played to him on the organ in the Chapel, where Catherine Howard and Catherine Parr had each been publicly acknowledged as Queen for the first time and where Cromwell's daughter was married to Lord Falconberg.

The last important visitor Cromwell received there was George Fox, who came to crave the Protector's mercy for his fellow-Quakers.

As if to make up for lack of glamour during the Protectorate, in the early years of Charles II's reign the Palace witnessed scenes of unparalleled elegance and splendour. The diary of Pepys and the *Mémoires* of the Comte de Grammont provide many fascinating descriptions and anecdotes of Charles II's court at the Palace.

Elizabeth Hamilton, whom Grammont wooed and won at Hampton Court, and several of the beautiful courtesans with whom the Merry Monarch associated, were painted by the brush of Sir Peter Lely, and their portraits may yet be seen in the Palace. One of them, Frances, Duchess of Richmond, was the original of the Britannia on English coinage. Another, the Duchess of Cleveland, was through her influence on the King, for many years one of the most influential women in the realm.

Scheme to Rival Versailles

William of Orange took his pleasures sadly, so that the air of gloom that had disappeared at Hampton Court during the Merry Monarch's reign reappeared again after the deposition of James II and the arrival of William's stolid compatriots.

The consuming passion of the Prince of Orange's life was his hatred of Louis XIV of France, and he thought to spite that monarch by transforming the creation of Wolsey and

Donald McLeish

HAMPTON COURT PALACE

Built by Cardinal Wolsey between 1515 and 1520, and later presented by him to Henry VIII, it was greatly enlarged by William III, who made it the largest and most splendid palace in England.

BANQUETING HOUSE OF WHITEHALL PALACE

Built by Inigo Jones in 1619 and intended as the nucleus of a palace of unparalleled magnificence. A tablet on the wall marks the point where Charles I emerged on his way to execution.

of Henry VIII into a palace that would rival Versailles, which Louis was then building. With this idea in view he employed Sir Christopher Wren, the architect of St. Paul's, to carry out the necessary alterations.

Wren's Unfinished Palace

There was never any real likelihood that his object would be achieved, for William, unlike Louis, had not the power to raise unlimited money from his subjects. Wren's ambitious design remained unfinished, but the austere building which now surrounds Fountain Court, with its impressive East and South Fronts, is one of the finest in England. It contains the great State Rooms with their marvellous collection of portraits. Verrio adorned the ceilings of some of them, and there much of Grinling Gibbons's best carving may be seen. The Old Court House which was given to Wren in payment of a debt of £100 for work done at the Palace is near the entrance.

Jean Tijou, a French Protestant, was another craftsman employed by William III. He was responsible for the beautiful wrought-iron screens in the South Garden.

Dutch gardeners were kept busy designing flower-beds, lawns and walks. The old accounts tell us how much they were paid for their work. A certain James Road received £234 11s. 9d. for collecting plants in Virginia; Herman Jansen got about a third of that sum for the carriage of orange trees.

"Little Gentleman in Black Velvet"

During 1695–96 two men were employed to catch moles in the grounds of Hampton Court. They failed to exterminate the vermin, and it was upon a mole-hill that William III's horse stumbled, throwing and fatally injuring the King, on March 8, 1702. In commemoration of this, to them, happy event, the Jacobites used thereafter to toast "the little gentleman in black velvet."

The first two Georges spent a good deal of their time at Hampton Court, but George III never lived there, he having conceived a distaste for the place after his grandfather had boxed his ears there when he was a boy. It was in his reign, however, that the famous vine was planted at the Palace. Although planted in 1768 and stated to be the oldest in existence, it still bears heavy crops of grapes, and constitutes a source of income to the Exchequer because as many as 300,000 people pay their pennies to see it in the course of a year. The sale of the fruit to the public helps towards the upkeep of the Palace, and a percentage goes to blind ex-Servicemen. The vine attracts rather more people than the Maze.

Royal Likes and Dislikes

During the nineteenth century the custom of granting apartments in the Palace to privileged persons who were not of Royal blood was gradually introduced. Queen Victoria can have had no great liking for the place, for she only visited it on three or four occasions, and she it was who threw it open to the public. Her son, Edward VII, is said to have considered taking up his residence there, but he finally decided not to do so for financial reasons. It was estimated that it would cost at least £500,000 to recondition the building.

Last Walk of a King

On January 30, 1649, at about ten o'clock in the morning, Charles I took his last walk through St. James's Park. He did not walk alone. There was a line of soldiers on either side, while before and behind him marched a troop of halberdiers with colours flying and drums beating. The procession ascended a flight of stairs at the place now known as the Horse Guards, and passing along the gallery which in those days spanned the thoroughfare of Whitehall, entered the Banqueting House of Whitehall Palace.

Four hours later the unhappy monarch stepped on to a wooden scaffold, where beside a block stood two masked executioners. Having said his prayers, he pulled off his doublet and,

INTERIOR OF BANQUETING HALL

Distributing Maundy Money in the Banqueting Hall. On the ceiling can be seen the paintings done by Rubens. The Hall was presented by Queen Victoria to the Royal United Services Institution in 1893.

EXECUTION OF CHARLES I

An old print showing the King on the scaffold erected outside Whitehall Palace. In the hall, on the inner side of a window, is preserved the pair of gloves handed to Bishop Juxon on the scaffold by Charles. It is said that the monarch's last words were, "To your power I must submit, but your authority I deny."

kneeling down, laid his head upon the block. A single blow of the axe sufficed. " Behold the head of a traitor! " cried the executioner.

Through Window or Hole?

There has been much controversy as to whether the King reached the scaffold through an open window or by means of a hole made in the wall. Jesse's evidence would appear conclusive. " It is perhaps sufficient to observe," he writes, " that at the renovation of the Banqueting Hall a few years since, a fact was made apparent which, I imagine, will be considered as setting the question at rest. Having curiosity enough to visit the interior of the building, the walls of which were then laid bare, a space was pointed out to me between the upper and lower centre windows of about seven feet in height and four in breadth, the bricks of which presented a broken and jagged appearance, and the brickwork introduced was evidently of a different date from that of the rest of the building. There can be little doubt that it was through this passage that Charles walked . . . ."

The building in which the martyred King spent the last hours of his life had been erected by order of his father, James I.

In 1619 a fire destroyed the greater part of Whitehall Palace, originally built by Hubert de Burgh, Earl of Kent, about 1240. Inigo Jones was immediately commissioned by the King to replace it. Two years later he had completed the Banqueting House, but for a variety of reasons no attempt was ever made to put the rest of his magnificent design into execution.

To Have Covered Twenty-four Acres

According to that invaluable gossip Horace Walpole, the new palace would have been " the most truly magnificent and beautiful fabric of any kind in Europe," and was to have covered twenty-four acres. The fine proportions of the Banqueting House are sufficient to justify Walpole's statement.

The main hall of the building is impressive enough in itself, but it is made doubly so by the beautiful paintings with which Rubens adorned the lofty ceiling, work for which the great painter was paid at the rate of £10 a yard.

It was proposed that his contemporary Vandyck should paint the sides of the hall, but unfortunately nothing came of the suggestion. This may have been because Charles I treated Vandyck most shabbily in money matters.

The palace which Inigo Jones intended to rebuild had been known as York Place before it was handed over to Henry VIII by Cardinal Wolsey. Shakespeare alludes to the change of name in the fourth act of his play *Henry VIII*:

"You must no more call it York Place—
that is past;
For since the Cardinal fell that title's lost;
'Tis now the King's, and called Whitehall."

Wolsey entered into residence there when he became Archbishop of York, the house having been settled on his successors in that office by Walter de Grey, one-time holder of it. The ambitious Cardinal determined to make York Place a worthy setting for his greatness, and in this he succeeded only too well, because the magnificence he displayed there aroused the envy of his royal master. Precisely the same thing happened in connection with Hampton Court Palace. To say that Wolsey lived in regal state is an understatement, for few kings carried Court etiquette to such extremes as he. Bishops tied the latchets of his shoes, while dukes commonly held the basin in which he washed his hands.

Henry VIII Meets Anne Boleyn

Henry VIII was frequently entertained at York Place and it was at a masque there that he first met Anne Boleyn. Not long after that fateful meeting Wolsey was in disgrace and, "taking a long farewell of all his greatness," he left Whitehall Stairs in the barge which took him to Esher.

The King lost no time in moving into the Lord Cardinal's residence, "because the old Palace nigh to the monastery of St. Peter is now, and has long before been in a state of ruin and decay." The Act of Parliament which legalised the appropriation says, concerning Wolsey, "he had lately, upon the soil of the said mansion-place and house and upon ground thereunto belonging, most sumptuously and curiously built and edified many and distinct beautiful, costly, and pleasant lodgings, buildings and mansions for his Grace's singular pleasure, comfort and commodity, to the honour of his highness and the realm; and thereunto adjoining had made a park, walled and environed with brick and stone; and then devised and ordained many and singular commodious things, pleasures and other necessaries, apt and convenient to appertain to so noble a prince for his pastime and pleasure."

The buildings of the palace extended from Westminster Bridge to Scotland Yard, and from the bank of the Thames to "the street leading from Charing Cross into the Sanctuary Gate at Westminster." Scotland Yard received its name from the apartments placed at the disposal of the Scottish monarchs when they made their annual visit to London to do homage and fealty to the English sovereign.

Neither his wives nor his homes satisfied Henry VIII, and he at once began to make a number of additions and improvements to the "mansion-place."

Holbein Kicks Peer Downstairs

In 1546 he commissioned Holbein to design a magnificent gateway, and when a nobleman protested to the King that the artist had kicked him downstairs because he had made a suggestion, Henry casually remarked, "Remember, of seven peasants I can make seven lords, but not one Holbein." The gateway was adorned with busts of some of the more distinguished men of the time, including Henry VIII himself and Bishop Fisher. It was demolished in 1750 when the thoroughfare from Charing Cross to Westminster was being widened, and its stones were used to repair the roads.

Near Holbein's Gateway, as it was always called, Henry caused a tennis-court, a tilt-yard, a cock-pit and a bowling-green to be laid out. The cock-pit occupied the site of 10 Downing Street, the official residence of the First Lord of the Treasury.

Holbein was given rooms in the palace and there he painted many portraits as well as his "Dance of Death." Henry had an affection for the arts, and after moving to Whitehall he collected a large number of pictures there.

"Revels and maskings and various other mummeries" enlivened Whitehall Palace during the reign of Elizabeth. There, with impressive ceremony, she received her distinguished suitors.

Such was the Queen's vanity that, when sixty-six years old and "with wrinkled face, red periwig, little eyes, hooked nose, skinny lips and black teeth," she delighted to sit in the tilt-yard of the Palace drinking in with eager ears the extravagant compliments of foreign ambassadors and her own courtiers.

In the days of her successor, James I, Whitehall was the scene of many a drunken revel. The King himself was no mean drinker, and he and his brother-in-law, King Christian IV of Denmark, celebrated the latter's arrival at Whitehall by a debauch which did nothing to improve the moral standard of Court society.

Intrigue at Whitehall

Macaulay tells us in a fine passage that when Charles II dwelt at Whitehall it was " the focus of political intrigue and of fashionable gaiety. Half the jobbing and half the flirting of the metropolis went on under his roof. Whoever could make himself agreeable to the prince, or could secure the good offices of the mistress, might hope to rise in the world without rendering any service to the government, without being even known by sight to any minister of state. This courtier got a frigate, and that a company; a third, the pardon of a rich offender; a fourth a lease of Crown land on easy terms. If the King notified his pleasure that a briefless lawyer should be made a judge, or that a libertine baronet should be made a peer, the gravest counsellors, after a little murmuring, submitted.

" Interest, therefore, drew a constant press of suitors to the gates of the Palace; and those gates always stood wide open. The King kept open house every day, and all day long, for the good society of London, the extreme Whigs only excepted. Hardly any gentleman had any difficulty in making his way to the royal presence. The levée was exactly what the word imports. Some men of quality came every morning to stand round their master, to chat with him while his wig was combed, and his cravat tied, and to accompany him in his early walk through the Park. All persons who had been properly introduced might, without any special invitation, go to see him, dine, sup, dance, and play at hazard. . . . Bystanders whom His Majesty recognised often came in for a courteous word. . . ."

Extraordinary scenes took place in Whitehall Palace early in February, 1685, when Charles II was seized with his last illness. " The palace had seldom presented a gayer or more scandalous appearance than on the evening of Sunday, the 1st of February." Ill as he was, the King held animated conversations with Lady Castlemaine, the Duchess of Portsmouth and the Duchess of Mazarin, while a boy " warbled some amatory verses " and twenty courtiers played cards.

When it became obvious on February 5 that there was no hope of Charles's survival, Father Huddleston, a Roman Catholic priest who had helped the King to escape after the Battle of Worcester, was sent for, at the suggestion of the Duchess of Portsmouth. The Duke of York introduced the priest to the King with the words, " Sir, this good man once saved your life. He now comes to save your soul." The priest listened to the King's confession, absolved him, administered extreme unction and then gave him the Sacrament.

Death of Charles II

During the night Charles said to James repeatedly, " Do not let poor Nelly (the celebrated Nell Gwynne) starve," but he did.

As dawn was breaking he smilingly begged the watchers at his bedside to forgive him for being " a most unconscionable time dying." The end came at noon.

With his death passed away the romantic glory of Whitehall. Before the end of the century the greater part of the Palace had been

PILLARED FRONT OF GREENWICH HOSPITAL

The birthplace of Henry VIII and of his daughters, Mary and Elizabeth, Greenwich Palace became in 1705 a hospital for retired sailors. In 1873 it was transformed into a naval training college

Donald McLeish

GREENWICH OBSERVATORY

Founded in 1675, the Royal Observatory stood in Greenwich Park, overlooking the Hospital. Through it runs the Greenwich Meridian. After 1946 the Observatory was removed in stages to Hurstmonceux.

destroyed and the Court had migrated to St. James's Palace. Fire exacted a heavy toll in 1691, and six years later the indefatigable Evelyn noted in his diary, " Whitehall burnt : nothing but walls and ruins left."

The Protestant Wind

On the roof of the Banqueting Hall, now the United Services Museum, is a weathervane. It has been there since 1688, and was put up by order of James II that he might get an inkling when William of Orange was likely to arrive. Crowds watched its movements, but none more intently than the unhappy monarch. For a week all went well from the point of view of the King, for the wind was blowing from a quarter that prevented the Dutch armada from sailing. Then the vane slowly but surely swung round to the north. The " Protestant wind " was blowing. It brought the stalwart of the faith to Brixham, and James's days in England were numbered.

Of all the royal palaces in or near London none has passed through so many vicissitudes as that of Greenwich. The abode of kings for about three hundred years, it became a hospital at the beginning of the eighteenth century and a naval training college in 1873.

The first palace, the favourite residence of Henry IV, was reconstructed by his son, Humphrey, Duke of Gloucester, on the present site of the Royal Naval College. Of it the crypt of the chapel alone remains. Added to by Henry VII, the building was known from the reign of his successor onwards as Placentia. It was the birthplace not only of Henry VIII but also of his daughters, Mary and Elizabeth. There, too, his unfortunate son, Edward VI, died—some say by poison.

On May 19, 1533, Anne Boleyn, whose marriage to Henry had just been made public, was escorted in great state up the river from Greenwich to London by the Lord Mayor and Aldermen of the City. According to Charles Mackay, " A foist, or large flat-bottomed boat, took the lead, impelled by several fellows dressed out to represent devils, who at intervals spouted out blue and red flames from their mouths, and threw balls of fire into the water. ' Terrible and monstrous wild men they were,' says Stow, ' and made a hideous noise. In the midst of them sat a great red dragon, moving itself continually about and discharging fire-balls of various colours into the air, whence they fell into the water with a hissing sound.' "

Unhappy Anne Boleyn

The King met the procession at Tower Stairs. Embracing Anne Boleyn, he kissed her with every outward sign of affection, in full view of the multitude of people who had assembled there to see the new Queen. Exactly three years later the blood of this unfortunate woman stained the block within the Tower precincts, hardly more than a stone's throw from the landing-place. She had been arrested at Placentia eighteen days before on a charge of infidelity.

It was at Placentia that Sir Walter Raleigh first gained the favour of the Virgin Queen by

ELTHAM PALACE RESTORED

A favourite country residence of medieval English monarchs, Eltham Palace was later allowed to fall into ruin. The ancient hall, seen left, has recently been most carefully restored.

placing his cloak on the ground so that Elizabeth's shoes might not be soiled. As a wit of the time remarked, his sacrifice of a cloak on that occasion gained him many a good suit later.

The famous Queen's House at Greenwich was begun at the instance of Anne of Denmark, upon whom her husband, James I, had settled both the Palace and the park. The Queen had Inigo Jones as her architect, but he did not finish the building until long after the death of his patroness. It was the property of each successive queen until 1805, when it was handed over to the governors of the Royal Hospital School. In 1933 a country home was built at Holbrook near Ipswich for that ancient academy, and in the following year the Queen's House became the National Maritime Museum.

Neglected by Cromwell

After the execution of Charles I, Parliament decided " that Greenwich House, park and lands should be immediately sold for ready money "; but for some reason this was not done, and in 1654 the Protector appropriated the palace as one of his residences. During his tenancy the buildings were so neglected that when Charles II took them over at the Restoration he decided to demolish them and erect a new and more spacious palace; but either for lack of money or want of interest, the work was discontinued after the completion of only a fragment of the design. Probably nothing more would have been done about it had not Mary, the consort of William III, hit upon the idea of erecting a great hospital for disabled seamen on the site of Placentia.

Plan for Greenwich Hospital

After her death, William hastily summoned Sir Christopher Wren and asked him to prepare plans for the hospital. It was thus, in Macaulay's phrase, to be " a memorial of the virtues of the good Queen Mary, of the love and sorrow of William, and of the great victory of La Hogue." That it served its treble function worthily no one can doubt. It is one of the finest specimens of classical architecture in Great Britain.

Evelyn, the celebrated diarist, was appointed treasurer to the hospital commissioners; and funds were raised partly by means of state lotteries. Wren, as Surveyor-General, was responsible for the layout of the design, but the details were mostly carried out by Sir John Vanbrugh and his two assistants, James, the architect of St. George's, Hanover Square, and Hawksmoor, the architect of St. George's, Bloomsbury.

In 1705 the work was far enough advanced to permit the admission to the premises of forty-two disabled seamen, and some thirty years later there were 1,000 in residence there, the number being subsequently increased to 3,000. For more than a century and a half the great building served the purpose for which it had been designed by its founder, but in 1865 Parliament passed an Act providing for the support as out-pensioners of the inmates of the hospital should they desire to leave it. The majority immediately accepted the offer. In 1869 the last of the pensioners said goodbye to the historic pile.

Four years later the great courtyards began to be crowded with sea-dogs of a different type—officers in search of nautical and scientific knowledge. It had been decided to make the buildings the home of the Royal Naval College, and they have been so ever since. The College could have been founded in no place more appropriate to its functions, for the Chapel and the Painted Hall with its ceiling pictures by Sir James Thornhill, famous for his frescoes on the dome of St. Paul's Cathedral, are for ever associated with the name of the greatest seaman of them all.

After it had been conveyed home from Trafalgar in a cask of spirits, Nelson's body lay in state in the Painted Hall, and thither thousands of people journeyed to pay a last tribute to him who had saved England from invasion by Napoleon. There may now be seen the most precious of the many Nelson relics that are preserved at Greenwich : the jacket and breeches which he was wearing when he was struck down by the sniper's bullet. The decorations that made him so conspicuous a mark for the rifleman on that occasion are still pinned to the breast of the jacket. Tarnished and tawdry they look : poor reminders of the honours which were heaped upon him. A nearby case contains his last will and testament, with its eulogy of Lady Hamilton. She died in poverty at Calais.

Over the Chapel door is suspended a representation of the royal arms which is claimed to be unique, for it contains in the bottom right-hand corner a white horse—the white horse of Hanover, home of George I.

The Naval Museum

In the great Naval Museum in the west wing may be seen the beautiful gold astrolabe which enabled Sir Francis Drake to find his way across the seven seas, the theodolite used by Captain Robert Scott on his expedition to the South Pole and the tragic relics of Sir John Franklin's expedition, as well as many other reminders of the intrepid seamen who have helped to make Britain what she is.

No more than a fragment, but that a very beautiful one, remains of Eltham Palace. The very name is attractive. It is a corruption of Eald-ham, which means the old home. Gone are the King's lodgings, the presence chamber, the apartments of the court, the tilt-yard, the water-towers and many another feature of a place that must have been very delightful in its prime, for it was a residence of English monarchs from Henry III to Henry VIII.

No one knows when the first palace on this site was built, though the soldier-bishop, Odo, half-brother of William the Conqueror, held the manor. Henry III kept Christmas there in 1270, and the amenities and good cheer were such that his example was followed by Richard II, Henry IV, Henry V and Henry VI. Edward IV surpassed them all in merry-making; during the Yuletide of 1482 he feasted 2,000 people daily. Here Edward III spent many of the last sad days of his long reign, doubtless with his mistress, Alice Perrers, who robbed the dying monarch of his ring. Eltham was the favourite residence of Henry VII. More than once Parliament met within its walls.

Eltham Deserted by Monarchs

Henry VIII neglected Eltham for nearby Greenwich, which was " through the benefite of the river, a seate of more commoditie." Queen Mary came occasionally, but early in her reign Queen Elizabeth conceived the notion that the stagnant waters of the moat rendered the palace unhealthy and decided against living there. James I paid it no more than a fleeting visit. Notable folk not of the blood royal occupied the place from time to time, including Sir John Gates, who took part in the plot to place Lady Jane Grey on the throne and lost his head as a consequence, and Sir Christopher Hatton, known as the Dancing Chancellor because he first attracted Elizabeth by his graceful performance at a ball. Then there were Robert Devereux, Earl of Essex, general of the Parliament, who died in the Palace, and Sir John Shaw, the befriender of Charles II when he was living in exile on the Continent.

During the Protectorate practically the whole of the palace, with the exception of the Banqueting Hall, built by Edward IV in 1476, was demolished for building materials. Many of the stately oaks in the park were cut down to furnish timber for ships and the deer were slaughtered for food. On the site of the old palace private houses were erected. Birds made their nests among the oak timbers of the magnificent hammer-beam roof, and weeds grew from the masonry of the decaying walls.

Not many years ago it seemed that this last reminder of the ancient glory of Eltham would soon disappear, but in 1933 Mr. Stephen Courtauld bought a ninety-nine-year lease of the palace and grounds. His first act on taking possession was to demolish all the modern buildings that encumbered the site. Then under expert guidance he began the work of restoring the ancient hall, and built beside it a dwelling-house which would not be out of keeping with the older building. Unluckily, the famous old hall was practically destroyed by German incendiary bombs during a raid in September, 1940.

There was much to recommend the restoration of Eltham, but few people regretted the demolition in 1863 of the Bridewell, which stood between Fleet Street and the Victoria Embankment, near the present Bridewell Lane.

BRIDEWELL PALACE
Built by Henry VIII it was given by Edward VI to the City of London, and later used as a prison.

Bridewell Palace was built by Henry VIII on the site of the Conqueror's Tower of Montfichet, and it was while living there that he first mentioned his uneasiness concerning the validity of his marriage to Katherine of Aragon.

In 1553 Edward VI presented Bridewell to the City authorities as a workhouse (the first known) or House of Correction for vagabonds and tramps. Apparently, it proved all too popular, for there were soon complaints that it was proving a drain on the City purse, and that it attracted idle and "masterless" people in large numbers.

The Great Fire laid the palace-workhouse in ruins. It was rebuilt in two quadrangles, and became definitely a gaol, though it was also a hospital for paupers and indigent folk. Some of the original building remained, including a room in which tradition said sentence of divorce was pronounced against Katherine of Aragon. During the seventeenth and eighteenth centuries the place became notorious for its floggings.

During the reign of Charles II a noted woman of infamous character died in the prison, leaving by will £10 for a funeral sermon, but the preacher was to say nothing but well of her. The cleric who undertook the job got neatly out of the difficulty.

"By the will of the deceased," he concluded his sermon, "it is expected that I should mention her, and say nothing but what was well of her. All that I shall say of her, therefore, is this. She was born well, she lived well, and she died well; for she was born with the name of Cresswell, she lived in Clerkenwell, and she died in Bridewell."

In 1860 the Bridewell and Bethlehem or "Bedlam" Hospitals were amalgamated, and with the exception of the hall and a few offices the grim old palace-prison was demolished.

In the year 1829 the greater part of old Lambeth House disappeared in a cloud of dust. Fiery Archbishop Baldwin, Primate from 1185 to 1190, with no more than nineteen places in which to lay his head, thought he would find a twentieth pillow here, but died in the Holy Land without having so much as seen his new home. In place of the venerable buildings so ruthlessly demolished, Edward Blore erected a mansion second only in size to Buckingham Palace and more suited to the taste of the time, which is not altogether a testimonial. It was of sham Gothic and cost some £60,000. As for the name, Lambeth means no more than "the muddy haven."

Certain parts of the old palace escaped destruction. They included the beautiful Norman crypt which Stephen Langton, one of the signatories of Magna Carta, knew well. The chapel above it, built in the reign of Henry III, was also spared, together with the Lollards' Tower, which dates from 1434. The massive Tudor gateway that was erected just after the Wars of the Roses, for defence if need be, was likewise reprieved.

If we except the crypt, the chapel is the most ancient part of the present buildings. Here in 1378 John Wyclif, "the morning star of the Reformation," appeared before a council of

LAMBETH PALACE FROM THE RIVER

Home of the Archbishops of Canterbury for seven centuries, it was severely damaged in the war. The Chapel, the Lollards' Tower, formerly a prison, and the Gatehouse survive from medieval days.

bishops, of whom the chief was Archbishop Sudbury, to offer a defence of his unorthodox doctrines. Foxe, the author of the *Book of Martyrs*, relates how Wyclif's followers, the Lollards, forced their way into the chapel, compelling the prelates to disperse in none too dignified a manner.

Wat Tyler Sacks Lambeth Palace

Three years later Wat Tyler, the self-appointed leader of the rebellion of the peasantry against the rapacious nobles, marched to Lambeth in the hope of capturing Archbishop Sudbury, who had more than once proved himself an enemy of the people. The Archbishop managed to escape to the Tower of London, but the peasants revenged themselves by plundering and wrecking the Palace, paying special attention to the well-stocked archi-episcopal wine-cellars. Some days later they seized the Tower and there beheaded the Archbishop.

So extensive was the damage inflicted on the Palace that repairs were still being carried out during the time of Chicheley, who took up his residence there in 1414. It was he who erected the Lollards' Tower, the very name of which was soon to strike terror into the hearts of any who questioned orthodox doctrine.

The tower contains a room known as the Lollards' Prison, in which most of the heretics condemned by Chicheley and his successors were lodged. This measures 12 feet by 9, and is lighted by two tiny windows. The floor, ceiling and walls are wainscoted with rough-hewn oak, which still bears inscriptions carved by the prisoners who were once confined there. A few feet from the floor are eight massive iron rings to which the unhappy inmates were bound. Among those who may have suffered was Lovelace, who out of the fullness of his heart wrote the often quoted couplet, " Stone walls do not a prison make, nor iron bars a cage."

Nearby is the post-room, so called because its ceiling is supported by a sturdy pillar, to which prisoners were secured before being whipped.

The great gateway at the Lambeth Bridge end of the Palace was erected about 1490 by Cardinal Morton, the author of the scheme known as " Morton's Fork " whereby Henry VII was enabled to wring much money from his subjects. Its sturdiness is a reminder of the troubled period which succeeded the Wars of the Roses, yet Christian charity was not altogether overlooked. Here for many years a farthing loaf, sufficient for a day's food, was distributed on Fridays and Sundays to every beggar who applied, and they frequently numbered 4,000 or more.

Puritans Demolish Great Hall

Like many things ecclesiastical, the Palace suffered much at the hands of Cromwell's followers, who for a time turned it into a prison for Royalists. They demolished the Great Hall and desecrated the chapel. They even broke into Archbishop Parker's tomb, opened his coffin and threw away the corpse. It was buried again after the restoration of Charles II.

After the Restoration, Juxon, who had as Bishop of London attended Charles I on the scaffold, became Primate. One of his first acts on taking up residence at Lambeth was to begin the rebuilding of the Great Hall, but it was not finished at his death. It now houses the great collection of printed books, pamphlets and manuscripts accumulated by successive archbishops from the time of Bancroft, who in 1610 bequeathed to his successors " for ever, a greate and famous library of bookes of divinity, and of many other sorts of learning." Removed first to Sion College and afterwards to Cambridge University, the collection was eventually restored to its original home, where it is available freely to any serious student.

The Bishop of London holds Fulham Palace by the oldest title in England, the manor of Fulham having been granted to Bishop Erkenwald and his successors for ever towards the end of the seventh century; and there is reason to believe that a manor-house existed there at the time of the Norman Conquest.

The oldest section of the present palace was built by Bishop Fitzjames during the reign of Henry VII, but since that time many additions have been made. Of Fitzjames's building the Hall is the most striking feature. It has associations with two of the great figures of the English Reformation : Bishop Bonner, whom the Pope wished to throw into a cauldron of molten lead but who died a natural death in Marshalsea prison; and his successor Ridley, who was burnt as a heretic in 1555.

Fulham's Famous Gardens

The gardens of the Palace have been famous since the sixteenth century, when Bishop Grindall grew fine grapes there; and according to Sir William Watson, an eighteenth-century botanist, " planted a greater variety of curious exotic plants and trees than had at any time been collected in any garden in England."

Donald McLeish

GREAT HALL OF FULHAM PALACE

Fulham Palace has been the official residence of the Bishops of London for about the same time that Lambeth has been of the Archbishops of Canterbury. The ancient moat, Danish or earlier, has been filled in.

WESTMINSTER PALACE FROM OLD PALACE YARD

The Royal Palace of Westminster extended from the Thames almost to the Abbey, covering part of the Old and New Palace Yards. The House of Commons, originally the chapel, occupied very nearly its present site. It dated from the thirteenth century and its walls were adorned with a series of frescoes.

EARLY HOME OF ENGLISH KINGS

The fire fiend was the terror of Old London. The first Palace of Westminster fell to its devouring fury about the year 1035. Little is known about the place except that it was the favourite residence of King Cnut, commonly called Canute. It was completely rebuilt by Edward the Confessor, partly on the present sites of Old Palace Yard and New Palace Yard.

There the Confessor held his court and entertained his cousin William, Duke of Normandy. There, too, the saintly but rather weak King breathed his last, muttering : " I shall not die, but live; and passing from the country of the dead, verily I hope to behold the good things of the Lord in the land of the living."

According to Stow, William the Conqueror found Westminster " farre inferiour to the building of princely palaces in France " and therefore made considerable alterations. The Palace also received an important addition when, during the first half of the twelfth century, King Stephen gave orders for the erection of the chapel which afterwards bore the name of his patron saint. This was badly damaged by fire about 1298, but was rebuilt during the second quarter of the fourteenth century in the style known as Decorated Gothic. Great labour and much skill were expended upon its interior decoration, the walls being adorned with a beautiful series of frescoes. These were covered up by wainscoting when Edward VI made the chapel the meeting-place of the Commons. After the Union of England and Ireland in 1800 the building was enlarged to make room for the representatives of the latter country, and on the removal of the wainscoting the frescoes were found in perfect condition. All but the crypt of the chapel was destroyed in the great fire of 1834.

The old House of Lords, which was also within the Palace, was not beautiful. Its principal treasures were a number of tapestries, depicting the rout of the Spanish Armada, which had been presented to Queen Elizabeth by the States of Holland.

Between the House of Lords and St. Stephen's Chapel was the Painted Chamber, in which

Edward the Confessor is supposed to have died. Like the chapel, its walls were decorated with a series of paintings, dating from the fourteenth century, and it was from these that it derived its name. They were chiefly battle pictures.

In this chamber witnesses at the trial of Charles I were examined, and here Oliver Cromwell and Henry Martin signed the King's death-warrant, indulging the while in ill-timed pleasantries.

The royal council chamber, commonly known as the Star Chamber, lay on the eastern side of New Palace Yard. It was probably so called because of stars that adorned the ceiling. At what date the Star Chamber became a court of justice is not definitely known, but it was probably in Henry VII's reign. This court had power to create and define the offences it punished, and its judges were also prosecutors, so that to say that "justice" was administered there is hardly correct. It could inflict any punishment except death. Some prisoners were merely heavily fined and imprisoned, but others were horribly mutilated, tortured, whipped and put in the pillory. Archbishop Laud succeeded in making the Star Chamber Court even more unpopular that it had been before Charles I's time, and it was abolished by Parliament in 1641.

Great Hall of William Rufus

All that now remains of the vanished glories of the ancient Palace is the Great Hall built by William Rufus in 1099. When it was completed its enormous size astonished the guests Rufus entertained there at the feast of Whitsuntide, but the arrogant king merely remarked, "It is but a bed-chamber to the palace that I will ere long raise up." In the following year, on August 2, William's lifeless body lay under a tree in the New Forest. About half a century later the Great Hall and the royal buildings that surrounded it had fallen into a state of ruin.

The whole of the palace was hastily repaired by Thomas Becket in the early years of Henry II's reign, and it was in the Great Hall that this monarch's son, Prince Henry, had a crown placed upon his head nearly twenty years before his father's death. At the feast which followed the coronation the King acted as his son's butler, which made the boy assume so arrogant an expression that the Archbishop of York, who was sitting near him, thought fit to reprove him, saying, "There is not another prince in the world who hath such a server at his table." To which Prince Henry haughtily retorted, "Why dost marvel at that? My father doing it thinketh it not more than becometh him; he, being born of princely blood only on the mother's side, serveth me that am a king born."

The tradition of using the Hall as a banqueting house, begun by its founder and kept up by Henry II, lasted for many hundreds of years. Henry III entertained 6,000 poor people there on New Year's Day, 1236, and Richard II feasted 10,000 there on more than one occasion.

In 1394, almost three hundred years after its foundation, Richard II decided to reconstruct the Hall, it having then been in a state of decay for nearly a century. The work was supervised by John Gedeney; but Hugh Herland, one of the King's master carpenters, was the probable architect and builder of the unique hammer-beam roof. It was, and still is, the only roof of its kind in the world. The Hall is 67½ feet broad and the roof stretches from wall to wall without any intermediate supports.

It is said that large quantities of black Irish oak, chosen because of its extraordinary durability, were used in the construction of the roof, which was covered with lead.

At the beginning of the nineteenth century the roof was adjudged to be unsafe, and it was thoroughly overhauled in 1819. Fifteen years later the great fire that destroyed the old Houses of Parliament threatened to devour the Hall, but fortunately at the last moment the wind changed and the flames were blown in another direction.

Oaks as Old as Roof

Just before the First World War an examination of the roof showed that the death-watch beetle had for many years been eating away the massive timbers. All that remained of some of the main rafters, purlins and collar beams were shells, their interiors having been completely destroyed.

When the question arose of purchasing new oak to replace the decayed beams the Office of Works discovered that a gentleman named Courthope, of Wadhurst, had supplied some of the original oak in 1394, and that one of his descendants, Sir George Courthope, Member of Parliament for Rye, possessed oak trees eminently suitable for the purpose. So they used his trees. They were over 600 years old,

THE STATELY HALL OF WESTMINSTER PALACE

Built by William Rufus, the hall was given a unique hammer-beam roof of oak during the reign of Richard II. First used as a banqueting room, the hall later became the scene of every important State trial during seven centuries. Here Charles I received his doom; a tablet on the steps marks the spot where he stood, silently defying his judges. In the fire of 1834 which destroyed the Houses of Parliament, the building was preserved by a change in the direction of the wind. The priceless roof was damaged by enemy bombs in 1941 and 1944.

TRIAL OF WARREN HASTINGS

For seven centuries every important State trial took place in Westminster Hall. That of Warren Hastings, first Governor-General of India, dragged on over seven years, from 1788 to 1795. It ended in his acquittal.

and must therefore have been standing when the original Courthope was alive. The less badly damaged beams were retained, being reinforced with steel girders, so placed as to be invisible. The work was finished in 1922.

Momentous State Trials

It is thought that William Rufus's primary object in building Westminster Hall was the provision of a suitable courthouse close to, yet distinct from, the private buildings of his palace. In those days it was customary for the Law Courts to sit wherever the King was in residence, but in 1244 Henry III ordered that they should sit permanently in Westminster Hall. Some of the courts sat in rooms adjoining the Hall until 1882, when they were removed to the Strand. Every important State trial held in England from the time of Rufus till the nineteenth century took place in Westminster Hall.

In 1517 occurred the trial, before Henry VIII, the Dukes of Norfolk and Suffolk and the Lord Mayor of London, as well as many other representatives of the nobility and the commonalty, of 480 men and eleven women who had taken part in the rising of the 'prentices on May Day. The prisoners were led into the Hall with ropes about their necks. Some of the judges wished to hang them all, but after Cardinal Wolsey and the Queens of England, Scotland and France—Katharine, Margaret and Mary—had interceded on their behalf the King pardoned them. The prisoners threw their halters into the air.

Sentenced to Death

Four years later the holder of the proud office of High Constable of England, Edward Stafford, Duke of Buckingham, heard sentence of death pronounced upon himself. He was a descendant of Edward III, and being "the infatuated victim of an astrologer's promise to the throne," had incurred the wrath not only of the King, but also of the all-powerful Wolsey.

In 1535 no less than three distinguished men stood their trials in the Hall. They were Sir Thomas More, Bishop John Fisher and

Lord Dacre. Both More and Fisher had refused to acknowledge Henry VIII's right to assume spiritual supremacy, and both were beheaded after enduring long terms of imprisonment. Dacre, who was accused of high treason, was the only state prisoner of Henry VIII's reign at whose trial the verdict "not guilty" was pronounced. Among the many exalted personages who were found guilty in this Hall during the sixteenth century may be mentioned the Protector Somerset, once "the darling of the people," Sir Thomas Wyatt, the Duke of Norfolk, the Earl of Arundel, and Robert Devereux, Earl of Essex.

Deserted by his King

In 1606 Guy Fawkes and his fellow-conspirators were there condemned to be hanged, drawn and quartered.

Thirty-four years later, Charles I having basely deserted him, Thomas Wentworth, Earl of Strafford, was tried on twenty-eight separate charges by the members of the House of Lords, the Commons being his accusers. The trial lasted for eighteen days, during which time Strafford defended himself with skill and courage. The King was present during the proceedings, the memory of which must vividly have haunted his mind when, in January, 1649, he himself stood in the selfsame hall vainly attempting to escape paying the terrible price Cromwell demanded for his folly; for it can hardly be gainsaid that when Charles signed the Bill of Attainder against Strafford he signed his own death warrant.

The final words of Strafford's defence were so eloquent that they touched even the hearts of his accusers. "My lords," he said, "I have now delayed your lordships longer than I should else have done but for the interest of these dear pledges"—here indicating his children who stood beside him—"which a departed saint in heaven has left me. I should be loth——" Here his voice broke with emotion. "What I forfeit for myself, it is nothing; but I confess, that my indiscretion should forfeit for them, it wounds me very deeply. You will be pleased to pardon my infirmity"—meaning his display of emotion. "Something I should have said, but I see I shall not be able, and therefore I leave it . . . And so, my lords, even so with all humility, and with all tranquillity of mind, I submit, clearly and freely, to your judgments: and whether that righteous doom shall be to life or death, I shall repose myself, full of gratitude and confidence, in the arms of the great Author of my existence. *Te deum laudamus.*"

Strafford's master was described by Cromwell's followers as the "tyrant, traitor and murderer, Charles Stuart." Nevertheless, he conducted himself with extraordinary dignity at the trial, refusing to plead since he denied the legality of the proceedings.

After the Restoration the heads of Cromwell, Ireton and Bradshaw were stuck on pikes and placed above the roof of Westminster Hall. Cromwell's body had been embalmed before burial. Consequently, although his head remained in position over the Hall for a quarter of a century, it was in good preservation when, after having been blown down in a storm, it was stolen by a sentry. It has been carefully preserved ever since, though it has passed through many hands, and was exhibited to a learned society in 1911.

Palace Used as Market

During the seventeenth and eighteenth centuries the Hall was used not only as a banqueting house and a court-room, but also as a market. Archbishop Laud, writing in 1631, tells of a fire which had its origin among the stalls and shops that lined the walls and which threatened to destroy the Hall. Nearly thirty years later Samuel Pepys recorded in his diary that a young bookseller had been buried in the Hall.

Tom Brown's Amusements (1700) has a vivid description of a visit to the Hall. It says, "On your left hand you hear a nimble-tongued painted sempstress with her charming treble invite you to buy some of her knick-knacks, and on your right a deep-mouthed cryer, commanding impossibilities, viz., silence to be kept among women and lawyers."

The shops and stalls were mostly those of publishers, booksellers, law stationers and milliners. The rents they paid—at least, in the seventeenth century—went to the Warden of the Fleet. That these tradesmen and tradeswomen carried on their business while the courts were sitting cannot be doubted.

Among those peers who were here tried for their parts in the Jacobite Rebellion of 1745 may be mentioned Lord Lovat, the most unprincipled scoundrel of his time. He was guilty of practically every crime but cowardice. After he had been sentenced to death, he turned to his judges and said, smilingly, "Good day, my lords; you and I shall never meet again in the same place."

A criminal of a very different type was Elizabeth Chudleigh, who in 1776 was tried in the Hall for having " married " the Duke of Kingston while her husband was yet alive. In such cases the prisoner, upon conviction, had her right hand branded upon the block, but the woman's beauty so affected her judges that they dismissed her on payment of costs.

Trial That Lasted for Years

One of the greatest trials of all time, that of Warren Hastings, first Governor-General of India, took place in Westminster Hall between 1788 and 1795, ending in the acquittal of the accused on all charges. Arrayed against the great administrator were the three most distinguished orators of the day—Burke, Sheridan, and Fox. The torrent of passionate indignation that fell from Burke's lips put the whole court into a state of frenzied excitement, and when Fox had had his say Hastings felt himself " the most culpable man on earth."

The president of the court, Lord Thurlow, habitually wore a somewhat owlish expression, which moved Fox to exclaim, " I wonder whether anyone ever was so wise as Thurlow looks."

That Hastings was to some extent guilty of the charges preferred against him there is little doubt, but the verdict was on the whole a just one. The length of his trial and the indignities to which his proud spirit was subjected were a sufficient punishment. Before the nineteenth century justice was very hard to come by, even in Westminster Hall. Ben Jonson refers to :

" The Great Hall of Westminster, the field where mutual frauds are fought and no side yield."

Peter the Great once visited the Hall, and the thing that impressed him most was the number of lawyers it contained. " Why," he exclaimed in astonishment, " I have but two lawyers in the whole of my dominions, and I mean to hang one of them the moment I return home."

PALACE YARD STAIRS
A print showing the busy landing stage in 1641.

To this ancient hall in May, 1898, was carried the coffin that held the body of Gladstone, and twelve years later that of Edward VII.

In 1923 King George V reopened the Hall after the completion of the repairs to the roof. On that occasion he said, " For centuries the Hall has witnessed the growth of the Constitution and has been, as it were, a link between the Crown and the people."

In May, 1935, on the occasion of his Silver Jubilee, he received the loyal congratulations of Parliament in Westminster Hall. " This, my Palace of Westminster," his Majesty remarked, " in the mighty heart of our Empire, is the very cradle of our envied Parliamentary institutions. Here is the anvil whereon our common law was forged, to become the joint inheritance of the United States of America and our own community of peoples."

Nobody foresaw that within a year the King would be lying in state in that very Hall, surrounded by an endless file of his mourning subjects; still less that only fifteen years afterwards the same sad, silent ceremony would be repeated for his son, King George VI.

But Westminster Hall has its glad occasions too. In November, 1954, the Hall was crowded with a distinguished company representing every shade of political opinion, who had come to witness the presentation by Parliament to Sir Winston Churchill of his portrait in oils—an event unique in British political history.

Westminster Hall suffered much during the German air raids. On May 10, 1941, its splendid roof was pierced by bombs. Three years later it was again damaged; but it still stands foursquare to all the world.

THE HOUSES OF PARLIAMENT

Designed by Sir Charles Barry, R.A., and erected between 1840 and 1857, they constitute the most beautiful modern Gothic structure in the world. To the left is the Victoria Tower, to the right the Clock Tower.

MOTHER OF PARLIAMENTS

At four o'clock on the afternoon of October 16, 1834, two gentlemen were being shown round the Houses of Parliament by Mrs. Wright, the deputy-housekeeper. On entering the House of Lords they found it unbearably hot, and so smoky that, as they said afterwards, they could not "see the throne from the Bar."

Later she found her own rooms growing uncomfortably warm. She made inquiry, and was told that, according to instructions, two workmen had been all day burning Exchequer tallies—the notched sticks on which, for eight hundred years down to 1826, the accounts of England had been kept—in the heating stove. There was no danger, she was assured.

At six o'clock a doorkeeper and his wife, Mr. and Mrs. Mullincamp, were setting out for the theatre, when they noticed a light under one of the doors. "Oh good God!" cried Mrs. Mullincamp, "the House of Lords is on fire."

The furnace feeders had done their job only too well. For hours they had gorged the furnace with tallies, and the tallies, dry as tinder, had burned with the stored-up energy of centuries. The flues had grown red-hot, and had first baked and finally ignited the aged panelling along which they ran.

The fire swept along passages, lobbies and staircases with appalling rapidity. By seven o'clock the ancient Palace of Westminster, historic seat of the Mother of Parliaments, was a raging mass of flame. The recently created London Fire-Engine Establishment rushed every man and every engine to the scene, but they were powerless to check its course. A host of ready volunteers, from Ministers of the Crown down to labourers, joined in frantic and heroic efforts to rescue the priceless documents, books, pictures and other historic relics stored in numberless rooms throughout the buildings.

Meanwhile from all over London, and beyond, people in countless thousands came flocking. The bridges were packed with seething masses, the river was alive with boats, even the roof of Westminster Abbey was black with spectators.

Few among the huge assembled crowds sincerely regretted the destruction of the Houses of Parliament; many openly rejoiced at it. When at eleven o'clock the roof of the House of Lords fell in with a resounding crash the mob is said to have raised a shout of joy.

Glory Sadly Tarnished

Nor was much more pity wasted on the greater part of the Palace of Westminster. Its glory had long since departed, and it had gathered round it a huddled mass of foul hovels, ramshackle sheds and villainous drinking dens—" ten acres of congestion," as one writer has put it.

But the magnificent old Hall of Westminster, built by William Rufus and roofed with British oak by Richard II—that was another matter. In that was represented the enduring spirit of England; it stood as a gorgeous symbol of England's might, majesty and power. It was inconceivable that it should perish. From many a heart never before that night moved by any spirit of reverence for the past there went up an ardent prayer that Westminster Hall might be rescued from the flames.

When dawn broke on the 17th an indescribable scene of desolation was revealed. Seven acres of buildings lay in smoking ruin; but to the unspeakable joy of everyone the historic Hall was untouched! At the moment of its greatest danger, the direction of the wind had changed.

Parliament was due to meet in six days. William IV, who with Queen Adelaide drove down to inspect the ruins, offered the use of Buckingham Palace to the Legislature. But the force of old habit was too strong; when Parliament met it sat among the ruins " in a temporary building, not unlike a barn."

Later, the famous Painted Chamber, which stood between the old Houses of Lords and Commons, was rendered habitable for the Peers; the Commons were installed in the old House of Lords, of which the walls had remained intact. In these makeshift premises the Commons at least were to meet for eighteen years, while round them the " New Palace of Westminster " grew slowly upon the ruins of the old.

New Palace of Westminster

There had been more than one suggestion for rebuilding the Houses of Parliament on a fresh site, either in Green Park, at Trafalgar Square, or within the City. But Wellington, the Iron Duke, to whose opinions many had deferred since Waterloo, vigorously opposed

RESTORATION OF ST. STEPHEN'S CRYPT

The Chapel of St. Mary Undercroft, as it used to be called, escaped the fire. Here Simon de Montfort married Henry III's sister Eleanor, and according to tradition Caxton presented his first book to Edward IV.

THE NEW HOUSE OF COMMONS

The new Chamber occupies the same position as the old one, but is much better equipped, and the galleries have been enlarged. The seats on the right of the Speaker's chair are occupied by the Government; before the chair is the table on which the Mace reposes when the House is sitting; above it are the Press and Ladies' Galleries. The Chamber is heated by concealed panels and has an elaborate air-conditioning system.

any suggestion of moving. The old site, he declared, was the only possible one, because with the river at its back Parliament could never be surrounded by a revolutionary mob!

It was finally decided to rebuild on the same spot. In June, 1835, architects were invited to submit competitive designs by November 1, for a new Palace of Westminster, "the Style to be Gothic or Elizabethan."

Ninety-seven architects responded to the invitation, submitting schemes comprised in a total of over 1,400 drawings. Four designs were selected for consideration by His Majesty, and finally plan No. 64 was chosen.

When the sealed packet containing the name of the successful competitor was opened it was found that the winning design had been sent in by Mr. Charles Barry, long known among architects for his delightful sketches, and already famous as the designer of the Royal Institute of Fine Arts at Manchester.

Barry had been born in Bridge Street, Westminster, and had grown up under the shadow of the old Palace. On the fateful night of the fire he had been travelling by coach from Brighton to London, and immediately he learned the meaning of the fearsome glow on the horizon which was exciting the curiosity of all, the thought came to him that it might fall to his lot to rebuild the Palace he remembered so well from boyhood days.

Designed on a Letter

When the competition was announced he toiled unsparingly to win it, cutting down his hours of sleep to a maximum of five a night in the effort to realise his ambition. His first rough sketch was drawn on the back of a letter, and from the main points of this original design he never deviated, but laboured throughout the six months at his disposal to enrich and amplify them. To perfect his plans he toured Belgium, visiting all its glorious medieval town halls to gain inspiration and glean suggestions.

Almost Superhuman Exertions

Strenuous as was this period of creation, Barry's real labours and vexations were to begin with the acceptance on February 29, 1836, of his design. The building of the New Palace of Westminster was to occupy him for the rest of his life—it was not indeed quite completed when he died suddenly of heart disease in 1860—and, in the words of the *Dictionary of National Biography*, " Had he not been of the toughest fibre, of almost superhuman industry, and still thirsting for fame, he never could have carried out in his lifetime so

THE RICHLY DECORATED HOUSE OF LORDS

Before the Thrones is the Woolsack, seat of the Lord Chancellor. The Bar of the House, at which the Commons assemble to hear the King's Speech and the Royal Assent to Bills, is beneath the near gallery

Donald McLeish

LORD PROTECTOR OF THE COMMONWEALTH

Cromwell stands before Westminster Hall, in which he was acclaimed Lord Protector of England in 1653. The statue was designed by Sir William Hamo Thornycroft (1850–1925), who was also responsible for the Gordon statue in Trafalgar Square and the Gladstone monument in the Strand. It was erected in 1899.

great a work as the Houses of Parliament." No words could be more true.

In addition to the colossal labour of directing and supervising the erection of so vast a structure, he had, continues the same authority, "to contend with conflicting opinions, some professional jealousy, visionary schemes, official interference, uneducated criticism in and out of Parliament, and the rancour of enemies whose malignity has even pursued his fame beyond the grave."

Slow Work but Sure

But Barry possessed all the qualities enumerated above, and he chose admirable assistants. At the time of the fire he was engaged in building the King Edward VI Grammar School at Birmingham, by many considered the most beautiful of all his works, and while engaged upon this he made the acquaintance of Augustus Welby Pugin, later celebrated as a builder of Catholic churches, and John Thomas, a sculptor of great ability. When he embarked upon the Palace of Westminster he appointed Thomas head of the stone-carving department and Pugin virtually second in command, though officially head of the wood-carving department.

The work proceeded slowly. The building of the river wall along the Thames was begun in 1837, but it was not until April 27, 1840, that the first stone of the new edifice was laid, quite privately, by Mrs. Barry. Seven years later the Lords were installed in their new chamber, and on February 3, 1852, Her Majesty Queen Victoria formally opened the Victoria Tower (then only half completed) and the Royal Gallery, conferring upon the architect the honour of knighthood.

The exterior of the New Palace of Westminster—familiarly known all over the world as the Houses of Parliament—is far too well known to require detailed description. Extending 940 feet along the river bank, the buildings, which occupy an area of eight acres, form an oblong block flanked by the Clock Tower and the Victoria Tower, with smaller but still substantial towers at the other extremities, and buttressed by Westminster Hall, which forms a slightly oblique central wing dividing the enclosed New Palace Yard from Old Palace Yard, the latter now little more than an angle of the roadway.

As it stands, the Palace is probably the largest and certainly one of the most beautiful Gothic structures in the world. Barry's design, until ruthlessly cut down by "official interference," would have made it even larger and

OVERHAULING BIG BEN

Removing an hour hand of the giant clock, the chimes of which are heard daily by radio listeners all over the world. This hand is only nine feet long, while the minute hand is fourteen feet long.

more impressive. He planned to have enclosed New Palace Yard with a range of buildings similar to those along the river front, completing the quadrangle with a magnificent gate-tower at the junction of Bridge Street with Parliament Square; and he meant to have made the Victoria Tower 100 feet square instead of 75 as it is now. Even in its truncated form the New Palace cost eventually three times the amount provided for in the original estimate, namely £2,198,000 instead of £700,000.

Constant Repairs to Fabric

Seeing that the beauty of the structure has received almost universal praise—an Emperor of Russia called it " a dream in stone "—it is all the more unfortunate that the building stone employed for the exterior walls—a magnesian limestone from quarries at Anston, near Sheffield in Yorkshire—has proved to be almost as unsuitable as it possibly could be, owing to its being of a type peculiarly liable to corrosion by the smoke-filled and acid atmosphere that is London's own.

Within a few years of the erection of the Palace signs of decay became manifest, and ever since such constant attention has been necessary to arrest deterioration in the fabric that for many years the Palace has rarely been free from scaffolding. In 1926 a comprehensive scheme of repair was embarked upon, to occupy between twelve and fifteen years, and estimated to cost £1,062,350—almost exactly half the cost of the original buildings.

Contains over Five Hundred Rooms

The interior of the Palace is much less well known, though Westminster Hall is open to the public daily, and the Houses of Parliament and other rooms can be seen on Saturdays. Many people seem to be under the impression that it consists chiefly of the Houses of Lord and Commons. The visitor who enters these august chambers is usually amazed at their extreme smallness.

Actually the Palace contains over five hundred rooms—of which the two Houses are by no means the largest—and eighteen residences, including those of the Speaker and the Serjeant-at-Arms.

By the happiest of inspirations Sir Charles Barry made the grand central entrance to the New Palace lead up through Westminster Hall and into St. Stephen's Hall, the room he built on the site of the ancient St. Stephen's

THE CLOCK TOWER

Its slender beauty is well revealed by floodlighting. It is 316 feet high and 40 feet square. The light situated at the top signifies that Parliament is sitting.

Chapel, for three centuries the meeting place of the Commons.

On the floor of this room may be seen brass studs marking the position of the Speaker's Chair and the great table in the days when Charles I attempted in vain to infringe the Commons' privileges by demanding the persons of the five members who had offended him.

The reply of Speaker Lenthall on that occasion is memorable. Falling on his knees before the King he declared, " Your Majesty, I have neither eyes to see nor tongue to say but as this House commands me."

When Sir Charles Barry built St. Stephen's Hall he intended that the panels beneath the windows should be filled with pictures. Ninety years were to elapse before his intention was realised.

On June 28, 1927, the Prime Minister, Mr. Stanley Baldwin, unveiled in the Hall a series of eight mural paintings illustrating the Building of Britain. Standing on the very spot where for centuries the Speaker sat and watched the growth of English liberty, Mr. Baldwin said, " The idea of the whole scheme . . . was the idea of how we in this country came to be what we are."

The historians and artists who combined to create the series, he added, " took for points of cardinal consideration the higher qualities of our race . . . the ideals which we all of us, quite irrespective of our party, cherish in our hearts and would fain live up to."

Gorgeous in colouring and impressive in design, the pictures represent King Alfred's fleet defeating the Danes, Richard Cœur de Lion sailing for the Crusade, the Barons and King John ratifying the Magna Carta at Runnymede, the Wyclif Bible read in secret meeting, the Speaker (Sir Thomas More) refusing to grant Cardinal Wolsey a Royal subsidy without debate, Queen Elizabeth commissioning Sir Walter Raleigh to " discover unknown countries," Sir Thomas Roe, the first British Envoy to India, at Ajmir before Jehangir, the Mogul Emperor in 1614 and

CROMWELL DISSOLVING THE LONG PARLIAMENT

The historic scene of April 20, 1653, when Cromwell turned Parliament out of doors. "You mistake, sir," said John Bradshaw, "if you think the Parliament dissolved. No power on earth can dissolve the Parliament but itself." Bradshaw, a friend of John Milton, was president at the trial of Charles I.

ROOM WHERE BRITAIN'S DESTINY IS SEALED

The Cabinet room at No. 10 Downing Street, scene of many historic discussions. Over the fireplace hangs a portrait of Sir Robert Walpole, first Prime Minister of England, who held office from 1721 to 1742.

Queen Anne giving Royal Assent to the Act of Union with Scotland.

From St. Stephen's Hall one passes into the octagonal Central Hall, the heart of the entire range of buildings. Sixty feet in diameter and 75 feet in height, this Hall has a fine vaulted stone roof inlaid with Venetian mosaics and crowned by the Central Tower, 300 feet high. Statues range the walls.

Origin of the Woolsack

To the right and left of the Central Hall are the Houses of Lords and Commons, each reached by a corridor and a lobby. The Peers' Chamber, lined with benches covered with red morocco leather and lit by twelve stained-glass windows containing portraits of English sovereigns since the Norman Conquest, gives an immediate impression of rich opulence. Beneath a gorgeous gilded canopy at the end of the Chamber stands the throne of the Queen of England, the back richly decorated with the Royal Arms, and surmounted by a crown. Beneath and immediately in front of the throne is the famous Woolsack, to-day a large square red-covered ottoman stuffed with wool and having a back in the exact centre.

The Woolsack, on which the Lord Chancellor sits, was first placed in the House of Lords by Edward III, to indicate to all that wool, and the woollen industry, was "the sovereign treasure of the Kingdom."

The House of Lords is 90 feet long, 45 feet wide and 45 feet high—not by any means a vast room for the number of peers entitled to meet on its floor. The House of Commons, which had to accommodate over 600 members, was considerably smaller, being only 75 feet long by 45 feet wide. It was destroyed by a German bomb, on May 10, 1941, and the Commons took up temporary residence in the House of Lords.

On May 26, 1948, the Speaker laid the foundation stone of the new House of Commons; and in a little over two years the five-storied structure, carried on a steel skeleton, was completed. The new Chamber maintains the traditional smallness and inadequate seating capacity of the old one, but in other respects is much improved. There are loud-speakers in the backs of the green leather benches; panel heating and air-conditioning are provided. The Press Gallery has been increased to almost twice its former size.

There are dining-rooms, refreshment rooms and libraries for the Commons, but only Cabinet Ministers have private offices, and ordinary members must receive deputations and see friends either in the public rooms or in crowded corridors.

At the far end of the House of Commons is the Speaker's chair. On the right of the Speaker are the Government benches, on the left the Opposition, the front row on each side being reserved respectively for the Ministers of the Crown and the leaders of the Opposition.

Between these redoubtable opponents is the Clerk's table, on which is placed the Mace. The present Mace dates from 1649, and is the same one (though redecorated and reornamented) concerning which Cromwell exclaimed "Take away that Fool's Bauble!" It is of wrought brass, highly burnished. No Parliamentary business can be conducted unless it is on the table, but directly the House goes into Committee it is removed.

No. 10 DOWNING STREET
Official residence of the First Lord of the Treasury, whose unofficial title is that of Prime Minister.

Customs of the House

The House of Commons is the scene of many ancient customs and usages. Every sitting is opened with prayers, read directly after the Speaker has marched in procession to his chair and the Mace has been placed on the table. No reporters are ever admitted until prayers are concluded.

Members of Parliament may not enter the House with their hats on—though this rule is relaxed in the case of women members—but they sometimes put them on when they are seated. An order of the day can be moved or seconded by a member raising his hat.

Every member on entering or leaving the House bows to the Speaker. This is a relic of the days when the Commons moved from the Chapter House in Westminster Abbey to St. Stephen's Chapel. The Speaker's chair was placed on the site of the altar, and members made obeisance to the chair as they would have done to the altar.

No Personalities Allowed

No member may in the House address another; all communications have to be made to "Mr. Speaker." Nor may a member be referred to by name; he is always "the honourable member for "—whatever constituency he represents.

It is one of the most stringent rules of the House that no personal imputations may be made upon members' characters. Only one member may be on his feet at one time : if another rises to interrupt a speaker, the first speaker immediately sits down, rising again to resume his speech when the interrupter has finished. And a member may not read his speech.

If he wishes to speak, a member must "catch the Speaker's eye"—often a matter of no little difficulty when competition is keen. The deference paid to the Speaker's authority and the ready obedience almost invariably accorded to his rulings are among the outstanding features of British Parliamentary procedure.

When the Speaker rises any member on his

OLD "INDIA" OFFICE FROM ST. JAMES'S PARK
This massive and dignified building, part of a quadrangle designed by Sir Gilbert Scott and erected 1863–73, formerly housed the famous India Office. Today it houses a number of Government departments.

feet sits down, and perfect silence reigns. In the rare cases when the Speaker's authority has been defied and it is necessary for him to request a member to withdraw from the House, it is the business of the Serjeant-at-Arms—in knee breeches and silk stockings, girt with a sword—to see the order carried out.

Turned Out for being Noisy

The office of the Speaker dates back at least six hundred years. When King Edward I sent the knights and burgesses (i.e., the Commons) into the Chapter House at Westminster Abbey to deliberate apart from the Lords because they were such a noisy lot, given to talking all at the same time, one among them was elected to report on their behalf. The Speaker is still the only M.P. entitled to speak "in Parliament assembled," that is, when Crown, Lords and Commons are met together.

When the House "divides," that is, votes upon any motion, a bell is rung throughout the building to call up members not in the chamber at the moment. When these have all assembled the doors are locked, and those in favour of the motion go into the "Aye" lobby behind the Government benches, those against into the "No" lobby on the opposite side. The House having been emptied, "tellers" take up their posts by the lobby doors and count members as they return to their seats.

"Who Goes Home?"

At the conclusion of every sitting the doorkeepers of the House throw open the doors, and down the corridors there echoes the cry, taken up by every policeman in the building, "Who goes home?" It is now but a signal that the House has adjourned, yet it reminds one of the times—not so long distant—when so many ruffians lurked in London streets that even members of Parliament were disinclined to go home alone, and used to set forth in groups attended by men bearing torches.

When the monarch comes in state to open or dissolve Parliament he enters the Palace by the Royal Entrance, a massive archway 50 feet high giving access to a vaulted porch beneath the colossal Victoria Tower. This latter, the highest Gothic tower in the world (336 feet), is surmounted by a flagstaff 110 feet high. On this gigantic pole, which weighs 16 tons, a Union Jack is flown throughout the days when Parliament is sitting. In the Victoria Tower is the Muniment Room, where after a general election the used voting papers are stored for a year and a day.

Largest Bell Cast in England

In spite of its size and stately dignity the Victoria Tower has never caught the popular imagination to anything like the same degree as the Clock Tower. The latter owes its fame, not to its extreme beauty—though it is one of the loveliest Gothic towers in existence—but to the ever-renowned "Big Ben," from the day of its installation one of the seven wonders of the modern world, and since the advent of broadcasting, become daily familiar to many millions of people.

Many people speak of "Big Ben" as if they were referring to the clock, but the name belongs strictly to the bell on which the hours are struck. The largest bell ever cast in England, it weighs 13½ tons, stands 7 feet 6 inches high and measures 9 feet across the mouth, cost £6,000 to install, and has been defective ever since it was hoisted into place in 1858.

"Big Ben" got its name from Sir Benjamin Hall, first Commissioner of Works in 1856, the year in which it was cast. Its early history is a record of misadventure. It emerged from the mould 16 tons in weight, or 2 tons more than had been agreed. Placed on board ship for transport from the Tees to London, it nearly sank the vessel on which it was loaded. The original 7-cwt. clapper provided for it was found inadequate to bring out the full tone, so a second, weighing 13 cwt., was provided. Not much later, the bell was found to be cracked, and a pretty controversy arose. The makers of the bell said it had been cracked by use of a too heavy clapper; their critics retorted that a bell which could not stand up to a clapper designed to bring out the full tone, could not be a very good one.

INSIDE THE FOREIGN OFFICE
The Locarno Room, so called since the signing there of the Locarno Pact on December 1, 1925.

Big Ben is Cracked

The upshot of it was that the bell was recast, but even this desperate remedy did not cure it of its fault. Within a very short time cracks again appeared; and though it was patched up "Big Ben" has remained a cracked bell ever since. Yet few people would have it replaced, for a new bell would not be "Big Ben."

No such criticism has ever attached to the clock which "Big Ben" serves. Since its installation in 1859 it has remained one of the most accurate timekeepers in the world. Checked continually at the Royal Observatory, it is rarely found to be more than one second at fault.

When so grave an error as a second is detected, an original method of correction is employed. Half-way down the pendulum a tray is fixed, and on this, if the clock is losing, a halfpenny or a penny is placed. If the clock is gaining, a coin is removed. The addition of one penny adds a second a day to the speed of the pendulum.

The four dials of the clock are each 22½ feet in diameter. The minute hands are 14 feet long, weigh 2 cwt., and travel a foot a minute. The hour hands are 9 feet long and the figures indicating the hours each 2 feet in length.

For many years one of London's most familiar figures was "The Man with the Telescope" who stood daily on Westminster Bridge beneath the statue of Queen Boadicea. Over 80 years of age when he died, he had occupied his pitch

CANADIAN HEADQUARTERS IN TRAFALGAR SQUARE *Donald McLeish*

Opened in 1925 by H.M. King George V, Canada House is a restoration of the Union Club built by Nash in 1826. It stands at the corner of Pall Mall on the west side of Trafalgar Square.

AUSTRALIA HOUSE FROM THE STRAND

Built on an island site at the east of Aldwych, it was opened by King George V in 1918, and is considered to be one of the finest buildings in this part of London. It is in Doric style.

INDIA HOUSE

Designed by Sir Herbert Baker and opened in 1930, it adjoins Bush House, Aldwych, on the west.

for so long that he had become as it were part of the scenery.

Fired in his youth by some lectures on astronomy, he bought a telescope and set up in business at New Cross, showing people the moon and stars. One night an Irishman came along and said, " I can see the moon any old time. Let's have a look at Big Ben."

" The Man with the Telescope " at once seized upon the idea. He moved first to Honor Oak Hill, where he enabled people to read the time at a distance of 4 miles, and later to Westminster Bridge, where he remained until his death.

While Parliament is sitting, a light gleams nightly from the Clock Tower : the life of the statesman is ever attended with publicity. That of the Civil Servant is passed in an obscurity that is rarely illuminated. In the ponderous but somewhat ragged range of buildings which lines Parliament Street and the lower half of Whitehall are men whose names are quite unknown to the public but whose counsels affect profoundly the nation's welfare.

Gloomy-looking structures many of the Government buildings are, but they possess for the most part a massive solidity which accords well with the English character and gives a not unmerited sense of security. Despite its reputation for red-tapeism and

Donald McLeish

NEW ZEALAND IN LONDON

The offices of the Dominion of New Zealand are in the Strand, adjoining the Adelphi Theatre.

circumlocution the British Civil Service is the finest in the world, with a reputation for integrity equalled by no other.

All the main Government departments have offices in Parliament Street or Whitehall. The solid block of buildings extending back from Parliament Street along Great George Street to St. James's Park housed the Board of Trade, the Board of Education and part of the Ministry of Health. Farther up Parliament Street on the same side the Home Office, Foreign Office, Dominions and Colonial Offices, are contained in a large quadrangular building designed by Sir Gilbert Scott. Formerly it also housed the old India Office.

SOUTH AFRICA HOUSE

Newest of the Dominion headquarters in London, this fine building faces Trafalgar Square and the Strand. Beside it is St. Martin-in-the-Fields Church.

The entrance to the Dominions Office is in Downing Street, the insignificant little *cul-de-sac* which since the days of Sir Robert Walpole has contained the official residence of the First Lord of the Treasury, that is, the Prime Minister. No. 10 Downing Street is a world-famous address, but the house—or its exterior, at least—typifies London domestic architecture at its worst.

How Downing Street got its Name

It and its neighbour No. 11, where resides the Chancellor of the Exchequer, are about as plain and drab a pair of houses as could well be imagined. The name of the thoroughfare perpetuates that of Sir George Downing, a successful political "trimmer" who served Cromwell and Charles II as Ambassador to The Hague and was heartily detested there.

On the north side of Downing Street are the Treasury (completely burnt out by a flying bomb in 1944, but since restored) and the Privy Council, with beyond them the Horse Guards—always a favourite resort of visitors, both young and old, on account of the mounted sentries and the daily ceremony of changing the guard.

Undoubtedly the best place for viewing all these Government offices is St. James's Park. From there they appear truly dignified and even pleasing, a massive and imposing range of buildings sweeping round the extensive Horse Guards Parade, from the Admiralty on the north, with its "nerve centre" bristling with wireless masts, to the Board of Trade on the south. A fine viewpoint is the bridge over the lake.

On the Thames side of Whitehall is the War Office; an immense irregular quadrangle (with not a single right angle), it contains a thousand rooms and has two and a half miles of corridors.

On the opposite side of Whitehall Place an immense but severely plain post-war office block houses part of the Air Ministry and Board of Trade. Its entrance is closed by two huge aluminium doors and is flanked on either side by a fleshy recumbent female nude, looking a trifle overfed and underworked (it is to be hoped, without any symbolic significance!). A second great office block is now being erected next door, which threatens to smother that relic of Victorian London, Richmond Terrace with its memories of Disraeli.

During the present century most of the British Dominions have built or acquired impressive buildings in London to serve as headquarters for the transaction of imperial and economic business. Since the passing of the Statute of Westminster in 1931 the British Parliament has, of course, no authority over the Dominions, which are now completely self-governing units owing allegiance only to the Crown, but the mutual interests of Motherland and Dominions are innumerable; and to ensure that these receive adequate attention each Dominion has a High Commissioner resident in London.

Australia House in the Strand, built in 1911–14, is literally a fragment of the Commonwealth deposited in London. It is faced with English Portland stone, but with this exception every block of stone in the building was brought from Australia.

In June, 1925, their Majesties King George V and Queen Mary drove to Trafalgar Square to open Canada House, where the Union Club had stood for a century. Eight years later their Majesties opened on the opposite side of the Square, next to St. Martin-in-the-Fields, the magnificent South Africa House.

Standing on what has been called " the finest site in Europe," this grand building has a central portico adorned with Corinthian columns in order to harmonise with the style of the National Gallery, and its front presents a series of symbolic carvings, including the springbok and the *Good Hope*, the ship of the first Governor of South Africa.

As with Australia House, native material was largely employed, including South African red granite, marble, teak and other woods. One of the most delightful features is the Travel Bureau, designed as a Dutch farmhouse interior, and paved with large red tiles.

For sheer beauty the interior of India House in Aldwych, opened by the King-Emperor in 1930, is perhaps unequalled by any other modern building in London. Every bit of the carved stonework and woodwork is Indian, and in the exhibition room are always to be seen exquisite examples of Indian craftsmanship in a variety of native materials.

Donald McLeish

ON GUARD

A Lifeguardsman on duty in Whitehall. The daily changing of the Guard attracts many spectators.

The premises of the other members of the British Commonwealth of Nations are at present scattered about central London, where they have to compete for attention with cinemas, shops and amusement arcades. One day, perhaps, there will arise in Whitehall a street worthy of the name, where alongside the offices of the mother nation those of her children may find fitting place.

When that day arrives, as surely it must, this part of London should present one of the most impressive and beautiful scenes in the world. The possibilities of the site are infinite; from Westminster Abbey the ground rises gently to Trafalgar Square, with on the one side the Thames, on the other the beautiful St. James's Park. An architect with courage and imagination would have an unrivalled opportunity.

THE LORD MAYOR RIDES IN STATE

The Lord Mayor's procession in November each year is one of London's time-honoured pageants. It originated in the ceremonial riding of the Mayor to be presented to the Monarch for approval.

RULERS OF THE SQUARE MILE

On the left-hand side of the steep hill leading up to Highgate village the curious passer-by may see on the pavement what appears to be a gravestone enclosed in an iron cage. It marks the spot where, according to legend, a poor ill-used kitchen boy who had run away from his master once sat to rest his aching limbs.

As he lingered there the far-off bells of Bow Church rang out, and it seemed to the listening boy that their peals formed into a rhyme, and that the rhyme ran :

Turn again Whittington,
Thrice Lord Mayor of London.

His weariness disappeared as the vision splendid inflamed his mind. Lord Mayor of London! Well, why not? Fired with courage, he resolved to return to his master, Hugh Fitzwarren, a wealthy mercer in the City. And from that moment Dame Fortune began to smile upon him.

Whittington prospered exceedingly, married his master's daughter, amassed great wealth, and, to justify the story, in actual fact thrice became Mayor of London.

He was actually Mayor—not Lord Mayor, for that title was not then used—four times. When Adam Bamme died in June, 1397, the King appointed Whittington to the mayoral chair for the remainder of the year; and the citizens elected him to be their cheif officer in 1398, 1406 and 1419.

A mercer, or dealer in cloth, by trade, Whittington became also banker to Henry IV and Henry V, both of whom borrowed large sums of money from him. To the victor of Agincourt it is said he once made a princely gift. During Whittington's last mayoralty Henry came in state with his Queen to dine with the Mayor, and at the banquet Whittington, having lit a fire of precious woods made fragrant with spices, threw into the flames bonds to the value of £60,000 (representing at least £1,000,000 to-day), thus cancelling all Henry's debts to him.

" Surely, never had King such a subject ! " cried the monarch, overwhelmed by such generosity. " Surely, sir," retorted Whittington with courtly grace, " never had subject such a King ! "

From very earliest days London had its own local government, though the tradition was not continuous. During the latter part of the Roman occupation it had two magistrates, a senate and a town council. The English did not like walled cities, and it is probable that after their coming London recovered its ancient position but slowly. It required the genius of Alfred the Great, who appointed his son-in-law Ethelred, Earl of the Mercians, as Governor

HENRY FITZAILWYN
First Mayor of London. From an original painting at Drapers' Hall. The likeness is doubtful.

of the City, to set it firmly upon its feet again. Thereafter it grew very rapidly in size and importance. It was governed by its bishop and a portreeve, the latter being an officer of the king who acted as civil magistrate and collected taxes and tolls, with the assistance of a number of subordinate officers. Every freeman claimed the right to partake in the government of the City, and all laws were made and criminal cases tried by assembly of the citizens, who were summoned by the tolling of the bell of St. Paul's Cathedral.

Charter Granted by William I

So powerful did the City become that it could bargain even with Norman William after he had conquered and slain Harold the Saxon; and it did not open its gates to him nor acknowledge him as king until he had agreed to the conditions it had laid down.

In the Guildhall is preserved the precious slip of parchment, six inches long and an inch broad, on which are written, in the language of our English forefathers, the words of the charter granted by William the Conqueror to the city he dared not besiege. They make up four and a quarter lines only, but they comprised all the citizens desired, and form the basis of the unique and exclusive status possessed to-day by the Lord Mayor and Corporation of the City of London.

The charter runs thus: "William, King, greets William, Bishop, and Gosfrith, Portreeve, and all the burghers within London, French and English, friendly; and I do you to wit that I will that ye be all law worthy that were in King Edward's day. And I will that every child be his father's heir after his father's day. And I will not endure that any man offer any wrong to you. God keep you."

William Rufus had little dealing with the City, but from Henry I, London obtained, probably in 1130, a charter of the first importance. In it the Conqueror's youngest son granted to the citizens the entire county of Middlesex, with the right to elect a sheriff over it; the right to elect their own justiciar, and the privilege of being subject to no jurisdiction save that of their own officers.

Henry II granted the City, which prospered greatly under his strong rule, a charter that was almost identical with that of Henry I except that he revoked the privilege of London to elect its own sheriff. It was probably during this reign that the citizens began to hanker after a *commune*, such as several great Continental cities possessed even at that time.

Beginning of City Corporation

Their opportunity to acquire this came in the reign of Richard I. That monarch having sailed as a soldier of the Cross to Palestine, England was left in the charge of his Chancellor and Justiciar, William de Longchamp, who soon made himself hated by all classes, because, besides being excessively haughty in his bearing, "he and his revellers had so exhausted the whole kingdom, that they did not leave a man his belt, a woman her necklace, a nobleman his ring, or anything of value even to a Jew. He . . . so utterly emptied the King's treasury, that in all the coffers and bags therein, nothing but the keys could be met with, after . . . two years."

Prince John, brother of the King, took up the cause of the people. London saw its opportunity to strike a profit[illegible] bargain. If John would recognise the ci[illegible]*mmune*, it would support him against Longchamp.

John agreed, and on October 8, 1191, the barons of England and the citizens of London met in the Chapter House of St. Paul's

Cathedral, deprived Longchamp of his post and appointed John regent of the country. "On that very day," says a contemporary writer, "was granted and instituted the Commune of the Londoners, and the magnates of the whole realm, even the bishops of the province itself, were compelled to swear to it." By that act London became possessed of its corporation—the oldest in the country, and older even than the Mother of Parliaments herself.

First Mayor of London

The first man named as Mayor of London was Henry FitzAilwyn. He held office for twenty-five years, though neither he nor the *Commune* was recognised by Richard I.

The reign of John proved London's greatest opportunity. In its first year the City got back the right to elect its sheriffs. When the barons rose against John, London sided with them and opened its gates to their army. The Mayor of London, though a commoner, was chosen as a member of the Council of Twenty-five Barons appointed to see that the terms of the charter John sealed at Runnymede on June 15, 1215, were carried out.

In that charter—the famous Magna Carta—are the words "Let the city of London have all its old liberties and its free customs, as well by land as by water."

Henry III Oppresses the City

There was one condition. Each newly elected mayor was to be presented to the king or his justiciar for royal approval before the appointment was confirmed. A troublesome condition this proved to be for some time; for example, in 1240 Gerard Bat, though he was elected for the second time (and so presumably was well known to the king) had to travel to Woodstock in Oxfordshire to be presented to Henry III, and was there told that the king would deal with the matter when he returned to London. This act was on a par with Henry's attitude towards the City, which, according to Sir Walter Besant, was "throughout this long

THE INDUSTRIOUS APPRENTICE BECOMES LORD MAYOR

From the original design by William Hogarth. Numerous poor boys have risen by hard work and business acumen to the position of first citizen of the oldest, wealthiest and most famous corporation.

LORD MAYOR'S SHOW ON THE THAMES

For four hundred years it was the custom for the Lord Mayor's procession to go part, if not all, the way from the City to Westminster by river to be presented to the King or to the Justices acting for him.

reign the unceasing object of the King's rapacity, tyranny, and hatred." On nine separate occasions he deposed the mayor; he taxed the City more grievously than ever before, and he imposed huge fines for most trivial causes. One can understand why London supported Simon de Montfort.

Out of the condition that the Mayor must be presented to the King for approval of his appointment—a condition which still holds good—arose that most popular of London pageants, the Lord Mayor's Show. Henry III gave permission for the Mayor to be presented, if he himself happened to be away, to the Barons of the Exchequer at Westminster; and it was only natural that the ceremonial "riding" of the newly elected Mayor to his presentation should be made an occasion for the pageantry that Londoners have always loved. But the idea seems to have developed slowly. At the beginning of the fifteenth century the "riding" appears to have been no more than a formal and stately procession. The Mayor, attended by the Sheriffs and the Beadle, was supported by the members of his guild, while minstrels played appropriate music.

In 1453 Sir John Norman was elected Mayor. The story goes that he was lame and could not mount on horseback, so as the Thames was then the great highway of London it was decided that he should proceed to Westminster by water. Sir John "caused a barge to be made at his own charge, and every company had several barges well decked and trimmed, to pass along with him."

There had been occasional processions by water before, but this one set a fashion which lasted for four hundred years. It was not until 1857 that it became again the established rule for the procession to go the whole distance by land.

During Tudor and Stuart days the Show increased in magnificence until it was one of the grandest pageants of the year. Visitors to Guildhall Museum will see a model which shows how gorgeous was the Lord Mayor's barge. Elaborate masques, written by eminent poets, enlivened the procession, and scores of barges and boats ablaze with colour attended the triumphal progress of the newly elected Lord Mayor.

Nor was this pageantry mere empty show; it reflected truly the importance of the first citizen of London. As a writer of Elizabeth's reign put it, " There is no public officer of any city in Europe that may compare in port (i.e., retinue) and countenance with the Lord Mayor of London during his time of office."

" My Lord the Mayor "

The Mayor had by this time become quite definitely Lord Mayor. Authorities disagree as to when the title was altered or whether there was any authority for the change. It is commonly held that it came about through the Mayor being addressed as " My Lord the Mayor," which became shortened to " My Lord Mayor." The latter title has been in regular use since about 1545. Some historians think it was used much earlier.

The Puritans did not approve of the Show, which they closed down between 1639 and 1655. Charles II revived it, but in rather tawdry fashion, according to Samuel Pepys. The revival was rudely interrupted by the years of plague and fire, and thereafter the Show steadily declined in grandeur and importance.

During the years of decay an innovation was made which has become so central a feature that without it we of to-day could hardly imagine the Show. In 1711 Sir Gilbert Heathcote was thrown by his horse, so a coach was built for the conveyance of the Lord Mayor to Westminster.

The original coach cost £1,065, the money being raised by subscriptions of £60 each levied upon the junior aldermen. A second coach was built in 1757; this was used until 1896, when a replica was constructed. The coach, with its elaborate allegorical carvings, painted panels and chariot-like wheels, is a massive affair weighing 3 tons 16 cwt., while each of the six horses pulling it carries nearly a hundredweight of harness. It has no springs, the body being suspended on four thick red leather straps secured by gilt buckles.

By 1850 the Lord Mayor's Show, like many another good old British institution, was practically dead, when a brilliant suggestion by a Mr. G. Godwin revived it in all its ancient splendour. He conceived the idea of set pageants, representing art, science, industry and commerce, and drawn on moving cars or floats. This idea has persisted right down to the present day.

The 1850 Show included Peace with her olive branch—this was the era when all men believed that war was to be no more—a huge car, drawn by six horses, bearing Britannia seated on a throne with Happiness at her feet, a ship in full sail, and cars representing the four quarters of the globe, laden with negroes, elephants, camels, deer and other exhibits. The procession was an unqualified success; it sent the London crowds into transports of delight.

Since that year the Lord Mayor's Show has steadily resumed its hold upon popular affection, and to-day, in spite of occasional grumbles that it dislocates traffic (which it certainly does), there are few who would willingly see it given up. Not a penny of its cost falls upon the ratepayers; the Lord Mayor and the Sheriffs foot the bill, which to-day amounts to about £4,000 or £5,000 annually.

The Lord Mayor's Banquet

Since the Courts of Law were transferred to the Strand in 1882, the Lord Mayor goes there, and not to Westminster, to be presented. On his journey he contrives to pass through as many as possible of the twenty-six wards into which the City is divided.

The Lord Mayor's Show is but one slight indication of the Lord Mayor's standing and importance. The status of the banquet which, by old-established custom, takes place at Guildhall on the evening of the same day is far more significant. Unless prevented by most urgent and important business of State, the Prime Minister is always present, and the occasion is made one for the delivery of a speech to which the whole world listens, because in it Britain's policy—especially in respect of international affairs—is reviewed

It would be difficult indeed to exaggerate the importance of the Lord Mayor of London.

GUILDHALL OF LONDON

The porch is fifteenth century, part of the original building begun in the fourteenth. The remainder of the front was rebuilt about 160 years ago. The main entrance leads directly to the Great Hall; to the right are the Art Gallery, Library and Museum, to the left the Guildhall Police Court. The roof of Guildhall, the rooms behind the Great Hall, the Art Gallery and 25,000 books in the library, were destroyed in the great fire raid of December 29, 1940. The interior of Guildhall has been completely restored since the war.

Within his city—the wealthiest and most powerful square mile in the world—he is in theory absolute, owing allegiance to none save his Monarch—and even the Sovereign must ask the Lord Mayor's permission before she may enter the City of London. This is done at Temple Bar, where the Lord Mayor hands the Monarch the Sword of State.

Status of Lord Mayor

As proof of his rank the Lord Mayor takes precedence in the City even over the heir to the throne. He is its Chief Justice, its Admiral and its General. On its behalf he has the right at any time to seek an audience with the Sovereign, and to present a petition at the Bar of the House of Commons. To him is sent each quarter, under the Monarch's Sign Manual, the password to Her Majesty's Tower of London. On the death of the Monarch—of which he is informed by the succeeding Sovereign—the Lord Mayor is the only Privy Councillor in the Realm until a Council is summoned to issue the Proclamation of the new Monarch. To this meeting the Lord Mayor is summoned, and he signs the Proclamation along with the Lords of the Privy Council.

The Lord Mayor summons and presides over the five courts of the City Corporation, those of the Aldermen, of Common Council, of Hustings (which dates from Saxon times), of Grand Wardmote and of the Common Hall. He is Coroner of London and Perpetual Escheator (i.e. officer registering reversion of property) of the City, Chairman of the Thames Conservancy and a Trustee of St. Paul's. His is the first name read out in the jealously guarded Commission of Oyer and Terminer (the commission empowering judges to hear and determine specified offences) by virtue of which the Central Criminal Court is located in London, and in this capacity he attends the opening session at the Old Bailey. No troops save the three units descended from the City Trained Bands—the 3rd Battalion of the Grenadier Guards, the Royal Marines, and the Buffs—may march through the City without his leave.

In addition to being the representative of the City, the guardian of its rights and the personification of its privileges, the Lord Mayor has a national standing of highest rank. He receives and entertains many of Britain's most distinguished foreign guests, while a Guildhall banquet in honour of a British subject is an acknowledgment of outstanding service to the State. It is the Lord Mayor's privilege to confer the Honorary Freedom of the City, a distinction very highly prized and only conferred in recognition of rare merit. One important function of the Lord Mayor is to act as Public Receiver and Almoner of Donations whenever any great disaster involving widespread distress occurs. A " Lord Mayor's Fund " may be opened on behalf of sufferers in any part of the world; France, Greece, Newfoundland, India, China and Australia are among the countries which have been aided in this manner.

The City of London is governed by the Lord Mayor, 26 Aldermen and 206 Common Councillors, the official title of the Corporation being " The Lord Mayor and Commonalty and Citizens of the City of London." To be eligible for election a citizen must hold the Freedom of the City.

The Aldermen are elected by and govern the Wards, which in far-gone days they owned and ruled as private domains. They constitute with the Lord Mayor the Court of Aldermen, which controls the City Police Force and approves regulations for vehicular traffic. The Court makes the final election of the Lord Mayor. In addition to other duties, each Alderman is a Justice of the Peace.

Courts of the City

Common Councillors are also elected by the citizens of the Wards. Each must be in occupation of premises within the City rated at not less than £10 per annum. The Court of Common Council, which consists of the Lord Mayor, Aldermen and Common Councillors, discusses and transacts the business of the City, much after the fashion of any other municipal corporation, with the important exception that politics is never allowed to obtrude. In this respect it is unique.

The Grand, or Great, Court of Wardmote meets annually on Plough Monday (about January 7), to receive the returns of the elections from the Wards and to hear petitions. It also admits to office the City Marshal and the Ward Beadles, the latter an ancient body of officials founded 600 years ago. They attend upon the Aldermen and carry the maces of the Wards. The ancient Court of Husting—literally " the Court held in a house "—meets every week, its chief duty being to enrol deeds and wills. It consists of the Lord Mayor,

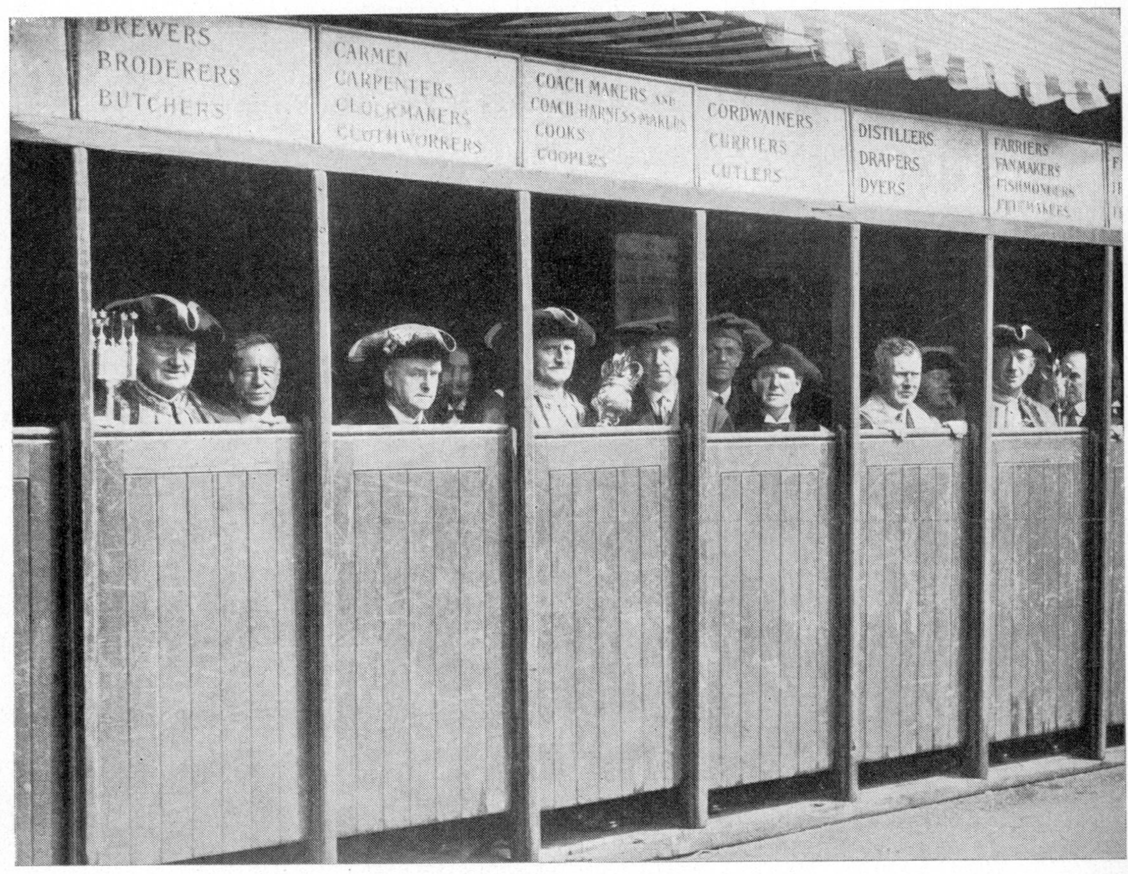

ELECTION DAY AT GUILDHALL

The Beadles of the City Wards, bearing their maces, wait for their Aldermen, who are in the Great Hall, in these boxes erected along the front of Guildhall. They are grouped according to their Companies.

Aldermen and Sheriffs as Judges, assisted by the Recorder, who sits as assessor and pronounces the judgment of the Court.

The full title of the Court of Common Hall is "The Meeting or Assembly of the Mayor, Aldermen and Liverymen of the several Companies of the City of London in Common Hall assembled." The court meets twice a year, on Midsummer Day and Michaelmas Day, to elect the Lord Mayor, Sheriffs, Chamberlain and other officers.

The Lord Mayor is elected on September 29. In the morning a short procession consisting of the Lord Mayor, his successor-to-be, and the officers of the Corporation, made its way to the church of St. Lawrence Jewry in Guildhall Yard, to attend the service with which the proceedings have for centuries commenced.

Each member of the procession carried a bunch of sweet-smelling English flowers—a reminder of the days when these were supposed to protect against the plague—and when at noon a return was made to Guildhall the floor of the Great Hall was strewn with sweet herbs.

It is to-day a foregone conclusion each year who will be elected Lord Mayor, but the election is carried out in time-honoured manner. Before he can be eligible for the office of Lord Mayor, a citizen must have been elected by his Ward as Alderman, and by the Livery (i.e., the City Companies—a reminder of the days when the powerful trading guilds almost got into their grasp the governance of the City) as Sheriff. After that it is a matter of seniority.

Usually about half a dozen names are submitted to the Court of Common Hall. To show that the election is free and unforced, the ruling Lord Mayor and the Aldermen who have "passed the chair" retire from the

Council Hall. The name of the Alderman next on the list for office is greeted with shouts of " All! " from the Livery, that of the one who will follow him with " Next year! " other names being greeted with " Later! " Occasions have been known when a name was received with cries of " Never! "

The first two names are then sent up to the Court of Aldermen, which selects one. The successful candidate returns to the Great Hall arm in arm with the Lord Mayor.

The Lord Mayor elect having been presented to the Lord Chancellor for approval by the Sovereign, he is sworn in at Guildhall on November 8, when he receives £12,500 for the expenses of his mayoral year (he usually has to spend more than twice that amount), and takes in his hand for a few moments the " Lord Mayor's Sceptre," the symbolic emblem of his sovereignty.

Gem of City's Regalia

Save for Royal Coronations, this is the only occasion on which this most precious and ancient piece of the City's regalia is seen. It is a small mace, consisting of a crystal shaft, eighteen inches long and possibly dating from Saxon times, engraved with a spiral thread and bearing gold fillets set with pearls. The gold head is ornamented with crosses and fleurs-de-lys, and supported by a band set with uncut rubies and sapphires.

On ordinary occasions the Lord Mayor is preceded by the " Great Mace," which is 5 feet 3 inches long and made of silver gilt. It is carried by the Common Cryer and Serjeant-at-Arms, whose office dates from 1364. In Common Council it is placed crosswise before the Lord Mayor, with athwart it the Sword of State, which is borne by the Sword-bearer. The Sword of State is to be distinguished from the " Pearl Sword," so-called because the scabbard is richly encrusted with pearls.

At his installation the Lord Mayor is invested with the mayoral chain of office, a rich chain of twenty-eight SS links made of gold and enamel, joined by alternate knots and roses in the same materials. The chain is clasped by a Tudor portcullis, from which hangs the famous City jewel, a cameo over three hundred years old, with an enamel band bearing the motto of the City—*Domine dirige nos* (O Lord direct us)—and surrounded by a wreath of roses, thistles and shamrocks composed of precious stones. The present chain (probably a copy of an earlier one—see the picture on page 118) was presented by Sir John Alen, a sixteenth-century Lord Mayor, who died in 1544.

Of the permanent officers of the Corporation, the first is the Recorder, who by the charter granted to the City in 1304 is constituted the spokesman of the Corporation in declaring and protecting its customs and privileges. Elected for life by the Court of Aldermen, he is the Senior Land Officer of the Corporation and a Judge of the Central Criminal Court.

The City Chamberlain, whose office dates from at least 1276, is the Treasurer of the City, and as such Keeper of " the City's Cash." All the accounts of the various departments of public works come under his supervision. He also keeps the Roll of Freemen, and has jurisdiction over all City apprentices.

The Town Clerk, formerly known as the " Common Clerk," is the Keeper of the City's charters, records and archives. He attends all meetings of the Court of Aldermen and the Court of Common Council, to advise on procedure and record the minutes; and he issues the precepts or writs for civic elections. His office dates from 1284.

The Common Serjeant, who is a Law Officer, is a junior judge to the Recorder, whose place he takes at the Central Criminal Court when the latter is absent. Usually, however, he takes his superior officer's place as President of the Lord Mayor's Court. Unlike all the other offices, this one is in the gift of the Crown.

Keeper of the Monument

The Comptroller and Vice-Chamberlain, who is also a Law Officer, has a most onerous and responsible task, for he has charge of the title deeds of the vast and profitable properties owned by the City, the rentals of which he controls. It is his province to execute all leases and agreements in connection with these estates. He is also Keeper of the Monument.

The Remembrancer has a multitude of various duties chiefly concerned with ceremonies, though one of his most important functions is to be present each day at the Houses of Parliament when they are in session, to watch over the City's interests. He issues the invitations to Guildhall Banquets and receives the guests prior to their presentation to the Lord Mayor, arranges the procession on Lord Mayor's day and has charge of arrangements when My Lord Mayor has to make a State visit or to present an address to the Crown.

The City Solicitor drafts the City's Acts, by-laws and regulations, prosecutes those who infringe them, and sues defaulting tenants for arrears of rent. One interesting duty he has is to appear every year before the Queen's Remembrancer at the Law Courts to perform suit and service for those lands the City holds of the Crown.

One very interesting point about this is that each year the City religiously hands over quit rent for two estates which it does not own, one of which it is never known to have occupied and the site of which has been forgotten. The quit rent in one case consists of horse-shoes and horse-shoe nails, in the other of a bill-hook and hatchet.

The titles of the Commissioner of the City Police and the City Surveyor indicate their duties. The Secondary is an officer to whom the Sheriffs delegate all their active functions, including the execution and return of writs and processes, levying and collecting of fines, preparation of the register of Parliamentary and borough electors, and conduct of Parliamentary and municipal elections.

The office of Sheriff is, as has been seen, considerably older than that of Lord Mayor. The right of election is now vested in the Livery Companies, and the two Sheriffs are elected in the Common Hall annually on June 24. Every Alderman is, by virtue of his position, liable to serve as Sheriff, but he may decline office. Many do so on the score of expense, as it costs £3,000 to £4,000 a year.

Duties of Sheriffs

The Sheriffs attend upon the Lord Mayor at most official functions, present petitions on behalf of the Corporation at the Bar of the Houses of Parliament, and have to attend each session of the Central Criminal Court.

The business of the City Corporation is conducted in Guildhall, which is one of the most interesting if not architecturally among the most distinguished of London's public buildings. The front was rebuilt in 1789 by George Dance, who, like other architects of his day, was struggling unhappily to combine in his work two completely contrasting styles of architecture, the Classic and the Gothic.

The gorgeous and lofty Great Hall, entered directly from the splendid central doorway, was begun in 1411, Sir Richard Whittington being one of those who contributed to the cost. The original roof was destroyed in the Great Fire, the walls were increased in height by Wren; the new roof dated from 1865 but was destroyed in the fire raid, December 29, 1940, but has now been rebuilt once more.

In this Hall the Lord Mayor is sworn into office, and here takes place each year the Guildhall banquet. Round the walls are monuments to Lord Mayor Beckford, who had the courage publicly to reprove his Sovereign; William Pitt, Earl of Chatham, William Pitt the Younger, Wellington and Nelson.

Giants of the Guildhall

In the gallery once stood the huge wooden figures Gog and Magog, which were carved by Captain Richard Saunders in 1708 to take the place of wicker and pasteboard reproductions always carried in the Lord Mayor's Show. According to legend, Gog and Magog were survivors of a race of giants, offspring of the wicked daughters of the Emperor Diocletian, who were brought to London in chains. Their high estate secured for them no more worthy position than that of porters at the King's palace. Gog was armed with bow and arrows, a sword and a spiked ball attached to a long pole by a chain. Magog, in the armour of a Roman soldier, had no more than a spear, a sword and a shield. They were destroyed in the fire raid of December, 1940 but, carved anew, now surmount in their wonted glory the beautifully restored Great Hall.

Beneath the Hall is a crypt, supported by pillars of Purbeck marble and architecturally

BECKFORD'S MONUMENT
Alderman Sir W. Beckford protested to George III at the monarch's language concerning the City.

GUILDHALL GIANTS WHICH ATTENDED THE LORD MAYOR'S SHOW
Gog and Magog, the two great wooden figures carved by Captain Saunders in 1708; long preserved in the gallery at the west end of the Great Hall, they were destroyed in the Fire Raid of December 29, 1940.

the most interesting feature of Guildhall. The Aldermen's Court Room was also destroyed in the fire raid.

The building on the right of Guildhall Yard houses the Library, Art Gallery and Museum, which are open daily to the public. The Library contained a magnificent collection of books, manuscripts and prints dealing with London and its history. The collection was modern, though the Library itself was begun by Sir Richard Whittington. The library and 25,000 of its books were also destroyed in the devastating fire raid by German bombers on the night of December 29, 1940.

How Londonderry Got Its Name

In the Museum, which is beneath the Library, may be traced the history of London since earliest days. There are many relics of the Roman occupation, and a goodly collection of the quaint and interesting tavern and shop signs which used to creak in every street of medieval London.

On the same side of Guildhall Yard are the " Irish Chambers," a reminder of the fact that Londonderry owes not only its name but its existence to the City of London.

It was in 1613 that " The Honourable the Irish Society " was granted a Royal Charter, and settled, on lands taken from Irish rebels, a number of English colonists, funds to the amount of £60,000 being raised by the twelve great Livery Companies. Thus it comes about that Londonderry still bears on its arms the red cross and sword of the City of London, and that the City Corporation possesses large estates in Northern Ireland.

The Lord Mayor's Church

On the left of the Guildhall Yard is the Guildhall Justice Room, while at the entrance stood the church of St. Lawrence Jewry-next-Guildhall, the official church of the Lord Mayor and Corporation. It was built by Wren to replace an earlier building destroyed in the Great Fire. In the porch could be seen printed copies of sermons preached before the Lord Mayor in the seventeenth century. The church also treasured a throne on which Charles II sat at the opening service; while the vestry with its elaborate carving by Grinling Gibbons, and its hand-plaster ceiling was considered to be the finest of its type. The church was almost wholly destroyed by bombing during the Second World War but is now being rebuilt.

Until the Great Fire the Lord Mayors lived during their year of office in their own houses. Then a house in New Court, Bow Lane, was presented for their use. The Mansion House was built between 1739 and 1753, the money being raised by fines on those who wished to avoid the office of Sheriff, a procedure which led a wit to say that the Mansion House was built for those who wished to become Lord Mayor out of the pockets of those who did not.

The chief room is the lofty and ornate Egyptian Hall in which the Lord Mayor feasts with becoming splendour, the distinguished guests who come his way. Appeals for Lord Mayor's Funds are sent out from the Mansion House, and the inauguration of any benevolent or charitable movement in a meeting there stamps that movement as of national character and worthy of national support.

Generosity of Whittington

It may well be imagined that with a roll going back nearly 750 years the City has been represented by a large number of able men, some more than ordinarily distinguished. Of Sir Richard Whittington mention has already been made, but it is not out of place to speak of him again, for among all the Lord Mayors of London he has been equalled by few and excelled by none.

"His generosity," says a nineteenth-century writer, "was like a well-spring; and being childless, he spent his life in deeds of charity and generosity." He was equally famed for his justice and his patriotism. He enlarged the nave of Westminster Abbey, founded the Church of St. Michael Royal, near which he lived and in which he was buried, restored St. Bartholomew's Hospital, endowed almshouses and built water conduits. And he was courageous enough to fine the Brewers' Company for selling bad beer!

Courage of another sort was required by Thomas FitzThomas, who in 1265 warned that weak and greedy monarch, Henry III, that "So long as unto us you will be a good lord and King, we will be faithful and duteous unto you." Henry read into the words an implied threat, threw FitzThomas into prison and deprived London of its Mayor for five years. The brave but unhappy defender of civic rights remained in a dungeon for the rest of his life.

History does not record the name of the Lord Mayor who was author of another famous rebuke to royalty. The story is placed indeed both in the reigns of Queen Mary I and James I. Concerning the latter monarch it is related that "being displeased with the City, because it would not lend him the money he required (he) had to him the Lord Mayor and Aldermen. Being somewhat transported (i.e. being very angry), he said he would remove his own Court, with all the records of the Tower and the Courts of Westminster to another place. The Lord Mayor calmly heard all, and at last answered: 'Your Majesty hath power to do what you please, and your City of London will obey accordingly, but she humbly desires that whenever Your Majesty shall remove your Courts, you would please to leave the Thames behind you.'"

Most people have heard the story of how Sir William Walworth slew Wat Tyler at Smithfield. It was long believed that the sword in the City's arms was added by Richard II in recognition of the Mayor's deed, but this is not the case. The sword is that of St. Paul, the patron saint of London.

Another of Richard II's mayors was Sir Nicholas Brembre, who secured his elections by packing Guildhall with armed men. He went too far when he tried to raise London on the side of his monarch: he was brought to trial, condemned to death and drawn on a hurdle to Tyburn to be hanged.

Debtor Who Became Lord Mayor

Very different was the story of Stephen Forster, who became Mayor in 1454. Legend says that in his youth he was confined in the debtors' prison at Ludgate. Being one day stationed at the grille where the wretched captives stood to beg for food of passers-by—their chief means of subsistence—he attracted the attention of a rich widow, who asked how much it would cost to set him free.

"Twenty pounds," he replied. The widow paid the money, and gave Forster a job in her business. He proved himself so industrious and capable that he gained his mistress's love. They married, and together amassed great wealth, with part of which they enlarged the prison and endowed there a chapel.

Curious tales are told of some of the medieval mayors. Bartholomew James in 1479 fined his Sheriff £50 for kneeling too close to him in St. Paul's and cursing him when spoken to. It appears that the worthy mayor was afraid of catching the plague!

When in 1444 Sir Simon Eyre was proposed as Mayor, he said he was not wealthy enough, whereupon an alderman retorted that "no citizen could be more capable than the man who had openly asserted that he broke his fast

LORD MAYOR'S OFFICIAL RESIDENCE

The Mansion House, which stands facing the Bank of England and the Royal Exchange across one of the busiest road junctions in London. It was built between 1739 and 1753 from the designs of George Dance.

every day on a table for which he would not take a thousand pounds."

Everybody became anxious to see this valuable table, and the Lord Mayor and two of the Aldermen invited themselves to dinner with Eyre. When they arrived at his home, Eyre told his wife to " prepare the little table." Mrs. Eyre was much embarrassed, but on her husband insisting she sat down on a stool, spread a cloth over her lap and put thereon a venison pasty.

" Behold," said Simon, " the table which I would not take a thousand pounds for ! "

Man Who Helped Wolsey

The reign of Henry VIII saw a number of distinguished mayors. Among them was Sir Richard Gresham, father of the builder of the Royal Exchange. The son probably got the idea from his father, who is said to have advocated it, and to have been the inventor of bills of exchange. Gresham risked disgrace by helping the fallen Cardinal Wolsey. So did William FitzWilliam, but Henry VIII, with characteristic unexpectedness, knighted him and made him a Privy Councillor, saying he had too few such loyal servants.

Sir Thomas White, founder of Tonbridge School and St. John's College, Oxford, kept London loyal to Queen Mary during Sir Thomas Wyat's rebellion in 1554. He was a poor boy who was left £100 by his master, and on this by diligence and thrift built up a fortune.

Apprentice Saves Mayor's Daughter

The most romantic story of all comes from the reign of Elizabeth. Sir William Hewet, Mayor in 1559, lived on London Bridge, and one day his little daughter Alice fell from a window into the raging current below.

Immediately a young apprentice named Osborne jumped from another window and gallantly saved the child. Years later Mistress Alice, grown to a fair lady, had many suitors because of her beauty and her father's great wealth. But Sir William refused them all. " No," he said, " Osborne saved her, and Osborne shall have her."

So the apprentice married the master's daughter and became wealthy and in his turn rose to be Lord Mayor of London.

Sir John Spencer, Lord Mayor in 1594, was less happy in his daughter. According to tradition, she left home concealed in a baker's basket in order to marry Lord Compton. A letter written by this young lady to her husband asks for an annuity of £2,200, the same amount for private expenses, £10,000 for jewellery, that her debts be paid and a coach and horses and female servants be provided for her. When her husband becomes an earl, she adds, he will no doubt allow her £1,000 more and double the number of her attendants. A modest request, considering the vastly greater value of money in those times!

Two Mayors Contrasted

The serene courage of Sir John Lawrence, who was Lord Mayor during the dreadful year of the Great Plague, must not be forgotten.

His successor, Sir Thomas Bludworth, was of very different kidney. Samuel Pepys has described how, when the Great Fire broke out, the wretched man ran about helplessly wailing "Lord, what can I do, what can I do?"

The story of Sir Robert Vyner is too good to miss. In the *Spectator* of the day you may read how, when Charles II came to dine with him, "The wine passed too freely, the guests growing noisy, and the mayor too familiar, the King, with a hint to the company to disregard ceremonial, began to steal off to his coach, which was waiting for him in Guildhall Yard.

"But the mayor, grown bold with wine, pursued the 'merry monarch,' and catching him by the hand, cried out, with a vehement oath, 'Sir, you shall stay and take t'other bottle.' The 'merry monarch' looked kindly at him over his shoulder, and with a smile and graceful air (for I saw him at the time, and do now) repeated the line of the old song, 'He that is drunk is as great as a King,' and immediately turned back and complied with his host's request."

As we approach our own times, the story of the mayoralty assumes a more prosaic character. Lord Mayors come and go, and each performs his duty honourably and with dignity, but without remarkable incident.

Yet there is still romance to be found in it. In November, 1935, Sir Percy Vincent succeeded to the chair. Fifty-four years previously he had come from a Norfolk home to be apprenticed at the age of thirteen to a draper in Stratford; and he recalled his country origin by presenting a pageant of the countryside and farming industries at his Show.

Curiously enough, his election was marked by an amusing but most appropriate incident. A starling entered the Great Hall, watched the proceedings from the Chatham memorial, and then, apparently to get a better view, flew on to the City Marshal's head, where it remained solemnly perched for at least two minutes.

First Overseas Visit

In April, 1936, Sir Percy Vincent set a precedent which his successors might well follow. He accepted an invitation to be present at the Jubilee celebrations of Vancouver in British Columbia, and thus became the first Lord Mayor of London to make an official visit to any part of the overseas Empire. In the five weeks he was away, the Lord Mayor travelled 12,000 miles, delivered over a hundred speeches, and was made a Freeman of five cities. On his return he said, "The visit has been a memorable one. All were interested in our civic pageantry; it is something they have dropped themselves, but they love it as being the tradition of their fathers."

The words are apt. London is the greatest city of the British Commonwealth of Nations and the fountain head of British traditions. The idea of its chief citizen becoming, after his Sovereign, ambassador-in-chief to the great Dominions, has an irresistible appeal.

SIR RICHARD WHITTINGTON
Four times Mayor of London. Though always called "Sir," there is no evidence that he was ever knighted.

FUN AT SOUTHWARK FAIR

From the original by Hogarth. In medieval days much trading was done at the great London fairs, and representatives of City Companies used to attend to test the quality of the goods and the fairness of measures.

MERCHANT ADVENTURERS

On November 2, 1932, H.R.H. the Prince of Wales (later King Edward VIII) attended a function unique in our times. He was present at the Mansion House as the first Master of the recently formed Worshipful and Honourable Company of Master Mariners, to receive for his Company from the Court of Aldermen the grant of Livery.

In making the presentation the Lord Mayor, Sir Maurice Jenks, said : " It is a matter for congratulation that the Master Mariners, in organising themselves, have taken as their model the very oldest and best type of guild rules. They are a new Company, but they have adopted the old tradition that a Company must be entirely identified with its craft . . . and set before themselves, in their own words, 'the maintenance of a high and honourable standard both of practical proficiency and of professional conduct.' "

The Lord Mayor's words carried his hearers back through the ages to the dim and distant days of London's turbulent youth. How far back it is impossible exactly to say, though it may be that the oldest City Companies have been part and parcel of the City's history since its rebirth in Saxon times. Certainly their origins are shrouded for ever in the mists of antiquity.

Long before the Norman Conquest there existed in England, as on the Continent, a number of guilds, or fraternities, bodies of men banded together in sworn brotherhood, vowed to common interests. Some of them had been founded purely for religious and charitable purposes. " This Society," say the ordinances of the Exeter guild, one of the earliest in Europe of which the regulations remain, " is assembled in Exeter for God's love and their souls' profit, both in regard to the prosperity of this life and the future."

The Frith guild was devoted to mutual protection against robbery and violence, and organised in some respects as a voluntary police force. There is preserved a complete code of a Frith guild written down in the reign of King Athelstan (A.D. 927–940), grandson of Alfred the Great, and the codes of the London guilds were put on paper at the same time. In the days of King Cnut there was formed in London the Cnihten Guild (Guild of Knights); this remained in existence for about a century, and was probably chiefly concerned with the defence of the City.

Religious Basis of Guilds

There is no certain evidence of the existence in London of merchant or craft guilds before the twelfth century, but it seems highly likely that some form of union for the protection and regulation of trade had been organised long before that time.

Whatever the main purpose, the organisation and rules of all these societies were markedly similar. Each had a religious basis, being formed under the ægis of a patron saint, whose name is retained in many of the titles of the present City Companies. The Drapers, for example, were (much later) incorporated as " The Master, Wardens, brethren and sisters of the guild or fraternity of the Blessed Mary the Virgin, of the mystery of Drapers," the Haberdashers as " The fraternity of St. Catharine the Virgin of the Haberdashers of the City of London."

GOLDSMITHS AT WORK
A quaint old print showing the different tools and methods of the medieval goldsmiths in London.

Members swore upon the relics of their saint to be faithful to each other, to succour any of the brotherhood in need or distress, and to obey the ruling of the master and wardens in all matters concerning the guild. They went ceremonially to church on their saint's day, attended *en masse* all members' funerals, and provided masses for their souls after death.

Every member paid an entrance fee and an annual subscription; it was probably by this token that the fraternities in England came to be called Guilds, though the old English word *gild* or *guild* had a variety of meanings, ranging from banquet to payment. It may have signified originally, societies which met or feasted together, for every guild held three or four business meetings each year, and partook of an annual banquet; but it seems more likely that it meant a body whose members made contribution to a common fund.

It is believed by some authorities that in the days before the Norman Conquest all the merchant guilds in London were united into a single guild, as happened in many other English towns, and that this body regulated the entire trade of the City. How it functioned—if, indeed, it ever existed—is not known, but later most if not all of its power seems to have passed to the Portreeve and the aldermen, who for a time acted in every way as a merchant guild.

The coming of the Normans greatly stimulated trade and industry in London, and it was not long after that definite trade and craft fraternities began to emerge.

Citizens' Meetings at St. Paul's

In view of London's early history, it could hardly have been otherwise. William I confirmed to the citizens all their civic rights, and in those days they governed the City in a very real sense. Three times a year, at Midsummer, Michaelmas and Christmas, every citizen had to attend the Folkmoot or Meeting of the People, at St. Paul's Cross; and whenever at other times a matter arose touching the whole community the great bell of St. Paul's boomed out to call the freemen to a Folkmoot; their decision on the matter under discussion, would be absolutely final.

The elders of the City met weekly in the Husting, or Hallmoot, to settle matters of law and administration, and presided as aldermen over the wardmoots which ruled despotically over the local wards into which the City was divided.

This tradition of meeting in common council was centuries old at the Conquest; so it was not surprising that the king's representative who had charge of the City's trade got into the habit of conferring with the "committees" representative of the various trades of London.

Company Levies Own Taxes

As early as the beginning of the twelfth century the Bakers and the Fishmongers had their own hallmoots: by 1155 the Bakers, having organised themselves and received royal recognition, were paying a yearly sum to the Exchequer for the privilege of levying their own taxes. The Fishmongers, though not officially recognised, early acquired extensive control of their trade. The guild of Tapestry and Cloth weavers received in 1160 a charter—the oldest known—having then had recognised existence for at least thirty years. The Pepperers, from whom sprang later the Grocers, and the Mercers, or dealers in all sorts of small wares from wigs and haberdashery to spices and drugs, were chartered not much, if at all, later.

With the exception of the Weavers and the Bakers, these early guilds had no legal standing. Yet they must have grown rapidly in number, for in 1179–80 no less than eighteen, including the Goldsmiths', Cloth Workers' and Butchers', were fined by Henry II as being adulterine, or unlicensed. The fines ranged from half a mark (6s. 8d.) to 45 marks (£30), and since the latter sum represents at least £1,000 in present-day currency, it is clear that some of the guilds were already wealthy.

That they were very independent is evidenced by the fact that these fines were never paid. Neither monarch's edicts nor repressive regulations could check the rapidly growing power and ambition of the London merchants and craftsmen. In their struggle for recognition they possessed the constant advantage that they always had money, and their sovereign frequently had none. It can scarcely have been coincidence that charters came the way of the earlier guilds most abundantly whenever the King of England had on his hands an expensive war.

It became the ultimate aim of every guild to receive a royal charter transforming it into an incorporated company. This not only gave it the right to own property and to amass

SIR WILLIAM WALWORTH
From the original statue in Fishmongers' Hall. Walworth, who slew Wat Tyler, was a Fishmonger.

revenues, but also vested in its officials complete control of the trade or craft (there is no very clear distinction between the two in medieval days) it represented.

Many of the guilds had to wait centuries before their ambition was realised. The Butchers, for example, were not incorporated until 1605, more than 400 years after the setting up of their guild. The Loriners, or bridle and bit makers, whose ordinances dating from 1269, are the oldest known of any craft save the Cappers, did not receive a charter of incorporation until the year 1712.

Crafts Which Died Out

Not a few of them never realised their ambition at all. Their crafts decayed or were merged in others before they received the coveted charter. How many people to-day have even heard of the Tapicers, who wove figured cloths or tapestries, the Tawyers, who made skins into leather, or the Hurrers, who made and dealt in hats and caps? Yet the members of these trades, together with the Brælers (belt-makers), Forcermakers (casket-makers), Whittawyers (saddlers), and a score or more of others, submitted their ordinances and regulations to the Mayor and Aldermen in the fourteenth century. One very curious and interesting survival is that of the Worshipful Company of Bowyers, which received its charter of incorporation only in 1620, by which time the musket had completely supplanted the bow as a military weapon.

Oldest Incorporated Companies

The long reign of Edward III was a golden period of prosperity for London, and offered an opportunity which the City merchants and craftsmen were quick to accept. The Goldsmiths and the Skinners (furriers) became incorporated companies in 1327, being thus the oldest, with the exception of the Weavers, the Bakers and the Saddlers—the two latter receiving charters in the reign of Edward I. The Carpenters followed in 1344, and the Grocers, or dealers *en gros*, who broke away from the Pepperers, in the following year. In addition to these a large number of trades and crafts, though not receiving incorporation, had their guild regulations confirmed by the Mayor and Aldermen, and thus acquired over their members considerable if not complete control.

THE LONDON 'PRENTICE
In medieval days every boy who wanted to learn a trade had to serve a bound apprenticeship.

While no guild could come to its full stature until it had been formally declared a corporation, the power, the prestige and wealth of these fraternities steadily advanced throughout the thirteenth and fourteenth centuries. The Fishmongers, for example, who were not incorporated as a united company until 1536, had been for at least two centuries previously among the wealthiest and most powerful bodies in the City. There were for long two guilds of fishmongers, the Salt-Fishmongers and the Stock Fishmongers, who dealt in fresh fish only. Each received Charters of Incorporation, the former in 1483, the latter in 1509.

In the reign of Edward III they twice contributed £40—a huge sum in those days—towards the expense of the war in France. They had more members than any other guild, and they sent six members to the Court of Common Council—a greater number than any other trade.

Despotic Power of Companies

The power possessed by a guild or company over its members became with time, almost despotic. The entry of new members was jealously scrutinized; every one had to pay a fee and to serve a bound apprenticeship of from seven to ten years, during which time he was to all intents and purposes the absolute property of his master, who had charge of his morals as well as his proficiency and could punish any delinquency by flogging or cancellation of indentures.

Every man who practised any trade or craft in the City had to belong to his guild or company. No outsiders were allowed, and to be expelled from the guild meant the loss of one's means of livelihood. Every tradesman or craftsman had therefore to live up to the regulations of his guild, and in the high standard of these is to be found one of the crowning glories of the system. There was, unhappily, another side to the medal. Power drifted inevitably into the hands of the master-craftsmen, and the journeymen gradually lost all semblance of rights and privileges. They were not allowed to form guilds or unions of their own, and the conditions under which they worked during the height of the guild system nearly approached those of slavery.

The guilds early obtained the right to inspect

COUNCIL CHAMBER OF VINTNERS' HALL
The Vintners' Company rose to importance through the desire of the Plantagenet sovereigns to increase overseas trade. They shipped English wool to France, receiving in exchange wine from Bordeaux.

all work done by their members, and to destroy any that was "false." This duty they performed with a scrupulous rectitude that was beyond praise, and often with a ceremony that must have made it terribly impressive.

Search for Bad Work

It was laid down of the Goldsmiths, for example, that "The wardens every quarter, once, or oftener, if need be, shall search in London, Southwark, and Westminster, that all the goldsmiths there dwelling work true gold and silver, according to the Act of Parliament, and shall also make due search for their weights."

So every quarter an imposing procession would set forth from Goldsmiths' Hall. First came the Beadle, in full uniform and bearing the insignia of his office. Then followed the Wardens, arrayed in bright-coloured livery—the long cloaks or hoods trimmed with fur which the guilds began to adopt in the reign of Edward I—and after them their Clerk, two renter wardens, two brokers, and a following of porters and attendants all dressed in the Company's livery. With stately step and solemn mien they proceeded on their way.

It was a procession such as must have struck terror into the hearts of any infringing the stringent rules of the craft, particularly as punishment could be not merely drastic, but to our modern way of thinking savagely so. For counterfeiting the "touch," or carat, of gold an Elizabethan craftsman had his ears nailed to the pillory and one cut off.

The Goldsmiths' standard of workmanship, always superlatively high, was triumphantly vindicated in 1465, when a trial of skill between English and foreign goldsmiths resulted in the victory for an Englishman.

Loaves Weighed Before Mayor

In the fourteenth century the size of loaves was regulated by the price of corn. To determine the standard size the Company of Bakers used to send four "sworn and discreet men" to purchase corn at the four markets of Grasschurch (where now stands Gracechurch Street), St Botolph, Bishopsgate, and Queenhithe. From the flour thus obtained two loaves of wheaten bread were baked, and these presented to the Mayor and Aldermen to be weighed, as the City Corporation retained control over the prices of bread, meat, drink and fuel.

In 1370 a baker detected selling loaves lighter than standard weight was dragged through the streets of London on a hurdle, with a fool's cap on his head and his loaves slung round his neck.

In 1396 it was discovered that certain greedy and unscrupulous persons were selling good ale in old soap and oil barrels. The Coopers' Guild at once appointed overseers to impound and destroy any barrels thus being used, " for the avoiding of such deceit, for the love of God, and as a work of charity." The wording of the charge reveals, to modern ears, a quaint but lofty sense of duty.

Spectacles Broken on London Stone

One of the most amusing records of the vigilance of a City Company on behalf of good workmanship comes from the books of the Spectacle Makers. The master and wardens one day seized " two and twenty dozen of English spectacles, all very badd both in glasse and frames, not fitt to be put on sale." Having after trial condemned these in no uncertain terms, they laid them, to end the matter, on "the remayning parts of London Stone, where the same were with the hammer broken all in pieces."

HEAPS OF MONEY
Every year the Goldsmiths test money from the Royal Mint. Coins in a machine at the Mint.

The authority of some of the Companies extended considerably beyond the City walls. The Pewterers were in 1534 empowered to inspect pewter ware " in all parts of the Kingdom." Forty years later the Tallow Chandlers were given the right to " search, examine, view and try " soap, butter, hops, oil and vinegar in the City and outside. The Coopers were authorised by Henry VIII to search and gauge all beer, ale and soap vessels in the City and for two miles round, and to make a charge of one farthing a cask. The Barber-Surgeons—how strange it seems to-day to couple the two arts!—held the monopoly of surgery within the City and for seven miles round. As early as the reign of Henry IV the Drapers were empowered to visit the great fairs of St. Bartholomew, Spitalfields and Southwark, examine the goods and measure them by the " Drapers' Ell." The Merchant Taylors had similar powers.

Perhaps the most generally known instance of powers exercised throughout the kingdom is that of the Goldsmiths, who were granted by Edward I the right to inspect, try and regulate all gold and silver wares, and to assay precious metals in the City and throughout the kingdom. It was ordained that all vessels of gold and silver had to be " gold of a certain touch (i.e. carat) and silver of the sterling alloy," and to this day the leopard's head of the Goldsmiths' Company is stamped on all such wares.

The right to assay precious metals led to the Goldsmiths being entrusted with a ceremonial " Trial of the Pyx," still held annually. Every year for centuries " The wardens of the Mistery of Goldsmiths of the City of London " have been summoned by the Lord Chancellor to form a jury, which must include their assay master, to try coins fresh from the Royal Mint.

How Coins from the Mint are Tested

The coins to be tested are delivered to the jury in a small box—the pyx—and consist of " one from each journey weight, the journey weight consisting of 15 lb. troy weight of gold coins (one out of every 2,000 pieces) and 60 lb. troy weight of silver coins." The jury has to ascertain both the number and weight of the coins, some of which are later melted into an ingot which is assayed to discover if the metal is " within the remedy as to fineness." In addition to coins from the Royal Mint, the Goldsmiths assay specimens sent to them from the mints in the Dominions and Colonies.

After assay, the Company reports to the Lord Chancellor, who hands its verdict to the King's Remembrancer, who files it "amongst the other records of his office." If it is a satisfactory one, the Master of the Mint receives his *quietus*, or certificate of accuracy.

This testing of coins used formerly to take place in Westminster Abbey, in an ancient vaulted chamber still called the "Chapel of the Pyx," and where visitors may see specimens of tested coins. The testing now takes place at the Goldsmiths' Hall.

"Entered at Stationers' Hall"

Another famous privilege was that formerly possessed by the Stationers, who were incorporated by Mary in 1557 in order to stop the spread of heretical publications. They were given power to "search in any shop, house, chamber or building of printer, binder or seller for books published contrary to statutes, acts and proclamations," and right down to 1923 virtually every book and pamphlet had to be "entered at Stationers' Hall." Publishers wishing to protect copyright may still register books and pictures there.

James I gave this Company the exclusive right of printing almanacs, primers, psalters, the A B C and catechisms. The Company also printed Bibles. In 1632 there was a tremendous row over an edition in which the word "not" was omitted from the commandment against adultery. Archbishop Laud arraigned the Company before the Star Chamber and had it heavily fined. On another occasion a Bible appeared in which the first verse of Psalm XIV ran "The fool hath said in his heart, There is *a* God." The substitution of *a* for *no* cost the printer £3,000.

As Corporations in absolute control of their trades and crafts—or "misteries" as the latter were usually called—the City Companies rose to their zenith in Tudor days. In their earlier days there had often been keen jealousy between them and bitter disputes over precedence. Sometimes these gave rise to fierce battles in the streets of London, the most memorable occasions being in 1267, when 500 Merchant Taylors fought 500 Goldsmiths and had to be separated by the Sheriff with "bows, swords and spears," and in 1340, when the Mayor himself, attempting to quell a fight in Cheapside between Fishmongers and Skinners, was seized by the throat and nearly had his head cut off.

STATIONERS' HALL BEFORE THE BLITZ
The Stationers' Company, founded in the fourteenth century, is still actively concerned with its craft.

In 1516 the Court of Aldermen, which by an Act of 1437 had acquired control over the Companies, met to settle once and for all the question of precedence. From this Court emerged the twelve "Great" Companies, namely the Mercers, Grocers, Drapers, Fishmongers, Goldsmiths, Skinners, Merchant Taylors, Haberdashers, Salters, Ironmongers, Vintners and Clothworkers.

Humble Origins of Companies

The origins of some of these proud Companies were humble enough. The Mercers were originally the Milliners or *Milaners*, so-called because many of their goods came from the Italian city of Milan. In their earliest days they were often pedlars, but their charter of incorporation provided that "No one who had carried packs through the country could be admitted as an apprentice."

The name "grocer" was at one time a by no means complimentary term, no doubt because of certain practices of those who dealt *en gros* and concerning whom a petition presented to Edward III complained that "Great mischief had newly arisen . . . from the merchants called Grocers (grossers), who engrossed all manner of merchandise vendible, and who suddenly raised the prices of such merchandise within the realm; putting to sale by covin (i.e., agreement between two or more people to defraud or injure a third), and by ordinances made amongst themselves . . . such merchandises as were most dear, and keeping in stores the others until times of dearth and scarcity."

Master Called a " Pilgrim "

The Merchant Taylors were described in their first charter as " Linen Armourers." Their master was called the " pilgrim," that is, the one who travelled on behalf of the whole Company, and their wardens were named " purveyors of dress." The Haberdashers were a branch of the Mercers which split into two guilds not united until 1487. The Cloth-workers broke away as Shearmen, or cutters of cloth, from the ancient guild of Weavers, and later united with the Fullers.

Had the City guilds been no more than trade corporations it is doubtful if they would have survived. There were other elements in their constitution which were more permanent. The religious basis persisted, to give a sense of spiritual union; the charitable activities of the Companies became ever more prominent; and the close connection from earliest days between the guilds and the City Corporation—of which at one period they almost assumed complete control—gave, together with the powers granted by royal authority, a dignity and sense of responsibility not easily shaken. Thus it is not surprising that the rise to power of the Companies and guilds was accompanied by a development of pomp and pageantry to a degree unequalled in the history of London or indeed of any other city. As soon as it could each guild acquired a hall. Many of these were glorious buildings, which in course of time became repositories of almost fabulous treasures, until ruthlessly plundered by Charles I and Cromwell, whose exactions almost ruined a number of Companies.

APOTHECARIES' HALL
The Society of Apothecaries grants diplomas for medicine and surgery and certificates to dispensers.

Why Goldsmiths Became Bankers

In this connection it is interesting to note that the Goldsmiths became the first bankers in England because Charles I stole their money. He applied to the Company for a large loan, and when he was refused coolly lifted the deposits they had placed in the Tower for safe keeping.

Having lost £200,000 by this barefaced piece of robbery, the Goldsmiths determined to keep their money in their own shops, from which it was an easy transition to lending it out at interest.

Forty years after Cromwell's death the Mercers were still crippled by debt, and in a desperate attempt to retrieve their fortunes they started the first life assurance office in England. Their example was followed by other business men, but the Mercers' scheme was too generous and, in 1745, the Company had to petition Parliament for relief as it then owed over £100,000. It was allowed to issue new bonds and to pay them off by a lottery held in its hall. This was so successful that it completely re-established the prosperity of the almost ruined Guild.

Most of the medieval halls were destroyed in the Great Fire of 1666 and many of those which survived were destroyed or badly damaged during the Second World War. That of the Merchant Taylors, said to be the largest of the thirty-five Companies' halls in London retained the crypt of the hall built in 1331. It was practically destroyed by German bombs. In this hall on June 7, 1607, the Merchant Taylors feasted James I and his son, Prince Henry.

Banquet for a King

The feast cost the Merchant Taylors over £1,000—a sum which may be multiplied by at least ten to give an idea of its value in modern currency. At its conclusion they showed the King a " role, wherein was registered the names of seaven Kinges, one queene, seventeene princes and dukes, two dutchesses, one archbishoppe, one and thirtie earles, five countesses, one viscount, fourteen byshoppes, sixtie and sixe barons, two ladies, seaven abbots, seaven priors, and one sub-prior, omitting a great number of knights, esquires, etc., who had been made free of that compagnie."

The Merchant Taylors can show upon their roll of honorary freemen more royal and noble names than any other City Company.

The Vintners commemorate by an annual banquet, the great day in 1363 when Henry Picard feasted five kings at the same board—Edward III of England, David of Scotland, John of France (the English king's prisoner), Valdemar of Denmark, and Amadeus, King of Cyprus.

The event is recalled in the time-honoured toast " The Vintners' Company, may it flourish root and branch for ever, *with Five;* and the Master," and by the five cheers that are raised when the toast is proclaimed.

Ceremony of the Cygnets

Ever since that memorable day, too, the Ceremony of the Cygnets has been observed, the Vintners sharing with the Dyers the privilege of keeping swans on the Thames. During the course of the banquet the Swan Warder, accompanied by his swan markers, uppers, and banner-bearer enters the hall and presents to the Master roast cygnets borne on high, while ancient music is played on wind instruments.

The right to keep swans on the river is a most jealously guarded privilege. Every year on the first Monday in August the Swan Wardens of the two Companies set out with their " uppers " or markers, to cut on the bills of their swans their distinguishing marks. The Dyers cut one nick, the Vintners two. It is from the Vintners' marks that there has come that strange name found on more than one London public house, " The Swan with Two Necks "—necks being a corruption of nicks.

The fifteenth-century Court Room of the Vintners' Hall is said to be the oldest remaining room in the City of London. In it is a famous painting by Rubens of " St. Martin dividing his cloak with a beggar "—St. Martin being the patron saint of the Company.

The hall of the Drapers' Company stands in Throgmorton Street. Part of the building dates from 1667, but what is of greater interest to most people is that here, in the densest and busiest part of the City, occupying ground estimated to be worth £5,000 a square foot, is a garden gay with flower beds, cooled by a fountain that falls into a pool in which grow water lilies, and containing an ancient mulberry tree and several young ones.

Fruit From City Garden

The fruit is bottled, and each year mulberry pie is served to the Drapers, who are thus in all probability the only people in the City of London who can boast of eating fruit grown in a City garden. The Girdlers have behind their hall in Basinghall Street a tiny garden containing a grape-vine and a mulberry tree; but the vine rarely bears fruit and the mulberry is so ancient that no one dares to gather its crop.

In former days many Companies, when they were not using their halls, used to make an honest penny by letting them for meetings and societies. One or two acquired history by this means. Until 1826 State lotteries used to be drawn in the Coopers' Hall in Basinghall Street. The Grocers' Hall was let to the Bank of England for forty years until the Bank built its premises in Threadneedle Street, and was used as a Lord Mayor's residence for over fifty years.

The old hall of the Founders, who had " power to search all brass weights and brass and copper wares within the City of London and three miles thereof," was in the eighteenth century a noted resort for political meetings, earning during the hectic days of the French Revolution the nickname of " The Cauldron of Sedition."

On May 29, 1780, the Protestant Association met in the Coachmakers' and Coach-Harness Makers' Hall in Noble Street, and there resolved to meet in St. George's Fields to accompany Lord George Gordon to the House of Commons to present his petition against Popery. This decision led directly to the fearful Gordon Riots-

GARDEN OF THE DRAPERS' HALL

Right in the heart of the City this tiny plot is preserved as a garden. Here with other vegetation mulberry trees are cultivated, the fruit being bottled and served to the Livery at their banquets.

The Salters' Hall was earlier equally famous as a meeting place for Dissenters. In 1719, when the Arian heresy was a burning religious question, there took place here a dramatic debate culminating in a cry of "You that are against persecution come up stairs," which was countered by another voice which shouted, "You that are for declaring your faith in the doctrine of the Trinity, stay below."

The heretics were in the majority. Fifty-seven people went up into the gallery; only fifty-three remained on the ground floor.

Finest of the City Halls

Among the modern halls that of the Goldsmiths, built in 1832–35, is reckoned the finest; and as befits its craft, this Company has a superb collection of plate, including a chandelier of chased gold weighing 1,000 ounces, two lovely old plates of gold bearing the arms of France quartered with those of England, and a gold cup from which Elizabeth I is said to have drunk at her coronation.

Many of the Companies are rich in plate, though owing to the exactions of Charles I and Cromwell, and to the havoc wrought by the Great Fire, which was a veritable melting-pot, most of it is comparatively modern. The Vintners possess a large silver-gilt salt cellar dating from the early years of Elizabeth's reign, but a more curious treasure is the "Milkmaid Cup," a seventeenth-century double drinking vessel so contrived that it is very difficult to drink from it without spilling its contents. In former days every Vintner had to celebrate his admission to the Company by "kissing the milkmaid." The Clothworkers treasure a richly chased silver loving-cup presented to them by Samuel Pepys, who was Master of the Company in 1677–78.

Picture of First Mayor

A catalogue of the famous pictures possessed by the Companies would fill a volume. Many of these are of royalties and noble personages who have become honorary freemen, and several show the grant of the royal charter to the Company. The Mercers have a somewhat doubtful portrait of Sir Richard Whittington, and an authentic one of Sir Thomas Gresham, both of whom were of the Company.

The Drapers treasure a painting of Henr FitzAilwyn, first Mayor of London, and picture of Mary Queen of Scots, with besid her James I as a boy of four or five. The Ironmongers, whose hall was demolished during an air raid, have a full-length portrait of Admiral Lord Hood, by Gainsborough.

The full-length portrait of Frederick, Prince of Wales, which hung in the Saddlers' Hall (now destroyed), recalled how in 1736 the then heir to the throne stole disguised into the City to see the Lord Mayor's Show as a private spectator. Recognised by some of the Saddlers, he was invited into their stand, where he got himself so liked that he was shortly afterwards chosen to be Master of the Company and presented with the Freedom of the City.

Carpenters' Unique Frescoes

The Carpenters possessed a unique set of frescoes of early sixteenth-century work, showing Josiah repairing the Temple of Solomon and mentioning that no money reckoning was made with carpenters and other workmen " because they dealt faithfully," Joseph working at his bench while the boy Jesus collects the chips from the floor, and Christ teaching in the synagogue with His audience asking " Is not this the carpenter's Son? " Carpenters' Hall and most of its contents were badly damaged during the air raids of the Second World War.

The Painter-Stainers—so called because a picture on canvas used to be designated a " stained cloth "—once possessed a notable collection of pictures. Before the Second World War there were over 150 pictures in their possession : but bombings destroyed all but two dozen and badly damaged their Hall.

Scorned Lover's Invention

In the possession of the Weavers is an old portrait of William Lee, the inventor of the stocking loom, bearing the following quaint inscription, " In the year 1589 the ingenious William Lee, Master of Arts, of St. John's College, Cambridge, devised this profitable art for stockings (but being despised went to France); yet of iron to himself, but to us and others of gold, in memory of whom this is here painted."

The story runs that Lee was deeply enamoured of a maiden who lived at Calverton, in Nottinghamshire, and used to visit her from Cambridge. But she would have none of him, and the more he pressed his suit the faster her knitting needles flashed in her work.

Despairing at last, Lee went away, and bent his energies to inventing a machine that should prevent anyone ever again having to knit stockings by hand. The story is commemorated

SCENE OF SPLENDOUR AT GOLDSMITHS' HALL

One of the gorgeous rooms at the Goldsmiths' Hall, reputed to be the finest modern City hall in London. Behind the centre table can be seen some of the marvellous plate which the Company possesses.

TREASURES AT GOLDSMITHS' HALL
The Court Room at Goldsmiths' Hall. Although the name "hall" is universally applied to the Livery Companies' buildings, these usually contain many rooms, which are adorned with pictures, plate, tapestries and other treasures. The Goldsmiths possess beautiful chandeliers in which candles are still used.

in the arms of the Framework Knitters, which show a gowned student of Cambridge sitting beside a young woman busily knitting.

Scriptural Coats of Arms

Another curious coat of arms is that of the Gardeners, which shows a man clad in skins digging, with beneath the motto, "In the sweat of thy brow shalt thou eate thy bread." The Fruiterers have also gone to Scripture for their arms, which show Adam and Eve beneath an apple tree round which the serpent has coiled. Incidentally, Genesis makes no mention of the species of tree.

In Fishmongers' Hall (also badly damaged) was a statue of William Walworth, the celebrated Lord Mayor who slew Wat Tyler. The Company also possesses a superb pall, in three pieces and in the shape of a cross, gorgeously worked with figures of Christ and Peter.

Among the numerous historic treasures possessed by the Companies none has a stranger or more gruesome story than the screen of stamped and gilded Levant leather owned by the Barbers. In 1740 the body of a criminal who had been hanged was sent to the Barber-Surgeons, who used such corpses for dissection.

They had actually started to work upon this body when they discovered that the man's heart was still beating! Hastily they suspended operations and bent their efforts to reviving him. Having accomplished this successfully, they hid him until he was completely recovered, and then raised between themselves sufficient funds to send him abroad.

The man went to the Levant, became there a prosperous merchant, and later sent them the screen as a thank-offering.

When Dead Bodies Revive

Apparently this sort of thing had happened before, for in the Company's papers under date July 13, 1587, is the following strange resolution: "It is agreed that if any body which shall at any time hereafter happen to be brought to our hall for the intent to be wrought upon by the anatomists of the Company, shall revive or come to life again, *as of late hath been seen*, the charges about the same body so reviving shall be borne, levied and sustained by such person or persons who shall so happen to bring home the body."

The readiness with which the Barbers agreed to pay in case of such happening illustrates the attitude of all the Companies towards charity. From earliest days it was the custom of every one to provide for any brother (or sister) who had fallen on evil days, and to look after the aged and the infirm.

Companies' Generous Charity

Throughout the centuries wealthier members left property and made bequests for charitable purposes, and to-day a large part of the vast accumulated wealth of the Companies is devoted to benevolent and charitable objects. There is no body of citizens in England, or indeed in the whole world, which gives so generously.

Roughly speaking, the objects of the Companies' benevolence may be grouped under three heads—trade, education, and the care of the aged, infirm and sick. Though it is not now necessary, nor even usual, for a freeman to belong to the trade or craft of his Company, the members of each take an active interest in promoting its welfare.

Active Interest in Trades

Some Companies—notably the Goldsmiths, Fishmongers, Apothecaries, Brewers, Gunmakers, and Stationers (who recently accepted the Newspaper Makers in their ranks)—still function actively in their trade capacity. Others, representative of long-vanished crafts, have transferred their affections to the modern equivalents; the Bowyers have "established prizes for rifle-shooting in the Army," the Patten Makers assist the galosh industry, the Coach Makers and Coach-Harness Makers are now interested in the making of motor-car bodies and aeroplanes.

Of the services of the Companies and Guilds to education, both pure and applied, it is impossible to speak fully. They maintain or assist

HALL OF THE BARBER-SURGEONS

A century-old picture showing the reception of a new member. The Barber-Surgeons used to receive the bodies of executed criminals for dissection. The Hall was destroyed during the Second World War.

six public schools and a number of others. It is estimated that during the past fifty years they have contributed at least £500,000 to the advancement of technical education. Goldsmiths' College at New Cross is said to have cost the Company altogether £100,000. The University of Leeds owes much to the Clothworkers, who assisted in the foundation of the Yorkshire College of Science out of which it grew; they spent roughly £250,000 on the establishment, enlargement and maintenance of the textiles and dyeing department, and make an annual grant of £7,000 towards the expenses of the cloth and silk departments.

Ancient Customs Still Practised

The charitable activities and donations of the Companies are innumerable. In London and throughout the country are to be found almshouses supported by their wealth; and hospitals, homes and benevolent institutions by the score have reason to bless them. In addition, it can be safely said that no national appeal for any cause that will ameliorate social conditions or relieve suffering ever fails to evoke a generous response from the Companies.

The former tradition of the City Liverymen as a body of corpulent elders chiefly devoted to lavish banqueting has long since ceased to have point or meaning. Yet the banquets persist, and at them may be seen strange and venerable customs which have been religiously handed down from century to century.

SAMUEL PEPYS
The famous diarist belonged to the Clothworkers Company, to which he presented a silver loving-cup.

The Shipwrights, who made King George VI, when Duke of York, a Freeman and their permanent Master, when they drink from their loving-cup, pass it along with both hands, and the one who has just partaken remains standing to guard from " treacherous attack " the one who holds the cup.

The annual election of Master and Wardens is always carried out in traditional style. A number of Companies " crown " their newly elected officers. The " crown " of the Master of the Girdlers is silk embroidered with gold.

Most of the ancient ceremonies preserved by the Companies to-day take place within their Halls, the gorgeous processions through the streets being now almost a thing of the past, though the Vintners still march in state to church each year preceded by their Tackle Porters, who, clad in white smocks and wielding besoms, sweep the roadway clean—a relic of the days when the filth and garbage of the London streets offered a real menace to their long fur-trimmed cloaks.

It is to-day the sunset of the City Companies, but it is a mellow and a lingering sunset, which all may hope will be prolonged indefinitely, since it is rich in blessing for many. Once upon a time the Liverymen grew so powerful that they aspired to rule the City, and almost succeeded in their design : to-day they are content to retain the formal right of electing the Lord Mayor, and to spend most of their energies in good works.

Royal Freemen of the City

They have gained none the less respect, but rather more, by abrogating many of their ancient rights. The greatest in the land regard it as an honour to be numbered in their ranks. " I am proud to come among you as a Fishmonger," said King Edward VIII when, as Prince of Wales, he became a Freeman of that Company. King George VI and Queen Elizabeth were both Shipwrights, and the King was also a Draper. The Duke of Gloucester is a Mercer.

To be a Freeman of the City of London has never been a mean privilege, and so long as the Companies maintain their tradition of dignity and benevolence the value of that privilege will not be lowered.

A SECTION OF LONDON'S VAST DOCKS

Five dock systems are included in the Port of London. They cover 4,246 acres, and deal yearly with ocean trade valued at about £500,000,000. This is over one-third of the overseas trade of Britain. London's dockland suffered terrible damage in the air raids which took place between 1940 and 1945.

LIQUID HISTORY

THE Thames made London. It was the easy way of approach from the Continent to England, more especially from Gaul, which we now call France. It is even whispered—for it is scarcely more than the shadow of a suggestion—that over 2,000 years ago enterprising traders with boatloads of gewgaws and other merchandise hugged the long coast from the Mediterranean and found a following wind that took them up the waterway. Their destination was the little hill settlement that is now the capital of an empire of 450,000,000 people.

There is little doubt that the Thames was the main thoroughfare from the east to the west of southern England long before the Romans paid their first visit to Britain in 55 B.C. Even so recently as two centuries ago it was the only reasonably safe highway from one end of London to the other, and it was certainly the busiest. The waves were no more deeply furrowed than the streets, and a few splashes of water did less harm than a fusillade of mud.

"Eastward ho!" and "Westward ho!" were as familiar cries at the water stairs as "Bank" and "Liverpool Street" were to be from the platforms of omnibuses at a later time.

Tacitus records that after the rebellion of Boudicca (Boadicea) in A.D. 61 the Roman general Suetonius Paulinus "marched amidst a hostile population to Londinium, which though undistinguished by the name of a colony, was much frequented by a number of merchants and trading vessels."

This, the earliest known reference to London, is valuable evidence that the place was an important centre of water-borne trade before it assumed significance as a centre of population.

About 150 years after Boudicca's fiery visit, London, according to the Greek writer

PANORAMIC VIEW OF LONDON

The City, the Thames, and Southwark as Shakespeare knew them. (1) Old St. Paul's. (2) St. Dunstan's Church. (3) The Temple. (4) St. Bride's. (5) St. Andrew's. (6) Baynard's Castle. (7) St. Sepulchre's. (8) Bow Church. (9) Guildhall. (10) St. Michael's. (11) St. Laurence Poultney. (12) The Old Swan.

Herodian, was " a great and wealthy city." Gildas, the British chronicler who died in 570, tells us that Britain "is enriched by the mouths of two noble rivers, the Thames and the Severn, as it were two arms, by which foreign luxuries were of old imported, and by other streams of less importance." Bede, the learned and pious monk of Jarrow, writing rather more than a century later, avows that London " is the mart of many nations resorting to it by sea and land."

Earliest Document Concerning Port

The earliest document still existing concerning the future metropolis has reference to it as a centre of shipping and bears the date 734. It grants leave by King Ethelbald to the Bishop of Rochester to send a ship without tax in or out of the port.

By the ninth century London was of sufficient importance to be the frequent object of Danish raids. In 895, during the reign of King Alfred, the invaders from the north towed their ships up the River Lea in an attempt to reach the city. Alfred built dams across the stream, which caused the Danish craft to be stranded, and their crews retreated overland towards the Severn, pursued by the Saxon army. It is related that " the men of London fetched the ships, and all that they could not lead away they broke up, and all that were worthy of capture they brought into the Port of London."

Ancient Tolls at Billingsgate

A parchment of the tenth century records the regulations made by King Ethelred for the tolls chargeable at Billingsgate for the use of a hithe : one halfpenny for a trading vessel without sails and one penny with them. Hithes were the ancestors of the docks of to-day. They were little backwaters wherein ships lay while their cargoes were unloaded on to landing stages. The name persists in Rotherhithe, and in a disguised form in Chelsea, which was originally Chealchyth, the Chalk hithe. To guard against piracy hithes were cut off from the main stream by means of gates—hence Billingsgate (traditionally named after Belin, a King of the Britons, though more probably after Biling, a medieval owner), which was situated on the northern side of the river, a short distance below the point at which the first stone bridge was built across the Thames between 1176 and 1209.

The construction of London Bridge, as it was

IN THE DAYS BEFORE THE FIRE
(13) London Bridge. (14) St. Dunstan's East. (15) Billingsgate. (16) Custom House. (17) The Tower. (18) Tower Wharf. (19) St. Olave's Church. (20) St. Mary Overies Church. (21) Winchester House. (22) The Globe Theatre. (23) The Bear Garden. (24) Hampstead. (25) Highgate. (26) Hackney.

called, had a considerable influence on the development of the port. It marked the limit of ocean navigation, for sea-going ships, unless very small, could not pass through the low, narrow arches. It is considered probable, too, that in the days when Peter of Colechurch built his famous bridge the ocean tides which surged up the estuary did not reach farther than this point. Similarly, river traffic tended to confine itself to the " above bridge " area, where the main hithe was Queenhithe, second only to Billingsgate in antiquity and importance. This distinction persists to-day. Ocean steamers are berthed right up to London Bridge, but they cannot pass it.

Foreigners Treated as Citizens

For a considerable period by far the greater part of London's sea-borne trade was carried on by foreigners. They were merchants of various cities of northern Germany, such as Lübeck and Hamburg, who afterwards banded together for mutual protection and commercial advantage, and became the powerful Hanseatic League. The enterprising Easterlings, as they were called and whose name is perpetuated in the word " sterling," made a start in London in 979, when Ethelred the Unready was king. The foreigners behaved themselves sufficiently well to be " judged worthy of the good laws, like to ourselves," and to be treated in every way as honest citizens.

Rent Remitted by Grateful King

In other words, little or no distinction was made between them and Londoners born. They were on terms of equality, although at Easter and Christmas the Easterlings presented to the City one piece of brown cloth, two pieces of grey cloth, five pairs of men's gloves, ten pounds of pepper and two barrels of vinegar. An annual rent of 2s. was exacted for the guildhall used by the men of Cologne, but even this was remitted by Richard I when he was released from imprisonment following his adventure in the Holy Land. He received so hearty a welcome from the largest and most prosperous city in Germany that he cancelled the payment and granted the Cologners the right to do business in all the markets of his realm.

The Hanseatics settled in the Steelyard in Thames Street in 1250, on the site now occupied by Cannon Street Station and Hotel. Privileges were almost showered on the ever-growing corporation in return for services rendered, and at one time they had trading centres in eight English towns in addition to London. The gate still called to mind by Bishopsgate was partly maintained by them in lieu of taxes for the upkeep of the City wall, London Bridge and the streets. A London alderman, chosen by them, represented the League in the City councils.

Edward III pawned his crown and jewels with the foreign magnates for a considerable sum of money, which he used in carrying out his French campaigns. Londoners were by no means enamoured of this monarchical fondness for foreigners, and there was much wrangling as a consequence. The growth of English sea-power and the rise of trading companies marked the beginning of the end, which came in 1598, when Elizabeth I, after a great deal of quarrelling and the capture of contraband in Hansa ships, peremptorily told the denizens of the Steelyard to clear out.

Regulations for Landing Goods

Forty years before this the Government had found it necessary to pass an Act to regulate the landing of goods in the Thames. From that time on it was an offence to discharge vessels except at twenty " legal quays " between sunrise and sunset. They were situated on the north bank of the river between London Bridge and the Tower, thus making the avoidance of the payment of Customs dues more difficult. Certain " sufferance wharves " were afterwards added, the word " sufferance " meaning permission granted by the Customs for the landing of merchandise.

In the early years of the seventeenth century the East India Company, which was destined to bring ever-increasing trade to London during the next two hundred years, established its headquarters at Blackwall. Samuel Pepys records a visit to this place in 1661, during which he saw the Company's wet dock, the first to be constructed on the Thames. It had at that time an area of 1½ acres, and was the pride of the East India Company.

Then, and for a hundred-odd years afterwards, the Thames was a great fishing river. Large numbers of people—many of whom came from Lambeth—lived by trawling in its waters. Regulations designed to preserve the fisheries were made as early as the reign of Richard I and were jealously enforced, in constantly changing form, from that time on. Edward I fixed the price of fresh salmon at 1s. 3d. each. A Dutch eel-boat has been moored off Billingsgate since the time of Charles I, who granted the Hollanders a charter giving them the right to sell eels off the market.

The Great Fire, which began within the Port's immediate environs, destroyed every wharf and warehouse from the Tower to the Temple Church. The work of rebuilding, begun in 1667, was mainly paid for by a tax on coal entering the port. In 1700 the tonnage of its shipping was 600,000, and the value of its imports and exports £10,000,000. The vessels were small, the average being 96 tons for vessels voyaging overseas and 50 tons for those engaged in the coastal trade.

The beginning of the eighteenth century saw the construction of the Howland Great Wet Dock on the south side of the river at Rotherhithe. Sanctioned in 1696, it was for close on a hundred years the largest dock on the Thames and remained in use until the end of the nineteenth century. London owed the enterprise to a woman, Mrs. Elizabeth Howland, of Streatham. The dock had an area of 10 acres, could accommodate over a hundred large merchantmen and was used mainly for repairing and refitting. Some sixty years after its completion it became a centre of the whaling industry, and for that reason the name was changed to the Greenland Dock.

From Pond to Ocean Dock

When about 1810 it began to be used by timber and corn merchants it was rechristened the Commercial Dock, and some years later was taken over by the Surrey Commercial Dock Company, which controlled all the docks on the south bank of the river. Modernised, the Commercial Dock is again known as the Greenland Dock, and as such it shelters liners up to 14,000 tons. " Big oaks from little acorns grow," but it is unusual for a pond only 6 feet deep to become a dock of 14 acres. Yet such is the story of the Quebec Dock, which is part of the system.

At the time of the construction of the Howland Dock the annual value of London's imports was under £5,000,000, but although this figure had swollen to over £12,000,000 in 1792, there was no appreciable increase in the dock area. London's trade was about three-fifths of that of the whole kingdom, yet the length of its legal quays was no greater than in the time of Charles II : they extended fo

PORT OF LONDON CUSTOM HOUSE
Situate in Lower Thames Street, it was built in 1814–17, and was the sixth Custom House to be erected on the site. It had later to be partly rebuilt owing to defective foundations. The front is 488 feet long.

little more than a quarter of a mile between London Bridge and the Tower. As for sufferance wharves, numerous abuses arose from their use, the principal one being that their owners levied exorbitant rates. Moreover, the warehouses connected with both the legal quays and the sufferance wharves could not receive more than a small proportion of the goods landed.

At that time all the larger vessels anchored in mid-stream and discharged their cargoes into lighters, which in turn discharged them at the quays and wharves. Because of the congested state of the river it often took ships three or four weeks to unload.

That such a state of affairs should have been allowed to persist is a matter for surprise, but it is easily accounted for : the activities of the port were controlled by monopolists who were only too well aware that reforms would reduce their swollen incomes.

Saving the Port of London

The port's most urgent need was an adequate system of docks. That this need was met was mainly due to the efforts of William Vaughan, the son of a London merchant. He had devoted much time to the study of naval architecture before publishing, in 1793, the first of a series of pamphlets on the question of how the Port of London could be improved. He insisted that unless an efficient dock system were quickly established London's trade would pass to such ports as Liverpool, Hull and Bristol, and suggested that the most suitable sites were at St. Katharine's Church, Wapping, the Isle of Dogs and Rotherhithe. At Wapping had stood Execution Dock, where pirates and others guilty of crime on the high seas were hanged and their bodies tied to poles in the river as a warning. As for the Isle of Dogs, it is said to have received its strange name because the royal folk who lived at Greenwich Palace had kept their hounds there. Tradition has it that in 1016 King Cnut dug a channel through the Rotherhithe marshes so that his fleet might pass to the west of London Bridge.

Opposition to Suggested Docks

Vaughan was instrumental in presenting a petition on the subject to Parliament, as the result of which a House of Commons Committee, under the chairmanship of Sir William Young, was set up to inquire into all the proposals that had recently been put forward for the port's improvement. Witnesses representing the East India Company, the Corporation of London, the Customs officials, Trinity House, the Admiralty, as well as many other interests, gave evidence before the Committee, which presented its report in May, 1796.

Never was there more conclusive proof that drastic reforms were imperative, and never were more determined efforts made to obstruct progress. The obstructionists included the proprietors of the legal quays and of the sufferance wharves, as well as the watermen, the lightermen, the City porters, the carmen and the Town Clerk. Opposition from every quarter was vigorously fought by the reformers, with the result that in 1799 Parliament passed a Bill providing for the establishment of docks at the Isle of Dogs between Limehouse and

Blackwall. The following year the scheme for docks at Wapping which had been originally suggested by William Vaughan was also approved. The sequel to this legislation was the completion of the West India Docks in August, 1802, and of the London Dock in January, 1805.

Docks Defended by Cannon

The West India Docks covered an area of some 54 acres, and their greatest depth of water was about 21 feet. An elaborate system of warehouses for the storage of sugar, rum and molasses, with a frontage of nearly three-quarters of a mile, was completed. For fear of attack there were outer and inner walls, a broad ditch, and 18-pounder guns. At the time of their erection the buildings were the finest of their kind, and even to-day they have few rivals for capaciousness. The Clock Gate erected to commemorate the beginning of work on the construction of the Dock on July 12, 1800, and its opening "for business"—to quote the inscription—on September 1, 1802, was demolished in 1932. The stone ship above it was removed to Poplar Recreation Ground.

The present "new" East India Dock was opened in 1806; the first part of the Surrey Dock system in 1807; the St. Katharine, so named because it covers the site of the Collegiate Church of St. Katharine by the Tower, in 1828; the Royal Victoria, where the first frozen meat warehouse in the United Kingdom was built, in 1855; the Millwall in 1868 and the Royal Albert in 1880. The Tilbury Docks, opposite Gravesend, begun in 1882 and opened in 1886, were a commercial failure for some years, which is not surprising seeing that they are 26 miles from London.

ANCIENT CLOCK GATE DISAPPEARS
Demolishing the 130-year-old Clock Gate at the West India Docks. The stone ship was preserved.

Towards the end of the century the increase both in the amount of trade handled by the port, and in the size and draught of the ships using it, made it a matter of supreme importance that large-scale improvements should be carried out. The cost was too great to be undertaken by any of the private companies which controlled the docks, and it soon became obvious that it would be necessary to set up a central authority of some sort. Such an authority would not only lead to the pooling of resources, but would also do away with the harmful competition in which the various interests were continuously indulging.

Port of London Authority

Matters were brought to a head in 1899 when the London and India Docks Joint Committee asked Parliament to grant them powers to make a charge on barges entering their docks for the purpose of loading or discharging goods, and also to levy a toll on such goods. The Government rejected the Bill but announced its intention of making a full inquiry into the matter. A Royal Commission recommended the establishment of a public trust which was to have complete control of the docks and to take over the duties of the Watermen's Company and of the Thames Conservancy Board below Teddington. The last mentioned had controlled the whole of the river since 1856. A Bill on these lines was presented to Parliament in 1903, but it met with no success, and several years elapsed before the Port of London Authority was established under the Port of London Act (1908).

Among the first activities of the P.L.A., as it is generally called, which began work on March 31, 1909, were the provision of new quays and sheds at the London, West India, East India, and Millwall Docks; the erection of new cold-storage warehouses for imported meat; an extension of the Tilbury Docks; and the installation of new cranes and pumping apparatus. The area of the Royal Albert and the Royal Victoria Docks, which are connected by waterways, was further increased in 192 when the new King George V Dock was linked with them.

London's vast dock area was one of the German airmen's main targets during the Second World War, when it suffered terrible damage. The very first raids, September 7–9, 1940, reduced the wharves on the Surrey Docks to a smouldering ruin. The story is told more fully in the chapter, " London at War."

By the time of the establishment of the P.L.A., shipbuilding, once one of London's most prosperous industries, had practically ceased on the shores of the Thames. The usual explanation given is that it was found impracticable to carry on a shipbuilding industry so far removed from the coal and iron mines.

Some Famous Old Shipyards

One of the most famous of London's bygone shipbuilding centres was the Royal Dockyard at Deptford Creek. Here Peter the Great picked up the rudiments of naval architecture and enjoyed many a night drinking beer in the local inn and discussing maritime matters with fellow-customers. Underneath the docks in the Isle of Dogs lies Joseph Somes's yard, where some of the finest of the old East Indiamen and not a few clippers came into being. The site of Money Wigram's yard, in which the celebrated Blackwall frigates were built, is now covered by a railway goods wharf.

A fair number of iron and steel ships were built on the Thames in the middle of last century. The most famous, the *Great Eastern*, came from Millwall. It was double the length of its nearest rival, and its tonnage six times that of the largest man-of-war then afloat. Bilbe & Perry of Rotherhithe produced some of the first composite ships (i.e., ships of wood and iron) in the 'fifties, and H.M.S. *Thunderer* left the yard of the Thames Ironworks Company in 1912. This fine battleship of 25,000 tons fought at Jutland.

In the days before coaches the Thames was London's main highway, and the watermen were its bus-drivers and cabbies combined. An old manuscript records how in 1293 people began to complain because the boatmen of Gravesend raised the fare to London from a halfpenny to a penny. Some years later the fare for the same journey was increased to twopence.

The lack of good land transport enabled the watermen to behave with all the customary high-handedness of monopolists. Samuel Pepys records that when his work as Secretary to the Admiralty made it necessary for him to use the river constantly, the watermen used frequently to overcharge him. He had his revenge by getting the press gang to apprehend some of the miscreants and send them to sea. In the second half of the sixteenth century, however, their monopoly was threatened by the coach; and by the reign of James I a bitter struggle was in progress between watermen and coach-owners. In 1614 the former were instrumental in introducing a Bill against " outrageous coaches " in the House of Commons, but it failed to pass through Parliament.

HEADQUARTERS OF P.L.A.
The Port of London Authority building. Completed in 1922, it stands in Trinity Square, and is 170 feet high. It was designed by Sir Edwin Cooper.

Watermen Appeal Against Coaches

The indignation of the watermen knew no bounds when hackney-carriages began to ply for hire. About 1645 the watermen decided to appeal to King Charles. In their petition they said : " Hackney coaches are so many in number that they pester and encumber the streets of London and Westminster, and, which is worst of all, they stand and ply in term time at the Temple gate . . . which doing of this doth undoe the Company of Watermen." The King was sympathetic and took steps to curtail the activities of the hackneys. Cromwell viewed the arrogant watermen with less favour, and further decreased their chance of custom by permitting the licensing of hackney coaches in the City up to a number of 200. The watermen then petitioned Parliament again, but the only result was a large increase in the number of hackneys. By 1685 there were 400, and nine years later a Bill to raise the number by 300 was successfully passed.

Thames Declines as a Highway

By the middle of the eighteenth century the monopolistic power of the watermen was a thing of the past; the Thames had ceased to be London's main throughfare. This revolution in the Londoner's means of transport had a tremendous effect on the layout of the City. Prior to the day of the coach little attention was paid to London's roads : they were merely means of access to the Thames. But the coach demanded main roads independent of the river, and these gradually came into being. From them have been evolved the thoroughfares of to-day.

DOGGETT'S COAT AND BADGE
Instituted in 1715 by Thomas Doggett, the watermen's race is a popular sporting event on the Thames.

Even after the coming of the coach, the power of one section of the watermen, those who manned the cargo-carrying barges, remained undiminished. Technically known as lightermen, their history may be said to date from the early years of the sixteenth century, when ships began to arrive in large numbers in the Thames. As trade increased congestion at the hithes also increased, so that it became customary for large merchantmen to anchor in mid-stream and have their cargoes taken ashore in barges called lighters.

The first lighters bore a superficial resemblance to Chinese junks, having tapering prows and being propelled by long oars called sweeps. These heavy and unwieldy instruments gradually ceased to be the only means of propulsion : first square mainsails were used, and then foresails, topsails and mizzens were introduced. To-day some of the larger Thames barges have a carrying capacity of about 400 tons, but at the end of the eighteenth century the capacity of the largest was probably less than 100 tons.

How to Become a Waterman

With the construction of numerous docks and deep-water jetties the sailing barge began to lose its importance. It was gradually supplanted by " dumb " lighters towed by steam tugs. To-day hundreds of tugs are employed on the Thames to convey lighter-borne goods from one wharf to another. The manually propelled lighter and the sailing barge have not yet entirely disappeared from the bosom of the mighty river, over whose destinies they once had such influence, but they have fallen from their high estate. Gone are the days when their ancestors proudly received the rare and costly products of an East Indiaman's long voyage to the Orient; the transport of refuse and ballast is now their humble lot. Even to-day it is not possible for any Tom, Dick or Harry to become a lighterman. He who covets a job as a lighterman has to study the practical problems of navigation in the Thames for a matter of two years before the question of granting him a licence will be considered by the Watermen's and Lightermen's Company

OXFORD *VERSUS* CAMBRIDGE
The University Boat Race has been rowed on the Thames since 1829, and is unique among sporting events in having no written rules. The umpire, who follows the crews in a launch, is in absolute charge.

For the lover of tradition, the watermen's race from London Bridge to Chelsea for Doggett's coat and badge must be one of the most interesting sporting events of the year. The race was instituted in 1715 by Thomas Doggett, the Irish Whig comedian, in commemoration of the " happy accession to the British Throne " of King George I, and for the encouragement of rowing among Thames watermen. Doggett bequeathed to the Fishmongers' Company, of which he was a member, a sum sufficient to purchase annually an orange-coloured coat, knee breeches, silk stockings and cap, and a silver badge bearing the white horse of Hanover, to be presented to the winner of the race. He did this because of his affection for the watermen who rowed him up and down the river, and who apparently were not in the habit of overcharging him as they did Pepys.

Race without any Rules

Of more popular appeal is the University Boat Race. The first race of this now annual event took place on June 10, 1829, the course being from Hambledon Lock to Henley Bridge, a distance of 2¼ miles. Eight-oared cutters with iron keels and without outriggers were used. No attempt was made to keep the course clear. Oxford won, but the next race, which was not rowed until seven years later, went to Cambridge. The course was changed in 1845 and now lies between Putney and Mortlake.

The Boat Race, which every spring attracts a million spectators to the banks of the Thames, is beyond doubt the most cleanly contested sporting event in the world. Though the university crews have met over one hundred times and for more than a hundred years, only one foul has ever been recorded. There are no rules for the race; the conditions under which each is to be rowed are agreed upon by the presidents of the university boat clubs, who also appoint the umpire. To this official is handed over complete and absolute charge of the race.

River Thieves and Cut-throats

Throughout the eighteenth century the necessity for large ships to discharge their cargoes into lighters in mid-stream brought into being a large army of thieves and cut-throats who lived by plundering such craft. This evil reached such proportions that the owners of ships trading to the West Indies were instrumental in the formation of a police force to protect their property. Constables were enrolled to act as watchmen while ships were being unloaded. Labourers were searched every evening before they left the ship, and were compelled to wear a type of uniform in which it was difficult to conceal stolen goods.

So incensed were the habitual thieves at this denial of their " right to plunder " that they organised an attack on the Police Office, and firearms had to be brought into use before the attackers dispersed.

The thieves were divided into gangs. The " River Pirates," who always went about fully armed, specialised in cutting lighters adrift at night and plundering them when they ran aground. The dishonest porters and labourers who handled the ships' cargoes were known as " Heavy Horsemen." They used to throw goods overboard at high tide, and at low tide such goods would be collected by the " Mud Larks." Scoundrelly watermen were known as " Night Plunderers," while their colleagues ashore were termed " Scuffle Hunters." As many of the revenue officials and ships' officers were in league with the various gangs, the prevention of smuggling and thieving was an extremely difficult task. When conditions were at their worst it was estimated that the gangs cost the merchants and the Government as much as £800,000 a year.

Work of Thames Police

As docks were constructed the evils assumed less formidable proportions. The establishment of an efficient police force in the metropolis in the second quarter of the nineteenth century soon made London the most law-abiding city in the world, and every year the " River Pirates " became fewer and much less venturesome.

Eventually a special department of the Metropolitan Police came into being for the protection of life and property on the Thames. The policemen, who dress in semi-nautical uniform, cruise up and down the river in motor launches, ever on the alert for irregularities. Their " beat," stretching from Long Reach to Barnes, is 36 miles long.

Markets on the Frozen Thames

On several occasions it has been possible to cross the Thames on foot. In 1434 the weather was so severe that the river was frozen from London Bridge to Gravesend, and it remained a solid mass for some fourteen weeks. Football was played on the ice between Westminster and London Bridge in 1564. Pepys records that in January, 1667, the Thames was " covered with ice," and in the winter of 1683–84 a frost fair was held. The frost began early in December and did not break until February 4. Within a few days of its commencement an animated scene was to be beheld on the river; the frozen surface of the Thames became a market-place, a social rendezvous, and a fun fair.

" I went acrosse the Thames on ice," Evelyn confides to his Diary on January 9, 1684, " now become so thick as to beare not only streetes of boothes, in which they roasted meate, and had divers shops of wares, quite

GUARDIANS OF THE THAMES

Thames River Police in the course of a routine tour of inspection. They patrol the river from Long Reach near Purfleet to Barnes, using swift motor launches, and wearing semi-nautical uniform.

acrosse as in a towne, but coaches, carts and horses passed over." Writing fifteen days later he notes : " The frost continuing more and more severe, the Thames, before London, was still planted with boothes in formal streetes, all sorts of trades and shops, furnished and full of commodities, even to a printing-press, where the people and ladies took a fancy to have their names printed, and the day and the year set down, when printed on the Thames : this humour took so universally, that it was estimated the printer gained five pounds a day, for printing a line only, at sixpence a name, besides what he got for ballads, etc. Coaches plied from Westminster to the Temple, and from other stairs to and fro, as in the streetes; sleds, sliding with skaites, a bull-baiting, horse and coach races, puppet-plays and interludes, cooks, tippling, and other lewd places; so that it seemed to be a bacchanalian triumph, or carnival on water; whilst it was a severe judgment on the land, the trees not only splitting as if lightning-struck, but men and cattle perishing in divers places, and the very seas so locked up with ice, that no vessels could stir out or come in! The fowls, fish, and birds, and all our exotic plants and greens, universally perishing. Many parks of deer were destroyed; and all sorts of fuel so dear, that there were great contributions to keep the poor alive!

" London, by reason of the excessive coldness of the air hindering the ascent of the smoke, was so filled with the fuliginous steam of the sea-coal, that hardly could anyone see across the streetes, and this filling the lungs with its gross particles, exceedingly obstructed the breast, so as one could scarcely breathe. There was no water to be had from the pipes and engines; nor could the brewers and divers other tradesmen work, and every moment was full of disastrous incidents."

Ox Roasted on the Thames

In 1716 an ox was roasted whole on the Thames, and the river was frozen again in 1740, 1789, 1814 and 1895, when the ice was so solid that a four-in-hand was driven across in perfect safety.

When London began to grow, the marshy nature of much of the surrounding land raised the difficult problem of how best to keep the Thames out so that the low-lying districts should not be subject to frequent flooding. The Victoria and Albert embankments are typical examples of substantial engineering works undertaken to serve the double purpose of holding the river within bounds and providing thoroughfares. Wharves, buildings and walls also form a part of the system, but in early times the Church also took a hand, particularly in the lower reaches, where it held much land. It took a leading part in enclosing its estates with embankments.

Reclaiming the Riverside

Apparently the retaining of the river within reasonable limits was regarded as of local rather than of national importance until the time of Edward II, when taxes—which are bugbears more ancient than is commonly supposed—were levied for the purpose. During the reign of Elizabeth and onwards quite a number of enterprising foreigners tackled the job of reclaiming acres from the ravenous river. It is no cause for surprise that the Dutch, whose native land is for the most part below sea-level, particularly distinguished themselves, and were usually happy to retain a part of the recovered property in lieu of a cash payment.

When excavations on the site of the Custom House were being made it was found that the earth consisted of three layers of considerable thickness and of different periods, and had evidently been taken from the bed of the river to prevent the encroachment of the water. Where a more substantial structure was not deemed necessary the usual method was to drive tiers of stakes into the bed of the river and back them with chalk or stone well rammed in.

To-day at least ten square miles of London lie below high-water mark, and so recently as 1928 the river burst its banks at Westminster, Putney and Hammersmith, causing the loss of fourteen lives and considerable damage to property. Two hundred and twenty years earlier the Thames broke through at Dagenham, flooded 1,000 acres and involved an expenditure of £40,472. On various occasions parts of Lambeth, Blackfriars, Vauxhall, Shadwell, Barking, Plumstead, Purfleet, Grays and Woolwich have been turned into miniature seas by floods, high tides and north-westerly gales.

The Thames is not London's only stream. Deep down below the streets and buildings are numerous streams, large and small, which now make their way to the Thames through conduits and sewers.

The most famous of London's lost rivers is the Fleet, which was once a very important commercial highway, and has given its name to one of the best known streets in the world. Rising in the Vale of Health, Hampstead, it passes under Kentish Town, Camden Town, King's Cross, Gray's Inn Road and Farringdon Road, to reach the Thames at Blackfriars Bridge. Near Clerkenwell it is joined by a tributary, which rises in Russell Square, and whose waters were disturbed when the foundations of the Imperial Hotel were being laid in 1902. Its upper reaches bore the name Holebourne, whence the modern thoroughfare and area, Holborn, is derived.

Ships on the Fleet River

After the Great Fire (1666) the Fleet was canalised between Holborn and Blackfriars and could be used by craft drawing 5 feet of water. It was then crossed by three bridges—the Holebourne, the Fleet and the Bridewell. By the end of the seventeenth century it had ceased to have any importance as a highway for the transport of goods, and as its foulness increased year by year, causing great offence to the citizens, in 1734–35 the stretch between Fleet Street and Holborn was covered in, and some thirty years later that from Fleet Street to the Thames was similarly dealt with. Until 1924 Ludgate Circus was mainly upheld by the arches of the old Fleet Bridge, which are only two or three feet beneath the surface of the street at this point.

WATCHING THE TIDES
A kiosk near Westminster Bridge containing meters and gauges to register the heights of tides.

It is still possible for those who attend to the sewers to wade along the course of the Fleet from Ludgate Circus as far as Flask Walk, Hampstead. At Holborn, where Sir Christopher Wren built an ornamental bridge over the river in 1674, a number of iron eyes, to which barges used to be moored, can be seen.

Another lost river which rises in Hampstead —at "Shepherds" o' Conduit Fields—is the Tybourne, which passes in its later stages under Marylebone Lane, Oxford Street, Brook Street, Grosvenor Street, Piccadilly, the Green Park and Buckingham Palace, to enter the Thames at Millbank. On autumn evenings a mist may be noticed hanging over the river's conduited course in the Green Park; and its waters may be seen pouring into the long pond in St. James's Park, near the Queen Victoria Memorial.

The Westbourne runs from Hampstead Heath to Hyde Park, where it feeds the famous Serpentine, the ornamental lake which George II's consort, Queen Caroline, ordered to be constructed. Thence it runs under the Albert Gate, Pont Street, Cliveden Place and the Court Theatre, passes over the railway at Sloane Square Station in a conduit, and proceeds beneath Holbein Place and Chelsea Bridge Road, to enter the Thames at a point near Chelsea Bridge.

Source of Fountains and Lakes

In the neighbourhood of Hyde Park the Westbourne throws off a branch called the Cranbourne, which feeds the lake in St. James's Park as well as the fountains in Trafalgar Square. Flowing under the street to which it gives its name, it passes by St. Martin's Lane and Whitehall, to enter the Thames under the House of Lords.

The Kilbourne, which had its source near the inn known as "Jack Straw's Castle" at Hampstead, flowed by old Watling Street and Kilburn Wells, where people used to take the waters only a hundred years ago.

The Wallbrook, which is formed by a number of tributary streams which meet near Finsbury, reaches the Thames at Dowgate Hill. In olden days it marked the dividing line between the eastern and western halves of the City.

Donald McLeish

VENICE IN LONDON

Paddington Broadwater, the point at which the Grand Junction and Regent's Canals unite. Browning, whose house overlooked it, was so charmed with its beauty that he called it "Venice in London."

John Stow, the sixteenth-century antiquarian, says that it was joined by the Langbourne near the site of the Bank of England, and that it passed down Lombard Street. It was vaulted over before Stow's time, but continues to give considerable trouble to builders in the City.

Another hidden stream that causes anxiety and, in times of flood, much damage, is the Effra, up which Queen Elizabeth I was rowed to visit Sir Walter Raleigh at Brixton. It rises in the Surrey Hills near Riddlesdown and joins the Thames at Nine Elms. It passes under Brixton Road, the Oval, Harleyford Road and Wandsworth Road. In April, 1923, it burst its bounds and poured water into the City and South London Railway, causing stoppages in the tube-train traffic at Stockwell and Clapham, and a tram stoppage in Stockwell Road. Long stretches at Kennington were as yet uncovered within living memory.

Long forgotten Streams

Other streams and wells are hidden beneath busy London. They remain forgotten until work is interrupted by an inrush of water from a source whose existence is not even suspected by the workmen. Then the antiquarian puts pen to paper and the story of the lost waterway is told in the correspondence columns of next day's newspaper.

Three waterways, all on the north side of the Thames, connect the Port of London with the Midlands. The oldest of these is the River Lea; the Grand Junction Canal and the Regent's Canal are purely artificial.

By means of the first mentioned, which was made navigable between Hertford and Ware in 1739 and thence to London in 1770, barges can travel from Blackwall to Hertford, passing through Edmonton, Ponder's End and Enfield Lock, and can then proceed from Hertford to Bishop's Stortford by the River Stort.

Canal Across London

The Regent's Canal, which was opened in 1820, having taken eight years to construct, runs northwards from Limehouse to Victoria Park, where the Hertford Union Canal, running north-east, connects it with the River Lea. Turning thence in a westerly direction it passes through Islington, and after flowing for three-quarters of a mile through Pentonville-hill by means of a tunnel, skirts the rear of King's Cross Station and makes for Regent's Park by way of Camden Town. At Paddington, which it reaches through St. John's Wood, it enters a wide basin adjacent to the Western Region railway station. This basin is also entered by a branch of the Grand Junction Canal, known as the Paddington Arm, which runs thence for 13 miles to Bull's Bridge, near Hayes, in Middlesex.

The Regent's Canal Dock at Limehouse, which has an area of 10 acres, is surrounded by wide quays and commodious warehouses; its cargo-handling facilities are excellent. It is the

London headquarters of many steamers trading to Norwegian, North German and French ports.

The Grand Junction Canal, which was first opened to traffic in 1805, runs for over 90 miles between Brentford on the Thames and Braunston near Daventry, where it joins the Oxford Canal. Including branches, which are numerous, its length is nearly 190 miles. Among other towns, it serves Slough, Uxbridge, Watford, Aylesbury, Leighton Buzzard, Fenny Stratford, Northampton and Leicester.

Fight for Proper Water Supply

The Grand Union Canal Company, which owns the Regent's Canal and the Grand Junction Canal as well as important canals in Warwickshire, controls altogether about 240 miles of artificial waterway between Limehouse and Birmingham.

The New River is a river by courtesy rather than by right and can no longer be regarded as new. It provided London's first effective water supply, and although it made its first official appearance in 1613, it continues its beneficent task. Its instigator was Hugh Myddelton, who received powers from the Corporation in 1609 and spent the intervening years in the tenacious pursuit of an extremely difficult task and in steadily but surely depleting his financial resources.

Hard pressed for money, the worried but dauntless pioneer was compelled by sheer force of adverse circumstances to apply to James I for assistance. The monarch was perfectly willing to help his subjects, but not as a philanthropist. He guaranteed half the cost and took thirty-six shares in the New River Company, a holding which he afterwards relinquished for an annuity of £500. Myddelton and twenty-eight other venturesome spirits also held thirty-six £100 shares between them, but when water from springs at Chadwell and Amwell in Hertfordshire eventually gushed into New River Head basin at Clerkenwell, Myddelton held no more than two.

He came up against vested interests at every turn. Londoners and farmers swore that the waterway would be " worse than an open ditch into which men and beasts would fall by the score in fine weather, and at every rainfall would overflow to the certain ruin of all the poor on its banks." Petitions to Parliament were numerous. Had they been attended to with moderate celerity the result would probably have been an enforced abandonment of the project. But those were the days when Parliament adjourned on occasion for years, and by the time it was ready to give serious attention to the matter Myddelton's work was completed.

Fabulous Value of Adventurers' Shares

For twenty years not a penny of dividend was earned. Then things improved, and the Adventurers' shares became so valuable that many were subdivided and split up into the strangest fractions. In 1897 a whole share was sold for £125,500, and when the Metropolitan Water Board took over the concern in 1904 the price paid to the New River Company for the seventy-two original shares and 5,000 new shares which had been issued of the nominal value of £100 each was £5,967,123.

The course of the channel has been altered considerably since Myddelton's day and the purity of the supply is safeguarded by more scientific means than documents sternly commanding all persons " that they or anie of them doe not hereafter cast or putt into the said new river anie earth rubbish soyle gravell stones dogges Catts or anie Cattle Carion or anie unwholesome or uncleane thinge nor shall wash nor clense anie clothes wooll or other thing in the said river."

SIR HUGH MYDDELTON
The seventeenth-century pioneer who fought for and secured an effective water supply for London.

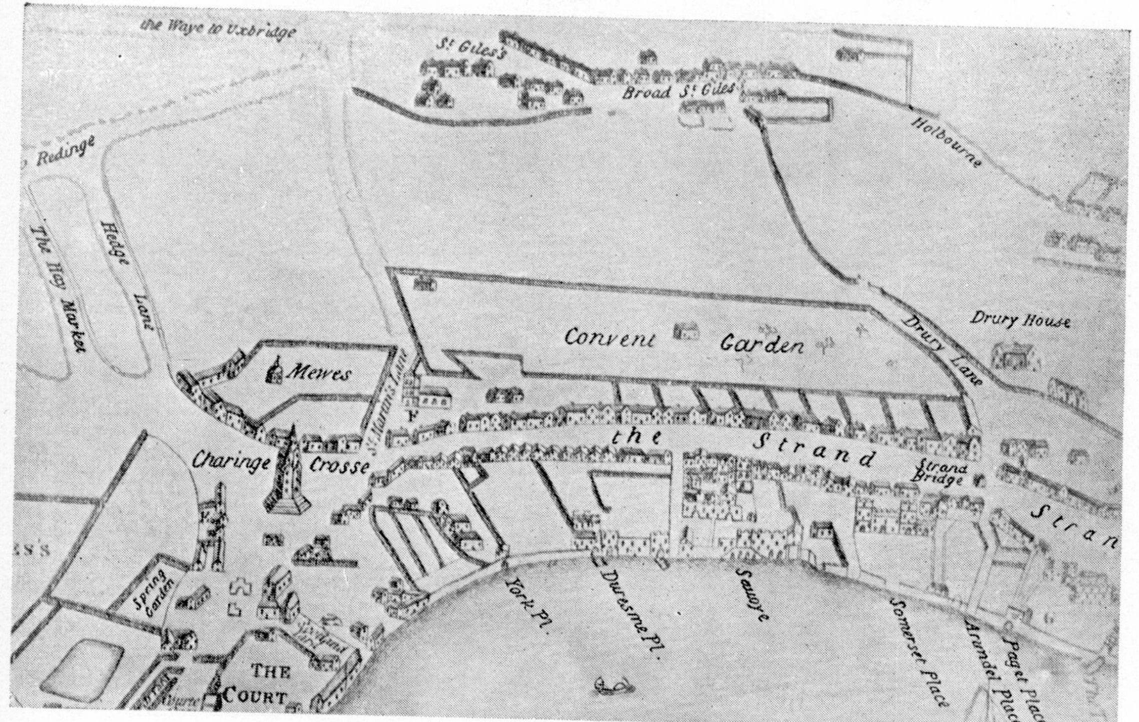

THE WAY FROM THE CITY TO WESTMINSTER

An old map showing the Strand and its environs in earlier days, when Covent Garden held a vineyard and Charing was a little village. The Strand developed from a bridle path along the river.

STORY OF THE STRAND

From Ludgate to Westminster was once a journey not to be undertaken without serious and almost prayerful consideration. It was both difficult and dangerous. The bridle path along the strand of the river was ill defined, and thickets afforded light-fingered but heavy-fisted gentry excellent cover. The Thames, considerably broader than it is to-day, resembled a miniature sea, and fields stretched out far away in their loneliness to the horizon of Harrow-on-the-Hill. A tiny village named Charing and a few scattered hovels were the only signs of human habitation.

Gradually the Strand developed into the main thoroughfare between London City, the centre of the nation's commerce, and Westminster, the centre of its political and religious life, and even in Elizabeth's time it was referred to in legal documents as the "High Street of Westminster."

By the sixteenth century bridle path and cart track had given place to a street of palaces. The south side of the Strand, from the City boundary to Charing, was lined with the mansions of peers of the realm and princes of the church. Each stately house stood amidst beautiful gardens that sloped gently down to the water's edge, where were landing-stages and water-gates, at which boats lay ready to take their lordships down to London Bridge or up to Whitehall Stairs. The family names of many of these noblemen have been given to the streets which cover the sites of their estates.

On the north side the passer-by would have seen the convent garden—now corrupted into Covent Garden—and the vineyard of the Abbey of Westminster, surrounded by the woods of Long Acre; and farther west, amidst green meadows, the church of St. Martin-in-the-Fields, a designation that seems strange now but then was literally true.

As the traveller made his way westward from Temple Bar, he would have had to cross a number of bridges, for at that time many streams made their free-and-easy way without let or hindrance from the north-side meadows to the river. The memory of one of these bridges is perpetuated in Ivy Bridge Lane, now a closed alley-way between Adam Street and Shell-Mex House; and we know that there was another opposite Strand Lane.

During the reign of Henry VIII the Strand was " full of pits and sloughs, very perilous and noisome," and it remained more or less in the same condition for many years after the death of that monarch.

Noise of Hackney Coaches

During the first half of the seventeenth century hackney coaches became very popular, much to the annoyance of the watermen, whose trade was, of course, adversely affected by them. Taylor, the " water poet," indignantly attacked the coach-owners, saying that they had " undone his poor trade." He writes, " I pray you look into the streets, and the chambers or lodgings in Fleet Street and the Strand, how they are pestered with them (coaches), especially after a mask or a play at the court, where even the very earth quakes and trembles, the casements shatter, tatter, and clatter, and such a confused noise is made, so that a man can neither sleep, speak, hear, write, nor eat his dinner or supper quiet for them." It would appear that the twentieth century is not unique in the matter of noise.

Donald McLeish

OLD TEMPLE BAR

The gate erected by Wren now stands at the entrance to Theobalds Park near Waltham Cross.

As late as the days of Dr. Johnson, the upkeep of the foot pavement in the Strand and other streets was left in the hands of the owners of the houses, each being supposed to attend to the space in front of his dwelling. All too often the arrangement began and ended as a supposition. While some stretches were kept in fairly good repair, others were left untouched for years at a time. The gutters were seldom cleaned out, and were filled with " all sorts of dirt and ashes, oyster-shells, the offals of fish, poultry, and other kinds of meat."

Dr. Johnson avowed that he thought " the full tide of human existence " was at Charing Cross, and Charles Lamb in the same vein once wrote, " I often shed tears in the motley Strand for fullness of joy at such multitude of life." Neither is an exaggeration, for at the beginning of the nineteenth century traffic congestion in the Strand was already a problem. The street was thronged with carriages and pedestrians, and because of its narrowness there were frequent " traffic-jams."

Strand Strewed with Flowers

The Strand has witnessed many historic state processions, but none so impressive and memorable as that which took place on May 29, 1660, when the Merry Monarch returned to the capital after many years of exile. That sturdy Royalist, John Evelyn, has pictured the scene in glowing words. He says that the procession included " above 20,000 horse and foot, brandishing their swords and shouting with inexpressible joy." He goes on to tell of "the ways strew'd with flowers, the bells ringing, the streets hung with tapestry, fountains running with wine . . . the windowes and balconies well set with ladies; trumpets, music, and myriads of people flocking even so far as from Rochester, so as they were seven hours in passing the city . . . I stood in the Strand and beheld it, and bless'd God. And all this was done without one drop of bloodshed, and by that very army that rebelled against him; but it was the Lord's doings, for such a restoration was never mentioned in any history, ancient or modern, since the return of the Jews from the Babylonish captivity; nor so joyful a day and so bright ever seen in this nation, this happening when to expect or effect it was past all human policy."

The event so enthusiastically described took place ten years before Sir Christopher Wren designed the new Temple Bar, which in 1672 was erected at the junction of Fleet Street and the Strand. It remained there until 1878, when it was removed, later to be set up in its present position at the entrance to Theobalds Park, Waltham Cross, some 14 miles away. For some years the stones remained dumped near Plumstead Marshes. Its site is now marked by a memorial, surmounted by the griffin or dragon of the City arms.

Viewing the Heads of Traitors

Originally no more than " posts, nails, and a chain," according to Maitland, Temple Bar marked a bound which no English King was allowed to pass without the Lord Mayor's consent. Not until that worthy had handed his sword to the monarch and the latter had returned it was he free to enter the City, and then only as a guest. The ancient custom obtains to this day. A gate-house was erected in the reign of James I, but this was taken down after the Great Fire and Wren's structure of Portland stone took its place. Statues of Charles I and II in Roman costume, and of James I and his Queen—or it may have been Elizabeth, because authorities disagree—occupied niches. On occasion the heads of traitors, real or supposed, were fixed on spikes above the centre gate. Horace Walpole writes that in August, 1746, he " passed under the new heads on Temple Bar, where people make a trade of letting spy-glasses at a halfpenny a look."

Taverns and Coffee-houses

In the seventeenth and eighteenth centuries the south side of the thoroughfare between Temple Bar and Essex Street was lined with taverns, coffee-houses and tea-rooms. One of the most celebrated of these was " Heycock's Ordinary," famous as a resort of Andrew Marvell, poet, wit and friend of John Milton. Marvell is alleged to have once remarked that he would never sell himself to the corrupt government of the time as long as he could get a good dinner for half a crown at " Heycock's."

At No. 216 may still be seen the sign of Messrs. Twining, a name familiar to London tea-drinkers since the days of Queen Anne. We can hardly doubt but that Dr. Johnson patronised this firm, for the immortal Doctor was passionately fond of the cup that cheers but not inebriates. Farther to the west and on the opposite side of the street is Shorts, " the oldest wine shop in London."

At the rear of Messrs. Twining's is Devereux Court, where stood " Tom's " and the "Grecian," two coffee-houses that were very popular among eighteenth-century literary men, including Goldsmith, Addison, Steele and Pope. If the coffee-houses were no longer " seminaries of sedition," as Charles II had called them in 1675 when he closed them all, they echoed all the talk of the town, scandalous and otherwise.

TEMPLE BAR
The monument which replaced the old gateway.

" Tom's " was named after its first proprietor, Thomas West. " After the play," says the author of *The Journey Through England*, published in 1714, " the best company generally go to Tom's or Wills's coffee-houses, near adjoining, where there is play at piquet and the best conversation till midnight. Here you will see blue or green ribbons, with stars, sitting familiarly and talking with the same freedom as if they had left their quality and degrees at home; and a stranger tastes with pleasure the universal liberty of speech of the English nation." The " Grecian " was the resort of the learned. One night a dispute arose as to the pronunciation of a certain Greek word, with the result that a duel was fought in the court and one of the contestants was killed.

Devereux Court is approached through Essex Street, part of which covers the site of Essex House, one of the most famous of the Strand's bygone mansions. Court, street and house derive their names from Robert Devereux, Earl of Essex, soldier and courtier of Elizabeth. The property was bequeathed to him by his father-in-law, the Earl of Leicester. It was from this house that Essex, then in disgrace, launched his ill-devised attempt to recover by force of arms the power he had once wielded. When it failed the place was surrounded and artillery placed in position to blow it to pieces should he refuse to surrender. He gave himself up, but his folly cost him his life.

Essex Street came into being a few years after the partial demolition, in 1682, of the mansion, the only tangible reminder of which is the Water Gate, built into the houses at the bottom of the street; this was largely destroyed by a German bomb in the Second World War.

Young Pretender's Secret Visit

To the Essex Street house of Lady Primrose, who had strong Jacobite leanings, Prince Charles Edward Stuart, nicknamed the Young Pretender, paid a dramatic visit in 1750. He had hastily crossed from the Continent with the intention of capturing the Tower of London. Without disguise and entirely unsuspected, he and a colleague named Colonel Brett had examined the defences and formed their plans. Nothing further was done, and the exile returned from whence he came. At the Essex Head Tavern Dr. Johnson founded "Sam's" Club, named not after himself but after Samuel Graves, the proprietor. The chair in which the great Cham of Literature sat is now at the "Cheshire Cheese" in Wine Office Court, Fleet Street.

Arundel House, residence of the Howards, Earls of Arundel and Dukes of Norfolk, stood westward of Milford Lane. John Evelyn, who frequently partook of the hospitality of the Howards, quaintly records that in July, 1662, he decided to take home from there his son John, "who had been much brought up amongst Mr. Howard's children here, for feare of their perverting him to the Catholic religion." There in 1635 died "Old Parr," said, at the time of his death, to have been 152 years old.

Arundel House was demolished in 1675 and three years later the street which is called after it came into being. There stood the Crown and Anchor Tavern, famous as the meeting place of the adherents of Fox, the leader of the opposition to William Pitt. In Approach Road, Arundel Street, is Electra House, the magnificent London headquarters of Cable and Wireless, and the Marconi Company.

Opposite St. Clement Danes Church is Strand Lane, formerly Strand Bridge Lane, which contains a well-preserved Roman bath dating from the second century of the Christian era. Measuring approximately sixteen feet by seven feet, it is built into the floor of a brick vault thirty feet beneath the level of the Strand.

Experts are of the opinion that for a long period during the Middle Ages the bath was hidden from sight beneath the ruins of neighbouring houses and that in course of time it was completely forgotten. However that may be, it seems fairly certain that it was known and used during the sixteenth century; but the first full description of it appeared in Knight's *London* (1841). Thereafter references to it occur fairly frequently. Charles Dickens makes David Copperfield tumble head foremost into it; and George Borrow, author of *Lavengro*, is known to have bathed there.

The streets in the neighbourhood of the bath have known many great men. Norfolk Street is associated with William Penn, the Quaker founder of Pennsylvania, and Peter the Great. Surrey Street knew William Congreve, one of the greatest writers of comedy, and Voltaire, the French philosopher.

The original Somerset House was built by the Lord Protector Somerset, who acted as regent during the reign of his nephew, Edward VI. The work of clearing the site involved the demolition of the palaces of five bishops as well as the church of St. Mary and many small houses. The owners of these properties were not, it would appear, compensated for the destruction of their property, but then Somerset was never remarkable for honest dealing in such matters. To obtain building materials he pulled down the charnel-house of Old St. Paul's, a good part of the church of St. John, Clerkenwell, and also an edifice in Pardon Churchyard, near the Charterhouse.

Palace of the Queens

The Lord Protector did not live long enough to enjoy the fruits of his rapacity. He was thrown into the Tower in 1548, only about a year after the commencement of the work, and though subsequently released, he was beheaded in 1552, when Somerset House became the property of the Crown and was renamed Denmark House.

It might well be described as the "Palace of the Queens" because the list of its tenants includes the names of Elizabeth; Anne, wife of James I; Henrietta Maria, wife of Charles I; Katherine of Braganza, consort of Charles II; and Charlotte, wife of the third George.

During Henrietta Maria's occupation a Roman Catholic Chapel was built there by Inigo Jones. The Queen regularly worshipped in it, and the Capuchin Fathers who ministered there gave much annoyance to Protestants.

In 1775 Parliament decided to settle Buckingham House upon Queen Charlotte, appropriating old Somerset House in exchange. Soon afterwards the work of demolishing the latter began. " When these apartments were visited by Sir William Chambers," writes Mark Lemon, " preparatory to the erection of the present building, he walked through rooms where foot had not intruded for nearly a hundred years, amid mouldering walls, broken casements, crumbling roofs, and decaying furniture. In one the chandelier still hung from the ceiling, and velvet curtains, tawny with age, fringed with a few shreds of gold and spangles, hung in tatters. In another were articles of different ages—broken couches and tattered hangings, screens, sconces, and fire-dogs, and the vestiges of a throne." In 1776 Chambers laid the foundations of the present edifice, of which the most striking feature is the river front, 600 feet long, with its broad terrace supported by arches, against which the river lapped prior to the construction of the Victoria Embankment.

Home of Learned Societies

Though the whole building with the exception of the East Wing is now occupied by Civil Servants, this was not always the case. The Royal Society, the Society of Antiquaries, and the Royal Astronomical and Geological Societies have all had rooms in Somerset House, while the Royal Academy held its annual exhibitions there for about sixty years after 1780.

It is at present used by the Board of Inland Revenue, the Principal Probate Registry and the Registrar-General of Births, Marriages and Deaths. In the central hall of the Probate Registry may be seen the wills of Shakespeare and Milton.

The East Wing, completed in 1829, houses King's College, which came into existence as the result of a Church of England protest against the non-denominational character of University College, Gower Street. In 1857 a new West Wing facing Lancaster Place was added. It is used by the Inland Revenue.

The church of St. Mary-le-Strand is so called in memory of the church demolished by Somerset when he was clearing the site for his new house. One of the fifty churches scheduled to be put up in Queen Anne's reign, it was consecrated in 1723, having taken nine years to build. Tradition asserts that in this church Prince Charles Edward Stuart, nicknamed " the Young Pretender," renounced Roman Catholicism in the hope of thereby increasing his chance of gaining the throne.

Strand Maypole

The present church occupies the site of the Strand Maypole, round which the populace used to dance on May Day, after they had garlanded it with flowers. It was 100 feet high and a source of great pride to the local inhabitants, but the Puritans regarded it as one of the " last remnants of vile heathenism " in the

WHERE WILLS ARE KEPT
Somerset House seen from the Strand Gate. The register of wills goes back over five centuries.

metropolis, and in 1644 they succeeded in having it destroyed, along with many others. Nearly twenty years before this the first stand for hackney-carriages had been established nearby.

In 1661 James, Duke of York, Lord High Admiral of England, supervised the erection by twelve seamen of a splendid new Maypole. This was taken down about 1710. It was purchased by Sir Isaac Newton and re-erected in Wanstead Park, where it supported the then largest telescope in Europe.

On Savoy Hill, some little distance westward of Somerset House, stood the Palace of Savoy, built by Simon de Montfort in the year 1245. It derived its name from Peter of Savoy, uncle of Queen Eleanor, to whom King Henry III granted it in the thirtieth year of his reign. Peter handed it over to the order of the Great St. Bernard in Savoy, but Queen Eleanor bought it back from this brotherhood and presented it to her son, the Earl of Lancaster, in the possession of whose successors the site has ever since remained.

In 1381 the followers of Wat Tyler, John Ball and Jack Straw, bent on proving that they represented the Commons of England, sacked the palace, then in the possession of John of Gaunt. Thirty-two of their number broached some of Gaunt's wine casks, with disastrous results. They " entered a cellar of the Savoy, where they drank so much of sweet wines, that they were not able to come out in time, but were shut in with wood and stones, that walled up the doors, where they were heard crying and calling seven days after, but none came to help them until they were dead."

Henry VII rebuilt the Savoy as a hospital but by 1793 the hospital was in a ruinous

Donald McLeish

THE NOBLE FRONT OF SOMERSET HOUSE

A view taken from Waterloo Bridge. Regarded as one of the finest examples of English classical architecture, this façade is 600 feet long. The centre of this front was destroyed by a German bomb.

ADELPHI TERRACE AND ARCHES

Built by the brothers Adam in 1768–70 on the site of Durham House, the Adelphi was considered one of London's finest blocks of buildings. After being the home of many great men, it was demolished in 1936.

state, and in the early years of the following century its remains were carted away to build up the approach to Waterloo Bridge. The British Broadcasting Corporation had its headquarters at Savoy Hill until May 14, 1932.

Chapel of the Savoy

The Chapel of the Savoy dates from the early years of the sixteenth century; but its interior was destroyed by fire in 1860, and a complete restoration was carried out within the next few years. The Savoy Hotel overshadows the tiny chapel. Near the Strand entrance to this hotel is Simpson's, a restaurant known all over the world for the high quality of its English cooking. Gourmets say that the best roast beef in England is to be had there.

Farther west is Shell-Mex House, a typical example of modern architecture. It occupies the site of the Hotel Cecil, demolished in 1931.

In Beaufort Buildings, westward of Savoy Hill, lived Henry Fielding, author of *Tom Jones*. The site was formerly occupied by Beaufort House, once the home of the Earls of Worcester, and the scene of a very unedifying quarrel. Stow tells us that " there being a very large walnut-tree growing in the garden, which much obstructed the eastern prospect of Salisbury House, near adjoining, it was proposed to the Earl of Worcester's gardener, by the Earl of Salisbury or his agent, that if he could prevail with his lord to cut down the said tree, he should have £100. The offer was told to the Earl of Worcester, who ordered him to do it and to take the £100, both which were performed to the great satisfaction of the Earl of Salisbury, as he thought; but there being no great kindness between the two earls the Earl of Worcester soon caused to be built in the place of the walnut-tree a large house of brick which took away all his prospect."

Palace Owned by Raleigh

To the west of Ivy Bridge Lane stood the London residence of the Bishops of Durham, one of the most celebrated of the Strand palaces. Like so many other buildings of its kind, Durham House fell into the hands of Henry VIII, who in 1540 held a great tournament there. Queen Elizabeth gave it to Sir Walter Raleigh, but at his fall it was handed back to its original owners.

In the reign of James I the stables were demolished, and in their place a building known as the New Exchange, or Britain's Bourse, was erected. It was not a success and it became a bazaar. Its upper floor was crowded with the shops of dressmakers and others, while the ground floor with its famous walk became a favourite *rendezvous* for gentlemen of fashion and their belles during the reign of the Merry Monarch.

A man named Gerard was one day lounging about in Britain's Bourse, turning over in his mind the details of a plot to murder Oliver Cromwell, when he was insulted by Don Pantaleon, brother of the Portuguese Ambassador. His reply infuriated the foreigner to such an extent that the latter engaged a gang of thugs to dispose of Gerard. The hirelings murdered another man by mistake, and Don Pantaleon was convicted and sentenced to death. In the meantime Gerard's design had come to light and he, too, was condemned. Their last meeting took place on the scaffold.

The Bourse was demolished in 1737, and about thirty years later the four brothers Adam purchased the site of Durham House and commenced to build the Adelphi. The word *Adelphi* is Greek for brothers, and the reason for its use in this connection is obvious, though the genius of Robert Adam far exceeded that of the other three members of the family.

The Adelphi Terrace was regarded by many people as the most beautiful and impressive block of houses in London, but neither their artistic excellence nor their historic memories availed to save them when the project of pulling them down was mooted. Even their foundations disappeared in 1936. Fortunately numerous examples of Robert Adam's work are still extant, not only in this neighbourhood but in other parts of London. The grim and cavernous Adelphi Arches, which led down to the river, used to bear a very unsavoury reputation as the haunt of individuals who lacked both money and morals. Later, the Arches became wine vaults and warehouses.

Less than a century ago, before the Victoria Embankment was built, a picturesque view could be seen through one of the Adelphi Arches, of a cottage more than two hundred years old, which stood on the Thames foreshore. On the site of Adelphi Terrace an enormous modern building was erected, which for most of its existence has been occupied by the Ministry of Supply.

Many famous people have resided in the Adelphi, including David Garrick, the actor; Benjamin Disraeli (Lord Beaconsfield), Prime

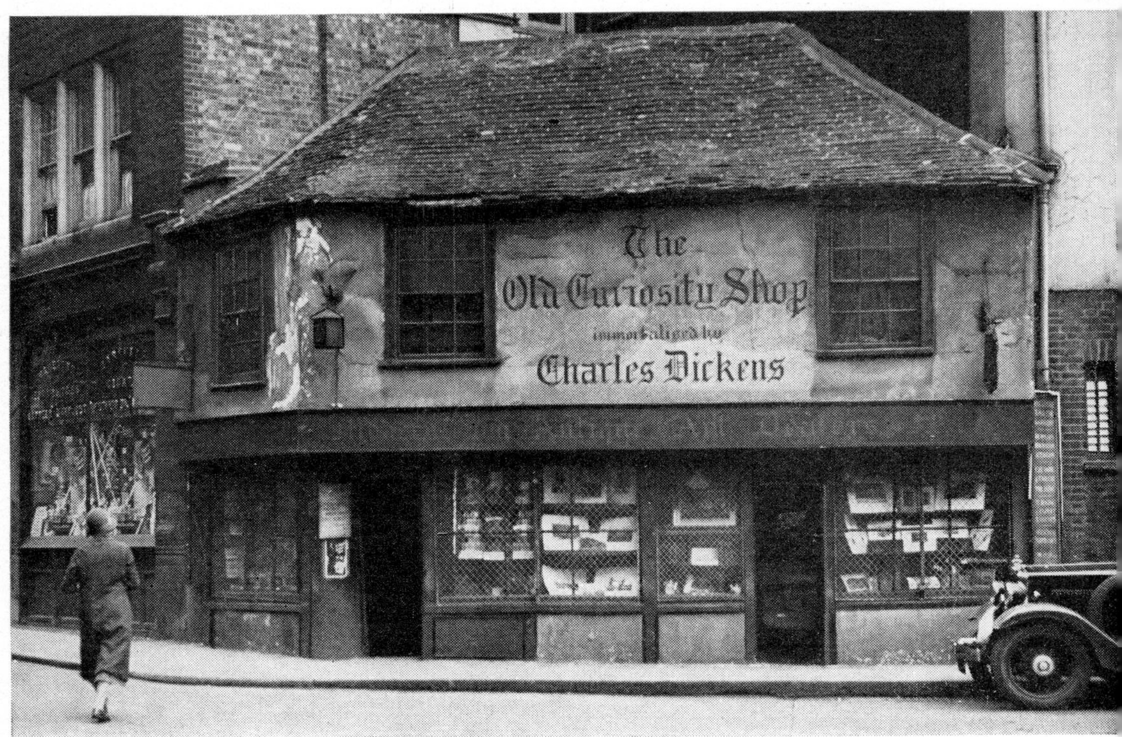

THE OLD CURIOSITY SHOP

Near to the Strand, this charming shop in Portugal Street attracts many visitors who believe it to be the spiritual home of Little Nell and her grandfather immortalised in Dickens's famous story.

Donald McLeish

ONLY RELIC OF ARCHBISHOPS' PALACE

The York, or Buckingham, Water Gate in the Victoria Embankment Gardens. Designed by Inigo Jones in 1625, it is all that remains of York House. Once boats were moored to its pillars.

Minister and opponent of Gladstone; and, in more recent times, George Bernard Shaw. There in 1824 died the King and Queen of the Sandwich Islands when on a visit to London.

Named After a Duke

Buckingham Street and Villiers Street are on part of the site of York House, the sixteenth-century residence of the Archbishops of that province. The house passed into lay hands during the reign of James I. At one time it was the home of Bacon, the philosopher, subsequently becoming the property of the Duke of Buckingham. In 1650 it was granted by Parliament to Lord Fairfax, Commander-in-chief of the New Model Army during the Civil War, whose daughter married George Villiers, second Duke of Buckingham, thereby bringing about the return of the property to her husband's family.

The extravagance of the second Duke so depleted his resources that he was forced to sell the historic mansion for building materials. A condition of the sale was that the streets which were to arise on the site would bear the Duke's name and title. Hence the names *George* Court, *Villiers* Street, *Duke* Street, *Of* Alley (now York Place) and *Buckingham* Street.

All that remains of York House today is the Water Gate at the foot of Buckingham Street.

Home of Famous Folk

Among the distinguished people who have lived in Buckingham Street may be mentioned Charles Dickens, Samuel Pepys, Peter the Great and William Etty, the painter. John Evelyn and Sir Richard Steele, of *Spectator* fame, both had apartments in Villiers Street.

Charing Cross railway station is on the site of Hungerford Market, demolished in 1862. Access to the market from the south side of the Thames was gained by means of a suspension bridge constructed by I. K. Brunel. It was removed to be replaced by one of the ugliest railway bridges in the world and part was re-erected at Clifton near Bristol. The market achieved lasting fame in the pages of *David Copperfield*, and the name Hungerford is perpetuated by the narrow footway which runs parallel with the railway track across the river.

In Craven Street, running down the west side of Charing Cross Station, lived Benjamin Franklin, distinguished American scientist and statesman, and Heine, the great German poet and democrat.

Statue Hidden for Forty Years

In the open space in front of Charing Cross Hotel is a reproduction of the original Cross which was set up by Edward I in memory of his wife, Queen Eleanor. It was one of the thirteen which the King raised to mark where his consort's body had rested on its journey from Grantham. The cross was among the many monuments that the Puritans objected to and was taken down by order of Parliament in 1647.

The site on which it stood is now occupied by an equestrian statue, by Hubert le Sœur, of Charles I. Cast in 1633, when the Civil War broke out, it came into the possession of a certain brazier called John Rivit. During the Cromwell régime Rivit carried on a steady trade in various metal articles alleged to have once formed part of the statue. His customers included both Royalists and Puritans, the former buying the articles out of respect for the martyred king's memory, and the latter doing so that they might boast of possessing an article that symbolised the destruction of the monarchical system.

Rivit was therefore in the happy position of making money out of members of both factions. But after the Restoration he solemnly announced that the statue had never been destroyed, but was hidden in his garden! Amidst scenes of great rejoicing it was in 1675 erected at Charing Cross, where it remains. A few years later it was found necessary to carry out a certain amount of restoration. The horse's tail was loose and the fore-legs were fractured. The statue is probably the finest of its kind in Great Britain.

It was on this site that the regicides, Harrison, Peters and Cook, paid the final penalty for their crime. Pepys was a witness of the executions. He says, "I went out to Charing Cross to see Major-General Harrison hanged, drawn, and quartered; which was done there, he looking as cheerful as any man could do in that condition. He was presently cut down and his head and heart shown to the people, at which there was great shouts of joy."

EXETER HALL
Once famous for its many religious gatherings.

After Harrison's body had been cut down his friend Peters was brought forward that he might see it being disembowelled. When the hangman, grinning horribly and rubbing his gory hands together with savage joy, asked Peters how he liked the sight, the reply was: "I am not terrified; do your worst." Before many minutes had passed this grim injunction had been obeyed.

In the account-books of the church of St. Martin-in-the-Fields there is an entry recording the payment of rent to the overseers by a certain Punchinello, a few years after the Reformation. It is possible that it was this Punchinello who brought Punch to England, for we know that about the year 1666 an Italian ran a puppet-show booth at Charing Cross.

Site of Dickens Hostelry

On part of the island site now occupied by the Government of the Union of South Africa, stood a famous old coaching inn known as the "Golden Cross." Charles Dickens makes Mr. Pickwick meet an eccentric cabman at the door of this hostelry. The name is perpetuated in Golden Cross House in Duncannon Street.

Charing Cross Hospital was founded in 1818 and built under the supervision of Decimus Burton. It was much enlarged in 1904.

How many of the thousands of people who walk past Rhodesia House at the junction of Agar Street and the Strand know that its outer walls are adorned with no fewer than eighteen statues by Jacob Epstein? When erected in 1908, by order of the British Medical Association, which at that time owned the building, they caused the first of the long series of Epstein sensations. There was a considerable agitation for their removal, but the clamour died down and the figures remained where they had been placed.

Between Bedford Street and Southampton Street is Exchange Court, where the Corps of Commissionaires has its headquarters. The Corps, recruited from the ranks of pensioned ex-servicemen and ex-policemen, was first formed in 1859. Its members act as messengers and in other similar capacities. They wear a distinctive uniform and are frequently to be seen in the streets of the central London area.

Inn Advertised by Pope

Southampton Street covers part of the site of the ancient residence of the Dukes of Bedford, and it is also famous as having contained an inn called the "Bedford Head." This latter was known to Alexander Pope, who extolled it in the line, " I'll have a party at the ' Bedford Head.' "

In Maiden Lane, running parallel with the Strand between Bedford Street and Southampton Street, Voltaire, Andrew Marvell and Turner, the painter, lived at different times.

Some few yards beyond the east corner of the Strand end of Bedford Street are the offices of the New Zealand Government, and beyond them is the striking black façade of the Adelphi Theatre, first erected in 1806 and rebuilt for the third time in 1930.

East of Southampton Street, between Exeter Street and Burleigh Street, is the Strand Palace Hotel, begun in 1907 on the site of Exeter Hall, once the headquarters of the Young Men's Christian Association.

Newspaper Offices in the Strand

During the eighteenth and nineteenth centuries the neighbourhood of that part of the Strand that lies between Exeter Street and the east end of Aldwych was crowded with the offices of newspapers and periodicals. There were published the *Illustrated London News*, the *Daily Telegraph*, the *Morning Post*, the *Morning Chronicle*, the *Sun*, the *Globe*, the *Observer*, the *Spectator*, the *Field*, the *Queen*, the *Graphic*, as well as numerous less well-known journals.

The Lyceum Theatre at the bottom of Wellington Street was the scene of the greatest triumphs of Sir Henry Irving and Ellen Terry, but it has been rebuilt since their time. Near the site of this theatre formerly stood Burleigh House, the residence of the great Elizabethan statesman of that name. Here he was visited by Queen Elizabeth, who remarked to an attendant anent the lowness of the threshold, " For your master's sake I will stoop, though I would not for the King of Spain." It was known as Exeter House for many years before its demolition, and was replaced by a building

GAVE PLACE TO ALDWYCH
Old houses in Wych Street, one of the thoroughfares demolished when Aldwych was built in 1900–05.

known as Exeter Change, which was in turn shop, exhibition hall, warehouse and menagerie. This latter disappeared in 1830.

Sir Edward Cecil, afterwards Viscount Wimbledon, a distinguished soldier of the early seventeenth century, had his residence, Wimbledon House, near the bottom of Catherine Street. Its site was afterwards occupied by a famous store known as D'Oyley's. Started by a French Protestant who had fled from his native land after the revocation in 1685 of the Edict of Nantes, the charter of Huguenot liberties, it was still in existence in the first half of the nineteenth century. There is reason to believe that the enterprising salesman introduced the ornamental mat known as a d'oyley, though it is spelt in a variety of ways.

Aldwych and Kingsway

The fine thoroughfares of Aldwych and the Kingsway came into being between 1900 and 1905. Their sites were previously occupied for the most part by a terrible slum.

The Aldwych island contains a number of fine buildings—Bush House, India House, the former Gaiety Theatre and Australia House. North of the island are the Waldorf Hotel, the Strand and Aldwych Theatres, part of the headquarters of the Air Ministry, and various fine blocks of shops and offices. Many of these were damaged by V-bombs in 1944, but have been restored—only the memory remains.

"Oranges and Lemons"

Beyond the eastern end of Aldwych, St. Clement Danes Church, immemorially associated with the nursery rhyme, "Oranges and Lemons," stands in the middle of the Strand. The latter part of the name recalls the probability that this district was inhabited by a colony of Danes in the days of King Alfred. The site has been occupied by a church from very early times, though the present edifice was not begun until 1680. Sir Christopher Wren supervised the work of construction, but the details were left in other hands. The steeple and clock-chamber were added by Gibbs in 1719. This famous old church was gutted by bombs in 1940 and left as a shell. It has now been adopted as the Church of the R.A.F. and is being restored. Dr. Johnson was a regular worshipper at this church; his fine statue, outside its eastern end, happily escaped the ruin which befell the church itself.

"LET'S ALL GO DOWN THE STRAND"

There is magic in the name of the Strand, and no visitor fails to visit the street that links the cities of London and Westminster. This view was taken looking east from Charing Cross towards Aldwych.

THE ROYAL EXCHANGE FLOODLIT

The present Royal Exchange is the third building on the same site. The first, built by Sir Thomas Gresham, perished in the Great Fire; the second was burned to the ground in January, 1838.

SIGN OF THE GRASSHOPPER

Sir Thomas Gresham, founder and builder of the Royal Exchange, came of " the right worshipful, ancient, pious, loyal and charitable family of Gresham of Gresham, in the county of Norfolk." He was born in London, the son of a knight, was educated at Cambridge University and served his apprenticeship under an uncle who was also a knight.

His famous sign, the grasshopper, had been in the family for at least a century. It was derived from a rather clumsy pun on the family name. " Gresham " is a corruption of *grass ham*, which means homestead or farm of grain.

Gresham, a clever business man and an astute financier, attracted the attention of royalty, and was appointed by Edward VI merchant factor, or agent, at Antwerp, then one of the greatest centres of commerce on the Continent. At Antwerp Gresham contrived, by methods not always over-scrupulous, to keep the royal coffers lined, and to raise English credit far above its previous level.

In the course of his negotiations he acquired an intimate knowledge of the Antwerp Bourse, or Exchange, the first institution in Europe where merchants could meet together to settle accounts, discount bills or arrange loans. The value of such a Bourse appears to have made a deep impression on him; and evidently he came to the conclusion that the merchants of his native city, itself no mean centre of commerce, ought to have a similar permanent meeting place for business, and not be compelled to use the streets " for the general making of bargains, contracts and commerce."

Other Londoners, including Gresham's father, had had similar ideas; in fact, the citizens had been talking about the desirability of a Bourse for at least thirty years. So when Gresham in 1563 offered to build one at his own expense if the Corporation would provide the land, the offer was promptly accepted.

A site was cleared in Cornhill, and with rather too exemplary rapidity the new Bourse was erected. The first stone was laid by Gresham on June 7, 1566, and the entire building was completed within eighteen months of that date. The " Great or Goodly Bourse," as it was first called, was a long, imposing edifice, with a lofty bell-tower next the main entrance, and containing on the ground floor a series of piazzas or covered arcades where merchants might make their deals undisturbed by the vagaries of the English weather.

Gresham certainly laid out a lot of money on his Bourse; equally certainly he expected to get it back. The two top storeys of his four-storey building were designed to house one hundred shops, and the cellars were constructed as warehouses. No doubt he calculated that the rentals of these properties would bring him a very fair return on his capital expenditure.

A gigantic grasshopper was erected on a tall column outside the north entrance. Not a single dormer window but had one of these insects on its peak, while over each corner of the building the Gresham grasshopper mounted guard. A statue of the donor was prominently placed near the north end of the western piazza.

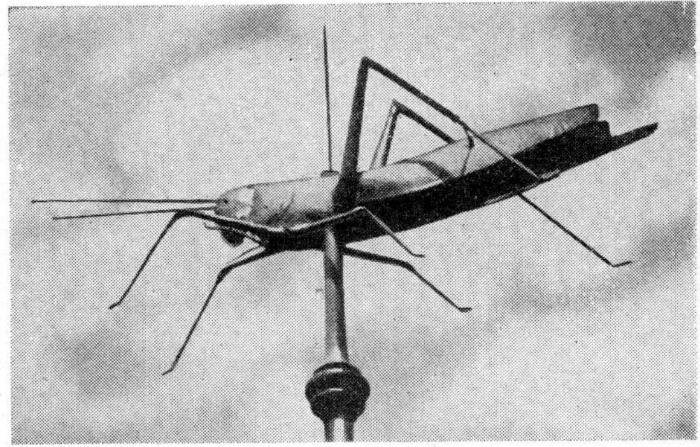

WORLD'S BIGGEST GRASSHOPPER
The famous Gresham grasshopper on the steeple surmounting the Royal Exchange. It is eleven feet long.

SIR THOMAS GRESHAM
Founder of the Royal Exchange. Born in London in 1519, he became the King's factor at Antwerp.

Unfortunately for the immediate success of Gresham's plans for profit, though the Bourse itself was extremely popular, the shops hung fire, and the cellars proved too damp for the storage of merchandise. Then in January, 1571, Queen Elizabeth decided to make a royal inspection of the building.

It would never do for Her Majesty to see empty shops, so Gresham did an extensive canvass, offering shops rent free for twelve months to all who would furnish them with wares and light them with wax candles. Naturally the vacant lots were eagerly snapped up on those terms; and the visit of the Queen was a huge success, so much so that she " caused the building to be proclaimed 'the Royal Exchange,' so to be called from henceforth, and not otherwise."

This gracious mark of royal favour started the shops off on a career of prosperity which was to last for a century and a half. Within a year or two Gresham was drawing rentals more than double those he had originally asked, and the " Eye of London," as the " pawns," or galleries containing the shops were nicknamed, fast developed into a vast bazaar which attracted all the fashionable world. Booksellers, apothecaries, milliners. mercers and haberdashers did excellent business.

Hawkers of fruit took up their stands at the gates, " amusing themselves in cursing and swearing, to the great annoyance and grief of the inhabitants and passers-by." Advertisers of bear-baiting exhibitions, then one of London's favourite pastimes, paraded with their fiddlers and their monkeys and their gaping, guffawing crowds up and down Cornhill, driving to distraction the honest merchants whom the great bell called to business each day at noon and 6 p.m.

On Sundays and holidays the Exchange became the resort of young hooligans and rapscallions, who would gather there and "shout and holloa, so that honest citizens cannot quietly walk there for their recreation, and the parishioners of St. Bartholomew could not hear the sermon."

To add to all these troubles, it was not long before the building itself began to fall into bad repair. Gresham died suddenly in 1579. He had, in accordance with his promise, bequeathed the Royal Exchange to the Corporation of London and the Mercers' Company (of which he was a member) after the death of his widow. On her death in 1596 the building was put into a state of much-needed repair and became once more a place of splendour and dignity. In 1641 John Evelyn could visit the Bourses at Amsterdam, Paris and Venice and proudly pronounce them all inferior to that of London.

During the period of civil strife in the seventeenth century the Exchange was not without its excitements. On May 30, 1648, someone threw down the statue of Charles I—the covered walks were decorated with statues of English sovereigns—and put up in its place a large board bearing the inscription *Exit tyrannorum ultimus* (Exit the last of the tyrants); and on May 28, 1661, the common hangman burnt on the steps of the Exchange Acts converting the English Monarchy into a Commonwealth.

During the dreadful days of the Great Plague grass grew in the deserted precincts of the Exchange, while huge fires were lit at the main entrances to purify the air for those few who continued to do business. In the following year the building perished in the mighty conflagration which swept away medieval London.

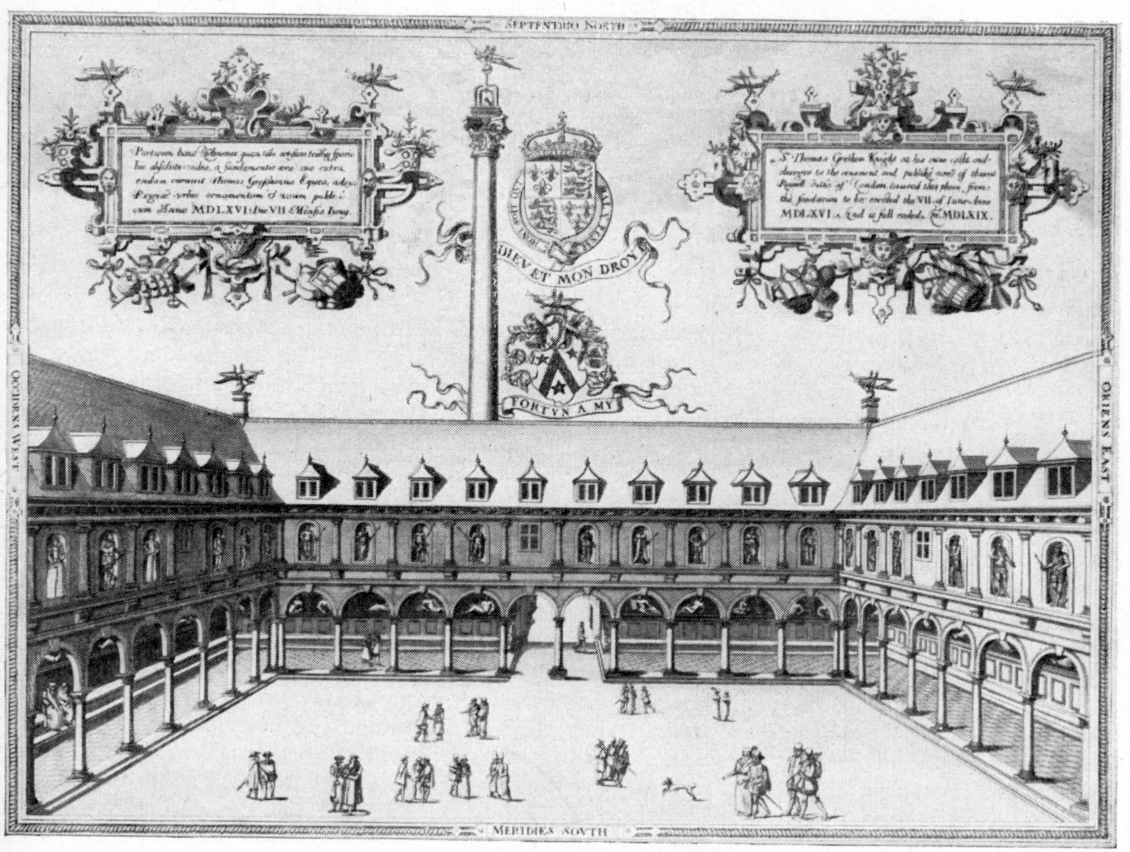

GRESHAM'S GOODLY BOURSE

The inscription states that "Sir Thomas Gresham Knight at his owne costs and charges to the ornament and publike use of this Royall Citie of London, caused this place from the fondacion to be erected."

THE SECOND ROYAL EXCHANGE
Built during the reign of Charles II, it contained an open court surrounded by an arcade of "walks." Over the arches were niches containing statues of British sovereigns. The central statue is of Charles II.

"How full of riches was that Royal Exchange!" exclaims a contemporary writer. "Rich men in the midst of it, rich goods both above and beneath. There men walked upon the top of a wealthy mine, considering what Eastern treasures, costly spices, and such like things were laid up in the bowels (I mean the cellars) of that place. As for the upper part of it, was it not the great storehouse whence the nobility and gentry of England were furnished with most of those costly things wherewith they did adorn either their closets or themselves? Here, if anywhere, might a man have seen the glory of the world in a moment. What artificial thing could entertain the senses, the fantasies of men, that was not there to be had? Such was the delight that many gallants took in that magazine of all curious varieties, that they could almost have dwelt there (going from shop to shop like bee from flower to flower) if they had but had a fountain of money that could not have been drawn dry."

In the stately London which Sir Christopher Wren planned to raise from the ashes of the old city, the Royal Exchange was to have been the central point, from which should radiate spacious avenues 60 feet wide. Vested interests defeated him; the City landholders would not give up a square inch of their precious sites save at exorbitant rates, and the new London which was actually built, though cleaner and healthier, was scarcely less cramped than its predecessor.

Even to gain a few extra feet for the new Exchange cost the City Corporation and the Mercers' Company many hundreds of pounds. Though it was shown that the proposed improvements would benefit the owner of the desired land, he demanded £1,000, and eventually, it is believed, got £700 for 783 superficial feet of ground and an area 25 feet by 12.

The Exchange was so necessary to the City that its rebuilding was pressed on as quickly as possible. The foundation stone was laid on May 6, 1667, and in October and November of that year Charles II, James, Duke of York, and Prince Rupert came to lay bases for columns at various points.

The Second Exchange, designed by Mr.

Jerman, one of the City surveyors, was an almost regular quadrangular building enclosing a spacious open court. Its main front, along Cornhill, was 210 feet in length, with an imposing central entrance behind which rose a three-storeyed wooden bell-tower.

In the lowest storey of the tower was a niche containing a statue of Gresham; in the second, which was octagonal, was a clock with four dials, in the third the Exchange bell. Above the tower rose a dome, and above the dome a pole bearing the famous grasshopper, which had been rescued from the flames.

Clock Plays Popular Tunes

The chimes of the clock in the tower played popular tunes four times daily, at nine, twelve, three and six. This practice has ever since been continued, though to-day the ceaseless din of the City traffic all but drowns the music of the bells, and he who would hear them properly must stand inside the building.

The area within the quadrangle, 144 feet by 117 feet, was paved with Turkey stones. This space was open to the elements, but at the sides were covered arcades very similar to cloisters. Sections of these arcades were speedily appropriated by merchants engaged in various trades. Thus on the south side were the Virginia, Jamaica, Spanish and Jews' " walks," on the west were the East India and the Norway " walks." In the centre of the area was a railed-off statue of Charles II attired as a Roman warrior.

HUMOURS OF 'CHANGE ALLEY
An early eighteenth-century opinion of the honesty of stockbrokers. The South Sea Bubble burst in 1720.

Though it was considerably larger than the first, the second Exchange quickly proved inadequate for the numbers wishing to transact business there; and in 1698 a most important event occurred. The money brokers migrated across the road to 'Change Alley, where they made their headquarters in a coffee-house called " Jonathan's." They have been a separate community ever since.

" There," wrote Colley Cibber of 'Change Alley in his play *The Refusal*, " you'll see a duke dangling after a director; here a peer and a 'prentice haggling for an eighth : there a Jew and a parson making up differences; there a young woman of quality buying bears of a Quaker; and there an old one selling refusals to a lieutenant of grenadiers."

Founder of Guy's Hospital

Among those who made their name during the early days in 'Change Alley was Thomas Guy, the founder of Guy's hospital. Sad to relate, he did not amass his fortune in too honourable a way, nor was he an over-nice person to know, being of miserly and penurious habits.

British sailors were in those days paid in promissory notes which, thanks to the unstable state of the national finances, they often found it exceedingly difficult to turn into ready money at the Government pay offices. Consequently they fell an easy prey to people like Guy, who would purchase their notes for cash—but at a huge discount—whenever they presented them. Guy and his like could afford to wait a favourable opportunity before parting with the notes to the Government; and they waxed fat on the proceeds. Thomas Guy died worth over £500,000, and made up for robbing the poor in his lifetime by leaving them £240,000 in his will.

Another famous character of " Old Jonathan's " was Sampson Gideon, of whom it was said when he died in 1762 that he was "worth more than the whole land of Canaan." Gideon's reputation for cynical wit was as great as his fortune. "Never grant a life annuity to an old woman," he would say. "Old women wither, but they never die."

Nine years after his death the following notice appeared in the paper: "Yesterday the brokers and others at 'New Jonathan's' came to a resolution, that instead of its being called 'New Jonathan's,' it should be called 'The Stock Exchange,' which is to be wrote over the door. The brokers then collected sixpence each, and christened the House with punch."

Countless stories could be told of the Stock Exchange, which to-day occupies premises just across Bartholomew Lane from the Bank of England, with the main entrance in Capel Court and other entrances in Throgmorton Street and Threadneedle Street. There is, for instance, the story of Nathan Rothschild, who, though unable to speak a word of English, came to England from Frankfurt in 1798 and avowed that in five years he multiplied his original capital 2,500 times. For many years he dominated the Stock Exchange.

N. M. ROTHSCHILD
Founder of London house of merchants and bankers.

Financiers' Gratitude for Kindness

Even Rothschild was not invariably successful in his speculations; on one occasion a rival caused him to lose in a single transaction about £250,000. Dealing on the Stock Exchange was a cut-throat business in those days. Abraham Goldsmith, the contemporary who came nearest to Rothschild in the scope and daring of his speculations, was utterly ruined by a group of financiers who banded against him, though personally he was the kindest and most charitably minded of men. Once having been nursed for a fortnight by a poor curate and his wife after an accident, he returned to London, invested £20,000 on behalf of his benefactors, and within a few weeks sent them a cheque for £1,500, the profit he had made on the transaction.

While the most famous of the "daughter" Exchanges was firmly establishing herself, history was being made in the parent building. For many years after the erection of the second Royal Exchange the shops continued to blaze with undiminished splendour and to attract the fashionable world as before. In 1720 rooms were rented in the building by the forerunners of a profession, then in its infancy, but destined to achieve in modern times colossal proportions. The practice of insurance against losses of various kinds had been carried on in England for nearly two centuries, but the Royal Exchange Assurance Corporation and the London Assurance Corporation, both of which were incorporated in 1720, were the first life insurance companies to be founded in Great Britain, if one excepts the Amicable Society for a Perpetual Assurance, which, founded fifteen years previously, was only a closed body sharing out funds yearly to representatives of deceased members of the Society.

The Royal Exchange Assurance Corporation has occupied offices in the Royal Exchange ever since its foundation, and to-day occupies the greater part of the building. It has a further title to distinction in that it was probably the first insurance office to have its own fire engines and fire-fighting staff, for its provision of these services dates from 1722.

A yet more famous "child" of the Royal Exchange is the association of underwriters known all over the world as Lloyd's. At what date the marine assurers, whose activities in England date from at least the middle of the sixteenth century, began to occupy quarters in the Exchange is not definitely known, but they were certainly there by 1627, for in that year a law was passed "for the sole making and registering of all manner of assurances, intimations and renunciations made upon any ship or ships, goods or merchandise in the Royal Exchange, or any other place within the City of London."

Lloyd's of Lombard Street

After the Great Fire, when everybody using the Exchange had to seek temporary quarters, the marine assurers first found a home near Cornhill, but they soon migrated from this to the coffee house of Mr. Lloyd in Lombard Street. At Lloyd's they remained for over a hundred years, and there built up the unique reputation which has ever since been theirs.

In 1774 Lloyd's returned to the Royal Exchange, which by this time had considerably altered in character. Throughout the long history of the building there had always been a tendency for the extraneous elements which were attracted there to drive out those for which it was originally intended. Earlier distractions have already been mentioned : in 1712 Sir Richard Steele wrote that " On evening 'Change, the mumpers (beggars), the halt, the blind, and the lame : your vendors of trash, apples, plums : your ragamuffins, rake-shames, and wenches—have jostled the greater number of honourable merchants, substantial tradesmen and knowing masters of ships, out of that place. So that, what with the din of squallings, oaths and cries of beggars, men of the greatest consequence in our City absent themselves from the Royal Exchange."

Lectures at Gresham College

The long reign of the shops in the galleries came to an end about 1739. In 1768 they were done away with completely, their places being taken by the offices of such businesses as the Royal Exchange Assurance Corporation, Lloyd's and the Merchant Seamen; by the Lord Mayor's Court Office and the Gresham Lecture Room. This last needs explanation. By his will Sir Thomas Gresham had made provision for lectures on divinity, astronomy, music, geometry, law, medicine, and rhetoric, to be delivered at the glorious mansion he had built himself in Bishopsgate. The lectures were commenced in 1597 when, after the death of Lady Gresham, the house passed into the hands of the Corporation of the City of London and the Mercers' Company, and they continued to be delivered in Bishopsgate until 1768, when the house, then known as Gresham College, was pulled down.

Birth of Royal Society

The lectures were transferred to the Royal Exchange, where they were read until 1838. Five years later a new Gresham College was erected in Basinghall Street. It was rebuilt in 1913. The Gresham lectures are now delivered in their fifth home.

It is interesting to note that it was largely as a result of the Gresham lectures that the Royal Society was born. For some time previous to 1660 philosophers had been meeting together in London; and on November 28 of that year, having gathered at Gresham College to hear Mr. Wren's lecture, " after the lecture was ended, they did, according to the usuall manner, withdraw for mutuall converse. Where amongst other matters that were discoursed of, something was offered about a

THE ORIGINAL GRESHAM COLLEGE

Sir Thomas Gresham left his house in Bishopsgate to the Corporation of London and the Mercers' Company for the purpose of lectures which he endowed. The house was demolished in 1768.

DESTRUCTION OF THE SECOND ROYAL EXCHANGE
The second Royal Exchange was burned down in January, 1838, on a night so cold that the hose-pipes of the fire engines froze. It is said that the fire originated in Lloyd's Coffee House.

designe of founding a Colledge for the promoting of Physico-Mathematicall Experimentall Learning." A scheme was drawn up and Gresham College was appointed as the meeting place. In 1661 Charles II became a member, and the following year "The Royal Society of London for Improving Natural Knowledge" was incorporated. The Society continued to meet in Gresham College until after the Great Fire, when it moved to Arundel House in the Strand; its headquarters are now Burlington House in Piccadilly.

Famous Hotel Owned by Foundling

It will be seen that the Royal Exchange has given parentage to many organisations of very varied character. Few visitors to Dublin can have failed to remark the Gresham Hotel in O'Connell (formerly Sackville) Street, to-day the largest and most luxurious hotel in the capital of the Republic of Ireland. The story of its founding is, appropriately, a romantic one.

On September 16, 1787, an infant boy, deserted by his parents, was discovered on the steps of the Royal Exchange. He was adopted by Mr. Samuel Birch, the confectioner, proprietor of a famous shop in Cornhill which until 1926 remained one of the sights of the City (the business is now in Old Broad Street, the original shop-front in the Victoria and Albert Museum). Named by his adoptive father Gresham after the founder of the Royal Exchange, and Michael from the parish in which he was found, the boy grew up clever and industrious, and made such a success of his hotel in Dublin that in 1830 he could sell it for £30,000. The hotel was destroyed during the Easter Rising of 1916, but has since been rebuilt in a modern and palatial style.

Exchange Again Destroyed by Fire

The second Royal Exchange, like the first was destroyed by fire. About 10.30 on the night of January 10, 1838, a bitter night o hard frost, flames were observed, and before midnight it became clear that the building was doomed. An hour later the bell-tower was alight. The fire set the chimes going, and appropriately enough, according to the story, they played first " Life let us cherish," then " God Save the Queen," and finally " There's nae Luck aboot the Hoose!"

Of the royal statues in the Exchange only that of Charles II survived; it may be seen in a corner of the present building. The Great Seal of the City was found uninjured in the Lord Mayor's Court Office, together with two bags each containing £200 in gold.

It was decided at once to rebuild the Exchange. Architects were invited to submit designs, and thirty responded; but no design entirely satisfied the judges, who were thus compelled to start designing themselves. Eventually the work was handed to Mr. (afterwards Sir) William Tite.

Tite decided to make the new building front west, and in order to add dignity wide open spaces were cleared both to west and east. In excavating for the foundations, a large and valuable discovery of Roman remains was made, ranging from coins to artificers' tools and sandals.

On January 17, 1842, the Prince Consort laid the first stone of the third Royal Exchange.

The century following the foundation of the new building has been a century of decline and fall for the Exchange itself. No longer are merchants to be seen pacing its ample walks; they have all migrated to other haunts, and the arcades are left to enquiring visitors and the hurrying clerks of the Royal Exchange Assurance Corporation.

Even Lloyd's have abandoned it. In 1928 the underwriters, having built themselves a palace in the modern style in Leadenhall Street, where they might live surrounded by the shipping companies upon which their existence is based, severed a connection with the Exchange which had lasted for over a century and a half.

One of the best known of the modern exchanges is the Baltic, or to give it its title in full, the Baltic Mercantile and Shipping Exchange, the headquarters of the dealers, shippers and brokers who trade in grain. It originated in the Baltic Coffee House in

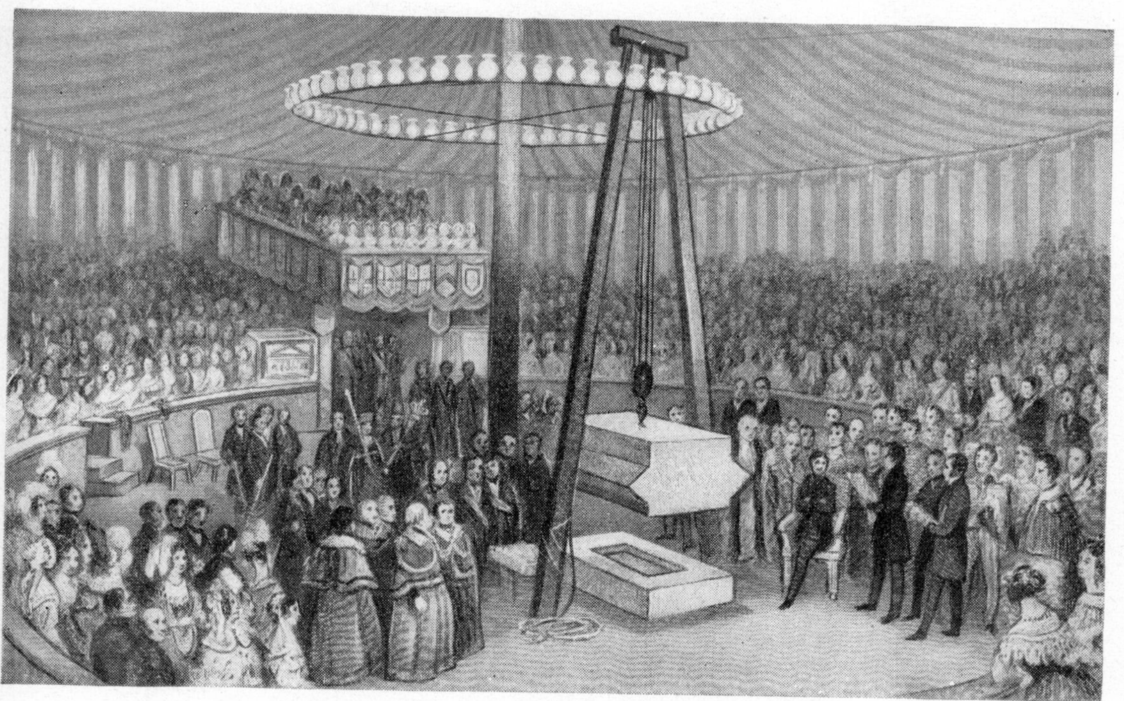

FIRST STONE OF THIRD ROYAL EXCHANGE

On January 17, 1842, H.R.H. Prince Albert, husband of Queen Victoria, laid the first stone of the present Royal Exchange. Coins and a Latin inscription were placed in a hollow in the stone.

Threadneedle Street, where the merchants and brokers concerned in the trade with Russia—hence the name—used to meet together. Sales of tallow, oil and hemp used to take place in an upper room. In 1903 a modern building was opened in St. Mary Axe.

Planted by Peter the Great

The present Coal Exchange is in Lower Thames Street, opposite the Billingsgate Fish Market. It is remarkable for its tower, which is over 100 feet high. During excavations preparatory to the erection of the Exchange, which was opened in 1849 by the Prince Consort, remains of a Roman villa were laid bare 13 feet below the level of the street. Part of the bath is shown, and in the building is preserved also a sword in the City arms, made of wood from a mulberry tree which tradition says was planted by Peter the Great of Russia while in England learning many useful arts but particularly, shipbuilding.

Two buildings in Mark Lane house the Corn Exchanges. The older of the two was opened in 1747, rebuilt in 1828 and enlarged in 1852; the new hall dates from 1881. Dealers in tea congregate in Mincing Lane, in fruit in the London Fruit Exchange erected by the Corporation of London in 1928–29 in Brushfield Street opposite Spitalfields Market.

The Royal Exchange, still surmounted by Gresham's famous grasshopper (which again survived the flames), has become one of the sights of London and is well worth a visit.

Within, the Exchange presents an ample courtyard, originally open to the sky but now covered by a glass roof, and paved with the original dark grey Turkey stones. In the centre is a statue of the youthful Queen Victoria as she appeared when on October 28, 1844, she declared the building open.

Frescoes in the Courtyard

For many people the chief attraction, apart from the historic traditions of the building, will be the fine series of mural paintings now adorning the walls of the covered walks surrounding the area. Depicting many stirring scenes in the history of England and London, these gorgeous panels make a superb display.

STOCKBROKERS IN THROGMORTON STREET

The buildings of the Stock Exchange are seen on the right. A great deal of business is done in the street, as only members can be admitted to the building. The main entrance is in Capel Court.

A BANK BUILT LIKE A FORTRESS

A view showing the Bank of England in 1827. Designed by George Sampson in 1734, the building was altered and enlarged fifty years later by Sir John Soane. For security it had no external windows.

THE OLD LADY AND THE BANK

IN the year 1680 Sir Dudley North, an Englishman who had lived many years abroad, was astonished to find on his return to London that whenever he went " on 'Change " members of the Goldsmiths' Company kept coming to him with the strange request that they might keep his money for him. His friends seemed apparently to think this quite in order, and they, too, persisted in asking where he kept his cash. " Where should I keep it," queried indignantly the puzzled baronet, " but in my own house? "

" In the reign of William (III)," wrote Lord Macaulay, who relates the above story in his *History of England*, " old men were still living who could remember the days when there was not a single banking house in the city of London." It was only during the reign of Charles II that the habit of entrusting one's money to a banker became general; and then only in face of much bitter opposition.

The die-hards, of whom Sir Dudley North was the last representative, looked upon banking as a risky form of gambling, and declared that the Goldsmiths, who held a virtual monopoly of the profession, " played at hazard with what had been earned by the industry and hoarded by the thrift of other men. If the dice turned up well, the knave who kept the cash became an alderman; if they turned up ill, the dupe who furnished the cash became a bankrupt."

There was more than a little truth in this unflattering description of the Goldsmiths : but banking had come to stay, and the more progressive among the economists were already beginning to discuss in earnest what had been mooted in 1660 and talked about even earlier, the foundation of a national bank after the style of the Bank of St. George at Genoa and the Bank of Amsterdam. Both these institutions had stood the test of time—the former for nearly three hundred years—and had proved their stability and inspired confidence in face of wars, revolutions and financial crises. England, it was argued, would profit immensely by possessing a similar reliable institution which, besides providing an absolutely safe deposit for private monies, could issue a dependable paper currency.

The accession of William III and Mary to the English throne, with its promise of a new political era, greatly stimulated interest in the

WILLIAM PATERSON
The clever Scotsman who founded the Bank of England. From a drawing in the British Museum.

proposal, and in 1691 a Scotsman, William Paterson, a merchant, placed before the Government an eminently practical scheme; but nothing was done about it for three years.

In 1693 the House of Commons voted £5,000,000 for the expenses of the army and navy during the coming year. To vote the sum was easy; to raise it proved beyond the power of the ablest brains in Parliament. Land and poll taxes were imposed; salt was taxed and stamp duties were levied. The London hackney coaches were taxed, in spite of the coachmen's wives, who marched to Westminster and mobbed the unfortunate M.P.s. Finally, a notorious professional gambler was invited to arrange a gigantic State lottery.

The lottery realised £1,000,000, but the Treasury was still short by a similar amount. At this desperate juncture Charles Montagu (later Earl of Halifax), one of the Lords of the Treasury, brought forward Paterson's scheme for a Bank of England. Having obtained the approval of the Commons, he incorporated it in a Tonnage Bill designed to raise money for the prosecution of war.

Briefly, Paterson's proposal was that he with other capitalists should raise a considerable sum of money and lend the whole of it to the Government at a moderate rate of interest, his Company to receive in return incorporation as the Governor and Company of the Bank of England, and the right of conducting a normal banking business.

"As soon as the plan became generally known," says Macaulay, ". . . the projectors who had failed to gain the ear of the Government fell like madmen on their more fortunate brother. All the goldsmiths and pawnbrokers set up a howl of rage."

The one sound criticism of the scheme, that the entire wealth of the nation and "the power of the purse, the one great security for all the rights of Englishmen" would pass from the House of Commons to the Bank of England, was met by a clause in the Bill forbidding the Bank to lend money to the Crown without the permission of Parliament.

Thus amended the Bill passed the Commons and went up to the Lords, where the real struggle began. The peers, many of whom had returned to London from the country to take part in the debate, argued from nine in the morning until six in the evening. Many feared "the danger of setting up a gigantic corporation which might soon give law to the King and the three estates of the Realm." More saw in the scheme a plan that would bring bankruptcy to the landed gentry.

Bill Passes the Lords

The upholders posed two questions. Dare the Lords amend a money bill, thus provoking a constitutional crisis by infringing the prerogative of the Commons? And dare they incur the responsibility, by refusing supplies, of leaving the English Channel without a fleet in time of war?

Their Lordships quailed before these questions, and the Bill was accepted by the narrow margin of 43 votes to 31.

The Company was pledged to raise a capital of £1,200,000, the whole of which was to be loaned immediately to the Government at 8 per cent. plus £4,000 for expenses : it was granted the privileges of a bank for twelve years, being allowed to deal in bullion or bills of exchange though not in merchandise, and having the right to issue notes up to the volume of its capital.

So doubtfully was the new venture regarded that the night before it began operations City men were betting heavily that not one-third of its capital would ever be subscribed. Officialdom had expressed a similar opinion by laying down the condition that if the £1,200,000—a vast sum in those days—were not subscribed by August, 1699, the Bank should cease to exist

These gloomy predictions were swiftly dissipated to the winds. On the first day £364,000 was subscribed; during the next two days another £300,000 came in, and in ten days the lists had to be closed.

"It was then," says Macaulay, "at least as difficult to raise a million at 8 per cent as it would be now to raise forty millions at 4 per cent." Macaulay wrote those words about a century ago, and his comparison, though striking, conveys little idea of the difficulty or the overwhelming success of the loan.

If comparison be possible, it is as if the City to-day, during a period of extreme financial stringency when credit was everywhere unstable, were to pour fifty to a hundred million pounds into an untried concern of very doubtful stability, and which the most sanguine hardly expected to last more than a few years.

Uneasy State of Country

The Bank was backed, it is true, by the Government; but the Government was already heavily in debt and, with the country at war, this debt was increasing at a rate which frightened everyone. Moreover, at least half the population quite expected, and probably nearly half hoped for, the restoration of the Stuart kings, an event which would almost certainly put an end to the new-founded Bank of England. The poverty of the Government may be judged from the fact that all the ordinary expedients for filling the Exchequer had failed, while the coinage of the realm was debased almost past belief. It was under such conditions that the infant Bank began its career.

National Bank in Single Room

It started modestly, hiring a room in the Mercers' Hall, from which it moved shortly to Grocers' Hall in the Poultry, where it remained for nearly forty years. "I looked into the great hall where the Bank is kept," wrote an essayist of the time, "and was not a little pleased to see the directors, secretaries and clerks, with all the other members of that wealthy corporation, ranged in their several stations according to the parts they hold in that just and regular economy."

Thus for long after it had got firmly on its feet the Bank of England carried on its business in a single room. During that period it passed through a succession of crises. Within two years of its foundation a deliberate attempt was made to smash it.

In 1696 cash was very short in England. The bad silver coins had been called in and the new ones were not yet issued. The value of gold soared, of securities fell. Bank of England stock dropped rapidly from 110 to 83.

WHERE THE BANK LIVED FOR FORTY YEARS

A contemporary engraving of the old hall of the Worshipful Company of Grocers, where the Bank of England was housed from 1694 to 1734. It was also used as the Lord Mayor's residence from 1681 to 1735.

WHEN BRITAIN WENT SPECULATION MAD

A scene in 'Change Alley during the days of the South Sea Bubble, when hundreds of thousands of pounds were lost in wild speculation. From the original by Edward Matthew Ward, R.A., in the Tate Gallery.

Seizing their opportunity, the Goldsmiths one day came in a body to the Bank to demand immediate payment in cash of huge sums. One man alone asked for £30,000.

Bank Survives Financial Crises

The Bank met the situation courageously. It continued to pay its ordinary creditors, but refused to cash the Goldsmiths' notes. Finally, since it found itself, on account of the number of frightened clients, unable to meet all demands, it called upon the proprietors to pay up 20 per cent of their subscription. With this money it handed out to every applicant 15 per cent of what he demanded and returned him his note with a minute on it that so much had been paid.

If the Bank had enemies, it had also friends. While its notes were at 20 per cent discount it was empowered to add £1,000,000 to its stock, and despite the discount the amount was readily subscribed. It survived the panic caused by the victories of Louis XIV of France between 1700 and 1704, and a threatened Jacobite invasion in 1707, even though on the latter occasion the Goldsmiths made a second concerted attempt to smash their hated rival. But the bitter hostility of the Bank's enemies only proved the loyalty of its friends. Members of the Whig nobility, including the famous Duke of Marlborough, loaded their coaches with bags of guineas and drove down to Grocers' Hall to pay them in. A man who had only £500 in the world lodged it with the Bank, an act of faith which so moved Queen Anne that she sent him a present of £100.

Granted Banking Monopoly

In 1709 the Bank's charter was renewed by Act of Parliament until 1732. The Act reduced the interest payable by the Government to 6 per cent, provided for an immediate loan of £400,000, and secured to the Government the right to ask the Bank to issue exchequer bills, that is, promissory bills backed by the authority of Parliament. In return, the Bank was granted the right to double its capital and its note issue, and was given a monopoly of joint-stock banking throughout England.

This monopoly it was to hold for one hundred

and seventeen years, which accounts for the fact that until 1826 all banking in England, except that done by the national bank, was carried on by private firms. The Bank of England, it will be seen, was a very different institution then from what it is now. To-day one of its main functions is to act the part of banker to the great joint-stock banks, while its private account business is relatively negligible. In the eighteenth and early nineteenth centuries it relied largely upon its private accounts, and could not play the part of central bank, simply because there was no ring of banks of which it could be the centre.

South Sea Bubble

So great was the confidence reposed in the Bank by 1709 that its new capital was heavily over-subscribed on the first day of issue. In the same year, however, it was in peril from rioters, following the arrest and trial of Dr. Henry Sacheverell for attacking Dissenters and the Whig Party. It was saved by the prompt action of Queen Anne, who at once despatched sufficient troops to overawe the mob.

A few years later the Bank triumphantly survived a far greater peril of a very different sort. In 1711 there was founded the celebrated South Sea Company, the purpose of which was to take over £10,000,000 of floating national debt at a rate of 6 per cent. In return for this undertaking the Company was incorporated and given a monopoly of trade to the South Seas.

The value of the monopoly proved to be far less than had been anticipated, and owing to prolonged negotiations with Spain the first Company vessel did not sail until 1717. In the same year the King mentioned his desire to reduce the national debt. The South Sea Company having increased their capital to £12,000,000, in January, 1720, offered to take over the entire debt, then standing at just over £30,000,000, at 5 per cent for seven years and afterwards at 4 per cent.

For this privilege they were prepared to pay £3,500,000. The Bank of England promptly offered £5,000,000, whereupon the South Sea Company raised their offer to £7,500,000. The offer was accepted, and a bill being laid before Parliament, the Company's stock rose by leaps and bounds to prodigious heights. In a single day it moved from 130 to 300. At the beginning of June it leapt 340 points in four days, and by August was quoted at over 1,000 per cent.

Excited by the boom, the entire country went speculation mad, and thousands of people quickly fell an easy prey to financial sharks of every description. Bubble companies were floated by the score; people fell over each other in their eagerness to subscribe. It did not matter how absurd the project was: no sooner was it mooted than the lists had to be closed. According to the *London Journal* "The constant cry was, 'For God's sake let us subscribe to something; we don't care what it is.'"

Parliament went as crazy as the rest of the nation. The South Sea Company Bill passed the Commons by 172 to 55, the Lords by 83 to 17. One clear-headed man alone opposed it—Britain's first Premier, Sir Robert Walpole; and he it was who had to clear up the mess when the bubble burst.

His proposal was to place £9,000,000 of South Sea Company stock with the Bank of England and £9,000,000 with the East India Company. Neither corporation was willing to take on so enormous a responsibility, but finally they and the Government came to terms.

Bank's Capital Again Increased

The Bank of England's capital was raised to nearly £9,000,000. The new stock sold immediately at 18 per cent premium—a striking testimony to public confidence in the Bank.

It was immediately after the South Sea Bubble that the Bank of England began to keep a reserve of capital—the famous "Rest" as it is called, which has ever since been the basis of its credit.

In 1734 the Bank moved into permanent quarters on the site in Threadneedle Street, now famous throughout the world. The house of the then Governor, Sir John Houblon, was acquired and on the ground occupied by this and the graveyard of St. Christopher-le-Stocks, George Sampson erected a small and modest building which remained for many years almost concealed by the surrounding houses. Part of the churchyard was converted into a pleasant fountain garden which survived until the reconstruction of the Bank began in 1925.

The march of the Young Pretender into England in 1745 caused a panic, and a run on the Bank; but by instructing its own employees to present notes, and paying them in sixpences, the crisis was tided over.

In 1750–51 the national debt was consolidated into one fund with a 3 per cent stock, which the Bank of England was requested to administer. This is the origin of "Consols" perhaps the best-known and certainly the most trusted Government stock in the world.

It was hardly to be expected that so notable an institution as the Bank of England could remain immune from the attentions of the forger, but it was not until 1758 that the first forged note was presented there.

Fortunes Made by Forgers

Though forgery was then punishable by death, the ease with which Richard William Vaughan, the first offender, had carried it out encouraged a flock of imitators, among whom John Mathison, "Old Patch," and Fauntleroy the banker stand pre-eminent. Vaughan, who was a linen draper, was betrayed by one of the men who had engraved the notes, which had been given to a young lady with whom Vaughan was in love as proof that he was not without worldly possessions.

Mathison began by forging the notes of the Darlington Bank. Detected in this, he fled north to practise on the Bank of Scotland. This proving profitable, he took a holiday, journeyed through England and came to London.

"OLD PATCH"
Master of disguises, Charles Price is said to have defrauded the Bank of England of over £200,000.

Mathison was a clever forger but an indiscreet man. He gave himself away by his lack of caution, and after vainly trying to bargain the secret of how he counterfeited the watermark against his life, suffered death by hanging.

Charles Price, familiarly known as "Old Patch," was a far more astute rogue. A master of disguises, he trusted no one but his mistress, and even went so far as to make his own ink and paper. To present his notes he engaged men off the street. It is estimated that by his forgeries he made over £200,000.

Even this gigantic sum was exceeded by Fauntleroy, who kept a bank in Berners Street. By means of forged powers of attorney he cost the Bank of England £360,000. He seems to have been inspired by a private grudge, for in his desk was discovered, with a list of his forgeries, a note saying : "The Bank first began to refuse our acceptances, thereby destroying the credit of our house. The Bank shall smart for it."

A forgery is said to have been indirectly the cause of the famous nickname, "the Old Lady of Threadneedle Street," by which the Bank of England is known.

In 1811 there was in the cashier's office at the Bank a young clerk named Philip Whitehead who lived so extravagantly that the directors, fearful of the consequences if he ran seriously into debt, called him before them and gave him a good talking to.

Sister Learns of Brother's End

Whitehead chose to be offended, threw up his job, and began to gamble heavily on the Stock Exchange. He was soon hopelessly involved, tried to clear himself by presenting a forged bill at the Bank, was arrested, condemned, and executed in the following November at Newgate Prison.

Out of consideration for her youth and beauty, friends concealed what had happened from his sister, Sarah Whitehead, then a girl of nineteen, who had for some time been acting as his housekeeper. They told her that her brother had been sent on a long journey on behalf of the Bank, and this story she believed until one day at the Bank an indiscreet clerk revealed to her the dreadful truth.

The shock sent her out of her mind. Every day for the next twenty-five years, dressed in black with a crape hood, she called at the Bank to ask " Is my brother here to-day? " Invariably she was told " No, miss, not to-day." She would stay chatting for a moment or two, and always concluded her visit by saying, " Give my love to him when he returns. I will call to morrow."

" The Bank Nun," or " The Black Nun," as she was dubbed, became an object of affectionate sympathy in the City. A group of business men bought her a small annuity, and every day, when at lunch time she repaired to a chop-house, someone immediately came forward and requested the honour of giving her a meal.

One day she was missing from her haunts. " Where is the Old Lady of Threadneedle Street? " City men enquired, not knowing that she had died suddenly; and the sobriquet in course of time became transferred to the Bank at which she had been so constant and pathetic a visitant.

This account of the origin of the nickname is denied by other writers, who declare that the term was in use many years previously, and was quite possibly applied to the original Bank building in Threadneedle Street.

Inkstands Made into Bullets

The home built by George Sampson for the Bank in 1734 had to be enlarged within twenty years; and in this state it remained until 1780. In that year occurred the dreadful Gordon Riots. The mob, " consisting of thieves of every species," burned Newgate prison and, reinforced by the criminals they had released, determined to assault the Bank.

But the authorities had taken adequate measures. Troops guarded the doors, and the roof was lined with clerks and volunteers armed with blunderbusses. In anticipation of an attack, the heavy pewter inkstands in use at the Bank had been melted down into bullets, and a supply of gunpowder had been laid in.

The mob charged twice, and twice was repulsed by volleys from the defenders. On the second occasion John Wilkes, the radical politician, led a sally from the Bank and with his own hands captured a number of the leading rioters.

Discomfited, the mob retired, and the Bank was not again molested. But the directors had received a severe fright, and they wisely decided that their property must never be exposed again to such danger. The military guard was retained, and to this day a squad of soldiers marches each evening to the Bank of England to mount guard over it until the following morning.

FAUNTLEROY THE BANKER
The most celebrated of all those who defrauded the Bank of England. His motive was spite.

The directors further decided to rebuild the Bank, and commissioned Sir John Soane to undertake the task. The old church of St. Christopher-le-Stocks was demolished, together with three taverns, lest these buildings might prove a rallying ground for any future rioters, and on an island site comprising the entire parish of the old church, Soane erected a one-storey building with grim fortress walls and lit by interior courts so that windows might be dispensed with.

" Soane's Money-Box "

The interior was richly decorated in the Adam style, and the courtyards were infinite in their variety. One of the most charming of the latter was the garden court, complete with trees and fountain, which occupied the site of the old churchyard. In the Threadneedle Street–Bartholomew Lane corner Soane erected a wonderful series of offices round a great circular dome, called the Rotunda, and at one time used as the Stock Exchange.

During the forty-five years (1788–1833) in which " Soane's Money-Box " was being built, the Bank emerged triumphantly from the gravest and most prolonged crisis it has ever experienced, the financial chaos caused by the Napoleonic Wars.

In 1796 the Radical Tom Paine alarmed many people by publishing a pamphlet to prove that the Bank's vaults could not hold more than £1,000,000 of gold, while bank-notes to the value of £60,000,000 were in circulation. His assertions were proved to be fantastically incorrect, but in the same year the amount of gold held fell dangerously low, the Bank was forced to suspend cash payments, and began to issue notes for denominations below £5.

Alarming Increase of Forgery

As one result of these measures, forgery increased at an alarming rate. Between 1797 and 1802 the Bank had to maintain an additional staff of seventy clerks merely to distinguish forged bank-notes from genuine ones, while each year thirty to forty people were hanged for forgery. But graver issues than this were at stake.

SARAH WHITEHEAD
Said to be the original of the nickname of the Bank, "The Old Lady of Threadneedle Street."

The Bank of England notes, though not legal tender, rapidly became in effect the national currency. War-time inflation brought high prices, and distress prevailed throughout the country. In 1810 Parliament appointed a Bullion Committee to investigate the relation between the rising price of gold and the issue of notes. The Committee in its report called for a resumption of cash payments, the suspension of which it declared had led to an excess issue of bank-notes, with consequent inflation. The report was rejected by the Commons, more inflation followed, and it was not until 1816 that the Bank itself took the initiative by declaring that it felt able to resume cash payments in part.

In 1819 Sir Robert Peel, who held that a national bank must always be prepared to pay out on demand gold for its notes, passed through Parliament a Currency Act securing a return to cash payments, and two years later the full gold standard was restored.

Even so, financial equilibrium was by no means established. The years 1824–25 saw a "boom" period in industry culminate in a slump which spelt disaster to large numbers of the old-fashioned private banks all over the country.

Forerunners of the "Big Five"

It became evident that the day of such institutions was passing. In 1826 an Act of Parliament sanctioned joint-stock banking anywhere in England more than 65 miles from London, and in 1833 this reserved area was abolished. In 1833–34 the forerunners of the present "Big Five" joint-stock banking concerns, the National Provincial, the London and Westminster, and the London and County Banks were founded.

The two acts of 1826 and 1833 radically altered the position of the Bank of England. Hitherto it had enjoyed a complete monopoly of joint-stock banking in the country. None of the numerous private banks could hope to compete with it. Each concern issued its own bank-notes, and the worth of these depended upon the reputation of the house. Cheques were little used as yet.

Now, however, the field of joint-stock banking was thrown open to all comers, and since newly founded companies were not to be allowed the right to issue notes, it was clear that they would concentrate on deposit banking, and might easily in this field become really serious rivals to the Bank of England.

The position was cleared up by Peel's Bank Act of 1844, which paved the way for the development of the Bank of England in its present character of a central bank. The Act strictly separated the Bank of England's functions of bank-note issue and deposit banking, and thus made it in effect two banks. It defined its relationship with the Government by fixing the limits of the Bank's fiduciary issue (i.e., that part of the issue of notes backed by Government) at £14,000,000 : all other Bank of England notes issued had to be backed by gold. Should any other bank forfeit the right of issue the Bank of England could take over the right up to two-thirds of the amount of the lapsed issue.

Suspension of the Bank Act

In time of emergency the Prime Minister and the Chancellor of the Exchequer might give the Bank permission to exceed the limit of the fiduciary issue. This permission, which has become famous in history as " Suspension of the Bank Act," has been granted only on four occasions, in 1847, 1857, 1866, and 1914. (The Bank's position was on a different footing in 1931, as will be told later.)

In 1847 and 1866 the mere act of suspension restored confidence, and on neither occasion did the Bank have to issue excess notes. It was far otherwise in 1857 when, largely owing to too rapid development and speculation in the United States, there was a world crisis. The Bank of England only just escaped having to close its doors, and was forced to issue nearly £1,000,000 of excess notes.

On the outbreak of war in August, 1914, unprecedented conditions supervened. There was a tremendous run on the Bank, with the result that the reserve dropped below £10,000,000. The Bank Act was suspended, the Bank Rate rose to 10 per cent, and a four days' Bank Holiday was proclaimed. England went off the gold standard, and the Treasury began to issue £1 and 10s. notes, a proceeding which virtually made the suspension of the Bank Act permanent.

The Act of 1844 initiated the transformation of the Bank of England from a privileged general banking concern into what may be called a " bankers' bank." The permission to open joint-stock banks was swiftly accepted, and the remainder of the nineteenth century is a history of numerous foundations accompanied by continual amalgamation, out of which has emerged quite recently the " Big Five "—Barclays, Lloyds, the Midland, the National Provincial and the Westminster Banks—which now hold a virtual monopoly of British banking.

DIVIDEND DAY
The interior of the Rotunda in the days when the Bank of England dealt largely in joint-stock.

Of these vast concerns Barclays was originally a private bank which in 1896 amalgamated with a score of others to become a joint-stock company. Lloyds also started as a private concern, but became a joint-stock company in 1865, since when it has absorbed (among others) the Capital and Counties, the National Bank of Scotland, and Messrs. Cox & Co., the service bankers.

Amalgamation of Many Banks

The Midland Bank dates from 1836; in 1918 it joined forces with the London Joint Stock Bank. The National Provincial Bank is three years older. It has taken over a great number of country banks, and in 1920 absorbed the famous Coutts and Company. The Westminster Bank is the result of the amalgamation of the London and Westminster and the London and County; among other concerns it has absorbed may be mentioned Parr's Bank, well known to innumerable Londoners until quite recently.

With the exception of the last-named group none of these banking giants is of London origin, though all have now their headquarters in the metropolis. Barclay's and Lloyd's operate from Lombard Street, so named from the merchants of Lombardy who settled there in the twelfth century to carry on what passed then for banking—largely, the lending of money at highly usurious rates. The others are all within a few moments of the Bank of England : the Midland right opposite it in Prince's Street, the National Provincial at the junction of Poultry and Prince's Street, and the Westminster just behind it in Lothbury.

The Banker's Bank

The Bank of England did not enter the lists as a competitor with the new joint-stock banks. From its birth it had accepted deposits from other banks, and as its position grew stronger this type of deposit tended to grow more and more important. From shortly after 1844 until 1914 the holding of bankers' deposits became, with the maintenance of a national gold reserve, one of its primary functions.

It is still possible to have a private account at the Bank of England, provided the account be not too small, but to all intents and purposes the Bank has retired from this sphere of activity in favour of the joint-stock concerns.

While the Bank of England is a " central " bank in that it is always in possession of large deposits from the joint-stock banks, it has nothing to do with the clearing of their cheques, bills and drafts. This is done by the Bankers' Clearing House, founded in the eighteenth century to save clerks the lengthy and laborious business of walking round to every different bank in the City in order to present cheques. The Bankers' Clearing House is to be found in Post Office Court, Lombard Street—so called because it was the site of the General Post Office from 1688 to 1829. In spite of its great importance and the huge volume of business there transacted, the Bankers' Clearing House is a most insignificant little building tucked away in a corner of the court and quite dwarfed in appearance by the very ordinary branch Post Office opposite.

After the First World War further changes were effected in the position of the Bank of England. In 1925 Great Britain returned to the Gold Standard—with reservations, the chief being that neither currency nor bank-notes were convertible into gold. The Bank of England was still bound to buy gold, but only to sell it in multiples of 400 oz.

In 1928 the issue of bank and currency notes was amalgamated, the combined issue being placed under the control of the Bank of England. That is why the present £1 and 10s. notes bear the words " Bank of England," and the promise to pay on demand is signed by the chief cashier of that institution. No other bank in the country now issues notes; the last right lapsed in 1920.

In consequence of the amalgamation the limit of the fiduciary issue of the Bank of England was increased from just over £19,000,000—to which amount it had grown by reason of lapsed issues—to £260,000,000. In emergency, the Bank could apply to the Treasury for permission to exceed this limit, such permission to be granted for a period of six months at a time, but not for longer than two years in all.

The financial crisis of 1931 proved the unassailable strength of the Bank of England. Faced with panic withdrawals amounting to many millions, it was able to fortify its position by credits of £25,000,000 each from the Bank of France and the Federal Reserve Bank of New York, and on August 1 obtained permission from the Treasury to increase its fiduciary note issue to £275,000,000.

Every creditor was paid in full, and at the very height of the crisis the Bank was able, after making provision for all contingencies, to declare its normal dividend of six per cent, less income tax.

Early in 1932 the credits from France and the United States were repaid, a few weeks later the Bank Rate was reduced, and in April a normal dividend was again declared. Gold flowed back to London, and in April, 1933, the fiduciary note issue reverted again to its normal figure of £260,000,000. During the Second World War, when the Emergency Powers Act gave the Government unlimited powers, this figure was multiplied almost five-fold; it reached the staggering total of £1,400,000,000 by the end of 1945.

Rebuilding the Bank

Throughout the years of strain and stress from 1914 onwards a physical revolution was taking place at the Bank. The old building having become quite inadequate, it was decided in 1925 to replace Sir John Soane's one-storey building by a mammoth three-storey erection

THE BANK OF ENGLAND TO-DAY

In 1925 was begun a reconstruction of the Bank which transformed it from a one-storey fortress into a three-storey palace guarded by fortress walls. Designed by Sir Herbert Baker and Mr. A. T. Scott, the alterations include new vaults, a large garden courtyard and a new Threadneedle Street entrance (seen above). Of the six carved figures above the entrance, two represent wealth and four custodianship.

The work, described as "the biggest, most secret, and most expensive operation ever undertaken in the City of London," cost over £20,000,000.

The vaults in which Britain's gold is now stored extend sixty feet below the street level, and can be flooded to protect them against fire, riot, invasion or bombardment. Standing on three floors, these bullion fortresses have reinforced concrete walls two feet thick protected on the interior with armour plating, and massive steel doors weighing many tons.

Man Who Got Into Bullion Room

So carefully is the bullion guarded that even directors wishing to enter the vaults must go in pairs.

The most romantic story told in connection with the old bullion room centres around an incident that happened many years ago. An anonymous letter was received stating that the writer had entered the place twice and inviting two of the directors to meet him there at midnight. This was followed by the arrival of a chest containing securities that were known to have been in the Bank's repository. The matter was too serious for the affair to be regarded as a practical joke, and the appointment was kept. A man duly presented himself and explained that it was his habit to enter the sewers in the hope of finding anything of value that might inadvertently have been washed into them. On one occasion he came across a disused drain, and on wandering along it found that by lifting a stone he was in the bullion room of the Bank of England. The man had taken nothing other than what he had returned as proof of his bona fides, and the directors rewarded him handsomely.

The new Bank of England is one of the largest and certainly the strongest block of office buildings in London. Erected on a framework of all-welded steel girders, it is virtually siege-proof, with its own supplies of water and electricity. Burglars, of course, the Bank has long been able to laugh at. It still retains the fortress-walls of Soane's old structure.

It is strange to think that the Bank of England, with its immense national and international responsibilities, its power of making decisions affecting Britain's credit, and even at times of dictating to Britain's rulers, remained for so long a private concern ruled by a very limited number of individuals.

Not even its stockholders had any power over it, its government and policy being in the hands of the Governor and twenty-four directors.

But the Second World War, during which the policy and affairs of the Bank were inextricably tied up with the decisions of the Treasury, decided the fate of the Bank of England. On October 20, 1945, the Labour Government brought in a Bill to nationalise the Bank. It became law in February, 1946.

The Bank is Nationalised

As Lord Catto said, "the Bill did little more than give statutory authority to what has long existed by custom and tradition." So "the old Man of the Treasury" and the "old Lady of Threadneedle Street" were legally married.

The Bank naturally works in close co-operation with the national banks of other countries, all of which have offices in London.

A short walk in the immediate neighbourhood will quickly emphasise the fact that London is the heart of world finance. Every corner of the world is represented in the crowded square mile of the City, and all watch intently every move of the "Old Lady of Threadneedle Street."

ONE OF THE "BIG FIVE"
The headquarters of the National Provincial Bank in Prince's Street, near the Bank of England.

NORTH LONDON'S PEOPLE'S THEATRE
Reopened after rebuilding in 1931, Sadler's Wells, like the prewar Old Vic in Waterloo Road, presents high-class drama and opera at popular prices. The spring that gave the place its name and fame is in the theatre.

PLAYHOUSES AND PLAY-ACTORS

It was in 1576 that James Burbage, a joiner by trade, built the first English playhouse, The Theatre, at Shoreditch. It cost £600. Two years after its erection it was referred to in terms of loathing by a preacher at Paul's Cross, but it did not long remain to excite the reverend gentleman's pious horror, being demolished in 1599. Its timbers were used to build the famous Globe Theatre.

It seems probable that James Burbage was also the builder of the Curtain Theatre, of which the first mention appears in 1577. It was within a very short distance of The Theatre, and its memory is preserved in the district in the name of Curtain Road. However this may be, he is certainly entitled to the honour of having built the Blackfriars, one of the most important of all the theatres of this period.

In a spiritual sense the father of the English stage, James Burbage was in the physical sense the father of the greatest actor of the Elizabethan era—Richard Burbage. The son was also a manager and he had as business partner, playwright and personal friend—Shakespeare himself. Together they controlled the Globe and the Blackfriars theatres, using the former for summer, and the latter for winter performances. As an actor, Richard Burbage excelled all his contemporaries, achieving his greatest triumphs in Shakespearean roles.

Both the Burbages lived and died in Shoreditch, although after the demolition of The Theatre the centre of London's dramatic life shifted from there to Bankside, on the south of the river between Blackfriars Bridge and Southwark Bridge. Besides the Globe and the Blackfriars, there were in that district the Rose, the Hope and the Swan theatres.

The Globe, for which Shakespeare wrote the greater number of his plays, stood where the Park Street brewery of Messrs. Barclay Perkins and Co. now is. A proclamation, issued early in the reign of James I, authorised " Our Servants, Lawrence Fletcher, William Shakespeare, Richard Burbage . . . freely to use and exercise the art and faculty of plays, comedies, tragedies, histories . . . within their now usual house called the Globe . . . or other convenient places."

This theatre caught fire one night in the year 1613 when Shakespeare's *King Henry the Eighth* was being played. A small cannon was accidentally discharged and set the thatched roof alight. The galleries quickly caught the flames and the place was destroyed. No lives were lost in the conflagration, " only one man had his breeches set on fire, that would perhaps have broyled him, if he had not, by the benefit of a provident wit, put it out with a bottle of ale." The theatre was rebuilt and stood until 1644, when it had to make way for tenements.

Puritans Get Theatres Closed

In 1632 William Prynne, a Puritan, published a long and bitter attack on the stage and everything connected with it. His book was called *Histrio Mastix: the Player's Scourge.* It was received with great indignation and the author was very severely dealt with, but within ten years the Puritan point of view had won so many adherents that Parliament passed an Act forbidding the production of public stage plays. The theatres were closed and not reopened until just before the Restoration.

The accession of Charles II marked the beginning of a period of intense theatrical activity, the symptom of a reaction against the dullness of life under the Puritans. The centre of this activity was Drury Lane, where in 1658 Sir William Davenant opened the Cockpit Theatre. The King's private playhouse was known as the Whitehall Cockpit.

THE GLOBE THEATRE

Opened about 1594, it had as sign a figure of Atlas supporting a globe. It was immortalised by its connection with William Shakespeare.

It was in the Old Drury Theatre in Drury Lane that Charles II was first captivated by the beauty of Nell Gwynne, who was there acting in one of Dryden's plays called *Tyrannic Love.* Prior to the year 1660, no women had acted on the English stage, their parts being taken by boys.

Nell Gwynne, with her bronze-red hair, blue eyes and winsome upturned nose, was by far the most famous of the Restoration actresses. Born, it is believed, in an alley called the Coal Yard near Drury Lane—though Hereford and Oxford have advanced claims—one of her first jobs was as an orange-seller in the pit of the King's Theatre, on the site of which Drury Lane Theatre was afterwards built. She became an actress at the age of fifteen, quickly made a great reputation, and at twenty-five left the boards for the more glamorous life of Whitehall and the embraces of the King. Samuel Pepys describes her as " pretty, witty Nell " and more than once pays tribute to her histrionic abilities. The great Dryden felt himself honoured to write plays for her. Charles II remembered his mistress on his death-bed, and James II was not unmindful of her. Her charming manner, boundless good nature and irrepressible high spirits won her countless admirers among rich and poor alike. Thousands of people attended her burial in St. Martin-in-the-Fields. She never put on airs and graces and remained at heart the denizen of the Coal Yard.

The beginning of the eighteenth century saw a great increase in the numbers of the London theatres. The most important were at Covent Garden and Drury Lane, but there were others in Lincoln's Inn Fields, Goodman's Fields and the Haymarket.

First Gas-lit Theatre

The Haymarket was probably the first theatre to be lighted by gas, that illuminant being one of the " vast improvements " made in 1843 in a house that will always be associated with Sir Squire and Lady Bancroft. The Savoy, which opened in 1881, was the first theatre to use electricity for illumination.

In 1741 an unknown actor called David Garrick made his first London appearance at Goodman's Fields, where he created such a sensation that playgoers deserted Drury Lane and Covent Garden to see him. For twenty-five years after that date Garrick remained the unchallenged leader of his profession, being not only head and shoulders over all his contemporaries in histrionic ability, but also a discriminating manager and a prolific, if mediocre, playwright. Unlike most actors, he played equally well in tragedy, comedy, and farce.

Garrick and Peg Woffington

In 1742 he went to Dublin with a native of that city, Peg Woffington, for whom he cherished a deep affection. This actress had made a considerable reputation in Ireland before she came, about the year 1740, to Covent Garden, where her charming impudence gained her many admirers. Her theatrical career was tragically terminated in 1757 when she was struck by paralysis while playing Rosalind in *As You Like It* at Covent Garden Theatre.

Covent Garden Theatre, at which Peg Woffington and many another eighteenth-century player charmed London audiences, was opened by a celebrated harlequin called John Rich in 1732. The first play to be staged there was Congreve's *The Way of the World*, which received such poor support that he swore he would write no more. An advertisement of this production stated that seats could be obtained at 10s. 6d., 5s., 2s. and 1s., which represented much more than corresponding charges to-day.

Handel, the great musical composer, resided in London for nearly fifty years, and it was at the Theatre Royal, Covent Garden, that the majority of his oratorios were produced.

DAVID GARRICK

Actor, manager and dramatist, he revolutionised the stage. Achieved success 1741, retired 1776.

NELL GWYNNE

Born 1650, she was orange-seller, actress, and favourite of King Charles II. She died in 1687.

Actor Tried for Murder

Charles Macklin, one of the most remarkable theatrical characters of the eighteenth century, made his first appearance at Covent Garden in 1733 and his last over fifty years later. Born in Ireland in 1697, he lived to be a hundred, and a good part of his long life was spent in or near this theatre. He stood trial for murder in 1735, having killed one of his colleagues in a quarrel. His memoirs tell us that during the first part of the eighteenth century the vast majority of stage folk lived within a few minutes' walk of Covent Garden. Garrick, for instance, lived in Southampton Street, and Wycherley in Bow Street.

In the year that Charles Macklin died in Tavistock Row the celebrated comedy actress, Mrs. Glover, made her first appearance at Covent Garden; and in 1803 Sarah Siddons, perhaps the greatest actress of all time, followed her brother, John Philip Kemble, when he deserted Drury Lane in favour of this theatre.

Covent Garden Theatre was destroyed by fire in 1808, after frantic attempts—involving the deaths of twenty-three firemen—had been made to put out the conflagration. The property was only insured for £50,000, whereas £150,000 worth of damage was done, so that the owners were faced with a dead loss of £100,000. They rebuilt it with amazing speed, however, and it was reopened in September of the following year. The foundation stone, a block of granite weighing three tons, bears the inscription : " Long live George, Prince of Wales," and is still in position. Then disaster threatened the enterprise, because the public were enraged at the high prices the management thought it necessary to charge for seats in the new theatre. They interrupted the play every night with cries of " Old prices," and with cat-calls, rattles and the beating of drums. Finally by these tactics, they succeeded in getting the prices lowered to their former level.

In 1833, the year in which Edmund Kean made his last appearance at this theatre, its management was amalgamated with that of Drury Lane, but the connection was soon severed. Four years later William Macready took over the theatre and for two seasons produced Shakespeare.

In 1847, after having been considerably altered, Covent Garden Theatre became the Royal Italian Opera House, much to the annoyance of the management of Her Majesty's, who claimed a monopoly of Italian opera in England; but this form of entertainment, though much appreciated by a vast public, failed to pay its way, and at the end of two seasons Edward Delafield, the lessee, went bankrupt. His losses totalled over £60,000.

Fire again attacked and destroyed the theatre while a masked ball was in progress, at five o'clock on the morning of March 5, 1856. The present building was opened just over two years later. The architect was E. M. Barry, and the cost £120,000. For twenty years after 1858 the

COVENT GARDEN THEATRE AGAIN DESTROYED BY FIRE

On March 5, 1856, at 5 a.m., just as a masked ball was concluding, fire broke out in Covent Garden Theatre, and within a few hours the splendid building was a devastated mass of smoking ruins.

theatre was extremely prosperous under the able management of Frederick Gye, a keen business man who saw that expenses were cut down to a minimum. When he died its fortunes steadily deteriorated until Sir Augustus Harris took charge. The latter revived interest in the opera and made Covent Garden one of the finest theatres of its kind. Melba first appeared there in 1888. In 1896, on the death of Sir Augustus, it was taken over by a syndicate.

Opening of Drury Lane

That other great London theatre, Drury Lane, was opened by John Killigrew in 1663, nearly seventy years before Rich built Covent Garden Theatre. Pepys tells us that he went to see the first play Killigrew presented there. It was a comedy by Beaumont and Fletcher, and the diarist thought it " a silly play." After it was over he was taken behind the scenes where he saw " Nelly (Gwynne), a most pretty woman, who acted the great part of 'Coelia' to-day, very fine, and did it pretty well. I kissed her, and so did my wife; and a mighty pretty soul she is."

The first Old Drury was burnt down in 1672, but was rebuilt within two years under the supervision of Sir Christopher Wren. Some thirty-five years later the new theatre was closed by order of the Lord Chamberlain because of the quarrels that were always taking place there between the owners and the players.

In 1747 Garrick, in partnership with Lacy, started a successful Shakespearean revival there.

First Appearance of Mrs. Siddons

Mrs. Siddons made her first appearance at Drury Lane in 1775, but she does not seem to have made much impression on her audience on this occasion. She afterwards became the theatre's leading light and when, in 1803, she left it along with her brothers, John and Charles Kemble, the management was in despair.

Between 1776 and 1778, Richard Brinsley Sheridan, helped by two friends, bought Drury Lane Theatre from Garrick for the sum of £80,000. *Pizarro*, the worst thing he ever wrote, brought him in £25,000 in five weeks. " At the time the house was overflowing, on the first night's performance of *Pizarro*," says the *Era Almanack*, " all that was written of the play was actually rehearsing; and incredible as it may appear, until the end of the fourth act, neither Mrs. Siddons, nor Charles Kemble, nor Barrymore, had all their speeches for the fifth. Mr. Sheridan was upstairs in the prompter's room, where he was writing the last part of the play while the earlier parts were acting, and every ten minutes he brought down as much of the dialogue as he had done, piecemeal, into the green-room, abusing himself and his negligence, and making a thousand winning and soothing apologies for having kept the performers so long in such painful suspense."

Despite the success of *Pizarro* and other productions, Sheridan died in great poverty.

Condemned as unfit to hold large audiences, the old theatre was pulled down in 1791. The new building, upon which an enormous sum of money had been expended, was opened in 1794, but was destroyed by fire fifteen years later.

When the fire broke out Sheridan was at the House of Commons, and when the news of it was received there an immediate adjournment was voted. The great orator made his way to Drury Lane and, having carelessly glanced at the fire, sat down in a neighbouring tavern and broached a bottle of port. A friend expressing surprise at this display of indifference, Sheridan remarked that " it was hard if a man could not drink a glass of wine by his own fire."

Early Days of Drury Lane

The history of Drury Lane Theatre for nearly seventy years after its reopening was not encouraging. The managers seem to have been continually at their wits' end to devise some means of filling the immense auditorium. It was used successively as a concert hall, an arena for wild beasts, and an opera house, with occasional intervals of real drama. Christmas pantomimes became a regular feature and drew large houses.

In 1879 the lease of the theatre was bought by Sir Augustus Harris, under whose management many spectacular successes were achieved.

Practically the whole of the building was reconstructed in 1921, the outer walls and the colonnade being preserved for sentimental reasons.

Samuel Phelps, manager of the Sadler's Wells Theatre from 1844 until 1862, deserves to be remembered by every playgoer, for while other London managers were concerning themselves solely about making money, he was working quietly and patiently at the task of presenting the masterpieces of the great English playwrights. No mean actor himself, he seems to have had a genius for selecting players of talent.

DAME ELLEN TERRY
As Beatrice in Shakespeare's *Much Ado About Nothing*. She played opposite Irving for twenty years.

Sadler's Wells derives its quaint name from a holy well that was once renowned for its healing waters.

The original building, Sadler's Musick House, became a theatre in 1753. Both Grimaldi the clown and Edmund Kean made their first appearances there, the former at the age of four years as a monkey. Reconstructed in 1930 when it was derelict, Sadler's Wells was re-opened in 1931 under the management of Miss Lilian Baylis, of the Old Vic.

It was at the Princess's Theatre that Henry Irving made his first London appearance in 1859, and Wilson Barrett thrilled packed audiences with *The Lights o' London* and *The Silver King*.

Irving at the Lyceum

Nearly twenty years afterwards Irving became manager of the Lyceum Theatre, where he remained acting constantly until 1899. Opened in 1772, " this muse-devoted dome " was originally an art gallery, became an exhibition of puppets, a grand museum, a school of eloquence, the home of Madame Tussaud's wax-works, and in 1809 a legitimate theatre. Destroyed by fire, it reappeared in 1834 as the Royal Lyceum Theatre and English Opera House.

In 1876, two years before she joined Irving at the Lyceum, Ellen Terry had been acting at the Court Theatre, where at the beginning of the present century the plays of George Bernard Shaw were first presented to large London audiences, and where, in 1905, she herself first acted in a Shavian production.

It is difficult for present-day playgoers to imagine what the coming of Shaw meant to theatrical circles in London at the end of the last century. It is not too much to say that he revolutionised the English theatre.

Long Wait for Recognition

Though his first play, *Widowers' Houses*, was produced in 1892, Shaw had to wait twelve years before the London stage accepted him. Between 1904 and 1907 three of his plays were enthusiastically received at the Court Theatre.

The capital remains as always the theatrical centre of the British Isles, providing entertainment to suit every type of mind. There were at least forty theatres within a short distance of Leicester Square about 1910, but several of them have now become palatial cinemas.

SIR HENRY IRVING
Real name, John Henry Brodribb. Born 1838, he dominated the English stage for over thirty years.

BURYING THE DEAD IN THE GREAT PLAGUE

It is estimated that 70,000 people died in London during the Great Plague of 1665. The work of burying the dead in mammoth pits was done at night by the poorest and meanest of the citizens.

LONDON'S BLACK DAYS

FROM lightning and tempest; from plague, pestilence and famine; from battle and murder, and from sudden death.

Good Lord, deliver us.

From all sedition, privy conspiracy, and rebellion; from all false doctrine, heresy and schism; from hardness of heart, and contempt of Thy word and commandment.

Good Lord, deliver us.

The common prayers of a people are wrought out of experience, and quaint though some of the above petitions from the Litany of the English Church may sound to modern ears, there is not a single phrase in them but has on countless occasions been pregnant with meaning to our forefathers. "Plague, pestilence and famine"—few of us to-day can fully understand these words, for of their reality we have no experience; but for a thousand years or more every Londoner as he thought of them must have felt cold fear clutch at his heart, for they were to him not vague and shadowy portents, but grim and deadly neighbours ever knocking at his door. And their call meant death—death in a score of terrifying and painful forms.

From earliest days until comparatively modern times London knew full well the ravages of that dreadful and loathsome medieval disease commonly called the plague. John Stow, the learned Elizabethan antiquary, tells how in the fifth century A.D., when the Britons were "continuing a lingering and doubtful war with the Scots . . . a bitter plague fell among them, consuming in short time such a multitude that the quick were not sufficient to bury the dead." Later historians are inclined to cast some doubt upon this story; but it is beyond question that between A.D. 952 and 1665 London suffered at least twenty grievous epidemics of plague, while, with the exception of a period of nearly two and a half centuries during which the City was apparently immune, there was scarce a year during which the dread disease did not make its appearance.

Everyone has heard of the Great Plague of 1665, but that of 1348–49, commonly known as the "Black Death" or the "Great Mortality," must have been equally terrible; in fact, considered in its world aspect, it was infinitely more so, for it swept the globe from China to the British Isles, accompanied by such a wave of earthquakes, thunderstorms, floods, drought and famine as humanity has never before nor since experienced.

50,000 in One Graveyard

No one knows the death roll. Many millions are said to have perished in China alone. India suffered frightfully. In Europe Italy lost half its population; entire villages were wiped out in France. Historians estimate that from one-third to one-half of the people of England died. Stow puts the mortality much higher, for he says that " scarce the tenth person of all sorts was left alive." He also relates—and the truth of his statement is amply testified—how in 1349 Sir Walter Manny, Mayor of London, because the City graveyards could admit no more dead, " purchased thirteen acres and a rod of ground " outside the walls where now stands Charterhouse Square, and that " In this plot of ground there were in that year more than fifty thousand persons buried."

Nor was this the only or even the first additional cemetery that had to be provided for the London victims of this dreadful visitation. Though the plague did not reach the City until the autumn of 1348, before the end of that same year the Bishop of London had to buy and consecrate " a piece of ground called No Man's Land," three acres in extent, lying north of the Charterhouse, while another plot of ground was purchased north-east of the Tower.

The Black Death was, so far as is known, the first serious outbreak of plague London had experienced since the year 1111. During the following two centuries the City was practically never entirely free of it; on at least fifteen occasions death swept the streets as a reaper mows down corn. Two of the worst outbreaks were those of 1603 and 1625; during the former there were 33,347 recorded deaths in London, during the latter 41,313 persons died within a twelvemonth.

Our ancestors lived, suffered and died in absolute ignorance of either the cause or the cure of the plague. They did what they could to stem its onslaughts, but they knew in their heart of hearts that all their efforts were futile, and the great blue or red crosses they painted on the doors of infected houses, with the pitiful appeal " Lord have mercy upon us," reflected their fatalistic submission to what they came to regard as a dread punishment inflicted by the Almighty to scourge them for their sins.

It was not until 1894 that the bacillus of the disease was discovered, and even more recently that it was definitely established that the bubonic plague was carried by fleas on rats.

Our worthy forefathers, so far as we know, never suspected the busy rodents who gnawed their wainscotings and not infrequently scampered squeaking across their beds, though they got as far as reasoning that animals might carry the infection, and more than once—greatly to the indignation of many good folk—ordered wholesale slaughters of dogs and cats.

The learned among them discussed earnestly what might be the cause of the plague. The majority inclined to the belief that the air was somehow poisoned, though others thought that the poison was in the soil. Knowing nothing of microbes, neither party could offer any valid theory, but those who accused the soil had much justice on their side, for the incredibly filthy condition of medieval London, with its open sewers and privies, its foul street kennels, its contaminated drinking supplies, its lice- and flea-ridden houses, together with the generally insanitary domestic habits of its people, provided, not indeed the cause of plague, but an ideal breeding ground for any and every variety of harmful microbes.

The common people, steeped in superstition, believed the most fantastic tales of the origin of the plague. The appearance of a raven portended it; a heron had alighted on a church, so pestilence was certain to follow; an ox had rung an alarm bell—that was an infallible sign.

Why Queen Elizabeth Fled

All, high and low, wise and ignorant, shared the same panic fear of the disease. In 1573 Queen Elizabeth, then in residence at Greenwich Palace, was talking with her maids of honour when one of them was stricken with sudden illness and expired. Within an hour her Majesty had packed up and was on her way to Westminster.

Elizabeth was no coward; she simply did what everyone did in those days when there was any reason to suspect the plague—got away as quickly as possible.

The so-called preventive measures of the day were wholly ineffective—some of them, in fact, actively assisted the spread of the disease. One order issued in 1665 provided that " As soon as any man shall be found . . . to be sick of the plague, he shall the same night be sequestered in the same house; and in case he be so sequestered, then, though he afterwards die not, the house wherein he sickened should be shut up for a month, after the use of the due preservatives taken by the rest."

By this rule whole families of perfectly healthy people were shut up with a single infected person, a procedure which frequently resulted in the slaughter of the entire household.

By August, 1665, when the plague was at its climax, the citizens of London were n such a state of despair that hey had given up all faith in emedies or preventive measures. " Now shutting up of visited houses (there being o many)," wrote the Rev. Thomas Vincent in a tract called " God's terrible Voice o the City," " is at an end, and most of the well are mingled amongst the sick." " The terror was so great at ast," says Defoe, " that he courage of the people appointed to carry away the lead began to fail them."

In September matters began to improve, but the plague ran its course hroughout 1665 and on into 666. So far as can be estimated, nearly 70,000 persons perished in London alone, while an unknown number of those who fled into the surrounding country lied of some other disease, tarvation or exposure.

THE FIRE OF LONDON

As pictured by Stanhope Forbes, R.A. The original painting is one of the magnificent series of mural decorations in the Royal Exchange.

There still stand in London one or two ittle-known memorials of the Great Plague.

Plague Memorials in London

In Seething Lane opposite Pepys Street is a ateway of St. Olave's Church bearing five grisly sculptured skulls, with bones beneath hem; and a somewhat similar gateway at St. Stephen's Church could be seen in Coleman Street, near the Bank of England. The Church was destroyed in the war. These mark graveyards of large numbers of victims of the plague.

That the plague would have returned to London but for the Great Fire is scarcely open to doubt. That mighty and terrible burning, which laid in ashes one of the leading cities of Europe, destroying 13,200 houses in four days and rendering some 200,000 people homeless, was perhaps the greatest blessing that

ESCAPING FROM THE FIRE

An unusual view of the Great Fire showing boats being loaded with refugees and household goods at London Bridge. On the hill stands old St. Paul's, untouched as yet by the flames

ever fell upon London. It swept away the filth of centuries, purified the disease-ridden soil, and buried beneath tons of debris the poisonous waters which menaced the health of the citizens.

Fire Believed to be God's Warning

At the time, of course, the citizens thought very differently. There was a widespread belief that both the Plague and the Fire were manifestations of the wrath of God against a disobedient and wicked people.

A London preacher, on the anniversary of the Great Fire, solemnly informed his congregation that " the calamity could not have been occasioned by the sin of blasphemy, for in that case it would have begun in Billingsgate : nor lewdness, for then Drury Lane had been the first on fire; nor lying, for then the flames had reached the City from Westminster Hall (Law Courts). No, my beloved, it was occasioned by the sin of gluttony, for it began at Pudding Lane, and ended at Pie Corner."

Less charitable people accused foreigners of having deliberately set the City on fire, and for some time it was quite unsafe for anyone of foreign extraction to be seen in the streets.

Tales of mythical fireballs inflamed the imagination of the Londoners and led to a number of tragi-comic episodes. People carrying parcels of eggs, potatoes or similar round objects were attacked, and the height of absurdity was reached when a poor widow, hastening away from her burning home with a brood of tiny chicks tied up in her apron, was set upon by the crowd and grievously ill-treated because her chickens were thought to be fireballs!

Hanged and then Proved Innocent

Finally, a self-appointed victim offered himself to assuage the wrath of the citizens. Robert Hubert, a poor lunatic Frenchman of Rouen, gave himself up to the justices, and an Old Bailey jury found that he, " not having the fear of God before his eyes, but moved and led away by the instigation of the devil," had maliciously set on fire the City of London.

There was not a scrap of evidence against Hubert. The judge who tried him did not believe a word of his confession, and was honest enough to tell King Charles so. The

Merry Monarch, who only the year before had "written to the Lord Mayor, Recorder and Aldermen, warning them of the peril of fire from the narrowness of the streets and alleys, and the overhanging houses built of wood," was equally sceptical of Hubert's guilt.

Nevertheless the poor wretch was hanged, and though it was afterwards clearly proved that he had not even been in London until two days after the Fire started, because he was a Catholic many people went to their graves believing the Fire of London to have been the result of a Popish conspiracy. Incredible though it may seem, it was not until 1830 that an inscription stating that the Fire had been caused by malice of the Roman Catholics was erased from the base of the Monument.

Great Fire Begun by Accident

Charles II and his counsellors came to the conclusion that the fire was due to "the hand of God upon us, a great wind, and the season so very dry." A modern Court of Inquiry would doubtless add "and to the complete inadequacy of the fire-fighting arrangements and appliances then obtaining."

That the Fire began by accident is quite certain. It started about 3 a.m. on Sunday morning, September 2, 1666, in the house of one Farynor or Farryner, a baker, who seems to have left a pile of faggots or brushwood too near the fire of his oven. Pudding Lane, in which he lived, was a street full of overhanging timber-built houses which could offer but slight resistance to the flames.

Panic Flight of Citizens

So swiftly did the fire spread that little at first was done to stop it; everyone was too intent on escape. Adjoining Farynor's house was the Star Inn, an old-fashioned hostelry with wooden galleries and stables full of straw and hay. This went up in a tremendous blaze, and from here the flames spread in every direction. By daybreak the fire had reached the river quays abutting on Thames Street.

Here was marvellous material for spreading the conflagration; large stocks of oil, tallow, timber, fodder, coal, butter, cheese, spirits, tar, pitch, rosin, brimstone, hemp, flax and other inflammable goods; and all the time a strong east wind kept blowing, causing the flames to leap from house to house and street to street in a manner that defied resistance. Nor, at first, were efforts organised to stop it.

Terror fell upon all who lived in the neighbourhood. The streets were choked with fleeing folk. Panic reigned at the City gates,

LONDON'S OTHER CASTLE

aynard's Castle, built in the reign of William I at the west end of London, never achieved the fame f the Tower, but it was the scene of some grim tragedies. It was destroyed in the Great Fire.

where wagons, hand-carts, barrows and people laden with bundles were jammed in inextricable confusion. Householders wildly offered huge sums for the removal of their goods, or even of their plate and jewels alone. Prices for the hire of horses and carts went up to fabulous heights; the profiteer, like the thieves and pickpockets who swiftly got to work, reaped a golden harvest.

Some people deposited their household treasures in churches, fondly imagining that these would be immune from the fire. The booksellers, who then as later congregated in Paternoster Row, rushed their volumes—to the value of £150,000—into the crypt of St. Paul's, where in a few hours they were buried beneath thousands of tons of burning debris.

Ten Thousand Houses Ablaze

For the first twenty-four hours the fire drove steadily westward along the river bank. Then the wind changed, and the flames rolled up Gracechurch Street towards the heart of the City. And then, remarks John Evelyn, the diarist—a staid and responsible man not given to emotion or exaggeration—" Oh, the miserable and calamitous spectacle! Such as haply the world had not seene the like since the foundation of it, nor be outdone till the universal conflagration thereof. All the skie was of a fiery aspect, like the top of a burning oven, and the light seene above 40 miles round for many nights. God grant mine eyes may never behold the like, who now saw above 10,000 houses all in one flame : the noise and cracking and thunder of the impetuous flames, the shrieking of women and children, the hurry of people, the fall of Towers, Houses and Churches, was like a hideous storm : and the aire all about so hot and inflamed that at the last one was not able to approach it, so that they were forced to stand still and let the flames burn on, which they did, for neere two miles in length and one in bredth."

An Incapable Lord Mayor

There was indeed only one practicable way of checking the fire once it had gained a firm hold—by destroying houses in its path and thus creating gaps it could not overleap. It was not until the Tuesday that this method was resolutely pursued.

Not realising the extent of the danger, people objected to having their houses demolished. The Lord Mayor, Sir Thomas Gludworth, was a

THE MONUMENT

Built by Wren, it stands near the spot where th Great Fire of 1666 started. It is 202 feet higl

weak ineffective creature incapable of rising to the emergency. Samuel Pepys relates how "the King commanded me to go to My Lord Mayor for him, and command him to spare no houses but to pull down before the fire every way. . . . At last met My Lord Mayor in Canning (Cannon) Street, like a man spent, with a handkercher about his neck. To the King's message, he cried, like a fainting woman, 'Lord, what can I do? I am spent; people will not obey me. I have been pulling down houses, but the fire overtakes us faster than we can do it.'"

Not an inspiring picture, but many a man equal to any ordinary occasion would have broken down in such case. The two outstanding heroes of the Fire were the royal brothers, Charles II and James, Duke of York, later James II. They summoned men from the royal dockyards to fight the flames and undertake demolition, and the Duke of York, who was in charge, "gained all hearts by his powerful labours in handing the buckets and giving orders."

Fine Example Set by King

As for Charles, he was, according to Mr. Walter Bell, "in the City on horseback from early morning. He rode from place to place . . . seeing that orders to man the stations were executed, passing to the very edge at which the Fire was burning, and by word and example encouraging those who toiled amid the oppressive heat to pull down houses or to throw water on the flames. . . . Laying regal dignity aside, the King alighted from his horse at some corner where falling buildings added to the common danger, and himself took a share in the work, handling spade and bucket and inspiring the courtiers about him to do the same. Bespattered with mud and dirt, his laced costume dripping with water, his hot face blackened with the universal fire dust, but himself alert and tireless—this was another monarch than he whom his people pictured dallying with his mistresses at Westminster."

The royal example had good effect; men "fell to work with effort, having soe good fellow labourers." By Wednesday the fire was checked, and though further small outbreaks occurred they were subdued without serious difficulty.

The labour of fighting the fire over, there came the dreadful task of surveying and estimating the damage. The total was appalling: 436 acres had been laid in ruins; 400 streets had been wiped out. St. Paul's Cathedral—one of the largest ecclesiastical buildings in Europe—the Royal Exchange, the Custom House, the Justice House and Sion College had all perished, together with 87 parish churches, 6 consecrated chapels, 50 companies' halls, hospitals, schools, almshouses, libraries and prisons. The total loss was estimated at nearly £11,000,000.

The homeless lay in scores of thousands beyond the City walls. "I then went towards Islington and Highgate," says John Evelyn, "where one might have seen 200,000 people of all ranks and degrees dispersed and lying along by their heaps of what they could save from the fire."

"Pitiful huts," says Maitland, the nineteenth-century historian, "were erected for their accommodation, and for their immediate needs the King sent a great quantity of bread from the Navy Stores to be distributed, and neighbouring Justices of the Peace were enjoined to send in all manner of victuals."

The boast was made after the Fire that London was rebuilt in three years. This is a pardonable exaggeration of a very wonderful performance. Long before the ruins were cold—in some cases they smouldered for months—the rebuilding of the City had begun, and within four years 10,000 houses had been erected. But for twenty years London bore patent marks of the ravages of the Fire, and it was thirty years before the rebuilding of the churches was complete—and even then only fifty-one were re-erected of the eighty-seven which perished.

It is one of the tragedies of London history that the plans for its rebuilding which Sir Christopher Wren laid before the King and his Council only five days after the Fire were never carried out. Had the great astronomer-architect had his way, a London of broad and spacious thoroughfares lined with stately buildings would have arisen, a very queen among cities. But it was not to be.

A New and Better London

Yet the new London was infinitely superior to the old, and the citizens patted themselves on the back (not without justice) at the improvement. Twenty-five years after the Fire, Thomas Delaune wrote, "As if the Fire had only purged the City, the buildings are infinitely more beautiful, more commodious, more solid, 'the three main virtues of all edifices,' than before. They have made their streets much more large and straight, paved on each side with smooth free stone, and guarded the same with many massy posts for the benefit of foot passengers: and whereas before they dwelt in low dark

ALMOST A GREAT DISASTER

Guy Fawkes and his fellow-conspirators discussing the Gunpowder Plot. What would have happened had their scheme succeeded? November 5, 1604, would have been counted one of London's most tragic days.

wooden houses, they now live in lofty, lightsome, uniform, and very stately brick buildings."

Though the Great Fire of 1666 was relatively the greatest conflagration London has ever known, the City has experienced many other serious outbreaks. In its early days it was not infrequently swept by devastating fires, so much so that the medieval chronicler Fitzstephen declared that " The only plagues of London are immoderate quaffing among the foolish sort, and often casualties by fire."

Roman London Swept by Fire

Visitors to Guildhall Museum can see a case containing fragments of Roman pottery, some of which have been fused together by heat. They constitute part of the evidence collected by Mr. Quintin Waddington, the Assistant Curator, to prove that about A.D. 125-130 a great fire, accidental in origin, raged in London, destroying in all probability about half the city.

Fitzstephen may have been an eyewitness of the terrible fire of 1136 which, according to Stow, " began in the house of one Ailewarde, near unto London Stone, which consumed east to Aldgate, and west to St. Erkenwald's shrine, in Powle's (Paul's) Church."

Fifty years previously St. Paul's had been consumed in a fire which destroyed all the houses from the West gate of the City to the East. In 1093 another great fire swept away a great part of the City, and in 1212 took place the fearful outbreak which, according to Stow and other medieval historians, trapped " an exceeding great multitude " on London Bridge, of whom " there were destroyed about three thousand persons, whose bodies were found in part, or half burnt, besides those that were wholly burnt to ashes, and could not be found."

Notwithstanding the stringent regulations laid down after the Great Fire, the following century saw a number of disastrous outbreaks, though it must be added that nearly all of these took place outside the City walls, and therefore in areas not under the jurisdiction of the City authorities.

Only ten years after the Great Fire Southwark was laid waste by a conflagration which destroyed the Town Hall, the Meat Market, the Prison of the Compter, and some 500 houses, including the famous Tabard and White Hart Inns.

Famous Coffee-houses Burned Down

In 1691 one hundred and fifty houses were burnt down in Whitehall : in 1748 nearly one hundred houses, including " Jonathan's," " Garraway's " and other well-known coffee-houses, were destroyed on Cornhill during a fire in which many people lost their lives and damage to the extent of £200,000 was done. In 1765 Cornhill was again devastated, nearly ninety houses in that thoroughfare and Threadneedle Street perishing.

Thirty years later, on July 22 and 23, over 600 houses and a warehouse belonging to the East India Company were burnt down at Ratcliffe Cross in Poplar. In November, 1832, a smaller but terrible fire in Long Acre wiped out fourteen houses in three hours.

Work of London Fire Brigade

With the vastly increased efficiency of modern fire-fighting appliances and organisation in modern times the danger of fires spreading over large areas has been diminished almost to vanishing point, though the actual number of outbreaks is still large. "But for the London Fire Brigade," a superintendent of that superb body has declared, "there would be a Great Fire of London about once a week."

In spite of all precautions it still happens that occasionally an outbreak of fire gets the upper hand of the fighters. Many people still living will remember the dreadful blaze in Cripplegate in January, 1898, when Well Street, Hamsell Street and Jewin Street were completely gutted and seventeen streets in all were affected. The rapidity with which in December, 1936, the Crystal Palace was devoured defied all efforts to save it.

London has suffered frequently from the malice of foreign foes, rebellious subjects and riotous citizens. The very first mention of *Londinium* is when in A.D. 61 it was sacked and burnt by Boudicca, Queen of the Iceni. Stow records that "This city of London having been destroyed and burnt by the Danes and other Pagan enemies, about the year of Christ 839, was by Alfred, King of the West Saxons, in the year 886, repaired, honourably restored, and made again habitable."

In 1381 the Kentish rebels under Wat Tyler, inflamed by the passionate harangues of the democratic preacher John Ball, entered the City and, uniting with the men of Essex under Jack Straw, burnt John of Gaunt's palace of the Savoy—the finest house in London—and the house of the Knights' Hospitallers in Clerkenwell, the Essex rebels having previously gutted in Highbury the residence of Sir Robert Hales, Lord Treasurer of England and Grand Prior of the Order of St. John of Jerusalem.

The night of Sunday, July 5, 1450, must have been one of terror for the inhabitants of London. The rebels led by Jack Cade had been three days previously admitted into the City, but having disgusted all by their open robberies, had been forced to retire to Southwark.

Cade swore that if he were not admitted again he would take the City by force, and the defences of London Bridge remaining closed against him he began a furious attack which lasted until nine o'clock on the Monday morning. The rebels fired the houses on the bridge, and "Alas!" laments the chronicler, "what sorrow it was to beholde that miserable chaunce : for some desyringe to eschew the fyre lept on hys enemies weapon, and so died : fearfull women, with chyldren in their armes, amased and appalled, lept into the river : other, doubtinge how to save them self betwene fyre, water and swourd, were in their houses suffocate and smoldered."

The abdication and flight of King James II was the signal for destructive rioting in London. Making the prevalent hatred of the Roman

JACK CADE AT LONDON STONE

Striking his sword upon the ancient London Stone, Cade declared himself Lord of the City.

Catholics their excuse, the mob fell upon and burnt Catholic churches and the residences of well-known Papists, as they were termed. The King's Printing House, because of the pro-Catholic literature printed there by James II, was given to the flames while a huge bonfire was made of its stocks of pamphlets and paper.

Even these scenes pale before the horrors of the Gordon riots, when for six days London lay at the mercy of a fanatical and murderous mob. In 1780, as in 1688, the cry of No Popery was the signal for outrage and rapine.

The actual march of the Protestant Association from St. George's Fields to the Houses of Parliament was orderly enough, but the procession attracted the riff-raff of all London, who began that night to ransack Catholic quarters in town.

On Sunday rioting broke out again, and on Monday his followers burnt before Lord George Gordon's house in Welbeck Street a large collection of Catholic images and vestments. By Tuesday evening the mob was ripe for any mischief.

"Then followed," says Sir Walter Besant, "the most terrible night in the whole history of London. Where were the Magistracy? Where was the Lord Mayor? Where were the soldiers? The mob was actually left entirely alone and undisturbed. Nobody seemed able to move. London was paralysed."

Donald McLeish

ST. JOHN'S GATE

Only surviving external portion of the Priory of the Knights of St. John of Jerusalem at Clerkenwell.

The sack and burning of Newgate Prison has been described by Charles Dickens in a passage of inimitable prose : "'Remember the prisoners!' . . . The cry ran through the mob. Hammers began to rattle on the walls, and every man strove to reach the prison and be among the foremost rank. . . . And now the strokes began to fall like hail upon the gate, and on the strong building; for those who could not reach the door spent their fierce rage on anything—even on the great blocks of stone, which shivered their weapons into fragments. . . . The clash of iron ringing upon iron, mingled with the deafening tumult and sounded high above it, as the great sledge-hammers rattled on the nailed and plated door. . . .

"While some brought all their energies to bear upon this toilsome task : and some, rearing ladders against the prison, tried to clamber to the summit of the walls they were too short to scale : and some again engaged a body of police a hundred strong, and beat them back and trod them under foot by force of numbers; others besieged the house on which the jailer had appeared, and driving in the door, brought out his furniture and piled it up against the prison gate, to make a bonfire which should burn it down. . . ."

Ken Wood Saved by Stratagem

Within an hour or two Newgate was ablaze from end to end, and the mob, reinforced by the 300 inmates of the gaol, was on its way to break open the new prison at Clerkenwell Lord Mansfield's house in Bloomsbury Square was burnt with all its treasures, and an attack upon his mansion at Ken Wood was only prevented by the cunning of the landlord of the Spaniards' Inn, who persuaded the rioters to stop and drink, while he secretly and swiftly sent for a detachment of the Horse Guards.

Meanwhile, other sections of the mob were spreading havoc throughout London. The Bank of England and the Temple resisted attack but every prison save one (the Poultry Compter said to have been preserved by Lord George himself because it had a ward for Jews) was burnt down, the toll gate on Blackfriars wa destroyed, and private houses were fired in every direction.

All Tuesday night, all Wednesday, and all Wednesday night the mob held sway. At one time thirty-six separate fires could be observed from London Bridge. No wonder Horace Walpole spoke of " the second conflagration of London by Lord George Gordon."

The culminating feat of the rioters was the destruction of Langdale's Brewery at Holborn Bridge. On Wednesday morning, Mr. Langdale, who was a Catholic, received notice that the mob intended to wreck his premises. On Wednesday evening they arrived to fulfil their promise.

After sacking the buildings and setting them on fire, the rioters fell to a bestial orgy on the looted liquor. Wine, spirits, gin flowed down the gutters of the street, and men, women and children flung themselves on hands and knees to lap it up. Numbers literally drank themselves to death : others, too intoxicated to realise their danger or to move if they did, perished in the flames.

DESTROYED IN AN AIR RAID
Odhams Press building in Long Acre, destroyed with fearful loss of life by a German 112 lb. incendiary bomb on January 28, 1918.

"At last," says Besant, "the troops arrived—Heavens! At last!—this time with orders to fire " (which before they had been forbidden to do). " Then from all quarters came the platoon firing of the soldiery. The citizens, not daring to leave their beds, listened with trembling satisfaction to the rattle of the muskets and amidst the roaring of the flames they thought they could hear the shrieks of the wounded."

Days of the Air Raids

London has never since known such scenes as these, but for universality of terror the nights and days of the air raids during the two world wars have never been exceeded. The sufferings, patience, endurance and heroic courage of the citizens between September, 1940, and April, 1945, surpassed anything in the history of crowded communities. They are dealt with specially in the chapter, " London at War."

In the course of the First World War, ten Zeppelins and about 130 aeroplanes made altogether twenty-five raids on London, dropping over 900 bombs, of which 355 were incendiary, killing 670 persons, injuring 1,962, and causing 224 fires.

Slaughter in London Streets

On September 8, 1915, a bus was blown to pieces outside Liverpool Street Station, only two people escaping alive; and between Noble Street and Aldermanbury damage to the value of £500,000 was done by fires started by incendiary bombs.

On June 13, 1917, fourteen aeroplanes appeared over London in the serene blue of a perfect summer morning, and before they were driven off 130 men, women and children had been slaughtered and 246 injured. In one office in Fenchurch Street nineteen people met their death, while eighteen innocent children were massacred at North Street School in Poplar.

On September 24 of the same year hostile aeroplanes rained bombs on Finsbury, Islington, King's Cross, Holborn, Soho and Piccadilly. Outside the Bedford Hotel in Southampton Row a bronze tablet records that " On and around these steps twelve persons were killed and many injured by bomb dropped from German aeroplane."

Tragedy in Long Acre

One of the most ghastly tragedies of the air raids occurred on the night of January 28, 1918, when a 112-lb. incendiary bomb crashed through the roof of Odhams' building in Long Acre, and tore its way down to the basement, where a large number of people from the surrounding district had taken shelter.

The building burst into flames, and all that night, while firemen fought the blaze, the bodies of the dead and injured were being extricated from the mass of smashed machines, fallen debris and burning timbers. Thirty-five people were killed and nearly one hundred injured in that appalling holocaust.

Yet after the war, when the full extent of the damage done in London by hostile aircraft became known, *The Times* could say, with all reason, that " In the last war, in fact, London was let off very lightly indeed." Subsequently, Viscount Trenchard declared in the House of Lords that : " I think I am not far wrong in saying that the few bombs which were dropped in this country in the Great War—in the whole of the four years—will be dropped in six hours (in the next war) continuously for five or six weeks."

This pregnant prophecy was only too speedily fulfilled; but even Lord Trenchard could not foresee the devastation and death which were to follow from H.E. bombs, incendiaries, flying bombs and rockets.

There was a total death roll of under 700 and material damage of just over £2,000,000 in London during the First World War. One proud boast the metropolis still holds, its immunity from foreign invasion. No soldiers of another country since those of William the Conqueror have entered it as invaders; and William's men did no damage to the City save that at the monarch's coronation they took alarm at the shouts of the English and fired the buildings round about Westminster Abbey.

Threats of invasion London has known both before and since that occasion. To such threats the citizens have on almost every occasion risen to surpassing heights of courage. The Danes, whose very name for centuries spread terror from the Shetlands to Gibraltar, time and again found the Londoners a match for them in prowess. In 994 Olaf Tryggvessön of Norway and Swegen of Denmark sailed with ninety-four ships right up to the walls of the City, but the citizens handled them so roughly that they retired discomfited and left London severely alone for fifteen years.

When in 1009 the Danes came again to London they were a second time repulsed, and even in 1013, when almost all the rest of England had fallen to the invaders from the north, " then would not the townsmen yield, but stood out against Swegen (Sweyn) with all their might."

In 1016 Canute, the mighty son of Swegen, came with his troops against the City, and dug a vast trench through Southwark to outflank the defenders on London Bridge, and " often did they (the Danes) fight against the town, but the citizens mightily withstood them." Canute retired, then returned to the assault, and once more, in the words of the pious chronicler, " the Almighty God delivered the city "—thanks largely, no doubt, to the invincible courage of its defenders.

Stout Fighting by Citizens

That courage was still in evidence in far more recent days. When in 1471 Thomas the Bastard of Falconbridge gathered ships and men in support of Henry VI, and dropped anchor near the Tower, he found the bank of the Thames bristling with fortifications. Refused admission to the City by the Lord Mayor, he assaulted Bishopsgate, Aldgate, London Bridge and the fortified bank of the Thames. At Aldgate he penetrated the defences, but the citizens, after dropping the portcullis and taking prisoner those of his force who had entered, raised it and rushed upon him with such vigour that they drove him as far as St. Botolph's, slaying some hundreds of his men.

During the Civil War, London sided with the Parliament, and when Charles I threatened to invade the City, men, women and children alike flew to its defence. The Trained Bands were mobilised; the trades and crafts turned

ENGLISH SHIPS BURNT IN THE MEDWAY

In 1667 the Dutch fleet sailed unopposed up the Medway and off Rochester sank three of the finest vessels in the English Navy, including the *Royal Charles*, seen in the foreground of this picture.

out *en masse* to dig trenches; guns were planted to command all approaches, and the entire City stood to arms.

Day after day London beheld the strange spectacle of now 6,000 tailors, now 5,000 shoemakers, or 5,000 felt makers and cappers, accompanied by their womenfolk and children, trudging with pick and shovel to raise defences against a tyrant king. At the west end of Piccadilly they made a fortification, " aided by the female population, and indeed, even ladies of high birth and blood lent a helping hand in the trenches, and in throwing up earthworks."

Women Work in Trenches

Samuel Butler in *Hudibras* says of the women that they

Marched rank and file, with drum and
 ensign
T'entrench the city for defence in :
Raised ramparts with their own soft hands,
To put the enemy to stand :
From ladies down to oyster wenches
Laboured like pioneers in trenches,
Fall'n to their pickaxes and tools,
And helped the men to dig like moles.

There was not so good a heart shown in 1667, when the Dutch fleet sailed into the Thames and destroyed three English warships in the Medway. " They (the citizens) look upon us as lost," wrote Pepys in his Diary, " and remove their families and rich goods in the City." But in 1745 the citizens of London made ready to defend themselves against the Young Pretender, even though their King was packing his goods in a panic and enquiring after the quickest route to the Continent.

Terrible Fourteenth-century Famine

As London has been fortunate in war, so it has generally been spared anything like prolonged distress from shortage of food. During the Middle Ages, certainly, dearths were not uncommon, and the City experienced more than one actual famine, but with the exception of the terrible one of 1314–15 these latter seem to have been of only moderate severity.

Famines are recorded in 1086, 1150 and 1195. In the early years of the fourteenth century there came a weary succession of wet summers with consequent bad or ruined harvests, after which " There followed this famine, a grievous mortalitie of people, so that the quick might unneath (scarcely) bury the dead. The Beastes and Cattell also by the corrupt Grasse whereof they fedde, dyed, whereby it came to passe that the eating of flesh was suspected of all men, for flesh of Beastes not corrupted was hard to find. Horseflesh was counted great delicates; the poore stole fatte Dogges to eate; some (as it was sayde) compelled through famine, in hidde places did eate the fleshe of their owne children, some stole others which they devoured. Thieves that were in prison did plucke in peeces those that were newly brought amongst them and greedily devoured them half alive." Happily, this state of affairs did not last long, for in 1316 there was " an early harvest, a bushel of wheat that had been sold for ten shillings, was now sold for ten pence."

In 1338, when another shortage threatened, the Mayor imported corn from abroad, and in later years it became the rule for the City Livery Companies to maintain adequate stocks of corn against emergencies. This rule was not always too well observed, for when in 1511 Roger Achley entered upon his mayoralty " there was not found one hundred quarters of wheat in all the garners of the city," with the result that " when the carts of Stratford came laden with bread to the city . . . there was such press about them, that one man was ready to destroy another, in striving to be served for their money."

Foreign Corn Purchased

Lord Mayor Achley soon put matters right, and stored up a huge reserve of corn in the Leaden Hall, which had for a long time been the chief storehouse in the City. Yet in 1521 the granaries were again almost empty, in 1546 two aldermen had to be specially detailed to see that adequate stocks were maintained, and in 1590 heavy purchases of foreign corn had to be made.

How near was the threat of scarcity to the citizens of medieval London may be judged from the fact that speculators in corn were regarded with the gravest apprehension, while " regraters," or those who held back supplies, were abhorred as ruthless enemies of the people.

The vast amount of daily charity dispensed in London until at least the sixteenth century shows how acute must have been the distress among the poorer folk. " I myself," records Stow, " in that declining time of charity, have oft seen at the Lord Cromwell's gate in London more than two hundred persons served twice every day with bread, meat and drink."

Henry II in 1171, doing penance for the murder of Thomas Becket, " daily fed and sustained " from April till harvest time 10,000 persons. Robert Winchelsey, Archbishop of Canterbury towards the close of the thirteenth century, gave a loaf of bread to every beggar who came to his gate at Lambeth on a Friday or Sunday and on alms days in time of scarcity fed 5,000 daily, on other days 4,000. This gives some idea of the number of beggars and of the wealth of the Church in those days.

All this implies a swarming mass of poverty-stricken folk, upon whom seasons of cold weather must have pressed very hard. That such seasons were not infrequent is evidenced by the numerous occasions upon which the Thames was frozen over. That it does not do so to-day is due to the increased rapidity of its flood caused by its embankments and the removal of the old many-arched London Bridge.

Jolly occasions were those on which the river became a solid mass of ice—jolly that is, for those who had warm enough clothes on their backs and their stomachs lined with good food. Oxen were roasted on the ice, and more than once a line of shops stretched from the Temple to Southwark. The gentry drove in coaches from bank to bank, while in 1683 they actually organised a fox-hunt on the ice.

But for those who had a sufficiency neither of food nor clothes those winters must have been truly terrible. In 1150 the Thames was frozen over from December to March. In 1281 five arches of London Bridge were swept away on the break-up of the ice. The year 1739 was long known as " the hard winter " because of the distress it caused among the poorer working classes.

Two Months of Frost

The frost, which was severe beyond all imagining, lasted from Christmas Day on into February, and was accompanied by high and destructive winds. Many people were killed in boats and wherries on the Thames through being caught in the ice and crushed. Street accidents were numerous, and old and infirm folk died off like flies owing to the bitterness of the weather.

The great frost of January–March, 1814, was ushered in by a dense fog lasting a week, during which time innumerable accidents occurred in the streets. The London fog is proverbial, especially that thick pea-soupy variety known as the " London particular," which, thanks to

LONDON WRAPPED IN GLOOM
One of the lions in Trafalgar Square looms up out of the fog which in February, 1936, covered practically the whole of Europe. For centuries London has been notorious for its thick, dirty-yellow fogs.

the decreased use of coal fires, is so rarely seen —or felt—to-day. It has been known for at least two centuries and a half. On January 24, 1684, John Evelyn recorded in his diary that " London was filled with the fuliginous steam of the sea-coal."

The comparatively sheltered position of London—lying as it does along a river valley between low hills to north and south—protects it from extremities of wind, though the Great Storm of November 26–27, 1703, was a terrible exception.

Fury of the Wind

A contemporary writer—possibly Daniel Defoe—penned a graphic description of this storm in which he says : " It did not blow so hard, till twelve o'clock at night, but that most families went to bed, though many of them with some concern at the terrible wind : but about one, or at least by two, few people, that were capable of any sense of danger, were so hardy as to lie in bed : the fury of the tempest increased to such a degree that most people expected the fall of their houses.

" And yet, in this general apprehension, nobody durst quit their tottering habitations; for whatever the danger was within doors, it was worse without : the bricks, tiles and stones from the tops of the houses flew with such force, and so thick in the streets, that no one thought fit to venture out, though their houses were nearly demolished."

The storm reached its height between five and six thirty in the morning, when " The fury of it was so exceedingly great . . . that had it not abated, nothing could have withstood its violence much longer."

Only four of all the ships anchored in the Thames rode out the storm : the others were blown down the river and piled one upon another on the shore. On land " practically all the roofs in London were stripped of their tiles "; twenty houses collapsed and two thousand chimney stacks were blown down.

The leaden roof of Westminster Abbey was stripped off : similar roofs on other churches were " rolled up like skins of parchment." Spires and turrets collapsed in great numbers, and thousands of trees were uprooted. Between thirty and forty people were killed, and some two hundred injured. In all reasonable probability London will never experience another tempest such as that one.

London's Earthquake Fiasco

The situation of England in the temperate zone precludes the likelihood of the more devastating natural phenomena, and the only notable earthquake recorded in London presents a story more comic than tragic. On February 8, 1750, a shock was felt. On March 8, precisely four weeks later, " at half-past five in the morning," relates a contemporary publication, " the sky being very clear and serene, and the air very warm, the inhabitants of London, and to a great extent round the City, were alarmed by the shock of an earthquake, that came with great violence, especially about Grosvenor Square. This was preceded, about five o'clock, by a continual though confused lightning, till within a minute or two of its being felt, when a noise was heard resembling the roaring of a great piece of ordnance, fired at a considerable distance, and then instantly the houses reeled, first sinking, as it were, to the south, and then to the north, and with a quick return to the centre."

Nothing very terrible, as will be seen; but unfortunately a half-demented soldier took to prophecy on the strength of these tremors, and predicted that on the morning of April 8 the real shock would come, and that it would lay in ruins London, Westminster and the suburbs. His ravings were given strength and substance by the attitude of many of the clergy, who with a zeal more passionate than wise informed their flocks that these unique phenomena were Divine warnings, sent to bid them give up their evil and vicious ways.

The Bishop of London lent his powerful aid to this attack, delivering a very plain-spoken address of which 40,000 copies were printed. It is hardly to be wondered at that people worked themselves up into a terrible state of fear, nor that the evening of April 7 should have beheld an unprecedented scene. London was a deserted city; in spite of the protests of the more responsible newspapers, practically all its inhabitants had fled into the fields beyond or to securer retreats in the Home Counties.

The country roads were thronged with carriages, in which sat trembling women waiting apprehensively for the fatal crack which was to spell the doom of London. The Thames was alive with boats, for curiously enough—in flat contradiction of all experience during a real earthquake—the citizens seem to have assumed that the river would be immune from the effects of any shock.

Shock That Did Not Happen

Greatly, no doubt, to the disappointment of the sensationally minded, nothing whatever happened, though the more fervent believers in prophecy remained alertly waiting until the last stroke of midday. Then they crept back shamefacedly into the City, and by way of recovering their self-esteem saw to it that the soldier who had deluded them was safely locked up in jail. History does not record that the Bishop of London was similarly treated.

There the matter ended, save that no doubt for many years country innkeepers and the Thames watermen remembered with gratification the huge profits they made that night. So perhaps did the enterprising haberdashers who brought out special lines in "warm earthquake gowns, for sitting up all night in!"

We know to-day, for science has advanced much, that earthquakes are not to be feared in Britain any more than are volcanoes, typhoons or tornadoes; but we have not by any means solved the problem of the floods which almost annually do vast damage to property and crops.

Rowing in Westminster Hall

They are no new problem. "In the year 1236," relates John Stow, "the River of Thames overflowing to the banks, caused the marshes about Woolwich to be all on a sea, wherein boats and other vessels were carried with the stream; so that besides cattle the greatest number of men, women and children inhabitants there were drowned; and in the great Palace of Westminster men did row with wherries in the midst of the Hall, being forced to ride to their chambers.

"Moreover, in the year 1242, the Thames overflowing the banks about Lambhithe (Lambeth) drowned houses and fields by the space of six miles, so that in the Great Hall at Westminster men took to their horses because the water ran over all."

In 1555 Westminster Hall was again flooded, and in 1579, after another inundation, "fishes were left upon the floor of the Hall by the subsiding stream."

On March 20, 1660, Samuel Pepys records that "At Westminster, by reason of rain and an easterly wind, the water was so high that there was boats rowed in King Street (Westminster), and all our yards was drowned, that one could not go to my house, so as no man has seen the like almost, and most houses full of water." Three days later, as he made his way by barge from the Tower to the Long Reach, he noted "the great breach which the late high water had made, to the loss of many £1,000 to the people about Limehouse."

On this occasion the wind and the high tides caused much destruction along the river from Maidenhead to the mouth of the estuary. In 1663 the Thames again overflowed its banks; on December 7 Pepys tells in his Diary that "I hear there was the last night the greatest tide that ever was remembered in England to have been in this river; all Whitehall having been drowned."

For a number of reasons the Thames is peculiarly liable to flood along its lower course.

SANDBAGGING THE EMBANKMENT

A scene at Westminster during the disastrous floods which occurred in the early days of January, 1928, when a heavy inrush of water from the North Sea was met by a huge volume of water pouring down the river. The Thames burst its banks in a number of places, drowning fourteen people.

London is situated on a plain two to three miles wide and nowhere as much as 25 feet high. Large areas are less than five feet above, and a good deal of land on the Surrey side is actually below, high-tide level.

The bed of the river is large enough to discharge some 4,500 million gallons of water in twenty-four hours. If, owing to heavy rains, the flood is greater than this, it has to overflow its banks. In 1894, during one of the greatest floods within recent years, over 20,000 million gallons poured past Teddington in twenty-four hours, with disastrous results.

Tidal Bore Devastates London

A high spring tide coinciding with a full moon can cause trouble, but the most dreaded factor is a gale in the North Sea during a period of heavy rain.

Early in January, 1928, London found itself ringed with floods. Many miles of road in the Thames valley were under water, hundreds of houses and shops were isolated, great lakes covered the countryside; and day after day the level of the river rose alarmingly.

In the early hours of January 7 disaster rushed upon the sleeping city. A phenomenally high tide from the North Sea—believed to be the worst ever known—surged up the estuary, met the huge volume of flood water pouring down, and before any warning could be given the river had burst its banks in a dozen places.

Westminster suffered worst. Two huge breaches were made in the embankment between Lambeth Bridge and Vauxhall Bridge, and the water poured in a devastating stream into the streets behind Grosvenor Road. Hundreds of basement homes were wrecked, and ten people, including four children, were actually trapped in basements and drowned.

Lives were lost also at Putney and Hammersmith. Desolation and ruin spread from Kew to the river mouth. The basement of the Tate Gallery, full of valuable pictures, was flooded up to the lintels of the doors. The subways under Westminster Bridge Road poured into New Palace Yard huge streams of flood water which penetrated to the vaults of the Houses of Parliament.

That part of Southwark where once stood Shakespeare's Globe Theatre suffered severely, and the basement of the old Lollard's Tower at Lambeth Palace was filled with water. Pitiful scenes were witnessed near Messrs. Doulton's Pottery Works in Lambeth; the old High Street was swept by the flood, and many poor people had to watch all their household possessions carried away by the swirling waters.

Dark Days in London Still

After this appalling disaster stringent precautions were taken to prevent a recurrence. The embankment was strengthened in many places, and the police have now a standing order to watch and report upon the height of the tides during any time of heavy continual rain.

Yet in spite of every precaution, the Thames remains a menace in times of winter floods.

"THE THAMES IS RISING"

The police patrolling the river bank have a standing order to watch the flow in rainy weather. Waves lash against the parapet at Millbank as the Thames rises towards the level of the busy thoroughfare.

ST. PAUL'S FROM THE AIR

The beautiful proportions of the great cathedral and the vast size of the dome are strikingly revealed from the air. The building of it, from foundation stone to ball and cross, took only thirty-seven years.

ST. PAUL'S—OLD AND NEW

WREN, working among the ruins of old St. Paul's, asked for a stone to mark the spot on the ground over which the centre of the dome of the new Cathedral would be. A workman brought him a fragment of a gravestone upon which was carved the single word *Resurgam*—" I shall rise again."

The incident meant nothing to the workman, but it meant a great deal to Wren. It is commemorated in the carving of a Phœnix which adorns the south door of the Cathedral. Phœnix-like, St. Paul's perished in the flames only to rise again. Yet another curious coincidence : the proceeds of a tax on coal—which is the food of fire—largely enabled Wren to bring the new St. Paul's to birth. It differs from all other cathedrals in that the money used to build it was mainly derived from taxation and not from the voluntary offerings of the pious.

The present building is the third Christian place of worship to occupy the same site at the top of Ludgate Hill, and some antiquaries are of the opinion that the first Christian church there replaced a much earlier pagan temple in which offerings were made to a Roman deity. This tradition that the site of St. Paul's Cathedral was once occupied by a temple to Diana is very ancient, but it was given fresh life by the distinguished Elizabethan antiquary, William Camden, who relates that an enormous quantity of stag-horns, boars' tusks and ox-skulls, as well as a number of sacrificial vessels, was dug up there in the reign of Edward III. Diana was the goddess of the hunt and the stag was frequently sacrificed to her.

John Selden confirms the tradition, even going the length of asserting that the name London was derived from the Welsh *Llan-den*, meaning temple of Diana. Sir William Dugdale, who outlived both the authorities cited, proved to his own satisfaction that in the early years of the fourth century, the Romans destroyed a Christian church which stood on Ludgate Hill and erected a temple to Diana on its ruins; and one of his contemporaries, Dr. Woodward, found a votive image of the goddess between St. Paul's Deanery and Blackfriars.

Some historians even allege that Diana worship was taken up by Christian priests, and that in very early times it was customary for them to carry a stag's head on a spear round St. Paul's, to the sound of horns. Sir Christopher Wren was inclined to ridicule the theories of these eminent antiquaries, but after his death a stone altar with an image of Diana was unearthed in Foster Lane, Cheapside.

How St. Paul's Got Its Name

The earliest church of St. Paul, Ludgate Hill, of which we have any definite knowledge, was that built in the seventh century by Ethelbert, King of Kent. It is also recorded that Mellitus, Bishop of London, preached in this place of worship. It was called St. Paul's because a legend existed that the great apostle visited England in the time of Boudicca.

William the Conqueror seems to have had a peculiar affection for St. Paul's, since he freed it from all services to the Crown; but in the last year of his reign (1087) it was burnt almost to the ground. The work of reconstruction was begun by Bishop Maurice and continued by his successor; but once again, in the unhappy reign of Stephen, fire attacked the church and partially destroyed it.

OLD ST. PAUL'S
Completed in the middle of the thirteenth century, it was the longest Christian church in the world.

The first Deanery was built about 1200 by Radulph de Diceto, himself a Dean. Later inhabited by John Colet, the founder of St. Paul's School, and the poet John Donne before it was destroyed in the Great Fire.

This church, which is always known as Old St. Paul's, was not finally completed until the middle of the thirteenth century. It was 586 feet long, the longest Christian church in the world, and the spire reached the amazing height of 489 feet, thereby creating a record in another direction. Salisbury Cathedral now boasts the tallest spire in England.

An extraordinary collection of holy relics, real or alleged, was housed in the Cathedral during the Middle Ages. Among them were the arms of Mellitus, the body of St. Erkenwald, a knife that had belonged to Christ, a lock of Mary Magdalene's hair, pieces of Thomas Becket's skull, and the head of King Ethelbert. These relics, which were said to have miraculous properties, afforded a considerable source of income for the numerous priests who attended to collect monetary offerings from pilgrims.

In the churchyard stood the Pulpit Cross at which, in the words of Dr. Sparrow Simpson, " folk-motes were gathered together, Bulls and Papal edicts were read, heretics were denounced, heresies abjured, excommunications published, great political changes made known to the people, penances performed." Built in 1191, but destroyed by an earthquake in 1382, it was re-erected by Bishop Kemp in 1449, and remained in position until 1643, when it was demolished by order of the Long Parliament. A memorial of St. Paul's Cross, designed by Sir Reginald Blomfield, was erected on its site in 1910.

The nave, which was always known as Paul's Walk, was used as a common thoroughfare and as a market-place. Bishop Corbet speaks of:

" The Walk
Where all our British sinners Swear and Talk,
Old hardy ruffians, bankrupts, soothsayers,
And youths whose cousenage (roguery) is old as Theirs."

A curious regulation provided that anyone who entered the Cathedral with spurs on had to pay a fee to the choristers, who were frequently to be seen in Paul's Walk waiting for an opportunity to demand their just due.

Fighting Forbidden in Cathedral

In 1553 the Common Council of London found it necessary to pass an Act forbidding the leading of horses and mules through the Cathedral, and Queen Elizabeth issued a proclamation forbidding fighting or the drawing of swords in the sacred building. Neither Act nor proclamation had much effect on the citizens. The walls of the church were covered with advertisements and its interior was a hiring-place for servants of all kinds. Street-women, thieves and cut-throats made the aisles their meeting-place.

ST. PAUL'S CROSS
The most notable gathering place in medieval London, it was removed in the seventeenth century.

In a book published in 1628, Bishop Earle lashes out in no uncertain language on this disgraceful state of affairs. " Paul's Walk is the land's epitome, or you may call it the lesser isle of Great Britain," he says. " The noise in it is like that of Bees . . . a kind of still roar. . . . It is the great exchange of all discourse, and no business whatsoever but is here stirring and afoot. . . . It is the general mint of all famous lies. . . . It is the thieves' sanctuary, who rob more safely in the crowd than a wilderness, whilst every searcher is a bush to hide them. It is the other expense of the day, after plays, tavern, and a bawdy-house; and men have still some oaths left to swear here."

Spire Bursts Into Flames

The third act of Ben Jonson's play *Every Man In His Humour*, is laid in the Cathedral, while Shakespeare makes Falstaff hire Bardolph there.

In 1561 an event occurred which many regarded as a judgment of God on the lack of piety displayed by Londoners. St. Martin's Church, Ludgate, was struck by lightning, and soon afterwards the great wooden spire of St. Paul's burst into flames. The spire was completely destroyed in four hours, and then the roof collapsed. Steps were immediately taken to restore the latter, but no attempt was made to build a new spire.

Married on Cathedral Roof

Nearly seventy years later Sir Thomas Gardyner, Recorder of London, complained that one of his daughters had made a runaway marriage. Without his consent, the irate father lamented, she mounted to the top of the Cathedral, " the nearer to Heaven, for to shewe God there howe wise shee was in her Actions, and there shee married unto Sir Henry Maynwaringe, and yet shee was not there taken upp

ON SITE OF ST. PAUL'S CROSS
The column erected in 1910 on the site of St. Paul's Cross. Designed by Sir Reginald Blomfield.

into Heaven, but came down againe upon Earth, here further to trouble mee before I die, although the greater Care and Charge I had in breedinge her upp did not deserve such disobedience."

Soon after his accession, James I attempted to coerce the Bishop and Chapter into undertaking the complete restoration of the church, but he met with no success. Then he appointed a commission, of which Inigo Jones, the famous architect who designed the Palace of Whitehall, was a member, to inquire into various questions concerning its reconstruction. The commissioners reported that the sum of £22,536 would be required, and a quantity of material was secured. George Villiers, Duke of Buckingham, who was at that time building himself a palace off the Strand, later on appropriated the stone. Some of it he used to build the water-gate which can still be seen in the Embankment Gardens.

Charles I's interest in St. Paul's was rather more practical than that of his father. When Inigo Jones submitted his design for the new portico, the King promised to pay for it himself. To make the approach to it more imposing many of the houses round the west front were demolished, while St. Gregory's Church, which was at the south-west wing, was removed. The fines obtained in the infamous High Commission Court, which inquired into heresy and other ecclesiastical offences, were set aside for the work, which included the erection of a new spire. When completed, the new portico, which was 162 feet high, lent to the whole edifice an imposing but somewhat incongruous aspect.

Choir Becomes Cavalry Barracks

Cromwell's seizure of power put an end to all hope for a reconstructed St. Paul's. Parliament confiscated £17,000 that had been raised for the work and proceeded to rob the Cathedral of any valuable metals it contained. The choir was turned into a cavalry barrack and the rooms above the portico were let to hucksters.

Three years after the Restoration, when the Dean and Chapter engaged Sir Christopher Wren to make a survey of the Cathedral, he reported that the pillars threatened to collapse and that the tower was leaning. He was of the opinion that it would be necessary to remodel practically the whole of it.

Hardly had he presented his report before the Great Fire broke out. It began on Sunday, September 2, 1666. Evelyn tells us that on the Monday the scaffolding round St. Paul's was on fire, on Tuesday melted lead from the roof ran in streams down Ludgate Hill, "the very pavements flowing with fiery rednesse, so that no horse nor man was able to tread on them," and that by Friday the whole edifice had been almost completely destroyed.

Wren's Rejected Design

Dean Sancroft immediately decided that the only possible course was to clear away the ruins and build a new cathedral, though as late as 1670 the Chapter still entertained hopes of rebuilding old St. Paul's. Charles II favoured a completely new structure, but he wanted the Frenchman, Claude Perrault, designer of the east front and colonnades of the Louvre, to be the architect, having apparently lost faith in the abilities of Wren. The Dean preferred Wren, whom in 1668 he asked to prepare a design for a new St. Paul's. Although this first design—or, rather, second, for Wren originally planned quite a small building—was approved by Charles and apparently highly thought of by the architect himself, it was not accepted.

It was in the form of a Greek cross—i.e., a

ST. PAUL'S IN FLAMES
It took five days to consume the mighty edifice which for so long had been the glory of London.

THE PARISH CHURCH OF THE EMPIRE

St. Paul's Cathedral from Ludgate Hill. Built by Sir Christopher Wren between 1675 and 1710, it has an exterior length of 515 feet and a width across the transepts of 250 feet. The height from the pavement of the church to the top of the cross is 365 feet. The diameter of the drum beneath the dome is 112 feet.

cross with four equal arms—surmounted by a massive dome. The design was rejected by the committee because they considered that it departed " too far from the Gothic."

Building for Eternity

After drawing up many other plans, the great architect finally succeeded in producing one which satisfied all concerned, but he was careful to obtain the King's permission to make any modifications he might think desirable as the work of building proceeded. Of this permission he availed himself freely during the following years, and the St. Paul's that we know differs in many important respects from that of the design originally approved. Wren himself laid the first stone of the new cathedral on June 21, 1675, several years having been spent preparing the site.

Wren at first used gunpowder to demolish the ruined walls of the old edifice, but an accident caused by an explosion having given rise to anxiety in the minds of the authorities, he abandoned it in favour of the old Roman battering-ram, which proved entirely successful.

The architect was not content to use any part of the old building, having determined to "build for eternity," and he spent much time in ensuring that the new foundations should be as firm as human ingenuity could make them.

The work proceeded so rapidly that the choir was opened for divine service on December 2, 1697, a day of thanksgiving for the Peace of Ryswick, by which France had agreed to recognise the results of the English Revolution of 1688. William III did not attend the service for fear that there might be armed Jacobites among the 300,000 people who were expected to line the streets.

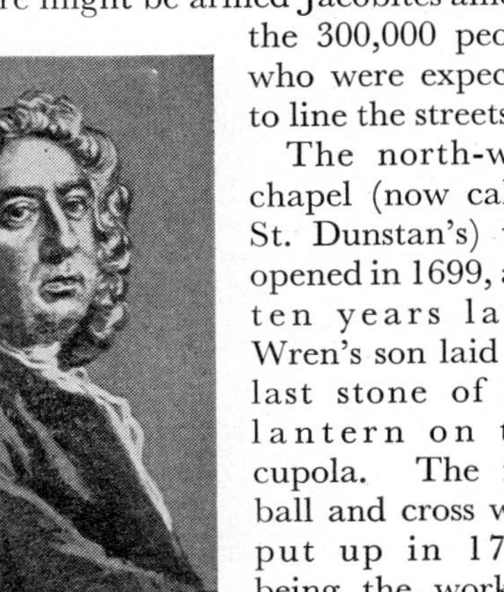

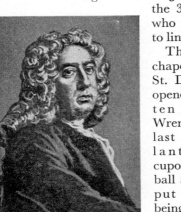

SIR JAMES THORNHILL
Painted the interior dome of the Cathedral for Wren.

The north-west chapel (now called St. Dunstan's) was opened in 1699, and ten years later Wren's son laid the last stone of the lantern on the cupola. The first ball and cross were put up in 1712, being the work of Andrew Niblett.

Thus, only forty-six years after old St. Paul's had perished in the flames of the Great Fire, a magnificent new building had arisen in its stead. The amazing achievements of the great architectural genius did not receive the acclamation they deserved. The critical and ungenerous spirit displayed by the Committee by whom his actions were controlled increased rather than diminished as the work proceeded. The men who served on it seemed determined to obstruct him in every possible way, even going to the length of forcing him against his better judgment to fall in with their ideas on technical details.

SIR CHRISTOPHER WREN
Born 1632. Mathematician, astronomer, architect. Designed St. Paul's and over fifty other churches.

Wren's Salary Withheld

The balustrade which surmounts the outside walls was entirely the Committee's idea, Wren opposing it vehemently. He also disapproved of the placing of the organ above the choir screen (removed in 1858), and to the erection round the churchyard of heavy iron railings, which were cast at Lamberhurst in Sussex when that county was famous for its smelting industry. Accusing Wren of corruption and of wilfully delaying the completion of the work, the Committee induced Parliament to grant them powers to withhold half of his salary of less than £4 a week until the task should be finished. It should be

MURAL DECORATIONS BY THORNHILL

n 1936 a complete cleaning and redecoration of the interior of St. Paul's was finished after five years' vork. The last task was the restoration of the dramatic but sombre Thornhill murals in the dome.

ıdded that money was then several times its ›resent value.

Court Favourite Given Wren's Post

They did not stop even at that point. In 718, when Wren was in his eighty-sixth year, ıaving held his post from the age of thirty-even, he was suddenly dismissed. His suc-essor was William Benson, whose only claim o such an honour rested on the fact that he vas a favourite at the Court of the Hanoverian King George I, who was suspicious of a man ike Wren who had received his office at the ıands of a Stuart.

Wren was by then too accustomed to "the lings and arrows of outrageous fortune" to e greatly perturbed, so he quietly retired to is house at Hampton Court, where he gave imself up to the study of philosophy. He assed away in 1723, at the age of ninety-one, "as well pleased to die in the shade as in the light." His was the first grave to be sunk in the new St. Paul's, but it was not marked by a conventional monument. The last words of his brief epitaph are, *Si Monumentum Requiris Circumspice* (If you seek his monument look around you).

Built on Coal and Wine

When the decision to rebuild St. Paul's was first arrived at, Charles II promised to contribute £1,000 a year towards the expenses, but there is no reason to suppose that he kept his promise. After the Great Fire a tax was imposed on all coal and wine entering the port of London, the proceeds being devoted to the reconstruction of the devastated areas of the City. St. Paul's had a handsome share of this tax—about £810,000—but, as has been wittily remarked, the coal had its revenge by defiling the stonework of the Cathedral. In addition to the money received from taxation, about £130,000 was subscribed by private individuals, so that the total cost may be put at about £1,000,000—a really enormous sum in the currency of those days.

Belated Decoration of Interior

It was Wren's desire that the dome should be lined with mosaics, but whether he had any other definite plans for the decoration of the interior is not known. During his lifetime the dome was painted by Sir James Thornhill, who was paid at the rate of 40s. per square yard, but it was not until one hundred and fifty years after Wren's death that any further decoration was attempted. In 1872 a thanksgiving service in the Cathedral for the recovery of the Prince of Wales (afterwards Edward VII) from a dangerous illness was associated with a fund for the decoration of the severely plain interior which had been started by Dean Milman. Public interest having been aroused, designs for mosaics in the spandrels beneath the dome were accepted, and in 1892 Sir William Richmond began the work.

Among the craftsmen who assisted Wren three at least will be remembered as long as the Cathedral stands. They are Grinling Gibbons, the wood-carver, whose most beautiful work may be seen in the stalls of the choir; Jean Tijou, a French iron-worker, who wrought so many of the exquisite gates and grilles; and Thomas Strong, the master-mason, who was constantly at work from the time of the laying of the foundation stone till the laying of the top-stone of the lantern. There were also Caius Gabriel Cibber, who carved the Phœnix over the South Door; Jonathan Maine, who assisted Gibbons with the wood-carving; and Francis Bird, who carved the Conversion of St. Paul in the Western tympanum.

The suggestion that monuments should be placed in St. Paul's was at first vigorously opposed by the Cathedral clergy, which accounts for the fact that the earliest statue admitted was that of John Howard, the prison reformer, who died in 1790. His statue faces that of Dr Johnson.

In the crypt rest the mortal remains of Nelson, Wellington, Roberts, Reynolds, Millais Sir Arthur Sullivan and many another whom the world deems great.

Painted in a Shroud

At its west end may be seen the six-wheeled funeral car upon which the body of the victor of Waterloo was brought to the church. It weighs eighteen tons and was made from melted-down cannon captured during the Napoleonic Wars. The names of the engagements in which the general distinguished himsel

THE WHISPERING GALLERY IN ST. PAUL'S
Below the dome, this gallery has the remarkable property of rendering the slightest whisper audible It is the only place from which the Thornhill murals, which are just above it, can be seen to advantage

are given on the sides. Nelson's sarcophagus was designed for Cardinal Wolsey. Recent additions to the busts in the crypt are those of George Washington and Colonel T. E. Lawrence (" Lawrence of Arabia "), whose exploits on the Palestine front during the First World War had become almost legendary by the time of his tragic death in 1935. His grave is not in the Cathedral.

The only complete monument which survived the Great Fire is that of John Donne, whose fame is based rather on his poetical works than on his having been Dean of St. Paul's.

A week or two before Donne died in 1631, he had himself wrapped in his winding sheet, with his eyes shut and his hands crossed like those of the dead. In this posture he was sketched, a sketch from which his marble monument was subsequently carved.

Spoiled Picture to Save Life

The true majesty of the great dome can be appreciated only from the vantage-point of the Whispering Gallery, and it is not possible from any other point except this to examine in detail Sir James Thornhill's paintings. There, one remembers the story of how Thornhill had a narrow escape from sudden death when he was working on a scaffolding scores of feet above the floor. Having put the finishing touches to the head of one of the apostles, he walked backwards so that he could see it in proper perspective. A friend who was with him, suddenly noticing that the artist's heel was suspended over the edge of the unrailed platform, snatched up a brush and daubed some paint on the face. Thornhill immediately rushed forward to save his painting exclaiming : " Bless my soul, what have you done?" " I have only saved your life!" his friend replied.

Having been initiated into the mysterious acoustic properties of the Whispering Gallery, which enable a softly spoken word to travel the complete circumference, the visitor will go out to the Stone Gallery, from which an amazing view of London can be seen. The roof and towers of the Cathedral can also be studied from this point. The southern tower contains the bell, known as Great Tom, which is used to broadcast time-signals when Big Ben is not working. Originally cast in the reign of Edward I, its first home was Westminster Hall. It is always tolled on the death of the Archbishop of Canterbury, the Bishop of London, the Dean, the Lord Mayor or in mourning for the death of a member of the Royal Family.

LAWRENCE OF ARABIA

The memorial bust in the crypt of St. Paul's to a great but unconventional hero of the First World War.

Beneath Great Tom is Great Paul, weighing seventeen and a half tons, which is tolled for five minutes every day at one o'clock. It took two traction engines a week to haul it to London. The peal of twelve bells in the north-west tower is considered the finest in England.

The Construction of the Dome

To reach the Golden Gallery which surrounds the outer base of the lantern, one ascends an iron staircase which is upheld by the timbers between the lead-covered dome visible from the streets and the hidden brick cone which supports both the outer dome and the lantern. The inner dome, or cupola, which one sees from the Whispering Gallery, is inside the brick cone. The weight of the dome is 67,270 tons. The dome was originally ordered to be covered with copper, but no competent coppersmith was available.

Above the lantern there is a little room called the Ball Room, through a hole in the floor of which one can gaze down, from a height of 300 feet, on the ant-like figures which move about on the floor beneath the dome. This view gives an awe-inspiring impression of the vast dimensions of the Cathedral.

The ascent from the Ball Room to the Ball itself is made by means of iron ladders, the last of which stands perpendicularly in a cylindrical space which is barely wide enough to take the body. Standing on the top rungs of the ladder, one gazes through wire-netting and the supports of the gilded ball at the City with its pall of smoke and the Thames winding its way like a snake past warehouses and under bridges. The top of the cross is 365 feet above the pavement.

Artist Who Lived Above Dome

The present ball was erected in 1821 when the original one became unsafe. The task of removing the first ball presented many difficulties, since it was fastened by immense copper bolts. After it had been lowered, it was rolled down Ludgate Hill, past hundreds of amused spectators, to the offices of the brass-founder who was making the new ball.

Before these operations were begun, one Thomas Horner had taken up quarters in the lantern for the purpose of making the drawings which enabled him to paint the famous Panorama of London which he displayed to the public in the Coliseum in Regent's Park in 1829. As soon as the authorities decided to remove the ball and cross, Horner obtained permission to erect a platform, several feet higher than the cross, and upon this he built an observatory, so that he might obtain a better view of the City. He worked up there all through the summer, starting at three o'clock in the morning before London had had time to clothe itself in its mantle of smoke. It was a bad summer and the observatory was often buffeted by gales which threatened to tear it from its scaffolding and send it flying over the roofs of the city.

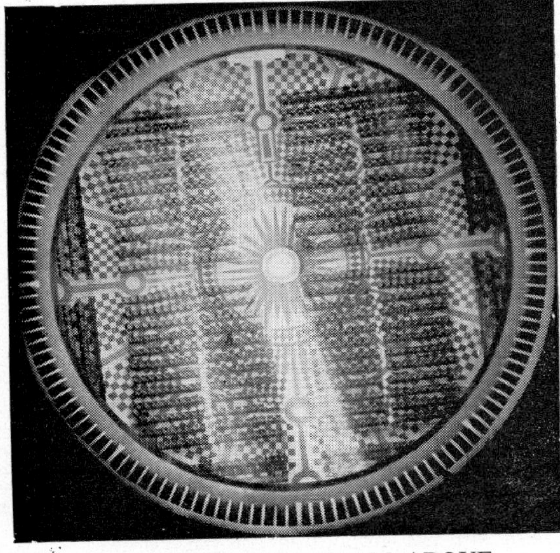

THE NAVE SEEN FROM ABOVE
View from the porthole in the Ball Room. The centre of the compass marks Lord Nelson's grave.

In describing "a squall more than usually severe," Horner says, "a great part of the circular framework erected above the gallery for the prevention of accidents was carried over the housetops to a considerable distance. At this moment a similar fate had nearly befallen the observatory, which was torn from its fastenings, turned partly over the edge of the platform, and its various contents thrown into utter confusion."

He passed the night in his observatory on one occasion, but so intense was the cold that he never repeated the experiment.

In his account of his work, Horner mentions the case of John Gwynne, the architect, who lost his foothold while engaged in measuring the dome. Fortunately, his fall was checked by a projecting piece of lead, and one of his assistants, who quickly discovered what had happened, rescued him.

The title of Cardinal is usually associated with the Roman Catholic Church, but the College of Minor Canons of St. Paul's annually elects a Custos or Warden, and those next to him in dignity are known as the Senior Cardinal and the Junior Cardinal respectively. The Pittanciary, who was once responsible for looking after the petty cash and conducting funerals, retains the title and continues to receive an annual fee of 3s. 4d.

Chapel Dedicated to Kitchener

In addition to the little Jesus Chapel in the apse behind the high altar and the St. Dunstan's Chapel already referred to, St. Paul's contains All Souls' Chapel, dedicated to the memory of Earl Kitchener, and the Chapel of the Order of St. Michael and St. George. This Order was instituted in 1818 by the Prince Regent, later George IV, to commemorate the placing of the Ionian Islands under the protection of Great Britain. Its members were originally limited to natives of the Ionian Islands and of Malta and British subjects holding high and confidential positions in the Mediterranean. The magnificent carving took twenty-five years to complete. A very human touch is afforded by the cherubs' heads on the reredos. The models were the children o

HORNER'S OBSERVATORY
Erected by the Corps of Royal Sappers and Miners to enable Horner to paint a panorama of London.

a British officer killed on Armistice Day, 1918. The altar in the Chapel of St. Christopher in the crypt is that erected by Wren in the choir before the present and more elaborate altar and reredos were placed in position.

St. Paul's in Danger

Like most cathedrals, St. Paul's has had structural troubles which none could foresee. Wren placed his great dome on four bastions and eight piers, the main weight falling on the latter. Unfortunately the piers were not built of solid material but of rubble encased in Portland stone only a few inches thick. For the most part their interiors were the sepulchre of odd bits and pieces of the old building mixed with mortar, and with the passing of time this filling tended to crumble and the piers to sink. Not one of the supports was other than out of the straight. In 1925 the pride of the City was designated a "dangerous structure," although steps had been taken for its preservation twelve years before and were still continuing.

Holes were drilled in the piers, bars of rustless steel were inserted, and liquid cement was introduced under pressure so as to make the interiors as solid as possible. As many of the old ones were found to be broken, new tie-bars and wall-plates, carefully hidden, were applied to connect the piers to the bastions. Cracks being discovered between the outer and inner drums or double circular walls which take the outward thrust of the brick cone on which the lantern stands, the inner dome and the lead-covered external dome had to be braced with steel bars and remedied in other ingenious ways. A mighty chain with links 15 feet in length and weighing 30 tons was placed round the outer drum. The task was difficult and lasted for five years; the cost was about £400,000. Wealthy and poor alike came to the rescue. Many thousands of pounds were contributed in pence by folk in humble circumstances.

Built on Sand and Water

Although the foundations of St. Paul's support a weight of nearly 270,000 tons they are only $4\frac{1}{2}$ feet deep. Below them is 6 feet of earth, and beneath that a bed of sand some 20 feet deep which is kept wet by springs. If the water were drained the Cathedral would almost certainly crash. That is why the Dean and Chapter view with disfavour any suggestions for building operations in the vicinity, for it would be only too easy, in excavating for foundations, accidently to drain away the running water which sustains St. Paul's. The Cathedral has no spacious Close like Salisbury, but it has a garden of its own, which is kept up by the Corporation of the City. It lies to the east of the Cathedral and contains a considerable variety of plants and shrubs, as well as some fine plane trees. Until 1874 St. Paul's had a far more imposing space in front of the West doors. In that year the Corporation of London paid £15,000 for part of the ground to improve the roadway. The statue of Queen Anne which stands in front of the steps is a replica. The original was removed in 1893 because it was somewhat worn, and is now at Holmhurst, near Hastings, Sussex.

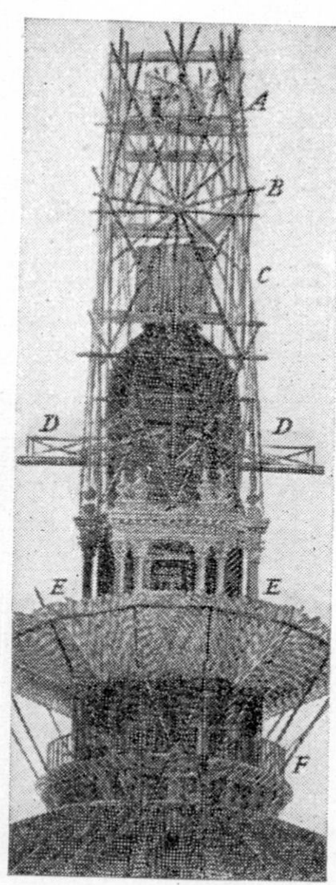

HOW IT LOOKED
A. — Hut. B. — Cross. C.—Ball. D.—Platform. E.—Net. F.—Gallery.

St. Paul's has been well named the Parish Church of the Empire. For long it has been the custom on occasions of Empire-wide thanksgiving or mourning for the greatest of the land to meet in solemn service in the Cathedral on Ludgate Hill.

Elizabeth went there to give thanks for the destruction of the Spanish Armada.

Thanks for victory in battle, prayers for aid in war, have ascended through the centuries to its noble dome. Particularly impressive were the funerals of Nelson and Wellington, Britain's greatest sailor hero and soldier duke.

Queen Victoria's Diamond Jubilee

Another memorable service marked Queen Victoria's Diamond Jubilee. A guard of honour composed of soldiers from every corner of the Empire was drawn up to receive her in the churchyard. Thunderous cheers had greeted her all along the route from Buckingham Palace to Ludgate Hill, but as she arrived at the steps of the Cathedral a great hush seemed to fall over the whole of London.

Then massed choirs sang the *Te Deum* and the Bishop of London uttered the special Thanksgiving Prayer. The short service ended with the pronouncement of the Benediction by the Archbishop of Canterbury, and then an extraordinary thing happened.

The colossal crowds in the churchyard and the streets north, south, east and west of the Cathedral suddenly, by one consent, took up the strains of the National Anthem. It seemed to those that heard it that the whole city was united in singing. When the deafening notes had died away the Archbishop stepped forward and called for three cheers for Her Majesty.

Queen Victoria's son was to have been crowned in Westminster Abbey on June 26, 1902, but at the last moment it was announced that the King was seriously ill and the ceremony would have to be postponed. At the hour at which the coronation was to have taken place, a service described "as an act of humble supplication to Almighty God for His Majesty King Edward VII in his sickness" was held at St. Paul's.

Some years later, on February 15, 1913, a vast congregation assembled in St. Paul's to mourn the sad fate of Captain R. F. Scott and his gallant companions, who perished on their way back from the South Pole. The King, the Prime Minister, and representatives of foreign states were present at the service.

National Thanksgiving

King George V attended national thanksgiving services in St. Paul's on no less than four occasions during his reign. Two such services were held in 1918; one in June, to celebrate their Majesties' silver wedding, and another in November in joyful thanksgiving for the Armistice and for victory.

His son, King George VI, ordered several days of prayer during the crisis of the Second World War; and he himself, with Mr. Churchill and his Ministers, attended the services held at St. Paul's on these occasions.

During these fateful years the Cathedral had its own crises; they are dealt with later in the outline of events of the war years.

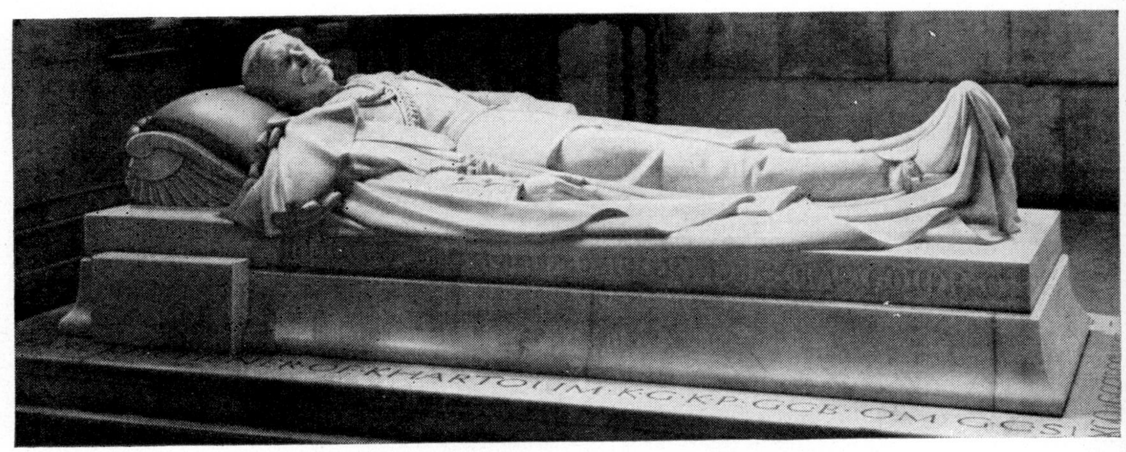

KITCHENER MEMORIAL IN ST. PAUL'S

All Souls' Chapel is dedicated to Kitchener of Khartoum. The effigy is by Sir William Reid Dick, R.A.

TRAFFIC JAM AT LUDGATE CIRCUS

'he congestion of London's streets is no new development due to the spread of motor transport. t has been a source of complaint for hundreds of years. A nineteenth-century scene of chaos.

TO AND FRO IN THE CITY

THE traffic jam is no new development in London. Throughout history it has been one of the City's major problems. Lon-loners of Elizabethan days complained bitterly f the congestion of their streets. No doubt heir ancestors complained with equal virulence. ondoners of to-day are still complaining. The roblem is yet unsolved. It grows rather than lecreases in intensity.

In the Middle Ages the citizens of London acked their confined area with buildings till t literally could hold no more. They econo-nised space by reducing the width of their treets until these were no more than alley-ways. Then they turned them into tunnels by piling verhanging upper storeys on their houses, nd finally they pressed economy to its utmost imits by making the tunnels serve the dual ourpose of highways and sewers, with the results hat stagger modern minds. There is record f one street in Plantagenet times being so eaped with garbage that it could be neither valked nor ridden through.

The confused network of sunless and filth-logged alleys which served medieval London as streets swarmed perpetually with men and animals. Of carts there were in early days but few, for the roads outside the City were quag-mires in winter and dust heaps in summer, while within the walls there were few thoroughfares wide enough to admit wheeled traffic. But pack-horses there were in plenty; and all the pageantry of medieval wayfaring.

Along one narrow lane rides a company of knights in gleaming armour; down another goes a great lord, for whose passing a way is cleared by his army of liveried retainers. Round a corner comes a company of pious pilgrlms, a confused and ambling medley of men and women, beasts and baggage; from out a church door emerges a procession of chanting priests. Porters stagger under burdens; housewives with their shopping baskets hurry home from the markets; servants run to fill their buckets at the public pump; stray dogs scratch in dung-heaps, and roaming pigs nuzzle in the gutters.

And all the while, along the side of every street the busy merchants range their wares, before which strut the 'prentices from dawn to dusk, deafening everyone with their chant of

CHAIR OF QUALITY
Scene from *The Rake's Progress* by Hogarth shows the sedan chair, popular for nearly two centuries.

" Buy! Buy! What d'ye lack? What d'ye lack? " Thronged as in an Oriental bazaar, the streets of medieval London were quite inadequate to meet the City's traffic needs. There remained the Thames to ease the strain.

Thames Alive with Boats

There was a time when boats and barges floated into London down that long-since buried stream, the Fleet. In Roman days sea-going vessels anchored in the Walbrook. Medieval London used its rivers as it did its streets—as dustbins and common sewers; the mouth of the Walbrook was so choked and the course of the Fleet so blocked with ordure that navigation on their waters early ceased.

Of the City streams the Thames alone defied all efforts to impede its flow; it became, and remained until quite modern times, London's leading highway. For hundreds of years its ample flood was alive with boats; by Shakespearean days the river traffic had grown to enormous proportions.

" After the players began to play on the Bankside," we read, " and to leave playing in London and Middlesex, for the most part, then there went such great concourse of people by water . . . that the number of watermen, and those that live and are maintained by them and by the only labour of the oar and the scull, betwixt the bridge of Windsor and Gravesend, cannot be fewer than forty thousand." Yet the total population of London at that time was only about 140,000.

Watermen Were Not Popular

Vital though the watermen were to London's well-being, they were far from popular, for though their fares were regulated by law, they never missed an opportunity to overcharge and many and bitter were the complaints raised against them.

No doubt many honest citizens rejoiced when, at the very height of their prosperity the watermen found their monopoly challenged. There is some dispute as to the exact date when coaches were introduced into the city but it is quite certain that the great struggle between land and water transport began during the second half of the sixteenth century.

By that time the main London thoroughfares had been considerably improved, though the lanes were as narrow and noisome as ever. Streets had been widened, paving with stone had begun in the fifteenth century, and the gutters had been moved from the centre to the sides of the roadway. Yet the pioneers who rode in the first coaches must have been adventurous and hardy souls, for the springless waggons (they were little more) must have jolted and bumped in cruel fashion over the ill-repaired and garbage-laden streets.

Besides coaches, other wheeled traffic had invaded London. The City had to be fed, and by no means all the food could come by water; so in spite of crippling turnpike tolls the farmers of Marylebone, Highgate, Hampstead, Stepney and other neighbouring villages daily drove their waggons within the walls.

The supplies they brought were welcome enough, but not the vehicles. Among the " enormities " of his day, " no less meet to be reformed," John Stow notes in 1598 that " the number of cars, drays, carts, and coaches, more than hath been accustomed, the streets and lanes being straitened, must be dangerous, as daily experience proveth."

In the year 1625 a certain Captain Bailey gave London its first vehicles for public hire. He posted four hackney coaches at the Maypole in the Strand (where now stands St

Mary's Church), with instructions to his drivers that they were to convey passengers to any part of the City. He charged by the hour —1s. 6d. the first hour, 1s. an hour afterwards.

The idea caught on. Other proprietors set up in the hackney coach line. By 1637 there were fifty of these vehicles on the London streets; by 1659 six times that number. Meanwhile the stage coach had been invented, and by 1663 was providing services from London to all parts of England and as far north as Edinburgh.

Great, clumsy, lumbering contrivances these coaches were. The first was a wagon, its successors slow, springless and uncomfortable. Even the hackneys had no windows for over thirty years, but perforated metal shutters.

The new forms of transport met with considerable opposition. " Whereas," states a royal decree of 1634, " the streets of our cities of London and Westminster, and their suburbs, are of late so much encumbered with the unnecessary multitude of coaches that many of our subjects are thereby exposed to great danger, and the necessary use of carts and carriages for provisions thereby much hindered; and Sir Saunders Duncombe's petition, representing that in many parts beyond sea people are much carried in chairs that are covered, whereby few coaches are used among them; wherefore we have granted to him the sole privilege to use, let or hire a number of the said covered chairs for fourteen years."

Duncombe's " Covered Chair "

Thus came to London the sedan chair, perhaps the most picturesque vehicle Britain has ever seen. It captured the heart of the " quality," and for nearly 200 years the fashionable world of the metropolis was carried to its routs and its balls and its banquets in the " covered chair " introduced by Sir Saunders Duncombe.

Yet it never ousted the hackney, and obviously it could not compete with the stage coach. How the latter vehicle ever survived its blundering and mishap-ridden youth is one of the mysteries of history, for it seems next to impossible to believe that anyone could welcome or even want to use a conveyance considered dashing if it averaged three miles an hour, and chronically liable to be bogged in the mud or overturned in the ditch.

It was not until the first half of the eighteenth century that popular indignation effected an improvement in the British roads, which till that time had been so indescribably bad as to strike terror into the heart of every traveller. There followed the golden age of the stage coach.

London became the national terminus. Numerous inns in the City rose to fame on the coaching trade. The amount of business some of them did was phenomenal. From the " George and Blue Boar " in Holborn, eighty-four coaches set out daily; from the " Old White Horse Cellar " in Piccadilly over fifty. Readers of Dickens will recall the names of the " Saracen's Head " on Snow Hill, the " Belle Sauvage " on Ludgate Hill, the " George " and the " White Hart " in the Borough.

London's Steam Coaches

From these and other inns set out " Short Stages " as well as long-distance coaches; four services daily were run from the " Old White Horse Cellar " to Richmond and Putney, and ten to Windsor and Eton. From other starting points in the City coaches ran to Hampstead, Ware, Enfield and St. Albans.

In town the hackney, though its numbers were limited by law, maintained an undiminished popularity. Better lighting and paving of the streets caused the decline of the sedan chair in the latter half of the eighteenth century, and by the early years of the nineteenth its long reign in the world of fashion was over.

SNUFFERS
Used by the link-boys who guided the sedans.

The modern story of London transport begins in the 1820s with a curious prologue. Between 1827 and 1836 the inhabitants of the City and its suburbs were hugely excited by the appearance on their roads of coaches propelled by steam.

In 1827 a Cornishman named Goldsworthy Gurney, inventor of the high-

TRAFFIC OF A BYGONE DAY

An early nineteenth-century picture of the Mansion House, showing typical traffic of the day; an omnibus —appropriately named *Civility*—a hansom cab, a private coach, a dray, a market porter and others.

pressure steam-jet which enabled George Stephenson's early locomotives to reach a higher speed, placed on the London to Bath service the *Royal Patriot*, a steam coach which ran at 15 miles an hour. In 1831, Walter Hancock began to operate a similar service between London and Stratford, and two years later he startled the metropolis with the *Enterprise*, a steam coach plying between Paddington and the City.

The Omnibus Comes to Town

In 1833 also August Maudsley began to run steam coaches between Lambeth and Croydon. His first vehicle created such a turmoil in the Croydon streets that his Majesty's judges were compelled to suspend the sitting of the assizes.

Hancock at least continued to maintain services by steam in and about London until 1836. His last coach, the *Automaton*, in October of that year ran from the City Road to Epping at an average speed of 11½ miles an hour, and entered the forest town " amidst the loud cheers of some thousands . . . and created much astonishment among many of the country folk, who had never seen such a vehicle before, and who could not imagine how it was moved without horses."

But Gurney, Maudsley and Hancock were in advance of their times. The steam coach disappeared from the London streets, and the advent of mechanical traction was postponed for another seventy years.

Meanwhile, the horse came into its own. On July 4, 1829, George Shillibeer appeared at the " Yorkshire Stingo," a licensed house on the Marylebone Road, with the *Omnibus*, " a handsome machine in the shape of a van," and " drawn by three beautiful bays abreast."

There are said to have been buses in the suburbs before this date, but to Shillibeer is generally given the credit of having introduced the omnibus to London. He was not its inventor; both the idea and the name are French, and it was in Paris that Shillibeer first learned to build omnibuses.

Learned His Trade in Long Acre

Yet London can claim at least part of the credit, for Shillibeer was a Londoner by birth, and had learned his trade in Long Acre—since the seventeenth century the headquarters of the coachbuilding industry—before setting up in business in the French metropolis.

His *Omnibus* " excited considerable notice, both from the novel form of the carriage and the elegance with which it is fitted out." With accommodation for from sixteen to eighteen passengers, all inside, it had a green body with yellow wheels, comfortable seats and—luxury of luxuries!—neat red curtains for its windows.

On the box sat Mr. Shillibeer, the driver, resplendent in a greatcoat of plum-coloured cloth, a rakish beaver hat and a green and blue cravat. To attract clients, collect fares, and in particular to give " every possible attention . . . to the accommodation of Ladies and Children," he had a conductor, " a person of great respectability," suitably attired in white trousers and a black jacket adorned with metal buttons.

New Standards of Courtesy

Shillibeer introduced not only a new type of public vehicle to London, but also new standards of courtesy and civility. The hackney coach drivers of the time were both rude and extortionate, and part—it may be much—of the success of the *Omnibus* was due to the fact that for the first time Londoners could travel about their streets cheaply, comfortably (according to the standards of 1829) and without being exposed to the indignity of gross insults and expletives from their conveyors.

Credit must be given to the first conductor, said to have been a " nautical friend " of Shillibeer's from France, for we read that he " captivated all the fair damsels of Paddington Green with his handsome figure and beautiful accent." To attract less impressionable clients, Shillibeer provided newspapers and books in his bus, but he was compelled later to withdraw this amenity because of the acquisitive habits of some of his patrons.

The *Omnibus* ran four times daily between Paddington and the Bank by way of the Marylebone Road, Somers Town, and the City Road. The fare from end to end was a shilling, from Paddington to Islington or Islington to the Bank sixpence.

Swift Growth of Bus Services

Shillibeer's service was an instant success, though unfortunately—like many pioneers—he made no fortune out of it. Within a short time there were many competitors on the road, and some idea of the swift growth of omnibus services may be gathered from traffic statistics collected in 1839. Of 5,515 wheeled vehicles which passed a given point in eighteen hours on

HANSOM CABS IN REGENT STREET

Hansom's " patent Safety Cab " was a profitable invention, for the inventor sold the design for £10,000. Originally the driver's seat was in front of the cab. Compare this picture with the one on page 362.

THE STRAND IN HORSE-BUS DAYS
How incredibly London has changed during the present century may be judged from this picture. The horse-bus is dead, landaus nearly extinct, and the Strand so much rebuilt it is here hardly recognisable.

Wednesday, January 16, about one in six were omnibuses.

The successors of George Shillibeer did not maintain his standard of courtesy. As the hosts of omnibus proprietors multiplied, a period of cut-throat competition ensued, during which, in their anxiety to secure custom, we are told that " Rival bus conductors sometimes left their vehicles when travelling at high speed, boarded a rival and fought on the step."

Colossal Profiteering Ramp

The climax of this era was reached in 1851, when the Great Exhibition was made by bus proprietors the occasion of a colossal profiteering ramp. Fares were everywhere raised, vehicles overcrowded, passengers carried on the roof (an illegal practice), while dozens of mushroom companies sprang into existence to make easy money by running only to and from Hyde Park.

In 1855 a move was made towards a coherent and comprehensive transport system for London. December of that year saw the birth of the Compagnie Générale des Omnibus de Londres, a French firm founded in Paris with a capital of 25,000,000 francs (£1,000,000) to buy up and amalgamate existing concerns.

" Keep the Frenchies Out ! "

The purpose of the Compagnie was at first misunderstood. It was thought to be competitive, and considerable hostility was organised against it. Its foreign origin was used to excite popular prejudice. " Keep the Frenchies out ! " shouted the bus drivers and conductors, while the proprietors placarded the City with posters protesting against the " foreign innovation."

When the Compagnie, which was in fact Anglo-French, five of its ten directors being

:nglish, made it clear that combination and not ompetition was its aim, and that the staffs of ll concerns taken over would be continued in ıeir posts, the opposition collapsed and malgamation proceeded rapidly and smoothly. Jevertheless, it was thought expedient two years ıter to re-register the Compagnie in London s the London General Omnibus Company.

Great Improvement in Services

The Compagnie set to work energetically. Within three months of its opening day," rote the *Illustrated London News* in April, 1856, " has so far extended its operations that it mploys fully 1,300 men and 5,000 horses." y the end of the summer it controlled 600 out f the 800 buses plying on the London streets.

The improvement in the services and ameni-es offered was immediate and marked. uses were made more comfortable, routes ere planned in organised fashion, and cheap ookings were introduced. The reproach of ıcivility was guarded against by the engage-ıent of ex-servicemen as conductors, so that,) quote the same journal again, " the unprotected female need be no longer a strong-minded individual to travel per bus; and even anxious parents will henceforth hazard their fond pledges of mutual affection without disagreeable associations connected with chimney sweeps or dealers in Norfolk sausages."

One thing the L.G.O.C. was unable to do—reduce the daily traffic jam on London's streets. To effect that reform involved the introduction of a form of transport not using the roads. In January, 1863, the first section of the Metropolitan Railway—from Paddington to Farringdon Street—was opened; it "brought instant and sensible relief to a most appalling street congestion."

World's First Underground Railway

There had been much opposition to the idea of an underground railway. People declared that the buildings along the route would be shaken from their foundations; that the passengers in the trains would be asphyxiated by noxious fumes, and that without a minimum interval of five minutes between trains there would be numerous and disastrous accidents.

LAST DAYS OF THE HORSE-BUS

xford Circus shortly before the First World War. One solitary horse-bus. A mass of motor transport. ıe motor-bus in the foreground is of the *Old Bill* type that did yeoman service in France between 1914 and 1918.

TROLLEY-BUS AND TRAM

This picture shows another stage in the evolution of London's transport. The last tram has now vanishe from the streets and even trolley-buses may soon give way to the more manœuvrable motor omnibuses

The promoters of the railway held to their project—though they were sufficiently intimidated by hostile criticism to promise a smokeless engine, which unfortunately no inventor was able to produce—and by having their way had the honour of giving London the first underground railway in the world.

Linking the Railway Termini

Strictly speaking, however, the Metropolitan is not a true underground railway. Civil engineering was not, in 1863, sufficiently advanced to bore a tube, and the Metropolitan was constructed on the "cut and cover" plan, that is, the line was laid in the floor of a deep cutting which was roofed over and covered to street level wherever road traffic rendered it necessary.

The idea behind the Metropolitan was to link the northern group of railway termini—Paddington, Euston, St. Pancras and King's Cross—with the City. Later, the eastern and southern main-line stations were included when the original section was extended to form what is to-day the Inner Circle of the Underground.

The tram was a very late comer to London but it is not only because the bus got ther first that trams were denied access to the hear of the metropolis. In fact, the L.G.O.C included a tram service between Notting Hi Gate and the Bank among its early schemes but the opposition was so hot that Parliamen refused its sanction.

In 1861 a tramway was actually laid dow along the Bayswater Road, but the projectin flanges of the rails proved dangerous to othe traffic, and the service was hardly begun befor it was abandoned. It was not until May, 187 that the Metropolitan Street Tramways Com pany and the North Metropolitan Tramway Company—in that order, but within a fe days of each other—began to run the firs permanent services.

Trams Not Admitted to City

From that start the tram spread north, sout east and west; but it never succeeded i penetrating more than the fringes of the Cit and Westminster. Streets in the former we too narrow, the buildings—or the inhabitan

—in the latter much too sacred. There was, it is true, one tramway through the heart of London, from the Embankment to Theobalds Road in Holborn; but it ran underground.

The years 1870 to 1885 saw no outstanding developments in London transport. During the 1880s a powerful competitor with the L.G.O.C. arose in the form of the London Road Car Company, which introduced the "garden seat" on the bus roof in place of the "knifeboard"—a fore and aft back-to-back seat invented to cope with the great Exhibition traffic—but otherwise these years formed a peaceful, if congested, prelude to a period of intense and far-reaching development.

In 1885 the Metropolitan Railway stretched out as far as Pinner, and during the following year was begun the boring of the first tube in the world. This, the City and South London, running from the Monument to Stockwell by way of Kennington, was opened for traffic by the Prince of Wales (later King Edward VII) in December, 1890, and was not only the first true underground but also the first electric railway.

It was followed by the Waterloo and City line in 1898, and the Central London—the original and famous "Twopenny Tube"—in 1900. Meanwhile, an even more momentous revolution in transport was being heralded.

Coming of the Motor-bus

The first motor-cars began to arrive in England about 1894, but until the passing of the Locomotives on Highways Act in 1896 all such vehicles were restricted to five miles an hour, and had to be preceded by a man bearing a red flag.

On Saturday, November 14, 1896—known in transport history as "Emancipation Day"—fifty-four mechanically propelled vehicles set out from London to Brighton. The first to arrive at the sea-coast town was a motor-bus.

In the following year an electrically propelled motor-bus, the *Radcliffe-Ward*, was licensed by Scotland Yard to ply for hire between Charing Cross and Victoria. Horse-bus drivers regarded it as a huge joke; and it must be confessed that this now almost forgotten pioneer vehicle had but a short and troubled life.

Nor had the first petrol bus much better success. This was put on the road late in 1899 by the Motor Traction Company, but soon withdrawn. It was followed in 1902 by a steam-propelled bus owned by the London Road Car Company.

It was not until 1904 that the L.G.O.C. began to operate its first motor-bus service. This late start did not imply a conservative or dilatory attitude on the part of the Company; on the contrary, it had been inquiring into the possibilities of mechanical traction since 1898, but with the due care and deliberation expected of a very large and responsible organisation. To such an extent were the interests of its patrons considered that over thirty different types of chassis were experimented with before one was selected as suitable for a standard motor vehicle.

Years of Fierce Competition

Actually, the first mechanically propelled omnibus placed in service by the L.G.O.C. was a steam car, a Clarkson single-decker, which plied between Hammersmith and Piccadilly Circus. The same year (1904) saw the inauguration of a regular motor-bus service.

Almost immediately the Company came up against stiff competition. The spearhead of this was the London Motor Omnibus Company, founded in 1905, and the parent of the Vanguard Company.

The Vanguard, unhampered by tradition, experimented daringly and with success. It introduced route numbers on its buses, opened up new routes and cut fares. Another formidable competitor was the Great Eastern London and Suburban Tramways and Omnibus Company, while even at this early date the name of Tilling was becoming well known.

The years 1905 to 1908 were intensely exciting and excessively competitive. All sorts of buses—steam, petrol and electric—appeared on the London streets, and almost every week saw a new variety of form or design. On one point only did the various companies seem agreed, that the mechanically propelled vehicle must be radically different from the horse-bus.

This brief period of confused and chaotic progress was brought to an end in 1908, when the Road Car and the Vanguard Companies were absorbed by the L.G.O.C. The united undertaking at once concentrated on the production of a standardised vehicle, and in October, 1910, after experiments with many types of chassis, produced the historic "B" type, of which the ever-famous war veteran *Old Bill* is an example.

On October 25, 1911, the last L.G.O.C. horse-bus was withdrawn from service. Few swifter revolutions in social life have ever been seen. In 1901 the horse-bus reigned supreme in London; within ten years it was swept from the streets of the largest city in the world.

A Colossal Change-over

The work involved in the change-over must have been colossal. Thousands of horses to be disposed of; thousands of men to be trained to new occupations; hundreds of buses to be scrapped or converted; hundreds more to be designed and built; scores of stables to be sold or transformed into garages; new premises to be acquired; a vast buying and distributing organisation, hitherto dealing in corn, straw, hay, beans, harness and the like, to learn the business of laying in and supplying stocks of petrol, oil and a large variety of mechanical spares. And all the time persistent and patient experimenting with engines, chassis and coach-work, not to mention development of new routes and—perhaps most exacting of all tasks—the readjustment of a mental attitude in face of an almost entirely novel situation.

The L.G.O.C. emerged triumphant from this struggle to be immediately immersed in another. No sooner had the technical and administrative problems posed by the advent of mechanical traction been resolved than the question of the co-ordination of the various forms of public transport in London became urgent.

LONDON TRANSPORT OFFICES
Headquarters of L.T.E., 55 Broadway, Westminster. A twelve-storey building completed 1929.

This particularly affected motor-buses and underground railways. They could no longer be allowed to run independently over virtually the same routes. In 1912 control of the L.G.O.C. passed to the Underground Electric Railways Company.

The latter company had been formed in 1902 as the Metropolitan District Electric Traction Company to carry out the electrification of the District Railway. By November, 1905, the District had become all-electric, and the Underground company had erected a huge power station at Chelsea.

It then acquired control of the City and South London, Central London, and the other tube railways, such as the Bakerloo (opened 1906), the Piccadilly, and the Hampstead, to which the twentieth century had given birth.

The 1914–18 War arrested all development. Hundreds of L.G.O.C. buses were sent to the battle-fronts; their drivers and conductors went with them, and the London services had to be rigorously curtailed.

A few even of the horse-buses were recalled; and no doubt many readers will recollect the passenger lorries, resembling enormous crates, which appeared in 1919, and for a few months supplemented the omnibus services.

Coming of the Motor Coach

The succeeding years were marked by a veritable orgy of progress, culminating in the formation of the London Passenger Transport Board in 1933. Perhaps the most appreciated advance in bus design has been the introduction of the roofed upper deck. This took place experimentally in 1923, when also the first pneumatic tyres were fitted. The roofed upper deck has been a permanent feature of the two-decker bus since October, 1925. The first bus designed by L.G.O.C. for pneumatic tyres was the LS (London Six) of 1927, the pioneer six-wheeler. Then followed the totally enclosed staircase and the diesel engine.

The first few years after the 1914–18 War saw in London and elsewhere an immense motor coach boom. Many of the companies concerned in it speedily went bankrupt or were bought up by larger concerns which, with the aid of the newly founded Ministry of Transport, gradually evolved some order out of chaos.

ENGLAND'S LARGEST COACH STATION

The Victoria Coach Station in Buckingham Palace Road, opened in 1932. Occupying 1½ acres of ground, it can accommodate eighty coaches at one time. Its amenities include a restaurant with a dance floor.

After some years of chaotic competition and not a little litigation the long-distance traffic between London and the provinces came into the hands of large independent combines, while the L.G.O.C. covered London, its suburbs and outlying districts.

Huge Motor-coach Stations

The coach combines early built themselves huge termini, notably at Victoria and King's Cross, comparable with the London main line railway stations. From these termini it is possible to travel in luxurious vehicles to any part of Great Britain.

So far as the L.G.O.C. was concerned, the most important development resulting from these years was the country bus serving the villages and towns outside London. The introduction of this service virtually necessitated the formation of a separate company, and in July, 1930, the Green Line came into being. It worked as an individual unit, but was financed by the L.G.O.C.

The Green Line operates for the most part outside the County of London. Thus the area that is covered to-day by the London Transport Executive—2,000 square miles—is considerably larger than that of the County of London or even of what is known as Greater London. It is estimated that its service caters for a population of 9,500,000.

The operating figures of London Transport Executive are astronomical. In 1954 they were as follows :

Type of Vehicle.	*Number Operating.*	*Passengers carried.*	*Miles covered.*
Buses and Coaches	7,300	2,712,100,000	339,300,000
Trolleybuses	1,600	718,000,000	71,200,000
Railway cars	3,300	671,400,000	192,300,000
Totals ..	12,200	4,101,500,000	602,800,000

Longest Tube Tunnel in the World

Not only have the underground railways been very considerably extended in the past, but further larger extensions are in hand. The longest continuous tube tunnel in the world is on the Northern Line, and runs from East Finchley via the Bank to Morden, a distance of 17¼ miles. Altogether, there are 253 miles of track. On these, 3,300 motor vehicles and carriages, comprising 478 trains, with a seating capacity of over 130,000, carry more than 1¾ million passengers daily.

Many of the underground stations have been

transformed, notable examples being Piccadilly Circus, the Bank, and Holborn (Kingsway). When the new Piccadilly Circus was opened in December, 1928, it was declared that there was "nothing else like it in any country." Half a dozen stairways from the street lead to two subways, the deeper 102 feet below ground level, which handle 1,500 trains a day and 50,000,000 passengers a year.

At Piccadilly Circus the platforms were illuminated at the beginning of 1946 by the new system of lighting, which made them almost as bright as day. This improvement is being applied progressively to other underground stations.

The large circular booking hall contains a brilliant arcade of shops. From this eleven escalators convey passengers to and from the trains. The escalator is a comparatively modern device, the first one on London's underground having been installed in 1911, though five years previously a spiral "moving staircase" was opened at Holloway Road on the Piccadilly line. The longest escalator in the world is in Leicester Square Station.

The newer suburban stations on ground level—most of the tubes come up to breathe towards the end of their journeys—are models of simplicity and modernity.

On July 1, 1933, the whole of the public passenger services in London and its surrounding districts came under the control of the London Passenger Transport Board, a public utility corporation formed to direct and co-ordinate bus, coach, tramway and underground railway services over an area of 2,000 sq. miles, and to co-operate with the main line railways in that area.

The Board had to tackle the biggest transport job in the world. It had in its charge an army of over 70,000 employees, and had to arrange for some 12,000,000,000 journeys every year. In addition it is organising vast extensions. In 1939–45, despite all the difficulties caused by black-outs, improvised labour and air attacks, the Board triumphantly maintained its services, although both buses and tube stations received direct hits. On January 1, 1948, the Board was replaced by the newly formed London Transport Executive.

Problem of the Rush-hour

The "rush-hours" provide the L.T.E. with a perennial problem.

In the hectic rush-hour periods the underground railways have to carry 400,000 persons into or out of Central London. As the maximum seating capacity of the utmost number of trains which can be rushed through in the periods is only a fraction of that number, it will be clear

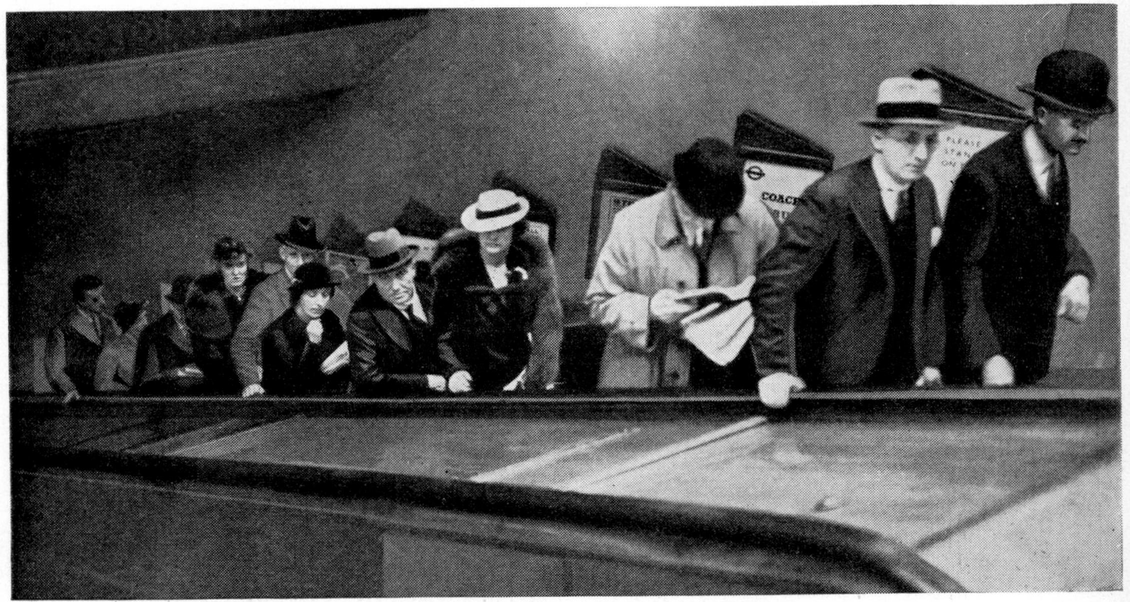

COMING UP THE ESCALATOR

At all modern underground stations in London escalators are now installed. At Leicester Square can be seen the longest in the world; other long and swift ones serve Hyde Park Corner and Holborn (Kingsway).

FROM LONDON TO THE NORTH

The "Night Scotsman" leaving King's Cross. In recent years there have been big developments on main line railways, but the problem of daily traffic to and from the suburbs remains unsolved.

why many have only "a standing seat."

The safety measures on the Underground have long been justly famous. Should the driver be taken ill while driving, the "dead man's handle" comes into operation. This is a handle with spring attached which he holds, so contrived that the moment the pressure of his hand relaxes the current is cut off and the brakes are applied. Should he by any chance pass a signal set at danger, a "trip-cock" strikes the brakes lever and brings the train to a standstill. If a breakdown occurs the driver has only to pinch together the two wires along the tunnel wall, and the current is cut off along the conductor rail, and the train and the walls are illuminated. The passengers walk through the train, descend at either end and make their way through the lighted tunnel in perfect safety while the driver telephones his plight to the nearest station.

Finest Drivers in the World

Equally stringent precautions are taken to ensure safety on the roads. London bus-drivers, admittedly the finest in the world, are recruited from men already experienced in street traffic, and are given a long and rigorous training. Bonuses are awarded to drivers who pilot vehicles for a year without grazing them. Vehicles are tested for skidding, overbalancing and other causes of accident, and are regularly overhauled to eliminate the risk of mechanical defect. In the last instance, however, the safety of any bus or coach must depend upon the driver, and for those in charge of London Transport vehicles no praise can be too high.

In considering the colossal number of passengers carried annually by the vehicles of the L.T.E., one must not overlook the parts played in London by the main line railways and privately owned road vehicles. Every day over 1,000,000 passengers are conveyed to or from London in the 10,000 trains provided by the national railways.

Failure of the "Penny Steamers"

Liverpool Street, serving the vast and populous areas east and north of the City, easily heads the list with approximately 250,000 passengers daily. London Bridge, Waterloo, Victoria and Broad Street all top the 100,000 mark. The numbers on all lines are increasing steadily as the population of the metropolis moves outwards.

It was this expansion which killed the last effort to revive the use of the Thames as a means of passenger transport. During the nineteenth century a determined attempt was made by four companies to provide services on the river for City workers. The cheapest fares in the world were offered; only a penny was charged for transit from London Bridge to Lambeth. The boats ran all the year round, and there were frequent services. But the suburbs moved steadily away from the river, and after successive amalgamations the enterprise closed down. A summer service of river buses, reintroduced in 1948, proved popular, however.

No survey of London's traffic can be complete without mention of the ubiquitous taxi. This appeared on the road about 1903 and speedily displaced the horse-drawn "hansom" and "growler," of which it was the lineal descendant.

For seventy years the two-wheeled hansom cab, which was named after its inventor, Joseph Aloysius Hansom, and the four-wheeled growler had been familiar features of London's streets. But, like the horse-drawn bus, they yielded swiftly to the onset of the mechanically propelled vehicle; both have already earned honoured places in our museums of antiquities.

Horse Banned from London Streets

The London taxi-driver is as unique as the bus-driver. He combines speed with safety, but his presence does not lessen the congestion of London, though few drivers can worm their way in and out of traffic with his skill. Truth to tell, in spite of every device so far tried to aid the circulation of traffic on the streets of the metropolis, the state of affairs grows worse instead of better.

The introduction of traffic lights at cross roads to some extent prevents lengthy jams, but tends to reduce average speed; one-way streets and roundabouts have the same effect. The horse has been banned from a number of thoroughfares, but for every horse which disappears two motor vehicles seem to appear. The post-war planners of the new metropolis were all agreed that a system of ring-roads, coupled with widened existing roads, was the only solution of the traffic problem.

London's Airports

Before the war, the air traffic to and from London was assuming formidable proportions, and the question of transit between the airports and the heart of the City seriously disturbed the authorities concerned. London's airports—Croydon, Gatwick, Heston and Gravesend—and airfields were all outside the county area, and much valuable time was lost getting to and from them. The replanning of London included a ring of airports at Blackbushe, Bovingdon, Croydon, Gatwick, Heath Row and Northolt. Work on the great airport at Heath Row began in May, 1944; now, as London Airport, it has become the greatest in the country. It is served by buses and coaches.

HEATH ROW, LONDON'S MAIN AIRPORT

London Airport in 1948. At this time construction of the aerodrome at Feltham, Middlesex, was in the second of three stages of development. Four runways out of nine planned had been completed.

BRITAIN'S LARGEST NATIONAL MUSEUM

The British Museum stands in Great Russell Street, Bloomsbury. Open every day of the year except Christmas Day and Good Friday, it is visited annually by over one million people from all over the world.

TREASURES WORTH MILLIONS

SOME years ago the value of the pictures in the National Gallery and the books in the British Museum was provisionally estimated at £40,000,000. As the literary collection is but a part of the immense treasure-house at Bloomsbury, and there are over fifty more collections in London, the worth of the whole of them is incalculable.

The British Museum is the largest national museum in Great Britain. To walk through all its rooms and corridors would take two hours, and the sightseer would have no time to take more than a fleeting glimpse. Every year well over 1,000,000 people visit the Museum. Admission is free, but the " invisible cost " to the State of each visitor is about 5s.

The Museum as we know it to-day is the result of the painstaking labour and the enthusiastic munificence of six generations of scholars and collectors. It owes its origin to Sir Hans Sloane, a native of Ireland who practised as a physician in Chelsea. He died in 1753, bequeathing to the nation a valuable collection of books, manuscripts and works of art, on condition that the sum of £20,000 should be paid to his family. This amount was less than half of what he had paid for the collection, being scarcely equal to the intrinsic value of the precious metals and stones contained in it. Parliament voted in favour of acceptance of Sloane's offer. By the same Act it made provision for the acquisition of the collection of manuscripts formed by Robert Harley, Earl of Oxford (known as the Harleian MSS.), and directed that the valuable Cottonian Library, given to the nation by Sir John Cotton during the reign of William III, and then inadequately housed in Ashburnham House, Dean's Yard, Westminster, should be amalgamated with the other two collections. Towards the cost of these transactions £100,000 was raised by means of a State lottery.

Montagu House, Bloomsbury, a magnificent mansion, was purchased for £10,250 in 1754 to house the collections, and was opened to the public in 1759 under the title of the British

THE BRITISH MUSEUM IN 1805

Montagu House, purchased in 1754 for the Sloane, Harleian and Cottonian Collections, was inadequate for the treasures which poured into the Museum. The present building was erected between 1823 and 1852.

Museum. Two years before this last event George II came forward with the gift of the Royal Library, formed by successive Kings and Queens of England from Henry VII to Charles II.

Library Bought with Navy Funds

In 1823 the Museum acquired the library of George III, containing some 120,000 volumes. At the time the public was informed that this was a gift from George IV. Such was not the case. "The First Gentleman in Europe," so far from entertaining any idea of giving the library to the nation, wanted to sell it abroad. Fortunately he was prevented from carrying out this project, and the books were "bought of him out of some Admiralty funds and so secured for the nation." Thus, by a curious chance, did the British nation gain a library at the expense of the Navy.

A special wing was built in 1828 to house this collection. It forms the eastern side of a quadrangle, the other sides of which were added later, Montagu House being demolished gradually as the new buildings arose. The main structure of the Museum as it stands to-day came into being between 1823 and 1852. Further extensions were made between the latter date and 1884, and in 1914 the north wing, known as the King Edward VII Galleries, was opened. A new gallery to house the Elgin Marbles was completed in 1939, and was the gift of Lord Duveen of Millbank.

Over Sixty Miles of Books

The most striking architectural features of the Museum are the portico with its massive columns and the lofty dome of the Reading Room. The latter, 140 feet in diameter and 106 feet high, is one of the largest in the world. The Reading Room was built in 1857 and

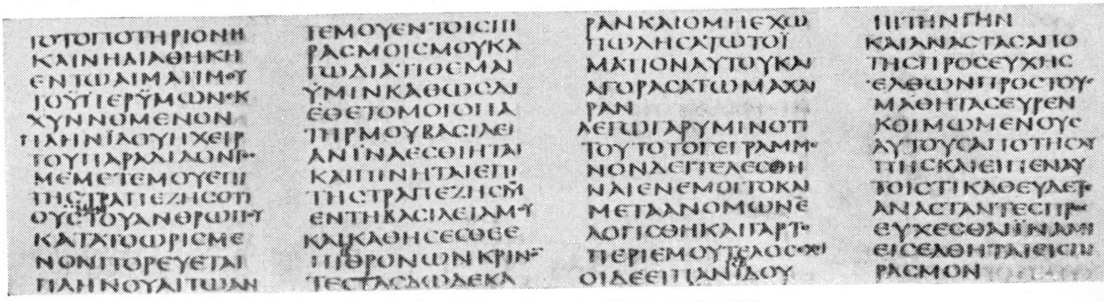

THE BOOK THAT COST £100,000

Part of a page of the *Codex Sinaiticus*, the fourth-century Greek manuscript of the Bible purchased by Great Britain in 1933 from the Soviet Government. The public was asked to subscribe half the cost.

BRITISH MUSEUM READING ROOM
Research workers and writers from all over the world are to be met in this room. Though it has accommodation for 500 readers, every seat is usually occupied by 11 a.m. It is open from 9 a.m. to 6 p.m.

afterwards extended. It has accommodation for some 500 readers, and the shelves round its walls contain over 80,000 volumes. No one knows the exact number of books in the Library, but it certainly exceeds 4,000,000 and increases at the rate of about 50,000 every twelve months. The volumes occupy well over sixty miles of shelving, which is extended at the rate of a mile a year.

The British Museum was entitled to a copy of every book published in the United Kingdom and the Irish Free State. It acquired this right in 1757, when George II's gift of the Royal Library was accompanied by the transference to the museum of the royal privilege of being given one copy of every work published in the King's dominions.

Catalogue to Cost £250,000

Specially trained workers are compiling a new catalogue, which will probably take a quarter of a century to complete. It is only the second of its kind, the first having been made between 1881 and 1905. Copies of this tremendous compilation are in great demand and have been known to fetch as much as £1,500. The new catalogue will be in some 250 volumes, each of which will have cost about £1,150.

20,000 Tons of Newspapers

The museum annually receives about 300,000 newspapers, which are sent to a special department at Colindale, in the northern suburb of Hendon. The fine modern building, completed in 1932, houses in easily accessible files copies of all the important national, provincial and foreign newspapers published since 1800. When first opened it contained 275,000 bound volumes, occupying fourteen miles of shelving. Half the storage accommodation was destroyed by a single bomb in 1940.

Tickets to the Reading Room at Bloomsbury, which place the whole of the immense library at the holder's disposal, are issued to those engaged on research. The authorities issue 3,000 fresh tickets, make 12,000 renewals and grant temporary admission to a further 12,000 people every year. From 3,000 to 3,500 volumes are taken out daily.

Countless distinguished people have made use of the Reading Room. There Thomas Carlyle toiled and Bernard Shaw educated himself by five years' reading, while Samuel Butler, the Victorian man of letters from whom he drew inspiration, sat at a desk three days a week for about a quarter of a century. Karl Marx, the inspirer of the revolutionary experiment that is being carried out in Russia, gathered information for his masterpiece *Das Kapital* in the Reading Room, in which Lenin, the instrument for the putting into practice of the Communist theory, also studied.

Finest Human Sculptures Extant

In the exhibition galleries the story of man is told by a record of his works, from the rough shaping of a flint when he could scarcely fumble, to the creation of the supremely beautiful.

Perhaps the most famous of its treasures is the collection of Greek sculpture known as the Elgin Marbles. They once formed part of the Parthenon, the temple of the virgin goddess Athena, at Athens, which was built in the fifth century before Christ. The sculptures, among which are the finest representations of the human body in existence, were brought to England by the Earl of Elgin in 1806–12, and they came into the possession of the museum shortly afterwards.

Stone that Explained Hieroglyphics

Fragments of the Mausoleum, one of the seven wonders of the world, are also to be seen in the Museum. It was the tomb of Mausolus, a prince of Caria in Asia Minor, who lived in the fourth century B.C.

In the Egyptian Sculpture Gallery, which contains objects made four or five thousand years ago, is a piece of black basalt which revealed an age-long secret. It was discovered by a French officer in 1798 at Rosetta in the Nile Delta, thirty miles west of Alexandria, and

MUMMIES THREE THOUSAND YEARS OLD

On the upper floor of the British Museum, several rooms are devoted to Egyptian antiquities, including a collection of mummies dating from approximately 1300 B.C. to A.D. 300. Animals are also represented.

STONE THAT DECIPHERED A LANGUAGE
When Napoleon Bonaparte sailed to Egypt in 1798 he took with him distinguished scholars and archæologists. They discovered the Rosetta Stone, which enabled the Egyptian picture-writing to be deciphered.

is therefore called the Rosetta Stone. Carved in 195 B.C., it bears inscriptions which enabled scholars to decipher the strange hieroglyphic writing of the ancient Egyptians, and thus to learn the history of the mighty race that was civilised 6,000 years ago.

Natural History and Science Museums

The Natural History department of the British Museum is in Cromwell Road, South Kensington. The building, designed by Alfred Waterhouse, took eight years to construct and was opened to the public in 1881. Every year this vast Noah's Ark gives pleasure to more than 650,000 sightseers, who can examine at leisure skeletons of mammoths and whales, see mounted specimens of the fiercest wild beasts in exact representations of their normal surroundings, and study the tiniest representatives of the animal kingdom.

Scientists from every quarter of the globe come to seek the advice of the staff on such questions as those relating to the protection of crops, property and human life against the ravages of insects. The museum officials are authorities on such pests as mosquitoes, which carry malaria and yellow fever, and the tsetse fly, the scourge of tropical Africa. There are about 2,500,000 species of insects, of which about one-tenth have been identified and named.

Behind the Natural History Museum, with its main entrance in Exhibition Road, is the Science Museum, a favourite resort of children of all ages, who troop there to the number of 1,300,000 a year. Its aim is to assist students of the development of science, and to illustrate the application of science to industry.

Special Gallery for Children

The history of the Science Museum began in 1857, when a large iron building was erected at South Kensington to house various scientific exhibits from the Great Exhibition of 1851, as well as some from Marlborough House. About seven years later the collections, then increased by the addition of a number of ship models and marine engines, were transferred to buildings on the present site, originally erected for the Exhibition of 1862. Parts of these buildings are still in use, but they are gradually being

Donald McLeish

NATURAL HISTORY MUSEUM
The most extensive of its kind in the world. Its exhibits illustrate every branch of natural history.

removed to make room for an immense modern structure, the Eastern Block of which was opened in 1928 by King George V.

In the basement there is a Children's Gallery, where scientific subjects are explained in a simple manner. A working demonstration of a rainbow attracts much attention. The development of transport by land, sea and air is illustrated in a series of perspective scenes; and that of methods of communication in a number of exhibits. This Gallery also contains a cinema, where films are shown three times a day.

Early Locomotive and Aeroplane

Among the more interesting of the many historical exhibits are the *Rocket* locomotive; the magnet which Faraday used in the experiments that gave birth to modern electrical engineering; a model of the Wright aeroplane of 1903, the first power-driven man-carrying machine to make a successful flight; the machinery of the *Turbinia* which made the *Queen Mary* possible; and the earliest motor-car.

Next door to the Science Museum is the Museum of Practical Geology. The building, which cost £220,000, was completed in 1933, just in time to be used as the meeting-place of the World Economic Conference. The exhibits were then housed in a building in Jermyn Street, Piccadilly, from where they were transferred in 1934.

Geology is not a subject that excites keen public interest, and before its removal the Museum was visited by an average of only 20,000 people a year, but the exhibits in their new home have been so skilfully arranged and so many more have been added that they attracted 159,000 people in the first six months following the opening.

Mount Vesuvius in Eruption

There is a fascinating series of dioramas of such subjects as Vesuvius in eruption, with the internal glow most realistically reflected on the clouds, a Glacier, Prehistoric Man in the Thames Valley, and Lulworth Cove. The central area of the ground floor is occupied by a collection of precious and semi-precious stones. On the first floor there is a large geological column, lighted internally, which makes many folk pause in astonishment. It shows the main events in geological history over a period of about 500,000,000 years.

The Victoria and Albert Museum, the colossal front of which adjoins that of the Natural History Museum, is the national museum of industrial art. Its beginning was the collection of objects of ornamental art formed first at

Donald McLeish

IMPERIAL INSTITUTE
Opened in 1893 as the national memorial of Queen Victoria's Jubilee, to give Empire information.

DUSTING THE DINOSAURUS
A plaster reproduction in the Natural History Museum of a dinosaurian reptile, from the original at Pittsburg, U.S.A. The skeleton is 84 ft. 9 in. long and 12 ft. 9½ in. high. The tail measures 49 ft. 2 in.

Marlborough House in 1852 after the Great Exhibition. This collection was moved to South Kensington in 1857, being housed in a building known as the South Kensington Museum, which was twice extended, and in 1899 was renamed the Victoria and Albert Museum by command of Queen Victoria.

World's Most Famous Carpet

Among its many treasures is the Ardabil carpet, the most famous carpet in the world. It is valued at about £50,000, but the Museum acquired it for one-twentieth of that amount. William Morris, the great Victorian artist and social reformer, was among the principal contributors to its cost. There is a unique collection of ceramics, English and foreign, ancient and modern. The magnificent stained glass from Ashridge Park was bought for £27,000 by an anonymous donor at an auction.

In the metalwork section may be seen the Campion cup. Made in London in the year 1500, it is the oldest known hall-marked example of its type. It was purchased in 1924 with a Parliamentary grant of £10,000. The silver censer from Ramsey Abbey was acquired in 1923. It had lain in Whittlesey Mere from the time of the suppression of the monasteries until 1850, when the Mere was drained.

The celebrated Raphael cartoons, perhaps the most valuable series of works of art in the world, are on loan from His Majesty the King. The Museum also possesses some extremely fine examples of Italian Renaissance sculpture, and many of the works of John Constable, who painted landscapes without fal-de-lal or fiddle-de-dee, as he expressed it.

Branch in East London

Collections illustrating the industrial arts of India, Ceylon, Afghanistan, Tibet, Siam, and Indonesia are housed in a separate building in Imperial Institute Road, South Kensington. There is another branch of this museum in Cambridge Road in the east of London. Known as the Bethnal Green Museum, it contains collections of pictures, textiles, pottery, modern industrial art and many books on art.

About the time that it gained the Geological Museum, South Kensington lost the Imperial War Museum, which was transferred to Lambeth Road, on the south side of the Thames, in 1935–36. It is housed in what used to be the Royal Bethlem Hospital for the insane, popularly known as "Bedlam."

Relics of the World Wars

The exhibition galleries of this museum show the means by which the World Wars were fought on land, at sea, and in the air. They cover every aspect of the conflicts. There may be seen guns and howitzers, the seaplane that took part in the Battle of Jutland, and the Sopwith Camel which brought down a Zeppelin over the North Sea in August, 1918, together with a flying bomb, a rocket, a jet engine, the cockpit of a heavy bomber, field and anti-tank guns, and models of landing craft and tanks used in the last war. There is also the War diary of the Duke of Windsor (then Prince of Wales), and the last letter of Nurse Cavell.

The Reference Department is probably the best of its kind in the world. Some 250,000 photographs are available for inspection by students, as well as a library of about 60,000 volumes which increases at the rate of between 400 and 500 books a year. It has also 700 official films taken during the conflicts.

In the fullness of time a similar but even more impressive collection will be made of all the weapons and inventions of the Second World War; but it will require a large museum for its housing.

The National Gallery in Trafalgar Square, opened in 1838, contains works by practically all the greatest masters of every period and of every country. It has the finest representative collection in the world.

It was fortunate in the time of its beginning. As a result of the French Revolution and the Napoleonic Wars, the Continent was seized by unrest and financial embarrassment, which caused the breaking up of many fine collections. England was comparatively secure and wealthy, and her connoisseurs found it easy to buy works of art at comparatively low prices.

Long Struggle for National Gallery

The formation of a National Gallery was suggested as long ago as 1777 by John Wilkes, who was never happy unless agitating. Edmund Burke had moved in Parliament that the grant to the British Museum should be increased, and Wilkes, in a speech supporting the motion, further suggested that the Government should purchase the famous Houghton collection of pictures, then in the market.

This suggestion was turned down, the works of art going to Russia, but nearly fifty years later the Julius Angerstein collection of thirty-eight

MUSEUM OF INDUSTRIAL ART

The Victoria and Albert Museum in South Kensington, seen from the air. The picture shows the frontage to Cromwell Road of the New Buildings, opened by King Edward VII and Queen Alexandra in 1909.

THE GEOLOGICAL AND SCIENCE MUSEUMS
The Geological Museum opened in 1934, after being used for the World Economic Conference in the previous year. In the Science Museum is a unique collection of machines, ships, locomotives and aeroplanes.

fine pictures was acquired for £57,000, and first exhibited to the public in a house in Pall Mall in 1824.

Gift of Italian Masters

The Gallery's first benefactor was Sir George Beaumont, friend of the poet Wordsworth and patron of Sir Thomas Lawrence, the painter. He presented fifteen pictures in 1826. Since that time it has been receiving a continuous succession of bequests. Perhaps the most important gift was the magnificent collection of Dr. Ludwig Mond, received in 1924. It consists of about forty works of Italian masters, including Murillo's "St. John the Baptist" and Raphael's magnificent "Crucifixion."

The Gallery's first keeper was William Séguier, who acted as art adviser to George IV when he was making the royal collection now at Buckingham Palace and Windsor. He acted in a similar capacity to Sir Robert Peel, the greater part of whose fine collection was acquired for the nation in 1871.

The post of director was instituted in 1855, when Sir Charles Eastlake, a man whose discernment in artistic matters was equalled by his energy and enthusiasm, was appointed. During his term of office, terminated by his death in 1865, he acquired no fewer than 139 pictures.

The value of the gems of art in the National Gallery can only be estimated approximately, but enormous sums have been paid for individual canvases. The "Cornaro Family," by Titian, the great Italian courtier-painter who lived to be ninety-nine years of age and to have every kind of honour conferred upon him, was purchased for £122,000 in 1929. Twenty-five years earlier his "Portrait of Ariosto" cost £30,000. His "Bacchus and Ariadne," considered by some critics to be the finest work in the Gallery, was offered to an Englishman travelling in Italy in the early years of the nineteenth century for £700. He was unable to find the money to buy it, and in 1826 the National Gallery had to pay 9,000 guineas for it and two others.

Fortunes Paid for Pictures

A large family group by Franz Hals was bought from Malahide Castle for £25,000, but the same artist's "Portrait of a Woman" cost only £105. Piero della Francesca's "Baptism" was also acquired at a low figure. It was bought at Uzielli (Italy) for £241 in 1861. Raphael's "Ansidei Madonna," so called

Donald McLeish

THE TATE GALLERY

Presented to the nation in 1899 by Sir Henry Tate to be a home for British art. It now includes also, a fine collection of modern foreign art.

because it was painted for the Ansidei family, was bought from the Duke of Marlborough for £170,000 in 1885. The famous Castle Howard Mabuse, "The Adoration of the Kings," cost £40,000, and Holbein's "Duchess of Milan," £72,000.

On the floor of the entrance hall of the Gallery there are three sets of curious mosaics. They are by Boris Anrep, a Russian artist.

That on the main centre landing, the " Awakening of the Muses," consists of portraits of well-known people. The original of Melpomene, the Tragic Muse, for instance, was Miss Greta Garbo, the film actress. To the right of this, up a short flight of stairs, is a mosaic of " Profane Love," round which is a series of medallions, including one showing a footballer and another a girl riding on the pillion of a motor-cycle. The third mosaic, to the left of the entrance, depicts the " Labours of Life."

Behind the National Gallery is the National Portrait Gallery. Although of less importance than its elder sister, it contains works by such masters as Van Dyck, Kneller, Romney and Gainsborough. The present building, the gift of William Henry Alexander, was completed in 1896; and a new wing, the gift of Lord Duveen, was added thirty-six years later.

The pictures are arranged according to the periods and professions of the subjects. The earliest are electrotypes taken from effigies on Royal tombs. The oldest painted portrait is that of the mother of Henry VII, Lady Margaret Beaufort. The latest portraits include those of King George V and Queen Mary, and groups of modern statesmen, admirals and generals.

The National Gallery of British Art, Millbank, popularly known as the Tate Gallery, contains,

THE NATIONAL GALLERY

Situated on the north side of Trafalgar Square, this century-old building houses the most representative collection of pictures in the world.

FORMER ALMSHOUSES BECOME MUSEUM
The beautiful exterior of the Geffrye Museum in Shoreditch. The building, erected in 1715, bears a statue of the founder, Sir Robert Geffrye, a Lord Mayor of London. The museum is noted for its old furniture.

curiously enough, an unrivalled collection of modern foreign art, but also a magnificent collection of works of the British School from the eighteenth century onwards.

It owes its popular designation to Sir Henry Tate, who not only presented the nation with the original gallery, opened in 1897 on the site of Millbank Prison, but he also contributed sixty-five pictures by British artists.

The building was enlarged in 1899, at Sir Henry's cost; and again in 1910, when the Turner wing was erected by Sir Joseph Duveen, father of Lord Duveen of Millbank. The latter presented the foreign rooms, as well as one for the works of John Singer Sargent.

Origin of the Foreign Collection

The nucleus of the foreign collection was the thirty-nine modern pictures known as the Lane Bequest. It has been largely increased through the munificence of Mr. Samuel Courtauld who, in 1923, gave £50,000 for the acquisition of works by modern foreign artists.

Hertford House, in Manchester Square, is the home of the small but priceless collection made by Richard, fourth Marquess of Hertford, and his reputed son Sir Richard Wallace. Bequeathed to the nation by Lady Wallace, it was opened to the public in 1900.

The Wallace Collection

The elder Wallace lived the life of a retired gentleman in Paris, there gradually gathering fine examples of French painting, sculpture, and furniture of the eighteenth century. His son, who resembled him in his appreciation of the arts, purchased a famous collection that had been formed by the Comte de Nieuwerkerke. All were transferred to their present abode in 1875.

Hertford House was built as a private residence by the Duke of Manchester in 1776–88. After his death it passed into the hands of the Spanish Ambassador, a fact that is commemorated in the neighbouring Spanish Place, where the Embassy Chapel (now a Roman Catholic church) stood. Later it became the residence in England of the representative of France, and after that of the Hertford family.

The National Maritime Museum, Greenwich, was established in July 1934 and was based upon the collections of the old Royal Naval Museum and the Painted Hall. To-day it is housed in the Queen's House (built by Inigo Jones) and the Caird Galleries and displays a collection of relics and records covering the Naval history and the maritime art of Great Britain from the earliest times.

Lancaster House

Lancaster House, St. James's, is another historic residence that became a national museum. The building was commenced by the order of the Duke of York in 1825. He died two years later, before the work was finished. Subsequently, the lease was acquired by the Duke of Sutherland, in whose family it remained until 1912. The following year Viscount Leverhulme purchased the lease and presented the mansion to the nation for the purpose of housing a collection of objects relating to the history of London, then inadequately exhibited at Kensington Palace. Lancaster House and the collection became known as the London Museum, but it was closed to the public during the war and in 1949 the collection was moved back again to Kensington Palace. The exhibits illustrate every aspect of London life through the ages. Lancaster House is used by the Government for important conferences.

There may be seen flint weapons used by the distant ancestors of Londoners, and leather sandals worn by Romans in London streets over 1,500 years ago. Realistic models of ancient buildings, spectacular dioramas showing phases in the development of civilisation from the Stone Age to the Middle Ages, and costumes queer, quaint and curious are included in this comprehensive collection.

Other London Museums

Among the many other London museums we must not forget the Public Record Office, in Chancery Lane, where Domesday Book is kept; the Guildhall Museum, with many relics of the City's history; the Soane Museum, overlooking beautiful Lincoln's Inn Fields; the Horniman Museum, Forest Hill, and Leighton House at Holland Park.

During the Second World War, most of the priceless pictures and other treasures were removed from London's museums; fortunately so because they suffered badly from bombing the British Museum and the Natural History Museum in particular.

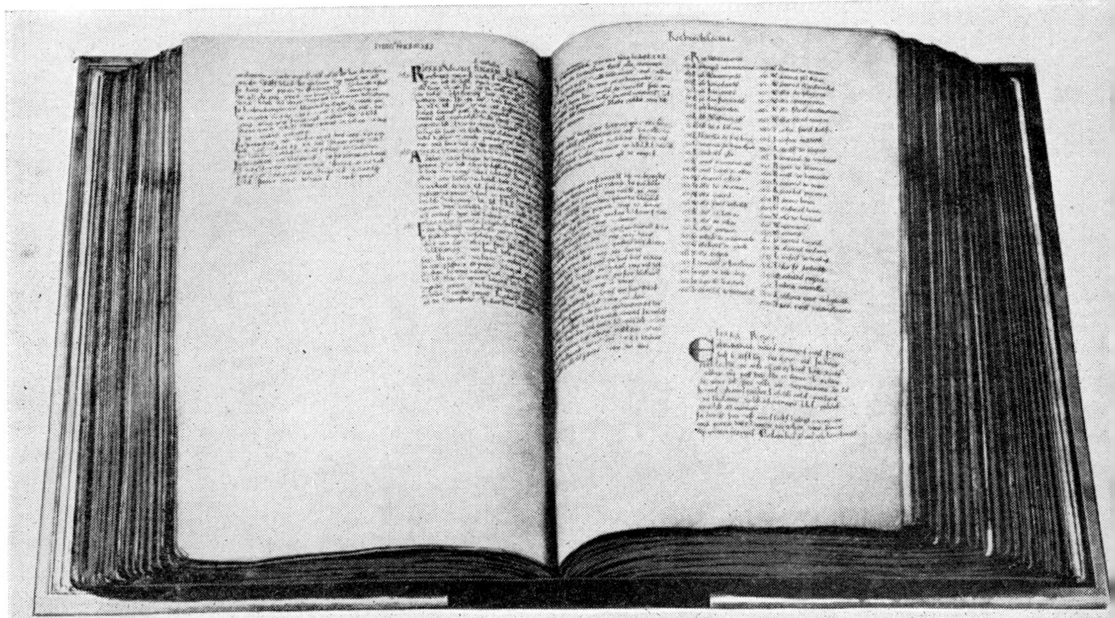

THE DOMESDAY BOOK OF WILLIAM I

Original manuscript of William the Conqueror's historic survey of England at the Public Record Office. Other treasures are Shakespeare letters, Guy Fawkes' signatures before and after torture, and Nelson's lo

HEADQUARTERS OF THE LONDON COUNTY COUNCIL

London County Hall stands on the south bank of the Thames adjoining Westminster Bridge. It was opened in 1922 by King George V, work on the site having been begun in 1909. It cost over £3,000,000.

HOW LONDON IS RUN

LONDON is a name with a multitude of meanings. There is the ancient City with its single square mile and night-time population of a mere 6,000, and there is the vast territory of the London Transport Executive, whose 2,000 square miles embrace a population of over 9,000,000. In between are such other Londons as the Administrative County, which covers only 117 square miles but includes almost half the population of the larger traffic area, being probably the most densely peopled area of this size on the earth's surface; " Water London," covering 573 square miles with a population of almost 7,500,000; and the Metropolitan Police District, with nearly 8,500,000 in an area of 734 square miles.

Thus nobody can say what London is, for the central area which is indubitably London all the time is surrounded by large tracts which are London for some purposes but not for others. But all these different Londons have one thing, at least, in common; on any definition London is immense. Think what these figures mean. The 9,000,000-odd population of " Traffic London " is greater than was the population of England and Wales combined so recently as the beginning of the nineteenth century; it is about 2,000,000 more than that of the Dominion of Australia at the present time. To regard London merely as a city puts in a wholly false perspective the problem of its administration. To govern London is a task equal to that of governing a fair-sized state.

In the course of time the government of London has come to be parcelled out between the City Corporation, the councils of twenty-eight Metropolitan Boroughs, a few special authorities and the London County Council. Of these the most important is undoubtedly the London County Council, which is the nearest thing the metropolis has achieved in the way of a central governing body. It is a comparatively youthful institution, largely because its creation, although urgently called for, was delayed owing to the opposition of the City Corporation and the unsympathetic attitude of Parliament. The London County Council is the fruit of a century-long struggle for unification denied to the metropolis alone among the cities of Great Britain.

This struggle arose out of the manner in which London grew up. Until as late as the beginning of the eighteenth century London was still more or less confined to the City boundaries. The majority of its inhabitants not only worked but also lived within the City walls. The square mile was terribly overcrowded, yet the population was already beginning to decline. This process of decline was to continue. The world of wealth and fashion drifted away to the West to form the new London which centred upon the coffee-houses of the Strand and the clubs of St. James's in order, as Petty says, to avoid " the fumes, steams and stinks of the whole Easterly pyle," the prevailing wind being from the west.

It was for a different reason that the exodus of the poorer people took place. Expansion of trade and commerce meant that premises within the City became more valuable as offices and counting-houses, places of business pure and simple, than as dwelling-houses. Unable to afford the higher rentals, ordinary folk were squeezed out on all sides and largely (in spite of the prevailing wind) towards the east, transforming the pleasant rural districts of Stepney and Whitechapel into densely peopled areas.

City Corporation Remains Aloof

London at this stage stood at the cross roads. Had the City Corporation chosen to extend its boundaries, and embrace the new suburbs which were the product of its own growth in wealth and power, it could have given some corporate unity to the teeming population which crowded round its walls and have helped London to develop as a real city. It preferred instead to remain aloof within its narrow boundaries, jealously guarding its ancient privileges.

Just as the power of the guilds, at first so democratic, gradually became concentrated in the aristocracy of the livery, so the wealth and privileges of London now became restricted to a small central area which was no longer a city in a real sense but a great market-place.

OLD-TIME LONDON LIGHTING
The watch, with their "cressets," or metal vessels mounted on poles, for holding oil or fat for lights.

It was a great misfortune for London that the City, which in national affairs had always been on the side of constitutional progress, championing the cause of Parliament against the King when it deemed such a course necessary, should have impeded progress towards the good government of London itself.

Repudiated by the ancient City, the new city without the walls became nothing but a cluster of habitations, the beginnings of what has been called "the Great Sprawl." The only form of government known to these new districts was that common to every village in the land, namely the parish or vestry, so called because its annual meeting was held in the vestry of the church or village hall. Everyone in the parish had the right to attend this yearly meeting, but it was a hopelessly inefficient method of running local affairs.

The officers of the parish, the constable, the surveyor of highways and the overseer of the poor were unpaid and often unwilling, and many of them either shirked their duties or turned them to personal profit. Even had they been prompted by the best intentions, the result would still have been chaos, for the parish was far too small a unit to deal with the big problems which had to be faced. How could one parish dispose of its sewage if the river were miles away? Why build good roads if they only joined up with the wretched cart-tracks of the parishes next door? For the solution of all such problems and a multitude of similar ones some central co-ordinating authority was needed.

Struggle for Central Authority

Throughout the nineteenth century th struggle went on to get some such centra administration for the whole area. In 183 the old close corporations were replace throughout the rest of England by municipa councils elected by the whole body of rate payers, but from the working of this Act th metropolis was excluded.

It was not until two years later that th Commissioners who had recommended thi measure presented their report on the Londo area. When they did they recommended i the strongest terms that London should have it municipal council just like any other city They could find "no circumstance justifyin the distinction of a small area within th municipal boundary (i.e., the City) from th rest," and insisted that a central administratio should be set up for the paving, sewage an

FIRE BRIGADE SERVICE
One of the most vital of the public utility services is the London Fire Brigade. An example of the modern equipment with which it operates is shown in this picture of a dual purpose fire-escape and pump.

lighting of streets, under the control either of the City or the State. But nothing at all was done for the next eighteen years.

In 1855 a Bill was passed which grouped the smaller parishes into larger districts and also set up the Metropolitan Board of Works. The setting-up of this Board left the power of the City Corporation untouched, for it consisted merely of delegates from the parishes and districts, combining to carry out certain specific services, notably drainage, which affected the area as a whole.

Metropolitan Board of Works

Although usually regarded as the ancestor of the present London County Council, the Metropolitan Board of Works was not a body elected by the whole of the ratepayers, but a mere piece of machinery. As the only piece of central machinery in existence, however, the Board was continually having imposed on it duties additional to the limited purposes for which it came into existence, notably the control of the fire brigade and the provision of parks and open spaces, which no single district would undertake on its own account for fear the ratepayers of the next parish would benefit as well as its own.

The Board could never become a real municipal government, and reformers were constantly pressing to secure a real central, democratically elected administration. Time and again their efforts were defeated by the City Corporation. Among the many Bills which foundered on this opposition was one sponsored by Lord Elcho in 1874 and having the backing of the Conservative party.

Another was that introduced by Sir William Harcourt ten years later, which aimed at extending the City boundaries and giving to all the ratepayers the right to elect a Common Council and Lord Mayor. Even though it provided that the old Common Council of the City should nominate forty-four members out of 240 on the new Corporation, the City was not to be appeased. Bullies were hired to break up meetings in favour of the Bill; the Lord Mayor exercised his right to take a seat in the House and led the agitation against the measure; and so, in the end, this Bill also suffered the fate of its many predecessors.

Ended by Financial Scandal

Reform came at last as the accidental result of a financial scandal. Rumours concerning the honesty of the Metropolitan Board of Works became so strong in 1887 that a Commission was set up to investigate. Its report incriminated some of the members and officials of the Board, and the Government concluded that the best thing would be to end its existence.

The chance came in the next year, when a

Bill was to be put through setting up County Councils for the whole of England. London was made an administrative county, with an elected London County Council, which took over the functions of the old Board of Works. Profiting from experience, the sponsors of the Bill did not try to build on the foundations of the City Corporation but to leave the jealously individual City as a separate entity and build the County round it.

The resulting situation is peculiar, for the administrative county embraces the City as well as the twenty-eight boroughs, while the City Corporation has the status of a county as well as of a city. The Act was passed in 1888, and the first London County Council came into being on January 31, 1889, even before the old Metropolitan Board of Works had ceased to exist. The area ruled by the Council covers 74,850 acres; it extends from Woolwich to Hammersmith and from Hackney to Wandsworth, and is bordered by Middlesex, Surrey, Kent and Essex.

Council's Many Duties

With the passing of time the London County Council has come to undertake a host of duties not dreamed of at its formation.

Two incidents in the history of London typify the results which are to be expected when a vast population is crowded together without the services rendered by local government authorities. Lacking the most elementary sanitation, the wooden houses in the narrow streets of the old City became a hotbed of filth and disease, resulting in successive epidemics of cholera, fever and other pestilences. These culminated in the Great Plague of 1665, which swept away 70,000 people. In the same way the Great Fire of the following year was but the most terrible of a series of conflagrations which, once started, destroyed large parts of the overcrowded town. One might summarise the work of the London County Council by saying that its task is to make such visitations not only impossible but unthinkable.

Let us consider some of the most important of the services which the Council operates, or helps to supervise.

First, one should take the prosaic question of sewerage, for this was not only the most urgent need of the early town, but being pre-eminently a problem for the area as a whole it provided the chief impetus towards centralisation. Chronologically, too, it was one of the first services to be set up, for Commissioners of Sewers were appointed as early as 1531, though it is not apparent that by modern standards they accomplished anything of importance.

Open Sewers in Streets

The one real achievement prior to the Great Fire was the covering in of the Fleet Ditch in 1637, which for long had been rendered impossible to navigation by the accumulation of filth and garbage which was emptied into it, poisoning the air of the streets through which it ran. For more than a century after that it was the custom for open sewers to flow through the crowded parishes, the sewage being received into wells and pumped into the kennels of the streets. Ultimately it found its way to the Thames, which at low tide gave off an unbearable stench, at times making business in the House of Commons impossible. Yet conditions in the City itself were such that the bridges were frequented by hundreds anxious for a breath of air!

At the time of Queen Victoria's accession in 1837 there was no sanitary legislation on the Statute Book. When the Bill setting up the borough councils was introduced in 1855 its sponsor stated that by 1847 the seven Commissioners of Sewers had attempted " only one great work—the Victoria Sewer, the estimate of which was £28,854 and the cost, so far as can be ascertained, £41,472; but this, it is said, falls far short of the cost." And the sewage still found its way into the Thames, polluting water drawn out for household purposes.

The system of main drainage was not even inaugurated until 1849, and it was only in 1855

FIREMEN IN STONE
Carving on the headquarters of the London Fire Brigade, Albert Embankment, near Lambeth Bridge.

that the creation of the Metropolitan Board of Works marked the beginning of better things. Then great main sewers were built, which carried the sewage underground to discharge itself into the river far outside London, at Barking on the north side and Crossness on the south.

But it was not long before the growth of the town extended to these districts also, so that in 1882 a Commission was set up to consider complaints from these neighbourhoods. It was then decided that the garbage in its crude state should not be discharged into the river at all. Treatment plants were set up to separate the solid from the liquid portions of the sewage, the former being carried away as sludge and deposited by barges far out at sea, and only a purified liquid, or effluent, being discharged into the river itself.

Together with the other functions of the Metropolitan Board of Works, main drainage was taken over in 1889 by the London County Council. At the present time the Council is responsible for the upkeep of some 400 miles of main sewers, these being additional to the 2,000 miles of local sewers maintained by the borough councils. Even the administrative county, with its area of 117 square miles, has proved too small a unit for this service. Twenty-two local authorities outside the county have made arrangements to use the London County Council drainage system, which thus serves a total area of 179 square miles. It handles 100,000 million gallons of sewage annually.

In the Middle Ages London drew its water chiefly from the local streams and wells, many of which, such as the Holywell and Clerk's Well, have left their trace in London place-names.

GUARDING HIS HEAD
Padded skeleton and mummified head of Jeremy Bentham the philosopher, at University College.

Failure of the Parish Pump

As early as 1236 the City obtained authority to build a channel for conducting the waters of the Tyburn from Paddington to the City. Towards the end of the century a conduit was erected in the West Cheap for distributing this water, and other conduits were built later which have also given names to London streets, such as the Lamb's Conduit in Bloomsbury. When the conduits fell into disrepair a class of water bearers grew up who earned a living by peddling the filthy water of the Thames from house to house in leathern panniers carried by horses.

Finally, in most parishes there was a parish pump. The supply from this source does not seem to have been particularly generous, for in 1855 the House of Commons was informed that in the Parish of St. Pancras the 472 Commissioners had only set up " fourteen public pumps for the use of 170,000 inhabitants, of which one is returned as out of order "—giving an average of over 12,000 inhabitants dependent for their water on each pump.

Water Wheels at London Bridge

In 1582 a Dutchman, named Peter Morrice, constructed water wheels at London Bridge worked by the action of the tides which caused a great sensation at their opening by generating enough power to throw a column of water over the steeple of St. Magnus's Church; in ordinary use they were made to serve the purpose of pumping water into the houses of some of the well-to-do citizens. The next really important addition to London's water supply came at the beginning of the seventeenth century, when Sir Hugh Myddleton brought water from Hertfordshire by means of the New River, which was completed in 1613.

In the following century there sprang up a number of water companies, of which the Chelsea Water Company was the first in 1721. Since the companies drew their water direct from the Thames, it was not surprising that epidemics of cholera continued. This practice was not quite so insanitary as it seems, for people drank beer rather than water.

Things tended to get worse rather than better, because after the foundation of the Chelsea Company the stimulus of competition was eliminated by a series of working agreements to divide London up between the different suppliers. It was not until 1852 that the Metropolis Water Act introduced even such an obviously needed regulation as to forbid the drawing of water below Teddington Lock. Many other regulations were enacted, but the companies were not too scrupulous in observing them and complaints continued.

Purest Water in the World

At various times throughout the latter half of the century Commissions recommended that London's water supply should be under the control of a central public body. An attempt by the London County Council to buy up the companies was opposed both by the companies and the local authorities. When action was at last taken, the twentieth century had already begun. The water companies were then taken over by a special body, the Metropolitan Water Board, with representatives of the borough councils, the councils of the Home Counties and the London County Council. To-day its water is claimed to be the purest in the world.

The Board supplies a population of 7,500,000 with an average of over fifty gallons each per day—twenty-five bucketsful per head. To do this it controls a vast network of 7,700 miles of water mains and about fifty reservoirs, or artificial lakes, which together form a sheet of water as large as Lake Windermere. Two-thirds of the water still comes from the Thames and a very large volume of the remainder from the River Lea.

The ever-growing size and population of the metropolis have in post-war days made it necessary to contemplate still more extensive schemes for an adequate water supply. At the beginning of 1946 the Metropolitan Water Board put out a plan for ensuring a supply of water free from pollution. The area to be covered was 2,754 square miles, extending from Hitchin to Guildford and from Gravesend to Maidenhead; it embraced a population of 10,700,000 using an average of 423,000,000 gallons per day. This scheme will take fifteen years to complete, at a cost of £37¼ millions.

Power to Clear Slum Areas

In all large cities the housing of the poor has always presented serious difficulties. This problem has been particularly acute in London where housing conditions did not begin to become tolerable by present-day standards until nearly the end of the nineteenth century. Then a number of Acts were passed which form the basis of the powers of local authorities to deal with insanitary houses.

The first important step was the Housing of the Working Classes Act of 1885, which was amended in 1890. A series of subsequent housing Acts has developed and extended the powers for housing and slum clearance, and the principle of assistance from the National Exchequer has been established. To-day the L.C.C. is mainly concerned with large schemes for slum clearance and housing and rehousing assistance, both within and outside the county. Borough Councils are responsible for individual bad houses and small slum areas within the area of each borough. In 1909 the Housing and Town Planning Act gave the council also the power to plan the development of unbuilt areas. A succession of Town and Country Planning Acts up to the present day has extended the council's powers, and it is now the planning authority for all kinds of development.

From its foundation the London County Council pursued a vigorous housing policy. It had been the practice of the old Metropolitan Board of Works to sell the sites which came under its control, subject to an undertaking on the part of the purchaser to erect working-class accommodation. The London County Council preferred to develop working-class estates, and because of the difficulty of finding suitable sites within its own area developed a number of areas on its outskirts.

Most spectacular of these ventures was the huge estate of Becontree, where no less than 25,000 houses were built to accommodate a population displaced from Central London of 115,000 to 130,000 people. £14,000,000 was required for the creation of this new town, which was completed in July, 1935, and formally opened by Dr. Christopher Addison.

These huge estates outside the County boundary created an anomalous position for the London County Council in that it undertook to subsidise the rentals of their tenants for a period of sixty years, while losing them as ratepayers. Since 1927 the London County Council has therefore adopted a policy of building huge five- or even eight-storey blocks of flats within the central area, which enabled the high ground rents to be paid without extravagantly raising the cost of the individual flat. These new structures are incomparably better than the slum housing which they replace, and are a distinctive feature of modern London.

Rehousing 400,000 People

Towards the end of 1936 the Council launched out upon its first large-scale experiment in town-planning; a scheme for the complete redevelopment of an area of forty-six acres in the densely populated district of Bethnal Green, involving the displacement and rehousing of 4,700 people at a cost of £1,750,000. Then came the Second World War with its air raids. The resulting devastation and the problems, as well as the splendid opportunities for rebuilding and rehousing London, are dealt with in the chapter "London at War." None the less, it is interesting here to record that in sixty-odd years the Council cleared over 400 acres of slums and built over 100,000 houses accommodating 440,000 persons.

It was not until 1866 that London possessed its own fire-fighting organisation. Until almost half-way through the nineteenth century the only organised protection against fire was that provided by the separate insurance companies, each of which maintained its own brigade.

It was only with insured premises that each particular office was concerned, and householders were given badges, or fire marks, to fix on the front of their houses so that passers-by should know which brigade should be summoned in case of fire. The company brigades were purely and simply for the protection of property. The only arrangements for the saving of life were independent fire escapes provided out of the voluntary contributions of charitable persons.

Fire Brigade Taken Over

In 1832 the insurance companies decided to pool their resources in this matter, and the separate brigades were merged into a single organisation prepared to attend any fires in its area in the centre of the metropolis; the parishes were supposed to provide protection in the rest. The brigade was taken over as a municipal service by the Metropolitan Board of Works in 1866, and thence passed under the control of the London County Council.

Tremendous strides have been made in the tech-

Donald McLeish

MOST BEAUTIFULLY SITUATED LONDON HOSPITAL

The seven detached buildings of St. Thomas's Hospital line the Albert Embankment. Several of the blocks were completely destroyed by enemy air attacks.

nique of fire fighting since the early days of the insurance company brigades. Until 1829 the water was still pumped by hand, but in that year the first steam-engine made its appearance, though it was not generally adopted until after 1850. Appliances were drawn by horses until well into the twentieth century, and the sight of the magnificent animals galloping breakneck through the streets gave an added thrill to the exciting spectacle of a fire which the present generation has lost with the introduction of the vastly more efficient, but less romantic, motor engines.

Donald McLeish

HOSPITAL FOUNDED BY A MISER

Guy's Hospital stands in Southwark near London Bridge. It was founded in 1721 by Thomas Guy, who atoned for a miserly life by a princely benefaction.

The equipment of the London brigade includes powerful fire-floats used for subduing fires on board ships in the river or in the huge wharves and warehouses which line its banks.

On the Way in Twenty Seconds

The question of time is, of course, of prime importance. On the average an escape leaves within twenty seconds, and a pump within forty seconds, of an outbreak being notified to the station. The brigade works as a homogeneous unit; if the officer first called to the scene of a fire decides that the outbreak is serious he signals back a district call, or even a brigade call, which brings another fifteen or thirty appliances on the scene. Meanwhile at headquarters, a pin representing each fire-engine has been moved on a map to indicate its whereabouts, and, if all the appliances of one district have been called to a big fire, reserves are shifted into position in case an outbreak should occur in a new area. In 1955 the London County Council brigade had over sixty stations with a staff of 2,400 and some 245 motor appliances. During the Second World War the L.F.B. was reinforced by a great number of mobile pumps, manned by the Auxiliary Fire Service. The vital part played by these "amateurs" in their heroic struggles with the ghastly fires of 1940–41 is told on another page.

During the war, too, the constant danger from incendiary bombs resulted in a tightening-up of the country's fire organisations, and the formation of a single National Fire Service. This was disbanded in 1948 and its work in London is once again carried out by the L.F.B.

Work of Pioneer School Societies

Education is one of the largest departments of the Council's services. Before 1833 only those children of poor families were likely to receive any instruction at all who chanced to live near a church which also ran a school. Two organisations had been started towards the beginning of the century for providing schooling for the poorer people, the British and Foreign School Society, founded in 1808, and the National Society, three years later.

Though the pioneering work of these societies was extremely valuable and formed the basis on which later education facilities were built, the people who started these organisations were primarily concerned with giving the children a knowledge of the Bible. Learning ıs such was purely incidental to their aims.

In 1844 the work of these institutions was upplemented by the setting up of the Ragged Schools Union. Yet as late as 1871 all the chools in London put together could not take nore than forty per cent. of the children. The conditions in some of them were abominable. An official report on one Ragged School n 1874 said there were " seventeen children n a small, filthy hovel. There were four, in act, but a few months old. The little ones vere quite naked. The woman who pretends o look after the school was engaged in a back ard, washing." Another observer states : " The masters and mistresses of ragged schools leclare that the children continually cry with unger and frequently fall exhausted from heir seats for want of food, and that it is mpossible to teach them in such a state."

London's Educational Ladder

From that time conditions began to improve, or in 1870 the Government laid the foundaions of a national system of education in the Forster Act, which in its application to London ave the citizens the right to elect a central uthority to control education within the netropolis. This was the origin of the London School Board, which did good work until it was absorbed by the London County Council in 1904.

Courtesy of the Postmaster-General

LONDON TRUNK EXCHANGE

Post Office telephone operators at the giant switchboard at Faraday Building in Queen Victoria Street.

The facilities offered provided a complete educational ladder, by means of which the scholarly child of the poorest parents is enabled to pass from a primary to a secondary school, and thence to a university. Special schools are provided for children physically or mentally defective, as well as special institutions for technical training and for the continuation of education by those who pass out of a primary or secondary school into industry.

The following figures will give some idea of the immense work which this implies : The Council maintains about 970 nursery and primary schools in which about 292,000 boys and girls are taught; it maintains, or helps to maintain, 326 secondary schools, attended by over 137,000 boys and girls, and also 129 technical and evening schools with 288,000 pupils; and it affords much assistance to the University of London.

Until July 5, 1948, the London County Council maintained over 100 hospitals with over 70,000 beds and dispensed poor relief. These services have now passed to Regional Hospital Boards and the National Assistance Board; but the Council retains a welfare service and has taken over many of the health duties of the twenty-eight borough councils. It still runs an ambulance service; maintains " ten bridges over the Thames and four tunnels under it " and upwards of 100 parks with a total area of about nine square miles; acts as a licensing authority for theatres, cinemas and other places of entertainment and for motor vehicles; enforces the Shop Acts; checks weights and measures; and so on.

Duties of Borough Councils

On the other hand, the Council is not entrusted with a great many functions which elsewhere are often performed by the municipality. The twenty-eight borough councils, for example, are responsible for the lighting, cleaning and repair of streets, and for the provision of libraries. The London County Council has no concern whatever with the policing of its administrative area, which is carried out by the Metropolitan Police Force under the direct control of the Home Secretary, or in the City by the independent City Police. Moreover the Council, as we have seen, has only an indirect interest, through its representation on the Metropolitan Water Board, in the supply of water, and it stands in the same relation, through its membership of the Port of London Authority, to the management of the Port of London. As the result of an early grant of monopoly the City Corporation remains the market authority for a radius of seven miles around its boundaries.

How the Council Works

Now as to the Council itself. The Parliamentary and County Council electoral divisions in London are the same; they were revised by the Representation of the People Act, 1948, and were used for the first time in the general County Council election of April, 1949. Each Parliamentary constituency elects three members. This gives the Council a total membership of 126 councillors. In addition, aldermen not exceeding one-sixth of the number of councillors are appointed by the Council. The Council, therefore, has twenty-one aldermen in addition to its councillors, giving it a total membership of 147. Councillors are elected for three years and aldermen appointed for six.

As is usual in municipal government, party politics play a large part in the regulation of the affairs of the Council. Thus it has become usual for the quota of aldermen to be divided between the chief parties in proportion to their strength on the Council. The same rule governs appointment to other offices. For example, the meetings of the Council are presided over by a junta of three, known collectively as " the Dais." The Dais consists of the Chairman, who is appointed by the majority party, not necessarily from among the elected councillors, the Vice-Chairman, also nominated by the majority, and the Deputy-Chairman, nominated by the opposition. The three Chairmen are not, however, during their year of office political leaders so much as ceremonial representatives of the whole Council. At Council debates there is a very salutary rule that no member shall speak for more than fifteen minutes, at the end of which period the Clerk hands to the Chairman a printed slip bearing the words " The hon. member has been speaking for fifteen minutes." An extension of time is often granted in the Council Chamber, but probably the member referred to does not mention this at home.

Committees Take on Routine

The routine work of the Council (work, that is, which does not normally involve any major question of policy) is carried on through Committees and sub-Committees, whose chairmen

FARADAY BUILDING
Headquarters of the Telephone Department of th G.P.O. The Telephone Service dates from 1892

are appointed from among the members of th majority party. This does not mean that th minority party is overridden, but is a mean of getting the work done more expeditiously as a chairman who has not a majority backin on a committee is in an anomalous position

Standing committees are appointed for a the chief services which the Council carrie out. They include, for example, an Educatio Committee, Parks, Town Planning and Hous ing Committees, and a Finance Committe whose task it is to examine and report upo the financial aspect of all proposals submitte by the spending committees. In addition there is a General Purposes Committee which acts as a co-ordinating body, including in its membership all the chairmen of the departmental committees. On the analogy between the vast population of London and that of many a state, the London County Council is often referred to as the "Parliament of London." Continuing the analogy, the Press refers to the Leader of the Council as the "Prime Minister" of London, and to the General Purposes Committee as the "Cabinet" of the Council.

Huge Staff of L.C.C.

The technical and administrative work of the Council is carried out by a large salaried staff. At the head of this stand the sixteen chief officers of the Council. Some of these, such as the Clerk, Comptroller and Solicitor act in various capacities "to" the Council, while others, such as the Education Officers or the Chief Officer of the Fire Brigade, are the responsible heads of the various services acting under the direction of the Council.

This democratically elected body must be one of the largest employers of labour, as well as one of the biggest landlords, in the country. On the clerical and administrative staff alone there were 6,750 people in 1955. Including those engaged in the various services no less than 62,350 persons were on the pay-roll. The post-war reorganisation of London may remove nearly a million people to the "outer ring," but the labour and supply needs of the London County Council will still remain gigantic.

GENERAL POST OFFICE

The G.P.O. occupies nine blocks of buildings near St. Martin's-le-Grand. The above picture shows the main post office, which is in King Edward Street.

Its annual "Budget" is of the order of £80,000,000. Only about two-fifths of this falls on the rates, the remainder being accounted for by Exchequer grants and other receipts. Education is by far the largest item each year and in the year 1955–56 was estimated to cost £36,563,000. The Administrative County has a rateable value of £60,000,000. Of the amount raised by the County on the rates the City contributes no less than one-ninth in payment for the various services administered by the Council in its area, which include such things as education, fire brigade, main drainage, hostels and relief for the aged, infirm and homeless.

The first offices of the Council were in the old County Hall in Spring Gardens, behind Whitehall. When the thoroughfare formed part of the grounds of the old Whitehall Palace, the placing of a foot on a step by a trespasser caused a spray of water to squirt out and remind him that the place was private property. Almost from the beginning the building was felt to be inadequate for the tremendous work to be carried out. Hence, in 1906, the Council obtained powers to construct a new dwelling for itself, and the site of the present County Hall beside Westminster Bridge, on the other side of the river, was decided upon.

County Hall Built on Raft

To secure adequate foundations for the immense structure which was to be erected it was necessary to reclaim two and a half acres of the Thames mud, and the building itself, which covers an area of six and a half acres, was erected upon a "raft" of concrete five feet deep. Building began in March, 1912, but was held up during the First World War and it was not until July, 1922, that the main part of the structure was completed and opened by King George V. The north wing has since been added, so that Londoners can now look with pride upon a fine symmetrical building, the chief feature of which is the central "crescent" colonnade, flanked by a wing on each side. The total cost was about £3,636,000.

Street lighting in London is believed to have been introduced by Henry III about 1253. For the purpose bonfires—originally termed bone-fires—carefully watched by a guard on account of the inflammable nature of the buildings, were made. Later, citizens displayed "lamps of glasse, with oyle burning in them all the night; some hung out branches of iron curiously wrought, containing hundreds of lamps lighted at once, which made a goodly shew, namely in New Fish Street, Thames Street, &c."

First Use of Gas and Electricity

The first gas-lamps were put up in Pall Mall in 1809, three years before the Gas Light and Coke Company began to supply London with its product. Gas-lighting became general in the streets of the capital in 1816, the year following the crowning victory of Waterloo. Indeed, the long-drawn-out agony of the Napoleonic Wars was commemorated by some of the lamp standards, the bases of which were cannon captured from the French during the conflict.

Electric light appeared in London in 1882, when T. A. Edison utiiised his invention in a few offices on Holborn Viaduct. Lord Randolph Churchill's house in Connaught Place was the first private residence in town to be lit with the new illuminant, the current being generated in the basement; and incandescent lamps were introduced as a novelty at the Savoy Theatre. The pioneer electric supply concern was the Kensington Court Company, established in 1886. To-day gigantic power-stations, such as that at Battersea, meet the needs of millions.

London had to wait many a long year for an efficient means of conveying messages. Now Faraday Building, Carter Lane, links the globe by telephone, radio and cable, and St Martin's-le-Grand by telegraph and post. At Mount Pleasant is the largest sorting office for postal packets in the world.

Beginning of the Post Office

The Post Office was originally started for conveying official dispatches, but a State service was begun in 1635, when a letter on a single sheet of paper could be sent a distance of eighty miles for twopence. Postage stamps made their first appearance in May 1841.

Donald McLei[sh]

UNIVERSITY COLLEGE

Founded to provide education in literature, science and the fine arts on a non-sectarian basis and at moderate cost. The building, opened in 1828, stands in Gower Street, Bloomsbury, near Euston Station

OLDEST ROMAN CATHOLIC CHURCH IN LONDON
The crypt of St. Etheldreda's, Ely Place, the only pre-Reformation church in London now held by Roman Catholics. This fine thirteenth-century building was formerly a private chapel of the Bishops of Ely.

WHERE LONDON WORSHIPS

In 1666, the year of the Great Fire, there were no fewer than 107 parish churches in the City, which means that there was at least one church to every seven acres. In 1939 the City had fifty-two old churches which either escaped the flames or were rebuilt shortly afterwards. By April, 1945, twenty of these had again been damaged or destroyed during the five and a half years' war with Germany. Their roofless walls stand naked to the sky. On their pavements the inscriptions have been filled in with rubbish. Between the stones willow-herbs and other weeds spring up. The priceless carvings, the choir stalls, the organs, the fonts, have been consumed by the flames. A few defaced monuments still adhere to the walls. Rows of pillars still mark the sites of the aisles, but the arches that they once supported have tumbled to the ground and been overgrown by grass. As features of London these churches exist no more; they might as well be pulled down and replaced by blue memorial plaques. But some have been restored, others will be repaired, a number will be converted to special purposes, and only a few will be entirely sacrificed.

The first church on the site of All Hallows, Barking-by-the-Tower, was probably built towards the end of the seventh century as a daughter church of the Abbey of Barking, some seven miles distant, hence the somewhat puzzling name. Rebuilt in the Norman style in the eleventh century and repaired in 1634, it was fortunate enough to escape destruction in the raging furnace of thirty-two years later. Destroyed during the last war, it is now being rebuilt.

William Penn, the Quaker founder of Pennsylvania, was born in Great Tower Street nearby and baptised in All Hallows.

It is the guild church of Toc H, an organisation for Christian Fellowship and social service which originated during the First World War at Poperinghe, in Belgium. " Toc H " was the army signaller's version of T.H., the original club being known as Talbot House. On the fifteenth-century tomb of Sir John Croke stood the " lamp of maintenance " given by the Duke of Windsor (then Prince of Wales) in 1922 in memory of his friends who fell in the conflict. Beneath the church, part of a Roman shop or villa, with tessellated pavement, was brought to light a few years ago. The Normans incorporated a section of the old Roman Wall in their building and the track worn by the feet of sentries is still evident.

Building on a Roman Bastion

There is another church of this dedication in the City—All Hallows-on-the-Wall—so called because it is said to have been built on one of the Roman bastions in London Wall. Built in the fifteenth century, it was demolished in 1764 and rebuilt shortly afterwards.

The Watch House to guard against body-snatchers in the churchyard of All-Hallows-the-Less still stands in Upper Thames Street though the church was destroyed in the Grea Fire of 1666.

WATCH HOUSE ON CHURCH SITE

Built in 1557 to guard graves from body-snatchers. The arched recess was for the watchman's bell.

Hidden amidst offices off Old Broad Street is Austin Friars Church, dating from the middle of the thirteenth century, when an Augustinian priory was formed there. Edward VI handed over the building "to the Dutch nation in London, to be their preaching place," and ever since then it has been used by the Dutch Reformed Church.

In 1550 it must have been a grand building "one of the beautifullest and rarest spectacles" in the City, we are told, with a fine spire choir, transepts and nave. This beautiful old church, once blitzed, has risen anew.

Christ Church, Newgate Street, claimed to be the widest City church. Built by Wren in 1687, it stands on the site of a Franciscan (Grey Friars) church which was begun in 1306. It, too, is now only a shell.

In the middle of the sixteenth century the buildings of the Grey Friars monastery were turned into a home for orphans which became known as Christ's Hospital. This fine effort was due to a sermon on charity. It was in 1552 that Nicholas Ridley, Bishop of London preached before Edward VI "a fruitful and godly exhortation to the rich to be merciful to the poor, and also to move such as are in authority to travail by some way or means to comfort and relieve them." "I think you mean me," said the King at the conclusion of the discourse, "for I am in the highest place." The Lord Mayor and the Corporation also helped, with the result that in the following year the house of the Grey Friars became "an hospital for fatherless children and for poor men's children, who can there find meat, drink clothes, lodging and learning."

Church of the Bluecoat Boys

After the new church was built, broad galleries were erected for the use of these children, the boys being familiarly known as "Bluecoat boys" on account of their quaint garb. The boys are now at Horsham and the girls at Hertford.

Wood Street, which boasts a plane-tree at the Cheapside end of it that marks the site of St. Peter in Chepe, also contains a church (now gutted) dedicated to St. Alban, Britain's first martyr. Rebuilt by Wren in 1685, it was remarkable in possessing the only Gothic tower that the great architect erected in the City

The Church of St. Andrew, Holborn, goes back to the Saxons. It escaped the Great Fire, but was in such bad repair that Wren found it necessary to demolish and re-erect it, with the exception of the tower, which only required refacing. It was burnt out during the war but is to be rebuilt.

A Church of Many Famous Men

The church has associations with more than one great name. John Webster, the dramatist, is buried there. The parish records contain the name of Thomas Chatterton, the youthful poet who committed suicide in a garret in Brooke Street, not far from the church. Colonel Hutchinson, of Civil War fame, married Lucy Apsley there in 1638, and William Hazlitt, the essayist, stood before the altar and wedded Sarah Stoddart in 1808, with Charles Lamb as best man. At the font the poet Savage and two famous statesmen, Benjamin Disraeli and Addington, were baptised.

Only a few yards away is the wreck of the City Temple, which was opened in 1874.

At the corner of St. Mary Axe is St. Andrew Undershaft, so called because in former times a " shaft " or maypole which overtopped the steeple stood before the south door. Chaucer refers to this shaft, and Stow, whose remains were buried in the church, tells us how he saw " the neighbours and tenants . . . after they had well dined, to make themselves strong," cut it in pieces, since preachers had denounced it as a pagan relic. " Thus was this idol . . . mangled, and after burned." The church was originally erected in 1326 and rebuilt in 1520, and was well known to Hans Holbein, who painted some of his finest pictures in London.

St. Augustine with St. Faith, in Watling Street, stands, a pitiful shell, under the shadow of St. Paul's Cathedral. It once had for its rector the Rev. R. H. Barham, the author of *The Ingoldsby Legends*.

St. Bartholomew the Great, Smithfield, was founded in 1123 by the monk Rahere, whose tomb is one of its chief treasures. He built his Priory on a swamp and to provide funds for the work was allowed by Henry II to hold a three-days Fair within the grounds. This became the famous Bartholomew Fair.

During the reign of Henry IV much of the Priory was rebuilt, there being planted in its grounds a mulberry garden, one of the first in England, and for long greatly famed. All trace of it has vanished, and its site is largely occupied by factories and offices, but the visitor may, as he finds his way round the curious wanderings of Bartholomew Close, try to picture the days when learned scholars argued fine points of logic beneath the leafy trees.

HISTORIAN OF LONDON
Bust of John Stow, the antiquarian, in the Church of St. Andrew Undershaft. The pen is renewed yearly.

Fortunes of St. Bartholomew's

In the sixteenth century Henry VIII laid covetous and destructive hands upon the religious houses of England, and St. Bartholomew's Priory was not more fortunate than the rest. Church and Priory were sold to Sir Richard Rich, but it is to be recorded in Henry's favour that in 1544 he founded a new hospital of St. Bartholomew, and when those he placed in charge mismanaged this, he established it a second time " for the continual relief and help of a hundred sore and diseased."

But the Priory buildings were thrown down, and the nave of the church. Only the chancel and part of the transepts were left to serve the needs of the surrounding parish. Thus the church stands now, although a boys' day school was once held in the north triforium, a blacksmith's forge stood in the north transept, and the Lady Chapel was at various times a fringe factory, a dancing saloon and a public house. A printing office was established in the sacred building, where Benjamin Franklin set type during his days in London. The cloisters were used as stables and the crypt as a wine and coal cellar.

St. Bartholomew the Great is the oldest parish church in London. It has been described as the " noblest monument of Norman ecclesiastical architecture in the capital," and the description is in no way exaggerated.

The massive round pillars and square piers separating the chancel from the aisles, the five semi-circular arches on each side, the columns of the triforium, and the arched and vaulted ceiling of the aisle surrounding the choir are all Norman work of the simplest and truest style, while the beautiful oriel window placed opposite the founder's tomb by the last of the priors must rejoice all who behold it. The panels in the choir-screen representing scenes in the life story of the minstrel-monk are the work of Mr. Frank Beresford, and were dedicated in 1932.

ST. BARTHOLOMEW THE GREAT
The church was founded in the twelfth century by the monk Rahere, who obtained money for the work from the subsequently famous Bartholomew Fair.

Sixpences for Widows

The nave covered what is now the graveyard, where a portion of its wall may still be seen. It extended to the beautiful Elizabethan gateway which, surmounted by a picturesque timbered gatehouse, now forms the entrance to the precincts from West Smithfield. In the churchyard is a flat tombstone on which every Good Friday twenty-one sixpences are laid, to be picked up by twenty-one aged widows of the City of London.

St. Benet's, Paul's Wharf, Upper Thames Street, has been for many years the church of the London Welsh. Built of red brick by Sir Christopher Wren, the present building is small and squat, but it has a simple beauty that is very attractive. Inigo Jones, the architect, was buried in the old church in 1652.

St. Bride's, Fleet Street, another war casualty, is known as the Journalists' Church, the saint from whom it takes its name being the patron of newspapermen. St. Bride (or Bridget) was Irish, and a disciple of St. Patrick. In her native land there are many holy wells bearing her name, and it is not surprising therefore to learn that a famous well near Fleet Street was called Bridewell. The name was later given to a king's palace which in its declining years became a notorious house of correction for erring females.

Where Pepys was Baptised

The present church is said to have been designed for Wren by his daughter, a woman who inherited her father's genius but died of consumption at an early age.

Samuel Richardson, usually regarded as the father of the English novel, wrote many of his early works in Salisbury Court, near at hand, and he and his two wives are buried in the church. Pepys was baptised there.

St. Clement's, in Eastcheap, is sometimes said to be the church referred to in " Oranges and lemons," but the majority of people support the rival claim of St. Clement Danes, Strand. Rebuilt by Wren after the Fire, the new place of worship so delighted the parishioners that they sent the architect a barrel of wine. On the list of organists is Edward Purcell, son of the famous composer Henry Purcell.

At the corner of Idol Lane and St. Dunstan's Hill is the church of St. Dunstan's in the East, not to be confused with the more famous St. Dunstan's in the West, Fleet Street.

The former is the last of the City churches built by Wren, and the architect has nothing finer to his credit than the steeple. The body of the church was pulled down and rebuilt early in the last century. Sir John Hawkins, the Elizabethan slave-trader and admiral, was buried in the old building.

St. Dunstan's in the West

High up on St. Dunstan's in the West there is a clock with two bells hanging in a porch, on either side of which stands a human figure. In their hands the two figures hold cudgels with which they strike the bells to mark the passing of each quarter of an hour. Declared to be "more admired by many of the populace on Sundays than the most elegant preacher from the pulpit within," they and the clock were removed in 1832 from the church, then being rebuilt, to the house of the Marquis of Hertford in Regent's Park. The price paid was £200.

The house, known thereafter as St. Dunstan's Lodge, gave its name to a famous organisation formed after the First World War to care for blinded British soldiers. There the giants, clock and bells remained until 1935, when they were returned to Fleet Street through the munificence of Lord Rothermere.

The present eight-sided church is the youngest of the City churches, but its predecessor was rich in historical associations. Its vicars included William Tyndale, translator of the New Testament, Thomas White, founder of Sion College, and John Donne, poet and Dean of St. Paul's.

While the last mentioned held office at St. Dunstan's, Izaak Walton, the author of *The Compleat Angler*, kept a shirt-shop two doors west of Chancery Lane and frequently attended service at the church. Tablets commemorate Hobson Judkin, "the Honest Solicitor" and Alexander Layton, "ye famed Swordsman."

St. Ethelburga, Bishopsgate, is called after the daughter of King Ethelbert, the first Saxon monarch to embrace Christianity. It is fitting, therefore, that it should claim to be the oldest foundation in London. It is also said to be the smallest church in the City. The present edifice appears to have been erected early in the fifteenth century. Two old shops, one built in 1570 and the other in 1641, stood in front of the church until recently.

Henry Hudson made his Communion at St. Ethelburga's before setting out on his first voyage in search of the North-west Passage. Stained-glass windows commemorate him and his companions.

St. Giles's, Cripplegate, one of the City's most historic churches, is to-day a ruin—another victim of the air raids.

In the churchyard are remains of a Roman bastion, from which an oval-shaped underground passage ran northwards to Barbican, where there was a fort. It is from this passage that the church derives its name : *cripple* is a corruption of the Anglo-Saxon *crepel*, or *crypele*, an underground way.

Oliver Cromwell was married in St. Giles's, and it contains the remains of John Milton, Sir Martin Frobisher, the navigator, John Foxe, the author of *The Book of Martyrs*, and John Speed, the historian.

The beautiful old church of St. Helen's, Bishopsgate, is often referred to as the Westminster Abbey of the City, because of the great number of memorials to distinguished citizens it contains. Chief among them is that to Sir Thomas Gresham, the founder of the Royal Exchange.

The Lord Mayor's Official Church

In 1598 there was a William Shakespeare living near the former church. He may have been the dramatist and have worshipped in St. Helen's, which is called after the Empress Helena, mother of Constantine the Great.

St. Lawrence Jewry, near the Guildhall, is the official church of the Lord Mayor and Corporation; it was destroyed in the fire raid, December 29, 1940, along with a large part of the Guildhall.

St. Magnus the Martyr, London Bridge, built by Wren in 1676, stands on the site of a church of which Miles Coverdale, who gave us the first complete English translation of the Bible, was rector. It was badly damaged in 1940, but services are still held in the crypt.

St. Martin's, Ludgate Hill, which rests on the Roman Wall, was rebuilt about the middle of the fifteenth century and again by Wren after the Great Fire. It had as rector in 1614 Samuel Purchas, the celebrated travel-writer, author of *Purchas his Pilgrimage*, and editor of some of Hakluyt's works.

On its seventeenth-century font are inscribed the Greek words, ΝΙΨΟΝ ΆΝΟΜΗΜΑ ΜΗ ΜΟΝΑΝ ΟΨΙΝ (Wash my guilt and not my face only). The letters form a palindrome, which is to say they read the same backwards as forwards. The sentence has formed a favourite inscription for fonts for about 1,000 years. It is inscribed in the Church of St. Sophia, Istanbul (Constantinople), in Notre Dame, Paris, and in at least four English churches.

The Chimes of Bow Bells

Everyone has heard of St. Mary-le-Bow, whose bells heartened Whittington when he was about to leave London in despair. Their chimes seemed to say, " Turn again, Whittington, Lord Mayor of London." To be born within sound of them is to be born a Cockney.

There has been a church on this site for nearly ten centuries, but the present edifice was erected by Wren. The steeple is remarkably fine, as perhaps it ought to be considering that it cost £7,388 of a total sum of £15,400 for the whole building. It is surmounted by an enormous gilded dragon, nine feet long and made of tin. Bow Church was gutted during the bombing, but is to be restored.

CLOCK FACE BECOMES BADGE
Badge of the Order of St. John of Jerusalem painted on the clock face of the chapel in Clerkenwell.

In the Church of St. Mary the Virgin, Aldermanbury, were buried John Heminge and Henrie Condell, the publishers of the first folio edition of Shakespeare's works, and also Judge Jeffreys, of unhappy memory. It was designed by Wren and was completed in 1677. During the first Zeppelin raid on London during the First World War, it had practically all its windows shattered by a bomb.

At the corner of Lombard Street and King William Street is the Church of St. Mary Woolnoth. The second name is possibly derived from a beam for weighing wool which stood in the churchyard of St. Mary's Woolchurch, the parish of which was incorporated with St. Mary's Woolnoth following the fire of 1666. Though not destroyed by the Great Fire, it was entirely rebuilt by Nicholas Hawksmoor between 1716 and 1727, and many years later its vaults were sold to make room for the Bank Underground Station. Its united twin towers are unique.

A lonely tower is all that remains of the Wren church of St. Mary Somerset, in Upper Thames Street, which was pulled down in 1868, but not before a band of ingenious thieves had helped themselves to the lead that covered the roof. Under the impression that the men were engaged in carrying out repairs, the police took no more than a cursory interest in the proceedings. In 1924 the tower became a rest-room for young women employed in the City. The porch of St. Alphage, London Wall, which dates from 1331, is used for a similar purpose. It is dedicated to a saint, an Archbishop of Canterbury who suffered martyrdom at the hands of the Danes.

Stow's Family Church in Cornhill

John Stow and his family attended the Church of St. Michael, Cornhill, which was rebuilt by Wren and many years later altered in some respects by Sir Gilbert Scott. It has a magnificent tower surmounted by lofty pinnacles which Wren erected almost half a century later than the church itself.

St. Olave's, Hart Street, by Mark Lane, is called after Olaf, the second Christian King of

Norway. The date of its erection is uncertain, but it escaped the Great Fire. Records show that a place of worship has occupied the site since 1100, if not earlier; the existing crypt is of the thirteenth century. Samuel Pepys was a parishioner, and he and his wife are buried in a vault there. Mrs. Pepys died first, and her sorrowing husband had a bust of her placed in such a position that its eyes were turned in the direction of the pew they once jointly occupied.

Curious Sanctuary Knocker

The gateway is crowned with skulls in memory of the victims of the Great Plague who were interred in the graveyard. Because of this Dickens called it St. Ghastly Grim.

A curious feature of this church is the sanctuary knocker on one of the doors. In former times the fugitive criminal who touched such knockers could not be seized by the civil authority, but he was forced to acknowledge his guilt and to leave the country.

Tradition states that St. Peter's on Cornhill was founded by Regulus Lucius in A.D. 179, but this is unlikely. Among its treasures, however, is an illuminated Bible which was given to St. Peter's in 1291 by the monk who produced it. The present edifice, one of the most beautiful in the City, was built by Wren some fourteen years after the Great Fire. Its predecessor was linked with St. Helen's, Bishopsgate, by an underground passage, part of which still remains.

The foundation of the church of St. Sepulchre, "over against Newgate, Holborn, London," dates from the First Crusade, hence the name. The present tower, rebuilt in the fifteenth century, escaped the conflagration of 1666. Its bells are those mentioned in the nursery rhyme as belonging to Old Bailey. For centuries the great bell of St. Sepulchre's was tolled as the condemned felons of Newgate prison started out for Tyburn; and, nearer our own times, before public executions outside the prison walls. As the Tyburn prisoners passed the church steps they were offered nosegays, and ale was given to them at St. Giles in the Fields.

To Americans St. Sepulchre's is particularly interesting since Captain John Smith, Governor of Virginia and Admiral of New England, is buried there.

Behind the Mansion House is St. Stephen's, Walbrook, Wren's own parish church and one upon which he is said to have lavished his great gifts to the fullest extent. Its handsome dome and roof suffered in the earlier air raids, but have now been rebuilt.

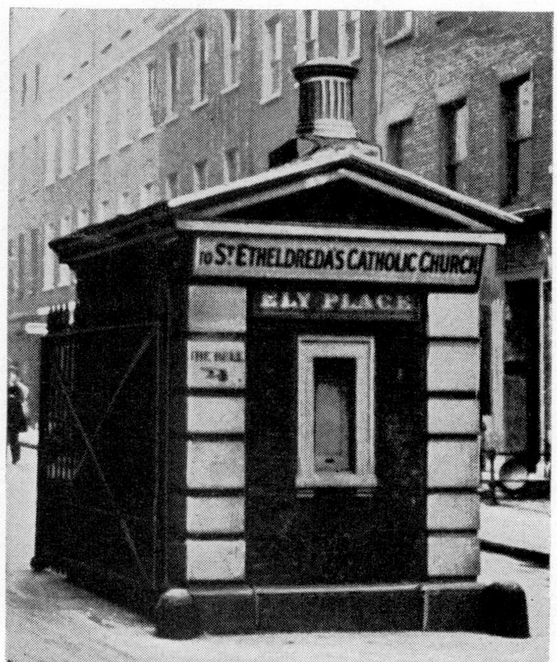

SITE OF BISHOP'S PALACE
Ely Place near Holborn Circus is private property. It is locked at night by the porter in charge.

One of Wren's colleagues, Sir John Vanbrugh, equally distinguished as an architect, and as a dramatist, is buried here.

Pendleton, alleged by some authorities to be the Vicar of Bray of the famous song, was once rector of St. Stephen's.

The Old City Monasteries

No account of the ecclesiastical life of the City would be complete without some reference to its bygone monasteries.

Whitefriars Street, off Fleet Street, preserves the memory of a Carmelite convent which once existed in that neighbourhood. Founded in the reign of Edward I, it was dissolved by Henry VIII, who gave the chapter-house to his physician. The refectory became the Whitefriars Theatre.

Farther east was the Blackfriars monastery, on which Edward I and Eleanor, his queen, bestowed many gifts. There Charles V of France lodged when on a visit, there Henry VIII held the Black Parliament which abolished the jurisdiction of the Pope of England, and there Katherine of Aragon was tried. The monastery

MOTHER CHURCH OF METHODISM

Wesley's Chapel, situated in the City Road, fronted by a statue of John Wesley, founder of Methodism, who laid the first stone of the chapel in 1777. The great divine now lies buried behind the chapel.

succumbed to Henry VIII's greed in 1538.

In the following year that rapacious monarch also confiscated the London headquarters of the Order of the Holy Cross, which stood at the western end of Crutched Friars Street, near Fenchurch Street Station. As the members of the Order were vowed to poverty, their property was of little value. They were called Crouched, Crutched or Crossed Friars from the cross they wore on their habits. The site of the friary was afterwards occupied by the Navy Office, where Samuel Pepys worked. He lived round the corner in Seething Lane.

Hospital of St. John of Jerusalem

The Grand Priory of the Venerable Order of the Hospital of St. John of Jerusalem has as its priory church that of St. John, Clerkenwell—outside the City—which until the end of 1930 served as a parish church. It then reverted to its old foundation previous to the Reformation. Heraclius, Patriarch of Jerusalem, who came to London to offer the crown of the Kingdom of Jerusalem to Henry II, laid the foundation of the original building in 1188, and traces of the circular nave are extant. Here the successors of the knights who defended the Holy Sepulchre, wearing the picturesque robes of the Order, hold an annual service. The St. John Ambulance Association and the St. John Ambulance Brigade, which the Order brought into being, have their headquarters nearby in St. John's Gate. This, the only remaining street gate in London, was built in 1504 by the Grand Prior, Thomas Docra.

Modern Life in Stained Glass

A little farther north, in Haggerston, is St. Augustine's Church. It is probably unique in that it possesses modern stained-glass windows depicting everyday life in the East End. One shows a working-class kitchen, with a range, an aspidistra in the window, two little children saying their prayers at their mother's knee, a sleeping cat and a teddy bear; another depicts boys playing cricket against a lamp-post near a public-house.

The mother church of Methodism, that

built by John Wesley in 1778, is in City Road, Finsbury, and the pulpit from which he preached is still in use. The remains of the great reformer rest near by. His house, now a Wesley museum, adjoins the chapel.

St. Blaise's Blessing

In Ely Place, off Hatton Garden, and almost a stone's throw from the City boundary, is the church of St. Etheldreda, first built about the year 1290, and for long part of the palace of the Bishops of Ely. It was in this palace that John of Gaunt, father of Henry IV, died in 1399, and it was to the garden there that Shakespeare referred in *Richard III* when he put the following words in Gloucester's mouth :

" My lord of Ely, when I was last in Holborn,
I saw good strawberries in your garden there;
I do beseech you send for some of them."

The chapel, as beautiful as it is ancient, was bought for £5,270 by the Roman Catholic Fathers of Charity in 1874. Here St. Blaise's blessing—the blessing of the throat—is administered on February 3. The saint was Bishop of Sebaste, Armenia, in the fourth century, and it is said that while he was on his way to martyrdom he miraculously cured a little boy of throat trouble.

Ely Place, being private property, is not under the jurisdiction of the Corporation. Every evening the gates are closed by a porter, who sings out, " Fine night, all's well."

Stow refers to Southwark Cathedral as the " fair church called St. Mary Over the Rie, or Overie, that is over the water." Further, " This church, or some other in place thereof was of old time, long before the Conquest a house of sisters, founded by a maiden named Mary; unto the which house and sisters she left (as was left to her by her parents) the oversight and profits of a cross ferry, or traverse ferry over the Thames, there kept before that any bridge was built."

It has associations with some of the greatest names in English literature. One of its benefactors was John Gower, distinguished poet and intimate friend of Chaucer, who is accepted as the father of English poetry. He was interred on the north side of the church, in the chapel of St. John.

The parish register contains the following entry : " 1607 December 31st . . . Edmund Shakespeare, a player buried in ye church with a forenoon knell of the great bell." Edmund was brother to the great William, who must have known the place well. John Harvard, the founder of the famous American University of that name, was baptised within its walls.

ST. MARTIN-IN-THE-FIELDS
Often called " the broadcast church," it was built in 1726. Nell Gwynne lies buried there.

The cathedral's chief architectural treasure is the Lady Chapel, a perfect example of the Early English style. For many years it was used as a court-room, but later, during the reign of Queen Elizabeth, became a bakery.

By far the best known church westward of the City is St. Martin-in-the-Fields, so called to distinguish it from the church of the same dedication on Ludgate Hill. Although a German bomb passed clean through the structure and killed a number of shelterers in the crypt, the church survived and still attracts large numbers of visitors.

History tells us that in Henry VIII's reign residents north of Whitehall " had no parish church, but did resort to the parish church of

St. Margaret's (Westminster), and were thereby found to bring their bodies by the Courtgate of Whitehall, which the said Henry then misliking, caused the church of St. Martin-in-the-Fields to be there erected."

The present edifice, of which James Gibbs was the architect, was erected in 1726. Having the greater part of Buckingham Palace in its parish, it keeps a pew for the Queen and the heir to the throne.

Jack Sheppard, the highwayman, Mrs. Turner, the murderess of Sir Thomas Overbury, and Nell Gwynne, mistress of Charles II, are buried there. Nell's funeral oration was preached by Dr. Thomas Tenison, later Archbishop of Canterbury, who eulogised her for her kindness.

Night Shelter under a Graveyard

The coffin of John Hunter, one of the world's most distinguished surgeons, was placed in the vaults of St. Martin's in 1793. Nearly seventy years later, Frank Buckland, a scientist who had a great admiration for Hunter, decided that the surgeon's remains deserved to rest in the Abbey, and began to explore the vaults for his coffin. The search was long and exhausting; it lasted sixteen days, and Buckland nearly died of the effects. In the end his courageous efforts were crowned with success and John Hunter now lies at Westminster.

In 1936 the parochial authorities of St. Martin's decided to clear the vaults of corpses in order that the large area they occupied might be used for social and welfare work. This space is under the graveyard, which is now paved over and used as a children's playground. For many years the crypt has been kept open as a night-shelter for "down-and-outs."

St. Paul's Church, Covent Garden, has a peculiar interest for lovers of the drama. There lie the remains of William Wycherley, the Restoration comedy-writer, and Charles Macklin, the actor, and there is a memorial to Dame Ellen Terry, the actress. The first scene of Bernard Shaw's *Pygmalion* is laid under the back porch.

Among other celebrities buried in the church or churchyard are Samuel Butler, author of *Hudibras*; Robert Boyle, the scientist; Sir Peter Lely, famous for his portraits of the beauties of Charles II's dissolute Court; Grinling Gibbons, sculptor and wood-carver; and possibly, Claude Duval, highwayman.

Farther north, off the Bloomsbury end of Shaftesbury Avenue, is the church of St. Giles-in-the-Fields, founded as a leper-hospital chapel during the reign of Henry I. The present building dates from 1734. In its safe keeping are the remains of George Chapman, who wrote the famous translation of Homer that gave the poet Keats so much pleasure, as are also those of Milton's friend, Andrew Marvell, and "Unparalleled Pendrell" who saved Charles II's life after the Battle of Worcester.

St. George's, Bloomsbury, is remarkable in possessing on top of its steeple a statue of George I in a Roman toga. When first erected it aroused a good deal of ridicule. One wit wrote:

"When Harry the Eighth left the Pope in the lurch
The people of England made him head of the Church;
But George's good subjects, the Bloomsbury people,
Instead of the Church made him head of the Steeple."

St. James's, in Piccadilly, is a Wren church that owes its existence to the purse of Henry Jermyn, Earl of St. Albans. It is of red brick, has an outdoor pulpit, and a stone font carved by Grinling Gibbons featuring Adam and Eve and Noah's Ark. This beautiful old building was reduced to a ruin by the air raids, but continued in service throughout the war. In 1946 a charming little Garden of Remembrance to those who worked and suffered so heroically in the *blitz* was opened facing Piccadilly.

St. Margaret's, Westminster

Adjoining Westminster Abbey is St. Margaret's, since 1614 the place of worship of the House of Commons. In that year the House gave up attending the Abbey officially because of what members regarded as the Papist tendencies of the clergy there.

Its literary interest is great. Chaucer gave evidence before the High Court of Chivalry there in 1387. Caxton, who had his press nearby, was for a number of years auditor of the parish accounts. There John Milton married his second wife, Katherine Woodcocke, whose remains—as also those of her infant daughter—are buried in the church. There, too, the headless body of Raleigh, the first man to attempt to colonise Virginia, was buried two years after Shakespeare's death. By a most callous order of Charles II the bodies of Blake, Pym and other leaders of the Common-

ENTHRONEMENT OF AN ARCHBISHOP

A striking scene in the vast and beautiful Westminster Cathedral, which has been described as " beyond all doubt the finest church that has been built for centuries." Although the foundation stone of the building was laid in 1895, the interior is yet far from being completely decorated. Parts of it are exquisite.

wealth were flung into a pit in the churchyard after his restoration.

The architecture of Westminster Cathedral, the foremost Roman Catholic place of worship in London, is Early Byzantine.

Designed by John Francis Bentley, the structure was begun in 1895 and completed in the remarkably short space of eight years. It covers the site of old Tothill Fields Prison. The two most impressive features are the great west front and the campanile, known as St. Edward's Tower. The latter, 284 feet high, has a metal-covered dome on which stands a huge bronze cross containing what is regarded as a fragment of the true cross. Visitors may ascend to the top by means of the highest passenger-lift in London.

THE ORATORY OF ST. PHILIP NERI

Familiarly known as Brompton Oratory, it is famous for its music. Built in the year 1884, it contains a seventeenth-century altar brought from Italy.

The colossal interior has many striking features. The rood or crucifix hanging from the sanctuary arch is thirty feet high. The High Altar, a block of grey Cornish granite weighing twelve tons, took three weeks to move from the west door to its present position. The Archbishop's throne is a copy on a smaller scale of that of the Pope's in St. John Lateran, Rome. The great Willis organ took twelve years to complete.

Beauty of Westminster Cathedral

The interior decoration is still far from finished, but there are many striking mosaics, and Eric Gill has contributed a remarkable series of stone carvings illustrating the Stations of the Cross. The beautiful marble columns came from many countries, including France, Greece, Switzerland, Italy, and Norway.

On the other side of the river, in Lambeth Road, there was another Roman Catholic Cathedral, opened in 1848, but it was gutted during an air raid. Its ruins stand close to Christ Church, the tower and spire of which constitute a memorial to Abraham Lincoln, and were paid for by American subscriptions.

The Church of the Oratory, Brompton Road, designed by H. Gribble in the Italian Renaissance style, was opened by Cardinal Manning in 1884. It is famous for its music.

Record of Famous Names

The marriage register of St. George's, Hanover Square, makes interesting reading. Among the many famous names recorded are Lady Hamilton, Benjamin Disraeli, "George Eliot," Theodore Roosevelt, and Lord Oxford and Asquith. The burial-ground, no longer used for its original purpose, is in Bayswater Road, some little distance from Marble Arch. There was interred Laurence Sterne, the lovable parson-author, who wrote *Tristram Shandy*. He did not long rest in peace, for two days after the funeral the corpse was dug up by body-snatchers and sold to an anatomist at Cambridge. Where once stood the mortuary chapel there is now the Chapel of the Ascension, built by Mrs. Russell Gurney as a place of rest and meditation.

PRISONERS AT NEWGATE GAOL

Criminals under sentence of transportation being marched from Newgate to Blackfriars. The transportation of felons to distant colonies was begun in the reign of Elizabeth, and ceased about 1860. North America was, until the War of Independence, their usual destination; after that, Australia.

CRIME AND PUNISHMENT

CRIME, like the poor, is always with us, but it is far less prevalent than was formerly the case. A glimpse at the history of London during the eighteenth and early nineteenth centuries proves this.

The Metropolitan Police Force was founded in 1829 by Sir Robert Peel to check a state of rampant criminality almost unbelievable to the modern mind. The establishment of the Force was at least 100 years overdue. " Violence and plunder," laments a writer in 1731, " are no longer confined to the highways . . . the streets of the City are now the places of danger; men are knocked down and robbed, nay, sometimes murdered at their own doors, and in passing and repassing from house to house, or from shop to shop."

Stage coaches, he added, were being held up in High Holborn, Pall Mall, Soho, Whitechapel, and every road leading to and from the City; hackney coaches and private carriages in Cheapside, St. Paul's Churchyard, the Strand, " and other the most crowded streets; and that even while the people in throngs are passing."

Thirteen years later the Lord Mayor was driven to present a petition to the King against the " evil-disposed persons " who, armed with every species of dangerous weapon, " infested not only the private lanes and passages, but likewise the public streets and places of usual concourse, committing most daring outrages upon his Majesty's subjects."

Henry Fielding, the novelist, who became a Westminster magistrate in 1748, wrote a pamphlet on crime in London in which he declared that the public was " affronted and alarmed with threats and execrations, endangered with loaded pistols, beat with bludgeons and hacked with cutlasses, of which the loss of health, of limbs and often of life, is the consequence, and all this without any respect to age, or dignity, or sex."

Highwaymen rode openly into Hyde Park at dusk, tied their horses to the railings, and sallied forth to rob " chairs, carriages and pedestrians " indiscriminately. In Kensington Gardens a bell was rung nightly to warn home-going promenaders to gather in large parties to defy attack. Members of Parliament were afraid to go home singly when the House adjourned at a late hour and the cry, "Who goes home?" still used to-day to denote the adjournment, was then a rallying call for members anxious to travel in parties.

Often the gentlemen of the road did not trouble to wait for dark to carry out their depredations. "One is forced to travel, even at noon, as if one were going to battle," wrote Horace Walpole, who narrowly escaped death from a highwayman's bullet in Hyde Park.

Highwaymen of Fact and Fiction

Imaginative novelists have in more recent years invented quite a pleasing type of highwayman, a dashing and romantic young blood with an eye for a pretty face and a leaning towards sentimental chivalry. "I have not found him," writes Charles G. Harper, after searching the criminal records of the eighteenth century, "but I have found plentiful evidence of the existence of innumerable ineffable blackguards and irreclaimable villains of the most sordid, unrelieved type; bestially immoral, tigerishly cruel, and cringing cowards."

Yet the highwaymen were the aristocrats of their profession. They were the heroes of a foul host of rogues and blackguards which day and night preyed upon the denizens of London and the strangers within her gates; and only too often of the beaux and belles of fashionable society, who flocked in crowds to visit them in prison, and pandered to their vanity by loading them with gifts and delicacies.

Districts Inhabited by Criminals

Every inn-yard was infested with luggage thieves, whose task was made the easier by the fact that the innkeeper and his servants, the stage-coach driver and guard, and the hackney coachman were usually in league with them. Pocket-picking had been reduced to a fine art. The light-fingered gentry plied their trade dexterously in every busy street, and actually staged street brawls to collect crowds and distract attention from their pilfering of watches, wallets and handkerchiefs. The footpad lurked in every side street and alley, enforcing his demands with brutal violence, secure in the knowledge that within a few yards there was sure to be a safe retreat or hiding place.

Whole areas of the town were inhabited solely by criminals. Alsatia, the district between Fleet Street and the Thames, was notorious: no honest man dared venture into that network of crooked lanes and fetid slums. The region round Covent Garden was studded with "night-houses," low taverns where every form of villainy was concocted and every variety of vice could be indulged in.

Saffron Hill, the home of Dickens's Fagin, abutted on Smithfield, which had a most unsavoury reputation. Between St. Katharine's Dock and Limehouse the riverside was lined with the haunts of the water-rats who robbed the shipping in the Thames to the tune of some £300,000 a year.

In all these districts, and many others, every street had its thieves' den, its receiving shop, and its brothel. In 1796 there were in London 3,000 old iron and rag shops, of which Besant says that "they were universally, and without exception, and notoriously receivers of stolen goods." At the same time the City contained over 5,000 public houses and beer-shops, many of which were little more than rendezvous for highwaymen, housebreakers, cardsharpers and counterfeit coiners.

Counterfeit Coining

Counterfeit coining was carried out on a prodigious scale. In 1790 there were in London forty or fifty mints engaged in this illicit industry. One alone is said to have produced £200,000 worth of bad half-crowns in seven years. The "smasher," or passer of counterfeit money, lurked near every inn-yard, while every hackney coachman had a base half-crown in his hand to return to the fare who was unwary enough to offer him a good one.

Burglary and housebreaking were daily occurrences, and the citizen's only defence was a stout cudgel or a brace of pistols. There was no police force, or at least none of any consequence. What there was, was both inefficient and corrupt. The watch which nightly patrolled the streets with staves and lanterns was for the most part composed of aged, decrepit or infirm dodderers, whom terrorism or bribery kept well out of the way when any villainy was toward.

Crime was discovered largely by means of the informer who sold criminals to the officers of justice for the sake of the official reward. There was a fixed scale of emoluments for the informer. He who landed in gaol a highway robber got £40, the horse, arms, furniture and money of the thief, and what was called a Tyburn ticket. This last was a certificate exempting the holder from all public office in his ward or parish. The actual recipient was

BRITAIN'S FOREMOST CRIMINAL COURT

The Central Criminal Court was established in 1834 as the "Old Bailey" sessions-house, and is still popularly known by that name. The present building, which stands on the site of Newgate Prison, was opened by King Edward VII in 1907. It has a magnificent marble and tiled central hall, off which are the four court rooms. The north-west corner of the building (now rebuilt) was destroyed by a bomb in 1940.

allowed to sell it, and usually did. Its market value was from £25 to £30.

A burglar or a housebreaker was worth £40 and a Tyburn ticket. A coiner of counterfeit money was valued at £40 if he dealt in gold or silver, but only £10 if he confined his attentions to copper. Tyburn tickets were given for the arrest of shop-lifters, warehouse pilferers and horse stealers.

Jonathan Wild the Thief-taker

This system naturally encouraged bribery on the one hand and double-crossing on the other. It culminated in the iniquitous profession of gangster-thief-taker, of which the most notorious member was Jonathan Wild, who for many years resided in Old Bailey Street, where he carried on a most profitable triple-sided business.

Neatly dressed in dark green and wearing a small plain sword, Wild was ostensibly in the services of the justices as a thief-taker. With this occupation he combined that of recoverer of stolen goods; and behind the cover of the two he kept in touch with almost every known criminal in London, and was organiser and head of one of the largest gangs of thieves and pickpockets ever known in the City.

ARREST OF JACK KETCH
Jack Ketch was an executioner in Charles II's reign. He beheaded the Duke of Monmouth. The name was passed on to succeeding hangmen.

The life of every man or woman in the gang was in his hands, for he could at any moment denounce an unwilling or insubordinate confederate. His word would always be taken before that of a criminal, and denunciation meant death by hanging, then the recognised punishment for a multitude of crimes.

Wild himself was sent to the gallows in 1725 for the comparatively venial offence of receiving money on false pretences; but many crimes less serious than this were punishable by death. Murder and treason have almost always been regarded as capital offences, and one can understand if not altogether agree with a code of law which demands the extreme penalty for arson, rape, piracy or highway robbery; but it seems a fantastic perversion of justice to condemn to death men, women and children (for babes of eight, nine and ten years suffered the extreme penalty) for picking pockets if the stolen goods were worth more than one shilling, for cutting down trees in a garden or damaging trees " planted for ornament," for stealing linen from bleaching grounds or ore from a black-lead mine, or for impersonating a Greenwich pensioner.

Two Hundred Crimes Punishable by Death

Yet such was the English law in the eighteenth century. Until Sir Robert Peel between 1825 and 1829 drastically reformed the criminal code over 200 offences were punishable by death. It might be thought that such comprehensive judicial savagery would effectually stamp out crime; actually, the reverse was the case.

The law terrified those who administered it more than those who fell foul of it. Thanks to the utter incompetency and venality of the police, only a very small proportion of crimes was detected; and of those criminals actually brought to justice relatively few suffered for their offences.

The Royal power of clemency was frequently exercised in favour of the condemned; judges pounced on every technical irregularity in counsel's cases as an excuse for acquittal; juries were reluctant to convict in face of any but the most damning evidence. Male convicts were pardoned in large numbers whenever

SESSIONS HOUSE AT THE OLD BAILEY

Situated in the street of the same name, it stood next to Newgate Gaol, whence prisoners were conducted to it by a passage known to them as "Birdcage Walk." In this passage executed prisoners were buried.

England was at war—as she was during the greater part of the eighteenth century—if they would enter either the Army or the Navy. Many of the soldiers and sailors who gave their blood to create the British Empire, and under Nelson and Wellington brought Napoleon to his knees, were gaol-birds of the deepest dye, bred in the London slums and reared on crime of the vilest description.

Bribery and Corruption Rampant

Of arrested criminals many never reached a prison cell. The constable in charge of the lock-up could be bribed; so could witnesses and jurymen. Magistrates were equally corrupt. Until 1792 all fines levied by Justices of the Peace went into their own pockets, and it can readily be understood why criminals with means sufficient to tempt gaoler or magistrate laughed at the gallows.

To such an extent was corruption carried that it is said constables went out into the streets and gave beggars pennies in order to arrest them and claim the £10 reward. One magistrate would issue sets of warrants, have every vagrant in the neighbourhood taken up, and then bail out all who could pay the necessary 2s. 4d.

In spite of the many loopholes by which criminals could evade justice, the London prisons were always full, and the hangman was kept perpetually busy.

The state of the prisons was foul beyond belief. Newgate, " the chief criminal gaol of London, through which passed an unending procession of vice, wickedness, innocence wrongly accused," was always the worst. Originally the " fifth principal gate in the City wall," according to Stow, it became a prison in the twelfth century, was repaired in the thirteenth, rebuilt in the fifteenth—out of money left for charity by Dick Whittington!—destroyed in the Great Fire and promptly rebuilt in stronger and grimmer fashion.

Humanity Outside, Pestilence Within

With a humour that seems altogether out of place, the rebuilders decorated the exterior of the new prison with statues of the most elevated virtues. Justice, Mercy and Truth looked down upon the City : Liberty (with Whittington's cat at her feet), Peace, Plenty and Concord gazed out upon the streets of Holborn.

The humanitarian sentiments thus expressed were reserved entirely for the outside of Newgate. Within, it was " a dark pestiferous den . . . perpetually ravaged by deadly diseases. Many died there in chains, worn out by the darkness and foulness of the place." Gaol fever killed far more than did the hangman's halter, and did not always confine its attentions to those in the cells. In a single session in 1750 it struck down the Lord Mayor, three judges, an under-sheriff, several counsel and a number of jurymen.

Foul Dens in Newgate

Among Newgate's blacker spots were the hold called Limbo, " a place underground, full of horrors, without light, and swarming with vermin and creeping things "; Tangier, " a large dark and stinking ward, occasioned so by the multitude of the prisoners in it and the filthiness of their lodgings "; Waterman's Hold, " terrible dark and stinking," which was reserved for women; and the Stone Hold, " a most terrible, stinking, dark, dismal place, situated underground, into which no daylight can come." In the Stone Hold were thrown those unfortunates who could pay nothing whatever for their keep, the accommodation in the prison varying according to the means of the prisoners.

TORTURE IN NEWGATE
William Spiggott enduring the *peine forte et dure* because he would not plead to his indictment.

Newgate was always overcrowded, being " fed by an incessant stream of the worst criminals in London," who were " lodged here pending their execution at Tyburn or (later) outside the Debtors' Door." There were in 1784 three floors of condemned cells, small vaulted boxes measuring about 9 feet by 6 feet, of which John Howard the prison reformer wrote that " Criminals who had affected an air of boldness during their trial, and appeared quite unconcerned at the pronouncing sentence upon them, were struck with horror, and shed tears, when brought to these darksome, solitary abodes." This was after two recent rebuildings of Newgate, in 1767 and following its destruction during the Gordon riots; and at a time when Howard could report not unfavourably on the remainder of the accommodation.

Escapes of Jack Sheppard

It was from Newgate that Jack Sheppard made his sensational escapes in 1724. On the first occasion he forced apart the bars of his cell, and two " female friends," " Edgeworth Bess " and Poll, pulled him through the window. Retaken at Finchley, he was handcuffed, his legs were loaded with fetters, and he was chained to the floor.

Again his friends came to his aid. They brought him a file, with which he first cut through his handcuffs and then detached a bar from the window. With the latter he levered the irons from his legs. Stripping Bess of her dress, he dropped the lady out of the window in her underclothes, followed her and was at liberty once more.

For some weeks he pursued an active career of crime, but in July was denounced by Jonathan Wild. Tried and sentenced to death, he was lodged in a condemned cell. On August 30 he escaped again.

The third escape resembled the first. The ever-present Bess and Poll dragged their hero

GALLOWS AT THE OLD BAILEY

The procession of the condemned to Tyburn was abolished in 1783, after which criminals were executed outside Newgate and other gaols until 1868. There was opposition to the abolition of public executions.

through the bars, clapped on his head a curly wig, arrayed him in a lady's scarlet riding cloak and marched him out. On this occasion, Sheppard had to break a way through half a dozen massive doors.

Fetters no Bar to Escape

Recaptured again within a fortnight, Sheppard was thrown into an innermost dungeon and secured with a mass of iron fetters weighing 300 lb. Even these were not proof against his genius for escape. The inevitable girl-friend passed him a file; he sent out his jailer to buy him some drinks, slipped his handcuffs, worked the staple which secured him out of the floor, climbed up the chimney, filing through an iron bar on his way, got on to the roof and was free once more.

It was his last escape. Sheppard's ingenuity in getting out of prison was only equalled by his stupidity once he was at liberty; only a few days elapsed before he was found dead drunk in Clare Market, and this time the authorities decided that no risks whatever were to be taken. Warders mounted guard over him day and night until on November 16 he was drawn to Tyburn and there hanged in the presence of 200,000 people. An attempted rescue was unsuccessful.

The weekly hangings at Tyburn during the eighteenth century were one of London's great public exhibitions. They took place on the Monday and were attended by vast crowds drawn largely from London's underworld. All along the route from Cheapside to the Marble Arch (the site of the gallows is indicated by a tablet on the railings of Hyde Park at the entrance to the Bayswater Road) were stalls where gin, nuts, apples and gingerbread could be purchased. Swarms of itinerant vendors hawked songs new-made about those who were about to be executed, together with last speeches and confessions—usually printed before they were delivered.

Last Day of Condemned

Drinking, singing, laughing, cursing, quarreling and fighting, the scum of the city awaited the arrival of the fatal carts in which those of their number who had been unlucky enough to be caught made their final journey upon earth. For the condemned the excitement began on Sunday.

At noon on that day they were led into the prison chapel, where, seated in the condemned cell with a coffin in their midst, they listened to the "condemned sermon," and looked as reckless as they could, being encouraged thereto by the other prisoners and by the presence of fashionable folk who crowded to this gruesome ceremony. There is record of one priestly criminal who preached his own sermon.

Tolling of St. Sepulchre's Bell

During the evening the sexton or beadle of St. Sepulchre's Church came to the gateway of the prison and in the course of a traditional adjuration besought them " to keep this night in watching and hearty prayer to God " for the salvation of their souls. At six the following morning the great bell of the church began to toll and continued for four hours. (This practice was continued until 1890.)

Early on Monday morning those about to die were assembled in the gatehouse. Their chains were knocked off, halters were placed round their necks, and their arms were bound at the elbows. They were then ushered into the carts, where they sat beside their coffins.

Outside St. Sepulchre's Church the sexton again exhorted the condemned to repentance, while their friends presented them with flowers to put in their coats. As the carts slowly trundled along Holborn and Oxford Street the crowd cheered, jeered at or abused their inmates according as they were popular or not.

The open space about the gallows was surrounded with stands and packed with people. No noble or tender emotion ever swayed that mob; it applauded or execrated, but never pitied. The condemned met their end in the atmosphere of a rowdy Bank Holiday. Dying was a lengthy business, for the scaffold had no drop. When the halters were adjusted the carts were moved from beneath the prisoners' feet. A strong man might live in his strangling noose, for half an hour.

" RESCUE WORK "
A policeman carries out a wide variety of jobs. Comforting a not too-happy young athlete.

A " PEELER " OF 1865
For many years the " New Police " enrolled by Sir Robert Peel performed their duties in top-hats.

It was largely due to Charles Dickens that public executions were abolished. In November, 1849, he spent the night among the crowd which was assembling to witness the hanging of two notorious murderers, a man and a woman, outside the gaol in Horsemonger Lane, and was horrified with what he saw and heard.

The last public execution in London took place on May 26, 1868, when Michael Barrett was hanged for blowing up the wall of Clerkenwell Prison in an endeavour to set at liberty two Fenians detained there.

Newgate Prison remained standing until 1902, when it was demolished to make way for the imposing buildings of the Central Criminal Court, familiarly known as the Old Bailey.

The Central Criminal Court was instituted in 1834. The present buildings were opened in February, 1907, by King Edward VII. When in 1814 Elizabeth Fry began her self-imposed task of bringing to the wretched women in Newgate some notion of decency and hope, she was confronted by a " swarm of drunken, mad, half-naked, starving women, living more like beasts than humans." So terrible were they that the governor of the prison was afraid to venture among them. Over the main door of the present Old Bailey are carved the words, " Defend the children of the poor, and punish the wrongdoer," while above the building gleams the figure of Justice, a drawn sword in her hand.

Within, the law is administered with inflexible integrity. His Majesty's judges sit in four small courts adjoining the magnificent central hall, lined with marble and tiles, which is the most imposing feature of the building. For prisoners awaiting trial there are ninety-six cells, all spotlessly clean; gone are the days when a hundred miserable wretches were crowded into two small rooms, the larger of which measured only 14 feet by 11 feet and was but 7 feet high.

The judges are still presented with nosegays of fresh English flowers, and the dock and desks are still sprinkled with rue; but these observances are now no more than traditional customs. Gaol fever has long since ceased to trouble the minds and vex the bodies of either accused or accuser.

Donald McLeish

ON TRAFFIC CONTROL

A mounted London policeman on duty at Hyde Park Corner, the most crowded of all traffic centres.

Gone, too, are the pillory and whipping post which once stood opposite the Old Court House. British justice has moved far from the days of the pillory, a sentence to which so often meant the death of the victim at the hands of the brutal mob. Flogging nowadays is virtually abolished, being reserved for convicted criminals in prison who mutiny or attack prison officers.

What has wrought this transformation? Partly the devoted labours of saintly prison reformers, among whom John Howard and Elizabeth Fry stand pre-eminent. Partly the penetration of thinkers who discerned, as did Jeremy Bentham, that crime would diminish when punishment became certain rather than savage. Partly the thoroughgoing reformation of the criminal law effected by Sir Robert Peel between 1825 and 1829. Partly the growing humanitarianism of the British people, developed by the diffusion of education, the labour of social workers, and the spread of domestic amenities. Partly, and not least, the increasing efficiency of the police.

Metropolitan and City Police

There are to-day no finer bodies of men in existence than the Metropolitan and City Police forces. They are respected and admired throughout the world—and not least of all by their fellow countrymen. It is generally admitted that no one excels the London policeman in controlling traffic, and he is seen at his best in handling a good-tempered crowd. His methods in dealing with an unruly one have at times been criticised, but it probably remains true that no one in the world is better at this difficult job than he.

To good-natured mockery the London police are inured. When the force was founded, its members were nicknamed " Peelers " and " Bobbies," and though the former epithet has passed out of currency, the latter is as popular as ever. For many years the public poked fun at the top-hats worn by Sir Robert Peel's force, and when these were given up, the bell-shaped helmets which superseded them came in for their share of raillery. Gilbert and Sullivan only reflected popular opinion when they made the police force a figure of fun in *The Pirates of Penzance*.

Not all criticism of the London police has been good-tempered. The " New Police " of 1829 met with much opposition and considerable hostility, not only from the mob but even from magistrates. This they overcame by producing results which could not be questioned, a rapid decrease in crime and increasing safety of life and property. Within seven years the area over which they had control—originally a radius of twelve miles from Charing Cross—was extended, and the River Police were brought into the new organisation.

New Scotland Yard

From the outset the police headquarters were in Scotland Yard. In 1891 new headquarters for the Metropolitan Police (from whom the City Police had always been separated) were erected at New Scotland Yard off Parliament Street. Here is the home of London's Criminal Investigation Department, familiarly known as the C.I.D., the finest and most famous detective force in the world.

NEW SCOTLAND YARD
Famous all over the world as the headquarters of the Metropolitan Police and the C.I.D.

The C.I.D. began in 1844, when Sir James Graham, successor to Sir Robert Peel, gave a dozen police sergeants the right to work in plain clothes. The innovation was bitterly resented by certain sections of the public, but thanks largely to Charles Dickens the opposition was broken down, and to-day " the Yard " has an organisation and personnel unrivalled for efficiency. One reason for this is that entry to the detective force is possible only by way of the uniformed ranks.

There was considerable opposition to a development of the Metropolitan Police Force, the institution in 1934, of the Metropolitan Police College at Hendon in Middlesex. This school was intended to take men of promise from the ranks and train them for higher executive and administrative posts. The scheme was discontinued in 1939. During the war, part of London's police force comprised special constables, who carried out their duties admirably.

London's Four Prisons

The Metropolitan Police Force has to-day an establishment of nearly 20,000 men and women. It controls an area of 700 square miles, which is divided into twenty-three districts, and comprises a population of 8,500,000. For the administration of summary justice there are in this area fourteen magistrates' courts, of which the best known is Bow Street, near Covent Garden. Under Orders in Council six Juvenile Courts for the trial of youthful offenders have been constituted.

The City of London Police Force, which has its headquarters in Old Jewry, has a strength of just over 1,100 and controls an area of 67[illegible] acres. During the day this area contains upwards of 500,000 people : at night the population falls to about 10,000. The magistrates courts are at the Mansion House, where the Lord Mayor and Aldermen officiate, and Guildhall.

There are in London four prisons, under the control of the Home Office. Pentonville erected in 1840 as the " Model Prison," is in the Caledonian Road. It contains 1,000 cells. Holloway Prison, in Parkhurst Road, which contains 436 cells, is now reserved for women. Brixton Prison is in south London, was purchased in 1853, and was formerly reserved for women under sentence of transportation o

POLICE TRAINING SCHOOL AT HENDON

Opened in 1934 as the "Police College," to train young constables and selected recruits from outside for higher posts in the Metropolitan Police Force, it became a normal training school for recruits after the War.

penal servitude. It is now used for prisoners awaiting trial on the capital charge, and for the detention of debtors who refuse to obey court orders as to payment of their debts.

Imprisonment for debt was abolished in 1869, again largely owing to the efforts of Charles Dickens, whose famous descriptions of the Marshalsea, the King's Bench and the Fleet prisons are well known. Dickens wrote from bitter experience : as a boy he knew the inside of a debtor's prison. To-day only those debtors who, in the judgment of the court, have had the means but have neglected to pay off their debts as ordered, can be committed to gaol, and then only for a maximum period of forty-two days.

Modern Prison Methods

Perhaps the most striking contrast between prison methods of to-day and those of yesterday is to be found at Wormwood Scrubs in west London, a large prison mainly occupied by first offenders and youthful delinquents. Here some of the more successful points in the Borstal system have been tried out, including the appointment of officers as "housemasters." The job of these officers is to move about among the convicts as friends and personal advisers, talk with them, explore the reasons which led them to crime, and by wise and sensible influence eradicate their inhibitions and complexes and return them to the world as normal citizens. These experiments show the modern attitude towards crime : it is regarded more as a mental disease than as sin.

The British are not usually regarded as a litigious race, though the fact that in the half-century between 1882, when on December 4 Queen Victoria opened the Royal Courts of Justice, commonly known as the Law Courts, in the Strand, and 1932 it is estimated that some 600,000 cases had been tried in these buildings, seems to suggest a contrary opinion.

Work of the Law Courts

The Law Courts have little to do with crime; they are mainly for the trial of civil cases. For hundreds of years the judges of the King's Bench and the Court of Common Pleas sat in Westminster, but by the nineteenth century their work had so grown in bulk that their premises were scattered all over London.

In 1858 a Royal Commission selected the present site for a building which should contain all the various courts, but several years elapsed before a start could be made upon it. Even then the work of demolition was so extensive that it was not until 1871 that the foundations of the Law Courts could be laid.

One of the worst quarters in London had to be swept away. Butcher Row, one of the alleys demolished, was described as a lane of "wretched fabrics, the receptacle of filth in every corner, the bane of old London, and a sort of nestling place for plagues and fevers." Tradition had it that the Gunpowder Plot was hatched in Butcher Row. It was a fit spot for so foul a crime.

The Law Courts were designed by G. E. Street, R.A., and have been described as the "final effort in London to make use of an ancient style for public buildings." They cover 5½ acres, and contain 1,100 rooms that are linked by 2½ miles of corridors with the magnificent Great Hall, which is 138 feet long, 38 feet wide and 80 feet high. In 1919 the Great Hall was for three weeks utilised as a dormitory for men of the American Navy.

Most Accurate Clock in London

The principal entrance to the Law Courts is in the Strand. It has a magnificent recessed archway which the close proximity of dense traffic makes it somewhat difficult to appreciate. In the Strand also is the clock tower, containing the only large public clock in London which does not require regular synchronisation with Greenwich time. It was made by a carpenter who could neither read nor write, and the secret of its perfect accuracy died with him.

Originally there were nineteen courts, to which in 1913 four more were added. In these rooms the curious member of the public may hear undefended divorce petitions disposed of at the average rate of one every seven minutes, or sit day after day while lawyers argue the apparently interminable complexities of a probate or chancery suit.

The administration of British justice has been considerably speeded up since the days when Dickens portrayed in *Bleak House* the suit of Jarndyce *v.* Jarndyce, but it is still not uncommon for twelve months to pass between the preparation and settlement of a case.

Street of Unfortunates

Possibly some of the unfortunates who have to find the way to Carey Street, where the Bankruptcy Court is situated, could wish even this time to be extended.

THE ROYAL COURTS OF JUSTICE

Opened in 1882 by Queen Victoria, the Law Courts face the Strand at the point where it links with Fleet Street. They contain twenty-three courts for the administration of civil justice. Criminals are not tried there.

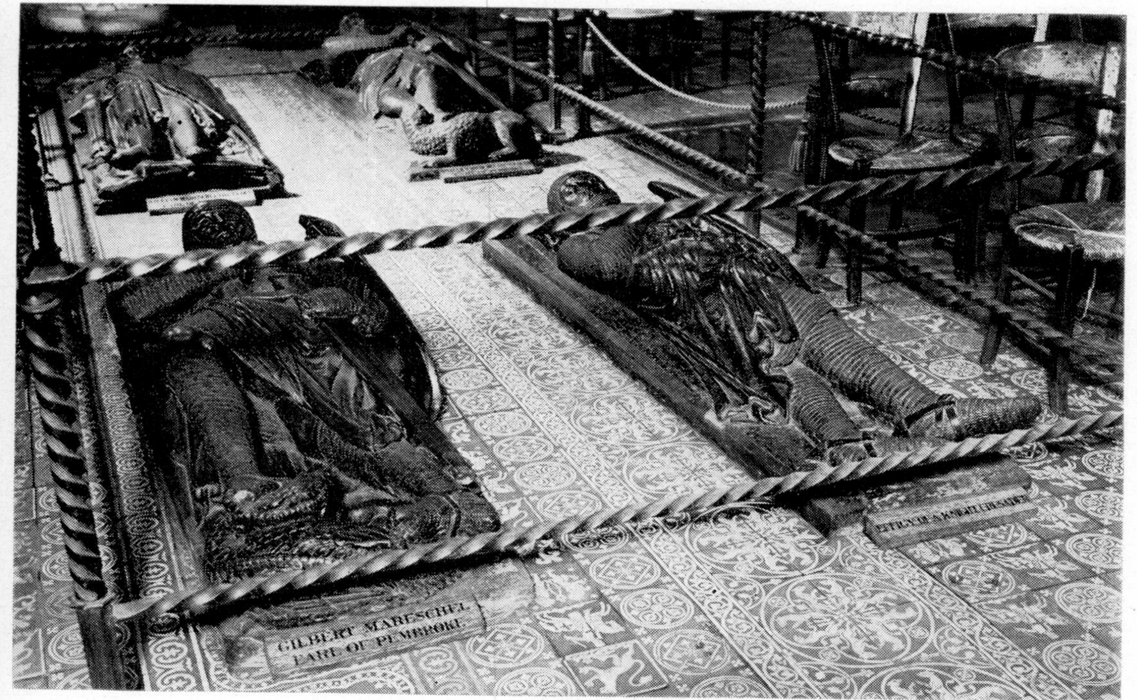

CRUSADERS IN THE TEMPLE CHURCH

Four of the nine mail-clad effigies of "Associates of the Temple" which rest in the Temple Church. The nearest is that of Gilbert Mareschel, Earl of Pembroke, who in 1241 was killed at a tournament.

ANCIENT CITY OF THE LAWYERS

THE Temple, once perhaps the most charming spot in London, was till lately a scene of ruin and desolation, for it suffered fearful devastation during the war. The Temple Church, a unique memorial of the early Middle Ages, was open to the sky; the famous Hall opposite was but a shell, and broken stones and stark walls ran right down to the river. These ruins embraced also the Essex water-gate and the adjacent houses.

The Temple is a city set within a city, inhabited by a single tribe, and though the general public is made free of its lanes and squares—though not of its gardens—the privilege is by sufferance, and the lawyer owners of the Temple could at any moment bar its gates and retire once again into the enclosed privacy it first enjoyed 750 years ago.

There were no lawyers in it then. In 1128 the militant "Order of the Poor Fellow-Soldiers of Jesus Christ and of the Temple of Solomon," founded by Baldwin, King of Jerusalem, in 1118 to guard the roads to the Holy City, and renowned in history as the Knights Templars, came to seek a home in England, and settled in Holborn near what is now called Chancery Lane. The Order grew rich and found its lodging poor and mean, so in the same century it purchased a large stretch of land between Fleet Street and the Thames, extending east and west from Whitefriars to Essex Street. On this ground was built a monastery, a church, a barrack and a council chamber, with residences for the prior and the knights, and a riverside terrace whereon the worthy Templars might indulge in religious meditation or exercise their chargers, as the mood seized them.

Of all the many buildings erected by the Templars in their riverside retreat but one remains, the Norman church which in 1185 Heraclius, Patriarch of Jerusalem, consecrated for them and dedicated to the Virgin Mary.

It was the custom of the Knights Templars to build their churches with round towers, modelling them upon the Church of the Holy

MIDDLE TEMPLE LANE
Leads from Fleet Street into the Middle Temple. Over the entrance is a gatehouse built by Wren.

Sepulchre in Jerusalem, the master of which was the head of their Order. Four such churches remain in England; the Temple, to which a rectangular choir in early English style of architecture was added in 1240, is the finest, most complete and most interesting.

The round church is entered by a superb Norman gateway, which is sheltered by a vaulted porch formerly communicating with the cloisters. Upon the floor of the church are the recumbent figures of nine Crusaders in full armour. This unique church was ruined by German bombs, but has now almost been rebuilt again.

Lawyers in the Temple

At what date lawyers first came to live in the Temple is uncertain, but it was probably during the early years of the fourteenth century. The Order of Knights Templars, having grown very wealthy and drawn upon itself the hatred of many enemies, who accused it of corrupt and evil practices, was dissolved by the Pope in 1312, whereupon the Temple estate, after being in private hands for some years, was leased by the King to the Knights Hospitallers of St. John, who as early as 1326 were renting houses in the churchyard to professors of the common law.

Communities of lawyers had begun to grow up in London not later than the thirteenth century. The earliest English lawyers were mainly priests, but in 1217 clerks in holy orders were instructed not to appear in civil courts, and in 1254 were forbidden by the Pope to lecture upon common law.

For many years in England a chaotic and frequently scandalous state of affairs resulted. Quite unqualified persons practised as lawyers, with the result that the administration of justice became exceedingly corrupt. At length, Edward I cleared up the muddle by ordering that only those appointed by the Chief Justice of the Common Pleas could plead in court.

Origin of the Inns of Court

Henceforth, to become a barrister it was necessary to study law, and at a recognised school. The present Inns of Court grew out of these medieval law schools.

It is probably that the " apt and eager " students of the common law who gathered round the feet of the " masters " who taught it lived first in hostels in Holborn, but that early in the fourteenth century they began to settle on the sites they now occupy.

For a long time the history of these legal communities is obscure. We have seen that by 1326 the Knights Hospitallers were renting houses in the Temple to " masters " of the law. Tradition asserts that about 1314 the Earl of Lincoln, " being a person well affected to the knowledge of the law," settled yet another community of masters and students somewhere near the present Lincoln's Inn, which was then the London residence of the Bishop of Chichester.

In 1294 Reginald de Grey, chief justice of Chester and first Lord Grey of Wilton, rented from the Dean and Chapter of St. Paul's the site of Gray's Inn, and in all probability gathered round him a number of law students.

Early in the fifteenth century all these communities, the vague beginnings of which are indicated here, emerge as fully fledged and vigorous institutions. In the Temple two societies appear to have existed side by side from earliest days. The Middle Temple is mentioned by name in a bequest of 1404, the Inner Temple is called a " college " in a letter dated 1440. The Outer Temple, between Fleet Street and Essex Street, was probably never occupied by the lawyers, though the Knights Templars had their residences there.

The records of Lincoln's Inn begin in 1422, and there is evidence that Gray's Inn was flourishing as a legal society many years before that.

Whatever the dates of their origin, it is quite certain that these four societies of lawyers are all over 500 years old, and that except for Lincoln's Inn, the present site of which was occupied in 1442, they have enjoyed virtually uninterrupted possession of the same estates throughout that time.

London is a city of the strangest contrasts, but there are few more remarkable than the hidden presence in one of its busiest and noisiest areas of the calmly serene, time-mellowed domains owned by the Inns of Court.

Donald McLeish

CLIFFORD'S INN

ldest and largest of the several Inns of Chancery, was demolished in 1934. It dated from 1344.

The Inns were not always thus pent within miles of bricks and mortar; when the masters of law settled in these quiet spots there were fields where now the Law Courts stand, Holborn was a country village, and their students hunted rabbits in Chancery Lane.

Each of the Inns of Chancery was more or less subject to one of the Inns of Court. Thus the Inner Temple looked upon Clifford's, Clement's and Lyon's Inns as its preparatory schools; the New Inn was subject to the Middle Temple, as were Furnival's and Thavies' Inns to Lincoln's Inn, Staple and Barnard's to Gray's Inn. There were in addition the two Serjeants' Inns, and a number of non-recognised Inns, including the Strand, St. George's and Scroope's.

Sites of Inns of Chancery

All the Inns of Chancery have now ceased to function and the buildings of most have been demolished. Street names mark the sites of Thavies' Inn on Holborn Viaduct and Clement's Inn opposite the Church of St. Clement Danes in the Strand. The fine modern thoroughfare of Aldwych preserves the name of Wych Street, where lived the students of New Inn after they had removed from St. George's Inn.

Lyon's Inn stood on the ground now occupied by the Globe Theatre in Shaftesbury Avenue; the buildings in a court on the south side of Fleet Street are still called Serjeant's Inn, but the older institution of that name, which stood in Chancery Lane just below the Public Record Office, has entirely disappeared. A notice let into the wall of the giant red-brick offices of the Prudential Assurance Company in High Holborn marks the site of Furnival's Inn, where once lived a youngster called Charles Dickens.

Of Clifford's Inn, which stood between Fleet Street and the Rolls Chapel, the ancient gateway and a seventeenth-century gatehouse have been preserved; the remainder was demolished in 1934 to make way for a massive block of flats and offices.

The Great Fire of London swept right up to but did not damage the ancient hall of Clifford's Inn, and here for three years Sir Matthew Hale and other judges sat to determine the innumerable boundary disputes which arose after the conflagration—an exacting task which alone made the rebuilding of London possible.

DUTCH GARDEN AT STAPLE INN

One of the loveliest spots in central London, it was reached through Staple Inn in High Holborn or from Chancery Lane. It was completely destroyed by a flying bomb in 1944 but has been largely rebuilt.

On the south side of Holborn, opposite the Prudential Building, is a short tiled passage leading to the Mercers' School, a royal foundation administered by the Honourable Company of Mercers. The dining-hall of the school was once the hall of Barnard's Inn.

Carefully rebuilt in 1931, this one-storey timber and brick building contains what is believed to be an original fireplace, early fifteenth century oak linen-panelling, and fine heraldic glass in the windows.

The Old Houses of Holborn

Farther west in Holborn is Staple Inn, so called because it traditionally occupies the site of an ancient wool market. This is one of the gems of older London. Few visitors to the city fail to admire the line of black and white timbered houses, with latticed and mullioned windows projecting over the street, which form its front. They have many times been restored, but nothing in all London more vividly recalls the aspect of the medieval city. The lovely Dutch garden behind it was destroyed by a flying bomb in 1944.

It is but a short walk from Staple Inn to Lincoln's Inn. Beyond question the right way to go is down Chancery Lane, so that you may enter the Inn by its "fair antient gatehouse," as Stow called it. Notice as you go in the fruit and sweet stand on the right. It seems incongruous, but its presence denotes a most jealously guarded privilege. There was an apple-woman by this gate in 1531, and fruit has been sold there ever since.

In Old Square, Lincoln's Inn

Pass through the gate, which was erected in 1518 and bears the escutcheons of Henry VIII and his Chancellor of the Exchequer, and you find yourself at once in medieval London. Old Square is a unique example of the great house such as noblemen delighted to build in Tudor days. On your left, on two sides, are old and mellow dwelling-houses; facing you is the original hall, built in the reign of Henry VIII; and on your right the chapel, designed by Inigo Jones and unique in being upstairs, above a crypt open to the air and between the arches of which you may wander at will.

If Gray's Inn gives the impression of peaceful seclusion, Lincoln's Inn gives that of vastness;

it is the most open of all the Inns. Beyond the first square is another, far bigger and wider, with on the right, built on high ground, a magnificent modern hall, which has been described as the finest large building created during the " revival " period of Gothic architecture.

Its gorgeous interior, full of carving and stained glass, includes a magnificent fresco by G. F. Watts entitled *The School of Legislation* and featuring the world's great law-givers from Moses to Edward I. This picture, which took the artist several years to paint, was done by him without fee, though on its completion he received a present of a gold cup and 500 sovereigns.

Next to the hall is the library, the largest of its kind in the world, containing 70,000 books, all about the law. Many of the older volumes " still retain attached to their covers the iron rings by which they were secured."

Priceless Legal Manuscripts

The library contains also a large number of legal manuscripts, many of them priceless because of their connection with eminent men who have been members of the Inn. To give anything like a complete list of the distinguished sons of Lincoln's Inn would be impossible here, for from earliest times the society has been a nursery of great law-givers and statesmen.

GATEWAY OF LINCOLN'S INN

The gateway leading from Chancery Lane to Old Square was built in 1518. The square is one of London's finest examples of Tudor architecture.

It is by way of Fountain Court—where the old fountain still plays—and Garden Court that one approaches that glory of the Temple, the Middle Temple Hall, the " finest and largest Elizabethan hall in London " and among the most superb in the country.

Middle Temple Hall

Completed about 1572 and said to have been opened by Queen Elizabeth in 1576, the Middle Temple Hall was not only a most glorious example of Tudor architecture but also a storehouse of priceless treasures. The hammer-beam oak roof is said to have been made from timber of Armada ships, the small serving table from Drake's famous ship the *Golden Hind*.

It is recorded that upon the same dais as the pre-war one in the Hall, on Candlemas night, 1602, " At our feast wee had a play called *Twelfth Night or What you Will*." On the dais was one of the most glorious tables in existence. Forty feet long and marvellously polished, it was cut from an oak in Windsor Great Park and presented by Elizabeth I to the benchers. Tradition says that upon it the Virgin Queen signed the death-warrant of Mary Queen of Scots. Above the dais hangs Van Dyck's celebrated picture of Charles I, whose face reflects the tragedy of his life and death. At the opposite end of the hall was a fine oaken screen.

The Inner Temple Hall is modern, but between it and the ancient Temple Church (almost destroyed during the Second World War) is a cloister square as old as the church itself.

" The Red Rose and the White "

Both halls overlook the beautiful Temple Gardens. Those of the Middle Temple date only from the middle of the seventeenth century, but the Inner Temple gardens are as old as the Temple itself, and centuries ago were famous for their roses. According to tradition, they were the scene of one of the most dramatic and fatal scenes in English history, the plucking by the rival nobles of red and white roses in the quarrel which led to twenty-five years of civil war in England. Warwick, in Shakespeare's *King Henry VI* declares that :

" . . . This brawl to-day,
Grown to this faction, in the Temple garden,
Shall send, between the red rose and the white,
A thousand souls to death, and deadly night."

No memorial of this event stands in the Temple gardens. Instead, the lawyers have chosen to commemorate the gentlest and most peaceful of the dwellers in their precincts. Beneath the trees, within sight of Lamb's birthplace, there stands in stone a little naked boy bearing in his hands an open book.

On the pages of that book are inscribed the words, " Lawyers were children once." Lamb wrote those words, and it is fitting that they be recorded. For the most charitable of us are inclined to look upon lawyers as a race apart, somewhat lacking in humanity, stiff as the parchment of their documents and stilted as their legal phraseology. An hour or two spent wandering through the ancient and beautiful city that has been theirs for so many centuries, and which they tend with such loving care, should correct that view.

Reminiscence of Charles Lamb

And, should you be lucky, you may see in Temple Gardens—as, no doubt, Lamb often saw—some bonny baby wake from sleep to stretch his tiny hands towards the aged trees. For even lawyers have children, like other folk.

As might be imagined of a place so venerable, the Temple preserves customs that have been handed down through the centuries. One of these is claimed to be the oldest in London.

One of London's Oldest Customs

Each evening during term time one of the warders of the Middle Temple goes to the strong room and takes thence a silver-mounted ox-horn kept there. Proceeding to Fountain Court, at 6.30 p.m. he blows there a long blast. It is to call the benchers to dinner.

The call is repeated in New Court, Essex Court, Brick Court, Pump Court, Elm Court, and Middle Temple Lane. It has been heard in these precincts since the days of the Knights Templars. Those gallant Crusaders had no clocks, though curiously enough it is said that it was from their deadly foes the Saracens that Europe learnt the art of clockmaking in the thirteenth century.

FRONT OF STAPLE INN

The timbered front of Staple Inn in Holborn is a unique and beautiful relic of Tudor London. In this building Dr. Johnson is said to have written in 1759 his romance *Rasselas* to pay for his mother's funeral.

IN THE HEART OF LONDON
The Foundling Hospital, founded in 1739 by Thomas Coram, having been moved to Berkhamsted in Hertfordshire, the site on which it stood in Lamb's Conduit Fields is now a children's playground.

PARKS, PLAYGROUNDS, EXHIBITIONS

In nothing is London more fortunate than in her parks and open spaces. Many people who do not know the metropolis appear to imagine that its inhabitants are divorced from all contact with the sight and sounds of nature. To such it will come as a surprise to learn that it is possible to walk three miles in a straight line through the very heart of London without touching street traffic or built-up areas for more than a few seconds. The route taken lies through St. James's Park, with its beautiful ornamental waters and wild fowl, the Green Park with its flocks of sheep, Hyde Park with its wild rabbits, its magnificent trees and its Lido, and Kensington Gardens with its brightly coloured flower-beds.

It must not be imagined that the West End is particularly favoured in this respect. Large splashes of green are evident on a colour map of London. Northward are Regent's Park and Hampstead Heath; southward, Battersea Park; and eastward Victoria Park, to mention only the best known.

The majority of the County of London's open spaces have become public property in a haphazard, almost accidental manner. The London County Council, however, are taking no chances with the future of the open spaces on the outskirts of the county.

In 1935, Mr. Herbert Morrison, then Labour leader of that body, announced that £2,000,000 would be set aside for the purpose of making grants to county councils and county borough councils towards the purchase of open spaces near London, so that in time the metropolis should be completely surrounded by a "Green Belt." Within less than two years of the commencement of the operation of this magnificent scheme nearly 30,000 acres had been saved from building. Ockham Common, Wisley, with its famous lake, is perhaps the most beautiful, though not the most extensive, of the areas thus acquired.

Another great scheme on which the London County Council was working before the war upset all educational plans was the provision of playing fields and open-air classrooms for school children who normally have to work and play amidst the roar of traffic. Eventually, there will be playing fields in the country for 250,000 London school children. Under this scheme free transport facilities would have to be provided to make it possible for each child to spend one day a week in the country. It would, therefore, be necessary to set aside for the purpose 740 buses, or their equivalent in trams or tube trains. Already open-air classrooms are available in seventy-two acres of fields at Hackney Marsh, Downham, Streatham Vale, Kidbrooke, Honor Oak and Bellingham.

The London County Council maintains over 6,500 acres of parks and open spaces, upon which there has been a gross capital expenditure of £3,000,000.

Hyde Park of the East End

The largest of these is Hainault Forest, two miles south-east of Chigwell, with an area of 1,108 acres. It has been common land from time immemorial and the London County Council acquired the right of administering 800 acres of it in 1903. A further 300 acres were acquired in 1934, and two eighteen-hole golf courses are available. Unfortunately many of the trees have been cut down and only about a third of the " Forest " is woodland.

Among the other parks and open spaces of the same authority are Hackney Marsh, Hampstead Heath, Battersea Park, Ken Wood, and Victoria Park. The last named is the Hyde Park of the East End. Its greatest attraction is an open-air swimming-pool erected at a cost of £25,000 and regarded as the finest in the world.

Hampstead Heath is universally known as the Cockney's pleasure-ground. On Sundays and Bank Holidays it is visited by enormous crowds from all over London. Its popularity is well deserved, for apart from its great natural beauty, the bracing quality of its air, its accessibility and its historical associations, it commands an unequalled view of the metropolis. To the north of it lies Ken Wood, in which is the mansion containing the fine collections of pictures and furniture known as the Iveagh Bequest.

The 270 acres of Blackheath Common are right on the other side of London, in Greenwich and Lewisham. There James I took his daily exercise, and there the game of golf was played for the first time in England by the King himself.

It is not now possible to play golf at Blackheath, but the public is at liberty to have a round on the London County Council's course at Beckenham Place Park, not far away.

The Government owns and administers no less than twenty-seven parks and open spaces in Greater London. They have a combined area of 6,218 acres and cost about £260,000 a year to maintain.

The largest is Richmond Park, with an area of 2,358 acres.

In the Park is White Lodge, built by George I and used by his successor as a hunting lodge. It was also the birthplace of the Duke of Windsor and for some years the residence of King George VI and Queen Elizabeth, when they were Duke and Duchess of York.

Chestnut Avenue in Bushy Park

On the other side of the Thames, a little over a mile away, is Bushy Park, with an area of 1,099 acres. Its most striking feature is the magnificent Chestnut Avenue which thousands

SATURDAY AFTERNOON FOOTBALL

The London County Council rents pitches for games to recognised clubs on its parks and open spaces A scene at Hackney Marsh, one of the largest open spaces, where scores of such pitches are provided

THE BROAD WALK IN KENSINGTON GARDENS

This beautiful chestnut-lined avenue, fifty feet in width, connects Gloucester Road on the south with Queen's Road on the north. At one end stands a marble statue of Queen Victoria by Princess Louise.

Donald McLeish

LAKELAND IN LONDON

A beautiful view of the Serpentine from the Marlborough Gate on the Bayswater Road. The Serpentine, which is fed by a well at this point, was formed out of the Westbourne stream and six small ponds.

flock to see when the 200-year-old trees are in bloom in May. This avenue leads almost to the gates of Hampton Court Park, with its beautiful gardens and historic palace.

Hyde Park and Westminster Abbey

Hyde Park, the most magnificent playground in the West End, covers 275 acres. It once belonged to Westminster Abbey, but Henry VIII made it into a deer park, and about a century later it was used as a race-course, the public having been given the right of entrance about 1635. The racing ceased long ago, but fashionable riders still frequent Rotten Row.

People of all classes make use of the bathing and basking facilities offered by the Lansbury Lido on the Serpentine, and refresh themselves in the Ring Tea House, a little farther north. Orators hold forth at the Marble Arch corner of the Park. There one may hear impassioned dissertations on almost every subject, political and religious. Nature-lovers enjoy the Bird Sanctuary near the Superintendent's House, and occasional glimpses of wild rabbits.

Amidst the leafy greenery of Kensington Gardens, the continuation of Hyde Park, streets and shops and noise seem very remote, though in reality they are quite near.

St. James's Park, to-day one of the most beautiful gardens in the world, was a swampy meadow before Henry VIII cast covetous eyes on the hospital which stood on the site of St. James's Palace. After building the palace he turned the swamp into a nursery for deer, but it remained in a wild state until Charles II had it laid out in walks and flower-beds.

The Merry Monarch spent much of his time in St. James's Park, talking to Nell Gwynne or another of his favourites, exercising his spaniels and feeding the ducks. It was he who introduced the ducks, and Pepys mentions that Charles also brought there " a great variety of water fowl," the like of which he had never seen before. It is said that many of the Park's present feathered inhabitants are descended from the original " great variety."

When Charles II Lost His Dog

The King, having lost his dog, issued the following quaint advertisement: " Lost four or five days since in St. James's Park, a Dogg of his Majestie's; full of blew spots, with a white cross on his forehead, and about the bigness of a Tumbler."

The public had always enjoyed certain rights in St. James's Park, but the imperious Queen Caroline, wife of George II, decided to make it into a palace pleasure ground. When she asked Sir Robert Walpole how much this would cost, he tersely replied: " Only three Crowns, Madam."

The Park was laid out almost as it appears

RIDERS IN ROTTEN ROW

Rotten Row, in Hyde Park, is a track one and a half miles long reserved for horse-riding and laid down with fine, loose gravel mixed with tan. For many years it was used exclusively by the wealthy aristocracy

REGENT'S PARK ONE HUNDRED YEARS AGO
An island on the lake and parts of Cornwall and Clarence Terraces. Originally known as Marylebone Park, Regent's Park was laid out about 1812 by Nash for the Prince Regent. It is 412 acres in extent.

to-day by Nash, the great architect, in 1829. The view from the bridge across the ornamental water looking towards Whitehall is said to be the finest in London, but it attracts less attention than the irresistibly comic pelicans and ducks whose weird antics amuse the public.

Palace that was Never Built

Still queerer antics may be witnessed in the Zoological Society's Gardens, Regent's Park, which are visited by more than 2,000,000 people a year. Many times that number use Regent's Park itself for recreational purposes. London owes this great open space to the Prince Regent, later George IV. His Royal Highness wished to build a palace somewhere on the site and he ordered Nash not only to build Regent's Street to connect the proposed palace with Carlton House, his St. James's Park mansion, but also to lay out this park. The palace was never built, but the park, designed in 1812, was completed by James Morgan, under Nash's supervision, some seven years later, and was opened to the public in 1838. Before the Prince Regent's time it was known as Old Marylebone Park, under which name Charles I pawned it for £2,300.

To-day the Park has many attractions for jaded workers. Its flower beds are often a mass of colour, and its chestnut avenue is a dream of beauty in spring. The extensive lake on the Baker Street side attracts hundreds of model-yacht enthusiasts.

The Royal Botanic Gardens at Kew, on the south-western outskirts of the County of London, are the finest of their kind. They contain practically every known species of tree, shrub and flower, some growing in the open and others in hothouses and conservatories.

Birthplace of the Rubber Industry

The services of Kew's staff of experts are available to farmers and horticulturists in every part of the world. Kew was the birthplace of the rubber industry. In 1875, 70,000 seeds of the Brazilian wild rubber tree were brought there by F. E. Wickham, acting under the orders of the India Office. About 2,500 germinated, and of these nearly 2,000 were sent to Ceylon, where they flourished. The great plantations of Para rubber to be found to-day in India and Malaya are the direct result of this experiment.

It was through Kew, also, that the quinine plant was brought from South America to India, where it has been the means of saving innumerable lives, particularly in districts where malaria is prevalent.

The City of London Corporation only maintains four acres of open spaces in the City itself, but it controls over 7,000 acres elsewhere. The smallest of its open spaces are Bridgewater Square in the City and Blackfriars Bridge Gardens in Southwark, each having an area of about one-tenth of an acre. The former was acquired in 1928, at a cost of £5,163. The largest is Epping Forest, the administration of which was taken over by the Corporation in 1882. The initial cost was £300,000 and £6,500 is annually spent on maintenance.

Custom Surviving from Norman Times

In the days of the Normans Epping Forest stretched all the way from London to Colchester, and special laws and customs were evolved to regulate its use. One of these ancient customs still survives in the periodical election for a term of four years of Verderers of the Forest, whose nominal business it is to see that the Forest suffers no injury. They must be "gentlemen of good account, ability, and living, wise and discreet men, and well learned in the laws of the forest."

Spelling of a Village Name

It was previously within their power to try people alleged to have committed offences against the laws of the Forest, but their last Court was held in 1854, and their position is now merely titular.

Not very long since people who lived in the Forest only a few miles from the outskirts of London were as far removed from the life of the metropolis as if their habitations were in Hampshire. When one of the first Government School Inspectors visited Theydon Bois, a village in the Forest, he was amazed to see over the door of one of the houses "Theydon Bois School." He turned to the Vicar and said, "It's high time we routed you up here, if that's the way you spell 'boys.'"

Another great woodland area controlled by

Donald McLeish

PELICANS IN ST. JAMES'S PARK

These quaintly dignified birds are very popular among visitors to the Park. They are among the numerous inhabitants of a sanctuary for wild fowl in the lake, which was made by King Charles II.

THE GREAT PALM HOUSE IN KEW GARDENS

This gigantic conservatory is 362 feet long, 100 feet broad, and 60 feet high. It contains specimens of palms of every kind from bamboo to banana, and its temperature is always maintained at 80° Fahrenheit.

the Corporation is Burnham Beeches, about four miles north of Slough. A relic of the ancient forest of Buckinghamshire, it was opened to the public in 1883, and now covers 480 acres.

In addition to those maintained by the three main bodies already mentioned—the London County Council, the Government and the City Corporation—a great number of parks and open spaces are controlled by metropolitan borough councils, and certain garden squares,

SHEEP IN HYDE PARK

In the heart of London it is possible to imagine oneself in the country; in both Hyde Park and the Green Park flocks of sheep are pastured. But the dull continuous roar of the London traffic never ceases.

THE HEADQUARTERS OF CRICKET

Lord's Cricket Ground in St. John's Wood, home since 1814 of the Marylebone Cricket Club, whose laws rule cricket throughout the world. Lord's takes its name from Thomas Lord, who in the nineteenth century made a cricket ground in what is now Dorset Square, and afterwards moved it to the present site.

LAWN TENNIS AT WIMBLEDON

The headquarters of the All-England Lawn Tennis and Croquet Club are in Wimbledon Park. Here every year in June take place championship matches which attract competitors from all over the world. The star games are played on the famous centre court. It was hit by a bomb in the air raids of 1940.

churchyards and disused burial-grounds are preserved for ever from building in the public interest. Altogether well over 20,000 acres, of which about 8,000 are within the County, are maintained at the public expense for the enjoyment of Londoners. No other city can make such a claim.

Cricket and Football Grounds

Among the sports grounds of private bodies in London the most famous is Lord's Cricket Ground, at St. John's Wood, the property of the Marylebone Cricket Club. It has an area of seven acres, and the magnificent pavilion, erected in 1890, cost £20,000. The annual match between Eton and Harrow, the great social event of the cricketing season, is played there. Test matches take place there and at the Oval, Kennington, the largest cricket ground in London and the headquarters of the Surrey Club.

Recent years have seen the erection of vast stadiums for professional football. The Cup Final ground at Wembley is referred to later in this chapter. On Highbury Hill the Arsenal Football Club have a ground with stands and terraces said to be capable of accommodating 90,000 people, while the open arena at Stamford Bridge, used by the Chelsea Football Club and noted for its national and international athletic sports meetings, can accommodate almost as many.

Rugby International matches are held at Twickenham, while during the present century the courts of the Lawn Tennis Association at Wimbledon have become world famous, the gaining of a championship here unofficially constituting a player champion of the world. The decisive games at Wimbledon are always played on the centre court, round which there is accommodation for 15,000 spectators.

Ice-hockey, a game which is steadily gaining in popularity, is played at Wembley, Harringay, Earl's Court and elsewhere.

Among other popular public spectacle sports in London, greyhound racing ranks first. On June 21, 1927, the White City Stadium held its first meeting before a crowd of 60,000 people; to-day over twenty-five London courses, including Stamford Bridge, Wembley, Harringay and West Ham, draw large crowds.

Early Failure of Greyhound Racing

Curiously enough, the first attempt to introduce greyhound racing to London was a dead failure. It took place in 1876, when a meeting was held at the Welsh Harp at Hendon. On that occasion the " hare " was drawn along a rail by means of a windlass.

Little public interest was aroused, and some fifty years were to elapse before Londoners were given a second opportunity to witness this sport.

Motor-cycle dirt-track racing, introduced about the same time as greyhound racing, has attained great popularity, " gates " of 70,000 to 80,000 at Wembley being not uncommon.

ATHLETES OF THE FUTURE

Battersea Park has an excellent sports ground on which athletes of every calibre may daily be seen training. Some clubs using the ground believe in catching their athletes young. A scene on the track.

FOOTBALL ASSOCIATION CUP FINAL AT WEMBLEY

For many years the Football Association Cup Final was played at the Crystal Palace. In 1924 it was transferred to the great Stadium at Wembley, built in connection with the British Empire Exhibition, and it has been held there ever since. The Stadium has an estimated accommodation for about 125,000.

THE CRYSTAL PALACE AS IT ONCE WAS

The Crystal Palace stood in extensive grounds covering an area of 200 acres and was laid out in terraces rising to the building. This aerial view shows it as it was before it was burnt out in 1936.

On the evening of November 30, 1936, the entire London Fire Brigade was rushed south to Sydenham Hill in Norwood. The Crystal Palace was on fire.

They could not save it. Within two hours the giant building was doomed; within three, only the two 282-foot towers remained standing.

When the great quarter-mile transept crashed to the ground the roar could be heard miles away. Flames leaped 500 feet into the air, and were seen from Devil's Dyke, near Brighton.

Story of the Crystal Palace

It would be interesting to know how many of the scores of thousands of people who were in at the death of the Crystal Palace could remember its birth, for the great building was eighty-six years old when it met its end.

Its story begins with the Prince Consort, husband of Queen Victoria, who in the 1840s dreamed a dream of a vast international exhibition, the first of its kind, from which "nothing great, or beautiful, or useful" was to be excluded, and which was to have as its aim the "promotion of universal happiness and brotherhood."

Being a practical man, he set to work to realise his dream, and in January, 1850, obtained the Royal sanction for his exhibition. A Royal Commission was appointed; it elected him as Chairman, and under his guidance pushed on with its gigantic task in face of incredible difficulties and all sorts of opposition.

As exhibits came pouring in it began to be realised that "no building on earth would be sufficiently large to contain a tithe" of the contents of the Exhibition. A special building would have to be erected.

The Exhibition Committee was dissatisfied with all the 233 designs sent in, but at the eleventh hour Providence stepped in—in the person of Joseph Paxton, head gardener, confidential secretary and personal friend of the eccentric Duke of Devonshire.

In June, 1850, Paxton had an idea which he thought might solve the difficulty. Three days later, at a railway board meeting, he sketched his idea on a sheet of blotting paper. Before the month was out Prince Albert had seen Paxton's rough plan and approved of it. The time was almost past for sending in tenders. The Committee allowed Paxton a fortnight to prepare his. In ten days of such labour as few men are capable of, Paxton worked out his scheme to the last nut and bolt, knew the cost to a penny, and had contractors ready to supply every girder and every pane of glass.

On July 16 the Exhibition Committee unanimously accepted Paxton's plans and tenders.

What Paxton proposed was, in brief, a huge conservatory. The exhibition hall was to be constructed entirely of glass supported by metal girders; no bricks were to be used. Lightness was to be combined with strength.

The moment his plans were accepted, Paxton got going at express speed, and unbelievable as it may sound, the entire work of construction was completed in seventeen weeks, though, as it stood in Hyde Park, the Crystal Palace was 1,851 feet long and 450 feet broad; contained 900,000 square feet of glass, or sufficient to cover twenty-five acres, and was supported by 33,000 iron columns and 2,224 girders. Thirty-four miles of guttering-tubes were required.

Chorus of Rapt Appreciation

Paxton used modern methods. His plan included " the first example of mass production on a large scale." All the material used was interchangeable : girders, columns, gutters, sash bars, were identical throughout.

The Great Exhibition was opened by Queen Victoria on June 10, 1851. It lasted five months and fifteen days, and was a huge success. Over 6,170,000 people came to see the goods displayed by 15,000 exhibitors on eight miles of tables. On the afternoon of October 7 there were 93,000 people actually assembled in the Palace at one time. Over £500,000 was taken in gate money, and the net profit was £213,300. Out of the profit came the Albert Hall and the Victoria and Albert Museum.

Fountains that Amazed the World

When the " World Fair " was over, no one knew quite what to do with the Crystal Palace. Everybody wanted it preserved; nobody wanted to bear the cost of preservation. At last a syndicate bought it, and removed it to Norwood. By the time they had re-erected it, they had spent £1,500,000. Then they launched out into fountains.

They determined to have better and bigger fountains than any in the world. They dug wells in the lowest part of the grounds; they made reservoirs in the middle, and they built towers at the top, to get a more powerful jet than had ever been known before. The first towers were not strong enough, so they tried putting tanks on the building itself. These had to be removed in a hurry.

Finally the directors succeeded. They built new towers, 282 feet high, put on each a tank holding 2,000 tons of water, and got at last their desire, the world's most stupendous fountains, two superb jets throwing water 280 feet into the air.

For all its attractions—and the display by 11,788 fountain jets, large and small, was only one among many—the Crystal Palace was not a financial success. Perhaps it was because it tried to educate as well as amuse; or perhaps because it was all so huge it rather stunned people.

Then someone suggested music. The first Handel festival was held in 1857; it attracted the Prince Consort, the King of the Belgians and an audience of 36,000. In 1860 the first great band competition was held. Whatever else failed at the Crystal Palace, Handel and the bands always remained popular. And the huge organ, installed in 1857 and renovated in 1920, was, till the fire, one of the seven wonders of the modern world.

Many Varieties of Exhibitions

During its long life the Crystal Palace was the home of a greater variety of exhibitions and shows than any other building ever erected. In 1861 Charles Haddon Spurgeon preached there to 43,000 people, and Blondin wheeled a barrow on a tight rope stretched between the towers. It was the scene of the Cup Final from 1894 to 1914. During the 1914–18 War, after it had been acquired for the nation, it became H.M.S. *Crystal Palace*, a naval depot where 125,000 men were trained. In 1920 it housed the Imperial War Museum, and during its last years the south tower was used as a short-wave television station, while a speedway track was built in the grounds. And one cannot omit mention of the gorgeous firework displays, so popular with thousands.

In 1946, elaborate plans were published for rebuilding the Crystal Palace, a work, however, which obviously had to await the demands of the immense rehousing programme.

The Alexandra Palace at Muswell Hill was, like the Crystal Palace, born of an International Exhibition, that of 1862. Intended to be a North London rival of its elder sister, it was constructed on a similar if smaller plan, and consisted of a nave 900 feet long, with three transepts, of which the centre one was 430 feet long and was crowned with a dome 170 feet in diameter and 220 feet high.

Opened on May 24, 1873, it lasted just over a fortnight, being on June 9 totally destroyed by fire. A red-hot coal fell from a brazier left by some workmen, and in an hour and a half only the walls and the gables of the transepts were left standing.

London's Great Television Station

Since its reopening in May, 1875, the Alexandra Palace has known a varied and somewhat hectic career. During the 1914–18 War it was used in turn for British troops, Belgian refugees and German prisoners. It later acquired fresh fame as the world's first public high-definition television transmission station.

In 1908 all the world and his wife travelled to Shepherd's Bush in West London to explore the Franco-British Exhibition—ripe fruit of the then recent Entente Cordiale between two peoples so long traditionally hostile.

Everyone wondered at the beauty of the glittering White City which had been erected to house the Exhibition, at its gorgeous pavilions, its ornamental gardens, its huge sports stadium and its gigantic fun fair.

The years passed. Other exhibitions came and went. Tired Marathon runners padded wearily round the stadium at the end of their twenty-six-mile run to the plaudits of assembled crowds : football matches, athletic sports and greyhound races attracted their supporters. Meanwhile the once gleaming White City grew drabber and dingier, and more of a problem to its owners. At last, in 1936, the London County Council acquired part of the site for the development of part of its housing scheme.

Fame of Earl's Court

Earl's Court, which is no more than a short ride from Shepherd's Bush, knew fame before

TELEVISION TOWER AT THE ALEXANDRA PALACE

The Alexandra Palace has been used for many purposes. In 1936 its television transmission mast was erected; closed down from 1939 to 1945, it reopened on June 7, 1946. At night a red light appears at the masthead.

the White City was dreamt of, died during the 1914–18 War, and has since risen from the grave to become once more an exhibition ground.

Earl's Court is inseparably connected with Buffalo Bill and his Wild West Show, Bostock's Circus, Boyton's waterchute and the Great Wheel. Once the Wheel got stuck, and several people were marooned all night high above London's roofs. Each received £5, as the directors had promised if ever such an accident occurred.

Olympia Saved by the Motor Show

The Exhibition was sold to the London General Omnibus Company in 1919. Few thought it would ever be used again, but in 1936 it was rebuilt. It covers twelve acres.

Olympia, during recent years more opulent than its neighbours the White City and Earl's Court, for long knew only too well the bitterness of failure.

Built in 1886 by the National Agricultural Hall Company, it was only saved in 1910 by the growth of the motor industry. Since that year the Motor Show has been held there annually. The Horse Show and the Ideal Homes Exhibition followed, the British Industries Fair made Olympia its London headquarters and the Royal Tournament set the seal upon Olympia's claim to be the aristocrat of London Exhibition halls. In 1923 large extensions were made to the buildings, the new hall along the Hammersmith Road being a triumph of the modern school of slab architecture.

In 1923 Wembley became the most talked-of exhibition ground in the world. Between April 23 and November 1, 1924, 17,305,620 persons visited the British Empire Exhibition—easily a world's record. Alongside the Exhibition was built a gigantic stadium, sixteen acres in extent (also a world's record), wherein were staged in that memorable year the Pageant of Empire, the Rodeo, the British Pageant, the Military Torchlight Tattoo, and the Cup Final. Wembley Exhibition has gone, but the Stadium remains. Now the permanent home of the Cup Final, it counts also to-day among its attractions a colossal swimming bath, an ice-skating rink, a greyhound and a speedway dirt-track.

Opposite Poles of Entertainment

No description of London's exhibitions, however brief, could possibly omit mention of those two aged but perennially popular attractions, the Zoo, and Madame Tussaud's. They are at the opposite poles of entertainment, yet they are the two shows never missed by an intelligent visitor to London.

MADAME TUSSAUD'S A CENTURY AGO

The famous waxworks exhibition now housed in the Marylebone Road was opened by Madame Tussaud in 1834 in Gray's Inn Road. It has been one of the most popular shows in London ever since.

LARGEST MARKET OF ITS KIND IN THE WORLD
The best time to visit Covent Garden is about five in the morning on a day in spring or early summer, when fresh flowers from all over the country can be seen in large and gorgeous heaps of loveliness.

SUPPLYING THE WORLD'S NEEDS

A MODERN store is divided into departments. Footwear, cutlery, books and so on have their own individual sections. When the City was confined more or less to the area within the encompassing walls, something of the same kind was attempted. Many streets bore the name of the trade with which they were specially associated, such as Bread Street, Milk Street, Poultry and Cornhill.

At Cornhill, according to Stow, a corn-market was " time out of mind, there holden." Since it adjoined the Stocks' Market, on the site of which the Mansion House now stands, and extended almost to Poultry, there is reason for the statement, but later Cornhill was better known as a centre of the old-clothes business. There, it has been said, one might even buy back a garment at small cost that not long before had formed part of the spoils of a robbery.

In the Middle Ages the most noticeable objects in Cornhill were the Tun, a round house or temporary prison for breakers of the law, and the Standard, a water conduit supplied by pumps from the Thames, which stood at the east end of the thoroughfare and was used as a point for the measurement of distances. In the fifteenth century the " Pope's Head " would probably have been better known than either of these landmarks, since there one could purchase for the small cost of a penny a full pint of refreshing wine, with bread thrown in.

The street to the west of Cornhill, on the other side of Stocks' Market, was Poultry, the early home of the poulterers. The fowls were dispatched to Scalding Alley near-by to be prepared for the table.

Poultry continued west as Chepe (now Cheapside), a busy market-place lined on both sides with booths or sheds stocked with a variety of wares of every kind, which overflowed into the streets passing north and south. Towards the end of the third quarter of the thirteenth century, candle-makers set up their sheds in Chepe, but they were not tolerated for long on account of the offensive odour given off by their wares, and were expelled at the instance of the citizens.

All sorts and conditions of wares were exhibited for sale in Chepe, and their marketing was apparently carried on throughout the day until, in the reign of Edward II, an ordinance was issued declaring that in future no person should "hold common market for merchandise in Chepe, or any other highway within the City, except Cornhill, after the hour of nones" (about three o'clock in the afternoon). The dealers in small wares were called mercers, and it was not until the fifteenth century that the name was applied to those who sold silks and velvets.

Dishonest Traders Stood in Pillory

It was not unusual for goods of a spurious kind to be offered for sale, and objection to such practice was sometimes raised by honest traders, an instance being a request by the hatters and haberdashers that search be made for traders selling "bad and cheating hats." When caught such dishonest traders were apt to be punished by a term in the pillory.

PLANE TREE OFF CHEAPSIDE
The tree marks the site of a church destroyed in the Great Fire. It shelters three ancient shops.

In the seventeenth century, when many of the houses in Cheapside had been replaced by business premises, and it had become the centre of the wealth of London, with a fine row of goldsmiths' shops, the traders began to take exception to the abuses of the market people, declaring that the encroachment of their stalls on the passages affected what they termed legitimate trading.

In Cheapside was one of the crosses which Edward I erected to mark the places where his wife's funeral *cortège* rested, and there Bishop Stapleton of Exeter was murdered and Lord Saye and Sele beheaded by Jack Cade. In happier vein the great conduit which stood in the thoroughfare was made to flow with wine when Edward III was born, and tournaments were held in the street when it was considerably wider than it is now.

Several of the tributary streets of Cheapside and Poultry were named from the character of the trading carried on there. Many of these names are still familiar, but not for their old trades. In Milk Street, the birthplace of Sir Thomas More, statesman, scholar and saint, was the milk-market of medieval London, and in Bread Street the market where bread was displayed, for in those days it was expressly forbidden for bakers to sell from their shops and houses. Later Bread Street became a residential quarter for many rich merchants.

Street Names with a Trading History

Ironmonger Lane, farther east, was the business quarter of the ironmongers. The fact that fishmongers dwelt there and served the Friday's Market is responsible for the naming of Friday Street, on the south side of Cheapside. Eastcheap owes its name to a meat-market held there as early as the reign of King John. Another thoroughfare named from its trading activities was Candlewick Street, since renamed Cannon Street, which was a centre of the candle-making industry.

The Stocks' Market was so called from its having been built where formerly had stood a pair of stocks.

In the Haymarket there was at one time a market in hay and straw, but this was transferred in the reign of George IV to Cumberland Market, Regent's Park.

Wood Street was named either after Thomas Wood, a sheriff of the fifteenth century, or from

MORNING FROLIC AT COVENT GARDEN

Covent Garden is as noted for its theatre, the Royal Opera House, as for its market. In the eighteenth century it was surrounded by a riotous and dissolute quarter. A scene before St. Paul's Church.

the wooden houses built there, contrary to the edict of Richard I that stone only should be used as a precaution against fire. A plane tree flourishes at the Cheapside end, and at the corner, facing the main thoroughfare, three little houses have stood since 1687. Each consists of a tiny shop with an equally tiny room above.

Cutler Street, so far as its recorded history shows, never shared in the industry that its name implies, nor is there any information to support a belief that Shoe Lane, where there was once a Roman cemetery, was ever the home of footwear manufacturers, or even of cobblers. It is scarcely likely that sea-going craft were ever built in Ship Yard, a tributary of Fleet Street and a locality that was once notorious for harbouring counterfeit coiners.

London's Wholesale Markets

London's great markets exist almost solely for wholesale supply, and they are mostly controlled by the Corporation. Three of them, the Central Meat Market at Smithfield, the fish market at Billingsgate, and the meat, poultry, game and fish market in Leadenhall Street, are actually within the City boundaries, while at Islington there is the Metropolitan Cattle Market, at Spitalfields a fruit, vegetable and flower market, and at Deptford the foreign cattle market. The principal fruit, flower and vegetable market is Covent Garden, a private undertaking. Most of these markets suffered damage from German air attacks during the war, more than 100 people being killed when a rocket struck Smithfield in March, 1945.

Story of Covent Garden

Covent Garden market, the largest of its kind in the world, covers an area of nearly six acres. It was built on the site of a convent garden which once belonged to the abbots and monks of Westminster, who cultivated it mainly for the benefit of the Benedictine community, and partly for public supply.

The land upon which the market stands came into the possession of the Russell family (the Dukes of Bedford) in 1552, and remained their property until after the First World War. The first market buildings were erected about 1631, and the greater part of the present edifice

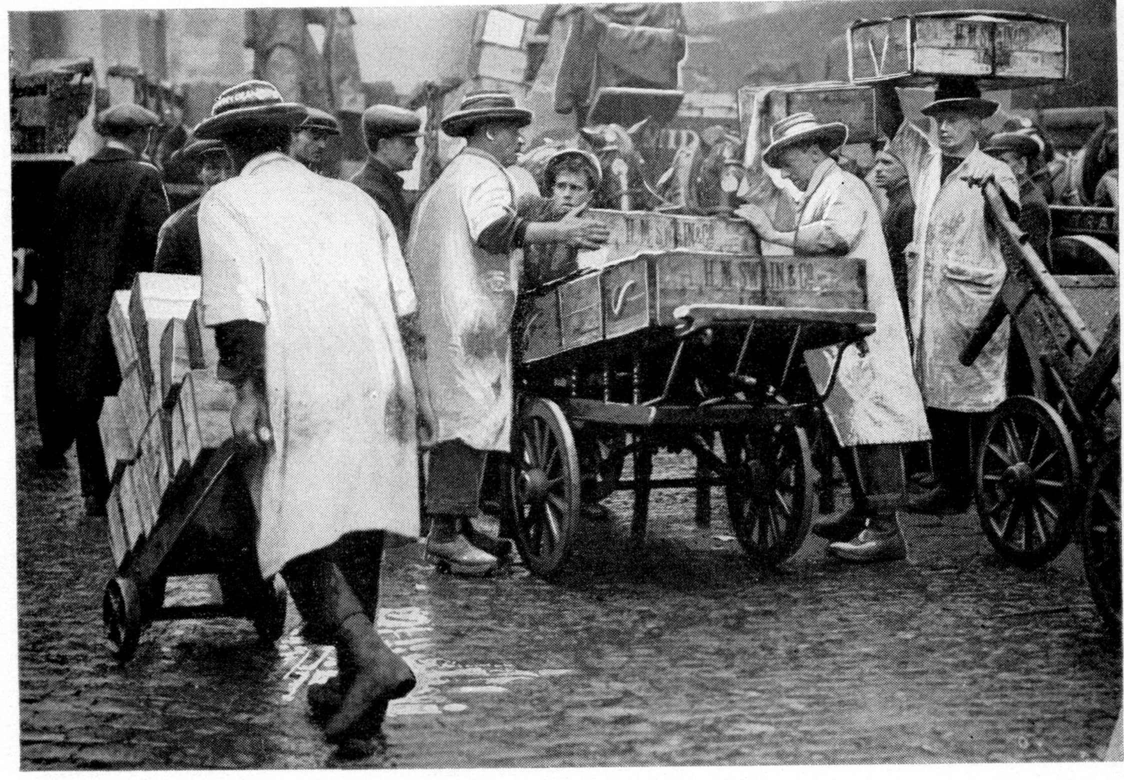

RUSH HOUR AT BILLINGSGATE

The Billingsgate Fish Market is in Lower Thames Street, close to London Bridge. The hats worn by the porters are said to have been modelled on those worn by the English archers at Agincourt.

two hundred years later. The market was established under a charter of Charles II in 1661. It now handles more than 1,000,000 tons of fruit and vegetables yearly.

Spitalfields and Borough Markets

Spitalfields Market, which was founded late in the seventeenth century, is situated in Stepney. For long it remained in private ownership, but in 1920 it was acquired by the Corporation, who two years later spent £2,000,000 on extending the buildings, widening the adjacent streets and rehousing the people displaced by the scheme of improvements. The new buildings were opened by Queen Mary in 1928, the original area of three acres having been increased to five. The London Fruit Exchange, occupying a total floor space of four acres, was completed in 1929, and six years later the new flower market was opened. The combined market trade exceeds 800,000 tons of vegetables and fruit yearly.

The Borough Market, covering an area of three and a half acres, dates from the time of Edward VI and occupies a site in Southwark where the Bishops of Winchester had their palace. It stood originally in the High Street, but when London Bridge was rebuilt it was removed to its present site, a more convenient position to the west. Some 300,000 tons of vegetables and fruit pass through the market every twelve months.

Legend of Billingsgate

There is an ancient legend connected with London's great fish market at Billingsgate. According to Geoffrey of Monmouth, Belin, a king of the Britons who ruled some 400 years before the birth of Christ, set up the gate and named it after himself, and on his death his body was burnt and the ashes placed in a brass casket and set upon a pinnacle of stone above the gate. It is more likely that the name owes its origin to the more prosaic fact that the wharf once belonged to a person of the name of Biling.

In its early days as a market it had rather an evil reputation for the tricks that were practised by some of the less reputable fish-sellers, who are alleged to have stooped to devious methods to secure higher prices for their fish, as for example, using pipes to blow out the cod-fish to a larger size, and putting dead eels in with the live ones.

As a " free and open market for all sorts of fish " Billingsgate dates from 1699. The present building, rather more than an acre in extent, was erected in 1877 by the Corporation, and extensions were made to it in 1920. It superseded one that had been built less than fifty years earlier. Altogether in recent years about £1,000,000 has been expended on improvements to the market, where upwards of 225,000 tons of fish are handled yearly.

Smithfield Meat Market

The Central Meat Market at Smithfield dates from 1868. It replaced the Metropolitan Cattle Market, which was transferred to Islington in 1855. Originally it covered about three acres, but periodical extensions have increased the area to some ten acres. The business of the old cattle market, in fact, was constantly outgrowing its capacity, which can readily be realised when it is stated that the number of animals sold in the middle of the eighteenth century was approximately twenty-five times greater than it had been a hundred years previously. There were exhibited at one time as many as 4,000 beasts and 30,000 sheep, apart from fifty pens of pigs, and the market for livestock was then the largest in the world.

Salesmen Never Used Scales

Scales were never used for ascertaining the weight of the animals sold, the salesmen estimating it by eye, and such was the accuracy they attained that they rarely miscalculated beyond a few pounds.

To-day the Central Meat Market conducts possibly the largest meat trade of any market in the world, besides disposing of an immense quantity of poultry, provisions, fish and vegetables. Between 400,000 and 500,000 tons of meat and provisions pass through the market every year. Hidden underground are immense cellars for storage.

Covering as it does some fifteen acres of

PRIME JOINTS AT SMITHFIELD

A 3 a.m. scene in the London Central Meat Market, showing porters in their distinctive uniforms carrying a massive side of beef. Most of the work of the market is done in the early hours of the morning.

LONDON THE IVORY MARKET OF THE WORLD
At sales of valuable ivory held periodically in London, quantities of tusks worth thousands of pounds change hands. Examining elephant and rhinoceros tusks at the Port of London ivory warehouse before a sale.

ground, including the public abattoirs, the Metropolitan Cattle Market at Islington surpasses all others in size. An attempt was made to establish a market here in 1833 by one John Perkins, who wished to obviate the danger of driving herds of cattle through the busy streets of London to Smithfield. He expended a sum of £100,000 on the project, but so strong was public opposition to the new venture that it proved a failure and had to be closed down. The unlucky Perkins was in advance of the times, for in 1852 when Smithfield was condemned on account of the noise and dangers of the place having become a nuisance, the Islington site was chosen as an alternative, and about three years later the transference took place.

£20,000 Pearls Bought for 7s. 6d.

The market has accommodation for about 6,000 cattle, 35,000 sheep, some 14,000 calves and nearly 10,000 pigs, and in addition there are abattoirs and cold storage facilities. On Fridays the market was formerly occupied by pedlars, who offered a remarkable collection of miscellaneous second-hand goods which attracted many visitors. It was the survival of the Pedlar's Market of old Bartholomew Fair.

It was not often that really valuable "finds" were made at the Caledonian Market, as it is called, but on one occasion a woman had a phenomenal piece of good fortune. Wishing to buy a row of beads to match the colour of a dress, and failing to do so elsewhere, she was induced to visit the market, and there purchased exactly what she required for 7s. 6d. The next evening a jeweller noticed the beads, and on examining them closely discovered them to be a string of genuine black pearls. Shortly afterwards they were sold for £20,000.

Market Bought from Whittington

Before becoming a centre of the poultry and vegetable trade, Leadenhall Market was used as a granary. A manor house, built in 1309 and belonging to Sir Hugh Neville, originally stood on the site, and this was converted into a store for corn, which later became first a market for meat and fish, and then for raw hides, wool and herbs.

A flourishing business has been carried on at the market for hundreds of years, and in the reign of Charles II the amount of business transacted so impressed the Spanish ambassador of the time that he declared there must be more meat sold in the market than in all the kingdom of Spain in a year.

The original market, which was acquired from Richard Whittington by the Corporation in 1411, was destroyed in the Great Fire. The present buildings, dating from 1881 and covering a little over one acre, were erected at a cost of nearly £100,000, the new approaches adding another £148,000 to that sum. In view of the association with the market of Whittington, it is of interest to record that until a few years ago cats were sold there, many destined for the hunting of rats in ships.

Where Russian Emperor Worked

At Deptford, in the south-east, is the Foreign Cattle Market, which stands on the site of the old Admiralty dockyard, where Peter the Great worked as a ship's carpenter in 1698. Under the Contagious Diseases (Animals) Act of 1869 it became necessary to obtain a site for the reception, slaughter and sale of foreign animals arriving at the port of London, and the Corporation at length decided on the disused Admiralty dock at Deptford, part of which was converted for the purpose. The market was opened towards the end of 1871 and occupies an area of about thirty acres.

Just as certain streets within the walls of medieval London were set apart for trade in specific wares, so many of the streets and districts of that much vaster London of to-day are similarly interested in particular trades and manufactures.

Haunts of the Booksellers

Holywell Street, on the north side of the Strand, better known as Booksellers' Row, disappeared long since at the demand of the builder, and for the second-hand volumes for which book-lovers frequented it a visit must now be paid to Charing Cross Road and the vicinity. Paternoster Row, near St. Paul's Cathedral, has enjoyed a reputation as a centre of the book trade for centuries; it was completely destroyed by bombing in 1940. Old St. Paul's was surrounded by a wall, and it is inferred that in former times the lane, when religious processions were in favour, was used for the purpose. Here they sang the Paternoster, hence the name. Ave Maria Lane perpetuates the chanting of the Ave Maria and Creed Lane that of the Creed.

Most of Great Portland Street is associated with motor-cars, and Bermondsey with leather and leather goods. The neighbourhood of City Road and Curtain Road, in Shoreditch,

A SALE AT THE LONDON FRUIT EXCHANGE

The London Fruit Exchange at Spitalfields Market was erected in 1929. Owned by the Corporation of the City of London, it covers a total floor space of four acres, and deals with vast quantities of fruit.

HANDLING THE EMPIRE'S WOOL

Examining bales of wool at the Port of London Authority Wool Warehouse. Large quantities of wool are landed every year at the London, St. Katharine, Victoria and Albert, and King George V Docks.

is a seat of cabinet-making and upholstery. Farther east in Bethnal Green and Stepney many hundreds of people follow the occupation of tailoring, an industry in which Jews predominate, and which is largely carried on in their homes. Hackney is concerned with the manufacture of boots and shoes, but this is not such a specialised trade of the district as it was formerly. Lambeth, Deptford and Millwall have extensive engineering works, the first-named being also noted for its potteries, while Bermondsey and Southwark are centres for soap-boiling and candle-making.

Riots of the Silk Weavers

When the decree granting religious freedom to French Huguenots was withdrawn in 1685 some 13,000 refugees sought a new home in London. Spitalfields became a hive of busy silk weavers, but to-day there is scarcely a trace of what was formerly a flourishing industry. During the reigns of Queen Anne, George I and George II, there was a considerable increase in the numbers employed, and at the height of the industry some 50,000 people were dependent upon the output of silk for their livelihood.

Peace did not always reign among the weavers, however, and the low wages earned were on more than one occasion the cause of a discontent which displayed itself in rioting. History records that the operatives once vented their wrath by tearing off the calico gown of every woman they happened to come across.

Home of the Diamond Trade

Another instance of their turbulent nature occurred in 1765, when they proceeded in procession to Parliament Square, carrying red flags and black banners, to present a petition to the House. The cause of their dissatisfaction was the importation of French silks, which they declared had reduced them almost to starvation. Such was the fury of their demonstration that Parliament deemed it wise to adjourn its sitting and call for the intervention of the Guards, who dispersed the rioters, many of whom sustained injuries.

Hatton Garden, named after Sir Christopher Hatton, a Lord Chancellor of Elizabeth's reign, is the home of the diamond trade and contains also the offices of several of the principal pottery manufacturers. Here formerly stood the palace of the Bishops of Ely, in which John of Gaunt, the father of Henry IV, died in 1399. In Hatton Garden there died also, in 1668, Dr. George Bate, the physician to Oliver Cromwell, whom he attended in his last illness. Later he regained favour with the royalists, which led to the suggestion, for which there was little foundation, that he had hastened the end of the Lord Protector by administering to him a dose of poison. Clerkenwell, to the north-east, has for long been the centre of the clock- and watch-makers' craft.

Import Centres in the City

The centre of the wholesale trade in tea, sugar, rubber and other colonial produce is Mincing Lane, at the eastward end of the City, where also, as in the adjacent Mark Lane, are huge wine vaults. The Wool Exchange, in Coleman Street, handles the wholesale disposal of wool. Grain dealings are centred in the Corn Exchange in Mark Lane, those for hops at the Hop Exchange in the Borough, for coal at the Coal Exchange in Lower Thames Street, and for metals at the Metal Exchange in Whittington Avenue.

The Baltic Mercantile and Shipping Exchange in St. Mary Axe deals with the grain imported from abroad, and is possibly the most important grain market in the world. Like the Stock Exchange and Lloyd's it started in a coffee-house—the " Virginia and Baltick " in

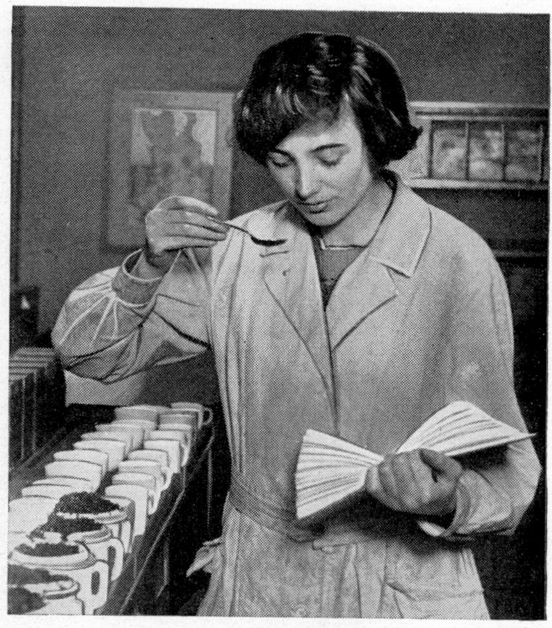

TEA TASTING

Tea tasting is a highly expert job demanding a very keen palate. Samples are taken of all incoming shipments of tea; these are tasted, and the teas graded according to quality before being sent out.

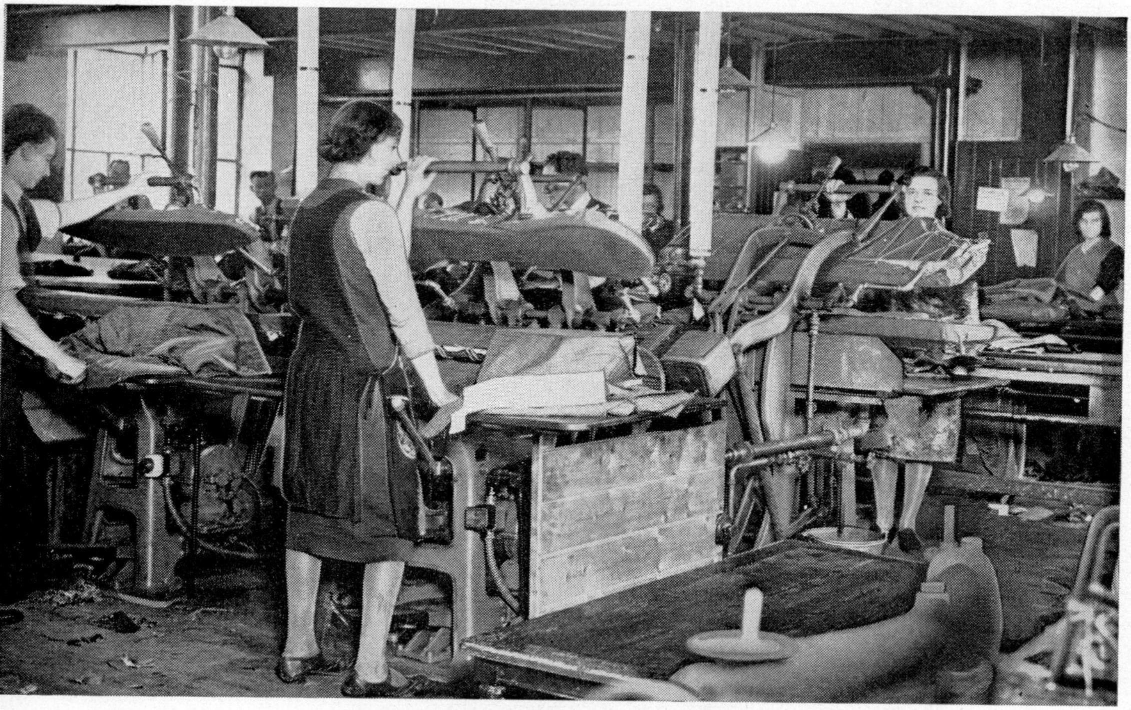

MASS-PRODUCTION TAILORING

Ready-made clothing is made in the East End of London, especially in Bethnal Green and Stepney. A scene in the pressing room of a mass-production factory. A good deal of work is done outside the factory.

FURNITURE FOR THE MILLION

The East End produces much furniture. The district round City Road and Curtain Road in Shoreditch is full of workshops, and any day loads of half-made furniture can be seen on the Bethnal Green Road.

Threadneedle Street, where "All Foreign and Domestick News are taken in; and all Letters or Parcels, directed to Captains in the Virginia or Baltick Trade, will be carefully delivered." There, in 1728, a negro boy was advertised to be sold.

Street of the Moneylenders

Lombard Street acquired its name from the Lombard moneylenders who settled there in the twelfth century. Ever since that time it has been associated with banking, and remains to-day the great money market of London.

The headquarters of many of the great shipping companies are located in Leadenhall Street, the eastward continuation of Cornhill, where also stands the new building of Lloyd's, the home of the mercantile underwriters who for so many years conducted their operations from the Royal Exchange. In other days Leadenhall Street was famed as the home of the old East India Company, which occupied the house of Sir William Craven from 1701 to 1726, when a new building was erected on the site. The company was dissolved in 1858, and a year later the building was sold and shortly afterwards demolished. Among other well-known people employed by the Company as clerks were Charles Lamb and John Stuart Mill, the former for over thirty years. Cockspur Street, off Trafalgar Square, is another centre of shipping interests.

London's principal shopping centre is the West End, and in Oxford Street, Regent Street, Piccadilly and Bond Street are found great stores and attractive shops where everything to delight the heart of man and woman alike may be obtained. Among other important shopping quarters of London are High Street (Kensington), Sloane Street, Brompton Road, Victoria Street and Queen's Road (Bayswater) in the south-west; the Strand and Holborn in the west-central district; and the neighbourhood of St. Paul's Churchyard and Cheapside in the east-central district.

Where Newspapers are Produced

For well over a century Fleet Street and the immediate neighbourhood have been associated with newspaper and periodical publishing, although *The Times*, launched by John Walter in 1785 as the *Daily Universal Register*, chose

Printing House Square, near Queen Victoria Street, which has remained its home to the present day. The site had previously been occupied by the King's printing office, from which were issued proclamations and other State documents. Within three years from the date of its foundation the *Register* adopted its present name.

Printing in Long Acre

In recent years Long Acre has also become intimately connected with the newspaper world. In it are situated the extensive offices of the *Daily Herald*, the *People*, *John Bull*, *Sporting Life*, and a host of other periodical publications issued by Odhams Press Ltd.

London has always been noted for its breweries, and according to one early writer there stood in the time of the Tudors, on the riverside below St. Katherine's, the great breweries of London, or the " bere house." Southwark was early famed for its strong ale, and a brewing name associated with the district for many years is that of Barclay Perkins. This business was acquired from Mrs. Thrale, the friend of Dr. Johnson; and the latter, as one of her husband's executors, helped to negotiate the sale. Other famous breweries were to be seen, and some of them may still be seen, in Spitalfields, Tottenham Court Road, Chiswell Street, Upper Thames Street, Castle Street, off Long Acre, Liquorpond Street, near Gray's Inn Road, and Mile End Road.

The street trading of the city of the Middle Ages is to some extent perpetuated in the street markets of the present day. Kerb markets still occur in many side streets, though sadly altered since the war. In main thoroughfares barrow-men are constantly " moved on."

In the Lambeth New Cut, for example, on any day of the week, one may obtain, if so desirous, a second-hand gramophone record, or a packet of washing powder, socks, " silk " stockings, spectacles, old bits of scientific apparatus, razor blades, grapes and oranges, plants and bulbs for the garden and second-hand books in great variety.

Well-known Street Markets

The New Cut is typical of many other kerbside " emporia " in north and south, east and west—Farringdon Road, Lower Marsh, Lambeth; Middlesex Street, Aldgate; Whitecross Street, St. Luke's; Rupert Street and Berwick Street, Soho, to mention only a few. Some of the street markets are specially productive of a good return for traders on Sunday morning, and this applies particularly to that of Middlesex Street, formerly called Petticoat Lane, and also to Club Row, in Bethnal Green,

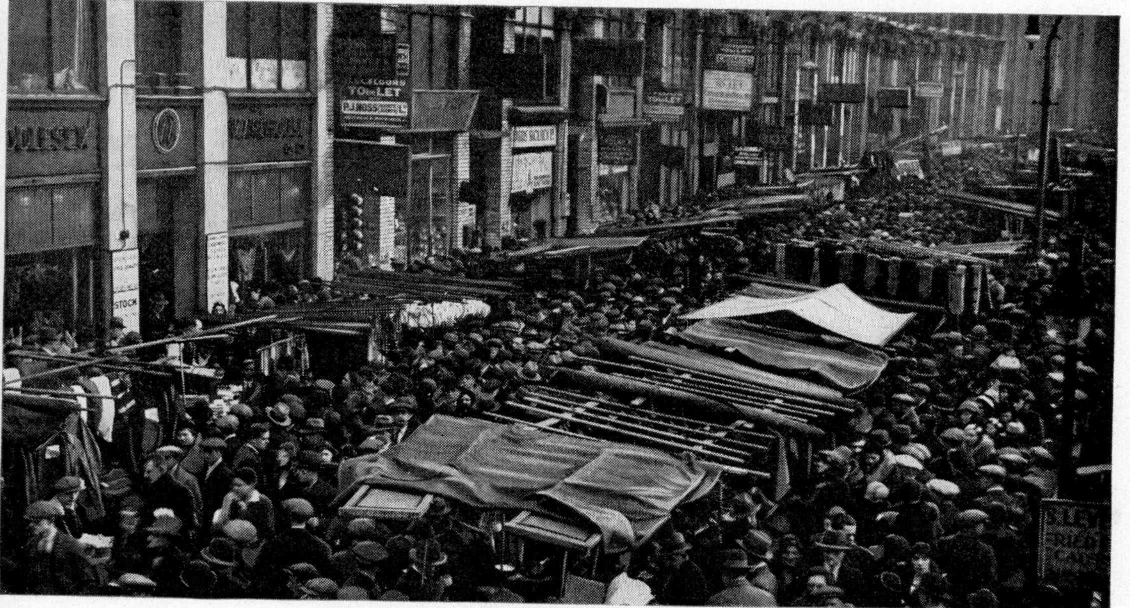

PETTICOAT LANE ON SUNDAY MORNING

Most famous of all London street markets is " Petticoat Lane," now known as Middlesex Street, off Bishopsgate. Almost every variety of goods is to be purchased there, frequently at bargain prices.

where, among other of one's needs, cage-birds and dogs may be bought at bargain prices.

South London Market

One of the largest and most popular of London's street markets is to be found in East Street, off the Walworth Road between the Elephant and Castle and Camberwell Green.

East Street rises to the acme of its glory on Sunday morning, when the stalls and stands overflow into half a dozen neighbouring thoroughfares, and for two or three hours, from about 11 a.m. till 1 or 2 p.m., a vast, good-natured crowd elbows and shoulders its way past them.

Even in the first century A.D., London was a great commercial port, if we can accept the description of Aulus Plautius. How then can it be described to-day when its few inhabitants of that far distant age have multiplied to more than 8,000,000 and its foreign trade has increased in proportion? In the last half-century there has been an increase of no less than fifty per cent in the number of ships entering and leaving the port; by 1939 their number annually exceeded 27,000. By 1953 the total net registered tonnage had become 33,393,000 and the annual value of the merchandise imported and exported was £2,140,000,000.

New Factories in Greater London

Through the long years London has held tenaciously to its proud position of the trade centre of the world. Meanwhile what is known as Greater London has become a great area of industrial development with an enormous range of factories of many kinds. These extend along most of the great trunk roads into the capital. Motor and engineering works are scattered along the Watling Street for miles, from Cricklewood to Edgware; similarly on the North Circular Road, the Great West Road and at Morden. Around these factories large new suburbs have grown up in the last twenty years.

NEWSPAPER-LAND

Fleet Street, popularly known among journalists as "the Street," contains the publishing offices of a number of national and many provincial newspapers. It has been connected with journalism for hundreds of years.

ST. LUCIA'S FESTIVAL AT ROTHERHITHE

The traditional ceremonies of the Feast of St. Lucia, honoured for centuries in Sweden, at the Swedish Seamen's Church at Rotherhithe. The "Lucia Bride" is pouring out the coffee she offers the household.

FOREIGN LONDON

ON October 18, 1685, a law was passed in France revoking the Edict of Nantes, thus depriving Louis XIV's Protestant subjects of all civil and religious liberty. Thousands of the Huguenots then fled from their native land and large numbers found their way to London, which city they greatly enriched, for they were honest, hard-working folk, highly skilled in many branches of industry, including the manufacture of silk, jewellery and crystal glass.

Many of them settled down in the area known as Soho, which has ever since been London's principal foreign quarter. They were not the first foreign settlers in that area, for a Greek Orthodox Church was built in Crown Street (now Charing Cross Road) in 1677.

Eleven years later James II granted Letters Patent for the erection of a chapel by the Soho Huguenots. It was built in Little Chapel Street in 1694 and was always called "the Patent." Many similar places of worship sprang up.

John Strype, the seventeenth-century ecclesiastical historian, refers to "chapels in these parts (Soho and its environs), for the use of the French nation; where our Liturgy, turned into French, is used, French ministers, that are refugees, episcopally ordained, officiating; several whereof are hereabouts seen walking in the canonical habit of the English clergy. Abundance of French People, many whereof are voluntary exiles for their religion, live in these streets and lanes, following honest trades; and some gentry of the same nation."

More than a century after the Revocation of the Edict of Nantes there was another great influx of refugees from France. Aristocrats fleeing from the excesses of the Revolution, they were totally unlike the Huguenots in character and upbringing. Nevertheless many of them chose Soho as their new home, mingling with the descendants of the men whom their ancestors had persecuted. These *émigrés*, as they were called, were incapable of enriching London industrially, like the Huguenots, but they probably helped to make social life more " civilised " in the French sense.

Formation of First International

There was a third influx of French refugees in 1851–52, when Napoleon III gave up the pretence of being a constitutional president, and with the help of the army suppressed the opposition of Republicans. Hundreds of liberal-minded Frenchmen fled to London, to be joined twenty years later by many of those who had fought for the Commune in the streets of Paris after the Franco-Prussian War. The latter had, as strange allies in Soho exile, hundreds of German Socialists, refugees from the wrath of Bismarck, the " Man of Iron."

Six years before the outbreak of the Franco-Prussian War London's habit of sheltering political refugees had given rise to the famous International Working Men's Association (the first " International "), which indirectly helped to bring the Paris Commune of 1871 into existence, and was the ancestor of the " Third International " of the Communist Party, which became famous in this century.

The first " International," formed under the leadership of Karl Marx and Friedrich Engels, originated from discussions in the " Hôtel de la Boule d'Or," in Percy Street. There French artisans who were in London at the suggestion of Napoleon III to inspect the mechanical exhibits of the Universal Exhibition of 1862, met the leaders of the English working-class movement to talk about means of bettering the conditions of workers in all countries. The " International " formed in 1864 was the immediate result of these deliberations.

Soup Kitchen for Exiles

In the seventies the " Boule d'Or " was the *rendezvous* of many distinguished Socialists, including Emile and Camille Barère, descendants of Bertrand Barère, a member of the Committee of Public Safety in 1793–94.

After the suppression of the Paris Commune,

A TYPICAL SCENE IN SOHO

These small shops and restaurants, with their rich assortment of French, Italian, Greek and other foreign goods, are peculiar to Soho, as is its population of many nationalities. It was a haunt of Charles Dickens.

FESTIVAL IN LITTLE ITALY
The procession of the Feast of Our Lady of Mount Carmel passing through one of the streets of Clerkenwell known as "Little Italy." There are probably more Italians in Soho than in Clerkenwell.

a soup kitchen, where anyone who had fought on the Communist side might obtain a meal for twopence, was established in Newman Street, near the eastern end of Oxford Street, by English sympathisers. The same charitable individuals established evening classes for French Communists in Francis Street, Tottenham Court Road. Some of them profited so much from the instruction they received that they preferred to remain in London rather than return to France when it was safe for them to do so.

Café Frequented by Karl Marx

In Charlotte Street were two or three cafés where Socialists of every nationality met. Perhaps the most famous was Audinet's Restaurant, frequented by Karl Marx and his sons-in-law, Longuet and La Fargue, among others.

The German Socialist, Rackow, who was forced to flee from his native land by Bismarck after he had just failed to secure a seat in the Reichstag, kept a tobacco shop in Charlotte Street for many years. Next door Lacassie, a well-known French revolutionary, had a hairdressing establishment.

Restaurant Famous in a Day

The northern end of Greek Street has many associations with political refugees. In a hotel there Marx and Engels used to meet Social Democratic members of the German Parliament, and there they prepared plans to force Bismarck to withdraw some of his anti-Socialist laws.

At the corner of Greek Street and Old Compton Street were two famous refugee hotels, the "Albergo de Venezia" and the "Hôtel des Bons Amis." The former was frequented by Italian revolutionary supporters of Garibaldi, and the latter by French Socialists.

Kettner's Restaurant, farther down the street, was started by an Austrian who catered for impoverished refugees, until one day an English journalist dropped in to have a meal and was so pleased with the food, the company and the picturesque air of the place that he wrote an article on it for *The Times*, with the result that the next day it was besieged by a large crowd. The restaurant was gradually enlarged, and to-day it is among the most famous in London.

In some parts of Soho and the district immediately north of it (the Charlotte Street area) the streets have a completely foreign air. It would appear at first sight that bits of France, Italy and Germany had been dropped into the heart of London.

Foreign Cafés in Soho

The French have played a leading part in " foreignising " this district. In Old Compton Street and its tributaries one sees French restaurants, cafés and shops every few yards. The cafés are quite unlike the ordinary London tea- or coffee-shops. They usually begin to get busy in the late hours of the evening, when the theatres are emptying. Amidst a haze compounded of tobacco smoke and the steam from urns, men and women of every nationality sit at little tables talking and drinking coffee. They seem rarely to eat.

There are large numbers of Italians in London. The majority used to live at the Holborn end of Clerkenwell Road, as many still do, but the war naturally affected their status and freedom, although many of them repudiated any connection with Fascism. Their restaurants and cafés, in many ways similar to those of the French, were scattered through Greek Street, Frith Street, Dean Street, and Charlotte Street. Many of the night clubs of which this area is full were also run by Italians.

In the summer of 1914 there were about 70,000 Germans in London, but shortly before August 4 large numbers of them left to fight for the Fatherland. History repeated itself in 1939! London's most famous German restaurant is on the west side of Charlotte Street. In the same street there is a small but celebrated Swiss restaurant in addition to French, Italian, Greek and Yiddish restaurants. There was a great influx of German political refugees after the Hitler " terror " of 1933. Many of these took up residence in Belsize Park and other parts of north London.

Negro and Indian Quarters

The Negro quarter of central London is also in Soho. New Compton Street is a favourite lodging place for coloured people, and at least one café there is used exclusively by Negroes.

Many Indians, mainly of the student class,

CHINESE SHOPS IN LIMEHOUSE

A visit to " Chinatown " is often suggested to visitors and tourists in London, but the Chinaman is very shy, hating nothing more than to be stared at. So a tour through Limehouse is apt to be disappointing

HOMES IN RAILWAY ARCHES

Limehouse is one of the poorest districts in London, and many of the houses leave a great deal to be desired. Here railway arches have been given a brick front and turned into dwelling houses.

have lodgings in the Bloomsbury area, north-east of Soho, which they make no attempt to penetrate. Gower Street in particular, being the street of University College, has many houses where they live; and there are Indian restaurants in the near neighbourhood.

Not many Chinese live in Soho, though they run several restaurants in the vicinity.

Unromantic Chinatown

The Chinatown of the romantic novelists is much farther east, in Limehouse. Those who imagine Limehouse as a place where evil-faced " Chinks " lurk in dark alleys, knife in hand, to rob and murder the innocent, will be sadly disappointed at the reality. There is little obvious romance in Chinatown, but there one may see many Chinese in streets of Chinese lodging-houses, laundries and chop-suey restaurants. The London Chinaman and his wife are hard-working and respectable.

Across the Thames from Limehouse is Rotherhithe, where there is a small Scandinavian quarter. It contains a church for Norwegian, and one for Swedish seamen.

The Jews have been living peaceably and industriously in London since the time of Cromwell, who tacitly permitted the lifting of the ban imposed upon them by Edward III. In many ways they are so much of London that they cannot be classed as foreigners in the ordinary sense, but the districts in which many of them live—Whitechapel, Stepney, Mile End and Bethnal Green—are in parts completely unlike the rest of the metropolitan area. In some streets Yiddish names and advertisements outnumber those in English. Within the last thirty years well-to-do Jews have tended to take up residence in outlying districts.

Refugees from Persecution

In the days of Elizabeth I Bethnal Green was populated to a large extent by Flemish weavers, refugees from the brutal persecutions of the Duke of Alva, who was at that time attempting to subdue the Netherlands for Spain. In more recent years Whitechapel witnessed a great influx of Polish-Russian Jews, also fugitives from persecution.

In medieval times the Bishop of London had the task of supervising and protecting foreign residents, and in 1571, Edwin Sandys, who then held that office, estimated the number of aliens in the City as 3,760, of whom 2,993 were "Duche." For many years now the interests of foreign nationals have been cared for by the diplomatic representatives of the various countries.

Embassies are Foreign Territory

The residences of ambassadors, many of which are situated in the south-west district, are regarded as foreign territory. In other words they are "in" the country their occupiers represent. Those who live in them are beyond the jurisdiction of English courts and can neither be arrested nor prosecuted.

All the great Powers have ambassadors and consulate-generals in London. The United States Embassy is at 1 Grosvenor Square; the French at 58 Knightsbridge; the Russian in Kensington Palace Gardens; the Netherlands at Hereford House, Park Street.

The smaller Powers are represented by ministers, whose residences are known as legations, and they also have consulate-generals in Canada.

The interests of the British Dominions are cared for by High Commissioners who enjoy many of the privileges of foreign ambassadors and ministers. They may, for instance, import for their personal use any of the products of the country they represent duty free.

Homes of Dominions Representatives

The High Commissioners for Canada, Australia, New Zealand, the Union of South Africa, India and Southern Rhodesia have magnificent premises in the Strand or its immediate neighbourhood.

The diplomatic representative of the Irish Republic has offices in York House, Regent Street, outside which hangs a large green, white and orange tricolour which no passer-by can fail to notice. London is truly a microcosm of the world.

RESIDENCE OF THE SOVIET AMBASSADOR

The Russian Embassy is on the west side of Kensington Palace Gardens, a spacious avenue running from Kensington High Street to Notting Hill High Street. It contains many fine Victorian mansions.

DR. JOHNSON AT THE " MITRE "

Johnson, Goldsmith and Boswell at the famous Fleet Street tavern. It was here that the " Scotch gentleman " who was to produce one of the finest biographies in the English language first met Dr. Johnson.

TAVERNS AND COFFEE-HOUSES

Of the old London taverns that are still standing to-day, the most celebrated is the " Cheshire Cheese," in Wine Office Court, off Fleet Street. Rebuilt in 1667, and since then little altered, it has retained an unspoiled eighteenth-century atmosphere.

As William Sawyer says : " There is nothing new, gaudy, flippant, or effeminately luxurious here. A small room with heavily timbered windows. A low planked ceiling. A huge projecting fireplace, with a great copper boiler always on the simmer. . . . High, stiff-backed, inflexible ' settles,' hard and grainy in texture, box off the guests half a dozen to a table. Sawdust covers the floor. . . ."

As a brass inscription tells us, the second " box " on the left is thought to be the place where Charles Dickens in the *Tale of Two Cities* put Darnay and Carton to dine after the former's trial.

Of all its bygone customers the " Cheese " is most proud of Dr. Johnson, who very frequently dined, drank, and held forth there. " There is no throne like a tavern chair," avowed the great literary dictator. He is the genius of the place. His friend, Oliver Goldsmith, lived a few doors away at No. 6 Wine Office Court, and we may be sure that as he passed the tavern entrance he would always drop in to see whether the portly doctor and his listeners were there.

Among the famous dishes served at the " Cheese " was " ye famous puddinge," consisting of rump steak, kidney, oyster and plover. Cheshire cheese is also on the menu.

A tablet in the wall on the south side of

Fleet Street, almost opposite the entrance to the Church of St. Dunstan-in-the-West, marks the site of the "Mitre," another tavern which Johnson frequented. It was there that James Boswell kept his first appointment with Johnson in June, 1763. "We had," he tells us, "a good supper and port wine, of which Johnson then sometimes drank a bottle." Boswell was delighted with the doctor's conversation, in the course of which he eulogised Oliver Goldsmith and expressed contempt for Gray, the writer of the *Elegy in a Country Churchyard.* When they parted near Inner Temple Lane, between one and two in the morning, Johnson sent Boswell into the seventh heaven by remarking, "Sir, I am glad we have met. I hope we shall pass many evenings, and mornings, too, together."

Johnson's Praise of London

It was at this tavern that Johnson uttered his much-quoted saying, "Sir, the happiness of London is not to be conceived but by those who have been in it. I will venture to say there is more learning and science within the circumference of ten miles from where we sit than in all the rest of the kingdom."

There are those who like to think that the "Mitre" was visited by Shakespeare, but this is doubtful. It ceased to be a tavern in 1788, and the building was pulled down some forty years later to make room for an extension of Hoare's Bank.

A bishop's mitre was once a very common tavern sign in London. Under date of September 18, 1660, Pepys writes that he went to "the 'Miter Taverne' in Wood Street (a house of the greatest note in London). . . ." This Wood Street is off Cheapside and is the same as that referred to in Wordsworth's *Reverie of Poor Susan* which begins, "At the corner of Wood Street, when daylight appears." In Mitre Court, between Hatton Garden and Ely Place, there stands to-day a Mitre Tavern which was established in 1546, when Henry VIII was king.

The present Cock Tavern, Fleet Street, is a spiritual descendant of an historic inn of the same name which stood on the north side of the street opposite the Temple. It was a fashionable haunt in the seventeenth and eighteenth centuries. Pepys knew it well, and he tells us how he went there one night with Mrs. Knipps, a lady of great charm, but of whom his wife strongly disapproved. They "drank, eat a lobster, and sang, and (were) mighty merry till almost midnight." That was not the only occasion on which he made merry with this lady. Finally his wife got so jealous about it all that one night when he was in bed she threatened to attack him with a pair of red-hot tongs.

Club Founded by Ben Jonson

Pepys's favourite tavern was the "Hercules Pillars," which used to stand on the south side of Fleet Street a few doors from the "Mitre."

Near the old "Cock" was the "Devil," which had for a sign St. Dunstan tweaking the Devil's nose. Here it was that Ben Jonson, Shakespeare's friend, started one of the first clubs in London. It was called the "Apollo," and a bust of that Olympian divinity adorned its entrance. The rules of membership were drawn up by Ben himself. They forbade the discussion of serious and sacred subjects, and the recitation of insipid verse. No moody lovers were to be allowed to depress the company by their sighing, and no quarrelsome people or street bullies were to be given the right of entrance.

We know that Swift was an *habitué* of the "Devil," since he mentions visiting it in his letters to Stella; and in 1751 Dr. Johnson, then engaged in the compilation of his famous dictionary, gave an all-night party at the tavern to celebrate the publication of the first novel of one of his lady friends. The "Devil" was demolished towards the end of the eighteenth century.

The Globe Tavern, which stood on the north side of Fleet Street, was a favourite haunt of Oliver Goldsmith. A story is told of how a pork butcher in the "Globe" used to shout to Oliver at the top of his voice: "Come, Noll, here's my service to you, old boy." This rudeness so annoyed the sensitive, good-natured poet that one day he turned on the man and rebuked him. This had no effect, so Goldsmith said to one of his friends: "I ought to have known before that there is no putting a pig in the right way."

The near neighbourhood of Fleet Street eastwards was very liberally supplied with taverns in the sixteenth and seventeenth centuries, but practically all of them were destroyed in the Great Fire of 1666. The most famous was the "Mermaid" in Cheapside.

There Raleigh is said to have founded the Mermaid Club, which, according to Gifford,

" BOAR'S HEAD " IN EASTCHEAP
Sign of Falstaff's tavern. The original is still in the possession of the Guildhall Museum.

" combined more talent and genius than ever met together before or since." The same author tells us that among its members were Shakespeare, Jonson, Beaumont, Fletcher, Selden, Cotton, Carew, Martin, and Donne, " whose names, even at this distant period, call up a mingled feeling of reverence and respect."

Of these days the playwright Beaumont says :

" . . . What things have we seen
Done at the ' Mermaid'? Heard words that have been
So nimble, and so full of subtle flame,
As if that every one from whence they came
Had meant to put his whole wit in a jest,
And had resolved to live a fool the rest
Of his dull life . . . "

The status of taverns in those days may be judged from the fact that many books were published from them. For example, *The Pastyme of the People* (1529) was " empryntyd in Chepesyde, at the sygne of the ' Mearemayd,' next to Pollys (St. Paul's) Gate."

" Boar's Head " in Eastcheap

Another tavern which Shakespeare is said to have frequented was the " Falcon," which stood near the end of Blackfriars Bridge. It enjoyed remarkable popularity as a coaching inn during the eighteenth century, but was demolished in 1808.

Readers of Shakespeare will remember that one of Falstaff's haunts was the " Boar's Head." This tavern stood on the north side of Eastcheap near St. Michael's Church. It was destroyed in the Great Fire of 1666, but a successor bearing the same name was still standing in 1831.

The burial-ground of St. Michael's contained the tomb of Robert Preston, one of the " barmen," or " drawers " as they were then called, at the " Boar's Head." His quaint epitaph was as follows :

" Bacchus, to give the toping world surprise,
Produc'd one sober son, and here he lies.
Tho' nurs'd among full hogsheads, he defy'd
The charm of wine, and every vice beside.
O reader, if to justice thou'rt inclined,
Keep honest Preston daily in thy mind.
He drew good wine, took care to fill his pots,
Had sundry virtues that outweighed his fauts.
You that on Bacchus have the like dependence
Pray copy Bob in measure and attendance."

Where Falstaff Caroused

Oliver Goldsmith once paid a visit to the "Boar's Head." He tells us how, " by a pleasant fire, in the very room where old Sir John Falstaff cracked his jokes, in the very chair which was sometimes honoured by Prince Henry, and sometimes polluted by his immoral merry companions, (he) sat and ruminated on the follies of youth, wished to be young again, but was resolved to make the best of life while it lasted, and now and then compared present and past times together. . . . I could have wished to know the history of a tavern that had such a long succession of customers. I could not help thinking that an account of this

GEOFFREY CHAUCER
First of England's line of poets and author of the immortal *Canterbury Tales*, was born a Londoner.

TABARDE INN IN CHAUCER'S DAYS

With the pilgrims of the *Canterbury Tales* setting out " the holy blissful martyr for to seek." It was the host of the " Tabarde " who made the suggestion that they should all tell stories to while away the time

kind would be a pleasing contrast of the manners of different ages. But my landlord could give me no information. . . ." The fact that the room where Falstaff drank and laughed had disappeared in the Great Fire does not lessen the interest of Goldsmith's thoughts.

In the Elizabethan era the area south of the river between Blackfriars Road and the Borough High Street was mainly given over to theatres, cock-pits, bear-gardens and taverns. The High Street itself, being the main road to the south of England, was lined with inns, as it had been for centuries. Stow mentions the " Spurre," " Christopher," " Bull," " Queen's Head," " Tabarde," " George," " Hart," " King's Head." " Amongst the which," he says, " the most ancient is the Tabarde."

Inn Where Chaucer's Pilgrims Met

The " Tabarde " occupies an important place in English literature, for did not Chaucer choose it for the scene of his *Canterbury Tales*? Built in 1307 by the Abbot of Hyde, the hostelry was much frequented by pilgrims on their way to the wonder-working shrine of Becket in the cathedral of the old Kentish city.

An inn called the " Tabard " still stands in the Borough High Street. Chaucer's inn was destroyed in the great Southwark fire of 1676, and although another was built on its site almost immediately its owners were so ignorant as to call it, not the " Tabarde," but the " Talbot." This latter name is to-day borne by the old " Tabarde's " yard.

Beautiful Courtyard of the " George "

By far the most picturesque and historic of Southwark's present-day inns is the " George," which stands with its famous galleried façade but a few yards from the site of the " Tabarde," in a little court off the High Street.

The earliest reference to it occurs in 1554 when a Mr. Colet, the Member of Parliament for Southwark, was the owner. It suffered the same fate as the " Tabarde " in 1676, but was rebuilt the following year. The present building has the distinction of being the only galleried inn in the county of London. It is almost exactly as it was in the seventeenth century, excepting that the hostelry once surrounded the courtyard on three sides. Two of the wings were demolished in 1889.

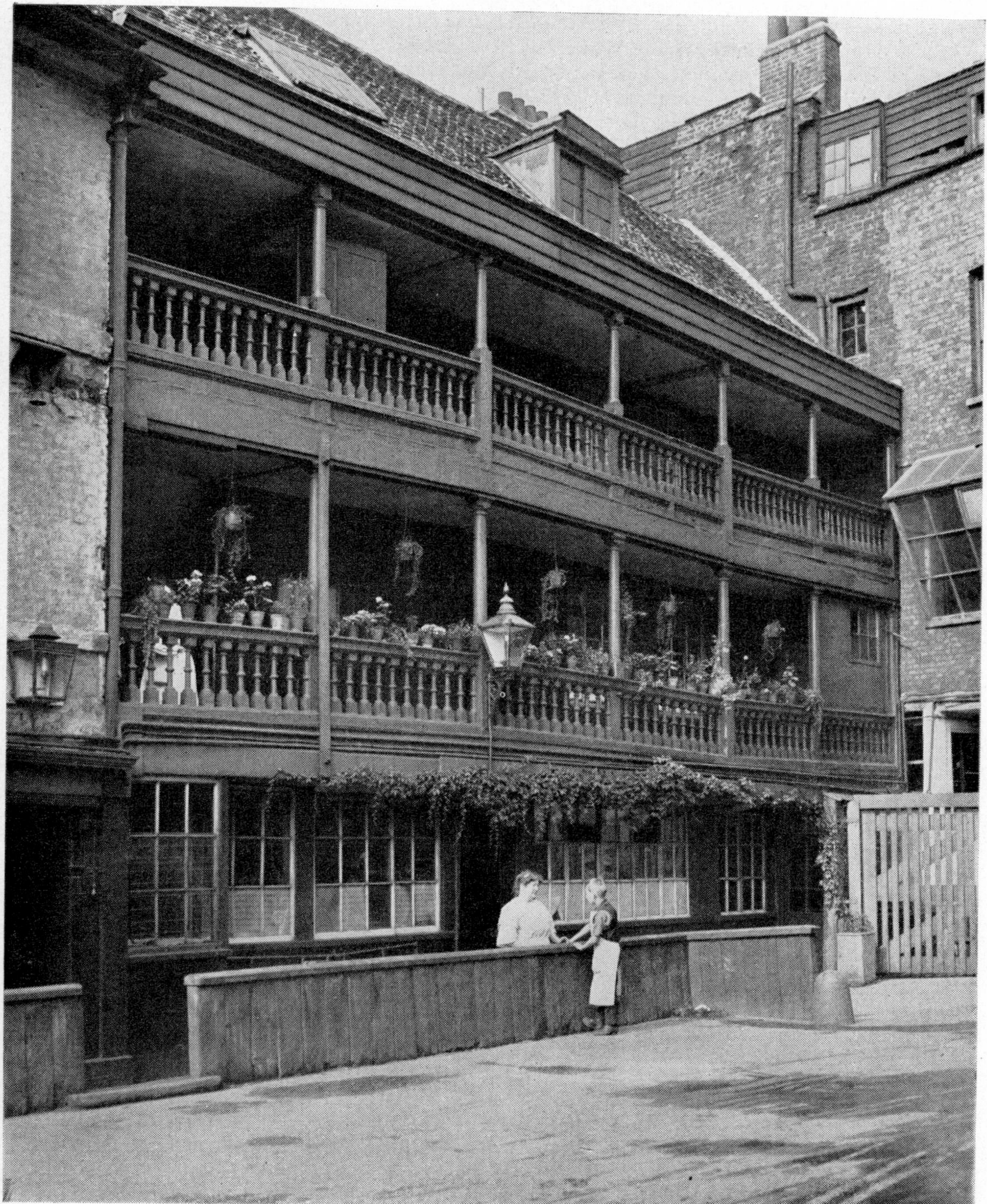

Donald McLeish

ONLY GALLERIED INN IN LONDON

The beautiful courtyard of the " George " in the Borough High Street, the sole surviving ancient inn in Southwark. The original tavern, mentioned by John Stow in 1554, was called the " St. George." This was largely damaged by fire in 1670 and completely gutted in 1676. The tavern was rebuilt on the same plan, with open wooden galleries surrounding the courtyard, and the doors of the guest-rooms opening on to the galleries. The " George " adjoined the " Tabarde," from whence Chaucer's pilgrims set out.

The memory of the "White Hart," mentioned by Stow, is preserved in the name White Hart Yard. It boasted the second largest signboard in London, and it was there that Jack Cade had his headquarters when he launched his attack on London. Fabyan's "Chronicles" tell us that "on July 1, 1450, Jack Cade arrived in Southwark where he lodged at the 'Hart' for he might not be suffered to enter the City."

Where Mr. Pickwick Met Sam Weller

Charles Dickens gives a fine description of the last "White Hart," demolished in 1889, in the *Pickwick Papers*.

"There are," he says by way of introduction, "in London several old inns, once the headquarters of celebrated coaches in the days when coaches performed their journeys in a graver and more solemn manner than they do in these times. . . . The reader would look in vain for any of these ancient hostelries, among the Golden Crosses and Bull and Mouths, which rear their stately fronts in the improved streets of London. If he would light upon any of these old places, he must direct his steps to the obscurer quarters of the town; and there in some secluded nooks he will find several, still standing with a kind of gloomy sturdiness, amidst the modern innovations which surround them.

SAM WELLER'S INN
The "White Hart" in the Borough as it appeared in 1827. Sam Weller was employed here as Boots.

"In the Borough especially, there still remain some half-dozen old inns. . . . Great rambling, queer old places they are, with galleries and passages, and staircases, wide enough and antiquated enough, to furnish materials for a hundred ghost stories. . . ."

He then goes on to describe the yard of the "White Hart."

It "presented none of that bustle and activity which are the usual characteristics of a large coach inn. Three or four lumbering waggons, each with a pile of goods beneath its ample canopy, about the height of the second-floor window of an ordinary house, were stowed away beneath a lofty roof which extended over one end of the yard; and another, which was probably to commence its journey that morning, was drawn out into the open space. A double tier of bedroom galleries, with old clumsy balustrades, ran round two sides of the straggling area, and a double row of bells to correspond, sheltered from the weather by a little sloping roof, hung over the door leading to the bar and coffee-room. . . . The occasional heavy tread of a cart-horse, or rattling of a chain at the further end of the yard announced to anybody who cared about the matter, that the stable lay in that direction. . . ."

First House Built after the Flood

At the southern end of London Bridge—popularly known as Bridge-foot—stood the "Bear," demolished in 1761, after having for more than three centuries enjoyed great popularity among Londoners. An amusing seventeenth-century rhyme states that the "Bear" was the first house built in Southwark after the Flood!

Pepys tells how in 1667 the Duke of Richmond fetched Mrs. Stuart "by a wile" to the "Bear," whence they "stole away into Kent without the King's leave," the lady, who had long been courted by Charles II, having resolved to marry any gentleman of £1,500 a year.

Hidden away amidst a cluster of mean houses behind Guy's Hospital is the "Ship and Shovel," named after Sir Cloudesley Shovel, the famous sailor. There medical students from the hospital assemble to quench their thirst and to discuss details of some "interesting" case.

The courts and alleys of the City contain many old taverns, but few are more ancient

Donald McLeish

"DIRTY DICK'S"

The famous tavern in Bishopsgate. Its underground tap-room is festooned with cobwebs.

than the "George and Vulture" in St. Michael's Alley, Cornhill. Stow refers to it in the following words: "This is said to have pertained to the Earl Ferrers, and was his London lodging in Lombard Street, and that in the year 1175, a brother of the said earl, being there privily slain in the night, was there thrown down into the dirty street. . . ." Charles Dickens mentions it as a resort of Pickwick and his friends, and there the Pickwick Club holds its meetings.

Old-fashioned Chop House

A few yards away is "Simpson's Chop House," one of the most delightful taverns in the City. Built in the year 1757, it has remained practically unaltered. A good deal of its charm arises from the fact that it is not in the least pretentious, making no claims to great antiquity nor yet to curious historical associations. There was another celebrated "Simpson's" in the City in Bird-in-Hand Court, Cheapside. It was utterly destroyed during the war. Established in 1723, it provided an "ordinary," a *table d'hôte* meal at which one could eat as much as one pleased.

The "ordinary" was a very common feature of London taverns as late as the first half of the nineteenth century. It is supposed to have been introduced in 1560 by Richard Tarleton, the actor and friend of Shakespeare, who kept a tavern called the "Castle" in Paternoster Row.

Prices for all Pockets

Shakespeare's England gives us the following information about ordinaries: "There were ordinaries of all ranks, the *table d'hôte* being the almost universal mode of dining among those who were visitors to London during the season, or term-time, as it was then called. There was the twelve penny ordinary, where you might meet justices of the peace and young knights; and the three penny ordinary, which was frequented by poor lieutenants and thrifty attorneys. . . . If a gallant entered the ordinary at about half-past eleven, or even a little earlier, he would find the room full of fashion-mongers, waiting for the meat to be served."

"Simpson's" of the Strand is famous all over the world for the high quality of its

Donald McLeish

"THE TIGER"

Stands opposite the entrance to the Tower of London. The original inn dated from 1500.

SIMPSON'S CHOP-HOUSE

Hidden away in St. Michael's Alley with all around it the huge ferro-concrete buildings of Cornhill and Lombard Street, this chop-house is pure eighteenth century. Close to it is the "George and Vulture."

English cooking, and its roast beef is notable. It has no connection with either of the other "Simpson's."

At Aldgate is the picturesque "Hoop and Grapes," built in the early years of the seventeenth century. In its cellars may be seen copper drums once used by smugglers of wine and spirits.

Fat Boy who Started Great Fire

At the corner of Cock Lane and Giltspur Street there formerly stood a tavern called the "Fortune of War," which had for a sign a charming statue of a fat boy, by whom, so tradition says, the Great Fire of 1666 was started. The statue now adorns the wall of a house at the corner of Cock Lane. The story says that while attempting to steal a pie from an oven the fat boy scattered some hot coals and thus started the fire.

Near the Tower are "The Tiger" and the "London," both of which claim Elizabethan associations. Farther east, at Wapping Old Stairs, is the "Town of Ramsgate," where the notorious and brutal Judge Jeffreys was caught disguised as a seaman when on the lookout for a ship to take him to Hamburg. His patron, James II, had fled the country, and the man who had sentenced hundreds of people to death was by no means anxious to fall into the hands of William of Orange. The tavern was then known as the "Red Cow," and it has since been rebuilt at least once.

Wapping High Street and Wapping Wall have always been fairly liberally supplied with taverns. In the middle of last century there were thirty-six, the most famous being the "Prospect of Whitby," which still stands on the waterfront.

Royal Carriage for Invalid

At Islington was the celebrated "Angel," once a recognised halt for travellers by coach on their way out of London. It was then, of course, well outside the metropolitan area. The old building was demolished in 1819, and on its site is now a restaurant, but its name is perpetuated as a London underground station.

Broad Court, Bow Street, the haunt of Dick Swiveller, one of Dickens's most famous or perhaps infamous characters, was the site of a tavern known as " The Wrekin." It was well patronised in the early days of Queen Victoria by devotees of the prize-ring. At a later phase of its history the place was bought by a Mr. Warner, who married the then popular tragedienne, Miss Huddart. When the latter fell ill a carriage from Buckingham Palace awaited the invalid every day and took her for a drive. This unusual mark of royal appreciation of the lady's talent was furthered on the lady's death by her widower being nominated by the Prince Consort for admission to the Charterhouse.

Dickens's Hampstead Resort

There are three very well-known taverns in Hampstead—the " Spaniards," the " Bull and Bush," and " Jack Straw's Castle."

The " Spaniards " had, at the time of the Gordon Riots, a landlord called Giles Thomas who has gone down to history as the saviour of Ken Wood House. How he effected this by offering his cellars to the mob and sending for soldiers is told in the chapter entitled " London's Dark Days." " Jack Straw's Castle " was a favourite haunt of Romney, Morland, Blake and Dickens. The great story-teller would often call in there after enjoying a walk over the Heath. It derives its name from Jack Straw, second in command to Wat Tyler, who is supposed to have had his headquarters in the near neighbourhood. His " castle " apparently consisted of a " mere hovel, or a hole in the hill-side." The " Bull and Bush," at which Hogarth and Addison were frequent visitors, has inspired a well-known drinking song.

First Coffee-house

The first London coffee-house was opened about the year 1652 in St. Michael's Alley, Cornhill, by Pasqua Rosee, " at the sign of his own head." Rosee was a native of Smyrna, and had been brought to England by Mr. Hodges, a Turkey merchant.

Like all new things, coffee was at first regarded with a great deal of suspicion. The vintners naturally hated it, and did all they could to induce the public to share their feelings, but in vain. The Londoner found coffee a pleasant drink and refused to give it up.

A MAD DOG IN A COFFEE-HOUSE

A caricature by Thomas Rowlandson (1756–1827). In the eighteenth century coffee-houses were all over London. They were great centres of political discussion; one government tried, but failed, to close them.

By the end of the seventeenth century the neighbourhood of Cornhill was plentifully supplied with coffee-houses. "Garaway's" in Exchange Alley enjoyed a great reputation. The author of *Robinson Crusoe*, writing in 1722, tells us that it was the rendezvous of many of the wealthier citizens; and Jonathan Swift mentions it in his satiric account of the South Sea Bubble. It was a tea-shop as well as a coffee-house—indeed, it was one of the first shops in London at which one could drink tea.

In 1675 the Government decided to suppress all coffee-houses, and even went so far as to issue a proclamation to that effect. Why did they dislike the coffee-houses? Simply because they had become centres where people met together to discuss politics, and to air their grievances. The newspaper was then in its infancy and most people relied on word-of-mouth for information about affairs of state. It became the general practice to adjourn to the coffee-house to garner such knowledge.

Donald McLeish

ON HAMPSTEAD HEATH

The "Spaniards," where Gordon Rioters collected to attack Ken Wood, and Mrs. Bardell was arrested.

A RIVERSIDE TAVERN

The picturesque old "Turk's Head" at Wapping, 400 years old. One licensee was an ex-pirate.

Scandalous Newspapers Forbidden

The Government's proclamation was received with such a storm of indignation that the retailers of coffee were permitted to open their houses to the public again on condition that they should "prevent all scandalous papers, books, and libels from being read in them, and hinder every person from declaring, uttering, or divulging all manner of false and scandalous reports against Government or the Ministers thereof." These terms were never observed. Coffee-houses sprang up all over London and attracted more and more customers, who spent their evenings sipping coffee instead of getting drunk in the tavern.

Many of the more famous eighteenth-century coffee-houses were in the Covent Garden area, near the two "patent" theatres, so called because they were exempt from the provisions

Donald McLeish

"YE OLDE BULL AND BUSH"

Frequented by countless holiday-makers on Hampstead Heath and the subject of a well-known popular song. The present building occupies the site of another tavern of the same name, in which at one time Hogarth the painter and pungent cartoonist lived. The inn stands on the North End Road, north of the Heath.

NAMED AFTER REBEL CHIEF

"Jack Straw's Castle," on Hampstead Heath, as it now appears following bomb damage in 1940. It is said to have been named after Wat Tyler's lieutenant, who had his headquarters near. Charles Dickens used frequently to take a walk across Hampstead Heath and lunch at the "Castle."

of the Disorderly Houses Act of 1751 which made a licence necessary. " Will's Coffee-house " stood at the intersection of Bow Street and Russell Street, and was kept by Will Urwin.

Resort of All the Wits

Alexander Pope tells us that " it was Dryden who made ' Will's Coffee-house ' the great resort of the wits of his time. After his death, Addison transferred this pre-eminence to ' Button's ' . . ." And we read in *The Journey through England* that " After the play, the best of the company go to ' Tom's ' and ' Will's ' Coffee-houses, near adjoining, where there is playing at picquet, and the best of conversation till midnight."

" Button's " was established in Russell Street by one of Joseph Addison's servants in the year 1712. Addison, Steele, and many other famous literary men spent most of their evenings at " Button's."

" Tom's " was first opened about 1700 and continued as a coffee-house for more than a hundred years. It appears to have been the haunt of the nobility and gentry in the reign of George III. At that time a club was formed there, having among its members Dr. Johnson, Garrick, Goldsmith, Lord Clive, and Lord Rodney.

After the decline of " Button's," the " Bedford," which stood not far away, became very popular. The *Connoisseur* of 1754 tells us that " This coffee-house is crowded every night with men of parts. Almost every one you meet is a polite scholar and a wit; jokes and *bon-mots* are echoed from box to box; every production of the press, or performance at the theatres, weighed and determined . . ."

COFFEE-HOUSE AND MUSEUM
Don Salters's coffee-house in Cheyne Walk, Chelsea, opened about 1690, and famous for its curiosities.

Sheridan, Garrick, Addison, Steele, and Pope all frequented it.

Farther west, near the corner of St. James's Street, stood the " St. James's Coffee-house," which remained throughout the eighteenth century one of the principal meeting-places of the Whig Party.

" That I might begin as near the fountain-head as possible," writes Addison, " I first of all called in at the ' St. James's,' where I found the whole outward room in a buzz of politics. . . . I heard there the whole Spanish monarchy disposed of, and all the line of the Bourbons provided for, in less than a quarter of an hour."

Clubs Take Place of Coffee-houses

One of the most famous coffee-houses in Fleet Street was " Dick's," demolished in 1875 after more than two centuries of popularity. In Charles II's time a haunt of dandies, it was frequented by the young lawyers of the Temple in the early eighteenth century and by literary men in the days of Johnson.

William Cowper knew it well, and it was there that the poet first displayed signs of mental instability. Having read something that upset him in a newspaper he went out and attempted to hang himself with a garter. He was unsuccessful, and shortly afterwards entered an asylum.

Most of these coffee-houses and tea-shops were clubs in all but name. Some of them gradually lost their coffee-house character altogether and developed into ultra-fashionable clubs. By the middle of the nineteenth century the coffee-house and the tavern had been completely superseded among the well-to-do by the club and the convenient restaurant.

Donald McLeish

ADMIRALTY ARCH IN THE MALL

Part of a memorial to Queen Victoria, this triple archway was designed by Sir Aston Webb and opened by Edward VII in 1910. Through it passes royalty on its state drives from Buckingham Palace to Westminster.

TO THE MEMORY OF THE GREAT

The Cenotaph, standing like a sentry in the middle of Whitehall opposite the Foreign Office, is by right the best-known of London's many memorials. Commemorating the million and more soldiers, sailors and airmen of the Empire who laid down their lives during the World Wars, it has a very real and personal significance for every British subject. There on Armistice Day the Queen, and representatives of the Government, the Dominions and Colonies, the Services and the Church, as well as enormous numbers of ordinary folk, assemble together to observe the two-minutes' silence.

The first Cenotaph was erected during the Peace celebrations in July, 1919. It was intended to be temporary, but it quickly became obvious to all that both site and design were aptly fitted to express the feelings of the Empire, and the present Cenotaph was set up and consecrated in 1920. Part of the original monument is preserved in the Imperial War Museum.

Designed by Sir Edwin Lutyens, this impressively simple monument was carved by craftsmen from the finest stone that Portland could provide. To make the Cenotaph applicable to both World Wars merely needed the addition of the date, " 1939–1945."

A little-known fact about the Cenotaph is that it is designed on the principle of curves and that none of its lines is perfectly straight. It is intended to symbolise infinity.

There is another notable Cenotaph not much more than a stone's throw from Whitehall. Facing the central archway of the Horse Guards, it commemorates the 14,760 members of the Guards Division who fell in the First World War. The strength of the Guards at the beginning of the conflict was less than half that number. Surrounding it are steel-helmeted figures of five guardsmen, made from the metal of German guns captured by this illustrious Division. One of the " guardsmen " had his leg pierced by a fragment of a bomb which burst in the Horse Guards Parade. The Cenotaph, which was designed by Gilbert Ledward and H. C. Bradshaw, is of Portland stone and weighs 170 tons. Set up over an ancient tributary of the Thames, it was found necessary, in order to make the foundations perfectly firm, to lay down a bed of concrete eight feet thick and containing six tons of steel.

On the Horse Guards' Parade are statues of Kitchener, Roberts and Wolseley, and at the corner of the Admiralty building is Sir Edwin Lutyen's beautiful memorial to the men of the Royal Naval Division. It is in the form of a fountain, the base of which bears lines written by Rupert Brooke, himself a member of the Division, who while on active service with the Dardanelles expedition fell ill at Lemnos and died on the Island of Scyros.

Gunners' Memorial by Gunnery Officer

The Royal Naval Volunteer Reserve Memorial, a bell supported by two dolphins, was unveiled in the grounds of the ill-fated Crystal Palace in 1931.

At Hyde Park Corner are the memorials of the Machine Gun Corps and the Royal Regiment of Artillery, the former by Derwent Wood and the latter by C. S. Jagger. A stubby 9·2 howitzer in stone dominates the Artillery Memorial, while four bronze figures of artillerymen and bas-reliefs showing guns and men in action are features of a very unusual conception, the work of a sculptor who served as a gunnery officer and realised the grim realities of war.

Donald McLeish

1914–18; 1939–45
The Cenotaph in Whitehall, Britain's memorial to the Empire's dead. Designed by Sir Edwin Lutyens.

Within the Stanhope Gate of Hyde Park the mounted figure of St. George, holding his sword aloft, and with a slain dragon beneath his horse, symbolises the sacrifices made by British cavalry regiments. It is by Captain Adrian Jones.

Opposite the entrance to the National Portrait Gallery a white-marble figure of Nurse Cavell stands against a yellow granite pillar, behind which is a lion on a serpent. Her inspired and inspiring words, "Patriotism is not enough, I must have no hatred or bitterness for anyone," are engraved in large letters near the base.

In Honour of London's Soldiers

In front of the Royal Exchange is the London Memorial, by Alfred Drury, in honour of all the Londoners who fell in the First World War. At Holborn Bars (the City boundary) a bronze soldier on a stone pedestal calls to mind the members of the City of London Regiment who served between 1914 and 1918.

There is a memorial to the Camel Corps in Victoria Embankment Gardens, and on the wall of the Embankment a bronze panel recalls the heroism of those who lost their lives while serving in submarines. On the same riverside terrace a tall column with an eagle poised as though about to strike, and the stirring motto (in Latin), "Through hardships to the stars," commemorates the Royal Air Force. It is near the monument erected by the Belgian people as a symbol of their gratitude for the hospitality accorded to their fugitive compatriots by Britain when their own country was overrun by the Germans in 1914.

Freemasons who made the supreme sacrifice are brought to mind by the impressive Masonic Peace Memorial in Great Queen Street, an imposing building which serves as headquarters for members of the craft throughout the British Empire. The idea was suggested by the Duke of Connaught, Grand Master of the United Lodge of England, on the day before the Treaty of Versailles was signed in 1919, and dedicated by him in 1933. The building contains fifteen

SOME MEMORIALS OF THE FIRST WORLD WAR

Top (left to right), the Cavalry Memorial in Hyde Park; the Nurse Cavell Statue near St. Martin's Lane; the Air Force Memorial on the Victoria Embankment. Bottom, the Artillery Memorial at Hyde Park Corner.

temples and is stated to have cost £1,000,000.

The London, Midland and Scottish Railway commemorated its heroes of the First World War outside Euston Station, and the Great Western Railway on the main departure platform of its London terminus at Paddington.

As regards the less bloody but even more desperate struggle against Nazism, King George VI suggested in 1946 that existing memorials be utilised, by simply adding the date, "1939–1945" (and, of course, the later Roll of Honour).

Nelson in Trafalgar Square

Monuments and memorials to heroes of other conflicts London has in plenty. Nearly 200 feet above the traffic of Trafalgar Square, Nelson towers over the "Grand Old Duke of York," who stands some little distance away on his pillar overlooking St. James's Park. We are told that the statue of Nelson is ugly, but, as Augustus Hare remarked, somewhat caustically, "that does not much signify, as it can only be properly seen from the top of the Duke of York's column, which no one ascends."

MASONIC TEMPLE
Front of the imposing Freemasons' Peace Memorial building in Great Queen Street, Holborn. It is reputed to have cost approximately £1,000,000.

The Nelson Monument took a long time in the making. A competition for designs, won by W. Railton, was opened in 1838, but the work was not completed until 1867. The capital of the column was made out of the metal of guns taken from the *Royal George*, which sank at Spithead in 1782. The bronze panels were cast from guns captured from the French.

Sir Edwin Landseer modelled the lions at the base. They cost £18,000, or nearly a third of the total expenditure on the monument. The statue itself, which is eighteen feet in height and weighs nearly eighteen tons, was the work of E. H. Baily, who used two blocks of stone from the Granton Quarry for the purpose. Before being placed in position it was on view to the public for two days, during which it was seen at close quarters by 100,000 persons.

The Trafalgar Square pigeons are prolific, but probably it occurs to few to wonder where they go to die. The men who clean the Nelson Column often find large numbers of dead pigeons on the ledge at the top, and they suggest that the ledge is used as the pigeons' "dying-place."

The Grand Old Duke of York

The pedestals near the base of the column are occupied by General Gordon, Sir Henry Havelock, Sir Charles Napier, all distinguished soldiers, and George IV.

The Duke of York's column, 124 feet in height, is one of London's "mystery" monuments. That is not to say that no one knows anything about it, but rather that very few do. There is no inscription on its base.

It commemorates Frederick, son of George III, who was for many years Commander-in-Chief of the British Army.

He had an income of £70,000 a year—a large sum in those days—but it proved insufficient for his needs, and he died owing £200,000. In consequence of this, some wit remarked that his statue was put up high so that he might be beyond the reach of his creditors.

The column is to remind us of the Duke's passionate, prolonged opposition to the emancipation of His Majesty's Roman Catholic subjects.

Donald McLeish

RICHARD CŒUR DE LION AT WESTMINSTER

This magnificent equestrian statue of the Crusader King stands in Old Palace Yard near the entrance to Westminster Hall. It was designed by the Italian sculptor, Carlo, Baron Marochetti, who after the revolution of 1848 in Paris, came to live in London. The sword was bent by blast from a bomb which fell in the Yard in 1940, but has since been repaired. Other examples of Marochetti's work may be seen in the Lord Clyde obelisk in Waterloo Place and the Inkerman Memorial in St. Paul's Cathedral.

On the east side of Waterloo Place, not many yards away, there is a statue of another member of the Services. Robert Falcon Scott lost his life and won undying fame not in a fight against his fellows but against Nature herself in Antarctica. Even the most unemotional person cannot fail to be stirred by the tragic memories that Lady Scott's (afterwards Lady Kennet) fine representation of her late husband evoke. Edward VII, Lord Clyde, Sir John Franklin, Lord Lawrence, and Sir John Burgoyne, also figure in sculpture in Waterloo Place. Edward the Peace-maker is in field-marshal's uniform and seated upon a high-spirited horse. The statue is the work of Sir Bertram Mackennal. There is a memorial to the King's consort, Queen Alexandra, in the wall of the gardens of Marlborough House.

The Lady of the Lamp

At the bottom of Regent Street are statues of Florence Nightingale and of Sidney Herbert (later Lord Herbert of Leigh), the Secretary of State for War who asked the heroic nurse to journey to Scutari to relieve the sufferings of sick and wounded soldiers in the Crimean War. Near-by is a memorial to the 2,000-odd officers and men of the Guards who died—mainly of disease—in the same tragic conflict. The guns are real ones, taken from the Russians at Sevastopol. Lord Edward Gleichen, no mean authority on London's outdoor statuary, said, perhaps unkindly, that this memorial looks best in a fog!

FLORENCE NIGHTINGALE
Heroine of the Crimea, where her pioneer nursing work saved thousands of British soldiers' lives.

The Duke of Wellington has many memorials in London. The most curious is the so-called Achilles statue in Hyde Park, erected in 1822 at the cost of £10,000 by the women of England in honour of the Iron Duke and his soldiers. It was cast from guns captured at the battles of Salamanca, Vittoria, Toulouse and Waterloo. Far from being an original effort, Sir Richard Westmacott copied it from a group in Rome.

Some little distance away, on an island in Piccadilly, opposite Apsley House, which was presented to him by the nation and where he lived, is a mounted statue of Wellington by Sir Joseph Edgar Boehm. For long the windows of Apsley House facing Rotten Row were obscured by shutters. On one occasion a mob which disliked the Duke's politics made its presence felt by breaking every pane of glass it could reach, with the sequel already mentioned. Opposite the Royal Exchange there is another equestrian statue of "the hero of a hundred fights." Designed by Sir Francis Chantrey, it is almost unique in having been erected during the lifetime of its subject. The Duke attended the unveiling.

From Triumph to Peace

The Constitution Hill arch, designed by Decimus Burton in 1828, used to carry an equestrian statue of the Duke of Wellington, but this was removed to Aldershot in 1883. The Quadriga which took its place is by Adrian Jones, and is a memorial to Edward VII. It represents Peace arresting the headlong rush of the chariot of war. Originally conceived as typifying Triumph, the artist changed his conception with the happiest result. The Quadriga weighs 38 tons, and is generally acknowledged to be one of the finest groups in London.

As we should naturally expect, in the neighbourhood of the War Office in Whitehall there are statues of men who have been connected with that department of the Government. The Duke of Cambridge, for nearly forty years Commander-in-Chief of the British

Army, quite literally rides his high horse there. Near him is the eighth Duke of Devonshire, twice Secretary of State for War. There is also an equestrian statue of Earl Haig, on a much-criticised conventional horse. Bronze busts of the Admirals Jellicoe and Beatty were set up on the north side of Trafalgar Square in 1948.

There are many ugly memorials in London. Among such must be reckoned that to the Westminster scholars who fell " in the Russian and Indian Wars, A.D. 1854–59." The list of distinguished names on the tablets includes that of Lord Raglan, Commander-in-Chief in the Crimea. The column occupies a conspicuous position opposite the west front of Westminster Abbey.

Queen Who Sacked London

John Tweed's Lord Clive, the hero of Plassey, in King Charles Street, off Whitehall, is among the best of London's soldier-statues. It was set up in its present position in 1917.

One of England's earliest warriors, Boudicca (Boadicea), has her memorial at the northern end of Westminster Bridge. The heroine is

QUADRIGA ON WELLINGTON ARCH
Placed at the entrance to the Green Park at Hyde Park Corner. Formerly bore statue of Wellington.

ACHILLES STATUE
Erected by the women of England to the Duke of Wellington. Stands in south-east of Hyde Park.

depicted standing upright in a two-horsed, scythed chariot. It has been pointed out by more than one critic that though the steeds are apparently travelling at a considerable speed there are no reins and very little harness.

As might be expected, the statues in Parliament Square all represent statesmen. That of Sir Robert Peel, the founder of the Police Force, is by Matthew Noble, and was erected in 1876. The bronze statue of the Earl of Derby (1779–1869) is by the same artist. Near-by is Thomas Woolner's Palmerston (1784–1865). Another statue of Peel, formerly in Cheapside, was removed to the Police College at Hendon in 1935.

Cromwell's Bible and Sword

Backed by Westminster Hall is a superb statue of Oliver Cromwell by Sir Hamo Thornycroft which was presented to the nation by Lord Rosebery. The lion at the foot is a poor specimen of the species. Although bombs fell all round him during the *blitz* the Protector escaped unscathed.

Disraeli, the Tory statesman, stands in bronze near St. Margaret's Church. On Primrose Day

Donald McLeish

ABRAHAM LINCOLN
This statue in Broad Sanctuary, Westminster, is an exact replica of the one in Lincoln Park, Chicago.

(April 19), sacred to his memory, his political disciples piously adorn the base of the monument with primroses, Lord Beaconsfield's favourite flower.

Lincoln and Washington

George Canning, the Foreign Secretary who " called the New World into existence to redress the balance of the Old " by recognising the independence of Spain's American colonies, occupies a position on the west side of Parliament Square. This statue is by Westmacott. While it was being fashioned in the sculptor's studio it fell and killed a man who was standing beside it.

With a due sense of fitness an excellent representation of Abraham Lincoln, President of the United States of America, the man who fought to preserve the Union and free the slaves, stands near that of Canning. It is a replica of one in Chicago by Augustus St. Gaudens. Given by the American people, it was erected in 1921. In the Royal Exchange is a fine bust of Lincoln.

Shortly after the First World War the State of Virginia presented a replica of Jean Houdon's statue of George Washington to the peoples of Great Britain and Ireland. This now stands in front of the National Gallery in Trafalgar Square. Washington is also represented by a bust in the crypt of St. Paul's Cathedral.

A bronze statue of a third American President, Franklin D. Roosevelt, now stands before the U.S. Embassy in Grosvenor Square. The Square itself has also been laid out as part of the memorial to this great statesman and friend.

London's Loveliest Statue

By common consent, Sir Alfred Gilbert's figure of Eros, which stands on tip-toe, bow in hand, above the rushing traffic of Piccadilly Circus, is the most beautiful of London's statues. It is a memorial to the 7th Earl of Shaftesbury, the great philanthropist who died in 1885. It is one of the very few aluminium figures in the capital.

Among other memorials to distinguished

GEORGE WASHINGTON
Presented to the peoples of Great Britain and Ireland by the Commonwealth of Virginia in 1921.

statesmen are the Gladstone group in front of St. Clement Danes Church, Strand, the bronze statue of William Pitt in Hanover Square, and the somewhat grotesque representation of Richard Cobden, the hero of Free Trade, in front of Mornington Crescent Underground Station. The last-mentioned was certainly not costly, for the bill amounted to only £320.

Of London's memorials to Royalty, those of Queen Victoria and her consort, Albert the Good, are the most conspicuous. The great Victoria Memorial, executed by Thomas Brock and Aston Webb, consists not only of the group immediately in front of Buckingham Palace but also of the Admiralty Arch at the eastern end of the Mall. The total cost was in the neighbourhood of £325,000.

The figure of the Queen was unveiled in 1911 by King George V, the German Emperor being present at the ceremony; but the monument was not completed until 1924.

In Kensington Gardens the Queen is represented in marble as she was at the age of eighteen. In the Royal Exchange, which she declared open in 1844, she stands in the height of youth. On the Victoria Embankment, near Blackfriars Bridge, she is seen in bronze as an elderly woman.

Much-criticised Memorial

The ornate Albert Memorial in Kensington Gardens has been subjected to more criticism than any other work of its kind in London. Standing 175 feet high, it cost £120,000 and took ten years to complete. It consists of an immense canopy underneath which sits Albert, gilded, and holding the catalogue of the Great Exhibition of 1851. The lovely marble groups arranged about the base are the work of Sir Hamo Thornycroft and were added much later.

We see the Prince in uniform, and on horseback, but with his cocked-hat lifted in unmilitary fashion, at Holborn Circus; and again in frock-coat, in the grounds of the Licensed Victuallers' Asylum off the Old Kent Road.

The best royal statues in London are those of James II, now set up in front of the National Gallery, and Charles II, in the grounds of Chelsea Hospital. Both are by Grinling Gibbons and both were paid for by Tobias Rustat, Under Keeper of Hampton Court Palace and Yeoman of the Robes to Charles II.

The statue of James II was first set up behind the Banqueting House in Whitehall, where it remained for over two hundred years. It was taken down in 1897 and erected alongside the west front of the Admiralty in 1903. The statue was removed during the Second World War and was set up on its present site in 1948. It is strangely garbed, for the king certainly never donned the dress of a Roman Emperor, in which he is represented. Another monarch wearing Roman costume is George I, whose bronze figure stands on the spire of St. George's Church, Hart Street, Bloomsbury.

There is a statue of Queen Elizabeth I, one of the oldest in the metropolis, over the vestry door of the Church of St. Dunstan-in-the-West, Fleet Street. It originally stood on Lud's Gate,

EROS IN PICCADILLY

This famous statue in Piccadilly Circus was set up about 1890 as a memorial to the Earl of Shaftesbury, an ardent advocate of social reform.

Ludgate Hill, which was pulled down in 1760.

Cleopatra's Needle has nothing whatever to do with the queen of that name. It was erected at Heliopolis by Thothmes III about 1500 years before she was born. Mehemet Ali, Viceroy of Egypt, presented it to England in 1819 and it was set up in London some sixty years later. Sealed up in the base of the pedestal are a newspaper, a copy of *Bradshaw's Railway Guide* and some English coins of the year 1878. The obelisk nearly got lost at sea while it was on the way to England and narrowly missed being destroyed by German bombs during both World Wars. The marks made by the splinters can still be seen.

London from the Monument

The Great Fire of London Monument, off King William Street, is the combined work of Sir Christopher Wren, Caius Gabriel Cibber and Edward Pierce. It was erected in 1675, and tradition says that Wren intended it as a telescope tube, but this is doubtful. It towers 202 feet above the City. From the platform at the top a magnificent view of London and the surrounding country can be obtained on clear days.

Donald McLeish

PETER PAN

Known and loved by thousands of visitors to Kensington Gardens, the statue of Peter Pan was designed by Sir George Frampton, R.A.

There are few outdoor statues of literary men in London. Shakespeare stands over a fountain in Leicester Square, surrounded at some little distance by Sir Joshua Reynolds, the artist, John Hunter, the surgeon, William Hogarth, the painter, and Sir Isaac Newton, the physicist.

There is a bust of the Bard of Avon on the portico of Drury Lane Theatre, and a marble statue, alongside similar figures of Chaucer and Milton, on the Poets' Fountain at the junction of Park Lane and Hamilton Place. This group has been removed to ease the traffic flow.

The bronze statue of Byron in Hyde Park bears little resemblance to the poet as he is usually depicted, and it is hard to believe that the author of *Don Juan* would ever have adopted such a pose as that which Richard Belt, the sculptor, has given him. The public contributed £3,500 towards the cost, while the Government of Greece, in gratitude for Byron's espousal of that country's cause in its war of independence against Turkey, presented marble for the pedestal.

Sir Henry Irving, wearing academic robes and hood, is pictured in bronze behind the National Portrait Gallery. It is usually conceded that Sir Thomas Brock secured a striking likeness, despite the unfamiliar dress. Yet it is correct enough, for the great actor was an honorary graduate of the Universities of Cambridge, Glasgow and Dublin. Like so many other London statues, Irving's was bricked in from 1939 onwards, but was much longer than most in emerging again.

Caused Controversy in Commons

In Hyde Park is Jacob Epstein's "Rima," a memorial to W. H. Hudson, naturalist and novelist. It depicts Nature, at once kind and cruel, beautiful and ugly, as a nude human figure. Her hair streams out in waves, and on either side of her are birds in upward flight. Abused by many and admired by some, the sculpture was on one occasion the subject of controversy in the House of Commons.

Sir George Frampton's "Peter Pan" in Kensington Gardens is in marked contrast to "Rima." It represents Sir James Barrie's most famous character, and attracts the attention of thousands by its beauty and winsomeness.

Edward Jenner, whose small-pox experiments led to the introduction of vaccination, sits in bronze not far away from "Peter Pan." The statue, removed from Trafalgar Square in 1862, is perhaps unique, in that it was paid for by international subscription.

Memorial to Boxer

There is a memorial to a boxer in Brompton Cemetery. It is the monumental tomb of John ("Gentleman") Jackson, who held the championship between 1795 and 1800. Remarkable as much for his polished manners as for pugilistic prowess, he numbered Byron among his pupils. A medallion of Jackson is surmounted by a recumbent lion.

Another unique memorial is Auguste Rodin's "Burghers of Calais," erected during the second year of the First World War in Westminster Palace Gardens, and paid for mainly by the National Arts Collection Fund. It is only a copy, the original being in the Place d'Armes at Calais. Few will like the situation, although it was chosen by the artist himself.

QUEEN ELIZABETH I
Stands over the vestry door of St. Dunstan-in-the-West. Originally erected on the old Lud Gate.

KING CHARLES I
Looks down Whitehall from an island site in Trafalgar Square. Hidden during Commonwealth.

Symbolical of the fact that Frenchmen and Englishmen had decided at the beginning of this century to forget the bitter memories of past disagreements and work together for "collective security," it brings to mind the Bush House memorial to the friendship of Britain and her former colonies in the New World.

Magnificently placed above the main entrance to Bush House, in Aldwych, the memorial consists of two figures representing the English and American peoples, holding aloft the torch of freedom. It looks most impressive at night, when the statues may be seen from the farther end of Kingsway, silhouetted against the curved ceiling of the great porch.

London has over 350 statues, but it does not boast of all of them. One, and that no more

Donald McLeish

EPSTEIN'S "RIMA" IN HYDE PARK

The memorial to W. H. Hudson in the Birds' Sanctuary. It depicts "Rima," the spirit of Nature. Some visitors to the Park disapprove of it, and several attempts have been made to disfigure it.

than a copy, has received universal admiration. It is the group called "Physical Energy," by G. F. Watts. The original is in Africa, far removed from Kensington Gardens, where the replica is placed, for it forms part of the noble Rhodes Memorial on the slope of Devil's Peak at Cape Town.

Two statues at least are without identity. Both are of women. One is in Smithfield, the other in Queen Square, Bloomsbury.

Donald McLeish

GIANTS OF ENGLISH LITERATURE

(Left to right.) Statue of Dr. Johnson in the churchyard of St. Clement Danes; of Thomas Carlyle at the foot of Cheyne Row, Chelsea; and that of John Milton in front of St. Giles, Cripplegate.

ONE OF LONDON'S FASHIONABLE SQUARES

Belgrave Square, which has given its name to the fashionable district of Belgravia, is in Westminster near Buckingham Palace. Built in 1827–28, it has always been a favourite residence of the aristocracy.

GHOSTS OF THE SQUARES

Many of the ghosts of London's famous folk, returning to the haunts of their earthly pilgrimage, would feel themselves strangers in a strange land. Gone are the once familiar fields, and all but a few outstanding landmarks. The spectres of others would find the streets readily enough, though not necessarily the houses. As to the City, it has retained the cramped thoroughfares and crooked passages of centuries.

Not a few shades would forgather in the squares, for the square is a London institution. Francis Russell, fourth Earl of Bedford, set the fashion in Covent Garden when Charles I was king, and Inigo Jones carried through the project for him so far as he was able. The Piazza or covered way became a fashionable promenade, and the houses above it highly desirable as residential quarters. Not until 1661 was a royal patent of licence granted for the purpose of holding a market, though stalls had made their appearance earlier.

Near-by was Bedford House, where the solemn-faced Earl toiled at his many interests, including the rebuilding of his Bedfordshire seat at Woburn, the development of his estates in the West Country, the draining of the fens and the writing of voluminous tomes on religious matters. Moreover he kept a careful eye on the great chest which held his money.

A sober enough man, the Earl could not refrain from making a passing joke on his death bed. Dr. John Craig and Sir John Cadman, physician to the King and Queen respectively, disagreed as to the exact nature of the patient's complaint, and were so unprofessional as to argue the point in the sick room. Whereupon the patient murmured that perhaps he had better die in order to please the doctors. The funeral made a substantial hole in the Bedford coffer, for it cost over £750, including £186 to the College of Arms for conducting it.

Among those who lived in Covent Garden was Lord Denzil Holles, who in 1629 helped to hold down the Speaker in his chair when he announced the adjournment of the House, and behind locked doors at which the King's guard hammered in vain, put to the vote three resolutions which were carried by acclamation.

Francis Russell, fifth Duke of Bedford, was the creator of Bloomsbury. Not a few legal luminaries lived in the tall and spacious houses of Russell Square. The most precocious of the lawyers must have been Alexander Wedderburn, who was called to the bar at the age of nineteen, and became successively Lord Loughborough and first Earl of Rosslyn. As he did not progress with the rapidity expected he entered Parliament, where he was an adherent of Lord Bute until the favourite of George III was driven from office. Asked by Lord North to become Solicitor-General, Wedderburn promptly accepted, although he had previously been in fierce opposition. He gradually climbed the rungs of the legal ladder until in 1793 he reached the top and was appointed Lord High Chancellor. According to Lord Brougham, " His decisions evince little of the learning of his profession, and do not even show a very legal structure of the understanding. They are frequently remarkable enough for clear and even felicitous statement, but in profound knowledge are evidently deficient."

MONMOUTH HOUSE IN SOHO SQUARE
Built by James, Duke of Monmouth, who rebelled against James II, it was demolished in 1773.

Other lawyers who lived in Russell Square

MANSION THAT BECAME ACADEMY
Old Burlington House as it appeared in 1804. Built as a private residence, it was purchased by the Government in 1854 to house the Royal Academy and various learned societies, and later rebuilt.

were Sir Vicary Gibbs, Lord Denman and Sir Thomas Talfourd. Denman was a sturdy opponent of the slave trade, and on a memorable occasion vindicated the rights of the subject against the alleged privileges of Parliament. Talfourd probably got more satisfaction when his drama *Ion* was staged by Macready than when he was appointed a judge. He died while addressing a jury. The chief claim to fame of Lord Tenterden, the son of a Canterbury barber who became Lord Chief Justice, is a learned treatise on maritime law.

Painted 900 Pictures

Sir Thomas Lawrence, another dweller in Russell Square, painted some 900 canvases, most of them portraits of eminent personages. His father was no more than an inn-keeper, and a thriftless fellow at that, but his son had indomitable perseverance and great belief in his own abilities, which time was not to prove mistaken. " Excepting Sir Joshua (Reynolds) " he remarked when he was no more than seventeen years of age, " for the painting of a head, I would risk my reputation with any painter in London." Setting up a studio in Leicester Square, then known as Leicester Fields, he had only just reached his majority when he received a commission to paint Queen Charlotte and one of her daughters. He became Painter in Ordinary to George III and from henceforth his success was assured.

Unfortunately Lawrence, like many another prince of the palette, was careless in business matters. The mere thought that he might have overcharged a sitter gave him insomnia. When he was President of the Royal Academy his income was not less than £20,000 a year, yet the spectre of debt haunted him. He called bills by the whimsical name of " casualties," and although several of his friends tried to straighten out his financial difficulties each in turn had to give up the task in despair. His ghost must have breathed a heavy sigh when the artist's " Pinkie " sold for 74,000 guineas in 1926, ninety-six years after the painter's death. It was a portrait of Mary Moulton Barrett, who became the aunt of Mrs. Elizabeth Barrett Browning, the poetess.

Man of Great Charm

Lawrence had love affairs, notably with Sally and Maria Siddons, but he never married. A man of great charm, Fanny Kemble admitted that he had a " very dangerous fascination,"

Donald McLeish

LONDON'S SMALLEST HOUSE

No. 10 Hyde Park Place. It consists of a door, a passage, and one small and narrow room above.

and added, " I think it not at all unlikely that had our intercourse continued, in spite of forty years' difference in our ages, I should have become in love with him myself." Among those whose portraits he painted were George IV, Francis I, Emperor of Austria, Sarah Siddons, William Pitt, Warren Hastings, Sir Walter Scott, Lady Hamilton and the Duke of Wellington.

Herbert Spencer, the engineer who turned philosopher, was another unmarried denizen of Russell Square. " After all," he remarked, " my celibate life has probably been the best for me, as well as the best for some unknown other." He devoted thirty-six years of toil, usually carried on in ill-health, to his *Synthetic Philosophy*. Small wonder that on occasion he almost despaired. " Even," he writes, "should it happen that, means and patience having sufficed, the goal is at length reached and applause gained, there will come nothing like the delights hoped for. Of literary distinction, as of so many other things which men pursue, it may be truly said that the game is not worth the candle. As contrasted with the aggregate of preceding pains, the achieved pleasure is insignificant."

Gained Bride but Lost Fellowship

Bedford Square, like Russell Square, has sheltered not a few eminent personages of wig and gown, including Lord Eldon, who began life as plain John Scott. Intended for the coal trade, his brother William, later to become an eminent judge and Lord Stowell, persuaded his father to allow John to proceed to Oxford. Elected a Fellow of University College, he had almost decided to forsake the choice made for him and become a clergyman when he fell in love with Elizabeth Surtees, daughter of a Newcastle banker. The young lady's father was obdurate; she was determined. One November night in 1772 she quietly left her home, and on the following day the couple were married.

Scott gained a bride but forfeited his Fellowship. Fortunately the parents on both sides took so lenient a view of the matter, despite their previous attitude, that they not only forgave the runaways but helped them financially. There was a suggestion that young Scott should go into partnership with a grocer, but he decided to enter the legal profession. He was so keen to make his way that he studied from four o'clock in the morning until late at night. Then by great good fortune he secured the post of Deputy to the Vinerian Professor of Law at Oxford, his task being to read the Professor's lectures. Ironically enough his first essay in this direction was to read a discourse on a statute dealing with the punishment of men who enticed away heiresses and married them. Eldon eventually became Lord Chancellor, and died in 1838.

Man Who Weighed the Earth

Of all the habitués of Bedford Square none was more brainy or eccentric than Henry Cavendish, the man who weighed the earth. He devoted the whole of his life to experimental philosophy, and his heir, to whom he left the substantial sum of £1,750,000, was only allowed to see him for half an hour once a year. So absorbed was he in his problems that on one occasion his banker called and suggested that as there was a balance of £80,000 to his credit perhaps he would like half of it invested. "Do so, do so," retorted Cavendish angrily, "and don't come here to trouble me, or I'll remove it."

Donald McLeish

WHERE CARLYLE LIVED

This house in Cheyne Row, Chelsea, was his home from 1834 until his death in 1881. Now a Museum.

One can well appreciate the opinion of Playfair, who was a fellow-member of the Royal Society Club. Cavendish, he tells us, "is of an awkward appearance, and has not much the look of a man of rank. He speaks likewise with great difficulty and hesitation, and very seldom. But the gleams of genius break often through this unpromising exterior. He never speaks at all but it is exceedingly to the purpose, and either brings some excellent information or draws some important conclusion."

Studied in a Tree-top

Cavendish did a great deal of his thinking perched on a tree-top in his garden at Clapham, where he had a laboratory, an observatory and a forge. His fine library he kept in another house. This was because he liked to lend his books to fellow-students but did not want to be bothered by them. There was one provision insisted upon. Borrowers had to give a receipt for every volume they took—a practice which the owner most religiously followed.

Donald McLeish

DICTIONARY-MAKER'S HOME

Dr. Johnson's house in Gough Square. Here he toiled at his Dictionary from 1748 to 1758.

Donald McLeish

BIRTHPLACE OF *VANITY FAIR*

The house in Young Street, Kensington, in which Thackeray wrote his novel. He lived here 1846–53.

Extremely shy, the great physicist usually communicated with his housekeeper in writing, and on the rare occasions when he entertained, a leg of mutton was invariably served. He varied neither the dish nor the cut of his clothes. Cavendish had left Cambridge University without a degree, but his name is commemorated in that ancient seat of learning by the Cavendish Laboratory for Experimental Research.

Friend of Charles Dickens

Bryan Waller Procter, the poet and friend of Charles Dickens, and his daughter Adelaide, whose simple verse had once great popular appeal, also lived in Bedford Square.

If ghosts haunt Bloomsbury Square their interests must be varied. There lived the widowed Lady Rachel Russell and Isaac Disraeli labouring at his bookish tasks. In the same square Richard Baxter, the Puritan divine "famous for weakness of body and strength of mind," was exposed to "obloquy and persecution," and Lord Ellenborough and the

Earl of Mansfield pored over legal tomes. There lived Mark Akenside who wooed the muse and sought to cure patients of divers diseases, Steele the essayist who "practised the lighter vices," and the fourth Earl of Chesterfield who was ambassador, wit, man of the world, and introducer of the Bill by which the new-style calendar of Pope Gregory XIII was introduced into England. "Give Dayrolles a chair," he whispered to his valet when a friend called to see him as he was dying. They were the last words of a man of great courtesy if not of high principle.

Refused a Bishopric

If wraiths smile that of Baxter must do so, for the divine lived in intolerant times and the present day is a golden age compared with his. Ordained a clergyman of the Church of England, he served as a chaplain in the Civil War, in which, he averred, "he was the most honourable who could kill most of his enemies," became a chaplain to Charles II, and was offered the bishopric of Hereford, which he declined. Then with 2,000 other ministers he left the fold for conscience' sake. For ten years he refrained from preaching publicly, but after the Declaration of Indulgence, which suspended all penal laws against nonconformists, his voice was heard frequently enough, though not for long because Charles II withdrew his Act of Toleration. It was illegal, said Parliament, and Parliament had its way.

Dying Man's Bed Sold

In that year, 1673, Baxter had removed from Totteridge to Bloomsbury Square and was preaching wherever and whenever he could. Constables, beadles and other Paul Prys watched his every movement. When he was ill, the bed on which he was lying was sold under him.

Baxter was committed to the King's Bench prison and brought before Judge Jeffreys. Jeffreys gave Baxter a number of choice names, including old schismatical rogue, hypocritical villain, old blockhead, and a conceited, stubborn, fanatical dog who deserved to be whipped through the City. The doughty champion of what he considered to be the truth went to prison for eighteen months, and was released under sureties. Shortly afterwards he went to live with a friend in Charterhouse Square, where he died in the closing month of 1691.

KEATS'S HOME AT HAMPSTEAD

Lawn Bank, at the foot of John Street, now Keats Grove, where the poet lived during the latter years of his life. In the garden he wrote the famous "Ode to a Nightingale." The house is now a Keats Museum.

UNIVERSITY OF LONDON: NEW BUILDINGS

One hundred years after its foundation, the University of London saw rising a home worthy of the leading academic institution in the greatest city of the world. The buildings are in Bloomsbury near the British Museum.

OLD GIVES PLACE TO NEW

NEVER since the fiery furnace of 1666 has there been so much tearing-down and putting-up in London as during the last few decades. Old has given place to new with a rapidity worthy of a mechanical age. Often enough no family likeness has been retained. Tradition has surrendered to experiment and decoration to severity.

There are several reasons for this state of affairs. The engineer has come to play an increasingly important part in the erection of buildings, and many materials hitherto little used for the purpose have been brought into service. An era of metal, glass and concrete has dawned. In the old days the bricklayer or stonemason patiently and skilfully built upward from the foundations. These necessary preliminaries continue to be laid because Science has not yet found how to do without them.

There the likeness ceases. A great steel skeleton is bolted or riveted together, and the top floor may be begun at the time the bottom floor is commenced if the contractor so pleases. The gaps between the framing are filled in with whatever material is chosen, be it brick, stone, wood or glass. A building may be "poured"; in other words made by pouring concrete into wooden moulds in which are placed steel rods to give added strength to the mixture. To quote Sir Giles Gilbert Scott, "Concrete, metal, glass and plywood are the 'big four' of modern architecture." London, while spreading earthward has also extended skyward.

Members of a family who are in daily contact are usually the last to perceive change and growth in the individuals that compose it. Much the same is true of Londoners and London city. Passing daily up and down its streets upon their business, they may notice casually the disappearance of familiar landmarks here and there, temporary gaps in the skyline, filled soon enough by new and shining structures. But the eye quickly accepts the strange outline, the atmosphere early tones down the tell-tale freshness, and in a short time it requires an effort of memory to recall that things were ever different.

But let a Londoner spend ten years away. Upon his return all the changes will break upon his consciousness at once, and he will experience astonishment at their extent and profundity. When the Bank of England—

symbol of permanence and conservatism—found it expedient to rebuild and enlarge its premises in order to come into line with current requirements, far-reaching changes on all hands were to be expected.

Factories Built on Marshes

London owes much to the Thames, and a trip upon the waters of that ancient highway, from the Pool of London upstream, would reveal an unmistakable impression of the extent to which the face of London has become changed. To the voyager coming in from the sea the change would be heralded even lower down, while he was still in London river, as sailors have immemorially termed that portion of the waterway which is navigable by sea-going vessels. Upon the Essex shore, where not many years ago were desolate, marshy flats, have arisen at Dagenham and thereabouts vast motor-car factories, huge oil depots and refineries as witnesses to the industrial invasion of the South.

Long before the Tower and Tower Bridge are reached, the great monolith of the Port of London Authority building, in Trinity Square, will have been seen, towering on the skyline above the wharf-side warehouses, and housing the immense staff needful to regulate shipping activities.

Not so far away, in Leadenhall Street, is the building wherein those same activities—and many others—are insured against loss. The new Lloyd's, designed by Sir Edwin Cooper in a Latin mood, solved several problems, among them those arising from an irregular site and how to give dignity to the "Room," ultimate successor to that apartment in Lloyd's Coffee-house from which the great institution takes its name.

Wharf in Reinforced Concrete

Hard by London Bridge, on the south bank, is a building that created something of a stir in architectural circles in 1932 when it was completed—Hay's Wharf. It is a plain, four-square structure in reinforced concrete, to which the designer, H. S. Goodhart-Rendel,

ADELAIDE HOUSE, BY LONDON BRIDGE

Built in 1920 on the site of the head office of the Pearl Assurance Company. The style is Egypto-Assyrian. During demolitions prior to its erection one of the arches of old London Bridge was discovered.

THAMES HOUSE AND IMPERIAL CHEMICAL HOUSE
Two of London's modern office buildings. Thames House (left), designed by Sir Frank Baines, has a frontage of 500 feet. Imperial Chemical House (right) overlooks Victoria Tower Gardens.

gave a distinctive character by placing round the central windows a massive frame bearing panels in gilded faience set against a background of black granite, the work of Frank Dobson.

Capital, Labour and Commerce are symbolised, but the general theme is "The Chain of Distribution," represented by such objects as crates, barrels, boxes and bales. Farther up on the South Bank stands the immense new Bankside Power Station, its single huge stack being 300 feet high, a challenge of modernity to the beautiful outline of St. Paul's Cathedral across the river.

The next bridge, that of Southwark, has acquired a new neighbour on the north in Vintry House, an office-building with a mansard roof, its vertical lines accentuated in the stone facing, and its horizontal lines in bronze panels. Its general aspect is typical of many buildings of similar purpose elsewhere.

Unilever House, with its curved, columnar façade of Portland stone rising upon the site

UNILEVER HOUSE, OPPOSITE BLACKFRIARS BRIDGE
Headquarters of Messrs. Lever Bros., it was opened by the Lord Mayor of London in 1932. Many interesting relics of old London quays and wharves were unearthed during the preparatory excavations.

of De Keyser's Hotel (demolished after a comparatively short span of life) at the northern approach to Blackfriars Bridge, was officially opened by the Lord Mayor of London in 1932. The rounded stone blocks rather suggest immense cakes of soap and the Ionic colonnade, mammoth candles—an appropriate and pleasing effect. Appealing features of the neighbouring building of Cable and Wireless, Ltd., are three enclosed porticos that relieve a certain monotony, as also do the terraced upper storeys.

Rennie's magnificent granite Waterloo Bridge, one of the most beautiful in the world, has been demolished and replaced by a severely utilitarian concrete bridge of five wide spans. Somerset House still guards the northern approach on its east flank, but many of its neighbours across the way have been rebuilt, notably Brettenham House, with its long horizontal bands of fretted stonework.

Not far beyond, towering high above the tree-tops of the Victoria Embankment, is the vast, many-windowed monolithic pile of Shell-Mex House, with its squat tower, housing a clock larger than Big Ben. This successor to the Hotel Cecil, which was demolished in 1931, has ten floors above the

DE KEYSER'S HOTEL
Now replaced by Unilever House. Opened in 1874 by a waiter who became Lord Mayor of London. No guest could secure accommodation in this hotel without a personal introduction.

GATES OF REMEMBRANCE IN TAVISTOCK SQUARE
These lovely gates, a memorial to the 574 members of the British Medical Association who fell in the First World War, were dedicated in 1925 by the Archbishop of Canterbury. They were designed by Sir Edwin Lutyens

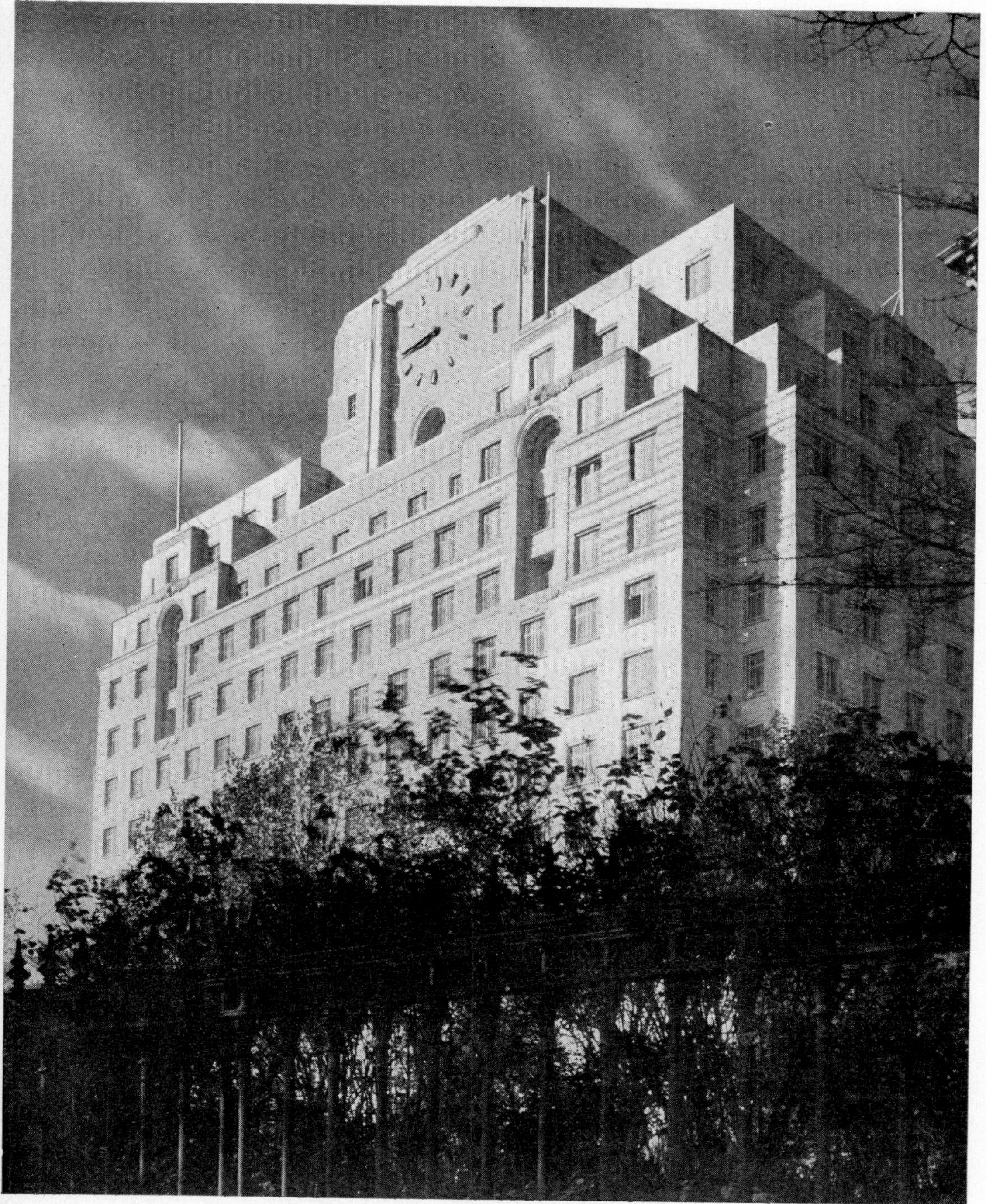

SHELL-MEX HOUSE FROM THE EMBANKMENT

This giant ten-storey building, which contains the London offices of the Shell-Mex Company, is the most prominent feature of the Victoria Embankment. Seen from a distance it has a massive dignity, though at close quarters it is rather overpowering. Within, it is a miracle of modernity and refinement, with electric lifts, air conditioners and fans, central heating and concealed lighting. In addition to the ten storeys above ground, there are four in the basement. The clock is the largest in the whole of London.

BATTERSEA POWER STATION
Designed by the architect of Liverpool Cathedral, it shows that an industrial building can be beautiful.

Strand level, built around two large internal courtyards, and four below; even below the Embankment level there are a semi-basement and sub-basement. And it is here, below ground, that one of the most significant changes in the new style of building, as compared with the old, can best be appreciated.

Skeleton of 6,500 Tons of Steel

In this, as in any other new pile of comparable size, the foundation floors house boilers, pumps, fans and other equipment that give them almost the appearance of ships' engine-rooms. A network of ducts, pipes and cables conveys conditioned air, hot and cold water for heating and other purposes, and electric power for lifts and lighting to the multitude of cells in the industrial hive. Some 6,500 tons of steel went into the making of the framework of this immense building. Adjoining it was the Adelphi, a notable relic of the eighteenth century until demolished in 1936.

The south bank on either side of Charing Cross railway bridge was transformed in 1951 by the erection of the Festival Gardens, with the Royal Festival Hall and a solid embankment which runs where only wharves and piles occurred before. Farther along is the London County Hall, the seat of the capital's municipal parliament. Seen by night from the Victoria Embankment, when greenly flood-lit, its colonnaded central block and two wings are extremely impressive. The design won the architect, Ralph Knott, the commission when he was in the twenties, but he did not live to see it completed.

Homes of Big Business

The next bridge above Westminster is of more recent construction—the elegant Lambeth Bridge, replacing in steel an obsolete iron structure of the suspension type. This groups most effectively, with Sir Frank Baines's two colossal blocks in the English Renaissance style —Imperial Chemical House and Thames House—on the river's left bank.

Fittingly included in the decorative details of the former building are Father Thames and Mercury, the patron of science and industry, and statuary representing agriculture, chemistry,

HOME OF MEDICINE
Headquarters of the British Medical Association in Tavistock Square. Built of red brick dressed with stone.

LUXURY FLATS OVERLOOKING HYDE PARK

Completed in June, 1932, Aldford House, which stands on an island site between Park Lane, Aldford Street, South Street and Park Street, consists of thirty-four super-luxury flats let at very high rentals. The majority of the flats comprise five bedrooms, two reception rooms, two bathrooms and a kitchen.

DORCHESTER HOTEL IN PARK LANE

Built in 1931 at a cost of £1,750,000, it is among the finest and most luxurious hotels in the West End It contains 400 rooms carefully sound-proofed, the bedrooms being lined with cork and the floors witl seaweed. It replaced Dorchester House, a magnificent private residence noted for its marble staircase

Donald McLeish

TYPICAL OF MODERN STYLE

The headquarters of the Royal Institute of British Architects in Portland Place. The interior is even more modern than the plain exterior, making fullest use of all the newer materials employed in building.

transport and building. The total weight of the structure is 250,000 tons. During the construction of Thames House the workmen created a record for Great Britain by putting up 1,080 tons of steel in a week, while 40,000 square feet of hollow tile flooring were laid in a similar period. The floor space is approximately 750,000 square feet.

Battersea Power Station

Rather more than a mile farther up stream is Battersea Power Station, a structure surprising to find so near the heart of the metropolis. Despite its four gigantic chimney stacks and its solid, uncompromising square walls, it nevertheless has a certain utilitarian grandeur and is a symbol of power and strength. It was designed by Sir Giles Gilbert Scott. Its brickwork, with its delicate touches of ornamentation, and the fluted vertical lines on the chimneys repay inspection at close quarters. A tall modern building, the Victoria Motor-coach Station, floor after floor horizontally emphasised, occupies a site not far away on the other side of the river.

Bronze and Glass Balustrades

Such are a few only of the newcomers on or near the banks of the Thames. Elsewhere in the capital the main arteries of traffic reveal changes on almost every hand. Symbolic of them all is the Royal Institute of British Architects, in Portland Place, a plainish, rectangular, flat-roofed building, very obviously newly arrived among classical neighbours. There was much discussion among architects when Grey Wornum's design was placed first in the competition for it, but its gesture towards modernism is now seen to be no bad thing. The interior reveals full use of the newer

BUSH HOUSE AND KINGSWAY

The top picture shows the impressive memorial at Bush House; the lower is a view of Kingsway to its junction with Aldwych. Both streets are 100 feet wide; Kingsway is 1,800 feet, Aldwych, 1,500 feet in length.

A BYGONE ENTERTAINMENT ARENA

Astley's Amphitheatre at Lambeth as it appeared in 1777. From 1768 to 1792 Philip Astley delighted audiences with displays of horsemanship and performing horses. Dickens described it in *Sketches by Boz.*

materials of building, including a staircase with balustrades of silver bronze and etched glass. The walls of the beautiful Henry Florence Memorial Hall are of polished stone carved to picture man and his buildings through the ages, and the ceiling reliefs illustrate the trades of the building industry. Some of the heads are portraits of men who helped to erect the structure. Among the subjects depicted on the massive bronze doors of the Institute are the Houses of Parliament, St. James's Palace, Guildhall, St. Paul's Cathedral, the Zoo, Waterloo Bridge, the Serpentine, and a London County Council tenement. The building was opened by King George V in 1934.

Farther south in Portland Place, looking like a battleship at anchor, is the impressive

PROVIDENCE HOUSE IN POPLAR

Designed and built by the Borough Council in 1935, this fine block contains eighty flats. It illustrates the balcony access design, which eliminates dark staircases. The architect was Mr. Rees Williams, A.M.I.C.E.

Donald McLeish

HOME OF BRITISH BROADCASTING

Broadcasting House, erected in 1930–31. It is a huge double shell with an inner sound-proof building. Behind it is the magnificent thoroughfare known as Portland Place, built by the Adam brothers.

bulk of Broadcasting House, completed in 1932. Another building notable for its peculiar shape is 55 Broadway, Westminster, the administrative headquarters of the London Transport Executive. Cruciform in shape and pyramidal in form, it has been likened to a kite. It is built of steel faced with Portland stone, 78,000 cubic feet of which was used; the face surfaces of the stone are just as they left the mason's chisel.

It is entirely without mouldings or projections, and the sole decorative features, other than those afforded by the Norwegian granite of the main doorways and the black Belgian

BALCONY FLATS IN THE EAST END

This block of workers' homes in Brunswick Street, Hackney, shows the transition from the old two-storey slum dwellings to the luxurious blocks of flats arising to-day. Flower-boxes are built into each balcony.

MODERN UNDERGROUND STATION

Opened in 1947, Gants Hill Station is a unique example of underground railway construction. It comprises a concourse, 150 feet long and surmounted by a 20-foot domed roof, which provides passengers with easy access to trains and street. The concourse is the largest drop-level structure of its kind in Britain.

THE ROYAL FESTIVAL HALL

The Royal Festival Hall, which was opened in 1951 for the Festival of Britain, is one of London's newest and most remarkable places of entertainment. The main concert hall is notable for its excellent acoustics.

marble of the capitals, are two symbolical groups and eight panels. The former, entitled "Day" and "Night," are by Jacob Epstein, and the latter, emblematic of the Winds, by Eric Gill and other sculptors. All were cut on the site. The ground now occupied by this immense building was formerly a slum known by the rather poetic name of Palmer's Village.

Luxury Flats and Hotels

One very striking feature of modern London is the great number of "luxury flats" and hotels that have been erected in residential areas. The Cumberland Hotel and Mount Royal have changed the aspect of Marble Arch. Not the least interesting feature of the former is the use of quartzite in the scheme of decoration. The stone was largely employed by monks, but had been neglected by architects until its qualities were rediscovered. While preparing the foundations a tributary of the Tyburn was exposed, together with wooden barrel-drains, thirty-five feet below the level of the street.

In Park Lane is Grosvenor House, built on the site of the historic home of the Dukes of Westminster, with the Italianate "pavilions" which Sir Edwin Lutyens so daringly perched atop of its jutting blocks to look out across the Park. Farther down is the inward-curving front of the Dorchester Hotel, as happy an essay in reinforced concrete as could be found.

It occupies the site of what was one of London's great houses, designed by Lewis Vulliamy somewhat on the lines of the Roman Villa of Farnesia. The external walls were four feet in thickness and sheltered a famous collection of old masters and first editions, the envied treasures of Mr. R. S. Holford. The grand staircase was unique, with walls of the rarest marbles and a roof of superb mosaic work. Within a mile radius of the Marble Arch there are literally scores of residential buildings to bear witness to the changed manner of living of Londoners.

Biggest Building in Empire

In the populous borough of Hammersmith, Olympia, the home of exhibitions, has 300,000 square feet of show space and is probably the biggest building in the Empire. Nearly opposite is a great modern office block, which houses the Ministry of Pensions. Of

HOME OF POPULAR ENTERTAINMENT
The Stoll Picture Theatre in Kingsway, formerly the London Opera House. As many theatres and music halls in London, it was converted into a cinema, but it still supports stage shows such as Ice Carnivals.

Earl's Court mention has been made already. It was rebuilt in 1935. At the older exhibition, Buffalo Bill's Wild West Show was held in 1887, and a bird's-eye view of London was afforded to patrons of the Big Wheel. Imre Kiralfy's representation of Venice, featuring picturesque canals and real gondolas, was for long the talk of the town.

Ever-changing Face of London

Many of the modern buildings illustrated in this chapter were erected between the two world wars; but the external aspect of the metropolis is forever changing, both at the centre and in the suburbs. Some of these changes, which were caused directly by the last war, will be noticed in the next chapter; but here it may be recalled that within the memory of many Londoners long lines of ancient, doddering roadside public-houses and decrepit cottages bordered the great trunk roads out of the capital, where to-day new suburbs have arisen, each with its Woolworth's, its branch Bank, its multiple grocers and tailors, its red brick town hall, in a pattern to be found all round the great city. To give but one example, only three years ago the Hatfield By-pass from Mill Hill outwards was bordered by green fields and open country. Now at least a dozen factories, large and small, jostle side by side within a half-mile stretch; and behind these factories are the new two-storey houses of the workers, the new one-storey, glass-faced schools, the new community centre and all the appurtenances of a new town. The increased value of land has also induced many a suburban property owner to sell part of his extensive garden for housebuilding development. Old, large, detached houses in many districts are also being pulled down and replaced by the latest types of modern villas. Everywhere, all the time, in London, old gives place to new.

THE NEW REGENT STREET

Regent Street is to-day one of the busiest of London's fashionable shopping centres. Opened in 1925 by King George V, it has been compared favourably with the thoroughfare Nash built a century before.

AFTER THE BLITZ
Ludgate Circus and Ludgate Hill after an all-night blitz on London. The capital suffered severe damage from incendiary and high-explosive bombs, flying-bombs and rockets from August, 1940, to March, 1945.

LONDON AT WAR—AND AFTER

WHEN the Second World War broke out, September 3, 1939, London already wore a strange and unfamiliar aspect; for the aerial massacres of the Spanish Civil War had pointed their own lesson, and the events of Munich and its sequel had made it vital to prepare against a surprise attack from Hitlerite Germany. The metropolis, although by no means ready for war, was in a fair state of partial preparedness against aerial attack from an enemy.

On that bright Sunday morning, three essential Civil Defence Services, the Street Wardens, the Auxiliary Fire Service and the Women's Voluntary Services, were already functioning. Novices at fire-fighting had been practising for months under the eyes of their professional colleagues, and now awaited events with a brave and growing array of portable pumps, resplendent in new grey paint and gleaming brasswork. The Police and wardens had been issued with steel helmets, and a street system of watchers had been organized but was still far from complete. Vast numbers of citizens possessed gas masks, for there was a wholesale dread that the enemy would attack with lethal gases. Steel pill-box shelters for one person had been set up at strategic points in most London boroughs; and the galvanized steel Anderson shelters, many as yet unassembled, disfigured suburban gardens or were stacked away in sheds. On walls and kerbs everywhere were streaks of bright yellow paint, by the discoloration of which the presence of gas could be detected. Notices directing the public to gas-cleansing centres and to the not very numerous underground air-raid shelters confronted the passer-by. Hospitals were holding wards empty in readiness for the expected thousands of casualties. A ring of weird, elephantine, stationary grey balloons waved unsteadily above the chimney-pots, and a very

GERMAN RAIDERS DAMAGE ST. PAUL'S

The City of London's great cathedral escaped irreparable damage during the bombing in the Second World War, although it was endangered many times by showers of incendiaries. A delayed-action bomb fell near-by in September, 1940, but was removed before it exploded. In October St. Paul's was again an objective for attack; a high-explosive bomb pierced the roof and damaged the High Altar.

few anti-aircraft guns had made their appearance in parks and suburbs, not a little to the delight of London's youth. Two temporary steel bridges had been thrown across the Thames, as an insurance against direct hits on the permanent ones. At night a horrible, Stygian blackness had suddenly descended upon everything, the illuminated signs flashed no more their red, green and blue invitations to Buy This or to Visit That, and pedestrians cautiously worked their way along in the gloom, dodging the mysterious lights of slowly moving vehicles, and inwardly cursing everything Teutonic. This black-out, in fact, had shrouded every building from the palace to the hovel, in funereal cloth, and life had thereby become very much more difficult for everyone.

Finally, during the past few days half a million children, together with many expectant mothers, old and mentally weak persons, had been evacuated by rail to "safe" places outside the metropolis, not without many a tear and protest. The greater part of this transport was done by volunteers, who accepted no payment and expected no thanks. Everybody dreaded what the advent of war might bring.

The Phoney War

It brought precisely nothing, beyond two false air-raid warnings, a spate of new government regulations, and a complete disillusionment as to the adequacy of the aerial defence. Measures were taken at once to improve the weak spots and fortunately time was allowed for this to be done; meanwhile many of the evacuees had found their way home, while Londoners generally had slipped back into their normal routine. Theatres and cinemas reopened their doors; only the hateful blackout remained. The A.F.S. foregathered in halls and requisitioned buildings, "wasting their time and public money," shortsighted people said; for nobody now (outside the privileged circles) expected what was really to happen.

Nevertheless precautions had been taken to preserve the many priceless objects of artistic and historic value which had been a great part of London's glory. The Throne had been removed from Westminster Abbey, priceless tombs and stained-glass windows had been bricked up (as well as a few statues), and irreplaceable pictures, manuscripts, libraries, *objets d'art* of all kinds, had been buried or dispersed.

The crash happened almost without warning. In April Hitler invaded Norway. In May Belgium and Holland were overwhelmed and within a few dreadful hours Rotterdam had been laid waste by bombs and many thousands of its citizens were dead. The French Army was crushed; the British, driven back to the Channel ports, died gloriously at Calais and escaped just as gloriously at Dunkirk, thanks largely to the aid of small craft from many a Thames creek and wharf. The triumphant foe stood where not all the blood and fury of the Great War had enabled him to stand, upon the shore looking across to the cliffs of Dover. Westminster Bridge was now scarcely half an hour away by air and London, the most obvious target for the next assault, stood squarely in the combat zone at last.

Home Guard

An invasion seemed imminent. The Chamberlain government fell and a Coalition headed by Mr. Winston Churchill accepted the charge of defending Britain against the greatest menace to her security since Napoleon. But there was no panic; inflexible resistance was the war-cry which rang from one end of the Island to the other. As if by magic, armed warriors sprang from the soil—milkmen, clerks, coal-heavers, Members of Parliament, shop assistants, to the number of $1\frac{1}{4}$ millions—almost over-night, as the "Local Defence Volunteers"; they were soon transformed into the Home Guard, an organization at which the Germans sneered, only to learn when their own turn came that they were unable to copy it. On the tops of convenient buildings, and in the City squares, these Londoners were drilled daily by ex-N.C.O.'s; the majority had only a most meagre equipment and all were entirely voluntary and unpaid. Rifle practice became a favourite sport—if one could get a rifle; the King himself could be seen practising on a miniature range. "What will you do if the Germans come?" a farm-hand was asked. "Shoot 'em," was his brief reply.

It seemed most likely that the enemy would make a great effort to secure the metropolis and that he might drop parachute troops in advance; therefore, while the special constabulary watched over waterworks, power stations and other important points, and armed guards stood within the closed gates of essential factories, all names were removed from road signs, railway stations, and advertisement signs, which would betray the position to an invader. Solid

WEST LONDON RAID DAMAGE
The King and Queen made many visits to badly damaged areas, giving sympathy and encouragement to those who suffered as the result of enemy action.

cubical tank-traps were also built across many roads, ready to seal off the inner capital at a moment's notice; by the side of these obstacles lay wicked-looking coils of barbed wire, and at strategic points were small stone forts, with slits for machine-gun posts. "The vast extent of London," said the new Prime Minister, "fought street by street could easily devour an entire hostile army; and we would rather see London laid in ruins and ashes than that it should be enslaved."

But the boasted invasion never happened. The Germans were as unready to exploit their success as their enemies had been to overcome their defeat, and by the time the ponderous war-machine was ready to move again it was too late. Spies reported to Berlin, and strategists there repeated, that "the Island had become one huge fortress. Invasion would be exceedingly difficult." Nevertheless the attempt had to be made. Hundreds of invasion barges were assembled, but they soon lay in littered ruin along the whole north coast of France, blasted and burned by the repeated hammerings of the R.A.F. Moreover the British still held the narrow seas unchallenged. Air attack was decided upon. It was determined first to soften up the English people by bombing their southern ports and destroying their aircraft on the Kentish airfields. Then would come mass raids on the capital. London, like Rotterdam, would be laid in ashes, the people would rush into the countryside panic-stricken, the Government would flee, the paratroops would drop; and while a part of the Luftwaffe kept the British Navy busy, invasion troops and tanks might get across. But at times of great danger the English people have always proved a sore disappointment to prophets. London was bombed, and bombed more unmercifully than any city up till then in the world's history; but the people did not panic, the Government did not run away, the Navy did not lose control of the sea even for an instant; and the baffled Hun turned East at last in his mad lust for conquest, to start there an adventure which in the end brought him to ruin.

First Aerial Attacks on London

The attacks on the capital, although continued throughout these five heroic years, were mainly concentrated into three periods, of which the first was by far the worst and the last by far the most dangerous. The first stage lasted from late in August, 1940, until the end of May, 1941, and involved the most terrible destruction of life and property. The second was short, from June to October, 1944, when the "Doodle-bug" menace was at its height; a time very trying to morale, but mere terrorism and in nowise affecting the course of the war. The third phase, which lasted from October, 1944, until the end of March, 1945, was the use of the rocket-bomb. It is not our intention to do more in this place than to indicate a few outstanding features of these unprecedented happenings in London's history.

The enemy, perhaps to salve his conscience, began by dropping leaflets. On August 2, 1940, "A last appeal to reason, by Adolf Hitler," floated down upon the muddy Thames and was floated away again by the next tide. Twenty-four hours later bombs began to fall in the estuary and the citizens heard the distant rumble of gunfire. After a short interlude, hundreds of hostile aircraft swept daily over the South-east coast, attacking ports and airfields, regardless of the barrage of anti-aircraft fire; the fighter planes of the R.A.F. tore into the enemy formations tirelessly, exacting a toll of two, three, even four to one, but were heavily outnumbered. On August 15, the enemy reached Croydon, part of the aerodrome being smashed, a number of small houses destroyed and many people killed. Next morning a large force of bombers came up the estuary and dropped their loads in South-west London, besides screaming down in power-dives and machine-gunning people in the streets. This was sheer murder and unjustified by any rule of war; it set the pattern by which reprisals could later exact a terrible vengeance. Meanwhile the defence hit back stubbornly, although woefully short of planes, men and guns.

The Struggle Intensifies

On September 7 came the first major blow. A great number of aircraft flew up the river, dropping high explosive and incendiary bombs, mainly on the docks on both sides; a tremendous fire broke out, three separate groups of warehouses being consumed, nor could the flames be extinguished. Barges moored alongside were burned to the water's edge. Amid the glare, the clang, the explosions and the smoke, every available fireman, regular and volunteer alike, worked like a hero, as did the heavy rescue squads; but before order had been restored the light from the fires had guided fresh swarms of the enemy to the same targets. Many innocent people in Poplar and West Ham were blown to bits, along with everything that they possessed. Other fires were started within the City, two schools were struck, and in all this terrible episode cost 306 people their lives, while 1,337 were seriously injured.

There was an immediate reaction within the capital. Instead of softening up, the public's temper hardened. More anti-aircraft guns were brought in, their fire being concentrated into a high curtain; so that on the night of the 10th the invaders ran into such an inferno of shells as no great city had ever witnessed. The Germans climbed to 22,000 ft. to get out of it, many turned back and at least nine were destroyed. The guns were in action all night; but next morning the tired gunners, with weapons cleaned although still hot, and with replenished ammunition, were ready at their posts.

Within the city, from the King and Queen in their palace down to the smallest errand-boy on his rounds, there was no thought but to hit back. If cowards there were (and some cowardice is inevitable in so great a multitude), they were shamed into endurance with the rest. The firemen and the police, the wardens and the rescue parties, the doctors and the noble self-sacrificing women of every rank of society, stood shoulder to shoulder undaunted, for London had met its crisis and survived: all knew that nothing could be much worse now. The public mentality at this time was shown by the souvenir hunters, who abounded and would repeatedly dart out into the street whatever the risk, in order to pick up a shell cap or a fragment of jagged, red-hot "shrapnel." Incendiary-bomb cases were also treasured prizes, to be stored in cupboards and drawers for future generations to ponder upon. London's peculiar brand of humour also broke out irrepressibly many a time. All these characteristics, which are so typical of the Londoner, have always been quite incomprehensible to outsiders; they

CHURCHILL SURVEYS THE HOUSE
Debris strews the debating chamber of the House of Commons, wrecked in the raid of May 10, 1941.

EAST END SHELTER VICTIM

After a lull of over seven weeks, enemy raiders returned to bomb London, and a shelter was hit. A.R.P. services worked for hours to free the injured who were trapped by the debris, and gave first-aid.

are part of a metropolitan outlook on life, steeled by struggle and tempered by adversity.

In the early raids Buckingham Palace was attacked several times. On the second occasion a bomb damaged the Queen's Suite and also the famous Chinese Chippendale Room. Then, on September 13, the Royal Chapel was wrecked; the King and Queen were in residence at the time, but escaped unhurt. They shared their losses throughout with the poorest of their subjects and were to be found daily among the smouldering ruins, consoling the survivors.

On September 12 the enemy tried new tactics, small formations of aircraft approaching from all quarters. One great bomb, 8 ft. long, fell just outside the north wall of St. Paul's Cathedral and buried itself 27 ft. in the ground, but fortunately it did not explode. A bomb disposal unit under Lieut. R. Davies dug out the bomb after three days of intense anxiety, during which it might have detonated at any moment. The streets were then cleared, and it was rushed by lorry to Hackney Marshes and destroyed. For this action Lieut. Davies and his chief assistant, Sapper G. C. Wylie, became the first two recipients of the George Cross, a decoration instituted soon afterwards as a civilian equivalent of the V.C.

A few weeks later the Cathedral was again in peril, sustaining a direct hit, when a bomb fell clean through the roof and damaged the High Altar.

Finally, on September 15, that famous Sunday when the blue sky above London was thick with warring planes, the enemy made his last great daylight attack, only to be utterly routed. The report issued that night (but subsequently shown to be exaggerated) was that 185 German planes were shot down, many by anti-aircraft fire; one even fell at Hyde Park Corner. The citizens knew that no air force in the world could stand such losses, and they were right; the enemy's heart for daylight raids was broken and never again did he venture in upon anything like the same scale. During this raid Buckingham Palace was struck once more, the roof of the House of Lords was set on fire, several City churches and a ward of St. Thomas's Hospital were destroyed, as was the famous old timber roof of Eltham Palace. Nevertheless Londoners everywhere regarded this day's event as a great victory. The author of these lines watched much of the conflict from a City doorway.

Tubes Opened as Shelters

Meanwhile the Lord Mayor had started a relief fund for the sufferers from air raids; within a week it reached £500,000 and by January amounted to £2,000,000.

The better to provide against casualties from the incessant attacks, stout double-brick shelters, with heavy concrete roofs, were erected on the pavement in many streets; but the shelter accommodation was still quite inadequate. In October, the Underground was opened as shelters. Bunks made from a framework of steel piping, with wire mattresses between, were erected along the station platforms. At any time during a raid, and normally from 9 o'clock in the evening until 6 o'clock next morning, these places were opened to the public. During the height of the Blitz from 100,000 to 140,000 people made their nightly homes in these places. Very largely women and children, elderly men, and so on, some with mattresses and blankets, others with suitcases, handbags or perhaps only an overcoat, they sought oblivion on the hard platforms, frequently overflowing into the approach passages, where late or early travellers —for the Underground still continued to open at about 5.30 a.m.—had to pick their way over the recumbent bodies of the sleeping people.

Even the Tube stations were not entirely safe and at least two of them suffered from direct hits. A bomb fell down the escalator at Camden Town Station and wrecked it; and the damage had only just been made good to the street outside when another bomb wrecked a bank next door. Far more serious was the disaster at the Bank Station, where the circular subway was hit when it was crowded with people, by one of a stick of bombs dropped in a line from Liverpool Street to Cheapside. Chaos resulted and days afterwards efforts were still being made to get out the bodies of the victims. This one stick of bombs killed 111 people, besides seriously injuring 433 more.

The King on His People

On another occasion Lincoln House, an office building in High Holborn, was struck by a bomb which unluckily burst the water main. Down in the basement more than a hundred people were sheltering, when the ruins fell on top of them, and many were drowned there. Really deep shelters hardly existed except in the Underground, and by and large the greatest security lay in dispersal; the figures quoted above show that by far the greatest part of London's population adopted this view and stayed in its own domestic shelters throughout the war.

On September 23 of this memorable year the King spoke to the nation. "In this battle for Britain," he said, "the mighty capital of the Empire occupies the forefront. Other cities are being subjected to barbarous attacks, but it is London that for the time being bears the brunt of the enemy's spite. I am speaking to you from Buckingham Palace, with its honourable scars, to Londoners first of all. The Queen and I have seen many of the places here which have been most heavily bombed and many of the people who have suffered and are suffering most. Their courage and cheerfulness are an inspiration to the rest of us to persevere. To the men and women of the A.R.P. Services I would like to say a special word of gratitude. The devotion of these civilian workers, firemen, salvage men and many others, in the face of grave and constant danger, has won a new renown for the British name. . . . The walls of London may be battered, but the spirit of the Londoner stands resolute and undismayed." He then announced the institution of the George Cross.

This high praise was fully deserved. Throughout the raids wartime policemen in steel helmets continued on their beat. In the darkest night, aided by nothing better than torches or the glare from a near-by fire, rescue parties crept in among fallen beams, bricks and jagged splinters of woodwork, tunnelling through the rubble at peril of their lives in order to reach the crushed and dazed victims inside.

There were 780 rest centres within the capital, where voluntary workers, mainly the W.V.S., took in the homeless and the lightly injured—bewildered, often almost naked, filthy with dust, bloody from scratches and cuts, soothed them, fed them, washed them, provided them with beds and shelter. After a few days funds were provided to set them on their feet again; rehousing officers found temporary homes for them; corporation officials collected such of their belongings as had escaped the wreck and stored them in empty schools until the beginnings of a fresh home could be made.

Fire-fighters, who eighteen months before had scarcely known one end of an engine from the other, now stood boldly on the top of 60-ft. ladders, playing great streams of water upon the flames, while far below others beat down wreckage with their axes and dragged out survivors, all the time in imminent peril of death from falling masonry; many of these brave men were in fact overwhelmed by collapsing walls, or caught by the flames and burnt to death. Meanwhile the piles of rubble, glass, smashed furniture, grew to such an extent that the Pioneer Corps had to be called in from the Army in order to cope with them.

Absence of Hysteria

Through and above all this complicated background of abnormal activities the ordinary citizen, walking past the charred doorway of what had yesterday been his tobacco shop, and stumbling over the snaky hoses which still encumbered the pavement, went to his work, sold his goods, entered his accounts, called on his customers, and then went home to a rationed meal and to listen for the next wail of the sirens—what time he was not getting ready for Home Guard drill or for his turn on the street-watching rota. Nor were his womenfolk less constant. There was everywhere an almost complete absence of hysteria. For the most part the people of London were much too deeply moved to be angry and much too busy to be afraid.

We have mentioned the women. Many of them shared all the perils of the raids, doing duty as porters, bus conductresses (for the buses made it a point of honour to continue running

BANK SUBWAY DISASTER

During a weekend blitz a high-explosive bomb made a direct hit on the Bank Underground Station, resulting in one of the major single bombing disasters of the war, with heavy loss of life and serious casualties.

SALVAGED HOMES

Despite constant attacks upon the poorer and thickly populated districts of London, the enemy failed to break the morale of the civilian population. Instead he engendered a spirit of increased stubbornness.

throughout, even though a number of them were hit), telephone girls, or nurses charged with the duty of getting helpless patients out when (as happened several times) a hospital ward was bombed. Other women, often quite frail and elderly, unflinchingly drove mobile canteens through the falling bombs and the shell-fire to the scene of an "incident" where, raid or no raid, they served out hot food and drink to the fire-fighters and demolition gangs, and saw such sights as were not meet for women's eyes.

The Great Fire Raid

The toll of property was appalling. Holland House, the Middle Temple Hall, with its beautiful oak screen and window tracery, the famous old Dutch Church in Austin Friars, St. Bartholomew's Medical School, the Stationers' Hall, the Centre Court at Wimbledon, Kensington Palace, St. Thomas's Hospital, St. Pancras Hospital, almost all the railway termini, the handsome headquarters of the Y.M.C.A., several great stores, were struck more or less severely. Up to November 5, 9,000 people had been killed, 16,000 seriously injured, and cases of minor injury (never reported) probably ran into six figures. In November and December the beautiful old Charterhouse, Australia House, the Records Office, Drury Lane Theatre, the fine old Church of St. James, Piccadilly, Broadcasting House and scores of other well-known spots had been added to the casualty list. But worse was to come.

On the night of December 29, 1940, the Germans made a deliberate and largely successful attempt to fire the City of London, by scattering thousands of incendiary bombs over an area from Old Street to the Bank and from Moorgate to Holborn. Much of this area was crowded with large five- and six-storeyed buildings, many of them crammed full of textiles and other inflammable goods and, for the most part, separated only by narrow lanes. The fire wiped everything out completely, leaving only a waste of broken stones and rusty girders, empty chimney holes, stairs that ran nowhere, and fragments of doors and arches, which still runs almost continuously from beyond Moorgate on one side to Cannon Street on the other, with Milton's old church of St. Giles, Cripplegate, arising from its centre.

This act, which was followed by another heavy incendiary attack a week later, was sheer vandalism and can never be either forgiven or forgotten; even though a terrible vengeance was taken for it by the R.A.F. in the subsequent bombings of Berlin.

The Raids of 1941

Two other chapters of this harrowing story must claim a word now.

There was a raid on the night of Saturday, April 16, 1941. It lasted for hours and the fires which were started could be seen long afterwards from the remotest suburbs, lighting up the heart of London. Scarcely a single district escaped some damage, for the enemy employed no fewer than 500 aircraft, using them skilfully in relays so that the fires which had been started by one set of raiders served as beacons for the next. Eight hospitals, several churches, two West End stores, a music-hall, two cinemas, a first-aid depot, and hundreds of houses and business premises were hit. Next morning many places were still ablaze. Unluckily a water main near the Bank of England had been hit and the firemen there had to depend on portable tanks, which were brought up by lorries. The corner of Wallbrook opposite the Mansion House was burning itself out, quite unaffected by the playing of several hoses upon it. As one tank was emptied another lorry drove in, and in the interval the flames could be seen visibly to gain ground. In Cheapside and Queen Victoria Street near-by, other firemen, perched at a dizzy height on ladders, were playing hoses upon the flames at the top of the tall buildings. Towards St. Paul's a great dark pall of smoke drifted, the dome showing fitfully above it from time to time. In Cannon Street St. Swithin's Church floor resembled a white-hot furnace hearth; but outside, set in the stout wall, old London Stone remained unharmed, and there it is still. Hoses, glass, water, ruins, bits of office furniture that had been frantically pulled out from the shops, filled almost all the narrow streets running down to the river. There were fires round the Cathedral, and at Cloth Fair and in Smithfield. To see these things was an unforgettable experience; one saw London at its worst and at its best.

Three weeks later (May 10), there came a particularly vicious assault from high-explosive bombs, and on this occasion Westminster suffered the most. The irreplaceable Chapel of Henry VII was damaged and the roof of the lantern in the Abbey also fell in; the historic Deanery was destroyed. Another bomb wrecked the Chamber of the House of Commons and the Members' Lobby, another fell into the House of Lords, but buried itself in the floor without exploding. Westminster Hall, the corner-stone of English history, also had its splendid oak roof pierced by bombs. Five hospitals were struck, one having to be evacuated at the height of the raid. The Mayors of Westminster and Bermondsey were both killed; and a distinguished exile, the Polish vice-premier, General Sosnowski, was among the many who were injured.

Rationing and Queues

After May things improved; for not only had the enemy other things to attract his attention, but the London barrage had become so formidable that the cost of a raid was a very serious matter and provincial cities were selected which offered easier and more profitable targets. Not until 1944 was the capital seriously afflicted again, although nuisance raids, each with its trail of death, loss and misery, were only too frequent.

Meanwhile the Londoners, who as a tribe have never been very ready to clear away rubbish, cleaned up those parts of their city which were needed and left the rest to the willow herb, the stray grass, the nettles and cats, which were to be its sole occupants for many a year. In some of the open basements quite substantial trees grew up; in others static water tanks were built, even though nothing much remained to be burnt. Partitions were erected across those parts of damaged shops which were still usable; and as glass had become scarce the retailer's goods could often be seen only through a small square let into a plywood panel. The lighting regulations naturally continued to be strict, but shopkeepers showed much ingenuity in getting round them. Householders were not so lucky. There was a shortage of steel scrap and throughout the vast metropolitan area countless railings and cast-iron gates were demolished and carted away, to be followed later by inadequate offers of compensation.

LONDON RESURGENT

Standing at the junction of Theobald's Road and Southampton Row, Sentinel House is one of the many post-war blocks of offices erected in London. Other examples are illustrated on later pages. The rebuilding of the capital, however, was delayed for years because of the shortage of labour, money and materials.

The populace of London (as of the whole country) had to endure yet another annoyance as the war years passed. Everything was becoming scarce. Long queues grew outside the shops and became quite a feature of London life; and yet, thanks to the excellent rationing system, there was never any real scarcity, and not a soul in Britain needed to go hungry throughout the war. But labour was also scarce; so that the butcher, for example, had to cut all his own joints, weigh them, pack them, take the money for them, and himself mark the ration book of every customer in turn. The queues grew almost as much out of this shortage of labour as from the natural desire to get the best of whatever might be available.

Another feature of London life was, that as clothes had been rationed, everyone from peer to porter was becoming shabby and reduced to a common level. The classes who hitherto had employed others to do their household work or upon odd jobs such as window cleaning and gardening, were compelled to do everything for themselves; for more than twenty million people—two-fifths of the nation—were now at work making things to defeat the enemy; and despite all inconveniences to individuals, this national effort far surpassed that of any other Allied nation. Nor did the petty annoyances really do John Citizen much harm; for many people now learned, perhaps for the first time, that all their neighbours were just like themselves; and in the great night clubs of the fire-watching brigade and the large shelter rough edges were worn away, new friendships were made, and a mutual respect was engendered between person and person which was all for the common good.

On June 13, 1944, just after "D-day," a new menace appeared, the V.1, flying-bomb or doodle-bug. Who among Londoners does not remember its curious deep-pitched pop-pop-pop; the sudden silence, the dreadful pause of seconds which seemed like eternity, and then the ear-splitting explosion and the tinkle of falling glass?

The flying-bombs were a "Revenge Weapon," a typical piece of terrorism intended solely for Londoners, and except in South-east England not many places were struck by them; the majority fell either in the metropolis or on the way thither. In one sense, every V.1 raid was alike. The bombs did not strike deep, rarely making much of a crater; but the blast effect was terrific and frequently broke windows half a mile away.

After a false start the enemy fairly got the range and continued to assail the capital for three months without a break; on one day 16 warnings were issued, and at first the menace seemed without a counter. The V.1 flew too low for the A.A. barrage to be effective, and too fast (400 to 450 miles per hour) for the ordinary defensive fighter planes to catch it. But eventually guns were massed in Kent, a great new barrage of balloons was sent up, and new and very fast fighter planes, now just coming into use, were put on patrol to shoot the missiles down. At first two bombs in three got through to London, but thanks to these successive measures the proportion fell to one in nine, or even less. The driving of the Germans out of Picardy practically ended the worst phase. This was fortunate, because the V.1 shook morale much more than any ordinary raids had done; it was not for nothing that General Eisenhower, who was himself in London at the time, called them "these damnable things."

Casualties From V.1

The first flying bomb fell on Coborn Road Bridge, near Bethnal Green. Subsequently many public buildings and other notable places were struck, including a terrible incident at the Guards' Chapel, Wellington Barracks. It was a Sunday morning in July and the service was taking place. A bomb was heard to approach; but the Colonel, Lord Edward Hay, of the Grenadiers, true to the Guards' tradition, took no notice. There were 180 people in the congregation. The bomb entered the Chapel, exploded, and hurled the limbs of the dead and dying around the sacred building. Colonel Hay himself, the Chaplain, and many officers and men were killed.

Arrival of V.2s

Much more deadly, though less nerve-racking, were the huge rocket bombs or V.2's (Revenge Weapon No. 2), at least 1,050 of which were aimed at London; many fell short or exploded in mid-air, but a high percentage found their mark. As they travelled very high and very fast, no warning was possible, and the first intimation of a bomb's arrival was the dreadful double-bang and the cloud of smoke above the spot where the missile had fallen.

The first V.2 fell at Chiswick on the evening of September 8, 1944, but the bombardment went on throughout the winter. During the second week in February 71 rockets fell; once seventeen fell in a single day. The last one dropped at Orpington at 4.54 p.m. on March 27, 1945, little more than a month before the German surrender, and when they could have had no effect whatever on the result of the war.

Some appalling disasters were brought about by these missiles. One of the worst was a direct hit on a Woolworth's store at New Cross, south of the river. It was the middle of the day, and both the store and the pavement outside were crowded with people, when without any warning they were blown to bits. 160 people were killed, 108 seriously injured. Two other bad smashes occurred at Smithfield Market and Whitefield's Tabernacle in Tottenham Court Road (March, 1945). At Smithfield, where people were gathered round the meat and flower stalls, the bomb crashed right through the floor to the railway beneath. The roof came down on the survivors, and bloodhounds had to be employed in order to detect victims buried under the debris. Here 110 people were killed, 123 injured. At Hughes Mansions, Stepney, where two blocks of flats were struck, 134 were killed and 49 injured.

The two "Revenge Weapons" between them cost the lives of 8,436 people and injured another 25,101. London's total civilian roll of honour from air raids throughout the war was 29,890 dead and 50,497 seriously hurt.

The war had now been won. The enemy was completely and utterly crushed. For a few brief hours London went en fête, but it was a hollow mockery of the relief which was felt

PROGRESS WITH HOUSING

In their drive to provide the accommodation so urgently required by thousands of Londoners after the war, Borough Councils and the L.C.C. put up large modern blocks of flats similar to the ones shown above at Finsbury Park. These flats, which were furnished with modern plumbing and other amenities, made it possible for many people to be better housed than before, besides conserving the available ground space.

NEW DUTCH CHURCH

The new Dutch Protestant Church at Austin Friars was opened in July, 1945, in the presence of Queen Juliana of the Netherlands. Its predecessor was destroyed by German bombs in 1940. This church is another instance of the people's invincible determination to maintain their old and cherished buildings.

on November 11, 1918; for the city was too battered by war, and grave problems of rehabilitation and the restoration of normality lay ahead.

People were flocking home, only to find that there was no home any more. Children returned, sometimes almost as strangers among their own families. There was an acute shortage of everything: houses, food, textiles, steel, building materials, but most of all, of men. Industry had to be got off a war-production schedule on to the normal basis of peace-time demands; machinery had to be adapted, railways repaired, and a hundred tasks taken up which only the most vital urgencies of the war had interrupted. London, being the focus of the nation's life, and itself a huge manufacturing city, had all these problems to face, besides some which were peculiar to itself.

Rehousing Problem

No fewer than 242,764 houses in Greater London had been destroyed or more or less seriously damaged, in addition to which some 700,000 had undergone first-aid repairs. The floating population was estimated to have risen to more than 10½ millions. Young people, returning home and hoping to get married, had to face the problem of spending all their savings and gratuities on essential but costly furniture, coupled with the virtual impossibility of finding anywhere in which to put it. Rents, and the value of property generally, rose at an alarming rate; and the Rents Tribunals had a long, stern struggle ahead to curb the extortionate demands of many unscrupulous landlords. Housing officers were constantly on the lookout for any premises which might be requisitioned, so that many people who wanted to move were afraid to do so lest their existing homes should be seized in the meantime. There was much hardship and annoyance all round.

To rectify this position builders good and bad, experts and beginners alike, were working seven days a week, without at first making the slightest impression; for every one of the twenty-eight metropolitan boroughs had the same urgent needs and the same long waiting lists of applicants for homes. A temporary compromise was found, in the shape of small structures which could be made by prefabricated methods and rapidly assembled on open sites; in this way the "Prefabs" came in, single-storey dwellings, or sometimes houses, with a few of two storeys. Made for the most part of steel sheets or concrete panels, and well supplied with modern fittings, the Prefabs met a real need; but they were expensive, costing on the average about £1,400 each, and they were designed only for a life of ten years.

The Squatters

Meanwhile general building was slow to get into its stride, mainly because of the acute shortage of materials and labour. The government and other bodies still held large numbers of properties which had been requisitioned for war purposes but which were now becoming empty; and they would not release them. There were also numerous large private houses the owners of which had not returned. Naturally such empty buildings, and likewise the rows of Nissen huts outside the capital which had been formerly occupied by troops, offered serious temptations to the homeless. A movement began in August, 1946, to occupy many of them; it spread rapidly throughout the country and included Barking, Dagenham and other places in outer London. The squatters moved in with their few belongings, closed the doors and refused to be turned out. On September 8 about 1,000 squatters from all over London took possession of Duchess of Bedford House, a large block of unoccupied flats in Kensington which was awaiting derequisitioning. Another 200 squatters moved on the same day into unoccupied flats and houses in Marylebone and Kensington; and on the 11th others moved into the empty Ivanhoe Hotel, Gower Street and Abbey Lodge, Regent's Park. This was sheer anarchy and they were threatened with prosecution; but the movement had aroused a good deal of public sympathy and large crowds demonstrated in the squatters' favour, by sitting down in the streets and holding up traffic. After further demonstrations several members of the Communist Party were arrested and were charged with conspiracy; as to the squatters, wherever possible facilities such as water and gas were cut off. The High Court having pronounced their action to be illegal, the squatters were induced to withdraw when the government offered temporary accommodation to those who did not resist. Most of these homeless people were eventually provided with some sort of shelter. As a necessary corollary of these events, rehousing became more than ever a first priority; and gradually—very gradually—the state of affairs improved.

Another disturbing feature of the immediate post-war years was the sharp increase in crime. Many lawless spirits had deserted from the armed forces, taking weapons with them, and had concealed themselves in the metropolis, where they lived by their wits. Crimes of violence in 1946 increased by 28 per cent; there was also a most serious rise in juvenile delinquency, due in large measure to the lack of control and education among children during the war years. The police, moreover, were woefully below strength, for the Metropolitan Police Force had fallen to 14,925, a shortage of 3,648 from its establishment. By sharp measures, by increasingly severe sentences for certain crimes, but mostly perhaps by the slow improvement in living conditions everywhere, the crime epidemic died away, though not for a considerable time.

Post-war Town Planning

In the midst of all these distractions, the planning of a new and better London went on. Planning was in the air everywhere; town plans sprang up all over the country and were as thick as the flakes of an April snow shower and not much more permanent. There was the gigantic Abercrombie Plan, the two City of London Plans, Borough Plans by the score. They often contained admirable features and some of them were wholly desirable; but the majority were hopelessly ill-timed, absurdly optimistic, and had not the slightest hope of being put into effect. Historians could have told these optimists that in similar circumstances similar drastic changes had been proposed before, only to be cast aside for the future admiration of antiquaries. After the Great Fire of 1666 Wren designed a much more commodious and sensible City of London than the one which the flames had consumed; but except for minor modifications the new city was built precisely where the old one had stood; and narrow passages such as Idol Lane, Dowgate Hill and many another street which had separated the old Elizabethan houses before the fire reappeared between the Carolingian houses that followed it.

Moreover, the planners of 1945 were to learn—just as their ancestors had done—that it is far easier to destroy a city than to rebuild one. After the Great Fire nearly nine years elapsed before any substantial steps were taken to rebuild the wildernesses of the City. Similarly, after 1945 another nine years were to elapse before any material inroad was made into the wildernesses which the war had caused. The planners failed to realize: (1) that property holders of valuable sites will cling to their land till the last instant; (2) that only sharp laws enforced by the firmest of governments can prevail against such opposition; (3) that planning is of no use without the money necessary to implement the plan; (4) that such money was not then available, either in credit or in cash, and could not be made available until several years of successful trading had permitted reserves to accumulate; and (5) that even if the capital had been there, other essentials such as bricks, cement, steel, glass, timber and labour were not and could not be had for a long while to come.

At least one important plan, however, survived the post-war stress, although in a much mutilated form, and has since been partially executed. This was the plan (or rather plans) of Sir Patrick Abercrombie, whose first scheme had been put forward as far back as 1943.

Abercrombie Plans

Since towns centre upon and are controlled by roads, he concentrated firstly on this aspect of the work, by proposing a series of concentric ring-roads around the city. The innermost, the "A" ring road, would link all the rail termini and would take in large stretches of the existing main roads; but many changes would be necessary, and it would also include a tunnel beneath the Thames near Tower Pier and another tunnel under Hyde Park. This, like most of the other Abercrombie proposals, was accepted by the government and adopted by the London County Council; but subsequent events caused first one part and then another to be whittled down or shelved. The "A" ring road was abandoned by the County Council in 1950, on the ground of the great expense and inconvenience, reasons which might have carried more weight in the first instance!

Outside this ring was to be a second or "B" ring road, an arterial thoroughfare up to 300 ft. wide, designed for fast motor traffic; it was to enclose the whole area bounded by Aldgate, the Elephant and Castle, Exhibition Road and the Angel. It would have no footways, pedestrians crossing by subways at intervals. This, too, is still a paper scheme, although the London County Council has at last (in 1956) decided to adopt a plan for improving the bottleneck at the Elephant, by a double roundabout and a good deal of rebuilding.

Farther out was to be a third or "C" ring road, which would run around the entire county. Beyond this, a Green Belt would provide permanent extra lung space for Londoners; and beyond that would stretch the outer belt of towns and suburbs, to which it was hoped to transfer many of the teeming thousands from the centre. The Green Belt was to be tied by strings of oases in the desert of bricks to the parks and playgrounds of the capital within. Radial roads from the centre would pass through all the rings into the great arteries leading across the country.

Sir Patrick Abercrombie envisaged the transference from London of about a million souls, many of whom he proposed to house in a series of satellite towns, each comprising a complete community, with its own businesses and factories, its own hospitals, schools, community centre. Out of this idea eventually grew the "new towns" of Stevenage, Harlow, Crawley, Basildon, besides the large urban centres now built at Borehamwood, Brentwood, Hatfield and so forth.

One feature of the Plans which has not materialized, and which is probably impracticable, was the creation of special areas called Precincts, across which no through traffic might pass; they included the Precinct of Westminster (centring upon the Abbey), a London University precinct, a medical centre, several shopping centres, and others.

He also proposed to sweep away completely the unsightly wharves and warehouses of the South Bank, from the County Hall to Southwark Cathedral, and to replace them by a noble embankment similar to that on the North Bank, but bordered by green lawns. An embankment of a kind has been built, but it is bordered by

NEW L.C.C. SCHOOL

Kidbrooke School, Greenwich, was opened by the London County Council in 1954. It cost more than £600,000 to build, has a staff of ninety teachers, and a population of nearly 2,000 pupils. A notable feature of post-war London is the large number of its excellent, well lighted and heated schools.

concrete for the most part. Opportunity was taken of the impending Festival of Britain in 1951 to sweep away the derelict old Lion Brewery and other familiar landmarks of that Dickensian shore, to build an embankment there, and to erect behind it the new Festival Hall and the foundations of a new National Theatre, at a cost in money far exceeding any nobility which the architects may claim for the buildings in question. Utilitarian questions also shouldered their way into this scheme, since there has been erected in Southwark the giant Bankside Power Station, with its single enormous square chimney 300 ft. high, despite many protests; the government having accepted the position that London's power supply must in 1960 be 100 per cent greater than it was in 1951. Other new power stations were also insisted upon as necessary to provide this power, sited at Rotherhithe, Blackwall, Croydon, Kingston, West Ham and Poplar.

Sir Patrick Abercrombie also envisaged the eventual electrification of all London's trains, which would enable Charing Cross and other North-side termini to go underground and the ugly railway bridges across the Thames to be demolished; this may well happen, but not for a good many years to come. He also proposed a great extension of the capital's airports. This also is under way and has, of course, resulted in the vast development of London Airport, now a favourite resort of the younger generation, who can watch entranced the giant transcontinental aircraft come and go throughout the day. But it still takes as long to get to the airport from town as it does from the airport to France, the provision of a helicopter service from Waterloo notwithstanding.

The City of London had its own post-war rebuilding plans. They have not yet borne much fruit. It is significant, however, that where rebuilding is now actively proceeding, in narrow streets such as St. Swithin's Lane and Wallbrook, those streets are just as narrow as they were before, canyons surrounded by Portland stone precipices.

Rebuilding of London

In the important matter of general rehousing, Abercrombie favoured large blocks of flats in some places, but varied by groups of smaller buildings. This idea has been widely adopted and is indeed both a necessity and a sound means of rehousing the people; but it will give to London a uniformity and barrack-like aspect which lovers of art and history must deplore. All over the capital great blocks of flats, each housing several hundred families, have been erected, almost entirely by the Borough Councils; and more are on the way. They include many amenities—central heating, baths, built-in cupboards, electric light, even ranges of small garages in the courts outside, which to the occupants must seem the height of luxury; but they are still barracks. For the most part these flats are let, at rentals which, although so low as to be uneconomic, are yet so high in some cases as to cause those on the waiting lists to refuse them. By these measures the County Council, and also the Borough Councils, have become landlords on the most gigantic scale; they are also public debtors to the same extent, for the new buildings will not be paid for, as a rule, until about sixty years have elapsed.

A pleasant feature of London's rebuilding is the skilful way in which some architects have taken out the interiors of small, old-fashioned but otherwise attractive houses and replaced them by designs incorporating all the latest improvements; an admirable thing, for in a great city nothing can be worse than uniformity.

Office Buildings

Large office buildings are now rising above the ruins, too, many of them intended for government servants. Such a one, Atlantic House, occupies the angle between Charterhouse Street and Holborn Viaduct; it is occupied by the Stationery Office and the Board of Trade. Another large block, St. Giles Court, fills the corner between Broad Street, St. Giles and Shaftesbury Avenue; its function is sufficiently indicated by the notice at the door, "All passes to be shown."

Among the industrial office buildings, a fine example is the new Gateway House, Cannon Street. The headquarters of a paper-manufacturing group, it overlooks the eastern end of St. Paul's Cathedral and the ornamental garden which has been laid out in perpetuity beside the ruined church of St. Augustine's.

So London grows almost daily, an insatiable monster, eating up bricks, mortar, steel, in one unending meal, rebuilding and pulling down, restoring and destroying, living and dying, in a perpetual kaleidoscope, the microcosm of a healthy, growing nation. So it has ever been; so it will remain (subject to the incidence of H-bomb warfare—which is not to be thought of!) for many a generation to come.

INDEX

References to pictures are printed in *italic* type.